PROFESSIONAL'S GUIDE TO

PUBLIC RELATIONS SERVICES

Other books by Richard Weiner:

Professional's Guide to Publicity

News Bureaus in the U.S.

Syndicated Columnists

Syndicated Columnists Directory

Military Publications

College Alumni Publications

Investment Newsletters

PROFESSIONAL'S GUIDE TO

PUBLIC RELATIONS SERVICES

SIXTH EDITION

RICHARD WEINER

amacom

American Management Association

This book is available at a special
discount when ordered in bulk quantities.
For information, contact Special Sales Department,
AMACOM, a division of American Management Association,
135 West 50th Street, New York, NY 10020.

Library of Congress Cataloging-in-Publication Data

Weiner, Richard, 1927–
    Professional's guide to public relations services.

    Includes index.
    1. Public relations—United States—Directories.
I. Title.
HD59.W38 1988   659.2′029′473   87-47829
ISBN 0-8144-5932-3

Printing number

10 9 8 7 6 5 4 3 2 1

Contents

Introduction

The public relations field is booming.

The spate of mergers, acquisitions, proxy battles and new issues has produced an impetus in financial relations activities. The stock market boom in 1986 and its collapse in late 1987 produced increased use of financial relations services.

The increased cost of advertising has stimulated marketers to consider other forms of promotion, notably public relations campaigns.

The value of public relations has been given increased recognition by many companies and organizations in the United States and other countries, in some cases for the first time.

In summary, public relations budgets are vastly increasing. Simultaneously, more new public relations techniques have been developed than ever before. It's extremely difficult for experienced public relations practitioners to keep up with the vast array of techniques, products and services, and it's even harder for neophytes! Furthermore, not even a multi-million dollar budget can buy every type of public relations service.

More than ever before, it's essential to know what's available, how to use the service and how to evaluate it.

Indeed, technology has arrived in the public relations field. For decades, professional communicators relied on the telephone and typewriter as their principal equipment. Communicators relied on conversation (in person or on the phone) or the printed word.

The arrival of television (the third T) increased the use of audiovisual communication, but public relations people remained oriented primarily to print and paper. Most communication has been via individually typed correspondence and printed news releases.

In the 70's, word processors and videotape recorders started to become popular in public relations offices, together with other new types of business equipment, notably copying machines and telephone facsimile devices.

The 80's are the decade of the business communications explosion. The computer has changed all of our lives. Major changes have resulted from the increased use of satellites, new types of telephone services and dozens of technological developments. Many of these involve computers.

The sixth edition of *Professional's Guide to Public Relations Services,* published in 1988, is much more than a major revision of the preceding edition, published in 1985. A new publisher—AMACOM, a division of the American Management Association—has provided a larger research staff and expanded

1

the scope of the book so that it now will be useful to an even larger number of associations, corporate and government executives, as well as public relations people.

Database research services were incidentally mentioned in previous editions. Now, the largest chapter is about research. The financial chapter has been greatly expanded. New chapters describe teleconferencing and the exciting array of telephone services.

Companies such as Federal Express, MCI, Mead's NEXIS and Xerox now are part of the standard way of doing business. In many cases, services have improved while prices have decreased!

For example, Dialcom and other companies described in the research chapter now provide an electronic clipping service. Clients can create a personal index of company names, key words or phrases and there ensues an instant one-time or continuing search of the current Associated Press and United Press newswires and other media.

The previous edition noted the importance of cable television, videotape and video cassette recorders. The video explosion has been phenomenal. VCRs now are in over 40 million homes and in just about every public relations office. Videotape has replaced film as the most common audiovisual medium for publicity. Cable TV now reaches half of all homes, though the major viewing still is of network and independent commercial stations, whether or not they are transmitted over-the-air or via cable. Thus, techniques to obtain publicity on television have not changed radically. In fact, news releases still are the most common type of publicity material, and their appearance has not changed. More publicity materials, notably news releases, are sent to the print media than to the broadcast media.

Material for the book was compiled from several thousand questionnaires, several thousand phone calls and interviews in person with about 100 experts. Invaluable, conscientious work was provided by a research team in the New York office of Doremus Porter Novelli, particularly Doris Lindell, Karen Parziale, Lynne Schaefer, Lisa Bershstein and Faith Tepper.

''I don't need any help from anyone.''

That proud boast of early publicists is now rarely heard, primarily because of the increased complexity and variety of public relations projects.

As the job has changed from press agent to public relations and communications executive, the measure of success has become not solely what an individual can do, but rather the total results which can be achieved, regardless of who does the work.

In short, a public relations job generally requires a team.

Having a good set of resources and suppliers, like a good staff, increases the power of the public relations practitioner to perform. You can get more done—often with better quality results and at lower cost—than if you tried doing everything yourself.

In recent years, companies and associations increased the size and stature of their public relations staffs in order to communicate their views about major issues and influence public policy. Others have increased their budgets to feature a greater and more creative variety of product and service publicity projects, special events and activities which are directly linked to marketing.

The public relations field now encompasses advertising, merchandising and promotion, as well as an array of techniques which include books, exhibitions, video and dozens of other forms of communication. As a result, public relations practitioners, whether they are a one-person operation or part of a large agency or department, must use ''outside services'' for assistance.

Increasingly, when sophisticated interviewers screen candidates for a public relations management position, an assessment is made not only of each candidate's skills and experience, but also of familiarity and knowledge about public relations services. Only through the judicious use of specialized services can one move from a primitive public relations practice into a more modern approach.

Ask yourself, as well as a job applicant, the following questions:

Which services do you use? Are they the most efficient and economical? Are they the best ones for the particular job? Or are they chosen through habit or haste or flattery? What were the results the last time you used this service? Can they be improved?

This book cannot tell you which services or combination of services are best for your organization, but it can and does give you solid factual information so you can make inquiries and arrive at these judgments in a rational, informed manner.

Experienced practitioners are familiar with mailing shops, messengers, printers, photographers and dozens of other companies which serve their day-to-day or occasional needs. But few professionals are familiar with the multitude of specialized services, which in some cases offer unique facilities. Furthermore, major clients of broadcast monitors, lecture bureaus, video distributors and publicity services often are unfamiliar with significant details of these and competing operations.

Decisions to use specific services often are reflective of the most persuasive or persistent sales pitch, rather than a careful analysis of rates, distribution, results and other precise aspects of the operation. Among the several hundred books on public relations and communications, this is the only guidebook which provides not only a list of names and addresses but also detailed descriptions of services. These include fees and other costs, personal observations and other data and comments which rarely are discussed in print. Included, for example, are branch office addresses, names of personnel to contact, phone numbers, information about quantity discounts and tips on cost-cutting.

When the first edition of this book was published in 1968, the concept was unique. A few directories now include listings, much like the classified phone book, without descriptions or evaluations. Some of these publishers sell classified and display advertising space, and a few list only advertisers.

With great pride, we note that Professional's Guide to Public Relations Services accepts no advertising and still is the *only* guidebook and reference source of public relations products and services.

This sixth edition contains many hundreds of deletions, revisions and additions, and is considerably expanded. New listings have been added for companies in Canada and the United Kingdom, though the book basically is a guide for U.S. practitioners. A few descriptions have been retained of pioneers in the public relations service field, though their companies no longer are in existence.

Following is a summary of new developments in public relations services.

The broadcast monitoring services are doing more business with publicity people than ever before. It used to be that the most common format was the typed transcript. Today, the most common format is the videotape, which generally is provided in ¾-inch form. The largest company serving the publicity field still is Radio-TV Reports, headquartered in New York. Among the new developments is the entry of Luce and Burrelle's clipping bureaus into the TV news videotape and transcript business.

Commercially sponsored sports and entertainment tours and other promotions involving celebrities are more popular now than ever before. In 1982, Crain Communications (publisher of *Advertising Age*) started a newsletter, *Special Events Reporter,* devoted to this field. Crain sold it in 1983 to Lesa Ukman, and she has developed the company, which now includes a major annual conference, into one of the important services in marketing communications.

Talent agencies which specialize in procuring celebrities for endorsements and other participation with public relations and advertising people are booming, particularly in New York and California. The lecture bureaus also are doing better than ever before, with widely publicized fees of $10,000 and up for celebrity speakers.

One of the most common frustrations among public relations people consists of the simple task of finding the correct address or phone number of a celebrity. Many have unlisted telephone numbers and their biographies, even if they are in *Who's Who in America* and other reference books, do not always include home addresses, but instead list their agents. It is surprising that many experienced publicists are not aware of such long-established companies as Celebrity Service and Roz Starr. Both provide subscribers, who pay relatively low monthly fees, with a tremendous amount of information, including the current location of specific celebrities.

The business of the three major national clipping services are considerably bigger than ever before. Each of them has its long-time fans, as well as critics. The critics sometimes become hysterical when a story goes out on a wire service and produces few or no clippings. There is a possibility that none of the subscribers to Associated Press or United Press used the particular story, though there's also a possibility that the clipping bureau was not as efficient as it proclaims. Be that as it may, clipping bureaus remain one of the most commonly used services in the public relations field, and the Big Three still are Bacon's, Burrelle's and Luce.

Bacon's also publishes several directories which are indispensable to many publicists. *Bacon's Publicity Checker,* Volume I, provides information about trade, business and consumer publications. Volume II is a directory of departmental editors at all daily and weekly newspapers, and Volume III (which is less frequently used) provides information about media outside of the United States. In 1985, Bacon's introduced a directory of special issues and, in 1986, launched a broadcasting directory.

Over 100 clipping bureaus provide local, regional and international coverage, with rates often so low that it is possible for a publicity client to retain more than one. However, rates have skyrocketed during the last few years, and the Big Three now charge well over $100 a month for the reading fee plus close to $1 a clipping.

Subscribers therefore are advised to be very specific in instructing clipping bureaus what to look for and what to omit. For example, an order can indicate that the service should be limited to specific regions or publications and can exclude specific media.

The analysis of clippings and other publicity is conducted on a very efficient basis by a few large companies and agencies. Many large companies reproduce clippings about their operations and competitors and distribute them to top management on a daily or weekly basis, sometimes with little or no analysis. Thus, the analysis of clippings has lagged behind the research services which exist in the advertising field.

Public relations people always are looking for speaking platforms. Undoubtedly the best single resource still is the *Encyclopedia of Associations,* published by Gale Research Company in Detroit. Another resource is the list of conventions which is published regularly in *Advertising Age* and many other trade and business publications.

Communications and image consultants is another major category which continues to expand. Many individuals and companies now provide various kinds of simulated interviews and other training to politicians, executives, authors and others. Many of these people formerly were broadcasters, while others have such professional credentials as speech therapy.

Though predictions about the use of optical scanners continue to be made, the servicing of news releases by using word processors to transmit material from the publicity source directly to the computer at the media still is rarely done. Furthermore, the various experiments with providing news releases in optical character recognition format still have not succeeded. Obviously, the media have become computerized, and very exciting changes have occurred with regard to the equipment used by the newswire services (PR Newswire and Business Wire remain the largest companies in this field), but the format of most news releases still looks the same as in past years.

Medialink, started in 1987, has installed newswires in TV stations to alert news directors about video news releases and other video materials. Medialink also transmits video news releases via satellite more efficiently and economically than was the case a few years ago.

More changes probably have taken place in the financial relations field during the last few years than in any other type of public relations. For example, companies now provide databases so that public relations practitioners can obtain everything from the latest stock quotations to extensive research information.

Many of these services, such as The Source or Dialog, can be obtained with just about any word processor or personal computer, simply by attaching a modem so that the information can be obtained over telephone lines. Dow Jones, Standard & Poor's, Moody's and other long-established financial information companies now provide daily access to their materials via database services. Financial relations specialists subscribe to the Dow Jones Newswire and other services, though even the largest companies are hard pressed to keep track of all the new directories, services and facilities.

The printers which specialize in 24-hour operations also reflect the boom in financial relations. This subject is covered in two chapters—financial and printing.

New material in the financial chapter includes a detailed description of The New York Society of Security Analysts, which can be extremely helpful to financial executives, as well as public relations and communications people.

The two largest publicity mailing services, Media Distribution Services and PR Aids, have invested hundreds of thousands of dollars in automation. In 1987, PR Aids expanded vastly and became PRA Information & Communications Group.

Large public relations departments and agencies still suffer in comparison to advertising operations with regard to providing a sufficient quantity of up-to-date resource materials. This is particularly evident with media directories. It is embarrassing to note that many well-known public relations agencies have an insufficient number of media directories or try to get by with editions that are a year or more outdated.

Two significant developments in 1987 were the acquisition of the venerable Ayer Directory of Publications by Gale Research Company in Detroit, and the introduction of several specialized media directories by Larimi Communications in New York.

It is confounding that many public relations agencies still do not subscribe to and are unfamiliar with two services which literally can be gold mines for them. They are *Party Line* and *Contacts*, which are weekly newsletter tip sheets devoted exclusively to publicity placement information and contact leads. *Party Line* is published by PR Aids, and *Contacts* is published by Larimi. Both are indispensable for any publicist organizing a media tour.

Messenger services still are an important part of public relations operations. In addition, few of us could operate without Federal Express and the other air courier services. These companies are extremely competitive in terms of prices and a large public relations operation often uses several of them, depending on the distance, city of destination and whether it is necessary to have delivery early in the morning, mid-morning, midday or the day after.

The U.S. Postal Service has joined this competitive fray, with a variety of services that are becoming increasingly useful to publicists, such as Express Mail. Electronic mail still is not widely used and is incompletely developed. However, it is an exciting aspect of the computer era, and a new section on this subject appears at the end of the chapter on mailing services.

16mm film has not been replaced by videotapes and Modern Talking Pictures (headquartered in St. Petersburg, FL) still is the largest distributor of sponsored films (and videotapes).

The word ''mats,'' which is short for matrices, still is used, though most of these publicity materials now are camera-ready for use by offset newspapers, rather than letterpress. Business is bigger than ever in this field. The largest company still is North American Precis Syndicate, headquartered in New York. Family Features in Shawnee Mission, KS, specializes in color layouts for newspapers.

In 1954, Herb Muschel created the public relations wire concept. Today, there's no public relations practitioner, particularly those in financial relations, who can operate without it. The two largest operations are PR Newswire, headquartered in New York, and Business Wire, headquartered in San Francisco. These scrappy competitors have made arrangements with hundreds of media throughout the country to receive their news advisories, news releases and other publicity materials. Because of this competition, as well as increased business and various efficiencies, prices actually have been reduced in some cases, such as for the New York City regional wire. Subscribers pay by the length, and therefore should be cautioned that it is not necessary to transmit news releases that run two, three or four pages, particularly since it's unlikely that they will be read in entirety.

The expanded chapter on television is due in part to the many new producers and distributors of video news releases. As TV stations begin to be deluged with VNRs, the percentage of actual broadcast diminishes. The choice of suppliers can be more important in this category than many other services, because of the high cost of TV production.

A new technique is the production of corporate and financial videotapes for showing to brokers (often via closed circuit), shareholders (at meetings and for home use on VCRs), potential investors (in their offices and at meetings) and other publics. The production of a video for an IPO (Initial Public Offering) presentation requires a knowledge of SEC and other regulations and guidelines, combined with communications skills. This specialty will be expanding during the next few years, as it is related to the increased use of VCRs in homes and offices. Several companies in this field are described in the chapters on motion pictures and television.

Thousands of art directors, editors (particularly of employee publications) and advertisers use the Bettmann Archive in New York and dozens of other stock photo and archive companies throughout the country. Surprisingly, public relations agencies rarely avail themselves of existing art and photos. For example, The Associated Press has several million news photos which are available for sale.

8 x 10 black-and-white glossy prints still are the most common form of visual publicity material, and hundreds of photo laboratories throughout the country specialize in low-cost, machine-made quantity prints. Prices and quality vary considerably, and public relations people should continually review these vendors, with an eye to making changes if necessary.

Many of the associations of newspaper publishers issue directories (often free), operate mailing services (generally at very low rates), place advertising, maintain clipping bureaus and, in general, provide a variety of services for local clients.

The annual and semi-annual press weeks of the American Home Economics Association, Men's Fashion Association of America and other groups provide excellent publicity opportunities. A counselor who is a specialist in a specific industry knows the major trade or professional conventions and appreciates that major media generally cover these meetings. For example, the Consumer Electronics Show and the Food Marketing Institute are among the major conventions at which to hold media events.

Major changes have taken place in the printing industry relating to the use of low-cost offset services provided by thousands of companies, such as Kwik-Kopy. The switch from letterpress to offset and the extensive use of photo-composition systems (many of which now are operated on the premises of major companies and a few public relations agencies) also has changed the production of news releases, booklets and other public relations materials.

TV game shows still are popular on daytime television and several companies specialize in providing prizes, with on-air mentions. Companies such as Don Jagoda also specialize in obtaining prizes for Broadway plays and contests, particularly sweepstakes promotions. The largest company that provides products for use in movies is Associated Films, operated by Robert Greenberg in Los Angeles.

Radio is still very much alive and well and presents an enormous array of publicity opportunities. Though audiences have shifted to FM stations, the largest number of interview programs still are on AM stations. Several companies specialize in producing and distributing records and tapes to radio stations, ranging from public service announcements to complete interviews. One of the largest and oldest in the field is Sheridan-Elson Communications in New York.

Several companies transmit news and interviews to radio stations via long-distance telephone and satellite. One of the largest is News/Radio Network in Milwaukee.

Every once in a while an imaginative publicist uses flexible records in annual reports, direct-mail, publicity or promotions. The largest manufacturer of these lightweight low-cost records is Eva-Tone in Clearwater, FL.

The research chapter has detailed descriptions of over 100 companies. No other publication has ever attempted to provide this amount of material about the public relations uses of database and other research services. Lest anyone become overwhelmed, keep in mind that the best research resource is available free—at your local library.

Public relations managers should provide each of their executives with a desk copy of a good dictionary and should stock their libraries with basic reference books, ranging from a thesaurus to an encyclopedia. It is a pleasure to report that public relations agencies and departments are doing a better job than ever before with regard to the purchase of research and reference materials and the use of research services, ranging from opinion research companies to online database services.

Many companies specialize in developing posters, teachers' guides, films and other materials for elementary, high school and college students and teachers. One of the most unusual is Rick Trow in New Hope, PA. Formerly called School Assembly Service, the company arranges for sponsored programs performed live in school assembly programs.

Just about every public relations firm now uses one or more of the reduced rate telephone services and telephone facsimile devices which provide transmission of printed material over telephone lines.

Television no longer is a medium only for publicists of consumer products and services. Financial, legislative, industrial and all types of public relations practitioners now utilize the television medium, and TV jargon is an essential part of our vocabulary. During the last few years the term "chroma key" slide has been heard with increasing frequency. Completely opaque—except for a small "window" in which a picture of your client's product appears—the chroma key slide makes the picture appear on the screen behind the newscaster or talk show hostess. By offering chroma key slides and a script, you can place a set of stills with quite a few TV stations.

Perhaps the most exciting use of television in the public relations field relates to video conferencing, in which one- and two-way communication can be set up for news conferences, meetings and special events so that groups can be linked in many cities throughout the world. Costs have come down considerably, as a result of extensive use of satellites, and public relations practitioners are advised to consider this technique even though it previously seemed to be prohibitive in cost. In Scottsdale, AZ, Michael Clifford operates Victory Communications International, a lively company with extensive experience in fund raising and other events conducted via satellite, using one- and two-way audio and video communication.

Whether or not you utilize satellite transmission, you must become familiar with the technology and terminology, as they are important in telephone communications, video conferences and other projects in all areas of business. If you know the definitions of the following words, you can go to the head of the class: bird, dish, downlink, earth station, footprint, microwave, geostationary orbit, transponder, uplink.

Many public relations people now work with media outside of the United States. It generally is wasteful to send news releases in English to non-English foreign media. Translation companies operate throughout the country. For example, Language Translation Services, Inc., which is located off the beaten track, in Lexington, KY, specializes in translation and production of marketing and technical materials in Spanish, French and German.

The preceding is a summary of the contents of this book. One change in this edition relates to price increases. Inevitably, some of the data, particularly fees, already are inaccurate. (A note about all prices—state and local sales taxes are additional. There is often a tendency to forget about this—until the bill arrives. In New York City, for example, the tax is over 8 percent.)

Many companies have local sales offices, and it sometimes is easier to call the local office instead of headquarters. However, the local office may be staffed by a part-time representative who is not able to provide complete or up-to-date rates or other data. Though no one likes to ''beat'' a sales representative out of a commission, in some cases it may be preferable to deal with the main office, in terms of speed, efficiency, accuracy, and, sometimes, price. At other times, a local representative can be extremely patient, helpful, creative, friendly and provide the perfect personal touch.

The author has tried to be as accurate and complete as is possible in a reference work of this type. Most of the services are recommended—provided they are utilized properly. Those companies not included in the book either are not recommended or, more likely, have been omitted due to lack of personal knowledge. In a sense, this is a personal guidebook, a ''consumer report'' from one professional public relations executive to another. All opinions and statements obviously are the responsibility of the author. Comments, and even rebuttals, information about new services or companies which inadvertently were omitted, and other changes and revisions are invited.

A few words about style. Several hundred titles of books and periodicals are mentioned in this book. For simplification, quotation marks have been omitted from titles, except where there may be ambiguity. For further ease of reading, address listings are not set in uniform style. States are omitted after major cities and, in a few cases, abbreviations are used for cities (notably N.Y. for Manhattan and L.A. for Los Angeles).

Also for simplicity, trademark registration symbols are omitted, though every attempt has been made to capitalize and respect all trademarks and copyrighted material.

Indicative of the increased importance of public relations in marketing is the inclusion of public relations news and commentary in Advertising Age, Adweek and other publications. Several industries, such as banking, health and travel, have publications on public relations subjects. The largest circulation publications are Public Relations Journal (published by Public Relations Society of America) and Communications World (published by International Association of Business Communicators). Both have redesigned their magazines to add vitality.

Jack O'Dwyer's Newsletter continues to have a refreshing independence and pithiness, which has stimulated some of the venerable publishers of public relations newsletters. In 1987, Jack O'Dwyer launched O'Dwyer's PRServices Report, a monthly magazine, which covers many of the same subjects as this book.

A weekly newsletter entitled pr reporter, published in Exeter, NH, frequently includes a supplementary Tips and Tactics sheet with practical tips on specific public relations problems.

Public Relations News, the weekly newsletter published by Denny Griswold in New York, devotes half of each issue to a case study which often includes procedural details.

As public relations becomes more extensive and complex, most practitioners tend to become ''generalists,'' and therefore must turn for assistance to specialists, outside vendors and intermediaries. However, with sufficient time and money, a practitioner could utilize all of the services described in this book and still not necessarily achieve the proper or desired public relations objectives and goals.

Each client must decide when and how to use these or any other specialized service. The objectives, concepts and other major decisions remain the responsibility of the public relations practitioner.

This book is not for amateurs who think that publicity is free and easy to obtain. It also is not for public relations professionals who think that they can, or must, do everything themselves and who sometimes resist the use of new techniques.

Unlimited budgets do not guarantee significant public relations results. This book is a compendium of techniques, sources and services which can be helpful to public relations practitioners. It generally does not deal with the concepts involved in public relations objectives and the relationship of public relations clients and services with the media and society. This broader subject certainly is of vast importance. For example, the chapter on clipping bureaus includes more information about how to collect clippings than ever before published, but the quantitative aspects of publicity certainly are less important than the qualitative analysis.

Why publicists strive to obtain clippings and how one clipping is evaluated in comparison with another are questions which are discussed in an incidental manner in this book. The author is aware that these and other introspective questions are more meaningful than which clipping bureau or any other technical service to use. However, there appears to be a void with regard to service data and a need for this ''encyclopedia.''

There now are so many different techniques and services available to public relations clients that it's almost impossible for a busy practitioner to keep track of them, let alone be in a position to provide evaluation.

In summary, Professional's Guide to Public Relations Services includes information, ranging from one-line listings to several pages, about over 1,000 products, companies, services and techniques. It really is a ''source file.''

It will help public relations practitioners to be more productive, particularly with regard to new techniques. There rarely is a guarantee of results, but each resource represents a public relations opportunity, when utilized efficiently. The results will be an increased awareness of many new types of public relations services and a realization of greater savings in time, effort and money in achieving important objectives.

Chapter 1

Broadcast Monitoring

More news, public affairs and interview programs are being broadcast on television stations than ever before. The large audiences of cable television (particularly Cable News Network), the introduction of "Live at Five" programs on dozens of major TV stations, the increased time devoted to morning, midday and evening news programs, the inauguration of late night and early morning network news programs and other recent developments have created more opportunities for publicists than ever before. As a result, broadcast monitoring services are one of the most widely used public relations services. At one time, every public relations practitioner knew about clipping bureaus but had considerably less familiarity with broadcast monitoring services. This no longer is the case.

During the last few years, the major national clipping bureaus and several local clipping bureaus entered the broadcast monitoring field. In addition, several new companies, many of them cottage industries operating in small markets, initiated various types of audio and video monitoring services.

The field has expanded so much that it now has its own association, The International Association of Broadcast Monitors.

The cheapest and quickest way to obtain a broadcast transcript is to work directly with the program producer or staff. Local stations often provide radio or television tapes at little or no cost. In many cases, the tape is given to an interview subject immediately after the broadcast. Even when there is a small charge involved, it may be worthwhile to obtain a tape and to request it in advance of the interview. Videotapes often can be used in a far more dramatic fashion than clippings, particularly at sales meetings and other presentations.

Clients from all areas of business, politics and the professions utilize the monitoring services to know and understand the broadcast-media handling of specific topics of interest to them. The recording and monitoring of news, commentary and discussion programs provide quick and convenient access to broadcast information often not available through any other means.

Verbatim transcripts and audio- and videotapes permit the study and evaluation of information exactly as it was presented to national and regional audiences. The effectiveness of publicity and promotional campaigns can be accurately measured, and continuing campaigns can be modified or reshaped according to current results. Erroneous information or incomplete stories can be corrected or supplemented, and broadcasters can be brought up-to-date on changes in information, as needed. In summary, monitoring services can keep you informed about what broadcasters are telling their audiences.

The 16mm kinescope has been replaced by the videotape as the most popular item ordered from TV monitoring services. Be sure to specify the tape width. Three-quarter inch is the size used by broadcasters and professionals, but if you have a ½-inch home video playback unit (a video cassette recorder or VCR), you'll need ½-inch tape.

When ordering audiotapes, be sure to specify single track, 7½ inches per second or whatever type and speed is compatible with your playback equipment.

Attempts sometimes are made to integrate photos taken off a television screen into the audio transcript. Though this results in a more dramatic and accurate presentation, the cost still is higher than some users can afford, particularly those who are accustomed to clipping service prices.

Another way to save money is to do-it-yourself. Though audiophiles may enjoy taping a broadcast, the mechanics of typing the manuscript, and the difficulties of an amateur photographer attempting to photograph a television screen, indicate that this can be an inefficient economy.

A professional broadcast-monitoring service offers speed, accuracy and efficiency. There also is an intangible value in presenting a transcript on the letterhead of a third party. The authenticity of the monitoring service imprimatur can have a merchandising impact.

In major cities, quite a few recording studios include facilities for off-the-air program recordings. If you are planning to make copies, you sometimes can save time and money by having the monitoring, editing and reproduction handled by a recording studio.

The largest company in the publicity broadcast-monitoring field is Radio-TV Reports. However, other large companies do extensive business with advertising clients and provide a variety of services, including several which specialize in same-day service and low prices.

A major new development is the entrance of clipping bureaus into the broadcast monitoring field. Burrelle's and Luce now provide extensive broadcast services.

In 1987, Bill Goodwill of Goodwill Communications, 1260 21 St., N.W., Wash., DC 20036, phone (202) 223-6123, introduced PUBSANS (Publicity and Public Service Advertising Analysis System), a unique computerized system that utilizes data from Broadcast Advertising Reports, clipping services and other sources to evaluate publicity and PSA campaigns.

1. Bowdens Radio/TV Monitoring

624 King Street West, Toronto, Ontario M5V 2X9, Canada
(416) 860-0794
Sal Culfraro, Gen. Mgr.

Branch Offices:
Ottawa (613) 236-7301
Montreal (514) 495-9434
Quebec City (418) 529-2932

A division of Bowdens (note no apostrophe) Information Services (clipping bureau, publisher, newswire monitoring and mailing house), the broadcast operation monitors most local Toronto, Montreal, Quebec City and Ottawa news and public affairs programs, and provides all audio and video formats and transcripts, as well as item summaries on a spot or subscription basis.

Monitoring service is $85 a month plus $21 per audio or videotape.

2. Broadcast Information Services, Inc.

7955 E. Arapahoe Ct., Englewood, CO 80112
(303) 721-8585
Robert Shapiro, Pres.
Frances Shapiro, V.P.
Galen Engh, V.P.

Branch Offices:
390 S. Potomac Way, Aurora, CO 80112
(303) 363-9500
Tyler Smith, Rocky Mountain Divisional Mgr.

746 Second St. Pike, Southampton, PA 18966
(215) 364-4343
Monica Weldon, Eastern Divisional Mgr.

7838 Big Bend Blvd., St. Louis, MO 63119
(314) 961-4113
Maryann Sexton, Midwestern Divisional Mgr.

Started in Denver in 1969, Broadcast Information Services opened a St. Louis office in 1977 and a Philadelphia office in 1979 and, in 1983, added New York news. This is a lively, efficient, personal operation which works on an assignment or standing-order basis. Tapes are retained for four weeks, enabling BIS to provide coverage of recent news and other programs. Reports are provided by telecopier, messenger or mail.

Typed transcripts are $20 up to 100 lines, plus 25 cents a line over 100. Public affairs programs are $50 for 15 minutes, $100 for 30 minutes and $150 for 60 minutes.

Audiotapes are $20 up to 10 minutes, $40 for 30 minutes and $75 for 60 minutes.

Video cassettes are $85 for 5 minutes, $95 for 10 minutes, $105 for 20 minutes and $155 for 60 minutes.

BIS monitors all network and local news and public affairs programs and talk shows which are broadcast in its areas. Though not located in New York or Los Angeles, many of its clients use BIS for its coverage of national programs. The Pennsylvania office picks up many New York stations. BIS also can make arrangements for taping in other markets.

In 1986, BIS introduced "NewsQuest," a computerized database of broadcast material appearing on radio and television. It includes summaries of network, cable and local news, as well as talk show and public affairs programming. NewsQuest's key word search enables clients, via desk computer and telephone modem, to locate any story of interest to them. Verbatim transcripts and new summaries can be viewed through and pulled from the computer.

3. Broadcast Newsclips
2100 Pillsbury Ave. S., Minneapolis, MN 55404
(612) 871-7201
Telex: 29-0306
TWX: 910-576-2770
Kit Hagan, Genl. Mgr.

A division of Publicity Central, Broadcast Newsclips monitors the radio and television stations in the Twin Cities of Minneapolis and St. Paul. Tapes are maintained for 30 days. Basic minimum charge is $50 for one segment on videotape. Radio minimum is $25.

4. Broadcast Quality
7800 Red Rd., South Miami, FL 33143
(305) 665-5416, (800) 330-2382
Ira Sochet, CEO
Diana Udel, V.P.

Started in 1978 as a film-to-tape transfer house, Broadcast Quality still handles 16mm mag and optical, super 8 and regular 8mm film, as well as all types of video production. On location production includes audio and videotapes.

Recently, as is common with several laboratory and production companies of this type in various major cities, B.Q. added seven-day-a-week video monitoring service. Their market includes Miami TV stations, via their own monitors. In Dade and Broward counties, the cost is $35 per air check. Tapes are maintained for 60 days. Tampa, Orlando and West Palm Beach stations are also available, at $50 per air check.

Burrell's Press Clipping Service
See listing under Video Monitoring Services of America.

5. Electronic News Services, Inc.
6575 W. Loop Dr., South, Houston, TX 77401
(713) 668-7551
Joe Gaston, Pres.
Bob Grimes, Dir. of Mktg.

Branch Office:
3922 Sherwood Forest, Dallas, TX 75220
(214) 351-1548
Bob Broxson

Joe Gaston is an experienced newspaper and television reporter, cameraman and public relations executive. In 1977, he formed Joe A. Gaston, Inc., and quickly became known as an expert on videotaping, notably news events such as oil well blowouts. This led to the formation in 1978 of a broadcast monitoring service, which has become a major regional operation.

In 1984, the name was changed from Broadcast News Services, Inc.

Radio or television monitoring is only $30 an hour. Transcripts are a minimum of $30 for the first 100 typewritten lines. Audio cassette recordings are a minimum of $30 for 5 minutes and video cassettes are a minimum of $60 for up to 5 minutes. Rates are additional for late night or weekends.

Electronic News Services also maintains a library which may be unique. Most items are retained for 2 to 4 weeks, but major newscasts are added to the permanent library, which has been in existence since 1979. Research in the library collection is at the rate of $35 an hour. You may go to the library and view material on your own at a cost of $30 an hour for material taped during the preceding month and $50 an hour for material which is older. To purchase material, one can indicate the exact program or go through the research procedure. The cost for up to 5 minutes ranges from $60 to $140, depending on how old the material is.

In 1987, the company launched TV News Link Services, an indexed compilation of network and local TV news in Houston, transmitted by computer in the early morning.

6. Information Quest
Box 750288, New Orleans, LA 70175
(504) 897-3715
Philip Davis
Monitors all local news and TV talk programs in the New Orleans area and retains tapes for one month. Videotapes (½- or ¾-inch) are $80 for New Orleans stations and $90 for Baton Rouge and Shreve-

port. Typed reports of New Orleans newscasts are 40 cents per line. Radio service ($35 per hour) is available on advance notice.

The company was formed in 1986 by Philip Davis, who previously was manager of another New Orleans monitoring service.

7. L.T.S., Incorporated
100 13 Ave., Ronkonkoma, NY 11779
(516) 467-3400
Robert A. Damers, Pres.

Founded in 1958, LTS is a sizable operation, particularly in the news and public relations field. Videotapes of news programs from network or any market can be ordered in advance at $65 for one to 10 minutes.

LTS also has a library of magazines dating back to the 1880s and also maintains a library of TV commercials.

8. Luce Press Clippings
42 South Center, Mesa, AZ 85210
(602) 834-4884, (800) 528-8226
William French, Pres.
Darrell A. Vincent, Customer Service Mgr.

Typed transcripts of network programs and programs on local stations in all major television markets are provided by Luce Press Clippings, which is one of the world's largest clipping bureaus. Luce provides computerized transcripts called Teleclips.

Lynch Transcription Service
See LTS.

9. Radio-TV Monitoring Service, Inc.
3408 Wisconsin Ave., N.W., Wash., DC 20016
(202) 244-1901
Robert E. Williamson, Pres.

Speedy service (often within 24 hours) is one of the strengths of this local (Washington area radio and TV) service, which provides typed transcripts and video cassettes of news and public affairs programs and commercials.

10. Radio-TV News Monitoring Service Ltd.
Box 153, Pointe Claire, Dorval, Quebec H9R 4N9, Canada
(514) 331-8904
John Hughes, Pres.

This key listening post, in suburban Montreal, monitors and tape records, in English and French, news and public affairs programs on all national Canadian radio and television networks and most of the regional networks, as well as special programs on assignment.

Typed transcripts are $36, up to 100 lines, plus 36 cents per line over 100. Audio cassettes are $36 up to one hour. Videotapes are $65 for the first items, $50 for each additional item on the same cassettes.

In addition to these low-cost, one-time rates, the company offers a monitoring service akin to a clipping bureau. The cost is $40 per month plus 36 cents per line for transcripts, $30 per audiotape and $50 per videotape. Subscribers may select transcript or tape, or vary the format in accordance with the length.

Broadcasts of over five minutes generally are cheaper on tape.

Transcripts are mailed or transmitted via telecopier; tapes are mailed promptly or transmitted via telephone.

11. Radio-TV Reports, Inc.

41 E. 42 St., N.Y. 10017
(212) 309-1400
Jerry Grady, Pres.

Branch Offices:
3636 W. Oakton St., Skokie, IL 60202
(312) 675-2180 (Chicago area)

24304 Meadowbrook Rd., Novi, MI 48050
(313) 478-4146 (Detroit area)

7033 Sunset Blvd., L.A. 90028
(213) 466-6124

4701 Willard Ave., Chevy Chase, MD 20815
(301) 656-4068 (Wash., DC area)

To some clients, broadcast-transcript services are synonymous with Radio-TV Reports, Inc., a national organization which pioneered this field in 1936. It is fascinating to visit the New York office of Radio-TV Reports, or its large branch offices, in order to watch the manner in which all major radio and television stations are monitored on a 24-hour, seven-day-a-week basis. Segments of particular programs can be obtained within a reasonable time after they have been broadcast, though it is preferable to order the service in advance, whenever possible.

A Field Monitoring Network covers many of the television markets in the country, a service used by many advertisers and advertising agencies. Public relations clients usually are more interested in the New York headquarters and the branch offices.

While most users of the service specify a particular program, it also is possible to request a ''standing order,'' in which all programs are monitored for client references. The advantage of this type of order is that there is no charge for the service, and the clients merely are called whenever a program has been monitored which would be of interest to them. The client then can accept or decline the proffered program. (Imagine the money you'd save if you could buy clippings this way!)

The manner in which the staff of Radio-TV Reports scans tapes is fascinating, and many aspects of their operation are similar to that of a clipping bureau—with earphones instead of eyeshades. Thousands of local and network radio-television programs are monitored each month. The most popular services consist of typed verbatim or summary transcripts, tape recordings and video cassettes. The prices vary, depending on length and other variables such as speed of delivery.

Seldom do two clients have the same needs and requirements and a variety of services and operating methods is often necessary to meet the exacting demands of a public relations customer. The staff of Radio-TV Reports, experienced in all phases of broadcast information, work with their clients to shape a combination of services designed to give maximum information in its most useful form.

Following are representative current prices in the five markets where Radio-TV Reports has its own offices.

Typed transcripts—25 cents a line (minimum), $5 to $10 for telecopy transmissions
Audiotape (cassette or reel)—$30 for 15 minutes
Videotape (½ or ¾ in.)—$95 for 10 minutes

In 1986, Radio-TV Reports was acquired by Control Data Corporation.

12. TV News Clips of Atlanta, Inc.
3680 Holcomb Bridge Rd., Norcross, GA 30092
(404) 263-9633
Carolyn Duncan, Pres.

Network and local TV news programs are monitored regularly. Tapes of other TV programs and radio stations in the Atlanta area also can be ordered in advance.

13. Target Video
Box 750044, New Orleans, LA 70175
(504) 456-6747
Emily McCulloch

Target Video monitors all news, talk and information programs on New Orleans TV stations, and supplies ½-inch and ¾-inch cassettes, which are retained for one month after the airdate. The company also provides transcripts and radio monitoring, with advance notice.

Television Monitoring Service
Acquired in 1985 by Video Monitoring Services of America.

14. Television News Index & Abstracts
Vanderbilt Television News Archive
419 21 Ave. S., Nashville, TN 37240
(615) 233-2927

The Heard Library at Vanderbilt University is one of the nation's outstanding resources of communications materials. In 1986, Vanderbilt started a monthly publication with descriptions of ABC, CBS and NBC evening newscasts. An annual subscription is $500 ($300 for nonprofit organizations). Note that it's a monthly publication. However, you also can borrow tapes of newscasts and other programs.

15. Tellex Monitors Ltd
47 Gray's Inn Road, London WCIX 8PR, United Kingdom
(01) 405-7151
Telex: 27688
Keith Grieve, Mng. Dir.
Brook Sinclair, Sales and Marketing Dir.

Formed in 1956, Tellex Monitors is the largest broadcast monitoring service in the United Kingdom. The company monitors 140 radio and TV stations, and provides typed transcripts and tapes, as well as summaries and other special services. Many clients pay an annual subscription fee, though reports also can be purchased on an ad-hoc basis, for about $50 each (as compared to about half-price to subscribers.)

Tellex is partly owned by Universal News Services, which is described in the chapter on newswires. Branch offices are in Edinburgh and other major cities. Tellex also publishes the annual Blue Book of British Broadcasting, with about 500 pages of data about the broadcasting industry in the U.K. It's about $20.

16. Universal News Services
Communications House, Gough Square, Fleet Street,
London EC4P 4DP, United Kingdom
(01) 353-5200
Robert Simpson, Mng. Dir.
UNS, which is a major company in the United Kingdom, is described in the chapter on newswires.

17. Video Monitoring Services of America, Inc.
330 W. 42 St., N.Y. 10036
(212) 736-2010
Robert J. Cohen, Gen. Mgr.

Branch Offices:
715 Boylston St., Boston 02116
(617) 266-2121, Brad Michaels, Gen. Mgr.

212 W. Superior St., Chicago 60610
(312) 649-1131, Michael Farley, Gen. Mgr.

8111 LBJ Freeway, Dallas 75025
(214) 424-6472, Jim Waggoner, Gen. Mgr.

190 E. 9 Ave., Denver 80203
(303) 861-7152, Ilene Lehmann, Gen. Mgr.

630 Oakwood Ave., W. Hartford, CT 06110
(203) 246-1889, Sue Loranger, Gen. Mgr.

3434 W. 6 St., L.A. 90020
(213) 380-5011, Joanne Berg-Quarm, Gen. Mgr.

2125 Biscayne Blvd., Miami 33137
(305) 576-3581, Sally Brown, Gen. Mgr.

1930 Chestnut St., Philadelphia 19103
(215) 569-4990, Bill Cowan, Gen. Mgr.

1951 4 Ave., San Diego 92101
(619) 544-1860, Dolores Canizales, Gen. Mgr.

577 Howard St., San Francisco 94105
(415) 543-3361, Lynn Cox, Gen. Mgr.

1066 Ntl. Press Bldg., Wash., DC 20045
(202) 393-7110, Jeff Friedman, Gen. Mgr.

Formed in 1981 as an affiliate of Burrelle's Press Clipping Service VMS has expanded with regional offices in many cities and monitoring and transcribing facilities in Livingston, NJ (headquarters of Burrelle's), Presque Isle, ME and Provo, UT.

Video coverage is provided, in just about any format (transcripts, audio and video cassettes) of programs in major cities, as well as commercial and cable networks. Tapes are held on file for a minimum of one month. Service is also provided of radio programs in major cities, with recordings held on file for a minimum of two weeks.

A videotape cassette (in any format) of one to ten minutes is $95 if the program is aired in a VMS market and $120 in other markets.

Audio cassettes of one to 30 minutes are $35 in the basic markets and $60 in others. Broadcast transcripts are $25 for the first 100 lines, with a minimum of $25 in the basic markets and $35 elsewhere.

Chapter 2

Calendars

Did you ever schedule a news conference or other event and wonder what else, of newsworthy interest or appealing to the same audience, would be going on at the same time?

One way to guard against picking a time which would be in conflict with one or more other major news conferences or events is to check with the banquet managers of the principal hotels and other places at which meetings are held. Sometimes members of the press, the chamber of commerce or other organizations can be queried for their knowledge about upcoming events.

A few years ago, Gary Wagner, a New York photographer, issued a monthly bulletin which listed forthcoming news conferences and events. Mr. Wagner discontinued the free service when he found it extremely difficult to obtain a sufficient amount of this information.

In 1985, publicist Norma Lee launched a similar publication, PR Clock, which is described in this chapter.

Another exciting development is the Metropolitan Day Book of PR Newswire in New York.

The most important development, however, is the access that many public relations people now have to the Day Books of The Associated Press and United Press via several database research services. This is discussed in the chapter on research.

AP and UPI issue daily calendars in New York, Chicago, Washington, DC and a few other cities. These listings are heavily relied on by news assignment editors, particularly at radio and TV stations. All you have to do to get your news conference or news event listed on the Day Book is call the Day Book Editor the day before. It's free!

About the PR Newswire Day Book, here's the way it works.

When a member uses PR Newswire to announce a news conference, photo opportunity or other press event, the announcement will be repeated at no additional charge on the day of the event in the PRN day book, which is transmitted to newsrooms between 8:30 and 9:00 A.M.

In addition, several news wire bureaus run ''recaps'' throughout the day to remind editors of stories that have moved on the wire, and enable them to request repeats if necessary. Repeats generally are sent at no extra charge on request from newsrooms or members. Recaps consist of a one-line summary of the story, and are moved in New York (for non-financial news), Los Angeles (for all news of West Coast interest), New England, Philadelphia, Pittsburgh and Baltimore.

Chase's Calendar of Annual Events, a listing of hundreds of special days, weeks and months, is published annually ($24.95) by Best Publications, 180 N. Michigan Ave., Chicago 60601.

In the fashion and theatrical fields, there are publications which are standard reference aids to many types of subscribers.

For example, the Fashion Calendar is a weekly publication which provides a comprehensive listing of forthcoming fashion and related events to subscribers who literally use it as a clearing house for fashion dates. The publication also includes information about major fashion events in other cities, but it is primarily New York-oriented.

Many trade publications publish calendars of forthcoming events, primarily conventions and meetings. Pollstar, 4838 N. Blackstone Ave., Fresno, CA 93726, is a weekly publication ($245/yr) in the entertainment (primarily music) industry. It's also available via computer network.

In 1987, Alliance for the Arts, 330 W. 42 St., N.Y. 10036, launched the Events Clearinghouse Calendar, a bimonthly list of benefit events in New York City. An annual subscription is $25 for nonprofit organizations and $100 for others.

1. EdVent

Timeplace, Inc.
460 Totten Pond Rd., Waltham, MA 02154
(617) 890-4636
Mark Dane, Pres.

A newcomer to electronic databases provides a comprehensive calendar of seminars, conferences, workshops and other continuing education programs. EdVent, as it is called, was designed as an efficient means of matching employee/corporation educational needs with continuing education offerings. It provides up-to-date information on over 120,000 programs in many fields of interest on any given day in the coming year.

The seminar information, including choices of programs, times and locations, costs and sponsor contacts, is available in the database through a simple telephone hook-up. Users can search seminar sponsor's catalogs in minutes and zero in on events of interest.

2. Fashion Calendar

185 E. 85 St., N.Y. 10028
(212) 289-0420
Ruth Finley, Publisher

The bright red cover of the Fashion Calendar is seen on the desks of hundreds of executives in the manufacturing, wholesale and retail-fashion industry, as well as related vendors, media and public relations people. Fashion Calendar has been issued since 1941. Each issue lists and describes public and private fashion openings, showings and other events of fashion significance for the forthcoming weeks. In addition, subscribers can call the Fashion Calendar in order to check future events and avoid conflicts of dates.

Rates for the Fashion Calendar are:

One year $300
Six months $200

In addition to fashion events, the publication also lists major conventions, benefits, theatrical and artistic functions, and other information about what's going on and what's planned to go on in New York City and other major markets. Thus, the publication is not only a dependable guide in planning events, but also a stimulant in promotional thinking.

For those not in the fashion field, it's still fascinating to read about the events of such organizations as the Chambre Syndicale de la Couture Parisienne and the Incorporated Society of London Designers.

Ruth Finley also publishes Fashion International, a monthly newsletter. An annual subscription is $85.

3. P.R. Clock
50 W. 41 St., N.Y. 10018
(212) 221-0410
Norma A. Lee, Editor
$105/yr.

Norma A. Lee Co., a public relations agency, publishes P.R. Clock, a biweekly listing of news conferences and events, mainly in the New York City area. Public relations practitioners can list their events free.

4. Theatre Information Bulletin
Proscenium Publications
4 Park Ave., N.Y. 10016
(212) 532-2570
Joan Marlowe and Betty Blake

Established in 1944, Theatre Information Bulletin is a weekly listing of Broadway and other shows, including data about casts, staffs, schedules, tickets and other facts of value to journalists, publicists, ticket brokers and others involved with show business, such as hotels and restaurants.

Rates are:

One year $100
Six months $55
Three months $35

A streamlined monthly summary is available for $35 a year.

From their tower suite, the T.I.B. proprietors also publish New York Theatre Critics' Reviews, a service that is popular with librarians and theatre buffs. The complete reviews of the New York theatre critics are reproduced verbatim for $100 a year, including a cheerful red binder. The media represented are The New York Times, New York Post, New York Daily News, New York Newsday, USA Today, The Wall Street Journal, WWD, Christian Science Monitor, Time, Newsweek and WABC-TV.

Indexes and back issues to 1940 are available in individual volumes. A combination price for the bulletin and the reviews is available for $170 a year.

5. The Theatrical Calendar
1780 Broadway, N.Y. 10019
(212) 757-7979
Frank Gehrecke, Editor

A semi-monthly listing of current and future shows and theatrical events, published by Celebrity Service International. The cost is $5 an issue, $100 a year.

Data for each show include theater, opening date, producer, publicist and phone numbers. A useful feature is the cast and travel schedule of future shows, which often provides celebrity tie-ins for public relations purposes.

The emphasis is on New York, but considerable information is included from other cities.

Celebrity Service also publishes The Social Calendar, a weekly bulletin ($100/yr.) edited by Donna Shor.

Editorial calendars are listed in the chapter on media directories.

Chapter 3

Celebrities and Speakers

H. L. Mencken once defined a celebrity as someone with an unlisted telephone number. This no longer is true, and it's difficult to define a celebrity. It's more difficult to locate and line up a celebrity for publicity and promotional tie-ins.

A celebrity is a famous or well-publicized person. The word itself comes from the Latin, *celebritas,* meaning "multitude" or "fame," but 20th-century-American society probably has made the celebrity concept more important than ever before. The greatest influences have been the mass media, which include theatrical motion pictures, television, gossip columnists, fan magazines and advertising.

It's often hard to determine whether a person becomes a celebrity as a result of deeds or simply from publicity exposure, and often the two factors are so intertwined that it's almost impossible to separate them. Whether our society is overly or falsely celebrity- and status-conscious is a matter for the sociologists. The thoughtful public relations practitioner usually deplores campaigns to "manufacture celebrities." However, celebrities do exist and not just in the entertainment field. Public figures, including political, literary and cultural leaders, are celebrities who can, by their participation and endorsement, function as authors, speakers and in other areas of public relations projects.

The celebrity realm therefore is not confined to press agents, though many lay people think that this is the exclusive domain of these publicists. The most successful Broadway or Hollywood press agent often has trouble arranging for a celebrity to appear at a commercial event, such as the groundbreaking of a new warehouse or the opening of a supermarket. Recognizing the difficulties involved in recruiting celebrities, publicists who are not involved in show business often try to stay away from projects involving celebrities, leaving commercial endorsements and related activities to the advertising agencies, agents, managers, attorneys and others who usually "get into the act."

The motto of many public relations practitioners often is, "Nothing is impossible." However, the client who asks a public relations agent to arrange for a top celebrity to speak at the dedication of a branch office in East Podunk is asking for something awfully hard to attain, at the very least. Sometimes success can be achieved by trying the most direct route. You may eliminate all of the intermediaries who are paid to say "no" by writing or calling directly to the celebrity.

The pioneer in the celebrity endorsement field was Endorsements International, Ltd., which was in business from 1945 to the late 70's. The company was so successful that its founder, Jules Alberti, also became a celebrity himself. The company supplied more than 20,000 endorsements for more than 15,000 products, using such celebrities as Bing Crosby, Mia Farrow, Wendy Vanderbilt and Mickey Spillane.

Endorsements International did not "control" celebrities but regularly worked with well-known personalities and their agents from the show business world, as well as prominent personalities in business, government, education, sports and other fields, including, of course, the Social Register.

A long-time producer of radio programs in Chicago (in the days when many network programs emanated from Chicago), Jules Robert Alberti was an expert on advertising, publicity and media, and thus was extremely helpful to public relations clients. One of his most successful advertising campaigns was the providing of celebrities to the Geer, DuBois agency for its Foster Grant sunglasses ads, in which Woody Allen, Julie Christie, Peter Sellers, Anthony Quinn and others were photographed.

One of Jules Alberti's mottos was, "If you have something uninteresting to say, better get someone interesting to say it."

He often is credited with originating the celebrity endorsement business. He in turn credited the late Danny Danker, who was active in the 30's and 40's.

There probably were Philadelphia lawyers in the 70's (1770's, that is) who tried to arrange for tie-ins with Ben Franklin and George Washington.

Federal officeholders and employees currently are limited by law to a maximum honorarium of $2,000 per appearance and an annual aggregate limit of 30 to 40 percent of their salaries. Travel expenses are not considered part of the honorarium, but they are limited to the actual cost of transportation, lodging and meals. As with all regulations, these fee structures may change. Check with the Federal Election Commission or ask the Federal officeholder.

Major U.S. Governmental officials sometimes can be obtained from The White House Speakers Bureau, Room 182, Wash., DC 20500, phone (202) 456-7560. Obviously, it's not likely that you'll obtain the President for a supermarket opening. One value of the Bureau is that its computer file can tell you about current and forthcoming speaking engagements of Government officials, and sometimes it's helpful if you can contact officials who are scheduled to come to your area.

Of course, if you're able to pay a fee, it may be preferable to get in touch with a talent agency, personal manager or lecture bureau. The largest companies in the field have offices in New York, Chicago, Los Angeles and other cities. They often are able to suggest celebrities other than the one you request and negotiate compensation and various details with considerable efficiency. The best-known talent agencies include:

Columbia Artists Management, Inc., 165 W. 57 St., N.Y. 10019
(212) 397-6900

International Creative Management, 40 W. 57 St., N.Y. 10019
(212) 556-5600

William Morris Agency, 1350 Ave. of the Americas, N.Y. 10019
(212) 586-5100

Among the theatrical talent agencies that provide one-person shows and lecturers are:

Associated Booking Corp., 1995 Broadway, N.Y. 10023
(212) 874-2400

Ray Bloch Productions, 1500 Broadway, N.Y. 10036
(212) 354-8900

Royce Carlton, Inc., 866 United Nations Plaza, N.Y. 10017
(212) 355-7700

Kolmar-Luth Entertainment, Inc., 1501 Broadway, N.Y. 10036
(212) 730-9500

Jack Morton Productions, Inc., 830 Third Ave., N.Y. 10022
(212) 758-8400

Podium Management Associates, Inc., 434 E. 52 St., N.Y. 10022
(212) 758-4558
(The Speakers' Group is the lecture division)

J. Franklyn Dickson, president of Ray Bloch Productions, stated in Public Relations Journal:

The increased use of entertainment in conjunction with business events has resulted in realizations that have shocked many executives. With the increase, there has also been a growth in the complexity of rules and regulations set up by unions, agents and Federal, state and local government agencies. And the ever-present fine print on a contract can make the business of entertainment a nightmare for the public relations person.

For example, certain standard contracts offered by musicians' unions and complex contracts offered by artists include such pitfalls as cancellation clauses, employer responsibilities, expense reimbursement, and others that can be confusing and expensive.

Is it necessary to feed an orchestra or performing artist? Who is responsible for withholding, Social Security and other taxes? What if a performer is hurt on stage? How can you, or your client, as buyers of talent, protect yourself?

Mr. Dickson's answer, not surprisingly, is to retain an "entertainment consultant," such as Ray Bloch Productions.

When setting up a lecture program, one of the first areas to explore is the business seminar field. Among the organizations which have a continuing need for speakers are the American Management Association, Advanced Management Research, Business and Professional Research Institute, Practising Law Institute, Public Relations Society of American and International Association of Business Communicators.

Information about these organizations is included in the Encyclopedia of Associations (Gale Research Co., Book Tower, Detroit 48226). The American Management Association is at 135 W. 50 St., N.Y. 10019, phone (212) 586-8100. The National Management Association, 2210 Arbor Blvd., Dayton, OH 45439, phone (513) 294-0421, publishes a Speakers Directory and conducts a Speakers Showcase during its annual convention.

Practising (note the s) Law Institute is at 810 Seventh Ave., N.Y. 10019, phone (212) 765-5700.

The AMA operates the Presidents Association, which conducts The Management Course for Presidents, held throughout the year at Boca Raton in Florida, the Homestead in Virginia, Quail Lodge in Carmel, California and other resorts in the United States and Europe.

Business & Professional Research Institute is at 353 Nassau St., Princeton, NJ 08540, (609) 394-5070.

Executive Enterprises, Inc., 22 W. 21 St., N.Y. 10010, conducts projects for several organizations, and operates the Banking Law Institute, which has a continuing series of seminars. The phone is (212) 645-7880.

Public relations people should be familiar with the Publicity Clubs in Boston, Chicago and Los

Angeles and other communications organizations. Benefits include participation as students, speakers, subscription to publications, access to libraries, employment services and dozens of other social and professional activities.

Public relations people often are interested in finding speakers for sales meetings and events, and, on the other side of the ledger, often are looking for "platforms" on which to place their own speakers.

Several business and trade publications conduct conferences, which are well attended and often are publicizable platforms for the speakers. Among those of particular interest to public relations clients are Advertising Age, Adweek, Computer World and Business Week.

Dottie Walters publishes a bimonthly magazine, Speakers & Meeting Planners Sharing Ideas. Advertisements and articles describe speakers and also products and services available to speakers, such as monthly joke services. It's $49.95 a year from Royal Publishing, Inc., Box 1120, 18825 Hicrest Rd., Glendora, CA 91740, (818) 335-8069.

Gale Research Company publishes a unique directory, Speakers and Lecturers: How to Find Them. The 1,358 page two-volume directory ($140) lists 6,400 speakers (free and fee) and 2,000 speakers and lecture bureaus. The book is published by Gale Research Company, Book Tower, Detroit, MI 48226.

A good source of lecturers are book publishers. Authors of new books sometimes are available free or at less than their regular fees.

The rosters of several lecture bureaus include retired athletes, politicians and other part-timers. These celebrities can be excellent speakers, but be cautious and selective as "no-shows" are a possibility.

Knowledge Industry Publications, which publishes video and education newsletters and other publications, conducts a variety of seminars and symposia, including the annual Video Expo, which is held in the fall in New York.

The smaller bureaus often are more interested in the specialized needs of public relations clients, who generally do not want a "canned speech."

Clients sometimes are confused about the different types of speakers bureaus, particularly since the same speaker sometimes is listed with several bureaus. It's akin to the multiple listings in the real estate field. Note that a speakers bureau is not an agent or a producer. An agent or manager generally has an exclusive contractual relationship with its speakers. A producer represents the speakers or performers for the specific programs or productions conducted by the producer.

Following is a list of several major bureaus.

Richard Fulton, Inc., 101 W. 57 St., N.Y. 10019
(212) 582-4099
Richard Fulton, Pres.

The Handley Management, 51 Church St., Boston 02116
(617) 542-2479
Mena Holmes

National Speakers Bureau, Inc., 222 Wisconsin Ave., Lake Forest, IL 60045
(312) 295-1122
John Palmer, Dir.

Harry Walker, Inc., 1 Penn Plaza, N.Y. 10119
(212) 563-0700, Telex 858282
Harry Walker, Chm.
Don Walker, Pres.
Formed in 1925.

In addition to the preceding, here are descriptions of several lecture bureaus.

1. American Program Bureau, Inc.

850 Boylston St., Chestnut Hill, MA 02167
(617) 731-0500, (800) 225-4575
Perry Steinberg, Pres.
Ken Eisenstein, V.P.

Founded in 1965, APB is one of the country's largest lecture bureaus.

2. Royce Carlton Inc.

866 United Nations Plaza, N.Y. 10017
(212) 355-7700
Carlton S. Sedgeley, Pres.

Exclusive agent for Dick Cavett, Nora Ephron, Douglas Fairbanks Jr., Father Andrew M. Greeley, Jeff Greenfield, David Halberstam, Vincent Price, George Sheehan, M.D., Simon Wiesenthal and others.

3. The Inc. Speakers Bureau

38 Commercial Wharf, Boston 02110
(617) 227-4700
Telex: (710) 321-0523
Ellen Kolton, Dir.

The Inc. Speakers Bureau, a division of Inc. (magazine) Publishing Co., represents journalists and executives, as speakers, primarily about growing companies.

4. Jordan International Enterprises/Success Leaders Speakers Service

Lenox Square, Box 18737, Atlanta, GA 30326
(404) 261-1122, (404) 231-2133, (800) ORATORS (672-8677)
Dr. DuPree Jordan Jr., Pres.
Margaret M. Jordan, Secretary/Treasurer

Margaret and DuPree Jordan have operated a group of family businesses since 1954, including an advertising and public relations firm, management training and educational consulting organization, speakers bureau and several publishing firms. They published a group of weekly newspapers in the Atlanta metropolitan area for ten years, and have published a business management/personal development newsletter, Success Orientation.

Their Success Leaders Speakers Service provides professional speakers, trainers, business consultants and resource people for management conferences, sales seminars, meetings and conventions all over the world.

Jordan Enterprises/SLSS conducted an annual Professional Speakers Showcase the first full week of May every year in Atlanta for 12 years, offering an opportunity for meeting planners to meet and hear potential speakers.

The Jordans are now offering a variety of personal tutoring programs at their new Jordan Communications Conference Center (JC^3) for Chief Executive Officers and other high ranking executives who want to improve public speaking and communications skills.

5. Keedick Lecture Bureau, Inc.

850 Boylston St., Chestnut Hill 02167
(800) 243-3228
Perry Steinberg, Pres.

Keedick is the oldest lecture bureau (established in 1907) in the U.S. The 1988 catalog includes such celebrities as Loretta Young, Eva Gabor, Norman Cousins, and Admiral Elmo Zumwalt. Keedick is a division of American Program Bureau.

6. Lecture Consultants, Inc.
Box 327, Mineola, NY 11501
(516) 741-0687
Frances S. Slotkin, Pres.
Helen Robbins, Marketing Dir.
    Fran Slotkin operates a speakers bureau, a women's fashion company and East Coast Communications Consultants, Inc., a video production company.

7. The Leigh Bureau (W. Colston Leigh, Inc.)
1000 Herrontown Rd., Princeton, NJ 08540
(609) 921-6141
Daniel R. Stern

Branch Office:
1801 Ave. of the Stars, L.A. 90067
(213) 277-5999
Fern Weber

    The largest and oldest exclusive lecture bureau in the country, The Leigh Bureau (in business since 1929) represents many celebrities. Among its clients are Alvin Toffler, Alex Haley, John Naisbitt, Gary Hart and other popular speakers.

8. Public Affairs Lecture Bureau
104 E. 40 St., N.Y. 10016
(212) 986-4456
Ms. V. K. Doyle
    About 4,000 speakers are available, including professors, experts in government, economics, sciences and the arts. The bureau is affiliated with Conway Associates, which is described in the chapter on translations.

9. Program Corporation of America
599 W. Hartsdale Ave., White Plains, NY 10607
(212) 365-3565, (914) 428-5840, (800) 431-2047
Alan Walker
    One of the major lecture management companies, PCA represents several thousand prominent speakers, with fees ranging from $1,000 to over $30,000.

10. Speakers Guild, Inc.
78 Old King's Highway, Sandwich, MA 02563
(617) 888-6702
Edward C. Larkin, Pres.

Branch Office:
11607 Stonewood Lane, Rockville, MD 20852
(301) 468-7778
Myrna Cooperstein

Founded in 1974, SG represents several hundred speakers and entertainers, who are available at fees from $1000 to $25,000.

11. Speakers International Inc.
51 W. Sherwood Terrace, Lake Bluff, IL 60044
(312) 295-5866
Telex: 270213
Cheryl L. Miller, Pres.

Formed in 1979 and located in suburban Chicago, Speakers International represents several hundred speakers in various fields.

12. Walters' International Speakers' Bureau
Box 1120, Glendora, CA 91740
(818) 335-8069, (800) 438-1242
Dottie Walters, Pres.
Lillet Walters, Exec. Dir.

A long-time professional speaker, Dottie Walters operates a speakers bureau and also is executive director of the International Group of Agents and Bureaus. She is the author of several books on selling to women, promoting your own business and other subjects. In 1988, Mrs. Walters and her daughter, Lillet, co-authored Speak and Grow Rich: The Handbook for Professional Speakers (Prentice Hall).

Publicists in the travel field and sponsors of tourism and other entertaining films should be familiar with Travelfilm Artists and Producers Guild (formerly Film Lecturers Association), 403 Lobos Marinos, San Clemente, CA 92672, phone (714) 492-2425. Thousands of college, club and other audiences attend film lectures, and many of these programs are conducted by members of this association.

If you want to find out which talent agency represents a particular entertainment celebrity, or if you want to contact the celebrity directly, you can read Variety or ask the headwaiter at Sardi's. Also—and this is preferable—you may subscribe to a service that provides publicists, editors and other clients with addresses, phone numbers and other information about how to contact celebrities. There also are several companies which specialize in the recruitment of celebrities for personal appearances, endorsements and other tie-ins. Keep in mind that a celebrity is a well-known person in the arts, business, education, politics, publishing, religion, science, society, sports and other fields and not just in stage, screen, radio and television.

Even if you are not in show business or do not regularly work with celebrities, there's a vicarious thrill in reading Celebrity Bulletin and Starr Report.

One issue of the Celebrity Bulletin, for example, noted the impending arrival and itinerary of H.R.H. Princess Margaret and the Earl of Snowdon (who, at that time, travelled together), Rod McKuen and others. The contact for the royal couple was listed as "B.I.S.," which to the non-Anglophile is British Information Services; for McKuen the liaison was simply "Buddah," which, one assumes, is Buddah Records. Sometimes, several contacts are listed, with a manager, agent, lecture bureau and press agent for the celebrity and the event all getting into the act.

If you're lucky enough to obtain a celebrity for a publicity appearance, you should remember to provide the full VIP treatment. However, first-class air travel, local limousines and hotel rooms cost more than ever before, and you and the celebrity should try to reach an understanding about all details involving money. Who will be responsible for actually paying the bills? Does the hotel bill include room service, barber or beauty salon, long-distance calls and other miscellaneous items? Who handles tipping?

Publicists often provide tour guides to handle all of these details and smooth the way, particularly when there is a hectic media schedule.

Press agents who represent celebrities often treasure, as their "stock-in-trade," lists of the home addresses or private offices of newspaper columnists. The movie "Sweet Smell of Success" helped to popularize the idea that the private secretary of a theatrical columnist can be a particularly valuable contact for a press agent. Many publicists frequently forget about columnists as major contacts for publicity. Among the columnists who are so prominent that they are celebrities themselves—and ideal for lectures and other projects—are "Abby," "Ann Landers," Jack Anderson, Art Buchwald, William Buckley, "Suzy," Sylvia Porter and many others.

Information about where to find several hundred columnists is a unique feature of the book, Syndicated Columnists, published by Larimi Communications, 5 West 37 St., N.Y. 10018.

The boom in sponsored special events and the tremendously increased use of celebrities in sales meetings and public relations projects has stimulated the publication of several new resources for finding celebrities. For example, Variety's Who's Who in Show Business is published by Garland Publishing, 136 Madison Ave., N.Y. 10016. It's $33 in hardcover and $20 in softcover. In 1986 the Putnam Publicity Group, 200 Madison Ave., N.Y. 10016, published The New Address Book (How to Reach Anyone Who's Anyone) by Michael Levine, which lists over 3,500 celebrities. And best news of all, it's only $7.95. Marquis Who's Who publications (3002 Glenview Rd., Wilmette, IL 60091) publishes the renowned Who's Who in America and Who's Who in Advertising (introduced in 1988, $225).

Once you've tracked down the celebrity, you (or your agent) will have to negotiate the arrangements. Sometimes, advertising, publicity or exposure to a large or important audience will enable you to obtain the celebrity at no cost. Nonprofit organizations and personal relationships have an edge in this area. Generally, a fee is involved.

The fee for the use of a celebrity depends on such factors as:

1. Advertising or publicity. The former generally calls for a higher fee, but not necessarily. Sometimes a performer wants the exposure or credit for a movie, play or book, and advertising is guaranteed, whereas publicity is speculative, and the ad rate in this case could be lower, or even waived.
2. The time required. A personal appearance is more costly than use of the name or existing photo.
3. The type of tie-in, time of year, personal need and other individual considerations.
4. Number of agents. Not all endorsement agencies have exclusive contracts; try to deal with the primary agent and not an intermediary.

Lloyd Kolmer, who operates a celebrity-endorsement company in New York, candidly states:

Prices quoted by agents or managers for stars, superstars and athletes are 'blue sky' numbers as there is no set price for talent. Each artist has a negotiable fee. It is our job to see that the performer is made aware of your interest and that such interest is properly transmitted through appropriate channels. In this way we have turned a vague, negative response into a positive reaction.

The following services can help you find the celebrities who can generate items in syndicated columns, create other publicity and also participate in public relations projects.

Many of the "talent brokers" are relentless, aggressive people, which aids in their pursuit of celebrities but sometimes makes them difficult as business associates. Several of the successful people in this field have become celebrities themselves, and they sometimes are snobbish toward low-fee public relations clients, as compared to advertising agencies.

1. Steve Arnold Enterprises
300 E. 40 St., N.Y. 10016
(212) 986-3188
Steve Arnold, Pres.
Arnold H. Arnold, V.P.
  Primarily a booking agency for professional athletes.

2. Athletes In Advertising
18 Tomney Rd., Greenwich, CT 06830
(203) 629-9098
Albert S. Kestnbaum, Pres.
  Formed in 1984 as a unit of Chestnut Communications, Inc., Athletes In Advertising provides creative promotional, production and marketing services to clients seeking sports personalities.

3. Blackman & Raber, Ltd.
545 Fifth Ave., N.Y. 10017
(212) 986-1420
Martin E. Blackman, Norman Raber
  In 1965, attorneys Martin Blackman and Steve Arnold, at that time each under 30, started Pro Sports Inc., a very successful company which negotiated several million dollars in contracts for its sports clients. The successor company, Blackman & Raber, specializes in sports, entertainment and leisure-time promotions, events, tournaments, sweepstakes, contests and also handles endorsements and appearances by athletes and entertainers.

4. Burns Sports Celebrity Service, Inc.
230 N. Michigan Ave., Chicago 60601
(312) 236-2377
David Burns
  A prominent athlete often is claimed to be represented by more than one talent agency, generally is available only during off-season and provides various complexities not encountered with other celebrities. Established in 1970, Burns can help to simplify some of these problems.

5. Capital Speakers Incorporated
770 Ntl. Press Bldg., Wash., DC 20045
(202) 393-0772
Frank E. McKenzie, Chm.
Phyllis Corbitt McKenzie, Pres.
  Formed in 1984, Capital Speakers is a full-service speakers bureau, representing speakers throughout the country, and not limited to the capital.

6. Celebrity Connection
8272 Sunset Blvd., L.A. 90046
(213) 650-0001
Barry Greenberg, Chm.
Rita Tateel, Pres.

Branch Office:
1001 Eagle Bay Dr., Ossining, NY 10562
(914) 941-6082

Celebrity Connection is a unique clearinghouse for celebrities wishing to become involved with charities, causes and political campaigns and for organizations looking for such celebrities. CC specializes in non-fee personal appearances, public service announcements, talent and the appointment of national spokespeople.

In addition, their Two Seas Productions unit, headed by Kelly Fitzpatrick, produces public service announcements with celebrities as spokespeople.

7. Celebrity Look-Alikes By Ron Smith

7060 Hollywood Blvd., L.A. 90028
(213) 467-3030
Ron Smith, Pres.

Branch Office:
235 E. 31 St., N.Y. 10016
(212) 532-7676

Started in 1976 by Hollywood producer Ron Smith, this company provides people who look and/or sound like celebrities. Fees range from $200 to $2,000 a day, depending on the popularity of the actual celebrity, the talent (singing, dancing or just appearing) of the look-alike and reason (advertising, publicity, charity) for the booking.

It's a clever idea and ideal for sales meetings, store openings and promotions, and who else can guarantee to deliver Elizabeth Taylor!

As a result of a tremendous amount of publicity, the company now has a roster of five thousand look-alikes and voice impressionists.

8. Celebrity Service International, Inc.

1780 Broadway, N.Y. 10019
(212) 245-1460
Vicki Bagley, Pres.
Bill Murray, Editor
Mara Sherwood, Marketing Dir., East Coast
Offices also in Paris, London, Rome and:
8732 Sunset Blvd., Hollywood, CA 90069
(213) 652-1700

In 1986, the company was acquired by Vicki Bagley. Mr. Blackwell, who has become a celebrity himself, remains as chairman. Ms. Bagley has made several changes, and also launched a new publication, the International Social Calendar ($500 a year).

Here's the way the Celebrity Service works:

In 1939, Earl Blackwell started a daily publication called Celebrity Bulletin, which lists celebrities who have just arrived in New York and other cities and gives their local addresses and telephone numbers, together with other information such as affiliations, press agents and other contacts. Also included is a "celebrity-of-the-day" biography, which is as delightful as any gossip column, except that the material always is favorable.

Celebrity Service screens clients in an attempt to eliminate those who might do damage with this kind of information. Publicists are eligible to profit from the information, however, for a monthly fee of $275 or $1650/year.

In addition to receiving the daily reports, subscribers can call the information service in order to obtain the biography or other information about thousands of public figures. This rapid, accurate and efficient service also is available to nonsubscribers, for a fee that varies according to the assignment, or $75 a month; $810 a year. The Bulletin alone is $165 a month and $1375 a year. Similarly, telephone service alone (limit of 5 calls/day) is $165/month and $1375/yr.

How Celebrity Service compiles its data (some of it cannot be obtained from any other source!) is a closely guarded treasure. Obviously, the reporters include travel agents, airline and hotel clerks, publishers and press agents.

Celebrity Service also can provide, for varying fees, lists of specially screened names of personalities to invite to parties, seminars, openings or other events, and assistance in creating the promotions and events and in obtaining the personalities. Knowing the individual preferences, taboos and availability of famous personalities enables Celebrity Service to make imaginative and valuable suggestions for any project involving endorsements, personal appearances, or anything else involving celebrities.

Celebrity Service is a well-organized operation. For example, subscribers must provide in writing the names (up to three) of people who can call in for information. Annual subscribers are entitled to information on up to 7 celebrities per day; short-term subscribers are limited to fewer requests.

Celebrity Service also issues two other publications:

Theatrical Calendar. Published since 1942, this biweekly digest lists the current and future director, press agent and company manager of hundreds of productions on and off Broadway. The editor is interested in receiving news releases about anything related to the theater. Subscription is $100 a year, or $10 an issue.

Contact Book. To anyone who works in the entertainment and allied fields, you can't function without a telephone, typewriter and this compact annual directory. For only $29 a copy you can buy the most comprehensive, up-to-date and accurate collection of names, addresses and phone numbers of producers, agents, nightclubs, ticket agents, publishers and others connected with international show business. The soft-cover book of about 7000 listings on 192 pages includes sections on New York, Los Angeles and London.

9. Celebrity Speakers Bureau
1105 17 Ave., S., Nashville, TN 37212
(615) 327-2395
Candace Brar, Pres.

Formed in 1979, CSB is located in the heart of "Music Row." Its clients include country music stars, plus dozens of other entertainers and speakers in all fields.

10. Garvey Marketing Group
4320 La Jolla Village Dr., San Diego 92122
(619) 453-6666
Steve Garvey, Pres.
John Boggs, CEO

Started in 1983 by baseball player Steve Garvey, the Garvey Marketing Group arranges for endorsements and appearances by athletes and also creates and conducts tournaments and other events. The group is a division of Steve Garvey, Inc.

11. Ingels Inc.
8111 Beverly Blvd. #308, Hollywood, CA 90048
(213) 852-0300
Curry Walls

Formed in 1975 by former comic actor Marty Ingels, this company moved quickly into the league of big-time celebrity finders. Born in Brooklyn in 1936, Marty Ingels was a partner in Tele-House, a company that sells records via television advertising, and he is a close friend of many celebrities. He married actress Shirley Jones in 1977. A few people still remember him for the mid-60's TV series, "I'm Dickens, He's Fenster." He was Fenster.

The company has a staff of about eight in Hollywood and representatives in New York and Nashville.

12. International Management Group

1 Eric Plaza, Cleveland 44114
(216) 522-1200
John Weil

The largest company in the world in sports promotion, IMG manages many superstars and consults on sports and leisure time marketing promotions.

13. Lippservice

305 W. 52 St., N.Y. 10019
(212) 757-0962
Ros Lipps

Ros Lipps, who was manager of Earl Blackwell's Celebrity Service for 15 years, started her own celebrity consulting service in 1987. She does not publish a bulletin.

Other services (hourly or project fees) include planning parties, sending out invitations and other glamorous and non-glamorous chores.

14. Lloyd Kolmer Enterprises, Inc.

65 W. 55 St., N.Y. 10019
(212) 582-4735

Lloyd Kolmer, who for 12 years was head of the commercial department of the William Morris Agency, heads one of the world's largest companies in the celebrity endorsement field. Born in 1930, he still has the youthful, fashionable appearance and manner of a show business agent.

He has set up many well-known advertising endorsements for such clients as MCI (Burt Lancaster, Merv Griffin, Joan Rivers), Atari (Alan Alda), Scoundrel Fragrance (Joan Collins), American Express (Karl Malden), Sweet 'n Low (Bill Crosby), Coca-Cola and Texaco (Bob Hope).

Kolmer generally charges less than 10 percent of the artist's compensation.

Kolmer also is very savvy about public relations and sympathetically appreciates that public relations clients generally have smaller budgets and different orientations than advertisers. For example, he often contacts a celebrity's publicist, rather than talent agent or manager, for low-budget (or no budget) public service or publicity projects.

15. Look Who's Talking

Box 7665, Newport Beach, CA 92658-7665
(714) 759-9304, (800) 433-2314
Mark Victor Hansen, Chm.
Jeanie Reilly, Program Coordinator

A popular speaker (motivational seminars with emphasis on humor), Mark Victor Hansen also operates a speakers bureau. He has written several books, including Future Diary, and recorded many cassettes. These activities are handled by his other company, Mark Victor Hansen and Associates.

16. Mattgo Enterprises, Inc.

185 E. 85 St., N.Y. 10028
(212) 427-4444
Matt Merola and Paul Goetz

Tom Seaver, Bob Griese, Reggie Jackson, Nolan Ryan, Gale Sayers, Gary Carter, Ron Darling, Cathy Rigby and other leading national and regional athletes, and sports greats such as Joe Frazier, are the specialty of this firm.

In case you haven't figured it out, Mattgo was concocted from the names of the proprietors.

17. Medical Speakers Agency, Inc.
271 Madison Ave., N.Y. 10016
(212) 683-6253
Anne Burton, Pres.

An unusual, specialized company, Medical Speakers Agency operates a computerized search service to find a well-qualified physician who is available as a spokesperson, lecturer, author and other public relations assignments. There is no fee. The physician pays 15% of the honorarium to Medical Speakers Agency.

18. Publicity Enterprises, Inc.
2175 Lemoine Ave., Fort Lee, NJ 07024
(201) 585-1500
Haskell Cohen, Pres.

Several publicists who represent famous people or regularly work with them often are available to help in the recruitment of celebrities for commercial or other sponsors.

Haskell Cohen, who was the public relations director of the National Basketball Association, has represented many athletic teams and sports enterprises for more than 30 years. He frequently is able to recruit sports celebrities at reasonable fees.

19. Ross Associates Speakers Bureau, Inc.
250 W. 57 St., N.Y. 10107
(212) 582-5700
Blanche Ross, Pres.

Branch Offices:
370 Cherry St., Denver, CO 80220
(303) 860-9400
Betty Naster, V.P.

1362 N. Doheny Dr., L.A. 90069
(213) 858-1944
Natalie Goodman, Pauline Buck, V.Ps.

Formed in 1981 by Blanche Ross and her cousin, Dee-Ann Mernit, Ross Associates specializes in women speakers, primarily for events at stores and women's groups. The company also has a men's division. It operates a speakers bureau for Working Woman magazine, featuring Kate Rand Lloyd and other editors.

20. Speakers Unlimited
Box 27225, Columbus, OH 43227
(614) 864-3703
D. Michael Frank

Founded in 1970, Speakers Unlimited provides speakers and also conducts seminars. Mike Frank is a former president of the National Speakers Association.

21. Roz Starr, Inc.
240 West End Ave., N.Y. 10023
(212) 354-5050
Roz Starr, Pres.

Formerly an employee of Earl Blackwell, Roz Starr has had her own business since 1960 and offers a service similar to that of Celebrity Service.

For a monthly fee of $80, Starr subscribers receive a daily report and have access by mail and phone to unlimited research involving such ''vital information'' as the name of the hotel at which Michael Jackson is staying during his visit to New York, the address of the apartment at which Frank Sinatra will be staying during his visit, and the telephone number of Elizabeth Taylor's press agent.

Publicists who do not regularly work with show business celebrities still will enjoy reading the Starr New York Report, since it's more fascinating than any newspaper gossip column. The report frequently states the business purpose of the celebrity's visit to the city.

A tip-off to the ''fly-by-night'' nature of some of the press agents and others who subscribe to Roz Starr's report can be gleaned from the fact that subscribers must pay their monthly fees in advance and, unlike almost all other publications, service is cut off immediately if payments are not received.

Miss Starr charges less than Celebrity Service and also includes research and other special services. Theatrical columnists and others who thrive on this data often subscribe to the publications and services of both firms.

The effervescent, efficacious Roz Starr also recruits celebrities and provides other promotional services, at modest fees.

The data bank of the Starr office consists of several dozen index card files, plus the amazing memory of Roz and her assistants. Roz had polio when she was two years old, but she has continued to race, and can handle more phone calls per hour than almost anyone else.

22. World Class Sports
9171 Wilshire Blvd., Beverly Hills, CA 90210
(213) 278-2010
Andrew Woolf

Branch Office:
110 E. 59 St., N.Y. 10022
(212) 593-6340
Jim Keller

Formed in 1983, WCSE is a sports marketing and talent agency.

Chapter 4

Clipping Bureaus

Probably no publicity service is more widely used by publicists than clipping bureaus and, at the same time, is the least understood and the most frequently criticized. Clipping bureaus provide vital information, and almost every publicist subscribes to one or more bureaus on a continuing or occasional basis. In addition, clipping bureaus are used by thousands of advertising and sales promotion directors, educators, Government officials and others who are interested in what's currently being published on subjects of importance to them.

Very few clipping bureau subscribers have ever visited the bureau with which they do business or any other bureau. Most subscribers are only vaguely aware of the mechanics of operating a clipping bureau and the large staffs and facilities involved in a national clipping bureau operation. Increased knowledge of the mechanics of a clipping bureau operation also may lead to valid suggestions by subscribers for improvements. For example, a few clipping bureaus identify those clippings that appeared on page one, which came about as a result of a suggestion from a client.

The major clipping bureaus issue booklets which include instructions and advice to subscribers. Subscribers are urged to send copies of news releases to the bureaus, together with an indication of where the releases were sent. Subscribers are also urged to be specific in their listing of companies, products and other names in which they are interested, and to issue this list to the bureau periodically as a means of updating it, as well as reminding the bureau's readers.

From time to time, a subscriber will retain two or three clipping bureaus, in an attempt to obtain more comprehensive coverage, and also to answer the question, "Which clipping bureau, if any, is completely efficient?"

The results of these studies seem to be inconclusive. Invariably, one clipping bureau will omit a major clipping from an important publication, and a second bureau will omit an equally important clipping from another source. It is terribly frustrating, though most of the bureaus do better than they are given credit. Furthermore, they are extremely competitive and continually attempt to improve their services.

A few major agencies and public relations departments retain two services in order to obtain more comprehensive clipping coverage. Bacon's reports that using a second bureau will generally result in a 25 percent increase in the unduplicated clippings received. One reason for this is the inability of the national services to obtain subscriptions to all of the *multiple* editions of daily newspapers. A bureau located in New York or Chicago can obtain all editions of the newspapers in its area, but not nationally. Thus, a bureau usually provides more complete coverage in its area of operation.

When the emphasis of the publicity program is directed to specific areas of the country or to the specialized business and trade press, the publicist should consider the strengths of the various services and, if the budget permits, select two services that complement each other. A combination of two of the five national services listed or a combination of a national service and a regional/state service are ways that the clipping return can be increased.

Clipping bureaus generally have a monthly reading or retainer fee plus a charge per clipping. Here's something you may not know. Articles of more than one page generally count as one clipping *per page*. Thus, your name may be incidentally mentioned within a 10-page magazine article, and you'll be charged for 10 clippings. Some bureaus are compassionate about this problem and charge one clipping for each two pages, if the pages are reproduced, rather than originals.

Among the misconceptions of many publicists:

1. Clipping bureaus are staffed by inefficient and visually handicapped people. Not true. "Readers" and "clippers" are extremely capable, but the clipping business—like the publicity business—is not as efficient as its proprietors claim.
2. Clipping bureaus get their publications free, and that's one reason they miss a lot. Not true. Except for a few bureaus associated with publisher's associations, clipping bureaus (including all of the national bureaus) pay for their subscriptions and subscribe to literally thousands of publications. This is extremely costly and makes clipping services a bargain that cannot be duplicated in-house.

Major users of clipping bureaus occasionally talk about forming their own clipping operation. Upon investigation into the enormous resources necessary to conduct a national publicity checking operation, these conversations invariably are terminated. The incoming mail of each of the large, national clipping bureaus totals more than a ton of newsprint, and more than 20,000 clippings are sent out—every day!

It is not essential to retain a clipping bureau in order to provide results of a publicity program, but the use of clipping bureaus has become almost a standard part of any publicity operation.

The key question remains: "Which bureau or bureaus should a publicist use?"

The two largest bureaus in the United States are Burrelle's and Luce, each with several thousand clients, several hundred employees and coverage of more than 15,000 publications. There are times, however, when a smaller or specialized bureau is more economical or efficient, or perhaps more convenient.

All bureaus issue credit for clippings marked in error which are returned within a reasonable period of time. The bureaus also are anxious to receive criticisms, complaints and suggestions for improved service.

Clients can help themselves and the clipping services by learning more about the companies with which they do business, as well as other bureaus.

Whichever service you retain, keep them advised of all news releases which you distribute and also of special restrictions and other "alerts."

In an article in Public Relations Journal, John P. French, Sr. V.P. and Treasurer of Luce Press Clipping Bureau, offered the following advice, which still is timely and helpful:

When restrictions must be made, the instruction should be tangible and stated in the negative. This leaves the least possible chance of readers missing desired clippings because of a misunderstanding.

For instance, never tell a bureau to "mark only financial news." What might seem financial news to one reader may in the mind of the one sitting next to her not to be financial news at all . . . and what might seem financial news in her judgment may not be in the client's opinion. The same is true about omitting something like "unfavorable news." It isn't tangible; it leaves too much to judgment . . .

A bureau must be kept abreast of publicity activities. Put the bureau on your mailing list to receive every release sent out. When received, these releases are checked and key words underlined—then passed among the readers so that they receive an extra reminder . . .

Return any clippings contrary to what was requested. These are analyzed at once. If any change in an order is required, it can be made quickly. If, on the other hand, it was a case of carelessness by the mailer, it can be taken up with the person at fault and, of course, the client's account credited.

One further suggestion: Whenever possible, advise the bureau immediately of any special placement which has appeared or is likely to appear. In the case of syndicated columns, wire service and Sunday supplement articles, you also may wish to save money by requesting only one, or a representative sampling, of the clippings.

As with all publicity services, clipping bureaus operate more efficiently if your instructions are complete and reflect a knowledge of their operation.

When you initiate service with a clipping bureau, consider whether or not you want to issue the following restrictions:

1. Omit listings in financial tables.
2. Omit specific publications (such as those you subscribe to).
3. Omit keyed mats (that is, the newspaper features distributed by the "mat services").
4. Provide only one edition of a chain of newspapers or magazines in which the same material appears in each edition.
5. Omit foreign publications.
6. Omit specific regions, such as areas in which the company does not operate.

Harold J. Gerberg, formerly of Burrelle's Clipping Bureau, stated that the biggest single cause of customer complaints arises from outmoded or incomplete instructions from the client, and offers nine major reasons why clipping bureaus may miss clippings:

1. There is the distinct possibility that even if the material were printed by various media, the key word or key phrase may have been deleted by the editors. This would make certain releases extremely difficult to recognize.
2. Frequently, an item is used in only one edition of a particular newspaper, and currently it is not practical for a clipping service to subscribe to every edition of ever newspaper in the country. Most bureaus, however, do subscribe to several editions of all the major papers.
3. The item may have appeared prior to the time the order was placed or prior to the time the bureau was advised that it should appear.
4. Occasionally, an item is printed two or three months after the bureau has been advised to be on the alert for it. Unless it is a constantly active subject in the press, the readers cannot be expected to recognize a photo or release which was shown to them months before it actually appeared in print.
5. While magazine and newspaper subscription lists are carefully maintained and checked, a certain percentage are lost in the mails despite all precautions.
6. (a) In the case of syndicated columns, a paragraph appearing in the newspaper in which it originated is frequently omitted in the out-of-town newspapers.
   (b) Syndicated columns, mat stories and feature items are often purchased in a "package deal"

but are used at the discretion of the editor. Consequently, the entire column or story containing mention of the subject requested may not appear.

7. National news of importance often crowds out items of local or limited interest which would normally have been allotted space. This would affect numerous releases.

8. Despite the fact that agencies receive requests from the editors, for additional information or glossy photos, later developments may preclude use of the material.

9. Last, but not least, thousands of expertly written, newsworthy releases, which entailed long hours of effort and research, are lost in the mountainous stacks of publicity from which each editor must select according to space needs.

One of the finest of the state clipping bureaus is the Michigan Press Reading Service. Its former manager, John E. Laycock, offered these two suggestions 15 years ago. They still are valid.

First, I find it helpful here in Michigan to explain to clients that this bureau, like most others, produces information by something akin to assembly line procedures. While readers can be incredibly selective in their marking (considering that our readers, for example, must be able to identify and correctly code more than 3,000 subjects, from memory), clients should be careful to make their instructions clear, concise and as simple as possible. Complicated orders loaded down with numerous restrictions delay production, and are the most frequent cause of "slow" clipping service (the industry's most common criticism).

And, second, clients should notify their bureau when errors are being made. It always amazes me how long, and in such silence, clipping clients are willing to endure unsatisfactory service. What they fail to realize is that most bureaus turn out tens of thousands of clips each week, and, in general, have only the most imperfect notion of what information is being sent to each client. If an error creeps into the system (most often a misunderstood instruction by one or more readers), that error can stand uncorrected for weeks or months. A reasonable complaint usually 1) corrects the misunderstanding, and 2) reminds readers to pay close attention to the client's order.

In general, then, most clients will obtain the best results if they maintain frequent contact with their bureau—first training the bureau's staff to their particular needs—and then alerting them to errors or special situations.

The first clipping bureau was started in Paris in 1876 and was called L'Argus de la Presse (The All-seeing Eye of the Newspapers). The field has developed considerably all over the world. Here is some information which you may not have known about more than 90 different clipping bureaus, all of which are in business to provide you with as many clippings as possible. As with other businesses, their current prices reflect the increased costs of labor, materials and postage.

A. NATIONAL CLIPPING SERVICES

Only two clipping bureaus offer a comprehensive, national service that includes most U.S. daily and weekly newspapers, consumer and business magazines and other publications. The basic services are similar in each of these bureaus, though each offers particular innovations and auxiliary services.

The two largest companies are Burrelle's and Luce. Both read major trade and business publications, in addition to almost all of the general-circulation newspapers and magazines published in the United States.

Many advertising and public relations agencies often ask clipping bureaus about quantity discounts. A few of the large agencies purchase several thousand dollars' worth of clipping services each month, so contract rates or other discounts could be a significant factor in doing business with a specific bureau. However, the bureaus claim that they operate on a very small profit margin and, for this reason, as well as others, do not provide any type of discount. An agency that retains a clipping bureau for several of its clients must pay a separate reading fee or service charge for each of the clients. One variation exists in the manner of billing, with some bureaus providing a single bill to an agency for all of its clients and others providing separate bills.

A minimum period of service generally is stipulated in the contract or letter of agreement. It usually is three months. The rates are similar but there are variations. Following is information about five of the largest clipping bureaus which offer national coverage.

1. ATP Clipping Bureau
5 Beekman St., N.Y. 10038
(212) 349-1177
Israel Fleiss

Formerly called American Trade Press Clipping Bureau, because it specialized in business publications, ATP now reads more than 10,000 publications, including daily newspapers and consumer magazines, as well as U.S. and foreign trade publications. In spite of its expanded coverage, ATP still is known as a trade press specialist. Industrial clients and others interested solely in trade and technical publications sometimes feel that ATP offers a better service in this area than the larger, general bureaus. Companies sometimes retain ATP in addition to one of the general clipping bureaus.

Competitors of ATP claim they read all of the publications covered by ATP with as much care and accuracy and cover an enormous number of additional publications, though at rates which are higher.
Rates: $175 per month plus 75 cents per clipping.

2. Bacon's Clipping Bureau
332 S. Michigan Ave., Chicago 60604
(312) 922-2400, (800) 621-0561
Patricia Clifford, Customer Services Mgr.

Established by R. H. Bacon Sr., in 1932, as the first clipping specialist in trade and technical publications, Bacon's now covers about 5,000 business, trade, consumer and farm magazines, all of which are listed in its well-known Bacon's Publicity Checkers. (Whether or not you use this service, these annual directories are essential aids and are described in the media directories section.)

In addition, Bacon's covers the top 500 daily newspapers. It does not read the remaining daily newspapers, nor does it cover any of the weekly newspapers, except in Illinois. Subscribers to Bacon's claim that this means the bureau can do a better job among the most important newspapers, while others may use Bacon's only when they are interested in magazine coverage.

Bacon's has developed a service called "Selected Subject Research," which has been adopted by other bureaus. Using this service, subscribers can get clippings on broad subjects, rather than limiting coverage to mentions of their own company or products. Bacon's also provides coverage of advertising and competitive checking.
Rates: $125 a month plus 79 cents a clipping.

3. Burrelle's Press Clipping Service
75 E. Northfield Ave., Livingston, NJ 07039
(212) 227-5570 (New York tie line), (201) 992-6600, (800) 631-1160
Arthur Wynne Jr., Robert Waggoner and Frederick Wynne, Partners

With a staff of over 1,000 employees, headquartered across the Hudson River from New York City in Livingston, NJ, Burrelle's probably is the largest clipping bureau in the world. Major reading facilities are also located in Provo, Utah, and Presque Isle, Maine.

Burrelle's coverage within the U.S. includes all (about 1,700) daily newspapers, all (about 8,300) weekly newspapers, and almost all (about 6,300) consumer and trade publications. If there is a publication that is not on Burrelle's list, notify them of your interest in the publication and the company will add it. The Latin American and Canadian services, for example, are unique among domestic clipping services and were added in response to requests from clients.

The company publishes a newsletter, Your Clipping Analyst, which is available to subscribers and potential clients. Though it is basically a promotion for Burrelle's, it often includes helpful advice and other articles of interest to publicists. A NewsClip Analysis Service provides monthly analyses of number of clippings, circulation, agate line measurement and summary of content.

Burrelle's NewsExpress provides same morning service, via telecopier, of 39 daily newspapers, 11 major magazines, and network and local broadcasts.

Burrelle's also has an Information Search Service, which includes all of the major database services, such as Nexis, Dialog, Vu/Text and Data Times.

Clippings are mailed twice a week, though a daily optional extra fee service also is available.

Rates: $172 per month service charge plus 92 cents per clipping. The usual minimum service is three months, but a one-month contract can be obtained if requested.

4. Luce Press Clippings, Inc.

42 South Center, Mesa, AZ 85210
(602) 834-4884, (800) 528-8226
William French, Pres.
Darrell A. Vincent, Customer Service Mgr.

Branch Offices:
407 S. Dearborn St., Chicago 60605
(312) 427-0906

912 Kansas Ave., Topeka, KS 66612
(913) 232-0201

420 Lexington Ave., N.Y. 10170
(212) 889-6711

Founded in 1881, Luce provides a comprehensive service, with coverage of daily and weekly newspapers, and several thousand trade and consumer magazines, totaling over 15,000 publications.

Luce maintains regional reading offices, primarily in Topeka and Mesa. This decentralization speeds mail delivery of publications into and out of the Luce office.

International service is provided on a subcontract basis, with the exception of many Canadian publications which are included as part of the regular service.

Luce has developed a computerized report which categorizes and tabulates clippings. This brings order out of chaos for some clients who receive large numbers of clippings, but a client generally must provide its own qualitative analysis of clippings because of the variety of subjective factors.

In 1979, Luce added an important new service, Teleclips, which are computer typed transcripts of television news programs. Luce currently monitors network news programs and local programs in major markets. The service is described in the broadcast monitoring chapter.

Rates: $169 per month plus 89 cents per clipping.

5. Press Intelligence, Inc.
1334 G St., N.W., Wash., DC 20005
(202) 783-5810
Esomor Krash, Pres.
J. Martin Jones, V.P.

Formed in 1949, this company has no reading or sales branch offices and operates with a smaller staff than other national bureaus. However, many of its subscribers state that the quality of service is excellent, and the firm's coverage does include 1,400 major daily newspapers, 4,000 weekly newspapers, business, trade, and consumer publications. Other users recommend the bureau because its rates are a bit less than its competitors.

Rates: $160 per month plus 74 cents per clipping.

Press Intelligence readers usually search for subject matter, rather than just company names or key words. Other special services include early morning Teletype service and telephone facsimile transmission to clients informing them of current news. This news is derived from 16 major daily newspapers that are read by Press Intelligence on the same day of publication.

Press Intelligence published a unique directory in 1957 and updated it in 1960. The directory has not been revised since then and is noteworthy only in an historical context. The Press Intelligence Directory took the 712 top daily newspapers in the country and provided data which is not included in any other book. For example, very few syndicates provide lists of their subscribers. Press Intelligence carefully went through 712 newspapers and then listed the specific newspapers which published each of the more than 200 different writers, from Joseph Alsop to Earl Wilson.

Most of the columnists in the 1960 directory no longer are columning, and it indeed would be useful if Press Intelligence or one of the clipping bureaus issued an update on this directory.

B. SPECIALIZED NATIONAL SERVICES

In addition to the five major national clipping services, several national bureaus offer specialized reading services.

1. American Press Clipping Service, Inc.
119 Nassau St., N.Y. 10038
(212) 962-3797
Scott Kelly

This bureau subscribes to major daily and weekly newspapers and trade publications, and also has arrangements with regional and state bureaus throughout the country. As a result, it can offer a comprehensive service, though its rate structure is different from the other national bureaus in that it offers an advance payment rate of $1650 for 1,200 clippings, or one year of service, which may include up to six subjects. An alternate rate plan, which includes up to two subjects, calls for a monthly reading fee of $125 plus 75 cents per clipping.

2. Home Economics Reading Service, Inc. (HERS)
733 15th St., N.W., #248, Wash., DC 20005
(202) 347-4763
Alice Brueck, Pres.
Gloria Hansen, V.P.

Started in 1958 as a unique specialized service for food and women's interest publicists, HERS reads *only* the women's sections of major newspapers, plus weeklies of important population areas. The readers are experienced home economists who follow all developments in foods, nutrition, consumer problems and home appliances and have an understanding of subscribers' aims. They are known for accuracy, reading "for sense", as well as company or product names as directed. They also clip advertising.

Rates: $140 per month plus 80 cents per clipping.

Reviews on File

In 1929, Estelle Boyd started Literary Clipping Service, a specialized clipping service of book reviews. The company was sold in 1960 to Burrelle's. Mrs. Boyd's daughter, Dorothy Brandt, retained the morgue of about two million clippings. Under the name of Reviews on File, she provided a unique service of original book reviews, at about 20 cents a clipping, for many years.

C. INTERNATIONAL CLIPPING SERVICES

Clients who are interested in clippings from publications outside of the U.S. can obtain these clippings in a variety of ways, depending on whether they want a representative survey or more comprehensive coverage. If one has a sufficiently large budget, the most efficient service probably can be provided by retaining clipping bureaus in each of the countries. Though many countries do not have clipping bureaus, the business is fairly well developed in most of the English-speaking countries and others in which publicity has become an important industry. For example, there are many large clipping bureaus in London, one of which publishes a directory similar to Bacon's Publicity Checker (P.R. Planner, published by Romeike & Curtice, Ltd.). The major British bureaus, which refer to their products as "cuttings," rather than clippings, are:

1. Durrant's Press Cutting Ltd.
103 Whitecross St. London ECIY 8QT
(01) 588-3671

Established in 1880, Durrant's is headed by T.W. Lorenzen and A.M. Kennedy. The cost for a minimum subscription of 100 cuttings or six months is about $120, depending on the exchange rate, with no reading fee. 1,000 cuttings cost about $830, a sizable saving.

2. International Press-Cutting Bureau
224/226 Walsworth Rd., London SE17 1JE
(01) 708-2113

A large operation, International Press-Cutting is headed by Robert Podro.

3. Newsclip Ltd.
52/53 Fetter Lane, London EC4A 1BL
(01) 353-7191

Newsclip was located for many years on Fleet Street, the hub of British journalism. The company is headed by Charles Goodman.

4. Romeike & Curtice Ltd. (also Media Information Group)
Green Lanes, London N13 5TP
(01) 882-0155

Affiliated with Bacon's, it is the oldest and largest U.K. clip bureau. The managing director is Paul J. Morgan.

A few U.S. bureaus include Canadian coverage, if specified. The major Canadian bureaus are:

1. Bowdens Press Clippings Ltd.
624 King St., W., Toronto, Ontario M5V 2X9
(416) 598-2625

Covers about 2,000 publications, including all daily and weekly newspapers, magazines and trade publications. The charge for unrestricted reading of every mention is $100 per month plus 55 cents per clipping, with a two-month minimum. Restricted, special instruction reading is extra.

More information about the extensive operation of Bowdens is described in a separate listing later in this section.

2. Canadian Press Clipping Services
4601 Yonge St., Toronto, Ontario M2N 5L9
(416) 221-1660
Joanne Crilly, Mgr.

Covers the Canadian daily and weekly newspapers and other publications. The company is a division of Maclean-Hunter Ltd. Rates are $120 a month reading charge plus 65 cents a clipping. All prices are Canadian dollars and include French and English service. Daily mailings (instead of weekly) are $37 a month additional. Major U.S. dailies are also available.

Maclean-Hunter publishes Maclean's, The Financial Post and several other business and consumer publications.

3. clip inc.
111 St. Urbain, Montreal, Quebec H2Z 1Y6
(514) 871-1466
Telex: (05) 267 371
Bernard Ozoux

The newest of the Canadian bureaus, clip inc. specializes in French publications, though it also reads major English-language newspapers and other publications.

4. John P. Stewart News Services
233 Dupras Ave., LaSalle, Quebec H8R 3S4
(514) 366-8410
John P. Stewart, Pres.

A small personal operation, Stewart reads Canadian newspapers and several hundred other publications, and also conducts research and editorial assignments. In 1987, he launched a monthly newsletter, Global Plastics Report.

5. Western Press Clipping Bureau
910-207 W. Hastings St., Vancouver, BC V6B 1H7
(604) 684-8928
Marjorie Stewart, Mgr.

Covers the provinces of British Columbia, the Yukon and Alberta Northwest Territories. Founded in 1947, this is an efficient regional operation. Charges are $95 per month plus 40 cents per clipping for "all mention" service, and $70 per month plus 40 cents per clipping for either of the provinces/territories.

The owner, Dean Miller, operates a public relations agency in Vancouver. Services include editorial and advertising clipping service, legislative research, opinion polling and news release distribution.

More information about foreign clipping services can be obtained from the International Federation of Press Clipping Bureaus, a trade association of about 50 companies from 30 countries. Founded in 1953, the Federation is headquartered at Streulistrasse 19, Zurich CH-8030, Switzerland. Formerly located in Paris, the exact name is Federation Internationale des Bureaux d'Extraits de Presse. Dieter Henne is Secretary-General. The members of FIBEP employ an estimated 2,350 people to read more than 50,000 publications published in about 30 countries. In summary, the clipping bureau business is not as "cut-and-dried" as one might think. Members of FIBEP outside of the U.S., Canada and Great Britain are (listed alphabetically by country):

1. Neville Jeffress/Pidler Pty. Ltd.
Prospect House, Blackburn Lane, Surry Hills 2010
Sydney 2002, Australia
A large operation with offices throughout Australia, the proprietors are June Pidler and Neville Jeffress. Monitors Australian print and broadcast media, publishes media guides and operates a mailing service.

2. Observer GMBH
Lessinggasse 21, 1020 Vienna, Austria
Herbert Laszlo, Brigette Eisenbacher, Katherina Gerwin

3. Auxipress SA (also Euro-Argus SA)
37-39 Quai Pierres de Taille
1000 Brussels, Belgium
Auxipress, founded in 1919, which covers Belgium and sends out clippings daily, and Euro-Argus, which covers Europe and is associated with bureaus elsewhere in the world, are both owned by Auxiliaire de la Presse, headed by Joachim V. Beust.

4. PRESSEklip
65 Glentevej
2400 Copenhagen NV, Denmark
Klemern K. Kirk, M.D.

5. Sita
Kasarmikatu 44
00130 Helsinki, Finland
Heikki Rikkonen
The exact name is Sanomalehtien Ilmoitustoimisto Oy, but you can call them Sita. The number to call is (358) 0175966; ask for Mrs. Melita Wilkman. Sita also does broadcast monitoring.

6. Agence Francaise d'Extraits de Presse
13 Avenue de l'Opera
Paris 75001, France
Pierre Bussac, Roland Dreyfus

7. Argus de la Presse
21 Boulevard Montmartre
Paris 75002, France
Bernard d'Aramon

8. Nouveau Courrier de la Presse Lit-Tout
15 Rue Colonel Driant
Paris 75001, France
Xavier de Monredon

9. Presse-Clearing
1 Rue Mirabeau
Paris 75016, France
(33-1) 4224 1356
Telecopier: (33-1) 4520 1454
F.M. d'Unienville, Gen. Mgr.
Operated by the Centre de Documentation Internationale, Presse-Clearing provides clipping service from about 80 countries, plus abstracts in English from Chinese, Danish, Dutch, French, German, Italian, Japanese, Norwegian, Spanish and Swedish.

10. Typos
Aristeidou 6
Athens 10559, Greece
Apostolos Douravaris

11. "Antal" Persknipseldienst
Waalsdorpesweg 122
The Hague, Holland (Netherlands)
Z.K. Berkes, M.G. Berkes

12. Persbureau Vas Dias N.V
Singel 91, Box 491
Amsterdam 1001, Holland (Netherlands)
Miss M. van Wyngaarden

13. Newscan Company Ltd.
26 Harbour Rd., Hong Kong
Located on the 38th floor of the China Resources Building, Newscan is headed by Berry Lo and Kenneth Chu. Services include public relations, monitoring and research, as well as a clipping bureau.

14. Mahir (Hungarian Publicity Company)
Box 76
Budapest H 10543, Hungary
Tamas Farago

15. Midlun
Box 155
Reykjavik 121, Iceland
Orn Thorisson

16. Indian Press Service and Business Information Bureau
16-a, Friends Colony
New Delhi 110065, India
P.L. Jhunjhunwals and Sudha Jhunjhunwala

Supplies business information and issues News Bulletins, Tender Service Bulletins and Parliamentary Digests.

17. Irish Press Cuttings Ltd.
7 Ely Place
Dublin 2, Ireland
Bill McHugh
Reads 110 newspapers and over 150 publications in the Republic of Ireland, Northern Ireland, and also monitors radio and TV.

18. Ifat Press Clippings, TV and Radio Monitoring
7 Dereh Petah-Tikva Street
Tel-Aviv 66181, Israel
Carlos Begas

19. L'Argo della Stampa (formerly L'Eco)
Via G. Compagnoni 28, Box 12094
20129 Milan, Italy
Sandra Colnaghi

20. Naigai Pressclipping Bureau Ltd.
14-4 Okubo, 3-Chome, Shinjuku-ku
Tokyo 160, Japan
Taro Ishihata
Founded in 1939, Naigai is a large operation. Its phone is (03) 208-5134.

21. Press Bureau Ltd.
Box 3711, Wellington, New Zealand

22. Norske Argus A/S
Storgt. 25, Postboks 1180 Sentrum 0107
Oslo 1 Norway
Stein Johansen

23. Pan Asia News (pvt) Limited
Box 5486, Ebrahim Bldg., W. Wharf Rd.
Karachi-2, Pakistan
Aijaz Haider, A.K. Ahmed
In business since 1963, Pan Asia is a sizeable bureau. The pvt in the name means it's a private company.

24. Biuro Wycinkow Prasowych "GLOB"
Al. Stanow Zjednoczonych 53
04-141 Warszawa, Poland
Marek Rasinski

25. Recorte
Av. Almirante Reis 19-20E, Apt. 2571
Lisbon, P-1114, Portugal
Ivo de Almeida

26. Peace Translation and Clipping Services Peace Centre
1, Sophia Road 05-35
Singapore 0922, Singapore
L.K. Chua
   Coverage of English, Malay and Chinese publications. $80 (Singapore) per month plus 80 cents per clipping. Coverage of Malaysia is additional.

27. S.A. Press Cutting Agency Pty. Ltd.
26 Pickering Street
Durban, Natal, South Africa 4001
   A long-time major operation—located on the second floor of Lionel House—the managing director is I.M.W. Rellie.

28. Agencia Internacional Camarasa, C.L.
Plaza Reyes Magos 12
Madrid 28007, Spain
Antonio Camarasa

29. AB Pressurklipp
Box 1510, 171 29 Solna, Sweden

30. International Argus der Presse AG
Streulistrasse 19
8030 Zurich, Switzerland
   Founded in 1896, Argus reads a selection of 300 international publications, plus all—about 1,500—Swiss publications.

31. United Pacific International Inc.
4th Floor, Yuan Chiang Bldg., 316 Nanking E. Rd.,
Box 81-417. Taipei, Taiwan
Chen Yih

32. Der Ausschnitt
Achterberg Gmbh & Co.
1000 Berlin 62, West Germany
Renate Achterbert

33. Hermes Zeitungsausschnittburo
Weberstrasse 92
D-5300
Bonn 1, West Germany
Rosemarie Severin

34. Metropol-Gesellschaft
Uhlandstrasse 184
1000 Berlin 12, West Germany
Manfred Matthes

35. Presse-Archiv
Tulpenweg 7
D6102 Pfungstadt 2, West Germany
Karl Spross

36. Pres-Kliping Novinska Dokumentacija
Box 95
Belgrade 11000, Yugoslavia

One of the problems that American clients may have in dealing with foreign bureaus is that the bureaus often correspond in their native languages and charge in local currency. Currency exchange rates fluctuate considerably. Foreign bureaus often require prepayments.

Several of the foreign bureaus, including Sita in Finland, provide broadcast monitoring and other services such as government documents and transcripts of legislative sessions.

Many of the clipping bureaus also provide advertising tear sheets and other advertising services, and several issue directories. For example, Press Research Bureau Ltd. in New Zealand (offices in Wellington and Auckland) publishes an annual Advertising Directory and Media Planner with data about over 550 publications in 21 classifications; a monthly Survey of National Advertising, with data about 35 newspapers and 13 magazines, and operates a mailing service called PR/Systems.

Many clipping bureaus have outstanding records of employing handicapped people as readers. In 1973, Irish Press Cuttings Ltd. acquired the press-cutting department of The Polio Fellowship of Ireland. Services also include broadcast monitoring.

The name of the clipping bureau operated by Metropol-Gesellschaft in Berlin is Zeitungsausschnitt-buro. Simple, if you're German or understand German. If not, it's one of the reasons to work with an international bureau in the U.S. or U.K.

A few clipping bureaus, such as GLOB in Poland, have reading fees that vary according to the subject. Obscure topics cost more than common items. It's fascinating to discuss this with the clipping experts at GLOB, but it's a lot simpler to place a foreign order through your regular U.S. or Canadian bureau.

Four bureaus in the U.S. specialize in international press clipping service. In addition, the Bowdens operation in Canada is described here, as it is the largest Canadian bureau and offers a variety of useful services.

1. Bacon's Information International, Inc.
332 S. Michigan Ave.
Chicago 60604
(312) 922-2400, (800) 621-0561
Patricia Clifford, Customer Service Mgr.

One of the largest international bureaus, Bacon's works with clipping bureaus throughout the world and is affiliated with Romeike & Curtice in London.

Rates for international service are based upon the number of countries to be covered and the material to be checked. The monthly service fee for each country (or subject) is $60 a month for the first country requested, $30 a month for each additional country, plus 80 cents a clipping.

Special rates for multi-country orders are available. A package rate for the 15 Western European countries, for example, costs $180 a month plus 80 cents a clipping.

The principal countries covered are: Australia, Austria, Belgium, Denmark, Finland, France, Germany, Hungary, India, Iran, Ireland, Israel, Italy, Japan, Mexico, the Netherlands, New Zealand, Norway, Poland, South Africa, Spain, Sweden, Switzerland, Turkey, the United Kingdom and East Asia.

In 1975, the company introduced Bacon's International Publicity Checker, which is described in the chapter on media directories.

2. Bowdens Press Clippings
624 King St. West, Toronto, Ontario M5V 2X9, Canada
(416) 860-0794
John Weinseis, Gen. Mgr.

The largest Canadian clipping bureau, Bowdens provides several major services to public relations clients.

The clipping service reads 2,000 Canadian publications and is an extremely efficient operation which includes readers and "scrutinizers" (who try to catch anything missed by the readers on the first reading). Cost is $105 a month plus 57 cents a clipping for all mentions.

Minimum service is two months. Daily first-class mailings (instead of weekly) are $30 a month additional.

Reminder: Prices are Canadian dollars.

Other Bowdens products and services are described in the chapters on broadcast monitoring, mailing, media directories and new wires. In particular, Bowdens operates a unique monitoring of news wires, which is described in the chapter on news wires.

3. International Press Clipping Bureau, Inc.
5 Beekman St., N.Y. 10038
(212) 267-5450
Irving E. Paley, Pres.

Branch Office:
1868 Columbia Rd., N.W., Wash., D.C. 20009
(202) 332-2000
Prescott Dennett, Mgr.

In addition to its foreign publication coverage, this bureau reads daily and weekly newspapers and other U.S. publications. A unique aspect of its coverage is the Anglo-Jewish press. Established in 1916, International Press also offers a "back search" service from its files of newspapers. TV and radio transcripts also are provided.

> *Rates: Domestic service—$105 per month plus 60 cents per clipping. A package plan is available which provides 1,200 clippings for $1375 for any period up to a year. Ads are included, for an additional fee.*
>
> *Foreign services—$1475 for 1,000 clippings for any period up to one year.*

4. Persburo Vaz Dias, B.V
Singel 91, Postbus 491, Amsterdam, Holland
Mrs. W. r.d. Bersselaar, Mgr.

With over 80 years of experience, Vaz Dias is the oldest international clipping service. It operates through a network of more than 50 bureaus. The Vaz Dias operation is principally an international advertising agency and Vaz Dias thus clips advertising as well as publicity.

The company is well organized to provide a variety of special services, including "caption and gist" translations of clippings and compilation and servicing of foreign media lists.

As with the other international clipping bureaus, rates are somewhat flexible in that higher rates may be applicable if coverage is to include countries where special arrangements are necessary.

Note: One advantage of dealing with a single bureau is to offset the complexities of currency exchanges and the constantly changing rates. For example, Australia, the Bahamas, Canada, Hong Kong, Jamaica, Malaysia, New Zealand, Singapore, Taiwan and the U.S. all use dollars, but of course, the value of each is different. Similarly, you'll find different values to the peso in Bolivia, Chile, Colombia, Mexico, the Philippines and Uruguay, as well as the pound in Great Britain, Israel and Lebanon, and the franc in Belgium, France and Switzerland.

D. REGIONAL SERVICES

A fairly sizable number of clipping bureaus scattered throughout the country provide services limited to publications in their area. For clients with limited geographical needs, these bureaus often can provide excellent services at low cost. Some of the bureaus are independent operations while others are adjuncts of state press associations.

Many of the state press associations maintain publicity mailing services and also place advertising. Public relations agencies and others who place advertising as a "sideline" often find these state press associations extremely helpful, and the charges are the regular, commissionable rates. A list is provided in the section on press associations.

A few of the companies have branch offices or affiliations, enabling them to provide regional, national or international services.

Major regional bureaus include: Allen's in California, Midwest Newsclip in Chicago, Mutual in Philadelphia, New England in Boston and Western in Minnesota.

Competition is keen in Minnesota, New York, Ohio and Texas, as these states each have two bureaus.

Because these operations usually are quite small, they attempt to offer more personalized service, frequently adapt the rates in accordance with the requirements of different clients, and usually permit one-month assignments. Following is brief information about most of the regional bureaus.

1. Alabama Press Association Clipping Bureau
Box 1800, Tuscaloosa, AL 35403
(205) 322-0380
William B. Keller, Exec. Dir.

$45 per month is the charge for the reading fee, which includes the first 100 clippings from about 140 daily and weekly newspapers and local magazines in Alabama. Additional clippings are only 15 cents each. An annual rate and data guidebook is $15. The Association was formed in 1871.

2. Allen's Press Clipping Bureau
657 Mission St., San Francisco 94105
(415) 392-2353
Philip N. McCombs, John N. McCombs

Branch Offices:
215 W. 6 St., L.A. 90013
(213) 628-4214
Al Catriz

519 S.W. 3 St., Portland 97204
(503) 223-7824
Ronald D. Schade

1331 Third Ave., Seattle 98101
(206) 622-8312
Trudy Gray

Established in 1888, Allen's is the oldest and largest regional clipping bureau. It clips all of the daily newspapers in the West, including different editions of the major newspapers, as well as all weeklies and most business publications. Service includes national and international daily, weekly and magazine coverage.

Rates vary according to the geographical coverage, and generally are less than the national bureaus. Service can be limited to individual states or regions.

3. Arkansas Press Association
1701 Broadway, Little Rock, AR 72206
(501) 374-1500
C. Dennis Schick, Exec. Dir.

$32 per month plus 25 cents per clipping provides coverage of all Arkansas daily and weekly newspapers.

The Arkansas Press Association also mails news releases to its members, providing the content is acceptable. The charge is $50 for a one-page release, and $10 for each additional page.

4. Carolina Clipping Service
1115 Hillsborough St., Raleigh, NC 27603
(919) 833-2079
Martin Greenwood, Mgr.

Founded in 1927, this service covers all daily and weekly newspapers in North Carolina and South Carolina. Charge is $40 per month for the first 100 clippings, plus postage for the weekly mailings.

5. Colorado Press Clipping Service
1336 Glenarm Pl., Denver, CO 80204
(303) 571-5117
Shawn Connelly, Clipping Supervisor

All Colorado daily and weekly newspapers are covered for $25 a month plus 25 cents a clipping.

The Service, operated by the Colorado Press Association (which, of course, is located in the Press Bldg.), reads daily and weekly newspapers in the state.

6. Empire State Press Clipping Service
455 Central Ave., Scarsdale, NY 10583
(914) 723-2792
Shirley Braudy

Formed in 1958, Empire State reads all daily and weekly newspapers in New York State. National coverage is also available.

7. Florida Clipping Service
Box 10278, Tampa, FL 33679
(813) 831-0961
E.C. Frick, Pres.

Established in 1930, Florida Clipping Service reads more than 600 publications, including all newspapers and magazines published in Florida. Mr. Frick and his daughter, Marjorie F. Diaz, direct a remarkable local operation that works with about 100,000 clippings a month on behalf of its 1,000 clients.

Rates are $40 a month plus 40 cents a clipping for Florida. The reading fee for Southeastern states is $10 more.

Advertisements also may be included. The company publishes a Florida Media List, which includes names and addresses of editors and publishers at a cost of $20. An affiliated company, Florida News Service, provides news releases and labels to Florida.

8. Georgia Press Association
1075 Spring St., N.W., Atlanta, GA 30309
(404) 872-2467
Kathy T. Chaffin, Exec. Mgr.

Most of the state press associations provide economical and efficient mailing services to their members, as well as advertising and publicity checking services. Many also publish annual newspaper directories.

The cost of the Georgia Press Association directory of all member newspapers in the state is $21. A one-page press release mailed to 250 newspapers is $95.

The Georgia newspaper clipping service is operated by The Rawson Company, 2 Northside 75, Atlanta, GA 30318. William C. Rawson is president and the phone is (404) 352-1777. Rates are $45 per subject, up to 50 clippings per month, plus 20 cents a clipping over 50. One-month-only service is $100.

9. Hawaii Clipping Service, Inc.
Box 10242, Honolulu, HI 96816
(808) 734-8124
Mrs. Elaine Fogg Stroup

Coverage includes about 20 daily and weekly newspapers and magazines. Charge is only $28 per month plus 10 cents per clipping in excess of 50, plus postage for the weekly mailings. No charge for the sincere aloha, which is included with all services.

10. Idaho Newspaper Association, Inc.
117 S. Sixth St., Box 1067, Boise, ID 83701
(208) 343-1671
Bob C. Hall

$35 per month covers up to 50 clippings; 25 cents per clipping 50 to 300. Coverage includes about 75 daily and weekly newspapers.

11. Indiana Newsclip
2102 E. 52 St., Indianapolis, IN 46205
(317) 253-8588
Mrs. Charlotte Allison

All (248) Indiana daily and weekly newspapers are read for $40 per month, plus 29 cents per clipping.

12. Iowa Newspaper Association

319 East Fifth St., Des Moines, IA 50309
(515) 244-2145
Bill Monroe, Exec. Dir.

This Association operates a mailing service and, like most of the other press associations, specifies that the text of the news releases must be acceptable to them.

Rates for the clipping service are $29 per month plus 29 cents per clipping.

13. Kansas Press Service Inc.

Box 1773, Topeka, KS 66601
(913) 271-5304
David L. Furnas, Exec. Dir.

$30 a month plus 25 cents per clipping for coverage of all newspapers in Kansas.

The company, which is affiliated with the Kansas Press Association (261 newspapers), provides mailing services ($110), advertising-placement services and publishes a directory ($18).

14. Kentucky Newsclip, Inc.

400 Sherburn Lane, Louisville, KY 40207
(502) 893-2449
Carol F. Shndll, Pres.
Elaine P. Burton, Office Mgr.

Founded in 1955, this service includes the 30 daily and 130 weekly newspapers in Kentucky and the Kentucky editions of the dailies in Cincinnati, Ohio, Evansville, Indiana, and Huntington, West Virginia. Charge is $55 per month plus 50 cents per clipping in excess of 100. Clippings also can be obtained from other states, via affiliated bureaus, at no additional cost.

15. Magnolia Clipping Service

Alabama Division
2600 8th St., Tuscaloosa, AL 35401
(205) 758-8610
Mary Anita Kofman, Mgr.

Complete coverage of newspapers, magazines and trade publications in Alabama, plus coverage of newspapers in Atlanta. Charge is $30 per month plus 30 cents per clipping.

16. Magnolia Clipping Service

Mississippi Division
Box 12463, Jackson, MS 39236
(601) 956-4221
Dred Porter, Exec. Dir.

Complete coverage of newspapers, magazines and trade publications in Mississippi, plus coverage of newspapers in New Orleans and Memphis. Charge is $30 per month plus 30 cents per clipping.

News release and scrapbook service is also available.

17. Metropolitan Press Clipping Bureau of Louisiana

5525 Galleria Dr., Baton Rouge, LA 70816
(504) 292-1715
Wayne Woodworth

All daily and weekly newspapers in Louisiana, plus several magazines, are covered for a $43 monthly fee plus 28 cents a clipping. The company also monitors TV news in New Orleans and Baton Rouge.

18. Michigan Press Reading Service

126 S. Putnam, Williamston, MI 48895
(517) 655-2116
Mrs. Betty Tratnik, Mgr.

A division of The Ohio Bureau Company, Cleveland, MPRS covers 53 Michigan dailies, more than 300 weeklies, and many legal, religious and university papers. Thirteen major dailies are included on the bureau's Rush List. Smaller circulation dailies and weeklies are normally processed within seven days.

MPRS was formerly part of the Michigan Press Association and was acquired by The Ohio News Bureau Company in 1969. In 1973, the bureau purchased the accounts of Michigan-Detroit Clipping Bureau, Royal Oak.

Monthly charge is $50, plus 35 cents a clipping.

19. Midwest Newsclip, Inc.

425 N. Michigan Ave., Chicago 60611
(312) 644-1720
Jordan Miller, Pres., Michael Buxbaum, Gen. Mgr.

This company covers all dailies and weeklies in the state of Illinois, and also black, ethnic and other publications

Founded in 1956, the company also publishes a directory, Illinois Media, which provides data about Illinois media at a cost of $95.

Monthly clipping service charge is $85 plus 60 cents per clipping.

National coverage is available through a network of 29 affiliated bureaus. Broadcast monitoring no longer is provided.

20. Minnesota Newspaper Association

84 S. Sixth St., Minneapolis, MN 55402
(612) 332-8844
Linda I. Falkman, Exec. Dir.

$23 per month plus 23 cents per clipping is the charge for coverage of all Minnesota daily and weekly newspapers.

Regional coverage from seven states is available for $20 a month, plus 30 cents per clipping.

The Association represents all general interest newspapers in the state and provides a variety of services, including a mailing service and advertising in its member newspapers.

21. Missouri Press Clipping Bureau

Eighth & Locust Sts., Columbia, MO 65201
(314) 449-4167
William A. Bray, Exec. Dir.

The charge is only $25 per month plus 25 cents per clipping for coverage of about 54 daily and 250 weekly newspapers in Missouri. Also available is the Missouri Bond and Construction News, a weekly compilation of bond issues, bid openings and other construction news, for $10 per month or $100 per year. As with many clipping bureaus, a mailing service to the media also is available.

22. Mutual Press Clipping Service, Inc.

1510 Chestnut St., Philadelphia 19102
(215) 569-4257
Alexander J. Schmerling, Pres.

56

One of the largest regional bureaus, Mutual provides coverage of all daily and weekly newspapers in Pennsylvania, New Jersey, Delaware, Maryland and Washington, D.C., at the rate of $70 per month, plus 55 cents per clipping.

An arrangement with an affiliated national clipping bureau enables subscribers to obtain additional coverage from more than 2,000 trade publications for $150 a month plus 83 cents per clipping.

23. Nevada Press Clipping Service
Box 7057, Reno, NV 89510
(702) 322-7431
Theresa Turner, Mgr.

Founded in 1964, the company covers all daily and weekly newspapers in Nevada for $50 a month for the first 100 clippings, plus 35 cents for each additional clipping. Daily mailing, instead of weekly, is $70 a month. Coverage of Lake Tahoe and other areas of California adjacent to Nevada is an additional $5 a month.

24. New England Newsclip Agency
5 Auburn St., Framingham, MA 01701
(617) 879-4460
Gail E. Milligan, V.P. and Gen. Mgr.

This bureau covers all daily and weekly newspapers in the six New England states, including all editions of the daily newspapers. Major newspapers in New York City and Washington, D.C., and all New England trade publications are covered.

The cost is $79 a month plus 54 cents a clipping. One-state coverage is less.

The Boston Newsclip, which New England Newsclip acquired in 1955, was founded in 1888.

New England Newsclip is owned by Burrelle's, which also owns clipping bureaus in New Jersey, New York and Pennsylvania. However, they operate from Burrelle's main office and therefore are not listed separately.

25. New Mexico Press Clipping Bureau, Inc.
Box NNN, Albuquerque, NM 87196
(505) 265-7858
Holly Mote, Mgr.

All dailies, weeklies and monthlies in New Mexico and a few nearby Texas newspapers are covered for $15.50 a month plus 28 cents a clipping.

The publication list ranges from Hatch Courier (circulation 935) to the Albuquerque Journal (circulation 137,000).

The Bureau was purchased in 1982 by the New Mexico Press Association.

26. The Ohio News Bureau, Inc.
1900 Euclid Ave., Cleveland, OH 44115
(216) 241-0675
Frances Tratnik, Pres.

Formed in 1898, the company was operated for many years by John Beach, who died in 1979, when Mrs. Tratnik took over the business.

This private organization issues an annual directory ($5) which provides extensive data about the daily and weekly newspapers in Ohio.

Monthly charge is $45 plus 35 cents a clipping.

27. Ohio Newspaper Services, Inc.

145 E. Rich St., Columbus, OH 43215

(614) 224-1648

Irene A. Litteral, Mgr.

A subsidiary of the Ohio Newspaper Association (formed in 1933), this company is the advertising representative for all Ohio weekly and daily newspapers. News release mailing service also is available.

An annual Directory of Ohio Newspapers is published for $30 a copy.

28. Oklahoma Press Clipping Bureau

3601 N. Lincoln, Oklahoma City, OK 73105

(405) 524-4421

Chris Johnson

$30 per month plus 30 cents per clipping covers all daily and weekly newspapers in Oklahoma. The bureau is a service of the Oklahoma Press Association. Page-one clippings are indicated. The bureau also publishes Oklahoma Bond and Construction News, a semiweekly construction report, for $30 a month or $330 a year.

29. Pacific Clipping Service

Box 11789, Santa Ana, CA 92711

(714) 542-7201

Gayl Kay

In business since 1959, Pacific is one of the most localized clipping services in the country. Coverage is limited to publications in Orange County. Monthly charge is $33.25 including up to 100 clippings, plus 26 cents for additional clippings.

30. Pressclips, Inc.

One Hillside Blvd., New Hyde Park, NY 11040

(516) 437-1047

N. Herbert Halberstadt, V.P.

All daily and weekly newspapers in New York City and Long Island, plus other publications in Nassau and Suffolk counties, are this bureau's specialty. $175 a month plus 70 cents per clipping, minimum of three months, is the national rate. Rates are lower for limited area coverage.

Subscribers receive a free Guide to Metro NYC Print Media, $15 a copy to nonsubscribers.

The company was founded in 1958 and has developed a devoted clientele.

31. Tennessee Press Association

Box 8123, Knoxville, TN 37996

(615) 974-5481

Don R. McNeil, Exec. Dir.

All of the state's daily and weekly newspapers are read for $25 per month plus 25 cents per clipping.

32. Texas Press Association

718 W. Fifth St., Austin, TX 78701

(512) 477-6755

Lyndell Williams, Exec. V.P.

The Association offers complete coverage of Texas for $30 a month plus 30 cents a clipping, with a minimum period of two weeks.

A subsidiary company, Texas Press Service, Inc., provides a mailing service to daily and weekly newspapers in the state. The total cost for mailing a two-page release is $170, plus postage.

33. Texas Press Clipping Bureau
109 N. Akard, Dallas, TX 75201
(214) 742-7628
A.D. Peterson, Gen. Mgr.

This independent company (established 1910) provides clipping service of most of the daily and weekly newspapers in the state. Rates vary according to subject and territory.

34. Utah Press Association
467 E. Third South, Salt Lake City, UT 84111
(801) 328-8678
Nancy White

About 54 weekly and six daily newspapers are read for $35 per month for up to 25 clippings, plus 25 cents each for additional clippings.

35. Virginia Press Services, Inc.
P.O. Box C-32015, Richmond, VA 23261-2015
(804) 798-2053
Tom Prentice, Executive Mgr.
Linda Cheek, Clipping Bureau Mgr.

A subsidiary of the Virginia Press Association, this Service reads all daily and weekly newspapers in Virginia.

Coverage also includes the Washington Post. The cost is $30 a month reading fee plus 22 cents a clipping, plus postage for mailing clippings in excess of 10 a month.

36. West Virginia Press Services, Inc.
101 Dee Drive, Charleston, WV 25311
(304) 342-6908
Bill Childress

An affiliate of the West Virginia Press Association, this Service covers all daily and weekly news-papers in the state for $25 per month plus 25 cents a clipping.

An annual directory ($10.00) includes extensive data about the 25 daily and 77 weekly newspapers and statistics about the 55 counties.

37. Western Press Clipping Services
8401 73 Ave. N., Brooklyn Park, MN 55428
(612) 537-5852
L. R. King

Established in 1983 and now part of Chapin Publishing Co., Inc., Western reads all daily and weekly newspapers in Minnesota, North Dakota and South Dakota. The company publishes an excellent monthly newsletter, the Media Messenger, which is filled with news confirming that the twin cities area (Minneapolis-St. Paul) has become a hub of public relations and media activities.

38. Wisconsin Newspaper Association
702 N. Midvale Blvd., Madison, WI 53705
(608) 238-7171
J. LeRoy Yorgason, Mgr.

Coverage of all Wisconsin daily and weekly newspapers is $35 for the first month and $30 a month thereafter, plus 26 cents per clipping.

News release mailings are sent weekly to all weekly newspapers in Wisconsin. The charge is $65 for the first page and $20 for each additional page, with news releases supplied by the client, plus $25 per page if printed by the Association.

39. Wyoming Newspaper Clipping Service
710 Garfield, Laramie, WY 82070
(307) 745-8144
Nancy Shelton, Mgr.

In 1984, this service became an affiliate of the Wyoming Press Association. It reads all daily and weekly newspapers in the state and several state trade journals. Founded in 1952 by Wallace R. Biggs, the service has maintained low rates—$20 a month reading fees plus 20 cents per clipping.

E. BACK ISSUES

The search for clippings has radically changed with the development and proliferation of database services, which literally are electronic clipping bureaus. These services are described in the research chapter.

However, it still is important to find the actual publication.

It ought to be simple, but it seems that one of the most frustrating activities experienced by journalists and publicists is the search for an article which appeared in a relatively recent issue of a well-known publication. The most logical place to begin such a search is the publication itself, but it seems that almost every publication has a different procedure for the purchase of back issues.

Take The New York Times, for example. This newspaper publishes two basic editions every day, as well as many changes within an edition. An article often will appear in the City edition but not in the Late Edition. Though The Times maintains a complete file of all editions, it usually is impossible to purchase the City Edition from the back issues department. Since this is the first edition which is mailed and delivered out-of-town, a publicist often will be frustrated when an out-of-town client has seen or heard about the article, but the publicist is unable to obtain it.

In fact, the business news and sports sections of most newspapers often are loaded with publicity material in the first edition which is replaced in late editions by quotations and game scores. Thus, the first edition frequently is most sought by publicists. However, the last edition is considered the "issue of record" and is the one which is indexed and filed.

The Times Square newsstands, particularly the ones at 42 St. and Seventh Ave. and 43 St. and Broadway, receive the first deliveries of The New York Times. Show press agents on opening night and other publicists start congregating at these locations shortly before 10 P.M., in order to grab the first copies (called the Bluebird/Condor flashes) which are hand-delivered.

Back issues of The New York Times can be obtained, but only as far back as three months (even then, some issues may not be available). Issues of the preceding few days can be obtained from the Times office at 229 W. 43 St. during regular business hours. Mail service is available, but it's a bit complicated.

Copies are 95 cents for dailies and $2.80 for Sunday editions. All orders take at least six weeks for arrival. Send the exact date of issue and cost to The New York Times, Box 508, Hackensack, NJ 07602.

University Microfilm International, 300 N. Zeeb Rd., Ann Arbor, MI 48106 (800-521-0600) provides any edition of the The New York Times from 1851 to present in a semi-gloss print in a variety of sizes (and will even frame the prints for an additional cost). University also provides the same type of service for over 2500 publications.

Other major publishers, such as the Chicago Tribune, the New York Daily News, McGraw-Hill and Time also maintain extensive back issue and reference services.

The first source for the obtaining of a back issue, therefore, generally should be the publication itself. Some publications maintain copies going back a few years, while others stock only relatively recent copies for sale. Some insist that the money be sent in advance, while others are willing to bill. As a result, one or more long-distance calls or the use of local messengers often is necessary to secure a back issue from the publication itself.

The reference departments of libraries represent another source, particularly the large branches, which have copying machines and thus are able to sell copies of magazine and newspaper articles. The Photographic Service of the New York Public Library, Fifth Avenue and 42nd Street, N.Y. 10018, handles telephone requests from charge account customers who deposit funds in advance.

Mail orders are accepted. However, there is a $3 fee per title for searching and cost-estimating for nondeposit account orders.

There is only one newspaper which really makes it easy to obtain back issues. The Christian Science Monitor is available in 2,500 reading rooms operated by the Christian Science Church in the U.S., plus 800 reading rooms in other countries. Of course, a complete file of recent issues of the Monitor is not available in every reading room, but a visit to one of these ''quiet rooms'' is such a pleasant experience that it's worthwhile to check this source, providing one is looking for a back issue of this particular newspaper.

Many public and university libraries have microfilm records of the Monitor and other major newspapers. The New York Public Library maintains an entire branch devoted to microfilm records of newspapers. It's at 521 W. 43 St., phone (212) 790-6351.

Advertising tear sheets and all types of back-dated clippings can be obtained from Packaged Facts, 274 Madison Ave., N.Y. 10016, phone (212) 532-5533. A description of this information research company appears in the research chapter.

In a few of the major cities, there are news dealers and other companies which specialize in the sale of back issues. Newsstands at airports, train terminals and major hotels often carry out-of-town newspapers.

A unique specialist in delivery of all types of current local and out-of-town newspapers and magazines is Mitchell's, Box 4040, G.P.O., NY 10163, phone (212) 686-7878.

News dealers and others who specialize in back issues usually are listed in the classified telephone pages under ''Magazines—Back Number.'' There also are several dealers who advertise in the classified columns of the Sunday book review sections of The New York Times, Washington Post, Chicago Tribune and Los Angeles Times. Following is a list of several specialists.

1. Grand Book Center

659-B Grand St., Brooklyn, NY 11211
(718) 384-4089
H. Somers

Old-time comic and magazine aficionados who prefer the quieter haunts of Brooklyn are familiar with the comic book collection of the Grand Book. The store also stocks books and posters.

2. Hotaling's News Agency Inc.

142 W. 42 St., N.Y. 10036
(212) 840-1868
Arthur Hotaling, Pres.
Susan Carey, V.P.

The Hotaling family operates what probably is the world's best-known newspaper stand. For many years it was under a shelter in front of the Allied Chemical Tower (the old Times Tower) at the south end of Times Square. Now it's a nearby store, east of Times Square, where Hotaling clerks sell daily newspapers from more than 350 American cities to many thousands of patrons. Clients who are eager to read out-of-town reviews or other articles can buy copies of most newspapers on the same day or a day or two after publication, usually for only 25 or 30 cents more than the regular price.

Hotaling's stocks more than 2,500 periodicals from 50 foreign countries. These English and foreign-language magazines and newspapers arrive anytime from the same day (by air) to a month after publication (by ship mail).

3. Jay Bee Magazines Stores, Inc.
134 W. 26 St., N.Y. 10001
(212) 675-1600
Henry Greenbaum, Pres.

New York's largest back-date magazine store, Jay Bee stocks more than five million magazines, including collections of many current and defunct American publications. Jay Bee also researches from its inventory.

4. LTS, Inc.
86 Terry Rd., Smithtown, NY 11787
(516) 265-0404
Robert A. Damers, Pres.

A major broadcast monitoring company, LTS (formerly Lynch Transcription Service) has an extensive library of about 100 years of magazine advertisements.

Over 500 daily newspapers and many other publications are read, primarily for advertisements. Rates are $60 per month plus 95 cents per tear sheet. LTS also prepares expenditure reports and handles searches and other assignments.

5. Magazine Center
1133 Broadway, N.Y. 10010
(212) 929-5255
H.B. Quoyoon

Thousands of back issues of magazines, notably 19th- and 20th-century American and foreign fashion magazines. Special emphasis on 1900-1960 general magazines, first magazine appearances of authors and photographers, compilation and research of author and subject bibliographies.

6. Packaged Facts Information Service
274 Madison Ave., N.Y. 10016
(212) 532-5533
David Ansel Weiss

Back-dated (as far back as 50 years) clippings and advertising tearsheets can be obtained from this unique information service organization. A fuller description appears in the chapter on research.

7. Pageant Book and Print Shop
109 E. 9 St., N.Y. 10003
(212) 674-5296
Shirley Solomon

Among the several bookstores still on or near lower Fourth Avenue is this antiquarian shop, which stocks about 500,000 old prints and manuscripts, as well as about 450,000 books and 750,000 prints, maps and other items. In business since 1945.

8. Princeton Antiques Bookservice

2917 Atlantic Ave., Atlantic City, NJ 08401
(609) 344-1943
Robert Ruffalo II

Robert Ruffalo operated a charming antique and art shop for many years at 175 Nassau Street in Princeton, NJ, near the campus. In 1969, he moved the business to Atlantic City, and two years later turned it over to his son, who has become a "servant of knowledge" (his motto) by collecting and selling rare and out-of-print books. The store now has over 150,000 books and periodicals in stock and functions as a reference library and search service. The publications are filed by author, subject and title, akin to a library. The odds that Bob Ruffalo will find your book are far better than at the nearby casino.

9. Howard Rogofsky

Box 107, Glen Oaks, NY 11004
(718) 723-0954 (after 6 PM)
Howard and Gail Rogofsky

The Rogofskys have a huge collection of old comic books, pulps and picture books and magazines, and miscellaneous hard-to-find items. There probably isn't too much professional interest in the Doc Savage magazine (Mr. Rogofsky has a 45-year collection), but you might be interested in the complete collection of TV Guide, Playboy and various toys, cereal premiums and movie press books, photos and posters. A 44-page catalog, issued three times a year, is $1.50. A special catalog for TV Guide (starting in 1951) is $1.50.

10. Topicator

Box 1009, Clackamas, OR 97015-1009
(503) 653-1007
Wendell Wolles

A bimonthly bibliography of articles in 19 publications in the advertising, broadcasting and marketing fields, plus an annual index. The publisher, Lakemoor Publishers, breaks the articles into 350 subheadings, so that the bimonthly service ($95) can be quite worthwhile, though the annual collection can be obtained singly for $60. The company was formed in 1965.

F. RELATED SERVICES

It's difficult to produce significant publicity results. It's easier to gather the clippings, broadcast transcripts, tapes and other results and then to present them in a meaningful fashion. And yet, this task is often neglected.

Undoubtedly, there are design studios and other organizations which can be retained to perform part of this service, on a one-time or continuing basis. Many large companies have full- or part-time individuals whose job is to maintain, organize, count, file and handle clippings.

Several large companies reproduce and analyze all or some of their clippings on a daily, weekly, monthly or other periodic basis. While a few of these presentations are done competently, most clients of clipping services do a poor job in the "merchandising" of their clippings. It can be discouraging to see agencies and companies in which there are loosely organized repositories of clippings, either in envelopes or mounted in scrapbooks. All too frequently the clippings gather dust and are discarded or sent to storage areas, with relatively little effort devoted to analyzing and circulating the clippings in a manner consistent with all of the effort which has gone into the securing of the clippings.

Albums, binders, covers, portfolios, scrapbooks and other items in which to store and display clippings can be purchased in stationery and office supply stores. A particularly comprehensive catalog of sales presentations and bindings can be obtained from John R. Cantelmo, President, Brewer-Cantelmo Co., Inc., 116 E. 27 St., N.Y. 10016, phone (212) 685-1200.

There have been a few recent attempts to analyze clippings by statisticians and sociologists who have evolved quantitative measurements, including the use of computers to tabulate clippings.

This type of service includes daily, weekly, monthly or other regularly issued compilations of the total number of publications which received the client's news releases; total number which used all or part of the release, with and without corporate or product credit; total circulation reached; percent of markets, and other arithmetic means of analyzing publicity effectiveness.

This analysis can be exciting, and useful, but some publicists believe that they cannot afford these services. Some public relations counselors believe that there is a greater need for *qualitative analyses,* and that this type of service can get bogged down in subjective evaluations and other seemingly intangible yardsticks.

In an article titled ''An Approach to Public Relations Measurement'' (PR Quarterly, Winter, 1965), J.N. Dumas of the General Electric Company concluded:

> One of the most common mistakes is the confusion of measurement with merchandising of public relations achievements . . . measurement is a management function and has three basic objectives—to control activity in process, to gauge the relative value of completed activity, and to improve the effectiveness of future activity. Merchandising is the effort to sell the function and its practitioners by presenting accomplishments in a favorable light. Not all merchandising constitutes measurement, but all sensible measurement has merchandising value.

Clipping analysis could become an important service in the public relations field. The subject is discussed in the research chapter.

The following section lists companies that have developed techniques to make the end product of the clipping services—clippings—meaningful forms of information.

1. The Advertising Checking Bureau, Inc.
2 Park Ave., N.Y. 10016
(212) 685-7300
Warren Grieb, Pres.
Brian McShane, V.P.

Though a few editorial clipping services include advertising checking, the major source for advertising coverage is the Advertising Checking Bureau. This is a huge operation which reads *all* daily newspapers in the country and also major weekly newspapers and general consumer magazines. ACB does *not* read editorial matter and is not a clipping bureau.

ACB can supply copies of a company's ads, competitor's ads, verification and analysis of all advertising in specific categories, and other services geared to the needs of advertisers and publishers. Rates therefore vary considerably. Special services include total retail lineage of the products of a company and its competitors, co-op advertising auditing, and other reports developed since the bureau was formed in 1917.

2. Bowdens Wire Service

130 Slater St., Ottawa K1P 6E2, Canada
(613) 236-7301

A unique service, introduced in 1974. Bowdens monitors the wires of the Canadian Press (which includes Associated Press and Reuters). Subscribers receive same-day or overnight delivery (by phone or mail) for about $85 per monthly monitoring charge, plus 55 cents per item.

3. Communications Management Systems

5813 Surrey St., Chevy Chase, MD 20015
(301) 656-5629
Paul M. Lewis, Pres.

A clipping bureau and academic background (co-founder of Press Intelligence; sociologist at Columbia University and University of Pennsylvania), combined with a technique for evaluating clippings as a function of communications policy, motivated Mr. Lewis to start this company in 1965. Ten years earlier, he coauthored an article titled "Some Methods of Measuring Press Attention" which appeared in the first issue (October 1955) of PR (now called PRQ).

CMS offers capabilities in press analysis systems to guide corporate staffs and meet communications policy objectives. The systems are individually designed and by contract only.

The company was previously called Communications Analysis Corporation. Note: It is *not* a clipping bureau.

4. Internews Media Services

1199 National Press Bldg., Wash., DC 20045
(202) 347-4575
Marie-Benoite Allizon, Dir.

A former Washington correspondent for Paris Match, Marie-Benoite Allizon formed Internews in 1976, primarily as a service to foreign correspondents, executives, lawyers and diplomats. The company has comprehensive files, including 11,000 biographies, and, since 1977, has published Internewsletter Afrique, a bimonthly newsletter *in French* which analyzes U.S. news coverage of African affairs and interviews of African specialists.

Related services include research, arranging for interviews, translation and interpreting.

For its clients, Internews provides a specialized clipping service, in which it reads 12 of America's top daily newspapers for $65 a month plus 25 cents per clipping. Internews also provides a French translation service for $70 per 1,000 words.

5. The National Research Bureau, Inc.

424 N. Third St., Burlington, IA 52601
(319) 752-5415
Milton Paule

One of the nation's largest advertising and public relations research organizations, NRB (founded 1933) operates a specialized advertising clipping service. Called the Ad-Clip Service, this NRB department subscribes to several hundred newspapers, from which it culls selected advertisements of particular interest to individual subscribers. For $133.75 per month, a client receives a weekly packet of 35 to 45 tear sheets, a folder of related advertising ideas and promotion suggestions and also access to NRB's reference files and other special services. The same service is available on a once-a-month basis for $39.75 per month. A nifty service, particularly useful to retailers and small advertisers.

6. National System, Inc.

8600 Manchester Rd., St. Louis, MO 63144
(314) 962-0761
Chase McKeague, Exec. V.P.

Established in 1919, this service monitors and researches advertising in over 300 newspapers in the U.S. and Canada. National publishes weekly and monthly portfolios, which reproduce and comment on advertising in 25 retail categories.

7. The News Analysis Institute

818 Liberty Ave., Pittsburgh, PA 15222
(412) 471-9411
Colleen P. Rodgers, V.P.

Founded in 1953 by public relations counselor William T. Schoyer, The News Analysis Institute pioneered the statistical and interpretive analysis of clippings. The company uses both computer and editorial techniques to measure the effectiveness of publicity programs.

Clippings are analyzed in prose, prose-statistical, or all statistical reports. News Analysis programs offer both quantitative and qualitative measurements of print communications through use of as many as 15 measurements, including reader exposure, space secured, advertising value, markets penetrated, key outlets, photo use, front page and magazine covers, full-length articles and type of distribution. Radio and television analysis also is available, plus special types of reports, including an assessment of negative news.

A brochure, reviewing the public relations background of analysis, value of various publicity measurements and types of reports currently in use, describes the service. The fees depend on the type of report and clipping volume.

Other services include preparation of clipping scrapbooks, sorting and maintenance of clip files and release distribution.

The company is affiliated with PR Aids and other organizations, so that it also provides a variety of publicity services. News Analysis Institute also produces Burrelle's Clipping Analyst, a four-page newsletter about outstanding publicity campaigns, which is sent to subscribers of Burrelle's Clipping Bureau.

8. PR Data Systems, Inc.

15 Oakwood Ave., Norwalk, CT 06850
(203) 847-0777
Jack E. Schoonover, Pres., William H. Wubbenhorst, Exec. V.P.

In 1964, PR Data Systems pioneered the use of computers in the measurement of public relations programs. Several major corporations since that time have used the techniques developed by Jack Schoonover to better evaluate the status of their external press relations programs.

The basis of the PRDS technique is to provide management with an indication of the PR "media buy." This reading is obtained through content analysis of all print and broadcast news clips, including an examination for one or more "copy points" or messages.

After identifying these messages, the computer generates reports which relate the message exposure to predetermined communications and/or corporate business objectives, and determines the degree of exposure to key audiences, such as stockholders, customers, Government officials and employees.

Raw "tonnage" figures also are accumulated in terms of total clips, inches or broadcast minutes, circulation, comparable advertising value (on an "if-purchased" basis), photographs, story treatment and other factors, including a comparison of "raw tonnage" and "message content" to the previous year-to-date period.

Included in the program is an option to trace news release distribution and usage. The computer maintains a record of each release distributed in terms of the specific publications receiving it. Clips that appear in print and a rate of return is developed for: 1. specific news release, 2. aggregate usage, and 3. individual media usage.

Fees are based on volume and report frequency and generally are several thousand dollars, though special one-time reports can cost less.

PR Data Systems also operates a computerized news release distribution service, which is described in the chapter on mailing services.

PR Data Systems continues to keep pace with changing computer technology. For example, in 1984 it combined basic components of press relations programs into a "Closed-Loop Communication System," which targets media so that these releases can be delivered more efficiently and results measured more accurately.

Several companies that provide electronic clipping services are described in the research chapter.

Chapter 5

Clubs and Conventions

Over 24 million people belong to the American Association of Retired Persons, a Washington-based organization with several hundred chapters. The Chicago-based National Congress of Parents and Teachers has six million members. Thousands of organizations—civic, fraternal, religious, educational, business, professional, patriotic—are listed in the Encyclopedia of Associations.

Though many of these organizations have specialized interests, quite a few are interested in corporate and association-sponsored programs, booklets, films, materials and speakers on such general-interest subjects as homemaking, family affairs, fashion and beauty.

Lists of clubs are difficult to compile and keep up-to-date, though a few national organizations supply names and addresses of local chapters. The San Francisco Chamber of Commerce, 465 California St., San Francisco 94104, publishes an annual Directory of San Francisco Area Clubs and Organizations ($5.33). Alternative America is an unusual annual directory of about 13,000 alternative, progressive and other off-beat and experimental organizations, book stores, media (including radio stations and publishers) and others in a variety of fields, particularly ecology, education, health care, nuclear energy and political and social action. A key aspect of the book consists of women's groups and publications, Alternative Press Syndicate members and other media. The cost is $19.95 and the publisher is Resources, Box 1067, Cambridge, MA 02238. The book is organized in three sections, a geographical listing (in zip code order, of each organization), an alphabetical listing, and an alphabetized listing of key words and subjects. The 1988 edition includes about 1,000 foreign entries.

Clubs with upscale members often are of considerable interest to public relations people, but are hard to find. Many such clubs, together with the names, addresses and phone numbers of about 33,000 individuals, are listed in the Social Register. This annual directory is quite well known, though relatively few people have ever seen a copy. In fact, it's hard to locate the publisher. Unlike Marquis (publisher of Who's Who books), the Social Register does not advertise.

A delightful article in The Wall Street Journal (November 14, 1984) about who's in and who's out of the Social Register omitted the name of the publisher and the city in which it's published. It's Carrie Pigeon, 40 Plimpton St., Boston 02118. The $54.50 price includes updates. Started about 100 years ago by Louis Keller, Edward Gardiner Thompson and Joseph L. Sullivan, the Social Register is now owned by Robert S. Beekman.

Many of the organizations listed in Gale's Encyclopedia of Associations publish directories of local chapters. In addition, many religious and other special interest publishers include lists of organizations in various directories. For example, the Jewish Publication Society, 1930 Chestnut St., Philadelphia 19103, publishes the American Jewish Year Book (continuous publication since 1889), which includes directories of Jewish organizations and periodicals, as well as a variety of articles and other data. It's issued in June and is $25.95.

A few years ago some people were predicting that changing habits, speed of air travel and other factors would result in fewer conventions and meetings. Such has not been the case. Though exhibit and hotel costs have increased considerably, there now are more conventions than ever before. Some of them, such as the Consumer Electronics Show (CES), are major events in which public relations people are heavily involved.

Exhibitor Magazine (Box 351, Rochester, MN 55903) publishes an annual Buyers Guide to Trade Show Displays ($49), with photos, prices and descriptions of 200 exhibit systems.

Successful Meetings (633 Third Ave., N.Y. 10017) publishes an annual International Convention Facilities Directory ($10, or free as part of a $49 annual subscription to this monthly magazine), and two publications of particular value to public relations people:

Exhibits Schedule. Over 11,000 trade and industrial shows, with current and future dates, locations, attendance, name and address of chief executive, sponsoring organization; three sections, by industry, geographically and chronologically. Annual book, includes July supplement. $95.

Directory of Conventions. Over 19,000 conventions in the U.S. and Canada listed geographically and chronologically, with chief executive, address, hotel, estimated attendance. Annual book, includes July supplement. $90.

Here's a great bargain. If you are responsible for arranging for meetings and conventions, you can get Successful Meetings free (including the big annual Convention Facilities Directory), as it's a controlled-circulation publication. Simply write to Successful Meetings, 633 Third Ave., N.Y. 10017.

Bowker (described in the research chapter) distributes the annual Tradeshow Week Data Book ($195), with information about nearly 4,000 exhibitions in the U.S. and Canada, and the annual Data Book ($145), with information about 1,800 exhibitions in the United Kingdom and Europe.

Following is a list of publications that cover the meeting and convention field. Most of these publications are free and many include annual directories. For example, the January issue of Meeting News is a Directory of Sites, Suppliers and Services.

Corporate Meetings and Incentives, 747 Third Avenue, N.Y. 10017
Medical Meetings, Box 700, Ayer, MA 01432
Meetings and Conventions, 1 Park Avenue, N.Y. 10016
Meetings & Incentive Travel, 1450 Don Mills Road, Don Mills, Ontario
 M3B 2X7, Canada
Meeting News, Gralla Publications, 1515 Broadway, N.Y. 10036
Physicians' Travel & Meeting Guide, Box 59, Quakertown, PA 18951
Successful Meetings, 633 Third Avenue, N.Y. 10017

With regard to working with clubs, associations and other groups, the best approach usually is to deal directly with the specific organizations. However, it often is considerably more economical, and quite efficient, to work with the program aids services which have been established to provide a link between public relations clients and clubs.

Afram (from African and American) Associates is an information/marketing firm in Harlem which distributes a Directory of National Organizations ($10) and other publications, and also operates a reference service and produces and distributes materials to schools, organizations and media, particularly fraternal organizations and clubs with black members. Headed by Preston Wilcox, Afram is located at 68 E. 131 St., N.Y. 10037, phone (212) 281-6000.

Distributors of materials to clubs are listed in the chapter on motion pictures. The largest company in this field is Modern Talking Picture Service. The chapter on mailing services includes several sources for purchasing mailing lists.

Chapter 6

Communications and Image Consultants

Media training (preparation of individuals before they are interviewed) now is a standard part of the public relations field. However, many corporate executives lack familiarity with this type of coaching and sometimes are skeptical, shy, frightened or apathetic.

For many years, presidents of countries and companies benefited from the personal counsel of communications and image consultants. Sometimes the advice was provided by public relations people and occasionally by television directors, speech writers, actors and other professional communicators. Roger Ailes and Robert Montgomery were publicized for their roles in advising Presidents.

Two major recent developments stimulated the growth of full-time speech and other communications consultants who are oriented to public relations needs. The first was television, with its increased use of company spokespeople, authors and other interviewees. And the second catalyst was the emergence of annual meetings of publicly owned companies as public forums.

The Effective Speech Writing Institute, Box 444, University of Richmond, Virginia 23173, conducts writing and speaking workshops and consulting services. Jerry Tarver is the director of the Institute, phone (804) 282-0388.

Several consultants operate under the name of Communication Associates or similar names, generally with the word Communication or Communications. Many of these people are actors, models, speech professors, public relations counselors and others who vary considerably in their experience, skills and orientation. Some are part-time consultants and freelancers who pretend to have their own full-time staffs and facilities. Often their primary assets are charisma and self-assertiveness, which are desirable, of course, but not necessarily transferable. This is a new field, and buyers must be cautious. Before you retain an "image consultant" (or any consultant), check with past clients and investigate several candidates.

Communications and image consultants are described in the Directory of Personal Image Consultants, a unique book ($30) published by Image Industry Publications, 10 Bay St. Landing, Staten Island, NY 10301. The biennial publication includes experts on speaking, dress and other aspects of personal public relations. Editor Jacqueline A. Thompson deserves praise for conceiving this in 1978, and expanding it since then.

She also is the author of Image Impact: The Aspiring Woman's Personal Packaging Program ($14.95), Image Impact: The Business and Professional Man's Personal Packaging Program ($16.95) and The Image Consulting Industry: A Statistical Profile ($10). The last is a pamphlet based on the data in the Directory of Personal Image Consultants. All are published by her Image Industry Publications (formerly called Editorial Services Co.), which also sells Image Consulting: The New Career ($10.45) by Joan Timberlake, which tells you how to become a personal image consultant, and is based on interviews with professional consultants.

One useful aspect of the directory is its inclusion of consultants throughout the country, including educators (psychology, speech, drama, communications, journalism, public relations and management are among the varied fields), actors, TV directors and others. Some are part-time and operate from their homes, and others have sizable staffs and operate from specially equipped studios and offices.

Communications is a monthly newsletter devoted to improving speaking and presentation skills, particularly for executives. Formerly called Decker Communications Report, it's now published ($59 a year) by Magna Publications, 2817 Dryden Dr., Madison, WI 53704.

Many sales-training and motivational-development companies, such as Dale Carnegie, include speech and communications skills in their courses. These companies are not included in this chapter, as they generally are not oriented to training interviewees to "meet the media" and other specialized needs of public relations clients.

Similarly, this chapter includes two dress consultants, though there are many others who often can be very helpful in preparing clients for public appearances and media interviews. Individuals and companies in this category include actresses, personal shoppers and other men and women who often are available themselves as spokespeople for media tours and also to coach others about grooming, fashion, voice and other aspects of personal image. If you're looking for someone in this category, ask a local beauty or fashion editor, television talk show host or hostess or other media person who can refer you to experts in your area.

1. Chester Burger Company
171 Madison Ave., N.Y. 10016
(212) 725-0000
Alfred Geduldig, Pres.
James E. Arnold, Exec. V.P.

Mr. Burger is the country's best known management communications consultant. His services are described at the end of the chapter on research (see CommuniCorp). Because of his broadcast background (he was director of CBS News) as well as his strong interest and experience in communications, Chet Burger developed interview training for corporate executives, including the use of video. A further extension of this service resulted in the pioneering use of video for corporate annual reports, including broadcast of annual meetings and other corporate communications on cable television. Chester Burger & Co. was formed on December 1, 1964. On its 20th anniversary, Chet Burger sold the company to Bill Cantor, a well known executive recruiter, and Alfred Geduldig. However, Chet Burger still is a full-time participant in the work of this unique company.

2. Chambers & Asher
1100 Spring St., N.W., Atlanta, GA 30367
(404) 897-1770
Wicke Chambers, Spring Asher

Media training and production of corporate videos.

3. Robert Chang
10 E. 40 St., N.Y. 10016
(212) 685-1060

Bob Chang knows about media, particularly TV, from many viewpoints. He was an NBC producer and writer, a public relations director at a company and a broadcast specialist at a major public relations agency. He started his own consultancy in 1979, specializing in video training and also produces video news releases. His fees are considerably lower than many larger companies and his happy clients include many public relations agencies, companies and associations.

4. Communispond, Inc.

485 Lexington Ave., N.Y. 10017
(212) 687-8040
Kevin R. Daley, Pres.
Charles J. Windhorst, Exec. V.P.
Edward M. Fuller, Sr. V.P.

Branch Offices:
676 N. St. Clair St., Chicago 60611
(312) 787-0484

12750 Merit Dr., Dallas 75251
(214) 385-0385

4665 MacArthur Ct., Newport Beach, CA 92660
(714) 851-9200

Conceived in 1969 by Kevin Daley and Charles Windhorst when they were account supervisors at the J. Walter Thompson advertising agency, Communispond has become the largest company in the executive communication field.

Messrs. Daley and Windhorst acquired full control of Communispond in 1976 and have expanded and diversified since then.

The program is so large that the basic program, called the Executive Communication Program, is conducted almost continuously. Programs ($950 per person) are weekly in New York and every other week in Chicago.

The company's Trainer Development Institute includes presentation, writing and interviewing techniques for company trainers.

A corporate program for up to 20 persons is $12,000. A special one-day program on business writing, called Speaking on Paper, is $450 for an individual or $4,900 for a corporate program for up to 15 individuals. A two-day version of the corporate program is $6,500. Individual counseling is available for $1,250 a half-day and $2,500 a complete day.

5. Communi-Vu, Inc.

1 Lincoln Plaza, N.Y. 10023
(212) 759-7343
Roslyn Bremer, Pres.

One of the pioneers in oral and written communication counseling, Roslyn Bremer is an expert in the writing and presentation of speeches and other materials. Ms. Bremer handles corporate training programs, train the trainer programs, preparation for television, radio and teleconference appearances. She has written several booklets, including:

How to Think on Your Feet and Say What you Mean . . . Effectively!
The Question and Answer Session Is Harder than You Think

What Every Good Panelist Should Know
How to Write a Speech—One that Talks

6. Duncliff's International

3662 Katella, Los Alamitos, CA 90720
(213) 596-5465
Charles H. Browning, Pres.
Beverley J. Browning, Exec. Dir.

Formed in 1979, Duncliff's specializes in image and communications coaching for physicians, attorneys, architects and other professionals. Charles Browning, Ph.D., is a clinical psychologist and thus can apply psychological concepts to his advertising and public relations work. The company conducts seminars throughout the country, generally conducted by Mrs. Browning, who also is a psychologist.

7. The Executive Television Workshop, Inc.

36 W. 44 St., N.Y. 10036
(212) 819-1633
Walter J. Pfister Jr., Pres.

The Executive Television Workshop provides oral communications training in public speaking, sales and management presentations, government testimony, videotaped appearances, teleconferencing, news media interviewing and crisis response. Custom workshops deal with content, issues, objectives and participants' experience level. Founded in 1978, the company is one of the most important in the communications coaching field. Wally Pfister is a renowned television specialist.

8. Executive Wardrobe Engineering

721 Shore Acres Drive, Mamaroneck, NY 10543
(914) 688-0721
Lois Fenton

Lois Fenton, a well known wardrobe consultant and lecturer, deals primarily with men, and has spoken at many associations and companies, specializing in seminars on achieving the successful executive look, with guidelines on cut, color coordination and quality. Her demonstrations do not use slides and concentrate on real clothing and audience involvement. She also provides personal advice about how to tie a necktie and dozens of other details, and has a twin program for women. Her fee, for up to half a day, is about $2500, plus travel expenses. Mrs. Fenton is the author, with Edward Olcott, of a book for men, Dress for Excellence ($19.95).

9. Dr. William Formaad

12702 Inverary Circle SE
Fort Myers, FL 33912
(813) 768-1451

Dr. Formaad was a professor of speech at Seton Hall University in South Orange, NJ and director of verbal communications of John Molloy's Dress for Success. In 1987, he moved to Florida. He still provides individual counseling and instruction on speech and voice improvement and speech delivery, and is a specialist on accent problems.

10. Going Public

28 E. 73 St., N.Y. 10021
(212) 734-0407
Pamela Zarit, Pres.

Pam Zarit has put her show business experience (actress, dialogue coach, talent booker) to work as a personal consultant to neophyte spokespeople and experienced performers. Her dynamic style is very personal, and includes video analysis and other techniques.

11. Hallstein and Associates
365 West End Ave., N.Y. 10024
(212) 496-6680
Philip Hallstein

An extraordinarily skilled speaker, Phil Hallstein has conducted workshops on presentation skills at many advertising and public relations agencies and departments. The workshops, generally for small groups, are delightfully entertaining, as well as extremely helpful. A former advertising agency executive, he knows the importance of content *and* style. He also does media training and related projects, including speech writing. Fees start at $2200 a day.

12. Jack Hilton Incorporated
230 Park Ave., N.Y. 10169
(212) 687-2002
Jack Hilton, Chm.

Started in 1976, Jack Hilton Incorporated now is one of the largest consultants in television and corporate communications. The staff includes full and part-time professionals, with particular concentration on television. The company has worked with over 20,000 executives in this capacity. Its TeleCounsel Course, which is held in professional studios with broadcast professionals as interviewers, is available in two formats. The two-day format for a maximum of six participants costs $12,000. A one-day format for two participants is $5,000.

An ExecuComm Course, which concentrates on professional speech and presentation training, is $3,000 a day for two people.

A subsidiary company, Jack Hilton Productions, headed by Stuart F. Sucherman, produces television programs. Another subsidiary is Hilton/Schmidt Incorporated, headed by J. Scott Schmidt, which is located at the Hilton western office, 1554 S. Sepulveda Blvd., L.A. 90025, phone (213) 477-5606.

13. Jacobi Voice Development
344 W. 72 St., N.Y. 10023
(212) 787-6721
Jeffrey Jacobi, Dir.

A speech coach to prominent actors, broadcasters and executives, Jeff Jacobi provides private instruction ($75 an hour) and six-hour seminars ($150 per person). His specialty is dialects and accents (generally to submerge or eliminate them and overcoming hoarseness, shrillness, nasality and other problems). The company was formed in 1939 by his father, Henry Jacobi.

14. Frederick Knapp Associates, Inc.
280 Madison Ave., N.Y. 10016
(212) 689-2299
Frederick Knapp, Pres.
Penny Leigh, V.P.

Founded in 1971, Fred Knapp heads an executive image and speech communications firm which provides seminars and training at its offices or elsewhere. Services include:

Media-Speak. Training on how to face the television camera and microphone, the professional way to sit and stand, when and how to get across the key points of the message, dealing with loaded questions and knowing how to buy time to think. Color videotapings throughout the one-day seminar. $695.

Execu-Image. The total image one projects. Emphasis is on executive dress, grooming style, inner and outer images, the executive way to communicate, executive style and the ability to persuade, executive body language, business manners and professional courtesies. Color videotapings throughout the two-day seminar. $745.

Execu-Speak. Concentrates on proven techniques that will help participants prepare and deliver successful presentations: speech organization, body language that communicates strength, key words, gestures to use and when to use them, professional use of visual aids, how to control nervousness, lectern and microphone techniques. Color videotapings throughout the seminar. $645.

Execu-Speak 500. For alumni of Execu-Speak or other business speaking courses. Concentrates on the professional speaking image, how you come across, controlling meetings, awards, media interviews, the art of being persuasive, thinking on your feet. Color videotapings throughout the two-day seminar. $745.

15. McAlinden Associates, Inc.
122 E. 42 St., N.Y. 10168
(212) 986-4950
Jack McAlinden, Anne McAlinden, Joel Wald

Founded in 1972, the firm was one of the pioneers in communication skills development for corporate senior management. Presentation and meeting skill programs include Building Communication Skills for up to six executives from the same company (two days and a one-day follow-up, beginning at $9,900); and Presenting for Results, an open workshop for up to ten people (two days, $950 a person). The writing programs vary in format and fees. Private instruction starts at $3,500 a day.

16. Media/Presentation Training
149 Madison Ave., N.Y. 10016
(212) 889-1327
Robert L. Kimmel, Dir.
Stephanie Mermin, Dir.

An experienced group of media coaches provide executive communication training in skills required for successful television, radio and print interviews, as well as public speaking. A division of Audio/TV Features, Inc.

17. New Image
14 E. 90 St., N.Y. 10128
(212) 289-7807
Emily Cho

One of the founders of the image consulting field, Emily Cho now is primarily a personal shopper and fashion advisor to women. She and her partner, Neila Fisher, charge $300 an hour for a unique service, which generally starts by visiting the client's home and analyzing her wardrobe. Then, Ms. Cho or one of her assistants takes the client on a whirlwind tour of specific stores where the new wardrobe is selected. Prominent executives, broadcasters and other clients look to Cho and Fisher for cosmetic, fashion and other guidance.

A psychology graduate of Cornell University, Emily Cho is the author of three books: *It's You, Looking Terrific* and *Looking, Working, Living Terrific 24 Hours a Day*. She also has been a spokesperson for Clairol and other companies.

18. Joyce Newman Communications
220 E. 63 St., N.Y. 10021
(212) 838-8371, (212) 964-0700

A licensed speech-language therapist, Ms. Newman has provided speech communications and image-building training since 1975. Private and group instruction includes video, rehearsal and speech rewriting services. She developed Speechright, a unique way to organize a speech on paper, and provides services to clients throughout the country. She is renowned for combining affable charm with astute critiques and advice, and has an extraordinary record of success in preparing individuals for investment meetings, news conferences, media tours, business presentations, speeches and other public relations projects.

19. Power/Speak
Box 1505, Bloomfield, NJ 07003
(201) 748-1077
Samuel S. Crandell, Pres.

Individual and group courses and also home study courses (with audio cassettes mailed to and from the client) are conducted by Sam Crandell on telephone performance and public speaking. The author of Power/Speak, a book on effective speaking, Mr. Crandell has given hundreds of training and motivational speeches and workshops.

20. Ready for Media
1900 South Sepulveda Blvd., L.A. 90025
(213) 473-7588
Anne Ready, Pres.

Since 1981, Ready for Media has expanded as a communications consulting firm to include not only preparing clients for television and print interviews, but also for speeches and presentations.

Because so many of its clients are corporations, crisis communication and strategy has played an increasing role in the company's work. "The best defense is still a strong offense," recommends founder and president Anne Ready.

Many of the clients are also taking advantage of Ready's background in television production for product introductions and video news releases in a new division called Videoworks.

21. Arthur Sager Associates, Inc.
Box 36, Topsfield, MA 01983
(617) 887-2886
Milton Archer, Pres.

The Executive Speech Seminar is a three-day program for a small group (generally 10 executives). Total cost for the group is $4,300, plus expenses. Sager also conducts an intensive one-day program.

22. Frank Sentry Group
7471 Melrose Ave., L.A. 90046
(213) 655-6099
Frank Sentry, Pres.

A long-time network radio and television producer, director and writer, Frank Sentry has operated his own company since 1971. The specialty is coaching for public speaking and media interviews. Fees are $1750 per day for an individual and $7000 for a three-day group program, with a maximum of eight participants.

Additional services include consultation on the design, training and operation of corporate speakers bureaus and the production of corporate annual and stockholders meetings, which includes directing, writing, editing and individual coaching for participants.

23. Speakeasy Inc.

830 Monarch Plaza, 3414 Peachtree Rd, N.E., Atlanta, GA 30326
(404) 261-4029
Sandy Linver, Pres.
Sally Langstaff, V.P.

Branch Office:
830 Montgomery-Washington Tower, 655 Montgomery St., San Francisco 94111
(415) 434-2682, (800) 221-7432

Started in 1973, Speakeasy specializes in providing business people with skills to make them more effective in any kind of speaking situation. In Speakeasy programs participants develop increased awareness of themselves and of their audience, and they are introduced to techniques that help them look and feel more in control when they speak.

Sandy Linver, president and founder of Speakeasy, is the author of *Speak Easy* (1979) and *Speak and Get Results* (1983), both published by Summit books. Nationally recognized as an expert on speaking, she travels throughout the United States coaching speakers, conducting seminars and speaking at meetings and conventions.

Services include a three-day Executive Seminar ($995 per person), an eight-week evening course for less experienced speakers ($350), private coaching services and in-house workshops and seminars.

24. Speaking Up

1750 Vallejo, San Francisco 94123
(415) 861-3059
Janet Stone

Formed in 1974 by Janet Stone and Jane Bachner (co-authors of *Speaking Up: A Book for Every Woman Who Wants to Speak Effectively*), Speaking Up is a specialist in employee training and development, particularly programs for women. Services include speech writing, coaching for broadcast appearances, and specialized "training the trainer" projects. These range from $2,300 to $2,600 per day.

The book ($6.95 in paperback) describes their techniques, which include a rigorous program in self-presentation skills. Ms. Stone and Ms. Bachner have extensive radio and television experience.

25. Speech Dynamics, Inc.

111 W. 57 St., N.Y. 10019
(212) 759-3996
Dorothy Sarnoff, Chm.

An independent subsidiary of the Ogilvy & Mather advertising agency, Speech Dynamics is one of the oldest (founded 1966) and largest companies in the personal communication field. The founder, Dorothy Sarnoff, is the most famous speech consultant. She has been a popular guest on TV talk shows and the subject of many major articles in The Wall Street Journal, The New York Times and other publications.

A former actress and singer, Miss Sarnoff has worked hard at developing techniques to transmit her communications skills to those who are less talented. Her impressive client list has included many thousands of politicians, executives, authors, performers and others who have participated in two-day seminars ($850 each) and corporate seminars ($5,500 to $7,000 per day).

Other courses, including private sessions, are available, such as a six-hour course for an individual, to be taken in three or four separate sessions, at a cost of about $3,500.

Miss Sarnoff, who is *not* related to the Sarnoff family at RCA, is the author of *Speech Can Change Your Life* (Doubleday). It has changed her life.

26. Speechworks

20 Hawkins Rd., Stony Brook, NY 11790
(516) 751-8549
Francine Berger, Pres.

A speech communication trainer for 20 years, Francine Berger started Speechworks in 1976 to assist people to develop the attitudes and learn the skills of persuasiveness and effective communication. A half-day program is $1,800 and a full-day program is about $2,400, depending on location and size of group. Private coaching is $200 an hour.

Speechworks techniques include lecture, demonstration, role playing, case study, coaching, visualization and videotape.

The most requested programs are: How to be an effective presenter, How to sell your ideas, How to be an assertive-responsive manager, How to listen for success, Body language—a key to your most secret thoughts, Image impact—conveying the look of power, Talk nice to yourself—the self-communication program for stress prevention, and How to get people to say "yes!" to you.

27. Spokesperson Services

4920 Van Nuys Blvd., Sherman Oaks, CA 91403
(818) 789-9881
Jan Bisgaard, Pres.

Founded in 1985, Spokesperson Services is an unusual operation created to fill a need of public relations people. For a $500 fee, Ms. Bisgaard will analyze a public relations program, determine the type of outside spokesperson who can handle the media tour, convention or other assignment, and then conduct a search. She then charges $500 for each spokesperson selected. For an additional fee, she provides training and other services, if needed.

28. Talk Lab Workshop

301 W. 53 St., N.Y. 10019
(212) 581-1840
Paul Kasander, Exec. Dir.

A division of Kay Korwin Inc., a personal-management company, Talk Lab Workshop conducts a confidential, executive speech-training program, with emphasis on increasing verbal effectiveness in *stress situations,* such as stockholder meetings, hostile audiences and press conferences. Mr. Kasander was a speech professor at Wayne University and held announcing and other positions at CBS and ABC. His associate, Shepherd Welsh, has coached many senators and members of Congress and worked for many years at advertising agencies.

29. Television Communicators

4626 Davenport St., N.W., Wash., DC 20016
(202) 966-6616
Robert D. Wechter, Pres.

A former TV news producer-reporter (WRC-TV in Washington), Bob Wechter provides individual and group media training, videotape evaluation and other related services.

30. Toastmasters International

Box 10400, 2200 N. Grand Ave., Santa Ana, CA 92711
(714) 542-6793
Terrence J. McCann, Exec. Dir.

Founded in 1924, Toastmasters International now has over 6,000 affiliated Toastmasters Clubs in the U.S. and 48 other countries. Many are sponsored by companies and government agencies to develop public speaking, leadership and communications skills. Dues are about $36 a year.

A company can establish an in-house club by contacting John A. Feudo, manager of membership and club extension. The charter fee is $75.

Members receive a monthly magazine and the opportunity to prepare, present and evaluate speeches in a friendly atmosphere.

An affiliated operation, Gavel Clubs, provides public speaking training in schools, prisons and other institutions, and often provides speaking opportunities for Toastmasters members.

31. Granville Toogood Associates

5 Salem Straits, Darien, CT 06820
(203) 655-5155
Granville Toogood, Pres.

Granville Toogood believes strongly that too many ''speech courses'' rely on a single training session. This program is spread over a period of months to insure continuity and reinforcement. Typically, a first session is devoted to teaching the executive how to read a speech verbatim, while appearing to be speaking extemporaneously or from notes. Subsequent sessions reinforce this and other skills. Courses also include television training for individuals and groups of executives.

The fee for a day with four executives is $2,500, plus expenses.

32. Video Consultants, Inc.

Box 13311, Tallahassee, Fl 32317-3311
(904) 668-1082
Clarence Jones, Pres.

Clarence Jones, who was an investigative reporter and newscaster at station WPLG-TV in Miami, formed this media consultant service in 1984. He teaches government and corporate executives effective media strategy and on-camera skills. He's located in northern Florida and provides consulting throughout the country.

33. You're On/Access to Television & Radio

19 Madison Ave., Beverly, MA 01915
(617) 927-6768
Richard M. Goldberg, Pres.

See listing in television chapter.

Pam Zaret
See listing under Going Public.

34. Arnold Zenker & Associates
99 High St., Boston, MA 02110
(617) 542-0220
Arnold Zenker, Pres.
Joan Quinn Eastman, V.P.

One of the country's best known media trainers, Arnold Zenker and his staff have developed several specialties, including crisis counseling and government testimony, particularly in the health care field. Fees for a one-day workshop range from $2,450 to $3,750, for two to several people. A two-day workshop is $695 per person, with a minimum of $7,450.

Other communications consultants, particularly experts on media training, are listed in the television chapter.

Chapter 7

Computerized News

Just as it has changed our business and personal lives, the computer has transformed journalism, news gathering and dissemination, media production and press relations. The wedding of the computer with advanced telecommunications also has given birth to a totally new medium—the powerful on-line, full-text news retrieval database.

As we try to grapple with accelerating change, the tide of technological innovation refuses to be staunched or stemmed. It now is obvious that PR practitioners must be "computer literate" and the sooner the better.

For more than a decade, David Steinberg (previously a prize-winning business writer for the New York Herald Tribune and now president of PR Newswire) has been analyzing and anticipating the impact on public relations of computerization at the news media. This chapter combines excerpts from his presentations to professional groups with comments from an interview with him and his associates at PR Newswire's impressively automated New York headquarters.

In the 80's, many public relations departments and agencies started to use computers extensively, though generally to a much smaller degree than they should. For many years, the use of computers by the media, particularly daily newspapers, has been far ahead of the public relations field.

The major wire services and newspapers now are computerized and America's leading radio and television stations are working to integrate computers into their news operations.

The hallmark of editorial computerization is the VDT (Video Display Terminal) screen, now perched comfortably on or beside editors' and reporters' desks all around the country. Only a few years ago, a VDT editing terminal was a menacing novelty in the newsroom. Reporters no longer are willing to share their terminals with other staff members.

What accounts for this proliferation of such expensive and sophisticated hardware?

Quite simply, apart from the necessary speed and production efficiency it embodies, the computer brings *order* to the newsroom. As modern communications techniques shrink the globe, the torrent of information flooding editorial offices has all but drowned the staff. Electronic processing makes the flood-tide manageable. Editors easily and quickly know what stories are on hand and can determine and find those they wish to use in the next edition.

The computer makes possible high-speed transmission and receipt of news and compact and instantaneously retrievable storage of countless pages of copy. With swift, silent efficiency, it reduces confusion, scales mountains of paper and even saves wastebaskets from overflowing.

Copy can be "deleted" from existence with a keystroke. Some systems, in fact, do not require anyone to strike a key. Stories ignored by editors for a set number of hours are automatically destroyed and you must hope your news release is not among them.

The ubiquitous VDT is the primary input device for original copy. Seated before its TV-like screen, a reporter can write and edit a story and correct spelling and typographical errors. The reporter can insert, delete or move individual characters, words, phrases, lines, sentences, paragraphs and even larger blocks of copy, can search through the text electronically to find, change, kill or replace certain words or phrases, and may make wholesale revisions or combine one story with another. In the newest systems, it is possible to "split" the screen with the story being written on one side and a "clip" from the paper's electronic "morgue" (or some other reference information) on the other side.

Correspondents in distant bureaus write, edit and transmit their reports to the main computer from bureau terminals, which usually are linked to the home office by private wire circuits. A reporter on out-of-town assignment or a sportswriter covering a game at a distant stadium may carry in a briefcase a miniature terminal with full editing features, a memory that can hold more than 100 pages of copy and the ability to transmit any, or all, of it back to the cityroom or the sports desk from the nearest telephone at 300 or 1200 words per minute (wpm).

Reports submitted by domestic and overseas stringers can flow by Telex straight into the computer system. Old-fashioned "hard copy" (typed on paper, like the venerable news release) can be entered into the computer system by tedious rekeyboarding or, if the investment has been made by the publication, by use of an optical scanner which reads certain typefaces and converts them into electronic pulses.

Staff-generated material is only part of the input. The publicist is competing with many other sources, such as the enormous quantity of news files received each day from the computers of the national and international wire services, syndicates and other general and specialized news and feature services to which a publication subscribes. Virtually all of this additional information arrives over high-speed circuits tied directly into the newspaper's own editorial computer. It is not unusual for a major daily newspaper to receive many hundreds of articles every day—hundreds of thousands of words—from all sources, including the public relations community.

But, now that the computer has transformed the mountains of urgent news to a staggering number of bits and bytes in its mysterious memory, how do editors know what they have to work with? Who sent what from where? Which items are most critical and which may be tackled later? Who should be assigned to what?

First, there is a primary monitor teleprinter, which slavishly prints a continuous index of everything entered into the system from any source. A single line tells the editor where each item came from, who wrote it, how long it is, when it was entered and when it may be published—but only five or six words with which to identify the subject. If an "abstract printer" is used, all the same information is presented along with about the first 30 words (the "lede") of the item. It is from these short or long indexes that editors make their selections. Each editor looks at a departmental directory, such as sports, politics, financial, world news and other departments.

In addition to monitoring input on index teleprinters, the editor may view any of these directories on a VDT, which now is much more than an exotic typewriter. In a flash, the editor also can retrieve on the screen the full text of any story of interest, can perform any required editing, or electronically pass it over to a staffer for rewrite on another screen. Of course, the editor may kill the item even faster than it was called up—with a single keystroke!

When a "story" passes editorial review, it may be forwarded electronically to the copy desk for final spelling, grammar, style and other revisions. Headlines may be composed on special terminals which display them in requested type sizes and column widths. There even are special VDTs designed to lay out full pages with all editorial content and advertising in position (a process known as "pagination").

The final step is a simple keyboard command which can whisk copy off the editor's screen at 9,600 or more words per minute for automatic typesetting equipment in another computer—which justifies margins to proper column widths, hyphenates words and checks itself for errors.

It is in this last step that automation of a news wire differs markedly from a newspaper. At the wire service, the last command from an editor is "send" or "transmit." Instantly, the words are off on a journey that may take them across the street by wire or around the world by satellite. At a few subscribing newspapers, magazines or broadcasting stations, the news may still clack out slowly on aging Teletype machines, whereas at others the news is received on silent high-speed teleprinters. At many major media offices, the material zips with lightning speed straight into the subscriber's own editorial computer.

From the VDT keyboard, the wire service editor controls the routing and destination of each piece of copy, and also can assign priorities to the items, change the order of stories queued up for transmission, break in with a bulletin, order a repeat, place a story on "hold" or slug it for later transmission.

We have come full cycle. We are back at the computerized newspaper, where the flood of urgent, time-critical material has not diminished. In fact, it may have grown exponentially. But, it has become comfortably controllable, eminently accessible and readily usable down to the very last moments before the presses roll out the next edition or the next news program goes on the air.

The crucial question for public relations practitioners in all this wizardry is: How will your news releases enter the complex circle of computerized news handling?

Increasingly, the media are giving greater emphasis and reliance on computer-compatible electronic copy—ready for prompt recall, review, revision, typesetting or transmission. The demand for electronic delivery has resulted in formulation of international text and transmission "standards." Copy sent and formatted to the specifications of The American Newspaper Publishers Association and The International Press Telecommunications Council is available to editors at computerized news media because their computers know precisely what to look for to receive, categorize and store copy and create the fateful indexes and abstracts that will guide these editors in their decisions.

How will you make certain that your news appears in these magical and decisive directories?

In some instances, the old methods will still work. In others, only the new will be acceptable. It is unlikely that an editor would refuse a good tip or worthy story because it was hand-delivered or possibly even handwritten. But, if your release must compete with all the other news of the day, it is preferable that it be there in the fastest and most compatible form.

It may be technically possible for you to deliver your news into some media computers by Telex or telephone dial-up from your own word-processor, personal or office computer system, or portable data communications terminal. But, you will be hard pressed, indeed, to deliver simultaneously to all relevant media, near and far, with the precise protocol, speed and format they require. Nor is it realistic to believe that newspapers and other media will build into their systems the additional computer ports and storage space that would be required for hundreds of corporations, government bureaus, public relations agencies and other news release sources to reach them individually.

At present, convenient, compatible access to the editorial computers of most major newspapers is available to public relations practitioners through the sophisticated communications facilities of some of the nation's "pr wires." PR Newswire, for example, transmits about 300 news releases by satellite every day to its nationwide network of "hard copy" teleprinters and also directly into more than 250 newsroom computers. The full text of every release is delivered simultaneously into other massive computer systems which are the heart of several different on-line databases specializing in news information.

These instantly-accessible and totally searchable electronic libraries have become vital resources for editors, reporters, financial analysts and corporate, academic, legal, governmental and other researchers. With nearly 2,000 databases now available, those offering national, world, sports and financial news are among the most heavily used. Prominent among them are NEXIS; Dow Jones News/Retrieval; NewsNet; NewSearch and the National Newspaper and the Trade and Industry Indexes of Dialog Information Service; Vu/Text; CompuServe, and The Source.

NEXIS, for instance, contains the full text of The New York Times, The Washington Post, News-week, Time, Forbes and over 100 other publications. It also houses verbatim files from AP, UPI, Reuters, six other wire services and every news release carried by PR Newswire since January 22, 1980—more than 500,000 news releases from more than 15,000 sources!

A poll of newspaper librarians indicates that approximately 75 percent of the nation's daily news-papers subscribe to one or more databases or otherwise have them accessible to their staffs. Use of databases by editors and reporters signals a revolution in newsgathering.

The inclusion in database archives of news releases in full, as originally written and issued by the source, heralds a new medium of "publication" for public relations and investor relations professionals. In a sense, for the first time you have some significant control over what is "published" simply by originating a release. Using PR Newswire, for example, your news release is retrievable within 15 min-utes of transmission in the PR Newswire file in Dialog and within two hours in NewsNet.

Databases keep your news release on call for days, weeks and possibly years by editors, reporters, investment analysts and others seeking knowledge of your company, your organization or your client. A journalist, when searching for background, or an analyst updating an industry, can find exactly what you said, and everything you said, even if only a small portion of your original release appeared in print in a minor publication. Because database searches can be conducted by broad subject as well as precise names or terms, searchers can discover what was said even if they didn't know you had issued a release. And they have your press contact name and phone number to call if they want more information.

The ability to retrieve so much valuable information so easily and quickly (an average NEXIS search takes only 20 seconds) can be as important to a public relations writer as a syndicated columnist. Many public relations agencies and departments now use "electronic news sourcing" to flesh out releases, watch what the competition is doing, prepare client and prospect presentations or simply as a handy "morgue" of all of their own previously issued news releases.

The sweeping changes brought to news operations and press relations by computers, advanced tele-communications and databases in the last few years are becoming evident everywhere. But, it is still too soon to discern their ultimate impact. It is not unlikely that technology will help determine where, when and how you distribute your news, and also how you write it as well.

For example, the beginning of this chapter discussed those decisive directories and 30-word abstracts which editors rely upon to make their story choices. Clearly, the first rule of good journalistic writing—"put the news in the lede"—has acquired new significance. In a paperless newsroom, if you want your release to be among the editor's choices, the news generally should be in the lede, or it may not be seen at all.

The media always can be expected to respond to a juicy news or feature release, whether it is delivered by satellite or semaphore. But, it also is only common sense for today's public relations profes-sionals to make certain they are "computer literate" and their output is "computer compatible."

One of the innovative leaders in establishing computerized public relations services is the 3M Co., which, in 1984, introduced an electronic service for journalists. Called the 3M Newsroom, the system is an electronic news and feature clearing house, which journalists can utilize via their personal computers. Reporters can receive up to the minute news releases and also ask questions and request exclusive mate-rial. The system is useful only for a large company such as 3M, which has many business units, each with its own public relations staffs.

Another sophisticated company is Philip Morris, which also makes extensive use of its word proces-sors in order to communicate computer-to-computer. One of its innovations pertains to the Virginia Slims Women's Tennis Tournament, sponsored by a Philip Morris brand, Virginia Slims. An enormous amount of data about women's tennis players is compiled daily in the Virginia Slims data bank.

Another area in which computers are beginning to play an exciting role is in the preparation of graphics for charts, reports, meetings and presentations. It now is possible to purchase software packages for use on personal computers and there now are better quality high resolution screens, fast computer speeds, and programs which create lucid, colorful and easy-to-comprehend graphics. The field is changing very rapidly, as is the case with all software, and the subject is not included in this book, except to note that there essentially are four types of graphics output devices which you'll need to prepare a computer generated graphics presentation. They are printers, plotters, slide-producing cameras and systems to project the image directly from your computer to a movie screen. The first is the simplest and the last is the most elaborate, and you should observe all of them in action before getting started in this arena. For example, you can print charts and graphs on a dot-matrix printer and then duplicate copies. The next step up, of course, is to add additional equipment, and software designed to reproduce graphics generated by your computer, such as line and bar graphs, pie charts and pictures.

More information about computerized news is included in the chapters on news wires and research.

Chapter 8

Editorials

The editorial page of a newspaper probably is more influential and has a higher impact than any other part of the publication. Political candidates, educational, civic, cultural, health, welfare and other nonprofit organizations therefore frequently provide news releases, pamphlets and research material to editorial writers and communicate with them by means of briefing sessions and individual meetings.

Many experienced public relations professionals, particularly those involved in commercial activities, usually ignore editorial writers. There sometimes is the feeling that the editorial department is a sacrosanct domain. All editors should be treated with respect, but that does not mean that publicists cannot deal with and provide a service to editorial writers in the same way that they work with other sections of the newspapers.

In this era of consumerism, companies and trade associations are more vulnerable than ever before to attack and criticisms by the media. There's hardly a commercial enterprise which is not involved with various types of governmental regulation and censure by Government agencies, and volunteer "watchdogs" are a constant threat, even to companies with the highest standards.

Editorials therefore should be considered as a publicity technique, for prevention and education, as well as for rebuttal and defense.

Several publicity services make mailings to editorial writers as part of their general operations, but there are very few editorial specialists. The pioneer in the sponsored editorial field was U.S. Press Association (USPA). Each week, from 1911 to 1973, the USPA sent a packet of six editorials, called Washington Exclusive, to about 1,000 editors of daily and weekly newspapers, mostly in small cities. In 1973, U.S. Press Association quietly disappeared. However, its unique service merits review, partly because it truly is part of the history of journalism and public relations, and also because quite possibly someone will resurrect the concept.

The heyday of USPA was in the 40's and 50's when the owner was Robert Taylor and his wife, Winnie. For about 25 years, they were the entire staff, and many clients treasured the charming notes, signed Winnie the Clipper, which accompanied each batch of clippings.

Bob Taylor was quite conservative and rejected clients with whom he did not agree or who he felt would not be compatible with his grass-roots, small-town editors. Each editor was considered a subscriber, even though the weekly collection of editorials was sent free and exclusive in each county. Some editors used the editorials as if they were a syndicated column under the title of Washington-Exclusive, but most published them as their own views, on page one or on the editorial page.

Bob Taylor sold USPA to Lyle Munson, who was succeeded by Herbert A. Philbrick. Both were active in ultraconservative political organizations, and Mr. Philbrick was best known as a former F.B.I. agent, author and lecturer.

USPA clearly stated its editorial policy with each mailing to editors, as follows:

> U.S. Press Association, Inc., believes that business is responsible for the atmosphere in which it functions. In cooperation with American business institutions, we present timely editorial comment on free enterprise achievements and problems. We fight for what we think is good for American business. We reject what we think is bad. Clients pay an established fee for editorial consultation. Political candidates, parties or groups are never accepted. Published each week exclusively for newspaper editors who have requested the service, the policies reflected and the opinions expressed are those of the publisher.
>
> We ask only that you place your name on your exchange list to receive every issue of your paper. We will be grateful for your comments, guidance and criticisms.
>
> At no time has the free enterprise system been subject to greater or more destructive attack than right now. Our sole purpose is to project and preserve that system. If you have an idea as to how we can better do that job, let us hear from you.

The USPA credo was reflected in editorials (many unsponsored) which were strongly critical of liquor, tobacco, motion picture, TV and other industries.

In a memo to editors, Mr. Munson stated:

"The inescapable impression is that Washington has come to be more and more isolated and unresponsive to what the voters across the land are saying and thinking. The emphasis in Washington is on influencing public attitudes rather than upon reflecting them.

"The flow in influence needs badly to be reversed. You can help to generate that reversal through your newspaper. I will try to send you some fuel each week."

Whether or not clients agreed with Messrs. Taylor, Munson and Philbrick, they usually respected their consistency and business fortitude. Their writing style was folksy and colloquial, but extremely literate and erudite.

And the results were extraordinary. For a fee of $700, USPA wrote the editorial, subject to client approval, produced and distributed it and provided an average of 100 clippings.

In 1973, Mr. Philbrick folded what had become an institution. Rising costs, other personal interests and increased competition from other publicity services were among the factors.

This left the field partly to E. Hofer & Sons of Hillsboro, Oregon, an editorial specialist from 1913 to 1975. For the journalism-public relations "record," here's an outline of the Hofer operation.

Each week, several thousand weekly and daily newspaper editors (all of the dailies *except* the majors) received a packet of pink, legal-size sheets, titled Industrial News Review, on which were crammed a variety of editorials, ranging from pithy one-sentence quotes to detailed analytic commentaries.

The editorials were provided free to the newspapers by Hofer and many published them regularly—complete and verbatim. The company (located near Portland) received its income solely from sponsors of the editorials. Most of the sponsors were associations, and companies were accepted only when their product dominated a field or was generic. Commercial credits generally were not included in the editorials.

Hofer wrote the editorial based on material provided by clients, but the editorial was *not* submitted to the client for approval prior to publication. The extraordinary modus operandi thus included the writing and distribution of editorials without submission to or approval by the sponsor, which is almost unheard of among publicity services.

For many years, the National Association of Manufacturers operated Industrial News Service, which provided the equivalent of sponsored editorials. However, this no longer is available.

So much for history. Now, here is a review of what's available.

Current and past copies of editorials from 150 major newspapers can be obtained from the Editorial Search Service of Facts on File Publications, which is described in the back issues section of the chapter on clipping bureaus.

Publicists can provide suggested editorials, fact kits, speech texts and other materials to editorial page editors, directly or via mailing services, and also can prepare and distribute "Op-ed" page features and editorial cartoons.

Many newspapers and other media subscribe to Editorial Research Reports, a weekly packet of materials produced by Congressional Quarterly Inc., 1414 22 St., N.W., Wash., DC 20037. Each 6,000-word report includes an in-depth analysis of a major issue plus a bibliography, maps, charts, graphs and other materials.

Public relations practitioners can provide backgrounders and other information to Editorial Research Reports, and also can subscribe to this unique service ($410/yr.), which includes The Weekly Report, plus a two-page summary, a newsletter titled News Futures about forthcoming events, and a telephone inquiry service.

Editorial Research Reports is a superb service that is unknown by many experienced public relations people. Richard M. Boeckel, who died in 1975, was editor for many years. The current editor is Hoyt Gimlin.

Additional information about Congressional Quarterly is included in the research chapter.

Derus Media Service, Inc., 500 N. Dearborn St., Chicago 60610, is a major distributor of packaged newspaper features. The company provides a congressional service in which it distributes materials, such as editorials, to its regular list of newspapers and then sends copies of the articles, together with a note (on the client's letterhead) to members of Congress. The cost is $3,300, including clipping service and replies from Congress.

Anytime you are involved in an editorial in a major publication, you may be able to put icing on this cake by sending the clipping to other publications. For example, just about every Senator and member of Congress puts out a newsletter and many of them look for editorials to reprint from their districts.

Another resource is to utilize a newspaper service which specializes in editorials. For example, North American Precis Syndicate produces and distributes a variety of articles and cartoons for all types of clients, with sponsor approval.

If you are in—or approaching—a situation where it is very important to you that millions of additional Americans should know some important facts about a question of public policy, you may want to do considerably more than a few editorials. You may want to get out a substantial number of features that will increase public awareness of your position.

There is "a rapidly evolving technology of public policy publicity," according to Ron Levy of North American Precis Syndicate. "Only a few years ago, the state of the art was to get out a set of editorials seeking fairness to the industry, damning the other side and making a point-by-point rebuttal of the opposing position on the issue. Today, the appeal of releases is fairness not to an industry but to the public interest. The readers may not care about your industry nor even about current events. But if he or she sees how a situation stands to raise prices or threaten jobs, he or she will care, and when enough millions of people care, you get an awful lot of letters to legislators," states Mr. Levy.

Editorials can be an extremely important part of the public relations efforts of trade, professional and other associations and organizations. Writing in a 1986 issue of Public Relations Quarterly and in several issues of Public Relations Journal, Ron Levy stated these basic principles.

1. Recognize that there is a "principle of primacy" in association PR: the side that gets to the newspapers first tends to be believed more; the side that comes second, and with contrary facts, is believed less by editors and readers who already "know better."

2. Going to the press with one basic story on The Issue, seeking fairness to your side, may not be the tactic of choice. This is because readers may care very little about The Issue—and reason that your side is rich enough to come out okay no matter how the issue is ultimately resolved.

3. A way more likely to win in the current environment is to go with stories on subjects that editors and readers care very much about—their own money, health and environment. If resolving the issue your way would mean genuine benefit to the readers, they will be interested to read about it. If the benefit to them could be substantial, they will care very substantially that your view should prevail.

4. Once the program plan has been approved, assign authority to clear releases to as small a group as possible. Those who wait for all the members to register their views sometimes wait for a very long time, and trying to conform to all details of all views can produce a program that is a monster.

5. Love thy lawyers as thyself. Using their affidavits, testimony and position papers can help you two ways: (a) as a source of well researched facts (using the same facts in publicity is like backing up the ad program with publicity); and (b) faster clearance by the lawyers who have already decided that the facts are correct and the language accurate.

6. Prepare extra copies of releases for member placement in plant town newspapers. It will mean not only more press coverage of your message, but also more involvement by the members. (Involved members are easier to deal with in getting approvals and budget, and often more enthusiastic in their appraisal of campaign results!)

7. Decide at the outset how you will evaluate results of the program, for especially if the program is being run by someone under you, how you measure will help determine what you get. A common error is to measure results only by the quantity of clippings and TV newscasts, for these tell you how much opportunity was obtained to do the persuading, not whether the persuading was done.

Editorials no longer are the only publicity tool when doing public policy publicity in the suburbs. A variety of features is also useful. A good set of releases may contain a background piece abstracted from testimony to help the public understand what's at stake . . . a "Believe-It-Or-Not" type cartoon to make a point with particular emphasis . . . a "Then & Now" release showing that there is already progress without unduly restrictive legislation . . . a "Test Your Knowledge" release . . . one or a set of Q&A releases . . . and more.

A point-by-point rebuttal is rarely used by veterans of public policy fights, for this would call the opposing position to the attention of many people who are not familiar with it. Instead, points are made positively without reference to the other side.

In a public policy contest, one side may decide on doing one set of 12 releases initially, and then a release or two each month until the issue is decided. Such a set of releases generates several thousand newspaper articles that get into Congressional issue files, stimulates letters to legislators, and helps to persuade both legislative aides in Washington and political leaders back home in the district. The cost is generally under $20,000.

Many public relations practitioners know that significant publicity can be obtained with bylined articles which appear on or opposite the editorial pages of major newspapers. Articles prepared for the editorial page or the op-ed page of The New York Times generally must be totally exclusive. Articles prepared for other major newspapers generally must be totally exclusive or exclusive in the area in which the newspaper is circulated. Smaller circulation newspapers, which still are important, often accept articles which appear elsewhere.

North American Precis Syndicate, Inc.
201 E. 42 St., N.Y. 10017
(212) 867-9000
Ronald N. Levy, Pres.
John Engel, Candy Lieberman, Francine Lucidon, Exec. V.P.s
Diane Mason, Marilyn Rosenfeld, Claudia Schiff, Jim Wicht, Sr. V.P.s
Kelly Lawrence, Dorothy Levy, Camilla Mendoza, V.P.s

Branch Offices:
333 N. Michigan Ave., Chicago 60601
(312) 558-1200
Jim Brosseau, Nora Lukas, Sr. V.P.s
Bonnie Cassidy Heller, V.P.

4209 Vantage Ave., Studio City, CA 91604
(818) 761-8400
Carol Balkin, V.P.

1025 Vermont Ave., N.W., Wash., DC 20005
(202) 347-7300
Jake Arnette, Sr. V.P.
Anne Barre, Monty Bodington, Wendy Sollod, V.P.s

North American Precis Syndicate (NAPS) is a packaged publicity service that produces and distributes newspaper "mats," TV slide scripts and camera-ready editorials. Ron Levy, the owner of NAPS, is one of the country's most articulate and knowledgeable public relations tacticians. He and the NAPS staff have analyzed the media and, among other innovations, adapted the newspaper mat technique to the needs of editorial page editors. Many clients send NAPS a speech or testimony, and NAPS converts this information into a set of proposed releases.

The offset proofs often are sent by NAPS under such standing headlines as Viewpoint, Background on Business and News of the Environment.

Coverage is to 1,000 daily and 2,800 weekly newspapers. Results generally are over 100 clippings, mostly on or opposite editorial pages, business and style pages.

The complete cost, including production, postage and clippings, is $2,000 to $2,600 per article, depending on size.

NAPS recommends a spot, or more, of art, to enhance readership, and also for a very practical concern of publicists. A symbol (NAPS' symbol is the letter T) is inserted in the right corner of a photo or drawing, and this is what the clipping bureau looks for.

A complete description of NAPS is in the chapter on newspaper services.

Chapter 9

Filmstrips and Slides

More than 60 million students and educators spend a good part of their lives in the 110,000 public and private schools in the United States. One of the most efficient means of communicating with these audiences, which range from nursery schools to universities, is by means of filmstrips and films.

Films are discussed in the chapters on motion pictures. The major film distributors, such as Modern Talking Pictures, distribute thousands of sponsored 16mm films to schools.

Posters, booklets, speakers and other means of communicating with students are discussed in several chapters, particularly the chapter about schools.

The focus of this chapter is on filmstrips, since they not only are a major public relations technique to reach the vast school market as efficiently and economically as possible, but filmstrips also are a popular technique in employee training programs, sales promotion and other public relations functions. Overhead projectors also are popular.

Filmstrip and slide projectors are vital pieces of equipment in almost every primary and secondary school classroom. Many thousands of business, government, religious and other organizations also own or have access to projectors. As a result, filmstrips and slides can play an important part in almost any public relations program. Government agencies, associations, companies and others have made a valuable educational contribution by distributing thousands of audiovisual kits to schools.

Slides still are one of the most widely used forms of communication (particularly in schools and at business meetings). They not only are relatively low in cost, but offer flexibility in terms of editing and revising and can be produced with and without sound and for use in a single tray or carousel on up to sophisticated shows with several projectors.

A slide projector, which costs about $350, should be in every major public relations office. You don't need additional equipment, though commonly used items are inexpensive, such as screen (about $35), viewer or light table ($25 to $300), storage carousels or decks (about $11), make-your-own-title kits (about $25) and 35mm camera with interchangeable lenses ($300 and up). Slide and filmstrip projectors are the work horses of audiovisual assisted instruction. Furthermore, they continue to hold an important place in the programs of community, religious, professional and other organizational groups, in part due to the fact that so many people have their own personal projectors for showings of their family and vacation slides. As a result, 35mm slides can play an important part in almost any public relations program.

Over the years, the filmstrip has gradually been replaced by the slide carousel. This is a result of the fact that slide projectors are more widely available and slide programs can be edited more easily than strips. However, filmstrips are a bit less expensive to produce and take up very little storage space compared to the relatively bulky slide tray.

Most motion picture producers and still photographers produce filmstrips and slide presentations. However, many public relations clients prefer to deal with filmstrip specialists, particularly since there are some companies which have established channels of distribution to schools and other key audiences.

Among the services provided to the sponsor by a filmstrip distributor are reports of numbers of showings, numbers of students, their ages, comments of the teachers and other data. One print of a filmstrip or set of slides often is viewed by more than 500 students during the first year of its use and frequently is used for several years.

The cost of a filmstrip depends a great deal on the amount and quality of photographs or artwork provided by the client. In most cases, it is necessary for the producer to create all of the photography and artwork, and also to write the script. A filmstrip accompanied by an audio cassette or record costs more than one accompanied by a printed script. The nature of the teacher's or speaker's guide and materials distributed to the audience also affects the production cost.

It therefore is impossible to estimate the cost of a filmstrip except that it costs considerably less than a motion picture of the same length. Among the variables contributing to the budget is whether the filmstrip is sold, donated on a permanent basis, or loaned but returned to the producer. If a loan system is to be employed for distribution of the program, bear in mind the logistical problems which such a system entails. Unfortunately, borrowers cannot be relied upon to return programs in a timely fashion, especially if they're not paying. If the next scheduled user does not receive the anticipated program, the negative reaction may outweigh the positive value of the program itself. The solution to this problem is to have a sufficient number of programs to insure backup and to allow lag time for anticipated late returns. If the budget allows, donating the program to schools for permanent use allows it to be utilized indefinitely.

In the school field, a good filmstrip should result in several thousand requests a year from schools throughout the country. Clients who are budget-conscious (who isn't?) can set a ceiling on the number of requests per year.

In producing a filmstrip for students or other audiences, it is generally recommended that the length not exceed 16 minutes. The reason is that teachers prefer to have time to prepare their classes for the program and conduct post-screening discussions or take a second look at portions of the program on which they want to concentrate. Here's a chart of average filmstrip time and length.

```
10 minutes . . . . . . . . . . . . . . . . . . . . . . . . . . . . .50 to 60 frames
12 minutes . . . . . . . . . . . . . . . . . . . . . . . . . . . . .70 to 80 frames
14–16 minutes . . . . . . . . . . . . . . . . . . . . . . . .100 to 120 frames
```

The minimum negative length generally is 2.75 feet, or 44 frames, including head and tail leader.

The International Communications Industries Association, 3150 Spring Street, Fairfax, VA 22031, conducts an annual trade show, publishes a membership directory and also the Equipment Directory of Audio-Visual, Computer and Video Products. It's $35 to members and $40 to non-members. The association, with about 1,400 members in the communications field, originally was the National Audio-Visual Association (NAVA).

Hundreds of sales promotion agencies, photographers and film producers produce filmstrips and slide shows. Following is a description of several which are primarily in the school field, as well as a few other related services.

Filmstrip programs contain much more than the filmstrip itself. For example, Knowledge Unlimited sells a kit to schools about economics. Here are the contents:

Six filmstrips, with Teacher's Guides and tapes
Three poster charts
Three-ring binder with activity sheets and glossary.

Slide shows are the most popular way to present a message to groups at sales meetings, trade shows, annual shareholder meetings, conventions and training sessions. Their advantage is that they can easily be updated simply by having new slides prepared and inserted. The temptation is to get carried away with the notion that your show should be a "Star Wars" type production complete with numerous special effects. This type of show is very expensive and usually involves 12-15 or more computerized projectors as well as other back-up equipment. It's very easy for your message to get lost in between the special effects with the result that your audience leaves with the impression that they have seen a great show but, unfortunately, they may have forgotten your message. Consider less exotic and more straightforward shows with dissolves and a high quality sound track. This type of two or three projector show can be dismantled and taken to another location with ease and it can be produced for less than half the cost of the multiprojector show.

Genigraphics Corporation, 620 Erie Blvd. W., Syracuse, NY 13204, a major manufacturer of photographic products, publishes the Genigraphics Custom Graphics Slide Guide, a magnificent catalog of "computer clip art" combined with excellent advice about preparing slides and overhead transparencies. The 64-page book is available at Genigraphics offices in major cities, including 500 N. Michigan Ave., Chicago 60611, 5028 Wilshire Blvd., Los Angeles 90036, 40 Broad St., N.Y. 10004 and 3 Ben Franklin Pky., Philadelphia 19102.

The following advice about slide presentations is excerpted from the Genigraphics book.

1. Simplify. Treat your slides like a billboard. Determine how much you really need. If it's difficult getting it all on one layout sheet without cramming, you probably have too much content for a single slide.
2. People read from left to right. Lay out your information so it conforms with the eye movements of your audience. Put your most critical, or most dramatic information at the top to maintain concentration.
3. Compatible layout. Be sure your layout is compatible with the colors you've chosen for the message you're sending.
4. Use a combination of slides. When possible, present your information using a combination of word slides, graphics, charts and graphs, and tabular charts to avoid monotony.
5. Text. Like a newspaper headline, use minimum space to put across maximum ideas. Avoid complete sentences. Consider building several different points one by one to keep your audience focused and prevent reading ahead.

Robert Cooke, Senior Vice President of Doremus Porter Novelli, New York, has produced many slide shows. "With regard to the text," says Bob Cooke, "most of the copy prepared by public relations people generally is much too long for slides".

Another tip from Mr. Cooke: Always take a spare bulb!

Companies that produce filmstrips and slides are listed in the photography and television chapter. Following are several companies of special interest.

1. Educational Enrichment Materials
Random House, Inc.
400 Hahn Rd., Westminster, MD 21157
(800) 638-6460

Formerly owned by The New York Times, Educational Enrichment Materials was bought by Random House in 1983. The division specializes in educational filmstrips and videos.

2. Hope Reports Inc.

1600 Lyell Ave., Rochester, NY 14606
(716) 458-4250
Thomas W. Hope, Chmn.
Vincent Hope, Pres.

If you are active in the audio visual and media communications fields, chances are you subscribe to one of Hope Reports publications. The founder, Thomas Hope, was an Army photo officer in the second world war and headed the Army Motion Picture School (AMPS). His broadcast experience includes converting the Lone Ranger radio program to television, in behalf of General Mills. In business since 1970, Hope Reports conducts market research in media communications and also publishes:

Hope Reports Briefing, a quarterly about audio visual and communications industry developments, $105.
Hope Reports Media and Market Trends, annual, $85.
Hope Reports Industry Quarterly, the marketing almanac in the audio visual and electronic media field, $1,500/yr.

3. Knowledge Unlimited Inc.

Box 52, Madison, WI 53701
(608) 836-6660, (800) 356-2303
Barbara Roberts, Catalog Director

Knowledge Unlimited produces and distributes filmstrips and other educational materials, primarily to schools and also to nursing homes, prisons and other facilities. The company now is operated by Judith DiPrima. In addition to a variety of filmstrips, which are sold via its catalog, Knowledge Unlimited produces NewsCurrents, a weekly news program distributed during the school year and consisting of 35 weekly news filmstrips with discussion guides written on three different vocabulary levels, so that they are suitable for elementary, and high school. Schools may purchase the program for $225 for the series. Several hundred newspapers for many years have provided the programs free to schools in their area, and commercial sponsorship sometimes also is available.

Over two million students see the weekly filmstrips throughout the year in over 10,000 schools.

KU also produces art posters and kits, generally consisting of filmstrips, tapes, posters, booklets and teacher's guides.

4. Visual Data Corporation

3755 Pennridge Dr., Bridgeton, MO 63044
(314) 739-7700, (800) 527-5605
Robert Kiehl

Visual Data provides a full range of filmstrip and slide services. It is best known as the manufacturer of VISDA Communication Packages, which incorporate one or more custom-produced 17.5mm or 35mm color filmstrips, a mailable plastic snap-up viewer (which uses available light—no power source necessary) and a custom-printed folder. The folder serves as a guide for the filmstrip and provides convenient storage for the viewer/filmstrip unit. Standard folder formats, as well as custom-designed folders, are available.

VISDA Packages can be used as a hand-out or mail-out piece for all types of corporate communication and school programs.

Information kits, containing samples, a detailed catalog and complete (net) pricing data on standard folder formats, are available at no cost. Pricing for a 13 picture filmstrip (17.5mm), viewer and two-color folder range from $1.00 up, depending on quantity.

Chapter 10

Financial

The stock market boom in the 60's produced a variety of financial public relations services, notably involving communications to analysts. Most of these services did not survive the subsequent recession.

In the 70's, many publicly owned companies assessed their financial relations programs and reduced, revised or eliminated mass mailings and other extravagant and inefficient operations.

Public relations counselors provided increased attention to the quality of annual reports and other materials and developed new uses for financial documents, such as distribution of the same or revised publications to employees, customers, legislators, media people and other publics.

In the 80's, financial relations services became more extensive and sophisticated than ever before. Years ago, a financial relations department looked different from other public relations facilities because of its Dow Jones news ticker or Quotron terminal. Today, all public relations operations are oriented to computers.

Proxy solicitation, annual reports, investment research and other financial services certainly require the use of financial experts. However, there is no need for a public relations generalist to be overwhelmed by technical jargon and the financial mystique. Attorneys, accountants and controllers must know about 10K's, 10Q's, 8K's, S-16's, N-1Q's and other S.E.C. filings, but a competent public relations person can function with professionalism without knowing these intricacies.

(The 10K is the annual report filed with the S.E.C. which is more detailed than the report sent to stockholders. The 10Q is the quarterly report filed with the S.E.C. and the 8K is a report of significant unscheduled events or corporate changes.)

If you are involved in financial relations, you probably cannot function without access to database research services. Some of these services are described in this chapter. Others are listed in the chapters on newswires, research and telephone services.

Closed circuit video, teleconferencing, corporate videotapes for distribution to brokers and investors and other new audiovisual dimensions to financial relations are described in the chapter on television.

Among the various databases with relevance to the financial community are American Banker, which carries the full text of selected articles from the American Banker newspaper and is updated daily; the IMS Weekly Marketeer, which has the full text of the newsletter of the insurance and financial services industry, and Financial Services Week, covering company profiles, corporate strategies and marketplace intelligence. The three databases are online for subscribers to NewsNet.

NAARS (National Automated Accounting Research System) has online files of annual reports for more than 1,500 public companies. Mead Data Central supplies the NAARS system. Mead also carries financial statements on more than 4,000 public companies in its Exchange database. Both NewsNet and Mead are described in the research chapter.

An expanded area in the 80's has been the hotly contested proxy fights, tender offers and other corporate battles. Some of the specialists in this arena are described in this chapter.

Not all of the companies are in Manhattan. For example, one of the major consultants on tender offer defenses, proxy solicitations and takeovers and buyouts is Skinner & Co., 660 Market St., San Francisco 94104, phone (415) 981-0970. Carlton Skinner is president and Martha Read is manager of Shareholder Locator Service, which helps to find lost stockholders and claimants in class action suits. The cable address appropriately and rhymingly is WINNER, SAN FRANCISCO.

Skinner's Directory of Security Dealer Name and Address Changes lists the complete genealogies of securities dealers who have changed addresses, merged with other dealers or gone out of business, with the name of the surviving entity.

A variety of free publications can be obtained from the New York Stock Exchange, American Stock Exchange and other exchanges. For example, the Chicago Mercantile Exchange publishes brochures on options, index futures and other investment instruments which include glossaries. The Chicago Mercantile Exchange is located at 30 Wacker Dr., Chicago 60606, phone (312) 930-1000 or (800) 843-6372. Their office in New York is at 67 Wall St., N.Y. 10005, phone (212) 363-7000.

Publications and conventions are among the services of the Securities Industry Association, 120 Broadway, N.Y. 10271.

10K's and other financial reports are available at many public libraries, including the Economic and Public Affairs Division of the New York Public Library at 42nd St. and Fifth Ave., Room 228, phone (212) 930-0724. Annual reports also are in the Business section on the fourth floor of the Mid-Manhattan Library, 40th St. at Fifth Ave., phone (212) 340-0884.

The offices of financial relations specialists now resemble those of stockbrokers in some of the equipment, particularly stock quotation machines of various kinds available from Bunker Ramo and other companies.

A few companies have news tickers, which can be rented from United Press International, Reuters, Dow Jones or The Associated Press.

Note: It is no longer necessary to have a separate terminal for each service. All you need is a computer terminal and a modem and you can access dozens of services. And each service is continually adding new databases.

In the case of Dow Jones, there are two News/Retrieval products. The first is the Dow Jones News Service (also known as "the Broadtape"), which is available through Quotron, ADP, Bunker Ramo and other vendors.

The Dow Jones News Service consists of every story that moves over the Broadtape within 90 seconds after it is transmitted and company news as far back as 90 days. In many cases, subscribers buy the Broadtape in a scrolling form, which means they see the stories as they move on the wire, while also buying the 90-day news database for near-term reference. This 90-day news database is the original Dow Jones News/Retrieval that Dow Jones developed along with Bunker Ramo in 1974.

The second product is an expanded version of the original database. In the late 1970s Dow Jones began offering related products, such as current and historical stock quotes, to the then fledgling personal computer market. A description of this service appears in the research chapter.

The Dow Jones News/Retrieval Service thus is a combination of reference library and stock quote monitor. Subscribers can query a data bank and obtain on a video screen news from the Dow Jones wire as recent as 90 seconds and as far back as 90 days, as well as stock quotes on over 6,000 companies. You can use a stationary or portable timesharing terminal to plug into the system, and costs depend on usage. Obviously, it's not cheap or for the casual investor. Dow Jones is headquartered at 200 Liberty St., N.Y. 10281, phone (212) 416-2000. Other Dow Jones sales offices are:

One So. Wacker Dr., Chicago 60606
(312) 750-4000

514 Shatto Pl., L.A. 90020
(213) 383-9090

201 California St., San Francisco 94111
(415) 986-6886

155 University Ave., Toronto M5H 3B7, Canada
(416) 364-0674

Before investing in any sophisticated system, it's a good idea to observe one or more competitive systems in actual use. Ask the sales representative for a list of nearby customers and visit their facilities.

Questions to ask Dow Jones, Western Union, Pitney Bowes, Xerox, IBM and other manufacturers and suppliers of systems and equipment:

1. Can it be purchased, initially, or at a later time?
2. What is the minimum rental period? What is the penalty for cancellation? How much notice must be given?
3. Who provides and pays for service? Materials? How much do materials cost (e.g., paper)? Can materials be purchased from other suppliers? (Get prices for contract and volume discounts.)
4. If leased, can it be replaced with newer or other models? If purchased, can it be traded in?

For financial uses—and many other uses—Western Union has several news services for telex subscribers.

FYI News—News (within 20 minutes of United Press International release), sports, scores, weather, commodity quotes and other reports, including ski conditions.

Stock Quote—Current prices and volume of all listed stocks.

News Alert—Major news bulletins from UPI delivered automatically on your telex/TWX terminal.

The News Alert Service is $10 a month or $100 a year. The other services are more expensive and depend on usage. For details, write to Western Union at 1 Lake St., Upper Saddle River, NJ 07458. Or, send them a telex!

ITT Update is a 24-hour news service with stock, bond and commodity prices, market reports, business and consumer news over ordinary telex machines. The news material is provided by United Press International, the financial data is from Bunker Ramo, airline information is supplied by D&B's Official Airline Guides, and there also is an interconnect with Dialcom, which is an ITT electronic mail service. To activate the service, the user calls the ITT Update telex number and enters a three-digit code to specify the desired information category. The cost is about 24 cents per minute for access to the Update database, plus the standard domestic telex rate of 35 cents per minute. The service was set up in 1984 by ITT Communications World, Inc., 67 Broad St., N.Y. 10005.

Among the text and reference books is Investor Relations Handbook, with chapters by 14 members of the National Investor Relations Institute. Published in 1974, the Handbook is $19.95 from AMACOM, a division of the American Management Association, 135 W. 50 St., N.Y. 10020.

The Investment Management Institute, 50 E. 42 St., N.Y. 10017, produces publications and conducts seminars in New York and other major cities.

Several directories are useful in any reference library but are of particular value to financial specialists. One of the major books is Standard & Poor's Register of Corporations, Directors and Executives ($425), published by Standard & Poor's Corporation, 25 Broadway, N.Y. 10004.

Hill and Knowlton, Inc., public relations agency at 420 Lexington Ave., N.Y. 10017, publishes What Non-U.S. Companies Need to Know About Financial Disclosure in the United States ($50) and The Annual ''Annual Report'' Report ($50).

Among the many financial newsletters is The Corporate Shareholder, $195 for 22 issues a year, from Edward Kulkowsky, editor/publisher, at 230 W. 41 St., N.Y. 10036.

In 1987, Dean Rotbart, a former Wall Street Journal reporter, launched TJFR, The Journalist & Financial Reporting, a unique semi-monthly newsletter with an analysis of business news and other investigative reporting about business and financial media. It's an extraordinary publication, and you may not agree with the author's opinions, but it indeed is lively reading; hampered, however, by the price—$520 a year, from TJFR Publishing Co., 82 Wall St., Suite 1105, N.Y. 10005.

W. R. Nelson & Company, 11 Elm Place, Rye, NY 10580, publishes ($249) Nelson's Directory of Wall Street Research, with 800 pages of data (360,000 listings) about security analysts and investment research sources at U.S., Canadian and other companies.

PIMS Financial Directory lists 7,000 security analysts, financial media and others in the United Kingdom. Updated quarterly, it's $90 a copy or $300 for an annual subscription, from PIMS London Ltd., PIMS House, 4 St. Johns Pl., London EC1B 1AB.

Several paper mills issue booklets, portfolios and books with colorful, useful material about preparing annual reports. You can get a free Publication Planning Guide from the Northwest Paper Division of the Potlatch Corporation, Box 510, Cloquet, MN 55720.

Among the graphics designers who specialize in annual reports are:

Corporate Annual Reports, 112 E. 31st St., N.Y. 10016 (212) 889-2450

Delphan Company Inc., 515 Madison Ave., N.Y. 10022, (212) 371-6700.

Shareholder Reports, Inc., 600 Third Ave., N.Y. 10016, (212) 686-9099.

Taylor & Ives, Inc., 1001 Ave. of the Americas, N.Y. 10018, (212) 921-9300. Contact Murray Balley, President, or Jay J. Coleen, V.P., for expert counsel. Formed in 1968, Taylor & Ives specializes in annual reports, corporate literature, financial advertising and corporate identity programs.

Another major creator, designer and producer in the graphics field, from a quarterly financial report to a sales meeting, is Anagraphics Inc., 104 W. 29 St., N.Y. 10001, phone (212) 279-2370.

The chapter on mailing services includes several publicity specialists who can handle the demands for speed and accuracy which are the rule in financial work. A ''rush expert'' in news releases and other printing and mailing is Associated Litho and Letter Service, 545 W. 45 St., N.Y. 10036, phone (212) 757-8775. Formed in 1919, Associated is headed by Joel M. Weiss.

Several printers specialize in overnight production of financial statements and other printing for the financial community. A few of these printers operate 24 hours a day, specialize in overnight service, have conference rooms and other facilities for clients to work on the premises and also maintain plants and regional sales offices throughout the country. Sorg Printing, for example, has major facilities at 650 West Washington Blvd., Chicago 60606, phone (312) 332-4730; 346 First St., San Francisco 94105, phone (415) 982-9663; and 515 S. Flower St., Los Angeles 90071, phone (213) 488-0024.

Following is a list of several major financial printers. Many also do general printing.

Anderson Lithograph, 3217 S. Garfield Ave., L.A. 90040, (213) 727-7767

Appeal Printing Co., (acquired by Sorg in 1985)

Bowne & Co., Inc., 345 Hudson St., N.Y. 10014, (212) 924-5500 (oldest and largest financial printer)

Bradley Printing Co., 2170 S. Mannheim Rd., Des Plaines, IL 60018, (312) 635-8000

Carpenter Reserve Printing Co., 7100 Euclid Ave., Cleveland 44103, (216) 431-0800

Corbett Press, Inc., 232 Amity Rd., Woodbridge, CT 06525, (203) 387-2551

R.R. Donnelley & Sons Co., 75 Park Place, N.Y. 10007, (212) 233-2611

Fine Arts Printing Co., 7100 N. Ridgeway Ave., Lincoln, IL 60645, (312) 674-3200

Graphics Arts Center, 2000 N.W. Wilson St., Portland, OR 97209, (503) 224-5311

Intelligencer Printing Company, 330 Eden Rd., Lancaster, PA 17603, (717) 291-3100

Moebius Printing Co., 300 N. Jefferson St., Milwaukee 53202, (414) 276-5311

Nelson Lithographing, 3731 Eastern Hills Lane, Cincinnati 45209, (513) 321-5200

Nies/Kaiser, 5900 Berthold Ave., St. Louis 63110, (314) 647-3400

Packard Press Corporation, 10th and Spring Garden Sts., Philadelphia 19123, (215) 236-2000

Pandick Press, 345 Hudson St., N.Y. 10014, (212) 741-5555

QuadGraphics, Pewaukee, WI 53072, (414) 691-9200

Sanders Printing Corp., 350 Hudson St., N.Y. 10014, (212) 691-1070

Shareholder Graphics, Inc., 6. E. 46 St., N.Y. 10017, (212) 661-1070

Sorg Printing Co., 111 Eighth Ave., N.Y. 10011, (212) 741-6600

Stephenson Incorporated, 5731 General Washington Ave., Alexandria, VA 22312, (703) 642-9000

Charles P. Young, Inc., 75 Varick St., N.Y. 10013, (212) 431-5300

Many stockholders, banks and other financial institutions publish newsletters, conduct meetings and other projects with public relations potential.

The New York Financial Writer's Association is at Box 21, Syosset, NY 11791, (516) 921-7766.

Financial World Magazine publishes the monthly Corporate Advertising Newsletter, which is available free (to prospective advertisers) from Financial World, 1450 Broadway, N.Y. 10018, (212) 869-1616.

Among the news conference facilities in Wash., DC, which are available to financial and other public relations clients are:

American News Women's Club, 1607 22 St., N.W., (202) 332-6770

National Press Club, 529 14 St., N.W., (202) 662-7502

The New York Stock Exchange and American Stock Exchange provide many services to their listed companies. For example, the American Stock Exchange handles all arrangements for CEO's to speak at Security Analyst Forums in New York, Boston, Chicago, Houston, San Francisco and Toronto. Companies pay the meeting costs plus a $500 fee. Meetings are breakfasts or luncheons.

Amex Clubs also conduct meetings in Boston, Chicago, Dallas, Houston, Atlanta, Jacksonville, Los Angeles, New York, Philadelphia, San Diego, San Francisco, Seattle, St. Louis, Washington, DC, Montreal, Toronto, London and other cities.

Information about Amex services can be obtained from Cheryl J. Schneider, American Stock Exchange, 86 Trinity Place, N.Y. 10006, phone (212) 306-1691.

Information about the New York Society of Security Analysts is in a separate listing in this chapter.

Many services in the financial field are described in other sections of this book. For example, the largest part of the business of the private newswire services is financial news, and the use of these services constitutes prompt, full disclosure.

The following is a partial list of financial relations services. For other companies, see, in particular, the chapter on research and the chapter on mailing services. Information about The Society of American Business Writers is included in the chapter on Press Weeks.

Who's Who in Financial Journalism, an annual directory of about 900 British journalists and financial correspondents based in the UK, is published (about $50) by Dewe Rogerson Limited, a public relations agency at 3Y2 London Wall Buildings, London EC2M 5SY.

1. ADP Network Services
175 Jackson Plaza, Ann Arbor, MI 48106
(313) 769-6800
Philip J. Griffiths, V.P.

A division of Automatic Data Processing Inc., ADP Network Services provides business-oriented computing and database services via a nation-wide proprietary teleprocessing network. Services include financial database information, project management software, facilities management and cash management services.

2. Bunker Ramo
2 Enterprise Dr., Shelton, CT 06484
(203) 337-1200
Carol Blaszczynski, Dir., Marketing Communications

Branch Offices:
5615 Highpoint Dr., Irving, TX 75038
(214) 550-5400

1165 Northchase Pky., Marietta, GA 30067
(404) 952-3898

655 Third Ave., N.Y. 10017
(212) 949-0950

100 Spear St., San Francisco 94105
(415) 974-5353

Bunker Ramo was founded in 1928 as The Teleregister Corp. The name was changed in the 1960's because of mergers with parts of the Bunker Ramo Corp. The original product was the Teleregister online stock quotation board system, serving brokerage firms in New York. It provided a network of electrically posted blackboards, which were activated from a transmitting station via telegraph lines. The boards were the first major advance in market information since the Edison ticker, and the system then stretched coast to coast, sending information to the securities industry well into the 1970's.

Today, Bunker Ramo (an Olivetti Co. since 1986) primarily provides automation systems to banks, including its Aladdin system.

3. CDA Investment Technologies, Inc.
11501 Georgia Ave., Silver Spring, MD 20902
(301) 942-1700
John J. Lewis, Marketing Dir.

Many clients use CDA's SPECTRUM Corporate Extracts to track the institutional ownership of their companies. SPECTRUM covers the 915 largest U.S. institutions, 685 U.S. investment company filings and the 565 largest European investment companies. With SPECTRUM Hardcopy Report, clients get weekly updates on all 13(f) institutional owners, with new filings "flagged" for easy identification. Data is also available via online or in micro-PC form.

4. The Carter Organization, Inc.
237 Park Ave., N.Y. 10017
(212) 883-8900
Donald C. Carter, Pres.

The Carter Organization is one of the major companies in proxy solicitation, investor relations and management advisory services. Carter is active in proxy contests, tender offers, exchange offers, stock surveillance, convertible security redemptions and the distribution of shareholder material. It is a subsidiary of the VPI Group plc.

5. Center for Business Research
Long Island University-C. W. Post Campus
Brookville, N.Y. 11548
(516) 299-2310
Mary McNierney Grant, Dir.

Many university libraries (and other libraries) provide reference and research services which can be extremely cost-efficient to public relations firms. One of the best is operated by Long Island University. Developed by Mary Grant in 1978, this excellent library, housed under an academic umbrella, provides information to the business and financial community on a for-payment basis. Part of C. W. Post's larger B. Davis Schwartz Memorial Library, it can utilize those resources as well. They include a general reference department, Government documents collection, the Media Center (which helps produce audiovisuals), and accounting and tax research library, special collections and a periodicals collection of 4,000 titles. The Center has over 1,400 current business periodicals and back issues, and more than 3,000 journals on microfilm.

Services include research, online searches (especially DIALOG and NEXIS), information packages, consultations and patent searches. Assignments vary from the Center's quick reference calls (15 minutes) to weeks or months. Same-day service is often available for documents if requests are received early in the day.

Clients with a deposit account are billed $55 per hour for research. Others pay $80 per hour. The library has evening and weekend hours.

6. The Chartmakers Inc.
33 W. 60 St., N.Y. 10023
(212) 247-7200
Joseph O'Hehir, Pres.

Founded in 1929, The Chartmakers is a major producer of materials for shareholders and sales meetings, including brochures, charts, videotapes and multi-image presentations.

7. Control Data/Business Information Services (BIS)
Box 7100, Greenwich, CT 06836
(203) 622-2455
Alan A. Caminti, Information Programs Mgr.

Control Data's far-ranging interests include Source Telecomputing Corporation and Arbitron Ratings Company, Ticketron and Business Information Services. BIS provides a variety of Government and industry management information services including X/MARKET, a database and reporting system that has data on 450,000 U.S. business establishments with 20 or more employees. Information is supplied by Trinet, a Control Data company. Price and historical data on 40,000 stocks, bonds and options traded on major U.S. and Canadian exchanges are available on MISTI II. Each record has 65 fields of information, some being updated daily reflecting market activity.

Prime-time rates for BIX are $16 per hour and nonprime-time and weekend rates are $6.40 per hour. There are some additional charges and a $200 per month minimum.

8. Corporate Studies, Inc.

366 North Broadway, Jericho, NY 11753
(516) 822-4422
Arnold I. Minsky, Pres.

Corporate Studies gives professional analyses of the ongoing trading in a company's stock; immediate contact with a client about unusual trading activity or news; sends monthly statistical and analytical reports; alerts a client to block accumulation or other "danger" signs. Assistance with IR programs, relating to trading. Investigative projects designed and implemented.

9. Disclosure Record

Box 639, Floral Park, NY 11001
(718) 347-1100
Telex 64-5475
Jack Lotto, Publisher

A weekly tabloid newspaper, distributed free to about 10,000 security analysts and others in the financial community.

Started in 1973 by Jack Lotto, Disclosure Record is the financial counterpart of a newspaper mat service in that it enables financial publicists to get their messages intact to investment professionals.

News releases are reproduced for $45 per 100 words, and advertising space is available for $700 a page.

A former International News Service editor and reporter, Mr. Lotto operated PR Wire Service from 1960 to 1971. The Long Island location is a bit far from Wall Street and is simply because he lives in nearby Bellerose.

However, telex and telephone facsimile enable Mr. Lotto to handle worldwide clients.

Nonanalysts can subscribe to Disclosure Record for $50 a year.

10. The Document Bank

Washington Service Bureau
655 15 St. N.W., Wash., DC 20005
(202) 833-9200, (800) 828-5354
Jeanne M. Carroll, Marketing Mgr.

The Washington Service Bureau has a library of Government documents available on a same-day basis. Documents include S.E.C. reports such as:

13D's—Williams Act Filings
10K's, 10Q's
Annual Reports, Proxies
Registration Statements
Prospectuses
Investment Company Act Filings
Releases and No-Action letters

This is not a subscription service and no deposit account is required. However, there can be extra charges for same-day service ($65), 24-hour service ($45) or one-week service ($35) and research ($60 per hour), and photocopying costs 65 cents per page.

Documents are 45 cents per page, $25 minimum.

A monitoring service is available to watch for periodic reports, registrations, tender offers and proxy contest materials. Information can be sent by facsimile. A daily watch costs $7.50 per day per company, a weekly watch is $30 and a monthly watch, $50.

11. Dow Jones & Company, Inc.
200 Liberty St., N.Y. 10281
(212) 416-2000
Lawrence Armour, Dir. of Corporate Relations

Dow Jones was formed in New York in 1882 by Charles Dow, Edward Jones and Charles Bergstresser, three young reporters from New England. Their office consisted of a small basement room near the New York Stock Exchange where they produced handwritten bulletins carrying the day's financial news.

This was the beginning of a worldwide news organization, at the center of which is The Wall Street Journal, now with over two-million subscribers and newsstand purchasers, a readership approaching seven million and the distinction of being the national daily with thorough coverage of business, economics and financial news, as well as consumer affairs, social issues, education, science, foreign affairs, leisure and the arts.

Back issues of The Wall Street Journal (going back one year to the day) can be obtained through the mail by writing Dow Jones & Co., Inc., Back Copy Dept., 200 Burnett Rd., Chicopee, MA 01021, phone (413) 592-7761, ext. 2124. The price is 50 cents plus postage.

If you need a photocopy of an article published in an issue of the Journal since 1889, contact the Inquiry Dept. on the fifth floor at 200 Liberty St., phone (212) 416-2676. The cost is $1 per article.

Dow Jones was the first private publishing company to own and operate satellite earth stations.

In 1975, The Journal created newspaper publishing history when it began printing the paper at a plant in Florida using full-page images transmitted by satellite from a composing plant in Massachusetts. The four U.S. regional editions are now printed in 18 plants throughout the U.S., all using satellite technology.

In 1983, Dow Jones added The Wall Street Journal/Europe, edited in Belgium and printed in the Netherlands and Switzerland daily for the European business community.

The Asian Wall Street Journal is the only English-language daily business publication covering all of Asia. The Asian Wall Street Journal Weekly is published in New York for North American and European readers.

Dow Jones has various other publishing interests, including Barron's National Business and Financial Weekly, which specializes in news of interest to the investment-oriented. Dow Jones News Services provides four business and financial newswires (including the "broadtape" or ticker) servicing subscribers in 850 North American cities. The Capital Markets Report newswire focuses coverage on fixed-income markets, the Dow Jones International News provides international wires for subscribers via electronic printers and video display units and the Professional Investor Report covers intra-day activity on the major U.S. stock exchanges.

In 1974, Barron's inaugurated Current Corporate Reports, a special advertising section for financial releases and "items of record." Contact the advertising department at Barron's, 420 Lexington Ave., N.Y. 10170, phone (212) 808-7242. Thursday, at 4 P.M., is the deadline for the issue on the newsstands Saturday.

Through its Dow Jones News/Retrieval Service, started in 1974 and now incorporating 42 databases, the firm is the leading provider of electronically delivered business and financial information. Among the services provided are Corporate Earnings Estimator; Weekly Economics Survey; Investext; business analysts reports; and Wall $treet Week Online, which reviews electronic transcripts of the most recent ''Wall $treet Week'' programs. See the research chapter for details on Dow Jones News/Retrieval Service.

12. DowPhone

Dow Jones & Company, Inc.
Box 300, Princeton, NJ 08543
(609) 520-4916, (800) 257-0437
William L. Dunn, Publisher, Information Services

Dow Jones (not hyphenated) & Company publishes The Wall Street Journal, Barron's and the Dow Jones News Service. It thus was logical for DJ to provide financial information services in nonprint formats. One of those is DowPhone, a service of Dow Jones & Company, Inc., for business professionals and investors who want to receive up-to-the-minute information throughout the day. DowPhone provides real-time stock quotes and business news selected by the subscriber. There's even a Portfolio feature allowing you to pre-code up to 64 company codes into personal ''portfolios'' for stock quotes and news stories.

With almost any push-button phone, DowPhone's voice reports on over 6,500 publicly owned companies and 300 business and financial subjects. The news stories are from The Wall Street Journal, Barron's, Dow Jones News Service and the international newswires. For a free demonstration, call the DowPhone Hot Line at (800) 257-0437.

The charge for DowPhone is 60 cents per minute and an annual subscription fee of $12.50. This does not include any local or long-distance charges from your telephone company. DowPhone also has an 800 ''convenience number.'' Customers using the service via this number are charged $1 per minute but incur no additional long-distance telephone charges. After signing up, you are issued your own Passport ID number and will receive a complete User's Guide including all company codes. The first $15 of usage is free.

13. Dun & Bradstreet International

299 Park Ave., N.Y. 10171
(212) 593-6800

The venerable Dun & Bradstreet offers its resources both in print and by electronic retrieval via DIALOG.

D&B, with 25 divisions and offices throughout the world, began in 1841 when Lewis Tappan formed the Mercantile Agency to provide credit reports on businesses and executive officers.

Among the early credit reporters, four were to become U.S. Presidents: Lincoln, Grant, Cleveland and McKinley. In 1870, the Mercantile Agency merged with Robert G. Dun & Co. of Cincinnati and, in 1933, with the Bradstreet Company.

D&B's online International Dun's Market Identifiers (file 518 on DIALOG) has been enhanced with considerable data on about 530,000 companies in 143 countries. Updated quarterly, it costs $100 per connect hour. Businesses in this file are chosen on the basis of international significance. The same company records are also available on magnetic tape or in printed list form.

In book form, the top 50,000 companies in the file are listed in Principal International Businesses (cost: $525).

Dun's Financial Records, produced jointly by Dun & Bradstreet Credit Services and Dun's Marketing Services, contains detailed financial information on approximately 700,000 public and private companies. Records include details of incorporation, company history and other information. DFR is $135 per connect hour plus record charges on DIALOG (file 519). It is updated quarterly.

Another database of interest is Dun's Reference Book of Corporate Management Online. It contains profiles of over 50,000 officers and directors from more than 12,000 U.S. companies. Professional histories are provided for more than 78,000 executives in both public and private companies. It is available on Infoline at $98 per hour plus record charges, and is updated annually.

Dun's Marketing Services are headquartered at 49 Old Bloomfield Ave., Mountain Lakes, NJ 07046, phone (201) 299-0181. Robert Clark is Director of Online Services.

14. The Financial Analysts Federation

5 Boar's Head Lane, Charlottesville, VA 22903
(804) 977-8977
Alfred Morley, Pres.

The membership directory of The Financial Analysts Federation is published annually (since 1948) and is available to nonmembers for $100 a copy. A supplement to the directory, listing analysts by industry and specialty, also is available for $90 per copy.

The 15,500 names are available on mailing lists. Permission to use the lists must be obtained from the Federation.

One-time use of the complete list, including labels, is $850.

The lists, which are revised semimonthly, also can be purchased by industry (81 categories), at a minimum of $200.

U.S. nonmembers may subscribe to The Financial Analysts Journal for $48 a year. Other items include the Society's monthly Program Calender ($45 a year), Corporate Information Committee Annual Report (summary of reporting practices of about 500 companies, $40), quarterly newsletter ($15), and Standards of Practice Handbook ($10). These items have a postage and handling charge.

15. Georgeson & Co.

Wall Street Plaza, 88 Pine St., N.Y. 10005
(212) 440-9800
Johnnie D. Johnson, John H. Jurgensen, Richard B. Nye, John C. Wilcox, Managing Directors

Founded in 1935, Georgeson was the first firm to provide professional proxy solicitation services and, since 1948, it has provided a broad range of services in the financial relations field.

Georgeson & Co. specializes in proxy solicitations, tender offers and other specialized aspects of investor relations, including bond holder consents. Georgeson publications include Georgeson Report, a quarterly newsletter, and Financial Executives' Guide to Writing.

Georgeson branch offices are:
2 N. LaSalle St., Chicago, 60602
(312) 346-7161
Rebecca Lahrmann

13777 N. Central Expressway, Dallas 75243
(214) 470-9009
Leona Hufstutler

4221 Wilshire Blvd., L.A. 90010
(213) 489-7000
Kate Ahern

482 Forbes Ave., Pittsburgh 15219
(412) 391-3146
Ernest J. Tonetti

16. Global Report
Citicorp
153 E. 53 St., N.Y. 10043
(800) 842-8405
Robert Haddock, V.P.

Financial and corporate information can be found online in a database from Citicorp called Global Report, which was introduced in late 1986. An information system available on your PC or terminal with 1,200 or 2,400 baud Hayes modem, Global Report gathers information from 14 sources, including Quotron, Standard & Poor's, Knight-Ridder, Dow Jones, Business International, ADP Bunker Ramo and the Financial Times.

Global Report concentrates on companies, markets, rates, industries, news, stock prices and in-depth profiles on over 10,000 companies from Standard & Poor's. Business International offers financial and economic information on 25 countries.

The system is searchable by subject, so that one can travel through the real-time and archival sources intent on one's topic rather than lots of menus. The basic subscription fee is $175 a month, plus $60 per hour.

17. InvesText
12 Farnsworth St., Boston, MA 02210
(617) 330-7878, (800) 662-7878
Josephine Ottman, Mgr., Marketing

InvesText provides online full-text financial research reports from leading investment banking firms in the U.S., Europe, Canada, Japan and Australia. They contain market share projections, earnings forecasts, research and development expenditures and related data. The database has reports on about 3,000 of the largest publicly traded U.S. corporations, about 5,000 smaller U.S. corporations and 2,000 large foreign companies.

InvesText is available in off-line print format and online computer via its own system and also BRS, DATA-STAR, DIALOG, Dow Jones News/Retrieval, KISCO, NewsNet and The Source.

18. D.F. King & Company, Inc.
60 Broad St., N.Y. 10004
(212) 269-5550
Neil J. Call, Exec. V.P.
Sima L. Nahum, V.P.

Founded in 1942, D.F. King & Co., Inc., is a financial relations consulting firm headquartered in New York, with offices in Chicago and Los Angeles. The company provides three basic shareholder related services:

Corporate Control Consulting—tender and exchange offers, proxy contests and counseling clients on strategies, outcomes, initiates, reactions and communications. Included in this service is a stock watch program.

Investor and Press Relations—annual and interim reports, financial community audits, press strategies, analyst meetings and investor programs.

Securityholder Solicitation—network of solicitors who contact institutional and individual holders with regard to annual or special meetings, bondholder consents, proxy contests, tender and exchange offers.

19. Kyodo News International, Inc.

50 Rockefeller Plaza, N.Y. 10020
(212) 586-0152
Makita Suito, Gen. Mgr.

The Japan Economic Newswire is published by Kyodo News International, Inc., a subsidiary of Kyodo News Service, Japan's largest international news agency and the Japanese equivalent of The Associated Press. While JEN has the responsibility for the content of Kyodo News, the bulletins are transmitted by Dow Jones' newswires, Monday through Friday, prior to the start of Dow Jones' daily transmission and printed out on the Extel printer that carries Dow Jones news.

JEN carries news of finance and industry, markets, the 136 Japanese corporations on Fortune's list of the 500 largest firms outside the U.S., news of 24 of the world's 100 largest banks, government news, forecasts, feature columns and a schedule of trade and industry meetings.

JEN can be transmitted to your office before 7 A.M., E.S.T., via Dow Jones, and complete data on the Japanese business day is available within two hours of its close because of the 13-hour time difference between Tokyo and New York. The news is satellite-fed from Tokyo, arriving in New York at 6 A.M.

A subscription to JEN, for printer subscribers to Dow Jones News Service, for one year, costs $50 a month.

20. Market Guide Inc.

49 Glen Head Rd., Glen Head, NY 11545
(516) 759-1253, (800) 642-3840
Scott Emerich, Pres.
Jack Kemeny, V.P., Marketing

In 1983, Scott Emerich (a former stockbroker) launched The Unlisted Market Guide, three-ring notebooks with reports on OTC companies. The slim sheets, which look like Standard & Poor's sheets, are crammed with information. It is now known as the Market Guide to better reflect its broadened coverage.

Companies pay $2,000 a year for the listing, which is updated quarterly. Renewals are $1,500 a term. (S&P lists—for free—the top OTC companies, plus about 600 others, which pay about $4,000). Subscribers pay $195 a year (S&P charges $685 for its OTC stock reports). New sheets are mailed weekly.

Listing in the Guide also includes distribution in the Market Screen database, which is available on Quotron, Dow Jones News/Retrieval, DIALOG and through other vendors.

21. Media Distribution Services

307 W. 36 St., N.Y. 10018
(212) 279-4800
Hymen Wagner, Pres.
Andy Guerzon, V.P.

MDS, the country's largest publicity mailing companies (described in the chapter on mailing services), introduced in 1987 a system to print financial news and deliver *by messenger* to financial analysts and others in the NYC financial community—all within two to three hours. Others outside of New York receive the material by mail.

News releases can be sent via computer or other means to MDS. In some ways, the system is similar to the analyst wires of PR Newswire and BusinessWire. MDS is different in that its lists are considerably larger and clients can select the specific names. In addition, MDS can print and mail the same news release to business editors and others from among the over 100,000 names in their Mediamatic System.

Media Distribution Services is represented in several cities outside of New York:

Chicago: Associated Release Service, Frank Bruni, (312) 726-8693
Minneapolis: Publicity Central, Marilyn Nipp, (612) 871-7201
Philadelphia: MediaLink, David Virtue, (215) 537-9010
Pittsburgh: Direct Mail Service, Ken Esch, (412) 471-6300
Washington, DC: Media Direct, Mitch Fanning, (202) 227-8232.

22. Media General Financial Services, Inc.

301 E. Grace St., Richmond, VA 23219
(804) 649-6587
Dennis H. Cartwright, Pres.

Media General Financial Services maintains a computer database of fundamental and technical data on more than 5,000 common stocks and special market and industry group databases.

23. Moody's Investors Service

99 Church St., N.Y. 10007
(212) 553-0300, (212) 553-0436, (800) 342-5647
Sean Devine, V.P. Sales

One of the "grand old names" in the financial information field, Moody's now provides business and financial data in both hard copy and electronic formats.

Moody's Corporate Profiles, online with DIALOG, offers financial and descriptive information on 4,200 public companies, including all companies on the New York and American Stock exchanges and about 1,800 of the most active emerging firms traded over-the-counter. Also included are five-year financial histories, key statistics and concise descriptions and more. The electronic file costs $60 per connect hour plus $4 per full record printed offline or displayed or typed online. More than 54 key fields are searchable. Also on DIALOG is Moody's Corporate News (covers 18,000 companies) and International Corporate News (covers 5,000 companies in 100 countries).

Moody's Industrial Manual, one of the staples of any business library, covers over 1,800 firms, including all industrial firms on the New York, American and regional stock exchanges. It provides company history and complete financial profile and costs $985 a year, including semiweekly News Reports. A companion, the OTC Industrial Manual, is the most complete reference source for the over-the-counter industrial firms. It contains information on over 3,000 companies not listed on major exchanges. Including semiweekly News Reports, the annual cost is $895. The newest addition is the OTC Unlisted Manual, which provides information on nearly 2,000 hard-to-find emerging companies not listed on any of the major or regional exchanges and not reported on the NASDAQ National Market. Including weekly News Reports, the annual cost is $810.

Moody's coverage ranges from public companies, including transportation and utilities companies, to municipal and government securities, and about 11,000 publicly held financial institutions, as well as foreign investments. In business since 1895, Moody's has been a wholly owned subsidiary of Dun & Bradstreet since 1962.

24. Morrow & Co., Inc.

345 Hudson St., N.Y. 10014
(212) 741-5511
Thomas J. Ficker, Pres.

Founded in 1972, this company offers financial services, including proxy solicitations for annual and special meetings and bond consents, tender and exchange offers, proxy fights for control, nominee identification and stock watch programs.

25. National Computer Network (NCN)
1929 N. Harlem Ave., Chicago 60635
(312) 622-6666
Charles Lizak, Dir., Software

Marketing Office:
175 W. Jackson, Chicago 60604
(312) 427-5125
Tom McDonald, Marketing Dir.

Formed in 1969, the National Computer Network (NCN) is an electronic timesharing source for inexpensive stock, bond, option and commodity market information from all major U.S. and Canadian exchanges. Price and volume information are available online both in real time (as they are occurring on the tickers) or historically dating back as far as 1975. NCN is known for having more historical information online than other similar services.

In addition, NCN offers custom programming services for technical traders (charting, predictors, indices, mathematical analysis), portfolio management (especially evaluating portfolio risk given expected market movement) and fundamental analysis which provides operating information about a company, its profile and the actual value of its stock.

NCN operates through ADP's Autonet network. Prime-time (8 A.M. to 6 P.M., Central time, Monday through Friday) costs $10 an hour plus $3 per CPU minute. NCN is available 24 hours a day, seven days a week and its nonprime-time rates are extremely competitive: $6 an hour plus $1.80 per CPU minute. There are surcharges for some of the proprietary databases, network charges ranging from $4 to $8 an hour and high speed (1,200 baud) communication surcharges.

The marketing office, headed by Tom McDonald, is at 175 W. Jackson St., across the street from the Chicago Board of Trade and Options Exchange.

26. The New York Society of Security Analysts, Inc.
71 Broadway, N.Y. 10006
(212) 344-8450

Founded in 1937, The New York Society of Security Analysts (NYSSA) has over 5,000 financial analysts and portfolio managers as members. One or more meetings are held on every business day. In addition to media coverage, NYSSA transmits the meetings via several technologies to large numbers of industries.

Members pay for their own lunches. NYSSA, which is a not-for-profit corporation, charges $7,950 for a company to make a presentation. The fee provides for telecasts, audiotapes, mailings and other services, as well as the meeting.

Located on the second floor of 71 Broadway (one block south of Wall Street), the NYSSA headquarters has been the scene of thousands of financial communications triumphs and disasters for about 50 years.

Companies scheduled to appear before NYSSA may not appear before any other analyst society or group within 30 days prior to the NYSSA meeting.

Luncheons are in their meeting rooms. Meetings at other times, including breakfast, mid-morning, cocktail reception and dinner, also are available.

Traditionally, companies are invited by a member of the program committee, though a company may solicit an invitation by contacting Judy Fontana.

The luncheon generally follows a set schedule:

11:45–12:15	Premeeting gathering for head table participants in the reception room
12:15–12:55	Luncheon
1:00–1:05	Formal remarks by company representatives consisting of the following five segments
1:05–1:10	Tight description of company's history
1:10–1:15	Dissection of company's major operating areas, including strategies and progress
1:15–1:20	Analysis of major external challenges and opportunities, raw materials supply, labor problems, and competition
1:25–1:30	Final summary Brief pause for attendees who wish to leave
1:30–2:00	Question and answer period
2:00	Formal adjournment

Maximum seating capacity for a luncheon meeting is 224. Auditorium seating can accomodate 400. The smallest room for lunch accomodates 35 people. Major seatings generally are held in room number one, which accomodates 150 people plus 10 to 12 people at the dais.

NYSSA gives one audiotape and videotape to each presentation company, and sells the tape to members and nonmembers ($15 for audio, $50 for video).

Some of the meetings are telecast daily. Com/Tech Communication Technologies Inc., 71 Broadway, N.Y. 10006, phone (212) 968-7315, produces the telecasts. Institutional Research Network, 215 Lexington Ave., N.Y. 10016, phone (212) 696-9476, handles the satellite transmission to the offices of institutional shareholders, analysts and others

Darome Inc., 140 Cedar St., N.Y. 11116, phone (212) 964-6968, provides telephone transmission to offices. Darome Connections is headquartered at 2100 M St., N.W., Washington DC 20037, phone (204) 331-3900, (800) 835-9700.

A printed transcript, prepared within two weeks, is distributed via several online services: EasyNet, BRS Information Technologies, ICC Information Group Ltd. (UK), Mead Data Central's Nexis, Wall Street Transcript, Dow-Jones News Retrieval, FIrst Call Investext, The Source, Dialogue, Newsnet and J/A Micropublishing.

Technimetrics handles mailings before and after each meeting, including information packets provided by each category.

27. H. F. Pearson & Co., Inc.
168 Main St. Huntington, NY 11743
(516) 427-3107
Frank Pearson, President

Pearson produces a service, called CORTRAC, which keeps investor relations professionals up to date with weekly reporting about institutional activity/holdings in a company stock.

28. Quotron Systems, Inc.
5454 Beethoven St., L.A. 90066
(213) 827-4600
George Levine, V.P., Marketing

Branch Offices:
100 Bush St., San Francisco 94104
(415) 981-0892

1515 N.W. 167 St., Miami 33169
(305) 620-4007

300 S. Riverside Plaza, Chicago 60606
(312) 559-3800

220 N. 4 St., St. Louis, MO 63102
(314) 621-8540

One Battery Park Plaza, N.Y. 10004
(212) 344-0400

49 E. 4 St., Cincinnati, OH 45202
(513) 621-3470

1500 First St., Portland, OR 97201
(503) 224-0340

121 S. Broad St., Philadelphia 19107
(215) 546-8700

500 S. Ervay St., Dallas 75201
(214) 747-3773

Thousands of stockbrokers and individual investors use the Quotron desktop machine to obtain information about current prices of stocks, options, commodities, bonds and other data. In addition, users have access to the Dow Jones News/Retrieval Service and other news services, as well as to about 20 third-party online databases of research and financial data.

Quotron provides an integrated services package consisting of communications, real-time market data, hardware and software, and maintenance.

Formed in Los Angeles in 1957 as Scantlin Electronics, the company became Quotron Systems in 1974. The information system has monthly fees ranging from $50 to $3,000 depending on the type and extent of information services used.

29. The Reuter Monitor
Reuters, Ltd.
2 Wall St., N.Y. 10005
(212) 603-3300

Paul Julius Reuter, in 1851, closed a gap in communications between Brussels and Aachen (Germany, near the Belgian border) by using carrier pigeons. He was able to reduce the time needed to send stock market prices from nine hours by rail to two hours by pigeon. He transferred to London when he heard that submarine cable was being put down from Dover to Calais, providing a connection from the European telegraphic network to London. He founded Reuters on October 14, 1851, at the Royal Exchange Buildings in London, and created a channel-crossing news service.

Reuter saw that a telegraphic information service was required by newspapers as well as the financial community. Seven years lapsed before London newspapers agreed and subscribed to Paul Julius Reuter's "electric news." From then on, these news editors were the first with scoops, getting news of President Lincoln's assassination two days before rivals. Establishing a telegraph line on the southwest corner of the Irish coast, he had mailboats from New York met by cutters sent out to pick up reports. He opened news bureaus around the world.

Now Reuters has 600 full-time staff journalists and 1,000 part-time correspondents. About 100 reporting bureaus are maintained, providing 90 news services in five languages. The largest editorial center is in London, where about five million words a day are processed. During the night, editorial control of Reuter news services moves from London to Hong Kong.

For subscribers, the Reuter Monitor video terminals have replaced teleprinters as their primary means of getting the news.

The Reuter Monitor carries essential information on securities, commodities, U.S. and international economics and finance, currency exchange rates and the energy industry. The Monitor provides 14 services from about 60 files, including investments and general news, money markets, metals and coins, and the tickers from American and international securities, options and futures exchanges. A "Contributed Information" section offers information from companies trading in markets that have no central exchange.

See the separate listing in the research chapter for the Reuter NewsFile, first developed by News Technology Corp., Mountainview, CA.

30. Securities and Exchange Commission
450 5th St., N.W., Wash., DC 20549
(202) 272-7450
Ms. Bonnie Westbrook Dir., Office of Consumer Affairs

The Securities and Exchange Commission has developed a program for its own online system called EDGAR (Electronic Data Gathering, Analysis and Retrieval) under the guidance of Arthur Anderson & Co., the accounting firm, with the participation of IBM and Dow Jones.

31. Select Information Exchange
2095 Broadway, N.Y. 10023
(212) 874-6408
George H. Wein, Pres.

Formed in 1965, Select Information Exchange sells hundreds of financial newsletters, books and services, primarily via an annual catalog sent to many thousands of investors. As a result of this sizable business, SIE has a variety of mailing lists, which are sold for $65 to $85 per thousand names.

SIE also advertises free annual reports in newspapers and its card packs and provides participating advertisers with individual requests for their annual reports. Payment is per inquiry (45 cents per gummed label), and there is no other charge.

32. Shareholder Communications Corporation
40 Exchange Place, N.Y. 10005
(212) 809-3600
Alexander B. Miller, Pres.

Founded in 1969, SCC provides specialized shareholder-related services, including proxy solicitations, address corrections, small shareholder buybacks and post-merger cleanups.

33. Shareholder Reports, Incorporated
600 Third Ave., N.Y. 10016
(212) 686-9099
Arthur Zelvin, Pres.

This graphic design firm, formed in 1961, writes, designs and produces corporate and financial literature and sales promotion materials for financial institutions.

34. Siegel & Gale Inc.
1185 Ave. of Americas, N.Y. 10036
(212) 730-0101
Alan Siegel, Chm.

Formed in 1969, Siegel & Gale now is one of the world's largest design and communications companies. The company is renowned for its language simplification work, particularly with loan applications, shareholder agreements, mortgages, insurance policies and other financial contracts, manuals, forms and documents.

Designer Bob Gale left in 1971 and Alan Siegel has become prominent with interviews on network television and in many major publications. Harold A. Pearson, president since 1983, also has an extensive background in advertising and other areas of communications.

The company literally has changed the content and appearance of significant financial and other forms and documents for several dozen major banks, financial institutions, companies and government agencies throughout the world.

Additional information is included in the chapter on literary services.

35. Standard & Poor's Corporation
25 Broadway, N.Y. 10004
(212) 208-8000
Candice Sherman, Media Relations Mgr.

Branch Offices:
4170 Ashford Dunwoody Rd., Atlanta 30319
(404) 252-0626

10 Milk St., Boston 02108
(617) 542-1301

625 N. Michigan Ave., Chicago 60606
(312) 263-4766

14701 Detroit Ave., Cleveland 44107
(216) 228-2425

10402 Little Patuxent Pky., Columbia, MD 21044
(301) 596-0394

401 Miracle Mile, Coral Gables, FL 33134
(305) 444-5657

211 N. Ervay St., Dallas 75201
(214) 742-3637

10880 Benson, Overland Park, KS 66210
(913) 451-9002

727 West Seventh St., L.A. 90017
(213) 622-1468

Three Parkway, Philadelphia 19102
(215) 568-5380

44 Montgomery St., San Francisco 94104
(415) 981-8660

For more than 125 years, Standard & Poor's has been one of the country's leading sources of authoritative financial information and analysis. Standard was originally Standard Statistics and Poor's was Poor's Publishing. They joined forces in 1941 and, since 1966, the company has been a wholly owned subsidiary of McGraw-Hill, Inc.

In 1860, Henry Varnum Poor, who was editor of the American Railroad Journal, published a 200-page book, The History of Railroads and Canals of the United States. The book was the predecessor of investment publications in this country and led to the formation, in 1867, of H.V. and H.W. Poor Company, a business publishing company primarily oriented to the railroads, formed by Henry Varnum Poor and his son, Henry William Poor.

By the beginning of the 20th century, financial publishing had become a thriving industry, which included such renowned names as John Moody, Roger Babson and Luthur L. Blake. Business operations of these men became intertwined. For example, when John Moody, a former newspaperman, formed Moody's Investors Service in 1913, Roy W. Porter took over Moody's former company, which published Moody's Manual. In 1919, Porter merged his company with Poor's Railroad Manual Company to form Poor's Publishing Company. In 1906, Luther Blake formed the Standard Statistics Bureau. Originally, the company compiled information on 100 companies and delivered via bellhop from the hotel in which they operated, cards on each of the companies to banks and brokerage houses. The company later provided subscribers of Moody's Manual with a daily update on the material in the Manual.

Roger Babson operated a similar card service and, in 1913, Blake acquired Babson's Stock and Bond System. For the next few decades, Poor's Publishing Company expanded considerably, but it never recovered from the depression of the 30's and declared bankruptcy. Paul T. Babson, a cousin of Roger W. Babson, took over the company and helped to bring about a merger with Standard Statistics in 1941, which resulted in the formation of Standard & Poor's Corporation. Paul Babson was the first board chairman. Actually, neither Standard nor Poor's were in great shape and the newly merged company struggled along for quite a few years, until the postwar boom in the late 40's and 50's. Today, the company can provide more data in minutes than its founder could in weeks or months of tedious work. The company's major publications are Standard & Poor's Corporation Records, which is issued in six volumes, and the Outlook.

Another division, Trendline Publications, publishes stock market charts. Other Standard & Poor's publications include Emerging and Special Situations, Industry Surveys and other investment information services. In addition to printed publications, Standard & Poor's provides information on microfilm and electronically. COMPMARK Data Services operates a databank with data from Poor's Register. COMPUSTAT is located in Englewood (Colorado) with sales offices in New York, San Francisco and Wash., DC. Another online service is MarketScope, which provides information about 4,700 companies.

Companies which are not covered by Standard & Poor's can pay to obtain a listing.

Many S&P services are available at local and university libraries. Among the S&P services with the broadest public relations applications are:

Corporation Records—A six-volume reference library of detailed business and financial information on more than 10,000 publicly held companies. Latest developments are reported five days a week in a seventh volume, Daily News. The cost to nonbrokers is $2,136 annually, including S&P's Daily News with continuous updates. The information also is available online through DIALOG Information Retrieval for business users and on DIALOG's Knowledge Index for after-hours home computers users. S&P's News on DIALOG, with daily updates, costs about $85 per online connect hour and 15 cents per full record printed offline. On Knowledge Index, it is about $24 per connect hour.

Industry Surveys—Comprehensive information and analysis on all major U.S. industries, including detailed financial data on more than 1,300 companies. For each major industry grouping, an annual Basic Survey and the quarterly Current Surveys are published during the year. The service also includes Trends & Projections—S&P's monthly economics letter—and a monthly Earnings Supplement. The service is $995 per year and is continuously updated.

Poor's Register—The S&P Register is widely considered the leading and most comprehensive directory of corporations and their executives. The publication provides listings on more than 45,000 companies, with the titles and duties of over 400,000 top executives. In addition to the business address and telephone numbers for all companies, the corporate listings include, in most cases, the company's accounting firm, primary bank and law firm, and the exchange on which its stock is traded. Approximate annual sales and number of employees are provided whenever possible. The cost is $425 annually, including three updates each year. If you purchase the Register around September, you will receive both this year's edition plus next year's edition for the one purchase price.

Data from the Register are available through S&P's COMPMARK service.

S&P Stock Reports—Two-page analytical reports on more than 3,600 publicly held companies, published in three four-volume sets covering the New York and American stock exchanges, as well as the Over-the-Counter market. Each report gives a succinct profile of the company's activities and financial position, supported by extensive statistics that facilitate quick year-to-year comparisons. Each company report is updated quarterly, or more frequently when significant developments occur. The New York Stock Exchange Reports is $820; the American Stock Exchange, $660, and the Over-the-Counter Reports, $660.

The Outlook, an investment advisory weekly with commentary on a wide range of securities, is $219 per year. As are many of S&P's publications, it is provided in loose-leaf format, with a binder.

S&P's Security Dealers of North America, a bound book, lists more than 11,000 brokerage and investment banking houses in the U.S. and Canada, along with their executive rosters and branch offices. It includes NASDAQ symbols; telex, telephone and teletype numbers; wire services facilities; and number of employees. This unique publication is issued twice a year with cumulative supplements provided every six weeks. The cost is $348 annually.

A catalog of S&P's services and publications is available by calling (212) 208-8786. S&P's COMPUSTAT Services are described in the chapter on research.

Note: Financial news releases should be sent as soon as available to Dave Mulcahy, Associate Editor, Daily News Desk, Standard & Poor's, 16th floor, 25 Broadway, N.Y. 10004, for inclusion in the S&P database. The automatic telecopier number is (212) 509-8994.

36. StreetSense
Citicorp Investment Bank
641 Lexington Ave., N.Y. 10043
(800) 241-2476
Kenneth Cirillo

StreetSense, a personal computer-based market information and order entry service, provides access to the Dow Jones News/Retrieval Service and other market data, as well as continuous monitoring of several thousand securities.

In 1987, a new feature was introduced to monitor late breaking news stories on selected companies and notify customers both audibly and visually of these stories. This ''Alert Window'' monitors block trades and total daily volume, in addition to upper and lower price levels on selected securities, so that it literally watches the market for its clients.

Available on an annual subscription basis, StreetSense functions through a standard personal comptuer with 512K memory, as well as on laptop computers.

37. Technical Data International
12 Farnsworth St., Boston, MA 02210
(617) 330-7878
Technical Data (previously called Business Research Corporation) is a pioneer in the electronic delivery of full text information of business and financial clients. Products include InvesText (Steve Keeble is sales manager at 800-662-7878) and StockGuard (Bruce Fader is sales manager at 800-447-1050).

38. Technimetrics, Inc.
80 South St., N.Y. 10038
(212) 509-5100
Carrie Thomas, V.P., Research

Branch Office:
4801 Woodway Dr., Houston 77056
(713) 965-9056
Ruth E. Flournoy

Since 1968, Technimetrics has provided specialist financial services to public corporations and brokerage firms primarily consisting of investment and research personnel at financial institutions around the world.

Custom-tailored services for reaching industry analysts, generalists, portfolio managers, directors of research and other key investment personnel at financial and brokerage firms are available in the basic program, which begins at $3,900 annually. It also provides access to European and Far East investment personnel. Information is available in various formats: mailing labels, magnetic computer tape and master listings, which include telephone numbers and asset sizes.

39. Telerate Systems, Incorporated
One World Trade Center, N.Y. 10048
(212) 938-5200
J. Ralph Hammock, Mgr. of Corp. Communications
Telerate's compact video terminal, installed in your office, permits continuous reference to a global storehouse of financial information contained in Telerate's central database and distributed through high-speed communications lines to subscriber terminals.

Telerate provides real-time, 24-hour, seven-day-per-week information on U.S. Government securities, U.S. and world money markets, foreign exchange, financial futures, mortgage-backed securities, Euromarkets, precious metals, energy markets, corporate markets, Federal Reserve statistics and Dow Jones news highlights.

Telerate also offers the Telerate Access Service (TAS), which enables subscribers to use their personal computers to access the Telerate system, as well as the Dow Jones News/Retrieval service; Telerate Broadcast, which transmits Telerate information via satellite or FM radio sideband; and several decision support products which enhance the trader's decision making ability through both fundamental and technical analysis.

The standard Telerate system, including screen, keyboard and controller, costs $660 per month on a two-year lease. One-time installation of the system is $700. Each optional service is quoted at an additional monthly fee. Telerate also is distributed outside North America.

40. Vickers Stock Research Corporation
266 New York Ave., Huntington, N.Y. 11743
(516) 423-7710, (800) 645-5043
Bruce Carlton

In 1983, Vickers Associates, a leader in the field of reporting institutional ownership of securities for more than 30 years, acquired Stock Research Corporation, a major supplier of corporate "insider" information. The new company, Vickers Stock Research Corporation, provides complete and timely databases of insider and institutional trading information.

The Vickers database contains information on transactions and holdings for more than 3,500 institutions that have positions in more than 8,500 common and preferred stocks, as well as similar information on publicly traded corporate bonds.

In addition to the Vickers on-line services, the company publishes a variety of directories and reports, including the following.

Stock Traders Guide. An alphabetical list of more than 8,500 common stocks and the identities of the institutions which hold them, as well as the transactions by those institutions in the most recent quarter, and the number of shares held by them. The Guide includes banks, colleges, investment companies, insurance companies and 13F money managers. Each report also contains the top 100 institutional holdings, sales, purchases, net sales and net purchases for each stock. Published quarterly in two bound volumes.

Bond Guide. A quarterly list of the holdings of U.S., Canadian and foreign institutions of corporate and convertible bonds, as well as preferred and convertible preferred stocks.

Facts on the Funds. A quarterly publication about the common stock holdings and transactions of more than 500 U.S. investment companies.

Directory of Institutional Investors. A detailed alphabetical listing of more than 3,500 U.S., Canadian and foreign institutional investors. Published semi-annually in one bound volume.

Other Vickers publications include quarterly looseleaf reports on investment companies, insurance companies, banks, colleges and money managers, as well as custom reports, and the following insider reports:

Transacting and Investing Report (semi-weekly)
Weekly Insider Report
Insider Options Report (biweekly)

41. Brendan Wood, Tutsch & Partners, Inc.
Suite 300, 100 Adelaide St. W., Toronto, Ontario M5H 1S3, Canada
(416) 863-6285
Paul Tutsch, Pres.

All types of financial research in Canada and elsewhere, including periodic syndicated studies of investor relations performance, investment banking, bond and money markets, retail financial consumers, institutional equity, corporate banking, middle market banking, corporate trust services, group insurance and pension fund management.

42. The Zehring Company
163 W. 74 St., N.Y. 10023
(212) 759-1972, (212) 496-0555
Karen Zehring, Exec. Editor

The Zehring Company, a subsidiary of Macmillan, Inc., is both an information medium and an information source. Begun in 1979, it specializes in products and services for the financial marketers to U.S. corporations, and retrieves and provides information to help marketers identify corporate prospects.

The Zehring database is a comprehensive source on the top financial strategists in the U.S. The database directories, The Corporate Finance Bluebook and The Corporate Finance Sourcebook are verified and updated each year. Data are available to clients as traditional reference books, on leased magnetic tapes, floppy disks, customized printouts and mailing labels.

Providing a "who's who" and a "who manages what" in the area of finance at the top 4,200 U.S. corporations, the hard-copy Bluebook sells for $395. Sortable computer tapes and labels are available.

The 900-page Sourcebook provides a compendium of sources of capital and financial services and costs $212. It lists over 2,200 firms and 10,000 names with phone numbers.

Chapter 11

Literary Services

From the age of about six, most people can write. Public relations professionals usually can write better than six-year-olds, but not always. Generally, they are adept in the writing of news releases, but few are capable of handling *all* types of journalism, such as speeches, technical reports, booklets and other types of writing which require more time, talent or expertise than any one person usually possesses.

Regardless of one's journalism experience, chances are insufficient attention is devoted to attempting to improve writing skills. In addition to attendance at courses and lectures, much can be learned from books and articles. A particularly useful book which also is quite entertaining is *The Careful Writer* by Theodore M. Bernstein (Atheneum). Other practical, useful, pleasurable books are *The Art of Readable Writing* by Dr. Rudolf Flesch (Harper & Row), The *Elements of Style* by William Strunk Jr. and E.B. White (Macmillan), and *Prentice-Hall Handbook for Writers* by Glen Leggett, David Mead and William Charvat (Prentice-Hall).

Several major newspapers publish "stylebooks." These guides are primarily for the use of their own writers but free copies often are available to publicists and other outsiders.

Many newspapers, particularly in small cities, publish free booklets with advice about writing wedding announcements, news releases about club meetings and other information for amateur publicists. The advice to civic volunteers often can be useful to professionals! For example, the Asbury Park Press, in Asbury Park, NJ, notes in its News Guide:

"Write 'cq' after an unusual spelling or anything that looks peculiar but is correct."

"When giving news over the phone, spell out names. Don't assume spellings of names. Pitfall letters are B, V, F, S, M, N, T and P."

Technical writers and typists should use specialized stylebooks, such as those published by the American Statistical Association, American Mathematical Society and other professional and scientific organizations.

Another useful tool for publication professionals is The Editorial Eye, a monthly newsletter ($49), which focuses on publications standards and practices. It is primarily for writers and editors and is a delightful mix of news and production tips, with letters, quizzes and editorials.

The publisher, Editorial Experts, Inc., 85 S. Bragg St., Alexandria, VA 22312, is described in a separate listing in this chapter.

The following description of the company's services is so detailed that it can be useful to anyone involved in the writing or production of a publication—whether or not you use this fine company.

Copyediting. Reviewing a manuscript for correct spelling, grammar, sentence construction, and consistency. May involve putting a manuscript into a specific editorial style; checking facts; checking accuracy and completeness of tables, charts, bibliographies, and footnotes; and preparing a style sheet.

Substantive editing. Copyediting a manuscript plus reviewing the content for accuracy and logic. May involve reorganizing the manuscript, writing transitions and summaries, eliminating wordiness, ensuring proper tone/approach for intended audience, and working with the author to clarify the text and incorporate the editor's suggestions.

Writing. Writing a manuscript for publication or audiovisual production, either from scratch or from an outline or notes already prepared. May include planning, interviewing, attending meetings, consulting with experts on the subject and performing various kinds of research. The writer may be expected to produce an outline and several drafts of the manuscript.

Publications Management. Helping plan publications programs and individual projects, organizing production schedules, coordinating staff, reducing costs and establishing policy.

Proofreading. Reading final copy, galleys, computer printouts, or other versions of a manuscript against a previous version, looking for and marking with standard proofreader's symbols any typographical errors, poor-quality type, deviations from typing or typesetting instructions, and querying blatant editorial errors and inconsistencies. Proofreading may be done by one person or by a team of two who read aloud to each other.

Editorial Proofreading. Reading material for typographical errors, format inconsistences, and moderate editorial and grammatical problems, and helping to impose a consistent editorial style throughout. Done by one person using no comparison copy.

Indexing. Reading text, noting important topics, and choosing concise words and phrases as index entries. Organizing the index with appropriate subheadings and cross references to meet user needs. Computer programs are used to manipulate entries in accordance with the requirements of the project and to sort and print the index in final form.

Abstracting. Selecting the important information from a research report or other publication and writing a succinct abstract, which includes a topic sentence, a brief description of methods, a summary of results, and a conclusion. Abstracting may include selection of key words or subject descriptors and coding for entry into a computer database.

Research. Collecting and verifying information. Searching databases and contacting information sources for answers to specific questions.

Design. Developing the visual treatment of a publication, including cover art, photographs or other illustrations, layout and typography. May include preparing rough sketches or comprehensives closely resembling the finished product.

Production. Supervising keyboarding, design, graphics and printing. May include production management of books, brochures, newsletters. May also include desktop publishing, computer-generated graphics, and slides.

Word Processing. Preparing draft or camera-ready copy on IBM-compatible computers using WordPerfect 4.2 software, and on stand-alone Wang OIS-115, NBI 3000, and Lexitron VT 1202 and 1303 word processing equipment. Capabilities include desktop publication and database creation and management. Printer capabilities range from dot-matrix to near-typeset quality laser printing, which incorporates various test and display typefaces in a range of sizes. EEI can accept and convert disks from other systems, and they will provide disks to clients for a minimal additional charge. IBM-compatible disks can be converterd to ASCII files at no extra cost.

Telecommunications. Transmitting copy via telecommunications modem to computerized databases or computerized typesetting equipment.

The most famous stylebook is *The New York Times Manual of Style and Usage,* which is only $6.95 (paperback), plus $1.50 shipping, from Times Books, 201 E. 50 St., N.Y. 10022. It's revised frequently and each edition is carefully read by editors, to note new style practices and also for the entertaining literary and other comments.

In 1960, The Associated Press and United Press International agreed to a joint style, but for many years, each published its own stylebook and sold them to nonstaffers for $1 each. In 1977, a long-awaited revised stylebook was published. Each service has added its own chapters to the basic text, and the book is revised frequently. Copies are $7.75, from The Associated Press, 50 Rockefeller Plaza, N.Y. 10020.

A few large public relations operations issue their own stylebooks and other editorial guides. Copies generally are available free to outsiders, but supplies usually are limited.

The Elements of Style is not a comprehensive stylebook, but it's required reading for almost every writer. The famous little book (85 pages) originally was written by William Strunk and was revised in 1979 by E.B. White. Published by Macmillan, the paperback is $3.25. Buy a few, as gifts, from your bookstore or Macmillan Publishing, Front & Brown St., Riverside, NJ 08075.

A useful book on scientific writing is *Why Not Say It Clearly?* The author is Lester S. King, M.S., former senior editor of the Journal of the American Medical Association. The publisher is Little, Brown and Company, 34 Beacon St., Boston 02108, and the price is $12.50.

The *U.S. Government Printing Office Style Manual,* an encyclopedia for cartographers, lexicographers and writers, is $11 (paperback) from the Superintendent of Documents, U.S. GPO, Washington, DC 20402. It's revised every few years.

Over 40 colleges in the U.S. and Canada now have grammar hotlines to enable editors and others to call with questions about grammar, usage, punctuation, spelling and related subjects. Among the hotlines are the Writing Center Hotline of Auburn University, Auburn, AL, National Grammar Hotline of Moorpark College, Moorpark, CA, Rewrite of York College of the City University of New York, NY, Writing Center Hotline of Cincinnati Technical College, Learning Line of San Antonio College and Grammar Hotline of Tidewater Community College, Virginia Beach, VA.

The University of Arkansas at Little Rock publishes *The Writers' Hotline Handbook,* which includes answers to the most commonly asked questions about subject-verb agreement, spelling, usage and punctuation.

You can get a directory of grammar hotlines, including their phone numbers and hours of service, by sending a stamped self-addressed envelope to the Grammar Hotline, Tidewater Community College, 1700 College Crescent, Virginia Beach, VA 23456. Donna Reiss Friedman is Director of the Writing Center and Grammar Hotline at Tidewater and you can call her from 10 A.M. to noon at (804) 427-7170.

Large public relations departments and agencies often include one or more full-time writers. Large and small operations often find it necessary, and desirable, to seek the assistance of professional freelance writers and agencies which specialize in literary services. These specialists are particularly useful in times of overload or other stress and also provide efficient, economical help for out-of-town and problem assignments.

In 1974, Jerry Buchanan started the TOWERS Club, USA Newsletter, a collection of ideas, tips, sources, direct marketing comments and other personal, useful material for writers, publishers and others. He's a very creative person and the monthly newsletter, which is oriented to the individual or small business, is a delight to read. $60 a year from Box 2038, Vancouver, WA 98668, phone (206) 574-3084. TOWERS is an acronym for The Original Writers' Educational Research Service.

A comprehensive list of communications periodicals appears at the end of the chapter on media directories. Included is the Maranto memo, a 116-page publication for writers, editors and business communicators. Launched in 1987, it's edited by Joe Marento, who was publications manager at Mobil Oil Corporation.

Many public relations periodicals, including several newsletters specifically for editors and writers, are described in the book, *Professional's Guide to Publicity* ($9.50), Public Relations Publishing Co., 888 Seventh Ave., N.Y. 10106.

Many freelance writers subscribe to The Source, the computer database service which is compatible with personal computers. It therefore is very easy to retain a freelance writer by simply using the message service of The Source. For example, you can insert an inquiry that you are looking for a writer who will be attending a convention or covering an event, and receive a response enabling you to deal directly with the writer, without paying an intermediary company. For information, contact The Source, 1616 Anderson Road, McLean, VA 22102. Information about The Source is included in the chapter on research.

Next time you prepare a speech or presentation, you might want to put it in a Script-Master, which is a special portfolio designed and sold by Brewer-Cantelmo Co., 116 E. 27 Street, N.Y. 10016. The cover is personalized with the user's name, and, more important, the interior enables the pages to be pushed aside rather than turned, which is helpful for some speakers in terms of eliminating page-turning distraction, as well as the inadequacies of a file holder, ring binders, note cards and other items used by speakers. Of course, it's still not as good as memorizing a speech or using a prompting device.

Several companies and many freelancers are adept at preparing speeches, annual reports, booklets and other projects which require extensive writing. Generally, good work is possible only when the writer knows and understands the company or spokesperson. Therefore, it sometimes is risky to work with a freelancer, particularly for the first time. Furthermore, freelancers and one-person businesses of this type can be peripatetic and unpredictable.

The most important part of any news release and many other public relations materials is the beginning. As noted in the chapter on computerized news, the era of news releases and summaries popping up in rapid succession on video display terminals has intensified the need for introductions that encourage editors to read for more than just a few seconds. In the electronic era, good writing is needed more than ever before!

"Will the Editor Read it?" is the title of a 1983 article in Public Relations Journal by Ronald N. Levy, president of North American Precis Syndicate. Following is the complete text.

An editor's interest can be either awakened or killed by opening sentences—the leads—of written material released by public relations practitioners.

How many types of leads are there? Surely, the number is almost infinite. But a study of stories—released by companies, public relations counsels, associations and advertising agencies—reveals ten basic story leads that seem highly effective in interesting editors.

1. *Question the reader*. The objective here is to involve the reader in the story as quickly as possible. Examples:

"Mister, have you a good head for business? The hat industry says you do. American men spend more than $100 million on headgear annually."

"Are you an American and a half? If so, the odds are that you will be taking a trip this year, for statistics indicate that 1.5 out of every two Americans will travel somewhere."

2. *The historical lead—with vigor*. This kind of lead helps avoid the trite notation of how many thousand years it's been since such-and-such began. Examples:

"Even before Jonah met that big-mouthed fish, people understood the importance of knowing how to swim."

"Ever since cavemen learned that there's more than one way to skin a tiger, forms of education have varied."

3. *The "inside story" lead*. This promises the reader that the story will give him facts which relatively few people know.

"Half of America's 10,000,000 diabetics don't know they have the disease, another

10,000,000 will one day get it—yet few people really understand what diabetes is . . . how it works . . . and what can be done to *avoid* it.''

"We eat it, wear it, even sleep on it—yet few people really *know* much about that fascinating fiber: cotton."

4. *The rhyming or alliterative lead.* This entertains not only because of the euphony but also builds up a bit of suspense as to what the subject is.

"Salesman and bailsman, office worker and soda jerker—these are a few of the jobs held by those millions of Americans who are now studying a foreign language." "Tool, tonic, sometimes symphonic, lighting plays a major role in determining your mood, comfort and appearance."

"Men have died for it, women have lied for it, billions of people have sighed for it. It's *love*—and what a history it has had!"

"Leaks? Squeaks? Drains? Mains? Which are the plumber's biggest headaches?"

5. *The prediction.* The usefulness of this lead isn't restricted to stories about the future. Often it can be used on a feature that dramatizes the importance of a recent innovation.

"If you are now in your 20's, or 30's, plan on living to be 80 or 90. Many children born now may well see the year 2080. That is the promise of hormone research going on right now."

"Consider the possibility of ski lifts, enclosed in clear plastic, connecting the tops of a city's tallest skycrapers . . . a municipal building one mile high . . . a whole city with walls of gleaming stainless steel."

6. *Entertaining sound.* Presently, leads of this type are among the freshest to cross an editor's desk.

"Thump! Thump! Thump! It happens over 100,000 times a day: your heart gulps in a few ounces of blood, then pumps out a fresh supply."

"Sing it: *meeeeeeee. Me-me-me-me-me!* The melody isn't important, but the word counts for a lot—it's the key to selecting good design."

7. *The quote.* Because so many writers use this lead, many feel that it's wise to use little known quotes.

" 'Beauty,' says an old Spanish proverb, 'is the compliment a wise woman pays to the man she loves'."

" 'The man who converseth well,' said Cato the Elder, 'may change his world'."

" 'One reason many people don't accomplish as much as they should,' says a top executive, 'is that they *work* too hard'."

8. *The pun.* Editors may wince at a pun, but often they grin—and bear it—to the composing room.

"If your grass is pleading, 'I want to be a-lawn,' here's down-to-earth advice."

"Any way you look at it, the female figure is impressive. Women vote 70 per cent of all corporate stock, spend 80 per cent of all family income, have ownership interest in 500,000 small businesses."

"Rug care needn't be rugged."

"Are you itching to scratch poison ivy from the list of problems you may run into this summer?"

9. *The "while you act" lead.* Like the question lead, this quickly involves the reader in the story—and is especially useful when the question would have to be one that the reader obviously can't answer.

"While you, at graduation ceremonies this year, are applauding your favorite senior, a Bantu tribesman will be painting his. The Eskimo student *paddles* his way to a diploma."

"Next time you drive under an over-the-highway bridge . . . or pause to admire a huge water-spanner . . . give a thought to the days—just 500 years ago—when most people thought a bridge could be built only with the help of the devil!"

10. *The promise.* This businesslike approach tells the reader quickly and plainly just how he will benefit by reading the story.

"Even if you're a skilled driver with more experience than average, the odds are that you can still cut car operating costs—save good money on gas, oil and tires—by keeping your car in more efficient condition."

"If you're carrying around too much *you,* take heart—50 million other Americans face the same weighty problem. If you'll settle for a weight loss of two pounds weekly, this diet will take a load off your mind also."

Though other types of leads are readily discernible—the statistic, the contrast, the simile, the anecdote and the definition are examples—it will probably never be possible to categorize all leads, nor to reduce lead-writing to a formula. This is a good thing. Would any practitioner want a formula for such creative activity?

The Council of Writers Organizations, which represents 23 organizations with about 40,000 members (many writers belong to more than one organization) is located at 160 West End Ave., Ste. 12 H, N.Y. 10023. Several of its organizations sell their membership directories, and a few accept public relations people who are part-time writers. The member organizations are:

Aviation/Space Writers Association
Boating Writers International
Chicago Women In Publishing
Dance Critics Association
Editorial Freelancers Association
Florida Freelance Writers Association
Independent Writers of Chicago
Independent Writers of Southern California
International Motor Press Association
Midwest Travel Writers Association
Mystery Writers of America
National Association of Science Writers
National Book Critics Circle
Outdoor Writers Association of America
Philadelphia Writers Organization
Science Fiction Writers of America
Society of American Travel Writers
St. Louis Writers Guild
Travel Journalists Guild
United States Ski Writers Association
Washington Independent Writers
Women In Communications
Writers Guild of America, East

Hundreds of literary services, including manuscript typists, writers and publishers, are listed in Literary Market Place. For example, the section on editorial services includes abstractions, bibliographies, fact checking, indexing, photo research, proofreading and research. (This excellent reference book is described in the section on media directories.)

Following is information about companies and associations which specialize in writing and publication services of public relations interest, with particular stress on those which are *not* in New York City.

1. The Alternative Research

Box 432, N.Y. 10156
(212) 683-3478
Don Wigal, Pres.

Formed in 1975, The Alternative Research provides writing and research services for non-publishers or self-publishers, as well as other clients. The company also operates The Institute for Independent Studies, which was formed in 1980. Dr. Wigal operates from his office at 4 Park Avenue.

2. Cambridge Associates

164 Canal St., Boston, MA 02114
(617) 423-5878
Kathryn Dinovo, V.P.

Many companies create and produce newsletters. A few have developed a spacialty of producing newsletters that are franchised, that is, the same newsletter is used by several "sponsors." Each sponsor appears to be the publisher, with its imprint on the top of page one and elsewhere, so that recipients (potential customers of the sponsors) may not be aware that the newsletter is not original. Depending on the number of copies, the franchise entitles the sponsor to exclusive distribution, in its geographical or industrial area.

Cambridge Associates (a division of the Dartnell Corp.) produces a variety of newsletters and is one of the leaders in this field. The monies involved in purchasing a newsletter obviously are much less than creating it yourself. For example, copies of a four-page newsletter, in quantities of 1,000, can cost about 30¢ each, complete with your masthead and other area for an advertisement, sales or public relations message. The cost of producing your own newsletter can be well over $1.00 a copy, when one has to allocate writing, typesetting and artwork costs to a small print run.

3. The Caruba Organization

Box 40, Maplewood, NJ 07040
(201) 763-6392
Alan Caruba

A writer, and public relations counselor, Alan Caruba is a frequent contributor to many magazines and newspapers. He provides diversified editorial services to a variety of public relations clients and agencies. He works on a set fee or retainer basis, with a minimum of $500 plus expenses.

4. Clipper Creative Art Service

Dynamic Graphics, Inc.
Box 1901, 6000 N. Forest Park Dr., Peoria, IL 61656

A monthly 24-page collection of camera-ready art on large-size (12½ × 19 inch) pages. Major illustrations are in different sizes, to save camera times and costs. Included are pictorial indexes and a supplement with how-to tips and short cuts. The cost is $29.50 a month.
Dynamic Graphics also publishes:

Print Media Service, monthly collection of camera-ready art oriented to the retailers, $39.75 a month.
Themed Art Packages, $49.50 to $89.50 each.
DeskTop Art, themed art collections for personal computers.
Step-By-Step Graphics Magazine, bimonthly, $42 a year.

5. The Comedy Center

700 Orange St., Wilmington, DE 19801
(302) 656-2209, (800) 441-7098
Lammot Copeland, Jr., Pres.
Robert Orben

A former writer for Red Skelton, Jack Paar and President Gerald Ford, Bob Orben probably is America's most prolific comedy writer. For many years, he worked from his home in the Flatbush section of Brooklyn, but in 1974, he moved his office from the joke capital to the corporate capital, where he operates The Comedy Center, and publishes the semimonthly Current Comedy ($72 a year). The material may not be reprinted and is for oral use only.

6. Creative Communications Services

Box 1007, 55 Encinitas Blvd., Encinitas, CA 92024
(619) 436-2279
Bob Fisher, Pres.

Formed in 1973, CCS is a business photojournalism service, with its own network of writers and photographers.

7. Creative Media Services

Box 5955, Berkeley, CA 94705
(415) 843-3408, (800) 272-0800
Linda Harris

Formed in 1970 by Phil Frank and Linda Harris, CMS publishes and distributes Clip Art books and captioned cartoons by syndicated cartoonist Phil Frank. Published annually, these materials are designed for newsletters, internal publications and advertising, and include topics for college, hospital and business communicators.

Current editions of Clip Art are $68 (64 pages) and past editions are $20–$40. Current Cartoon series are $35 and past editions are $15.

8. Creative Resource Group

990 Avenue of the Americas, N.Y. 10018
(212) 629-0062
Leo J. Northart and Peg Dardenne

An editorial services and counseling firm, CRG handles all types of writing and editing assignments, including design and production. Mr. Northart was editor for many years of Public Relations Journal.

Dartnell's Cambridge Associates

See listing under Cambridge Associates.

9. Editorial Experts, Inc.

85 S. Bragg St., Alexandria, VA 22312
(703) 642-3040
Claire Kincaid

Founded by Laura Horowitz in Washington, D.C., in 1972, Editorial Experts, Inc. (EEI) has become the largest publications services business in the metropolitan area, providing writing, editing, publications management, indexing, abstracting, database management, proofreading, production, design, graphics, keyboarding and telecommunications services to government agencies, consulting firms, national associations, corporations and other clients. The company is renowned for its high quality work. Its monthly newsletter, The Editorial Eye, focuses on publications standards and practices.

126

Its other publications include *Mark My Words,* a textbook on proofreading; *Stet! Tricks of the Trade for Writers and Editors,* an anthology of articles from the newsletter; and the biennial *Directory of Editorial Resources.*

Through its temporary placement service, Editorial Experts provides editors, writers, proofreaders, and graphics specialists to work onsite in clients' offices, with a minimum charge of five hours per person per day.

Editorial Experts also conducts workshops on publications skills, which are held in the Washington, D.C. area, Chicago and San Francisco.

10. Folio Publishing Corporation

Box 4949, 6 River Bend, Stamford, CT 06907
(203) 358-9900
Barbara Love, Editor

Folio, a magnificent magazine about magazines, is published by a company that, since 1975, has conducted the Folio Publishing Conference and Exhibition. Several times a year, these meetings provide exhibit space, speaking opportunities, and other services relevant to public relations people in the book and periodical fields.

11. Fillers for Publications

1220 Maple Ave., L.A. 90015
(213) 747-6541
John Raydell, Editor

A variety of noncommercial items, articles, cartoons, puzzles and clip art, ideal for house organ fillers, can be purchased for $148 a year. Subscribers receive a monthly packet. The editorial copy, cartoons, puzzels and clip art can be purchased separately for $64 each, any two for $98, three for $128 and all for $148.

12. First Draft

Box 574, Winnetka, IL 60093
(312) 441-7473
Louis C. Williams Jr., Publisher
Karen C. Weeder, Mgr. Ed.

Started in 1984, First Draft is a news and feature article service for editors of employee publications. Subscribers, who may choose from among 12 articles each month, pay $550 for up to 60 articles a year. The company is owned by L.C. Williams & Associates, Inc., 320 N. Michigan Ave., Chicago 60601.

13. The Huenefeld Company, Inc.

Box U, Bedford, MA 01730
(617) 861-9650
John Huenefeld, Pres.

Established in 1968, The Huenefeld Company counsels new and small book publishers on all aspects of management, production and marketing, and publishes The Huenefeld Guide to Book Publishing ($185), an encyclopedia which literally can put you into the book publishing business, and The Huenefeld Report ($88), a biweekly newsletter.

14. The Jokesmith

44 Queen's View Rd., Marlborough, MA 01752
(617) 481-0979
Edward C. McManus

Ed McManus, a long-time ghost writer of business speeches on the lighter side, and Bill Nicholas, a specialist in audio-visual presentations, are the authors of "We're Roasting Harry Tuesday Night . . . How to Plan, Write and Conduct the Business/Social Roast" ($15.95). In 1983, they started The Jokesmith, a quarterly newsletter ($35 a year, $10 for a sample issue).

15. Michael Larsen and Elizabeth Pomada
1029 Jones St., San Francisco 94109
(415) 673-0939

This charming, creative couple created Metro California Media, operated a public relations agency and now are literary agents. Because of their super-energy and public relations orientation, they actually help to develop book concepts, as well as market manuscripts. Before emigrating to San Francisco in 1970, they worked for several publishers in New York.

Mr. Larsen and Ms. Pomada have formulated The Nidy (Non-Institutional Do-It-Yourself) Gritty School of Writing, and suggest the following checklist for prospective writers:

1. Something to say.
2. The compulsive need to say it.
3. Talent: the gift of forming words, characters and situations and knowing when they are "right."
4. Discipline.
5. Trust in your instincts.
6. Faith in your work.
7. Patience with your talent and others' appreciation of it.
8. Reading.
9. *The Elements of Style.*
10. The need to grow as a writer and the experience with art and life to do so.
11. Allowing nothing—especially waiting for success or achieving it—to interfere with the rest of the checklist.

16. Media Resource Service
355 Lexington Ave., N.Y. 10017
(212) 661-9110

A program of the Scientists' Institute for Public Information, Media Resource Service provides journalists with the names of scientists, engineers and other experts who can provide information free. Over 20,000 experts are listed in the data bank.

17. Multi-Ad Services, Inc.
1720 W. Detweiller Dr., Peoria, IL 61615
(309) 692-1530, (800) 447-1950

Multi-Ad provides a variety of packaged art services, including Kwikee INHOUSE Graphic Services, a syndicated monthly eletronic art and layout service.

18. National Writers Club
1450 S. Havana St., Aurora, CO 80012
(303) 751-7844
James L. Young, Exec. Dir.

The National Writers Club, which represents about 5,000 freelance writers, publishes annually The Professional Freelance Writers directory ($10) which includes NWC professional members who are available for assignments and members of the Associated Business Writers of America.

19. Newsletters Unlimited
The Newsletter Clearinghouse
44 W. Market St., Box 311, Rhinebeck, NY 12572
(914) 876-2081
Howard Penn Hudson

Mr. Hudson, a prominent author and public relations counselor, also operates a service which handles part or all aspects of newsletters, from creation to mailing, and publishes a newsletter and The Newsletter Yearbook Directory.

20. Palazzo & Associates Inc.
155 E. 55 St., N.Y. 10022
(212) 826-6481

Renowned for his graphics work at Forbes, the New York Herald Tribune, Chicago Daily News, Family Circle, Family Weekly and other publications, Peter Palazzo is the person to contact about the aesthetic rejuvenation of any type of company publication.

21. Para Publishing
Box 4232–4041 Santa Barbara, CA 93140
(805) 968-7277
Dan Poynter

The author of 20 books (mostly about publishing), Dan Poynter is a consultant to publishers and conducts workshops on book marketing. Book promotion services of Para Publishing include:

Reviewer's Choice. Semi-annual mailing of a brochure about books to in-house corporate magazines. Editors can request review copies. Cost to publishers is $150 per listing, plus books.

Author/Expert Interview Service. Mailing about interviewees to radio and TV talk shows. $165 per listing.

Journalists' Resource. Mailing to freelance writers. $165 per listing.

Publishing Poynters. Monthly newsletter on book promotion. Free.

22. John Peter Associates, Inc.
233 E. 50 St., N.Y. 10022
(212) 355-4252
John Peter, Pres.
Stephanie L. Jackson, V.P.

A former art director of McCall's Magazine and an editor of Life and Look, Mr. Peter is a management consultant in the publications field who specializes in magazine design and development.

23. Lawrence Ragan Communications, Inc.
407 South Dearborn St., Chicago 60605
(312) 922-8245
Lawrence Ragan, Publisher

Founded in 1970, Lawrence Ragan is a renowned expert on communications, particularly employee publications. His company conducts over 200 annual workshops in writing, design, photography and other aspects of public relations and communications, publishes several books, provides critiques ($250 each) of organizational publications, and publishes five periodicals:

The Ragan Report, the flagship publication, weekly, $139.
Speechwriter's Newsletter, weekly, $158.

The Bottom Line Communicator, monthly, $49.
Editor's Workshop Newsletter, monthly, $69.
Corporate Annual Report Newsletter, monthly, $197.

24. Wm. A. Ries & Associates
Box 2350, Kill Devil Hills, NC 27948
(919) 441-3141
Frances K. Ries, Pres.

Founded in 1975, as a local advertising agency in the Outer Banks of North Carolina, Wm. Ries now produces two services for communications clients throughout the country. Both are located at Box 529, Kitty Hawk, NC 27949.

Hospital Graphics (started in 1981) is a monthly collection of clip art especially for hospitals. It's $27.95 a month, $311.40 a year.

Editor's Choice (started in 1985) is a quarterly collection of clip art for in-house publications. It's $48 a quarter, $172 a year.

25. Herbert Schwartz, Inc.
One Penn Plaza, Suite 100, N.Y. 10119
(212) 947-4078

A long-time successful writer of speeches, booklets, annual reports and other corporate communications materials, Herb Schwartz works for companies and agencies throughout the country.

26. Sidebar/Chicago News Service
Box A-3945, Chicago 60690
(312) 784-0724
Donald V. Radcliffe, Mgr.

Sidebar/Chicago handles interviews, photography, case histories and other assignments. Fees vary in accordance with the time, geography and other details. Specialties include medical and business subjects. Mr. Radcliffe is renowned for his expertise in the hearing field and other medical and scientific areas.

27. Siegel & Gale, Inc.
1185 Ave. of Americas, N.Y. 10036
(212) 730-0101
Alan Siegel, Chm.
Kenneth Morris, Tim King, Exec. V.P.'s

Formed in 1969, Siegel & Gale has become one of America's leading design firms, specialising in corporate identification and advertising, packaging, architectural graphics and publications, including editorial services. Alan Siegel's well-rounded background includes BBDO (advertising), Ruder & Finn (public relations) and Sandgren & Murtha (designers). Designer Robert Gale left in 1971. The company was acquired by Saatchi & Saatchi in 1985.

The company is best known for its language-simplification work, and Alan Siegel is the country's number-one expert on this subject. Siegel & Gale has redesigned and rewritten loan agreements, insurance policies and other contracts, forms and documents for Citibank, St. Paul Fire & Marine, Fidelity Union Life Insurance Co. and other companies, as well as government agencies and associations throughout the world. Alan Siegel is a much-sought-after speaker at conferences of lawyers, accountants, public relations and other executives concerned with consumerism, language-simplification laws and regulations which require drastic changes in existing materials.

A handsome athlete, Alan Siegel is a photographer, writer, artist—a multimedia star who has been profiled in People, The New York Times and other media, and has appeared on the Today Show and many TV programs.

28. Robert Uchitelle, Inc.
655 Irving Park Rd., Chicago 60613
(312) 472-7071

In business since 1961, Mr. Uchitelle has handled hundreds of writing assignments in the Chicago area and elsewhere. He is renowned for business articles, case histories and speeches. He specializes in writing newsletters and provided a camera-ready service at a per-page price.

29. Katheryn Ullmen
2022 Grove Avenue, Quincy, IL 62301
(217) 222-0492

A puzzle expert for over 20 years, Katheryn Ullmen creates camera ready crossword, word search and other puzzles and quizzes, customized to order or nonexclusive on safety, business, holiday and other themes from an extensive list.

30. Carlson Wade Agency
Room 4K, 49 Bokee Ct., Brooklyn, NY 11223
(718) 743-6983

Mr. Wade's specialty is writing on food, nutrition and health topics, as well as medical articles, booklets, books and speeches.

31. Washington Independent Writers
220 Woodward Bldg., 733 15 St., N.W., Wash., DC 20005
(202) 347-4973

Nearly 2,000 writers in the nation's capital are members of this organization ($55 a year dues) and thus receive a variety of publications as well as other services, including workshops and a job bank. Nonmembers can obtain the membership directory ($15 including postage), A Writer's Guide to Washington ($7.95 plus $1.00 postage) and the member's newsletter ($30 a year).

32. Writers Alliance Ltd.
104 E. 40 St., N.Y. 10016
(212) 986-2830
Robert L. Johns, Pres.

Offers complete editorial services, from research and writing to copy and line editing, proofreading and placement with media. Writers Alliance also provides literary agency assistance and representation.

33. Writers: Free-Lance, Inc.
12 Cavalier Dr., Ambler, PA 19002
(215) 646-7550
Robert M.Cullers, Pres.

Funded in 1961 by James Eysler, this organization has become a leading source for professional writers, editors, researchers, artists and photographers around the world. More than 3,000 pros are registered for specific assignments and pinpointed according to their field of knowledge, specialties and locations. Bob Cullers formerly was managing editor of employee publications at a major oil company.

34. The Writing Company
1130 Bedford Rd., Pleasantville, NY 10570
(914) 769-2160, (203) 431-8280
Jane Johnson, Ph.D., Lea Lane, Mgr. Partners

Writing, editing and training services. Formed in 1979. Dr. Johnson has taught proposal writing and other writing techniques, particularly for non-profit organizations. Lea Lane is a former journalist and book editor. She is the author of the book, *Steps to Better Writing.*

Most literary services involve a few hours or days of an editorial specialist's time. Occasionally, a public relations project involves the commissioning of a lengthy booklet or even a book. Such projects often entail working with publishers and require a familiarity with the publishing business.

Not many people read nonfiction books (as compared to newspapers and magazines). Fewer than 30 percent of adult Americans regularly read books, which is considerably less than other forms of communications such as newspapers, magazines, radio and television. American publishers put out more than 40,000 new books or new editions of old books each year. How many are read?

There are a few books which sell more than a million copies, but less than 50,000 copies of the average new book are sold each year, and a book often is considered successful if more than 5,000 copies are sold.

So if not many people read nonfiction books, and book publishing is a highly speculative kind of business, why bother?

It is possible that the numbers are deceiving and that books can be, and often are, the most influential communications medium. A book such as Ralph Nader's *Unsafe at Any Speed* is capable of changing an entire industry, not necessarily because of the number of people who actually read the book.

The greatest value of a book often is not the number of copies which are sold, but rather the content of the book, who reads it, and who reads or hears about it. Radio and TV appearances by authors are a vital part of book-marketing.

In short, a thoughtful, well-written book can present new ideas and influence society in a lasting, significant manner, by itself and abetted by publicity.

A busy executive or official may want to write a book to expand on a theme or idea, but require assistance from a public relations practitioner with regard to research, writing, publishing and distribution. Such assistance does not necessarily mean going to a ''vanity press'' or dealing directly with a printer.

A public relations practitioner can function as a literary agent, in a completely ethical manner, with any legitimate book publisher. Sometimes it will be necessary to retain a professional or make a commitment to purchase a specified number of copies, and, in this sense, the book is dubbed a ''sponsored book.'' In other cases, the idea for the book may have sufficient sales potential so that there is no need for any financial guarantee, and therefore it is no different from novels, plays or other literary works which have no public relations involvement.

Though the primary objective of a sponsored book often is not mass audiences, public relations executives and publishers, working together, continue to amaze themselves with the fact that an obviously commercial book can become a best seller.

Take a look at *Verse by the Side of the Road.* Written by Frank Rowsome and published by Stephen Greene Press. The book basically is a history and collection of the jingles and poems used by the Burma Shave Company on its roadside advertising signs.

The Burma Shave Company did *not* pay for the services of the writer, nor did it make a commitment to buy copies of the book. It simply provided access to its files.

Many thousands of people paid $3.95 to buy copies of this interesting, nostalgic book, making the publisher quite happy. Burma Shave also benefited from the hundreds of news articles and favorable reviews acquired by the book—but not quite enough, as the company, and its signs, faded away a few years ago.

There are many other examples, though, of books which have company names in their titles and yet are not vanity or giveaway items.

The *Guinness Book of Records* has established publishing records in the United Kingdom and other countries. Other publishing successes include *The Michelin Guide, Mobil Travel Guides, Johnson & Johnson First Aid Book* and *The Fannie Farmer Cook Book.* The number-one best-selling travel guide in the United Kingdom is published by Egon Ronay and sponsored by Lucas, an automotive parts company.

There have been other books which were noncommercial in content, but involved some type of corporate participation. Clairol provided color transparancies of its art collection and bought several thousand copies of *Mother and Child in Modern Art,* published by Duell, Sloan & Pearce. The Mead Corporation did the same thing with *Artist and Advocate,* published by Renaissance Editions.

In an article in The Director (a British magazine), titled "Companies in Search of an Author," Mr. J. A. Maxtone Graham wrote:

> Certainly the company history still has a place, but the tendency nowadays is to have it so written and produced that it is of interest not only to those directly connected with the firm, but also to others in the trade and sometimes to the general public. Very often—as with The History of Unilever by Charles Wilson and The History of Vickers by J. D. Scott—the company history has become a work of serious scholarship.

On this side of the Atlantic, *My Years with General Motors* by Alfred P. Sloan and *Confessions of an Advertising Man* by David Ogilvy were best sellers. In 1984 and 1985, the number one book was Lee Iacocca's autobiography, written with William Novak. However, these were not sponsored books. *Oil for the World,* sponsored by Standard Oil of New Jersey, ran through three paperback editions and was translated into seven languages.

Subsidized books can backfire and embarrass or cause other problems for the sponsor. An example was the subsidization by a Rockefeller intermediary of the Arlington House biography of Arthur Goldberg during the 1970 New York gubernatorial election.

The book was a flop. On the other extreme, in 1960, a Barry Goldwater intermediary agreed to pay a publisher part of the production costs of *The Conscience of a Conservative.* Over a million copies have been sold, and the book still is selling.

TV-producer Chuck Barris was miffed with Harper's Magazine Press, and vice versa, but the book, *You and Me, Babe,* became a best seller. One version of the story is that Mr. Barris agreed to buy the book's reprint rights for $35,000 and paid for extensive promotion.

Books which are published by major companies as part of agreements in which the author or sponsor agreed to buy a minimum number (generally 10,000) of copies include *The First Five Years of Life* (by Dr. Arthur Gesell; Harper & Row), *The Human Environment and Business* (speeches by Henry Ford; Holt, Rinehart and Winston), *A Peace Policy for Europe* (Willy Brandt; Weybright and Talley), *A Matter of Life and Death* (Connecticut Mutual Life Insurance Co.; Random House), *A Foot in the Door* (Fuller Brush Co.; McGraw-Hill), *A Whale of a Territory* (General Tire & Rubber Co.; McGraw-Hill), *Gun Controls* (by Robert Kukla, sponsored by National Rifle Association; Stackpole Books).

In summary, you don't have to go to a vanity publisher, such as Exposition Press, or a local printer in order to arrange for a book. The exciting aspect of all of this is that most of the aforementioned books sold well above the minimum purchased or guaranteed by the sponsor, so that everyone, including the publisher, benefited.

Not surprisingly, cookbooks and travel guides are the largest categories of sponsored publications.

133

For more information about self-published, sponsored books and other aspects of book publishing, buy a copy of *How to Get Happily Published* (Harper & Row) by Judith Appelbaum and Nancy Evans.

O.K., so you're convinced. Books can be a very successful public relations tool. How do you get started?

As with any other project, you first should have an idea. The place to discuss your idea probably is New York City, the heart of the publishing industry in America. But you can start by going to almost any publisher, anywhere in the country.

Another involvement of public relations and publishing executives could be the creation of books or the purchase of existing titles, for use as premiums, gifts, sales incentives and other advertising and promotion techniques.

Harry N. Abrams, Inc., 100 Fifth Ave., N.Y. 10011, phone (212) 206-7715, and other art book publishers offer substantial discounts for books and color reproductions used as premiums. The annual catalog includes full-page color reproductions of paintings and other artworks, suitable for framing. The person to call is Paul Gottlieb.

Write to Thomas Murray at the Premium Department of Doubleday & Company, Inc., 245 Park Ave., N.Y. 10167, phone (212) 953-4788, for a brochure.

Map, travel guide, reference and financial publishers offer a variety of promotion and public relations opportunities for banks, airlines, travel agencies, utilities and other organizations. The leaders in this field are Rand McNally & Co., 8255 N. Central Park Ave., Skokie, IL 60076, phone (312) 673-9100; Hammond Incorporated, Maplewood, NJ 07040, phone (201) 763-6000 and (212) 962-0120, and Gousha Publications, Box 6227, San Jose, CA 95150, phone (408) 296-1060. Contact Maryann Braun at Gousha about customized full-color magazines, including creation, printing and mailing.

Hammond, which has been making maps since the turn of the century, has expanded and diversified into other publishing projects and now markets hundreds of titles. There still is a Hammond family and you can talk to Kathleen or Dean Hammond about creating a publication.

In addition to its maps, McNally handles books, diaries and other premiums, which include creating custom publications. William Priebe is the contact.

Other lucrative promotional sources are the comic book publishers and comic syndicates. One of the leaders is King Features Syndicate, 235 E. 45 St., N.Y. 10017, phone (212) 682-5600, which publishes comic books used by career counselors and for other school uses.

Encyclopedia and reference book publishers provide another avenue of literary exploration. In addition to Americana, Britannica, Compton's, Grolier, World and other well-known companies in this field, there are several publishers which specialize in reference book premiums.

Prentice-Hall offers public relations opportunities involving all types of books. Contact Prentice-Hall, Inc., Englewood Cliffs, NJ 07632. This firm also publishes the excellent *Public Relations Handbook* by Philip Lesly.

Note: McGraw-Hill publishes the *Handbook of Public Relations* edited by Howard Stephenson, $45. The 1987 edition of *Dartnell's Public Relations Handbook,* edited by Dan Forrestal and Robert Dilenschneider, is available for $49.95 from Dartnell, 4660 Ravenswood Ave., Chicago 60640.

Chilton Book Company, Radnor, PA 19089, specializes in automotive, hobby and other instructional books.

If you go into the publishing business, you may wish to register your copyright claim of the book, magazine, or other publication or recording with the Copyright Office, Library of Congress, Wash., DC 20559. The application form for a book is Form TX. For a periodical, it's Form SE.

For information about facts of copyright registrations, consult the Catalog of Copyright Enties, published by the Copyright Office and available at major libraries. The Copyright Office can conduct a search for you for an hourly fee, but is prohibited from giving legal advice or opinions.

If you need copyright application forms in a hurry, you may call (202) 287-9100 at any time to leave your request as a recorded message on the Hot Line of the Copyright Office.

If you're in a rush to protect your song or other work of art, copyright forms may be obtained by telephoning (202) 287-8700 or at Room 401, First and Independence Ave., S.E., Wash., DC 20559. The office is open Monday through Friday, 8:30 A.M. to 5 P.M. The Copyright Office has no branch offices.

Back to book publishing: There is a world of difference between the creation of an original book and the purchase of an existing book. In between are such adaptations as special covers, title pages and inserts. An original or existing book can be individualized with imprinting on the binding or elsewhere or use of bookmarks, bookplates and other labels.

All of which adds up to not trying to do-it-yourself. The simplest way often is to contact a major publisher. You may find that it is more efficient to deal with a company which specializes in "subsidized books," that is, books which are sponsored by companies or in various other ways are used as public relations and promotional tools.

Here are several specialists who can help you transform your book idea into a reality.

1. The Benjamin Company, Inc.
One Westchester Plaza, Elmsford, NY 10523
(914) 592-8088
Roy Benjamin, Chm., Ted Benjamin, Pres.

Branch Office:
1200 W. Park Pl., Milwaukee 53224
(414) 466-2120

This company, which is the largest in the field of sponsored books, provides two basic types of services. The first consists of specially written books. In these cases, publisher Benjamin brings together a "project team" which may include an author, a distributor and, most important, a sponsor.

A small part of Benjamin's activities involves books and booklets which already are in existence. The Benjamin catalog lists thousands of books, booklets, prints, records and maps published by Simon and Schuster, Pocket Books, Scribner's, Harper & Row, and many other publishers. These books are available as published, or with the addition of special deluxe bindings, cover and insert advertising or imprints, and other means of identifying and promoting the sponsor.

Where special printing is not required, the prices generally are about 40 to 50 percent off the book's original retail price. The price thus can vary from a few cents to several dollars.

The minimum quantities for special cover printings and other means of sponsor identification usually are about 25,000 copies for paperbound and 5,000 for hardback. Books used as premiums or in promotions are sold to advertising agencies or directly to advertisers. Former advertising executive Roy Benjamin also is interested in attracting business from public relations people, particularly where it involves a book which might have a large sales potential.

Benjamin has many of its books on display in its attractive office and also publishes a free newsletter, The Benjamin Publishing/Marketing Report. Formed in 1953, Benjamin also creates booklets, audio and video cassettes.

2. James Peter Associates Incorporated
Box 772, 151 Sunset Lane, Tenafly, NJ 07670
(201) 568-0760
Herbert F. Holtje, Pres.

135

Formed in 1972 by Bert Holtje, a psychologist who is the author of many books, the firm provides ghost writing and creative services to a variety of companies and other clients throughout the country. In addition, the company creates and produces sponsored books and other publications, and also creates a variety of training projects, including programmed instruction and multi-media programs through an affiliated company.

Renaissance Corinthian Editions

This company no longer is publishing sponsored books. Formed in 1966 as Renaissance Editions, its founder, Burton Richard Wolf, sold the company in 1968 to the Corinthian Broadcasting Company. The listing is included here because several Renaissance and Corinthian sponsored books received a great amount of publicity, and helped to develop a greater interest in this field. Among the Renaissance-Corinthian titles were the *Hertz Survival Manual for Traveling Businessmen* and *How to Survive in New York with Children* (sponsored by Citibank).

3. The Rosen Publishing Group

29 E. 21 St., N.Y. 10010
(212) 777-3017
Roger Rosen, Pres.

Formed by Mr. and Mrs. Richard Rosen, the company now is operated by their son, Roger. The company publishes several lines of unusual public relations value, including the Careers in Depth series—more than 400 books, from accounting to X-ray technology, each authored by a prominent person in the field. Other series include the Military, Theatre Student, Coping and Student Journalist series.

Mr. Rosen is constantly searching for successful executives and other potential authors. A large market of teachers, students, librarians and other buyers already has been established for these series. Since standard royalties are paid to authors, a company president, association director or other author can promote a greater interest in her or his field and also receive an income from book sales over a period of years. Rosen also publishes corporate histories and sponsored books.

4. Sensible Solutions Incorporated

6. E. 39 St., N.Y. 10016
(212) 532-5280
Judith Appelbaum, Florence Janovic, Managing Directors

Started in 1981 to help writers and publishers succeed with nonblockbuster books, Sensible Solutions now provides all types of literary services, including concept and manuscript development, attracting offers from publishers, editing, design, marketing and other counseling. Judith Appelbaum was managing editor of Publishers Weekly, a columnist at The New York Times Book Review and co-author of *How to Get Happily Published*. Florence Janovic was an executive at advertising agencies specializing in books.

Though most of their clients are writers and publishers, Sensible Solutions can be extremely helpful to public relations people who are contemplating sponsored books or other publishing projects.

5. Snibbe Publishing Co.

1115 Ponce de Leon, Clearwater, FL 33616
(813) 586-1779

Formed in 1963 by Bob Snibbe, the company is the largest publisher of low-cost booklets for advertising, sales promotion and public relations purposes, such as traffic builders, giveaways, write-ins, in-packs, on-packs and mail enclosures. All are 16 pages, 3x5 inches. Quantity prices range from 8 cents for 1,000,000 to 16 cents for 50,000, and include custom front and/or back color covers. Titles include Golf, Baseball, Tennis, Football, Bowling, Pro Basketball, and others.

BOOKLETS

Public relations practitioners usually are more familiar with booklets than full-length books as a means of communication.

A four-page folder listing recipes can be published by a food manufacturer at a few cents a copy. A 16-page booklet describing career opportunities can be printed for a dime a copy. An annual report to stockholders or a deluxe brochure, describing the history or overall organization of a business, can cost a dollar, or considerably more, a copy.

Public relations people often are involved in the writing and production of booklets and are capable of handling these responsibilities. Distribution of booklets, however, often proves to be a problem.

Consumer Reports, Good Housekeeping, Changing Times and McCall's Magazine are a few of the major magazines which regularly list free booklets.

A listing in any one of these publications usually results in more than 5,000 requests for the booklet. And that's where the problem sometimes begins. The price of success revolves around the cost of the envelope, addressing and postage. It may cost 30 cents or more to send a booklet which had cost only a dime to produce, and sponsors sometimes forget to include distribution in their budget plans.

In addition to the magazines, many newspapers regularly offer booklets to their readers, usually on their style pages. There also are syndicated columns devoted partly or entirely to booklet listings. They are listed in the book, *Syndicated Columnists.*

Magazines and newspaper columns often will include booklets which are not absolutely free; that is, those which are available for a stamped, self-addressed envelope or a small price, such as 50 cents.

Occasionally, a newspaper columnist or broadcaster will offer booklets. Readers and listeners are invited to send in stamped envelopes in order to obtain booklets from manufacturers who provide them to the media in bulk.

National Syndications, Inc., 230 Fifth Ave., N.Y. 10001, produces a page called The Information Center, which appears several times a year in the Sunday newspaper supplements Parade and USA Weekend. It consists of brief descriptions of booklets and other items. The "advertiser" pays only for the number of responses from the listing—50 cents each for free items and $2 each for items with a charge. The names are provided on pressure-sensitive labels.

It's a terrific deal, as you can expect to receive 15,000 to 30,000 inquiries. However, be prepared to spend $10,000 to receive, for example, 20,000 address labels, plus the cost of mailing, including postage.

Kathleen Ryan at National Syndications, phone (212) 686-8680, can describe advertorials, catalog pages and other promotions.

It would appear that there is a need for companies which specialize in the distribution of free booklets. There are a few companies which provide booklets for the employee reading racks of factories, but their booklets generally are restricted to those written by these services, and must be noncommercial and institutional. The major company in this field is:

National Research Bureau
424 N. 3 St., Burlington, IA 52601
(319) 752-5415

National Research Bureau publishes Working Press of the Nation, Shopping Center Directory and other publications, including dozens of magazines, newsletters and booklets which are distributed to office and factory workers as part of its Employee Communication Service. Monthly magazines, including *Supervision*, are supplemented by sports handbooks and a variety of booklets about courtesy, exercise, diet and other subjects.

Companies which subscribe to the program receive several booklets each month, and pay per booklet, depending on quantity.

National Research Bureau is a division of Automated Marketing Systems, Inc., 310 S. Michigan Ave., Chicago 60604, phone (312) 663-5580.

Chapter 12

Mailing Services

Everyone in the communications industries has access to mailing facilities or uses letter shops and mailing services, usually located nearby. Today's public relations executive must have some familiarity with automatic typewriters and other printing machines, photocopy and other duplicating equipment, computer addressing, Cheshire machines and a variety of other equipment and processes involved in the mailing of news releases, reports and other materials.

Several companies specialize in public relations mailing services, with stress on accuracy, speed and other unique requirements of the field. A few of these companies maintain extensive media lists, which are computerized or on plates, and thus provide unique research facilities combined with their abilities to print and mail publicity materials. Most are in New York City, but their mailing lists are so extensive that they are utilized by clients throughout the country. Many of the large mailing houses maintain plants and branch offices separate from their executive offices, so check addresses before shipping envelopes or other materials.

In 1988, the choice of how to transmit a message is more varied than ever before. Hardcopy services includes the U.S. Postal Service, the overnight air courier companies, telegrams, Mailgrams, telex, cables and computerized letters. Electronic services include Voice Mail, Telemail, Quick-Comm and other companies described in this chapter.

Several public relations and advertising periodicals rent their subscriber lists or permit (for a fee) enclosures with their mailings. The Gallagher Report has a prime list of 50,000 executives. You can test the list with a minimum order of 5,000 names at $60 a thousand by contacting Cynthia Billings at Gallagher, 230 Park Ave., N.Y. 10017, phone (212) 661-5000.

A directory of mailing and list suppliers is included in every issue of Direct Marketing (monthly magazine), 224 Seventh St., Garden City, NY 11530. Postal rates and regulations change frequently, and it is wise to consult with a direct mail specialist, even if you handle most of your mailings in your own mailroom.

Major direct mail users and frequent buyers of mailing lists should consult the Directory of Mailing List Houses, a directory of over 3,000 list specialists, published by B. Klein Publications, Inc., Box 8503, Coral Springs, FL 33065. The book is $65 and the complete list on gummed labels in ZIP code order is $150.

Of course, the content is more important than the list, and directories and mailing services are not substitutes for direct mail expertise.

Many list brokers provide a 20 percent commission to other brokers and a 15 percent commission to letter shops, advertising and public relations agencies.

Reminder: The address for materials for mailing often is different from the sales office, so before you send them to the mailing house, check with the list broker or mailing house.

In the public relations field, the most commonly mailed items (other than letters and correspondence) are news releases. The printing and mailing of news releases probably is the largest expenditure in the publicity business. Production and distribution costs vary considerably. A two-page release to 100 publications costs about $100 including postage.

An essential reference book for *every* office, regardless of the size of the mailings, is the official U.S. Postal Service National ZIP Code and Post Office Directory, with over 2,000 pages of streets, with their ZIP codes, and other postal data. ZIP codes change, so it's a good idea to use a current directory. It's published annually and can be purchased from your local post office or by mail from the Superintendent of Documents, U.S. Government Printing Office, Washington, DC 20402. The actual name of the book is the National Five Digit ZIP code and Post Office Directory.

About 40,000 ZIP Codes arranged by Congressional Districts are the basis for the Congressional District/ZIP Code Directory, published by Tyson Capitol Institute, 7735 Old Georgetown Rd., Bethesda, MD 20814. It's $1,245 on magnetic tape.

Increased postal costs and problems with regard to delivery have stimulated many clients to take a hard look at their mailing procedures. The resulting efficiencies can save considerable time and money.

Here are several pointers for your mailroom personnel.

1. Check accuracy of your scales—be sure only authorized personnel have access and only those who know how to use equipment properly.
2. Mark mail plainly as to class so right amounts of postage are affixed.
3. Use meters when possible—date imprint permits post office to skip a step in processing and move such mail a day or so faster.
4. Check local post office for new services that can save time and money.
5. 1st class: Mail *early* on Monday morning. Aim for Tuesday delivery, when mail is lightest. 3rd class: Mail Friday, avoid the end-of-week pile-ups this slower mail invites.
6. If it's not essential, don't send it.
7. Consider using the phone (unless a hard copy is needed). It's faster, cheaper and affords two-way instant communication. Another possibility is telephone facsimile.
8. Purge that mailing list! Delete obsolete or marginally important names; check addresses.
9. Try to be brief. A five-page release may require additional postage.
10. Review enclosures. Are they necessary? Can you use a lighter stiffener?

Here are more mailing tips from Publicist, the bimonthly newsletter of PRA:

If time is not critical, consider third class or bulk business mail (formerly 3rd class bulk.) However, most publicists often fail to realize that 1st and regular 3rd class rates are identical through the first four ounces.

For larger and/or heavier mailings, the use of bulk business mail can offer potential savings. There are several considerations in addition to time of delivery, however. First there is the minimum piece requirement of 200 identical items. You must pay a $40.00 annual bulk business mail permit fee and, if using the permit imprint system (indicia), have on account with the post office sufficient postage to cover the expense of your mailing.

Business mail must be sorted according to zip-codes, which while not affecting the actual postage expense, does add to the overall mailing costs and lengthens the preparation time. Generally, any project involving over two ounces of 600 pieces would warrant consideration of bulk business mail.

Envelope size also affects the cost of postage. Under most circumstances, you can mail up to five pages in a #10 business envelope for one ounce of postage. Anything over five pages should go in a

9×12 envelope where the materials can lay flat and not cost any more postage than if mailed in a #10 envelope.

Avoid non-standard mail. Any piece weighing less than one ounce will receive a surcharge if it exceeds any of these standards: height more than 6⅛ inches, length more than 11½ inches, or thickness more than ¼ inch.

Pieces that are ¼ inch or less in thickness can be mailed *only* if they are rectangular, at least 3½ inches high, at least 5 inches long and at least .007 inch thick (about the thickness of a postal card).

So, avoid cute invitations and other envelopes that will be returned to the sender!

Following are additional personal recommendations.

1. The Post Office claims that mail deposited *before* 5 P.M. is very likely to be delivered to other locations in the same city and many other cities the following morning. This may be debatable, but, in any case, it's a good idea to get out the mail as it's done, in batches, rather than waiting until the end of the day.
2. Special delivery often slows up delivery because, instead of going out on a regular morning route, it is delayed and sent via a later special route.
3. Mail deposited at the main Post Office (in Manhattan, it's at 8th Ave. & 33 St.) before 5 P.M. may be delivered the following morning to most major cities. The Post Office does *guarantee* overnight delivery via its Express Mail and has set up hundreds of special pickup boxes in major cities.
4. Books, records, films and manuscripts can be mailed at various special fourth-class rates.
5. When mailing to a dual address, that is, a street address and a post office box, put the box number below the street address and above the ZIP Code, or omit the street address.
6. Minimum first-class postage covers almost all releases, including, for example, a three-page release and cover letter. However, adding a picture can triple the postage cost, as well as adding other costs, such as the photo, caption, chipboard, large-size mailing envelope. For example, the *total* cost of addressing, printing, paper, envelopes, mailing and postage of 100 copies of a two-page news release is about $100, whereas the *total* cost of 100 copies of a two-page release with one captioned 8×10 photo is about $240.

The U.S. Postal Service is testing many new types of services. Contact your local post office to get on their mailing list for new announcements, including rate changes.

Among the many free publications available from your local post office or the U.S. Postal Service, Washington, DC 20260-6320, are A Consumer's Directory of Postal Services and Products (Publication 201), Packaging for Mailing (Publication 2), How to Prepare and Wrap Packages (Publication 227).

You know this, of course, but here's a quick summary of the basic U.S. postal services.

First-class mail—letters
Second-class mail—available only to publishers and registered news agents
Third-class mail—bulk business mail, including printed material. Single pieces can be mailed at this low rate.
Fourth-class mail—parcel post 1 to 70 pounds and up to 108 inches in length and girth combined
Priority mail—first-class mail 12 ounces to 70 pounds
Certified mail—provides sender with a mailing receipt and, for an additional fee, proof of delivery
Express mail—fastest service
Collect-on-Delivery (C.O.D.)—first-class, third-class or parcel post up to $500
Registered mail—first class mail valued up to $25,000
Special delivery—all classes, except bulk third-class

For information about special handling, insurance, return receipts and other services, ask at your local post office.

PRA has compiled these additional tips on how to save money on news releases.

What about release stationery? Design a simple all-black heading and have only a few hundred copies printed. Type release copy camera-ready on this preprinted form, then have it reproduced by photolithography. In this way the heading is printed with the text at no extra cost. And, you'll never run short of letterheads.

Cut a page of copy from all long releases. A release running over two or three pages that can't be edited down is rare. You'll save substantially on printing, collating and possibly postage costs.

If you're mailing reference material, consider printing on both sides of the paper (never do this in the case of a release). On a six-page fact sheet this would save over $125 per 500 copies including postage. You can save almost half, too, by single-spacing reference material.

To save on mailing of photographs: Switch from labels to preprinted 9×12 envelopes. In quantities of 5,000 or more, printing your return address on 9×12s can save at least $100 per 1,000 over the total cost of plain envelopes plus labels and label affixing. A photograph added to a release mailing triples the cost, so a little extra care is worth it. Use a mailing list coded on the basis of whether the publication uses photographs (e.g., The Wall Street Journal doesn't). This saves money and avoids irritating editors who don't use photos.

Another suggestion: Consider whether all the types of media getting the release really need to get the photograph. It may be that only media in the primary field covered by the release are likely to use the photograph. You'll save two-thirds in costs on the other media if you send them only the release.

Mail a 4×5 head shot with a personnel release rather than the customary 8×10. Not only are the pictures less costly, but you'll save two-thirds in mailing costs because they can be mailed in a #10 envelope.

When a caption only identifies someone or something, use a strip-in caption. A strip-in caption is a typewritten line printed in the bottom border of the photograph. This saves printing captions and the labor cost of pasting them on. Many editors say they prefer the strip-in caption. For one thing, it can't become detached from the photograph.

Following is a summary of some of the preceding budget-stretching tips (which bear repeating!), plus a few new techniques for improving efficiency and also saving money.

Consider whether the release really is necessary. Are you doing it merely out of habit, or so you can show copies to the executive mentioned in it?

Omit expensive enclosures—photos, brochures, etc.—from the portion of the mailing going to non-media lists. In many cases, these people need only the release text, since they already have received the other material through different channels.

Use a black letterhead without half-tones. This image can be reproduced along with the typewritten release text each time you do a mailing. This saves the cost of a separate press run to print black letterheads.

Cut down long releases. Rarely should a release exceed two or three pages. Overlong texts not only waste money, but also alienate the editors who must read them.

Single-space reference material and print it on both sides of the paper. Only material intended for publication needs to be doublespaced.

If you use a lot of large envelopes, pre-print your return address on a supply of them. In quantities of 5,000 or more, pre-printing 9×12 envelopes can save at least $425 over the cost of plain envelopes plus labels and label-affixing.

Use third-class postage. If your mailing piece weighs more than four ounces, the savings can be substantial. The slight delay in delivery does no harm if you are sending out feature material or background information.

Send the release without photograph to some media categories. When money is tight and your photo routine, you should send it only to media categories with a strong interest in the subject-matter.

Mail 4×5 photo prints rather than the customary 8×10. Many publicists today use 4×5 prints for routine personnel head shots. The savings are substantial, because the smaller prints can be mailed in ordinary #10 envelopes.

Use strip-in captions. If a photo caption is very brief (e.g., merely a person's name), strip it into the bottom border when making prints for your mailing. This saves the cost of printing and affixing captions, and may save on postage as well.

One of the buzz words in the 80's is electronic mail. Several companies entered this new field, and others undoubtedly will follow. Each has its own trade name and variation. In one version, letters or other printed materials are sent via high speed facsimile transmission. Thus, if you have a telephone facsimile machine, you already are in this business. However, the recipient of a specific document may not have a telephone facsimile machine, or for various reasons you may prefer to have it handled by an outside service. The procedure generally involves pick-up of the documents, which are then taken to a local office where facsimile copies are transmitted to the office nearest the recipient so that the transmitted document then can be delivered.

Electronic mail still is being developed, and it is not a major factor in the public relations field. Federal Express invested several million dollars in its Zapmail, and dropped it in 1986. The Postal Service and the ITT Corporation also dropped out of this business. ITT calls its service Faxpack and others in this business include DHL Worldwide Courier Express.

An extension of facsimile transmission consists of "Computer Mailboxes", in which messages are typed into a computer and then sent to one of the services, which transmits the text to the recipient's computer. If the recipient does not have a compatible computer or if the client prefers delivery of the "hardcopy", it can be printed out for hand delivery.

Electronic record-keeping originated in World War II and was first used as a means of inventory control. The sending and receiving of electronic mail, or digitized messages, has existed for a number of years within major companies and government agencies. Facsimile, Telex and TWX have served as earlier and slower forms of electronic mail.

As a few companies have perfected their in-house electronic mail systems, they have offered them to the public. The popularity of personal computers has increased the usage of these electronic mailboxes.

And now several companies are in this business. For example, MCI (the David which originally challenged the Goliath, AT&T) now offers MCI Mail, in competition with the U.S. Postal Service.

Electronic mail is simply the instant transmission of text to one or many locations, terminal to terminal via telephone lines.

Some electronic mail services claim it costs one-third as much to send a letter electronically. Telephone bills and time spent on phone calls also may be reduced.

The more computers and workstations in existence, the more electronic messaging will be relied on and specializations within the service (such as GTE's Phycom for the medical profession) will become extensive. Some of the electronic mail services are Western Union's EasyLink, OnTyme, MCI Mail, ITT's Dialcom, GTE's Telemail, CompuServe's InfoPlex and QUICK-COMM.

One drawback with some of the services is that they are designed for within-corporation use and a secondary vendor may be required for other deliveries. Another possible drawback is that letters sent electronically are unsigned.

Information about electronic mail services is included in this chapter, and also in the chapter on research.

Western Union and the U.S. Postal Service are linked in the Mailgram service, which also provides for guaranteed overnight delivery. However, the message must be transmitted by phone (toll-free) or other means (messenger, Telex, computer tape) to Western Union.

If you have a Telex or TWX terminal, contact The Western Union Telegraph Company and obtain a portfolio of booklets which describe services of specific use to public relations customers. Western Union is headquartered at 1 Lake St., Upper Saddle River, NJ 07458.

Examples:

Transmit Mailgrams, Telegrams and International Cablegrams individually or in bulk via computer addressing at regular rates or reduced Nite Cost rates.

News Alert for receipt of United Press bulletins (only $100 a year!).

FYI News-Stock Quote.

A major difference between Telex and TWX is that the former provides direct service between the U.S. and Mexico, and between "continental U.S." and Alaska. TWX does not. Western Union is a domestic carrier and only has offices in the 48 contiguous states.

Another major company in global communications services is RCA Global Communications, Inc. (RCA Globcom), which provides international and domestic communications services to users in the continental United States, Hawaii, Guam, Puerto Rico and the Dominican Republic. The company's major services are telex, telegram, data and facsimile transmission, leased channels, marine telegram and marine telex. In addition, RCA Globcom provides long distance service from Guam.

Since 1982, RCA Globcom has offered domestic telex service, international digital and voice leased channel service and domestic ExpressNet (up to 1,200 bits per second) leased channel service. It recently launched an electronic mail service (RCA Mail) and formed a partnership, Radio PageAmerica, to introduce a radio messaging service.

Two of RCA Globcom's popular services are its Computer to Telex service and "Hotline" information service, available worldwide over the company's telex network. Computer to Telex allows computer users in the United States to send and receive telex messages, both in real time and store and forward, with any other public telex network in the world.

Public relations clients are likely to be particularly interested in Datalink, which provides U.S. access to overseas database research services (described in the research chapter) and Computer to Telex.

The Computer to Telex service offers no registration charge, no minimum charge and all RCA Globcom's telex service options. Computer to Telex costs are simply the regular cost of sending a telex as though it had been sent from a telex terminal. The only additional cost option of Computer to Telex service is DataBank (mailbox) service. This costs $15/month. Computer to Telex service is especially useful for computers and word processors. The cost of leased telex equipment is saved and productivity is often increased since messages do not have to be retyped.

In 1987, the General Electric Company, which had acquired RCA, sold RCA Global Communications to MCI Communications Corporation, which combined RCA Global, Piscataway, NJ, with MCI International Inc., Ryebrook, NY.

The two largest publicity mailing houses are PR Aids (now called PRA Information & Communications Group) and Media Distribution Services. Both are headquartered in New York and operate in a similar manner. Each maintains the names and addresses of many thousands of editors, writers, broadcasters and other media people. They are divided into more than 2,500 editorial-interest categories and cross-classified by geographic scope of editorial coverage, types of release materials used (e.g., photos), frequency of publication, etc.

Through this system, you can reach *by name* the person at The New York Times who covers foreign trade, the writer on professional basketball at Sports Illustrated, the part-time book editor of a biology journal, the editorial-page editors of all newspapers read in a particular county in Ohio—to cite just a few examples.

Each company has complete reproduction and mailing facilities, organized exclusively for public relations customers. They produce and distribute, not only releases, but also captioned photo prints, press kits, personalized letters, television and radio materials, newsletters and reports. They offer dozens of other printing and distribution services.

In addition to using the media lists of PR Aids or Media Distribution Services, customers can have them computerize special administrative lists—branch offices, sales representatives, etc.—which are to receive information copies of releases at the same time as the media. These companies also help to develop entire direct-mail programs aimed at sales prospects, investors, members, voters, legislators, civic leaders and others.

Customers also can access the mailing house services direct from microcomputers and word processors in their own offices.

Following is information about PR Aids and Media Distribution Services, as well as other major mailing houses and related services in the U.S. and Canada.

1. Adcraft Business Mail
719 S. Hoover, L.A. 90005
(213) 386-6245 (FUN-MAIL)
Myron Crespin, Alan Bailey

Located in Wilshire Center since 1956, Adcraft is a specialist in publicity, advertising and direct mail, including printing and mailing news releases, press kits and other publicity items. The last digits of its phone number spells MAIL.

2. Bacon's Publicity Distribution Service
332 S. Michigan Ave., Chicago 60604
(312) 922-2400 (800) 651-0561
Rob Bacon

In the early 70's, Bacon's Clipping Bureau entered the publicity mailing business with quite a splash by putting all of the listings in its Publicity Checker on Addressograph plates. The company can be utilized for addressing media lists or complete news release production and mailing labels, to consumer and trade publications and daily and weekly newspapers.

In 1978, Bacon's began offering computerized media selection and list-compiling through its own media bank of over 100,000 print media names. Users of Bacon's Publicity Checker are familiar with the print media categories.

In 1986, Bacon's launched a broadcasting directory and these lists also are available.

Bacon's Information Services thus provide a logical, efficient correlation of Bacon's Publicity Checker and Bacon's Publicity Checking Services.

Bacon's Information International (a joint venture with Romeike & Curtice, Ltd., of London) provides news release distribution, translation clipping service and other publicity services in Europe, the United Kingdom, Mexico, Australia, Japan and other countries.

3. Bowdens Print/Mail
624 King St. West, Toronto, Ontario M5V 2X9, Canada
(416) 860-0794
Blair Enman, Mgr.

Branch Office:
130 Slater St., Ottawa, Ontario KIP 6E2, Canada
(613) 236-7301

Bowdens Information Services, Inc., is one of the world's largest public relations service companies, which includes a clipping bureau and broadcast monitoring services.

The Bowdens Print/Mail Distribution Center prints and mails news releases and other publicity materials to its media bank of more than 6,000 editors and broadcasters or to computer lists maintained for clients by Bowdens.

4. R. R. Bowker Company
245 W. 17 St., N.Y. 10011
(212) 337-6900
Ira Siegel

The Bowker literary directories are available on mailing lists, and the company also provides a complete mailing service. In many cases, the prices are lower than the identical lists available from mailing list brokers, as Bowker is the source. Lists can be purchased in a variety of categories. For example, here's the breakdown of America's major libraries.

By Book Budget:
Over $1,000
Over $5,000
Over $10,000
Over $25,000
Over $50,000

By Type of Collection:
Libraries with Filmstrips
    Film Collections
    Record Collections
    Audio Tapes
    Black Literature Collections
    Spanish Language Books
    Videotapes

And these are only the major libraries—there are over 31,000 libraries in the U.S. and about 3,576 in Canada.

Here's the breakdown of America's retail book outlets.

Stores Handling:
Art & Museum Books
Second-Hand Books (Used Books)
Remainder Books
Rare Books (Out of Print)
College Books
Paperback Books
Religious Books
    Protestant Books
    Catholic Books
    Jewish Books
    Metaphysical Books

Law, Medical & Technical Books
  Law Books
  Medical Books
  Technical Books
Juvenile Books
New Hard Cover Books (All Subjects)
Black Studies Books
Spanish Language Books

The basic price for master lists is $55 per thousand. Selections from the master list are $5 extra and pressure-sensitive labels are $8 extra.

5. Ed Burnett Consultants, Inc.

99 W. Sheffield Ave., Englewood, NJ 07631
(201) 871-1100, (800) 223-7777

Formed in 1959, Ed Burnett Consultants is one of the pioneers in list management and direct mail consultation. The free catalog has about 7,000 categories. Lists are provided on Cheshire labels, though other formats are available, including peel-and-stick labels, gummed perforate, heat sensitive, heat transfer, magnetic tape and floppy discs.

6. CMG Information Services (formerly College Marketing Group)

50 Cross St., Winchester, MA 01890
(617) 729-7865
Bob Scott, Sales Mgr.

A mailing list company that offers:

1. A response list of more than 2.6 million people who have purchased professional-level books through direct mail pieces from over 40 leading publishers. There are over 2,700 subject area selects to choose from, as well as recency, gender, home vs. office address to enable a mailer to reach specific target markets. This list is updated quarterly. $70/M.

2. A compiled list of more than 600,000 professors, administrators and librarians at over 3,000 colleges and universities in the U.S. and Canada. It is the most comprehensive, most highly segmented list (over 4,600 course category selects) in the industry.

This list is updated continuously. $55/M

3. A full complement of computer services, which includes merge/purge, list maintenance, data entry, zip code correction/verification, carrier route coding, and bad debt suppression.

7. Chase Direct Mail Corp.

275 Seventh Ave., N.Y. 10001
(212) 929-7400
Richard S. Post, Pres.

Having served public relations and advertising clients since 1948, the Chase people are well schooled in the workings of publicity and promotion. That means they know the meaning of a deadline and appreciate the daily crises which often are involved in mailings. You not only may expect folding, inserting, sealing, stamping, labeling, collating, stapling, but also a knowledgeable and sympathetic ear and other things that money cannot buy, as well as word processing and other computerization. As Mr. Post puts it:

So, when on Friday afternoon at 3:45 it develops that you're flying to Detroit and must have some releases there on Monday morning which you've just dictated to your secretary but which will have indicated copy changes in paragraphs three and seven on part of the run and paragraph nine deleted on another—well, it wouldn't be Friday if it didn't happen, and we wouldn't be Chase if we didn't get caught up in the excitement of it. And evidently that feeling shows in our work and that's why we get such nice phone calls.

8. Chittenden News Service
1265 National Press Bldg., Wash., DC 20045
(202) 737-4434
Bob Chittenden, Pres.

Distribution of news releases in Washington is this company's only business. 450 copies of a news release delivered to the news media is only $55, including copies to the bureaus in the National Press Building, the National Press Club, Senate and House Press Galleries, and each of many other correspondents. This bargain price has hardly changed in many years.

The company was formed in 1945 as Washington News Service.

Chittenden can also mail you each day's batch of news releases from the U.S. Congressional Press Galleries for the same low price. (Washington subscribers receive them daily by messenger.) A similar service is $75 a month for news releases from all U.S. government agencies. Other messenger and mail services are available.

9. Churchill Communications Corporation
500 Eighth Ave., N.Y. 10018
(212) 563-5000
Mark Roter, Pres.

A pioneer in computerized communications, Churchill has many clients in direct marketing, public relations, fund raising and other fields. Its services (some are unique) make use of voice mail, telex, TWX, telegrams, mailgrams, computer-based messaging systems and other electronic mail.

Churchill can counsel you about the best way to handle a proxy fight, product recall or other "instant communications" project, and then handle all of it, including use of Western Union, MCI, Graphnet, Telenet, AT&T mail and other companies.

10. Cogliano Benedict Photographics, Inc.
1472 Broadway, N.Y. 10036
(212) 391-0141

Primarily a photo production company, CBP has expanded its facilities to a complete publicity mailing operation, including printing and mailing news releases and press kits.

11. Direct Mail Promotions Inc.
342 Madison Ave., N.Y. 10173
(212) 687-1910
L. Joseph Morton

Cooperative mailings are the Morton's specialty—mailings of several clients in the same envelope, particularly book publishers to schools and libraries. For example, a mailing to 5,000 librarians is only $600. Of course, the client must provide the single-sheet mailing piece. Morton also produces a ¼-page (4×5 inches) advertisement on a bulletin, at a total cost of $150 to 2,500 college libraries, $200 to 5,000 libraries and $250 to 5,000 school libraries.

A Morton special for $300 (4×5) goes to 5,000 public libraries and 2,500 college libraries.

148

12. Dunhill International List Company, Inc.

1100 Park Central Blvd., S., Pompano Beach, FL 33064
(305) 974-7800
Robert Dunhill, Pres.

Branch Office:
419 Park Avenue South, N.Y. 10016
(212) 686-3700
Andy Dunhill

Dunhill is one of the nation's largest mailing list houses, with over 15 million names stored on magnetic tape. Formerly headquartered in New York, the company now has its main office in Florida, with computer facilities there and in New York, and sales offices in several cities. The specialty is professional, executive and investor lists.

More than 1,900 mailing list categories are featured in its free catalog.

Minimum order on any list is $150, with a 95 percent guarantee on accuracy and a postage refund on each undeliverable item in excess of 5 percent. Lists are provided on magnetic tape, pressure-sensitive labels or Cheshire ungummed labels, which require special mailing equipment, and generally cost $30 to $40 a thousand.

Note: If you are doing the mailing yourself and do not have special equipment, specify self-adhesive labels, which are available at about $6 additional per thousand. You also may want a copy of the list, available at half-price, but remember that lists are provided for one-time use only.

The basic charge is five cents per name for general disciplines, six cents per name for specific course titles. Other lists include journals and associations in the field of higher education, book-buyers and libraries. The company was acquired by Dun's Marketing Services in 1986.

13. Hugo Dunhill Mailing Lists, Inc.

630 Third Ave., N.Y. 10017
(212) 682-8030, (800) 223-6454

In addition to operating one of America's largest mailing list companies, Hugo Dunhill publishes The Complete Catalog of Mailing Lists. It's free and also includes articles and mailing tips. To subscribe, call Editor Sandy Kaiman or visit Dunhill on the 11th floor.

Among the lists of relevance to public relations people are:

Advertising and public relations
Alumni
Associations and clubs
Colleges and schools
Donors
Executives (arranged in hundreds of categories)
Government officials and agencies
Prominent people
Wealthy people (e.g., yacht owners)

Note: Hugo Dunhill Mailing Lists, Inc., is *not* affiliated with Dunhill International, except that Hugo and Robert Dunhill are brothers.

14. The E-Z Addressing Service Corp.
80 Washington St., N.Y. 10006
(212) 422-9448
Mike Gentile, V.P.

E-Z has been serving Wall Street since 1927, and has mailed many thousands of black- and red-ink annual reports, market letters, announcements, offering circulars, as well as news releases.

E-Z maintains lists of all brokers, banks, security analysts and others in the financial field, arranged by state and numerous other categories. Most of the lists cost $40 per thousand for addressing. Among the lists of particular public relations interest are market letter publishers and presidents of leading companies.

15. George-Mann Associates
Box 930, 403 Mercer St., Hightstown, NJ 08520
(609) 443-1330
George Sharoff, Pres.

Renowned for its boating and self-improvement lists, this company also compiles many specialized lists which appeal to fund raisers and public relations mailers. For example, the George-Mann Directory describes the following lists, which are available (@ $45 a thousand) through all recognized list brokers:

325,000 art and civic contributors
455,000 alumni contributors
127,000 hospital contributors
 74,000 attorneys at home addresses
240,000 country club members
 62,000 doctors at home addresses

16. David M. Grant Software, Inc.
485 Lexington Ave., N.Y. 10017
(212) 687-8600
Telex: 6501138571
David M. Grant, Pres.

The head of a successful public relations agency, David Grant developed a computer system to manage his firm's mailings. In 1987, he decided to share this extraordinary resource with other public relations practitioners.

Called PR 6-in-1, the software has these functions:

1. Maintain media lists.
2. Edit lists on screen or paper.
3. Print labels and envelopes.
4. Help merge text of letters.
5. Produce mailing records.
6. Produce media directory.

The software costs $1,000, plus $100 per professional user in the customer's office. The package includes a 3,300-name database of newspapers and business publications. It requires an MS DOS operating system, including 256K RAM, and hard disk.

17. Market Compilation and Research Bureau, Inc.

11633 Victory Blvd., N. Hollywood, CA 91609
(213) 877-5384
Stephen L. Allen, Pres.
James Parish, V.P. of Marketing Services

Branch Offices:
Chicago: 2500 W. Higgins Rd., Hoffman Estates, IL 60195
(312) 310-0800
Jim Price

New York: 60 E. 42 St., N.Y. 10165
(212) 661-1250
John Ferrini

Washington-Baltimore: 7075 Oakland Mills Rd., Columbia, MD 21045
(301) 598-5775
Rachel Manning

Founded in 1947, MCRB is one of the nation's leading direct marketing organizations, with such services as compiling and maintaining lists, fulfillment distribution and other packaged insert programs.

18. Media Distribution Services, Inc.

307 W. 36 St., N.Y. 10018
(212) 249-4800
Hymen V. Wagner, Pres.

Hy Wagner set up his organization of public relations media and mailing specialists in 1964. Media Distribution Services has grown rapidly, expanding the facilities of its "release distribution center" to a point where it services more than 1,500 public relations agencies and major corporation public relations departments throughout the country.

The company's "Mediamatic System" has a computer data bank with more than 100,000 editors and broadcasters *by name,* and thus is one of the most comprehensive publicity mailing services in the country.

The media system provides access to all of the trade, technical and professional journals, daily and weekly newspapers, wire services, syndicates and syndicated writers, consumer magazines and radio and television stations in the U.S. and Canada. All media and editors have been classified by their specific editorial interests.

In addition to its mailing lists, the company maintains printing, photo reproduction and other letter-shop facilities geared to the unique requirements of the public relations field.

Clients are provided with a file organized into media sections, which enables them to mark appropriate media sheets with selected categories to go with any special instructions. The service is easy to use and enables clients to pinpoint mailings by media locality and subject interest. Security analysts also are included.

Through telephone calls, questionnaires and examination of literally thousands of publications, Media Distribution Services is able to maintain lists which are far more accurate and up-to-date than those in any directory.

In addition, they publish the Mediamatic Calendar of Special Editorial Issues three times a year at an annual cost of $90. This is a compilation of the subjects that publications plan to write about during the upcoming period and includes the editorial and advertising closing dates, editors' names, addresses and telephone numbers.

The company issues a free Pocket Media Guide, a handy 33-page collection of names, addresses and phone numbers of the major print and broadcast media. Organizations that are licensed to access the Mediamatic System are Associated Release Service in Chicago, Publicity Central in Minneapolis, Direct Mail Service in Pittsburgh, MediaDirect in Washington, DC, and Media Link Distribution Service in Philadelphia.

In 1987, MDS introduced a special service to security analysts which is described in the Media Distribution Services listing in the financial chapter.

19. National Register Publishing Co., Inc.

3004 Glenview Rd., Wilmette, IL 60091
(312) 256-6067
Jeanne Owen

Sales Offices:
3400 Peachtree Rd., N.E., Atlanta 30326
(404) 233-6493
George McLaren

333 N. Michigan Ave., Chicago 60601
(312) 726-5744
Jerry Marconi

6300 Wilshire Blvd., L.A. 90048
(213) 478-1557
John Sienkiewicz

866 Third Avenue, N.Y. 10022
(212) 702-6885
Russ Brown

A subsidiary of Standard Rate & Data Service, National Register has converted the data in its directories to mailing lists. These include the Standard Directory of Advertising Agencies ($55 a thousand), Standard Directory of Advertisers ($60 a thousand), Directory of Corporate Affiliations ($55), and The Official Museum Directory ($50 a thousand). The costs for the advertiser lists are a bit higher than most mailing lists, but they are extremely accurate. As might be expected, agency commissions are paid.

20. PNA Services Ltd.

13-19 Curtain Rd, London EC2A 3LT
(01) 377-2521
Bill Gibbs, Mgr. Dir.

One of the largest publicity mailing services in the United Kingdom, PNA has a computerized media system, word processing and other state-of-the-art facilities.

Another major company is PIMS, Faber Court, 4 St. John's Place, London EC1M 4AH, phone (01) 250-0870. PIMS provides four-color printing, word processing and couriers. Julien Henchley is managing director.

21. PR Data Systems, Inc.

15 Oakwood Ave., Norwalk, CT 06850
(203) 847-0777
Jack E. Schoonover, Pres.
William W. Wubbenhorst, Exec. V.P.

Branch Office:
156 Fifth Ave., N.Y. 10010
(212) 645-8040
Mark Weiner, V.P.

In 1974, after 15 years of experience in evaluating publicity, PR Data Systems installed a computerized news release distribution system which can print and mail any type of material to all major media in the U.S. and Canada.

In the area of media list development, PR Data offers an extensive and very sophisticated computerized system of media selection. From the file of 35,000 media, users can build their own customized and proprietary versions, as well as private and internal lists, to focus on key target audiences. Lists may be accessed by computer for updating, reference and printing. The company also produces computer-generated localized releases featuring local datelines, names and other individualized references.

PR Data reproduces releases, b&w and color photographs, newsletters, press kit covers and other release materials for assembly and distribution. Text may be submitted by computer to computer and routine releases are mailed the same day they are received at no additional cost. A free follow-up printout, featuring media name, location and telephone number, is provided after each mailing.

Jack Schoonover is one of the pioneers in publicity analysis and this aspect of the operation is described in the chapter on clipping bureaus.

22. PRA Information & Communications Group (formerly called Public Relations Aids, Inc.)

330 W. 34 St., N.Y. 10001
(212) 947-7733
Richard Toohey, Pres.
John Pirrone, Sr. V.P. Production
Wick Taylor, Michael Hagerty,
Mark Glickman, V.P.s

Branch Offices:
161 Spring St., Atlanta 30303
(404) 523-2515

35 Morrissey Blvd., Boston 02107
(617) 482-6245

1 E. Huron St., Chicago 60611
(312) 943-9410

1801 S. Hill St., L.A. 90015
(213) 749-7383

818 Liberty Ave., Pittsburgh 15222
(412) 471-9411

24500 Southfield Rd., Southfield, MI 48075
(313) 557-7500

1615 L St., N.W., Wash., DC 20036
(202) 659-0627

The concept of PR Aids was developed in 1957 by two public relations executives—Richard Toohey and Lee Levitt—who found existing press release methods time-consuming and inefficient.

A survey they made among various public relations organizations in the New York area revealed similar dissatisfaction, centering on two problems: (1) as much as 30 percent of a public relations executive's time was being consumed by the "production" activity necessary to get out a press release; (2) no matter how much effort was expended, an uncertainty always existed as to whether the releases were reaching the right editors.

What was needed was an entirely new concept in press release procedures, which would free the executive from the noncreative nuisance details clogging his day, and, at the same time, fully guarantee the accuracy of a press release mailing.

The result: PR Aids, one of the world's largest public relations service organizations—handling press release operations for more than 4,000 agencies, corporate and institutional public relations departments.

Representing an investment of more than $900,000 and costing over $350,000 a year to maintain, the on-line database system developed by PR Aids is one of the most comprehensive, flexible and up-to-date listing of editors. A research staff makes more than 700 changes every day in order to keep the "living directory", called MediaBase, up-to-date and enable users to reach media people all over the world, with pinpointed accuracy.

The company maintains extensive release and photo reproduction and mailing facilities, all organized exclusively for public relations customers. PR Aids also publishes Party Line (a unique weekly newsletter which provides practical, useful placement information, including what editors are looking for and who to contact). In addition, the company publishes Publicist, a bimonthly tip sheet on publicity techniques, distributed free.

In April 1974, 305 East 45 Street, the building in which PR Aids had been located for many years, was almost destroyed by an early morning explosion. No one was hurt and, miraculously, PR Aids salvaged its computer disks so that it was back in business within hours, and within weeks, moved to magnificent, new larger offices. In 1983, the company moved again, this time to a building across the street from the main post office, where it occupies 40,000 square feet on the 7th floor. The premises include a conference room and PR Aids is very generous about its use by groups.

The price of every mailing job at PR Aids is different, depending on number of pages, number of addresses and many other variables. For example, if the first page is printed on your letterhead, but PR Aids provides paper for the remaining pages, there's a deduction. There is no membership fee or monthly minimum.

Routine scheduling provides for most jobs in one day and out the next day. Same-day charges are extra, generally 50 to 100 percent.

Rates vary considerably, of course. For example, clients who provide release and envelopes pay $60 for a one-page release to 100 publications; $150 for a two-page release to 300 publications and $250 for a three-page release to 500 publications. *Postage, paper, envelopes and other supplies (e.g., chipboard with photos) are extra.*

PR Aids has extensive graphics and printing operations, and often produces news release letterheads and envelopes for its clients.

In 1986, PR Aids opened a 40,000 sq. ft. plant at 70 Washington St. in the Fulton Landing seaport area of Brooklyn. Worth a visit, just for the spectacular view.

In 1987, the company name was changed to PRA Information & Communications Group and the company started a tremendous expansion and diversification program, with new "service centers" in many cities and a PRA Broadcast Center in Washington, DC.

Also launched was Targeter, a desktop communications system to link clients to the nearest PRA office to access the PRA Mediabase and other facilities.

23. Public Relations Production Company, Inc.
301 E. 57 St., N.Y. 10022
(212) 593-6480
Michael Cannata, Pres.

PR Production is a subsidiary of Ruder Finn & Rotman, a major public relations agency, and thus if ever there was a mailing service that is public relations-oriented, this is it. The office is in the same building and the plant is on the other side of the 59th Street Bridge in Long Island City.

Though its principal business is with the agency's clients, it also provides complete lettershop and mailing services to other companies. The cost of 100 copies of a two-page news release is:

Printing $24.60
Collating 7.15
Folding 6.60
Inserting 3.35
Addressing. 23.00

Thus, the mailing would cost $64.10 plus taxes and postage, assuming the client already had provided the media names (cost for making each listing is 75 cents) and provided the envelopes. Same-day service is 50 percent extra, and 100 percent extra for service within five hours.

24. Radio Information Center
675 Third Ave., N.Y. 10017
(212) 818-9060
Daniel R. Taylor, Sales Mgr.

A specialized mailing service, called Bullseye, that provides labels to U.S. radio stations in many formats, such as addressed to department heads by name or title.

25. Signed, Sealed & Delivered, Inc.
516 W. 25 St., NY 10001
(212) 633-0113
Ed Bahnatka

Handwritten envelopes, particularly for invitations, often are very effective, and the "proper" thing to do. In 1983, two enterprising men started Signed, Sealed, & Delivered, Inc., which provides signatures, addressing and other personalization and mailing of corporate announcements, invitations, greeting cards and other items.

26. Western Union Corporation
One Lake St., Upper Saddle River, NJ 07458
(201) 825-5000

Western Union, for over 100 years a major company in the telecommunications field, remains a leader in the industry. With over 10,000 consumer offices and agencies, the company is omnipresent.

The majority of its services are provided through its principal subsidiary, The Western Union Telegraph Company, a leading carrier of recorded message and data traffic. Western Union operates a nation-wide communications network that includes communications satellites, a transcontinental microwave system, electronic switching centers and local transmission lines in major metropolitan areas.

Public relations professionals use Western Union's services to increase traffic at trade shows with announcements to preregistrants; to alert media of upcoming materials, and to send overnight invitations to news conferences and other events.

Following is a summary of Western Union "products".

Western Union Telegram. Provides same-day message delivery and is a recognized legal document.

Cablegram. (Overseas Telegram) Message destined outside North America.

Personal Opinion Message. A reduced-rate Telegram sent to officials of state and Federal governments, foreign embassies in Washington, DC, and missions to the United Nations in New York.

Mailgram Message. Messages are sent electronically to 143 post offices in the continental United States, Canada and Puerto Rico for delivery in the next business day's mail. Mailgram messages may be originated by several different methods: by Telex subscribers through their teletypewriter terminals; by EasyLink subscribers; from a communicating word processor; by magnetic tape; by large volume users directly through their computers; and by the public generally either by telephoning Western Union or delivering the message over the counter at a Western Union office or agency. The Spanish-speaking population can send messages by dialing an 800 number to reach Spanish-speaking operators. A subsidiary, Western Union Electronic Mail, Inc., serves business customers who need to send a large volume of Mailgram messages. Mailgram message services include: business reply enclosures, certified delivery, and confirmation copies.

Scheduled Mailgram. A cost-effective way to send 25,000 or more Mailgram messages at a discount price; arrangements must be made at lease five days in advance.

Worldwide Mailgram. Current locations include the United Kingdom, Argentina, Philippines, Netherlands, Chile; contact Western Union to obtain more information about additional locations.

Priority Letter. Provides two-day service; an economic service for regularly scheduled communications.

Computer Letter. An economical, high-volume oriented service, which offers enclosure capabilities for brochures and literature.

Action Hotline. Western Union's special service designed to provide communications medium through which to implement and effect a successful lobbying effort. Action Hotline is utilized easily by calling Western Union toll-free and setting up a designated operator number. Next, the organization/membership is notified of the issue, and provided with procedural information. (Western Union products can be used for this initial contact.) The individuals respond by calling Western Union's toll-free number and asking for their designated operator, at which time they can dictate their own message or select one provided by the Hotline sponsor.

27. Fred Woolf List Co., Inc.
280 N. Central Ave., Hartsdale, NY 10530
(212) 679-4311, (914) 946-0336, (800) 431-1557
Fred Woolf, Pres.

The free catalog of Fred Woolf has over 20,000 lists with about 100 million names.

28. Zeller & Letica Inc.
15 E. 26 St., N.Y. 10010
(212) 685-7512, (800) 221-4112
Fran Green, V.P.

Z&L is one of the country's leading list compilers, managers and brokers, with lists of over nine million businesses and 75 million consumer households.

ELECTRONIC MAIL

In the 70's, a few large companies developed private electronic mail systems for use between their offices. In the 80's, MCI, Western Union and others launched public electronic mail services. Some of these suppliers, such as General Electric, previously limited these services to their own employees.

All of the services operate in a similar manner in which a subscriber can send text (messages, letters, documents) via telephone lines to one or more electronic mail boxes. The sending and receiving is on the keyboard of a computer (such as a word processor or personal computer) or even a modified electronic typewriter equipped with software and a modem.

In addition to computer-to-computer communication, several companies, such as MCI, Telenet and Western Union, can convert the text to hard copy (paper) and deliver via telex, Mailgram or messenger. RCA, Western Union and other E-mail service providers can deliver telex and computer-based message copy to fax machines.

Current and proposed E-Mail and videotex operators in the U.S. and other countries are listed in the annual Telecom Factbook ($125), published by Television Digest, Inc., 1836 Jefferson Place, N.W., Washington, DC 20036.

Here are the views of Mark Roter, president of Churchill Communications Corporation, 500 Eighth Ave., N.Y 10018, about trends in electronic mail:

> Paper-based electronic mail messages will see an explosive growth by the end of this decade, although the number of carriers of such messages will be reduced to those three or four major-league players who are capable of making the commitment required to provide efficient, effective, and timely processing and delivery through sophisticated (and flexible) distribution facilities. Delivery options will still equate speed with dollars, with the most expensive messages being those delivered the fastest.
>
> Telegram, Cable, Telex/TWX, will still provide users with the fastest method of getting a message delivered, but at a premium price. Mailgram, MCI Mail and Telenet Telemail Xpress will provide senders with the best delivery options.
>
> For two-day or longer delivery, while maintaining the electronic mail "look," some of the more performance-effective computer letters will preserve their market share. Some will still be produced under the logo of their parent company, while others will be produced by the majors in "private-labeled" form.
>
> What will change most dramatically is the way in which users will originate their messages. Many more messages will be voice-originated, utilizing lists of stored addressees, and telephone systems like the Rolm PhoneMail, which will by then be capable of collecting messages in bulk and transmitting them for processing and distribution to the end-carrier. This will parallel the growth of computer-based messaging systems with access to hard copy delivery services.
>
> All of the "closed" public systems, such as The Source, CompuServe, and private corporate systems, will have had to develop access to the major carriers and their message offerings, which will be accomplished most efficiently by the use of a value-added carrier such as Churchill Communications.

A description of Churchill Communications appears earlier in this chapter. Following are descriptions of specialists in electronic mail.

1. Dialcom, Inc.
6120 Executive Blvd., Rockville, MD 20852
(301) 881-9020, (800) 435-7342
Founded in 1970, Dialcom was acquired by ITT in 1982 and bought by British Telecom in 1986.

Subscribers in about 1,000 cities can use a local telephone number or an 800 number. Cost is only $19 an hour, weekdays from 8 A.M. to 6 P.M. and $13.50 an hour at other times, with no start-up fee. However, there is a $100 per month account fee. After six months, an additional $500 a month minimum also applies.

2. EasyLink
Western Union Telegraph Co.
One Lake St., Upper Saddle River, NJ 07458
(201) 825-5000
Started in 1982, EasyLink has been heavily promoted by Western Union and is now the most widely used public electronic mail service.

It provides a low-cost electronic messaging service. Press releases and other copy can be transmitted. If you use local access (paying for the call) and 300–1,200 baud, rates vary from 35 cents to 50 cents per minute. Using WATS lines, charges are about 65 cents to 80 cents per minute.

Subscribers can send the message via telex, overnight mail, mailgram or computer-to-computer, and also can receive various news services, through EasyLink's InfoMaster and FYI News.

3. EasyPlex/InfoPlex
CompuServe Information Services (CIS)
Box 20212, 5000 Arlington Centre Blvd., Columbus, OH 43220
(614) 457-8600
Dave Bezaire, Mktg.
CompuServe, which started in 1969 as a timesharing service and began offering its videotext services in 1979, now has over 380,000 subscribers and is the foremost interactive online videotext system. (See listing in research chapter.) CIS offers an electronic mail service called EasyPlex, which is an easy-to-use, flexible and sophisticated electronic communications system.

EasyPlex is designed for the individual consumer. A $39.95 one-time subscription fee applies, plus a flat usage rate of 10 cents a minute or 20 cents, depending on transmission speed. It has a two-level security system.

InfoPlex provides instant messaging within a corporation or other organization. Hardcopy delivery capability is available through one or more other vendors. The system provides integrated electronic mailbox access and is available in hundreds of cities around the world through CompuServe's Network Service. It can distribute, receive and store information and has 24-hour accessibility and security that allows users to distribute information confidentially. InfoPlex mailboxes are protected by four-level security.

Among other features is the use of ordinary terminology, such as "Compose," "Scan," "Receive," "Send" and "File." Computer-assisted instruction is available, augmented by an online "Help" command.

InfoPlex training classes are given in CompuServe's local offices. The InfoPlex user maintains the system and has the ability to define privileges and control access.

InfoPlex has two pricing options. One is Transaction Pricing, which requires a $500 initiation fee and, after the first four months, a $500 minimum per month. The Pilot Program costs $5,000 for three months of unlimited usage, then the standard Transaction $500 minimum applies. To compose a message costs 45 cents and to send a message costs 35 cents per recipient.

4. Infonet Division
Computer Sciences Corp.
707 Westchester Ave., White Plains, NY 10604
(914) 683-5320
John Hoffman, V.P.

Branch Office:
530 Fifth Ave., N.Y. 10036
(212) 398-2828
Michael Binder, Eastern Region

Computer Sciences Corp. (formed in 1959) created Infonet in 1969. It now provides computer data networking and international messaging services to major corporations. Fees are based on connect time and the number of characters transmitted electronically and there is a minimum of $1,000 per month.

5. MCI Communications Corporation
1133 19 St., N.W., Wash., DC 20036
(800) 444-6245

Annual fee is $18. The services include Instant Letter—electronically sent to a compatible device for about $1 per "ounce" (7500 characters or about four pages). MCI Mail has laser printers that will print your company logo and your signature on each letter. It can send to CompuServe electronic mailboxes.

Customers can access Dow Jones News/Retrieval Service.

6. OnTyme
Applied Communications Systems
McDonnell Douglas Corp.
2560 N. First St., San Jose, CA 95161
(408) 446-7420 (800) 435-8880
Lynne Edwards, Product Mgr.

A computer-based message system, OnTyme is a business-oriented electronic mail system for personal computer word processors and host computer users. This system is designed for communications among the offices of a company or organization.

OnTyme is not difficult to use and is available through Tymnet in about 500 metropolitan areas in the U.S. and 56 abroad. Incoming communications are stored temporarily, with permanent storage available in multilevel electronic files. This service is not for the occasional user. The subscription fee is $300 per month plus $4.50 per hour for connect time, plus 25 cents for each 1,000 characters output or input. After three months, minimum billing of $500 applies.

7. QUIK-COMM System
GE Information Services
401 N. Washington St., Rockville, MD 20850
(301) 340-4494, (800) 433-3683
Steve Haracznak, Mgr., Press Relations

GE (General Electric) Information Services has a myriad of computing services, including the QUIK-COMM System electronic mailbox service, which was originally introduced within the company's offices in 1969.

Messages can be sent to a set of addresses held on the user's system and contact is made using a terminal or PC linked to GE's computers via a local telephone call to the GE Information Services Network.

Pricing is in three classes. The first is a "note" consisting of one to 300 characters. The offline creation charge is 35 cents; additional copies, 20 cents each; intercountry sending, an additional five cents, and additional recipients, 20 cents each.

The second class is a "memo" containing 301 to 1,500 characters. The offline creation costs 70 cents; each additional copy is 40 cents; intercountry sending is 15 cents, and additional recipients, 40 cents each.

The third class is a "document" of 1,501 to 3,000 characters. Offline creation costs $1; additional copies, 60 cents; intercountry sending, 25 cents; additional recipients, 60 cents; additional pages, 80 cents for the first copy, and additional copies, 50 cents.

User charges are a minimum of 10 cents per session. A mailbox costs $1 per address per month, and to be listed in the QUIK-COMM directory costs 25 cents. The month-to-date on-screen usage inquiry is 25 cents, and 800 number usage is charged at $20 per hour.

The QUIK-COMM System also offers a hard copy E-Mail product called QUIK-GRAM, telex access, and dial-up interfaces to IBM's PROFS and DISOSS in-house electronic mail services.

8. RCA Mail

RCA Global Communications, Inc.
201 Centennial Ave., Piscataway, N.J. 08854
(800) 526-3969

Launched in 1984, RCA mail uses upper and lower case letters, a full 80-character width screen and simple one-word commands. The cost includes a $140 monthly charge per user organization, online time of between $4 and $14 an hour depending on time of access, 5 cents per every 1,000 characters transmitted and .007 cents for every 1,000 characters held in storage beyond five days.

RCA Mail provides worldwide access, with features including distribution lists, bulletin board, filing and storage and interface with worldwide telex network, as well as a variety of special message-sending features such as "Urgent," which sends the message to the top of the incoming mail list.

9. Sourcemail

The Source Telecomputing Corp.
1616 Anderson Road, McLean, VA 22102
(703) 734-7500

Founded in 1979 and acquired by Welsh, Carson, Anderson & Stowe in 1987. Available via a local telephone number in 1,200 U.S. cities and an 800 number.

$49.95 registration plus $10 monthly minimum, applied towards usage. 300, 1,200 and 2,400 baud per-minute pricing.

10. Telemail

Telenet Communications Corp.
12490 Sunrise Valley Dr., Reston,VA 22096
(703) 689-6000, (800) 336-0437

One of the services of Telenet, Telemail, a CBMS (Computer-Based Message System) is on the Telenet telecommunications network. One of the earliest electronic mail systems, Telemail offers a variety of options such as delivery through telex or TWX (teletypewriter exchange at 110 baud), filing of incoming messages, online directory information, distribution lists and special security.

Telemail's monthly corporate account is $140, regardless of usage, plus connect hour rates of $14 during the business day and $7 after 6 P.M., plus 5 cents for each 1,000 characters transmitted. After 90 days, there's a monthly billing minimum of $500.

11. Telepost

1951 Kidwell Dr., Vienna, VA 22180
(703) 790-0410, (800) 368-4045
Michael Lune, Sales Mgr.

Formed in 1976, Telepost is a division of Telecommunications Industries, Inc. The Telepost electronic mail system includes laser printing, data processing and other state-of-the-art facilities.

12. United Wire Service

2400 W. Altorfer, Peoria, IL 61615
(309) 686-1900
Cathy Beers, V.P.
Steve Lambert, Ntl. Sales Mgr.

A division of Customer Development Corporation, United Wire Service (no connection with the United Press International newswire) is a licensed reseller of Western Union Computer Letter and also handles other services that are part of "priority" dispatch message programs.

Western Union Corporation
See listing earlier in this chapter and also EasyLink earlier in this section.

Note: Additional material about electronic mail is included in the research and telecommunications chapters.

Chapter 13

Media Directories

Gone are the days of the press agent who operated on a first-name basis with dozens of columnists and other media people, supplemented by a little black book of addresses and telephone numbers. Today's public relations practitioner must know about literally thousands of publications and other media, most of which are continually changing their personnel.

It is impossible to keep a personal directory of all media people, and it's also extremely difficult to keep track of the directories and other sources for tracking down this information. Following is a detailed description of the contents and price of more than 100 media directories. There are only a handful of public relations libraries which house all of these directories. Everyone has special media directory needs, which vary from time to time. There is a fairly sizable cost involved in purchasing all of these directories, particularly since most of them are issued annually. Furthermore, there is some overlap in the information included in many of the directories. The following descriptions, therefore, can aid in choosing the directories which can be most helpful to you.

It is embarrassing to note that many publicists waste hundreds of dollars in time and mailing costs by sending news releases and other publicity material to nonexistent publications or misaddressed publications. No media directory can be completely accurate and up-to-date, but almost all of the following directories are extremely reliable and can save time and money many times beyond their cost.

The prices of several long-established media directories have been radically increased in recent years and there is a temptation to do without them or make do with the previous edition. Most of the media directories are fairly priced, particularly in view of the vast research required to produce them and their relatively limited market.

Your best source for the most comprehensive media information cannot be found in any directory, but rather by reading a current issue of the specific publication or listening to the particular radio or TV station. A few publications provide lists of their editorial personnel.

It is not likely that a public relations agency or department, or even a library, college or reference service, stocks every one of these dozens of media directories. One of the most frequently asked questions by publicists is "which are the one or two best 'all-purpose' media directories?"

A few years ago, this directory author surveyed 90 public relations departments and agencies about current and past editions of media directories which they own. Here are the results.

The most "popular" books are Bacon's Publicity Checker, which topped the list closely followed by Editor & Publisher International Year Book and Gale Directory of Publications. Other widely owned books are Working Press of the Nation, New York Publicity Outlets and Broadcasting Yearbook.

Though evaluations were not requested in the mail questionnaires, a few respondents noted their opinions. Laudatory remarks were made about Hudson's Washington News Media Contacts Directory, TV Publicity Outlets, News Bureaus in the U.S., Party Line, and the Larimi books and newsletters, particularly Contacts.

The public relations agencies generally reported owning more reference books than the public relations departments of companies and associations. More companies than agencies "make do" with last year's, or older, editions of directories, particularly the Broadcasting Yearbook.

It is shocking to see back-issue directories, such as two- and three-year-old editions of Gale being used by prominent publicists. Regardless of your prominence and affluence, you probably should be investing more heavily in current editions of all major directories, and then keep the books up-to-date and make use of them. Bigger expenditures and greater respect for the tools of the trade can produce substantial efficiencies and economies. And there are other benefits. The Editor & Publisher Year Book, for example, is a veritable encyclopedia of information. Other media directories provide similar bonuses.

Whether you buy a few or all of these media directories, you should be familiar with their contents, attempt to keep them up-to-date, annotate their pages with your personal additions and revisions, and use them "often and well." Several publishers issue supplements and revision sheets. If you use a directory frequently, it is worthwhile to take the time to go through the book and pencil in all additions and changes, rather than inserting the supplement inside the cover.

Several new directories were launched in the 70's and 80's, and it now is possible to choose from two or more competitors which cover the same or similar fields. Active publicists sometimes purchase more than one directory in the same field, such as broadcasting, because of the frequent changes and the need for comprehensive information.

One of the problems in compiling any directory is the necessary reliance on questionnaires and large amounts of data provided by mail. The tendency is to collate the data and publish them without further investigation, particularly if the editor or researcher is not a publicist or journalist. It is a pleasure to note that several publishers, notably Bacon's and Larimi, now provide updating services throughout the year.

A few directories have dropped by the wayside. The declining number of black newspapers is one of the reasons for the current omission of a directory for this category. The Black Press Periodical Directory, and its publisher, the Black Press Clipping Bureau folded in the mid-70's. Black newspapers are included in Gale, Editor & Publisher, N.Y. Publicity Outlets and other directories.

Alliance Publishers, Box 25004, Fort Lauderdale, FL 33320, publishes directories of media in California, Illinois, New England, New York and Texas. The New York Media Directory is $60 and the others are $50.

The big news in late 1986 was the purchase by Gale Research Company of the venerable IMS/Ayer Directory of Publications.

In 1987, Standard Rate and Data Service, a company renowned for its advertising directories, introduced its first directory specifically for publicists, SRDS Print Media Editorial Calendars. The books are described in the SRDS listing in this chapter.

Are you familiar with Hudson's Newsletter Yearbook Directory? Newsletters have relatively small circulations (sometimes a few hundred, generally a few thousand) and publicists often ignore this medium. However, newsletter readers often are extremely influential and responsive to what they read. Many editors, broadcasters and freelance writers look to newsletters for tips on trends and other news leads, and thus the sophisticated publicist can use newsletters to gain the "inside track."

Newsletters require a special expertise, which few publicists possess. A neophyte in the cosmetics field noted that many people referred to "The Rose Sheet," but he was unable to find this publication listed in any directory. The explanation is that a few specialized publications, which are absolute "must reading" in their fields, have alternate or nicknames. For example, F-D-C Reports, Inc., founded in 1939, is the authoritative source of news about the drug, cosmetic and related industries. The newsletters, printed on pink and other color sheets, are published at 5550 Friendship Blvd., Chevy Chase, MD 20815. An annual subscription to the publication known as "The Pink Sheet," for the prescription and OTC pharmaceuticals industries, is $470. F-D-C Reports publishes a rainbow of information—Health Policy & Biomedical Research ("The Blue Sheet"); Toiletries, Fragrances and Skin Care ("The Rose Sheet"); Medical Devices, Diagnostics and Instrumentation Reports ("The Gray Sheet"); Weekly Pharmacy Reports ("The Green Sheet"); and Quality Control Reports ("The Gold Sheet").

There is one way to save a small amount of money. A few publishers offer pre-publication discounts, and, in some cases, a standing order for each new edition is available. This is useful not just for the economy, but also to guarantee early delivery. Payment with order generally produces a savings in the postage or handling charge, and occasionally discounts are available to purchasers of multiple copies.

Chambers of commerce, Jaycees and other civic and business organizations publish free media guides to their areas, and a few publications and stations publish media guides as a community service and for promotional purposes. Several of these publications are listed in this chapter or are mentioned elsewhere in the book.

Radio station KNX (CBS), 6121 Sunset Blvd., Hollywood, CA 90028, publishes a free directory of media and advertising agencies in the Los Angeles area.

The Counselors Academy of the Public Relations Society of America provides its members with a Resource Reference Bibliography.

Several associations publish directories that include media in the specific subject area of the group. The New York chapter of the National Academy of TV Arts and Services publishes a directory of its members, plus related services and practices. It's $15 from them at 110 W. 57th St., N.Y. 10019.

Many annual directories are published in January. However, don't assume that a directory with the preceding year on its cover is outdated. Several major directories are issued later in the year, either because the publisher plans it that way or for other unplanned reasons. For example, the Broadcasting Yearbook for many years was issued in January. Then it was shifted to February, and now it's March. The Editor & Publisher Year Book is issued in the spring or summer; the date is not precise.

Here's a tip: Before ordering a directory, find out when the next issue will be published. It may be worthwhile to wait a few days or weeks for the new issue.

Armed with all of this pontifical advice, you still may ask, "If I am not a media buff, and assuming 'average' publicity needs, isn't there a basic publicity library, a sort of five-foot shelf package?"

It is impossible to pinpoint the single most indispensable directory. Possibly if a publicist were absolutely restricted to owning only one directory, the choice would be Gale.

However, the choice would depend on the type of work, and the active publicist cannot function with only one directory.

Following is a recommended *"basic"* library of media directories. It should be supplemented by other books and services, in accordance with one's needs and method of operation.

One final note. Any evaluation is not totally objective. This evaluator has two prejudices. First, he's a media directory buff. And, second, the list includes two of the media directories written by this author.

Bacon's Publicity Checker
Broadcasting Yearbook
Contacts
Editor & Publisher International Year Book
Gale Directory of Publications
Hudson's Washington News Media Contacts Directory
Literary Market Place
Media News Keys
National Radio Publicity Outlets

New York Publicity Outlets
News Bureaus in the U.S.
Party Line
Radio Contacts
Radio-Television Contact Cards
Syndicated Columnists
TV Publicity Outlets
Television Contacts

In summary, all media directories can be valuable and a few are indispensable. Yet, many publicists attempt to function with a minimum of assistance in this area. Following is information about more than 100 media directories, including quite a few which are free or cost only a few dollars. Regardless of the investment cost, all of them are recommended for consideration as vital "tools of the trade."

Reminder: Most publishers add shipping costs to the price of their books.

1. All-TV Publicity Outlets-Nationwide
Public Relations Plus, Inc.
Drawer 1197, New Milford, CT 06776
Harold D. Hansen, Editor
$159.50

Anyone who books guests on local TV programs or distributes scripts, slides or films to TV stations will find this loose-leaf binder to be a unique bargain. (And, the competitor costs much more.) First issued in 1970, the service includes information about over 4,400 television programs, with revisions twice a year. Cable TV programs, previously listed in a separate directory, are included.

A tremendous amount of data are crammed into each listing, including program, station, address, time, host, contact, telephone, audience size, major interest of program (e.g., guests, slides, film) and even whether booklets are offered. The price actually is an annual subscription, as a completely new directory is issued every six months.

Mr. Hansen, who also publishes New York Publicity Outlets, metro California media, National Radio Publicity Outlets and The Family Page Directory, no longer is a New Yorker, but can be reached easily at (203) 354-9361.

2. American Society of Journalists and Authors Membership Directory
1501 Broadway, Suite 1907, N.Y. 10036
$50

Formerly called the Society of Magazine Writers, the ASJA represents the cream of the nation's nonfiction freelance writers. Obviously, approaches to these writers must be on an individual basis, and it is wasteful and annoying to flood them with mass mailings of news releases.

The membership directory is the only source for complete biographical information about these writers: home address, phone number, agent, magazines they regularly write for, books they have published, subject specialties and interests. Members are listed geographically, by specialty and areas of expertise.

It is not easy to interest ASJA members in writing a magazine article involving a "publicity angle." But it's worth trying, because this can lead to articles in the Reader's Digest, McCall's and other mass media which often are otherwise unattainable.

ASJA members also sometimes are available to write booklets, annual reports, speeches and other freelance assignments. Contact Alexandra Cantor, executive secretary, at (212) 997-0947, or call Dial-A-Writer at (212) 398-1934.

165

The ASJA Membership Directory is a unique compilation of information about major freelance writers. Magazine writers are included in Volume IV of Working Press but with considerably less data about each writer.

There are so many freelance journalists and writers in California that a 430-page directory exists, which is described under Rothman's Guide to Freelance Writers.

The 190-page membership roster of the Society of American Travel Writers is available for $50 from the Society at 1120 Connecticut Ave., N.W., Wash., DC 20036.

Robert Scott Milne, a prolific travel writer who is a member of the Society of American Travel Writers, American Society of Journalists and Authors and other organizations, publishes the monthly Travelwriter Marketletter at 1723 Plaza Hotel, N.Y. 10019. The newsletter ($40 a year) provides market information for travel writers and photographers and lists free trips for professionals.

In 1984, Author Aid/Research Associates International introduced Freelancers of North America, a softcover book with about 6,000 freelance writers and editorial services. It's available for $32.95 from 340 E. 52 St., N.Y. 10022.

A directory of about 180 freelance writers is available for $10 from National Writers Club, 1450 S. Havana St., Aurora, CO 80012. James Young is director of the organization.

PIN OAK, Inc., 604 W. Marshall St., Norristown, PA 19401, publishes an annual Directory for Advertisers ($16.95) with data about major consumer publications.

In the San Francisco Bay area, Media Alliance (an organization of freelancers and media people) publishes People Behind the News, with profiles of 500 local journalists. It's only $12.15 from Media Alliance, Fort Mason Center Building D, San Francisco 94123.

The National Association of Science Writers, Inc., also provides pressure-sensitive labels or Cheshire 4-up labels, in ZIP code order. The active members labels (about 685) are $125. The entire membership list (about 1,300) is $175. Contact Mrs. Diane McGurgan, administrative secretary, Box 294, Greenlawn, NY 11740.

3. Asian Rates and Data Service
Asian Business Press
17 Tractor Rd., Jurong, Singapore 2262
$68 a copy, $190 a year

Advertising and editorial information about print media in several countries. Published quarterly. The Asian Press and Media Directory no longer is published.

4. Audit Bureau of Circulations
900 N. Meacham Rd., Schaumburg, IL 60173
M. David Keil, Pres.
Meg Laidlaw, Mgr. of Communications

The Audit Bureau of Circulations (note the s) is a not-for-profit, tripartite association of advertisers, advertising agencies and publishers. Its main function is to audit the circulation figures of its member publications and to disseminate that information to media buyers.

Formed in 1914, ABC moved in 1980 from downtown Chicago to a suburb near O'Hare Airport.

Branch offices are at 420 Lexington Ave., N.Y. 10170 and 151 Bloor St., Toronto, Ontario M5S 1S4, Canada. Publications available to nonmembers include:

U.S. Daily Newspaper FAS-FAX, circulation data on ABC member newspapers $40
Periodical FAS-FAX, circulation data on ABC member periodicals $40
Canadian Factbook, circulation data on all Canadian daily and weekly newspaper
    ABC members by market and county $60

Newspaper Circulation Rate Book, single-copy and home delivery rates of all ABC member daily newspapers $10
Prices to ABC members are considerably lower.

Ayer Directory of Publications
See listing under Gale Directory of Publications.

5. Bacon's Media Alerts
Bacon's Publishing Company
332 S. Michigan Ave., Chicago 60604
$155

Established in 1983, this companion directory to Bacon's Publicity Checker alerts users to editorial features and special issues up-coming in more than 1,900 key magazines and over 200 major daily newspapers. The annual edition of Media Alerts gives editorial deadlines for both feature stories and general news releases, in addition to ad closing dates and editorial profiles for each listing.

An important feature of Media Alerts is Bacon's unique cross index of subjects and products. Each issue lists hundreds of product lines, industrial and consumer-interest subjects that will be featured in up-coming issues of magazines and trade papers. While the index shows regularly-featured subjects in publications where you would expect to find them, its primary purpose is to alert you to those subjects featured in publications outside the main market group. It tells you, for example, that a women's interest magazine is planning an in-depth look at car stereo products . . . or that a publication serving the hotel/motel industry is planning an extensive feature on security systems.

A bonus newsletter entitled Bacon's Media Update (which is included with each issue), provides editorial profiles on new and to-be published magazines, and alerts subscribers to changes in publication status.

6. Bacon's Publicity Checker
Bacon's Publishing Company
332 S. Michigan Ave., Chicago 60604
$155

Bacon's Publicity Checker has been published annually since 1951. Beginning with the 1978 edition, the Publicity Checker was expanded with the addition of more publications (e.g., all daily and weekly newspapers), and it now is published in two coil-bound volumes.

Volume I-Magazines. Lists more than 7,000 U.S. and Canadian business, trade, industrial, farm and consumer magazines and newsletters categorized by market classification (e.g., accounting, advertising, automotive). Each publication is coded by its editor to show the types of publicity desired (new products, personnel news, trade literature). Each listing includes the name of publication, editorial address, phone number, editor, circulation, frequency and publisher. Useful codes indicate whether publicity photos are used and if there is a charge for engravings.

Volume II—Newspapers. Lists all daily, weekly and semiweekly newspapers in the U.S. and all daily newspapers in Canada. Daily newspaper listings include the names of the editor, managing editor and city editor, as well as 22 departmental editors. Weekly newspaper section includes information on reaching the chains. Special marketing lists include news services, black press, top 100 metro markets, all papers over 50,000 circulation and other useful groupings.

The Publicity Checker is published annually in October and both volumes are kept up-to-date throughout the year with revisions in January, April and July. The $155 price includes the revisions, which are supplied on easy-to-use gummed labels.

In 1975, Bacon's introduced its long-awaited, much-needed Bacon's International Publicity Checker-

Western European Edition. This 850-page, coil-bound volume is published annually in February and is arranged in a format similar to the U.S. edition. About 11,500 business and trade magazines are arranged by country and also by market classification. The countries are Austria, Belgium, Denmark, Finland, France, Germany, Ireland, Italy, the Netherlands, Norway, Portugal, Spain, Sweden, Switzerland and the United Kingdom. Over 1,000 national and regional daily newspapers also are listed. The largest number of publications (over 2,000 magazines and 200 newspapers) are in the United Kingdom section. In each country, the publications are grouped by classifications, such as financial, architecture, banking and other categories akin to Bacon's U.S. Checker. A major feature is an indication as to whether translation is required from English, and the specific language or languages. This magnificent research effort also includes maps and useful facts on each country. The price is $165.

If you're in a rush, you can call Bacon's toll free at (800) 621-0561. In Illinois, the number is (312) 922-2400.

7. Bacon's Radio/TV Directory
Bacon's Publishing Company
332 S. Michigan Ave., Chicago 60604
$155

Introduced in 1987, this directory is what you would expect from the Bacon's organization. Its 920 pages is crammed with data about 9,000 radio and 1,300 TV stations. The spiral-bound book provides the names, contacts and information about the news and talk shows on each station, plus maps for the 25 top markets and other features.

8. Benn's Media Directory
Benn Business Information Services, Ltd.
Box 20, Sovereign Way, Tonbridge, Kent TN9 1RQ, England
Patricia Dunkin Wedd, Production Editor
$165 (2 volumes)

First published in 1846 as the Newspaper Press Directory, Benn's now is an annual two-volume set, which can be purchased together or individually. Purchased individually, each volume is about $95. Note: The price of the English pound, as with all foreign currencies, varies considerably in terms of U.S. equivalent.

The United Kingdom volume describes close to 1,800 newspapers, over 8,500 consumer, trade, technical and professional publications, advertising and public relations agencies and services, and broadcasting and other media organizations. The International volume lists over 30,000 newspapers and other publications in 197 countries, including the United Kingdom. This encyclopedia also includes information about embassies, news agencies, broadcasting and other media associations.

9. Bowdens Media Directory
Bowdens Information Services
624 King St. West, Toronto, Ontario M5V 2X9, Canada
Erica Waldman, Editor
$175

Canada's most comprehensive media directory, this excellent book lists over 11,000 names, addresses and phone numbers of editors, feature writers, columnists, newscasters and broadcast personalities at all daily and weekly newspapers, consumer and business publications, local and network radio and TV stations and other media, including the national and provincial press galleries. All addresses are available on labels. (See mailing services.)

The price includes three revisions within the year and a monthly bulletin of updates.

10. Broadcasting/Cablecasting Yearbook

Broadcasting Publications
1705 DeSales St., N.W., Wash., DC 20036
$105

Published by the same organization which produces the weekly Broadcasting ($70 a year), this annual directory is *the* source of information about radio and television stations in the United States and Canada.

Issued every March, the Broadcasting/Cablecasting Yearbook is the electronic counterpart to Editor & Publisher, in that it not only includes extensive data about *all* stations, cable systems and satellites, but also is an encyclopedia of information about advertising representatives, FCC rules, producers, equipment, associations and other aspects of the industry.

Prepaid advance orders are $90 a copy.

Television/Radio Age publishes an annual pocket-size 12 City Directory with over 6,000 listings of stations, agencies, advertisers, associations, media, program distributors, hotels, restaurants and other categories in New York, Chicago, Los Angeles, San Francisco, Detroit, Atlanta, Dallas-Fort Worth, St. Louis, Philadelphia, Minneapolis-St. Paul, Washington and Boston. $10 from Television/Radio Age, 1270 Avenue of the Americas, N.Y. 10020.

In the United Kingdom, an equivalent encyclopedia of about 500 pages is published annually by Tellex Monitors, a broadcast monitoring service partly owned by Universal News Service. It's called the Blue Book of Broadcasting, and is about $20.

11. Business and Financial News Media

Larriston Communications
Box 20229, N.Y. 10025
$80

First published in 1983, this annual looseleaf directory provides data about business editors at over 300 daily newspapers, plus syndicates and other media. The price includes a midyear update.

12. Cable Contacts Yearbook

Larimi Communications Associates
5 W. 37 St., N.Y. 10018
Michael M. Smith, Publisher
$171

Cable Contacts is an annual 450-page directory with about 750 cable systems in the U.S., satellite networks, independent producers, news services and multiple system operators. Local cable system listings include address, personnel, satellite networks carried, data channel information, public access channel descriptions, local origination programming personnel and address, number of systems and subscribers served, program listings, guest/information requirements and contact persons. Independently produced programs, indexed by network and producer, includes guest information/product usage, technical and visual support material requirements, subscriber figures and pre-produced segment placement or joint production opportunities. Larimi publishes several directories and newsletters, including Contacts. The subscription price includes monthly updates.

Cable TV Publicity Outlets—Nationwide

In 1982, Harold Hansen (publisher of New York Publicity Outlets) introduced this specialized directory, a reflection of the growth of cable TV. In 1986, it was incorporated into the company's National TV Publicity Outlets, which is described later in this chapter.

13. California Media

Public Relations Plus, Inc.
Drawer 1197, New Milford, CT 06776
Harold Hansen, Editor
$89.50

California is our largest state (in population) and this directory reflects it, with data about 114 daily newspapers, 533 weekly newspapers, 324 magazines, 103 TV networks and stations, 518 radio networks and stations, 109 bureaus and 115 syndicated writers, arranged in 22 metropolitan areas.

If you're wondering why a California media directory is published in a little town in Connecticut, here's the explanation:

In 1972, Michael Larsen and Elizabeth Pomada launched California Publicity Outlets and published it for a few years. One of its distinctive features was elaborate printing, including a colorful cover.

In 1978, Harold Hansen took it over and vastly updated and improved the directory. The spiral-bound format is similar to Mr. Hansen's basic publication, New York Publicity Outlets. A former New Yorker, Harold Hansen operates a very efficient media directory publishing company in Connecticut, phone (203) 354-9361. The full name of the book is metro California media, and it's a detailed listing of personnel at daily and weekly newspapers, and other local, regional and national publications, as well as radio and TV stations. The price includes a mid-year revision edition.

If you're headquartered in California or have a special interest in California media, this book is indispensable. For others, it's extremely useful, though some of the material can be found in various other national directories.

14. Catholic Press Directory

Catholic Press Association
119 N. Park Ave., Rockville Centre, NY 11570
James A. Doyle, Editor, Regina Salzmann, Mng. Ed.
$25

Since 1951, the Catholic Press Association has published an annual reference guide to all recognized Catholic publications in the United States, Canada and the Caribbean. Extensive advertising, production and editorial data is provided about more than 600 newspapers, magazines and directories with a total circulation of about 28 million.

Many of these publications use publicity material, particularly if it involves a Catholic or religious orientation. The directory also includes such influential and large circulation general-interest national magazines as America, Catholic Digest and Columbia, as well as such special-interest publications as Religion Teacher's Journal and Hospital Progress.

The Catholic Press Association, which started in 1912, represents Catholic publications and publishers. It also publishes The Catholic Journalist, a monthly newspaper.

15. Channels

PR Publishing Company, Inc.
Box 600, Exeter, NH 03833
$40

Channels started as the membership publication of the National Public Relations Council of Health and Welfare Services (formed in 1922), which became the National Communication Council for Human Services in 1975 and then consolidated its membership with the Public Relations Society of America in 1977. Don Bates, former executive director of the Council, continued to edit Channels, until he left PRSA in 1979, and now is a contributing editor.

In 1983, PR Publishing Company took over Channels and continued it as a monthly newsletter for non-profit organizations. PR Publishing Company is headed by Otto Lerbinger, the renowned educator (professor at the Boston University School of Communications) and Patrick Jackson, public relations practitioner who was president of PRSA. The company also publishes *pr reporter,* the weekly newsletter.

16. Chicago Publicity Club

Suite 110, 1441 Shermer Rd., Northbrook, IL 60062
$75

Annual directory, including members of the Publicity Club of Chicago; lists personnel at Chicago daily newspapers, wire services, radio and TV stations, magazines, community and suburban newspapers, freelance writers, professional reference sources and suppliers.

Signs of our times: The Publicity Club of Chicago has its office in a suburb! In fact, the club is managed by Direct Connection, Inc., a professional association management company.

17. College Alumni and Military Publications

Larimi Communications Associates, Ltd.
5 W. 37 St., N.Y. 10018
$75

In 1980, Richard Weiner introduced two unique directories, College Alumni Publications and Military Publications. In 1987, Larimi Communications took over Weiner's media directories and made a tremendous research investment. One result was a new book that combines College Alumni and Military Publications. The unusual book was introduced at a lower price than other Larimi directories in order to encourage publicists to become familiar with these specialized media.

The college section has data about 500 alumni publications.

The Military Publications section also has been thoroughly revised. This unique book provides circulation, advertising rates and other data about 500 Government and civilian newspapers and magazines for U.S. military personnel and their families.

Easy-to-use listings are by state, plus an outside-the-U.S. section and an alphabetical index.

Army, Navy, Air Force and Marine publications are distributed to over two million U.S. military personnel. There also are publications for their families, as well as for veterans, reservists, suppliers and others with military links.

Veterans' publications, ranging from such well-known general magazines as American Legion, DAV, VFW, National Amvet and Jewish Veteran, to such local publications as Minnesota Legionnaire, also are included, but the emphasis of the book is on base newspapers and other military publications that are not listed in any other directory.

18. College Student Press in America

Oxbridge Communications, Inc.
150 Fifth Ave., N.Y. 10011
Dr. Dario Politella, Editor
$75

Over 5,500 periodicals (newspapers, yearbooks and magazines) published by students on about 2,500 campuses, are listed in this biennial 300-page directory. The full name of this book is Directory of the College Student Press in America.

The directory includes advertising and subscription rates, description of contents, frequency, circulation, method of financing (often supported by the college) and other data, but not the name of the editor or other editorial staff data. News releases generally are not used by college newspapers, except if the release relates to a local event or has a strong student appeal (e.g., contest for students). Sixth edition (1986) includes radio & TV stations.

19. Computer Media Directory

2211 Norfolk, Ste. 700, Houston 77098-9985
$169.95

The Computer Age is reflected in the size (over 500 pages) of this extraordinary directory. Each computer publication is described on a separate page, with such information as type of publicity used, staff members, bureaus and correspondents. Also included are newspapers and general publications which use computer news. Loose-leaf updates are provided quarterly.

The binder is divided into seven categories:

1. Basic computer and end-user oriented publications.
2. Publications aimed at computer industry manufacturers, technicians and theoreticians.
3. Magazines and newsletters for those in the computer distribution cycle, from corporate marketing directors to retailers.
4. Vertical publications with computer news.
5. General, business and noncomputer trade magazines, newspapers and news services that carry computer news.
6. Freelance writers.
7. Computer industry analysts.

20. Congressional Directory

Compiled by the Joint Committee on Printing
U.S. Government Printing Office
Wash., DC 20402
$15 (paper), $20 (cloth)

The more than 1,000 pages of this directory contain biographies and other data about the members of the U.S. Congress and a tremendous amount of information about Government agencies. Additional material includes the staffs of international organizations with headquarters or offices in Washington, D.C.; U.S. embassies and diplomatic offices throughout the world and foreign diplomatic offices in the U.S.

The 100-page media section includes the business and home addresses of all U.S. and foreign journalists entitled to admission to the Senate and House Press Galleries.

The Congressional Directory is published biennially and can be obtained by mail from the Superintendent of Documents, U.S. Government Printing Office, Wash., DC 20402.

Other versions of the Congressional Directory include a thumb index edition ($23), and a pictorial directory in paper ($4) and cloth ($12).

Additional material about Congress is included in the Congressional Staff Directory. This annual directory does not include media information. However, many public relations people find this book extremely valuable, particularly since its format makes it easy to use.

Congressional Staff Directory is published by Charles B. Brownson, who was a Congressman for eight years, and can be obtained for $45 from the publisher at Box 62, Mt. Vernon, VA 22121. The annual book is issued in May, but if you can't wait, a 500-page Advance Locator paperback is available in February for $12. The Directory includes about 3,200 hard-to-find staff biographies.

Formed in 1959, Congressional Staff Directory Ltd. also publishes the Federal Staff Directory ($45) each December and the Judicial Staff Directory ($45) each October, introduced in 1987.

Columbia Books, Inc., 1350 New York Ave., N.W., Wash., DC 20005, publishes directories of lobbyists and other information relevant to our nation's capital. Founded in 1966, this small specialized publisher is headed by Arthur C. Close, President, and Craig Colgate, Jr., Chairman. Its major publication is a directory of national trade and professional associations.

The most comprehensive compilation of the Washington press corps appears in Hudson's Washington News Media Contact Directory, described later in this section. Media Distribution Services maintains mailing lists of Government officials, business leaders and others who comprise its Special Target Audiences. Information about Media Distribution Services, and other sources of lists of Government officials, is included in the chapter on mailing services.

21. Contacts
Larimi Communications Associates, Ltd.
5 W. 37 St., N.Y. 10018
Michael M. Smith, Publisher
$297/year

A four-page weekly newsletter with news about new publications and programs and media changes of specific value to publicists. The publication is patterned after Party Line, but there are notable differences. Contacts is four pages (Party Line is two pages), and the center pages are used to describe a specific publication or a media category in a primer manner which is particularly helpful to beginners.

The center pages, called Between the Lines, often consist of an in-depth profile or a survey of a media category, such as inflight magazines and op-ed pages, which is extremely helpful to publicists on all levels.

Contacts rarely lists requests from freelance writers and leaves these nuggets to Party Line. However, Contacts includes more media data and news about media personnel changes.

Many professional publicists subscribe to Party Line and Contacts. If you want to subscribe to only one, try a short-term subscription or inspect free sample copies.

22. Dati & Tariffe Pubblicitarie
P. Le Cantore, 12
20123 Milano, Italy

A bimonthly directory (in Italian) with extensive data (dati) about print media in Italy. The company also publishes the bimonthly Media Help.

23. Editor & Publisher International Year Book
The Editor & Publisher Co., Inc.
11 W. 19 St., N.Y. 10011
Robert U. Brown, President, Ferdinand C. Teubner, Publisher
$70

Editor & Publisher, the nation's oldest news magazine about publishing and advertising, has issued a yearbook since 1921. The directory is the most complete and authentic record of the newspaper business, and is used by thousands of advertisers, publishers and librarians. It should be used by more public relations practitioners, particularly since there is far more journalistic information (as compared to advertising and production) than is generally known.

More than half of its 650-page book is devoted to comprehensive information about each of the daily newspapers in the U.S. and Canada, including all personnel.

Other sections of the book include information about every weekly newspaper in the U.S.; major black newspapers; all college, industry, foreign language, special-interest daily newspapers, and national and regional supplements.

The international section includes varying amounts of information about almost all of the daily newspapers of the world, their advertising and editorial staffs and representatives in the U.S.

The syndicate section includes a large number of feature, news and picture syndicates, but the names of individual columnists and bylined writers are not listed.

The final sections list U.S. and Canadian advertising and journalism schools, clubs and associations, and recent books, films and awards related to the newspaper business.

Even the advertising in the Editor & Publisher International Year Book includes helpful information, such as photos of editorial personnel!

Editor & Publisher devotes its last issue in July to syndicates. This valuable directory of newspaper columnists can be obtained for $5, or as part of an annual $40 subscription to the magazine.

24. Edpress Membership Roster and Free-Lance Directory

Educational Press Association of America
Glassboro State College
Glassboro, NJ 08028
Donald R. Stoll, Exec. Dir.
$22.95

America's Educational Press, a directory with information about over 2,300 education periodicals (including many newsletters and journals not listed in any other directory) has been discontinued. The 33rd edition was published in 1976 by the Educational Press Association of America.

The Association does publish an annual Membership Roster of about 600 members. The book is $22.95 to nonmembers and free to members (dues are $40 to $150 a year).

25. The Family Page Directory

Public Relations Plus, Inc.
Drawer 1197, New Milford, CT 06776
Harold Hansen, Editor
$60

Started in 1968, this unique directory lists the beauty, food, fashion, home furnishings and other specific editors of the ''family pages'' (formerly called women's pages) of the largest daily newspapers (over 500).

All newspapers with circulation in excess of 24,500 are ranked so that publicists easily can select the top 100 or any other grouping. Included is an indication of the editor's preference for Ms., Miss or Mrs. (or Mr.)

Instead of issuing corrections or supplements, Harold Hansen provides subscribers with an entire new directory twice a year, so the $60 annual cost is quite reasonable.

26. Finderbinder Media Directories

4679 Vista St., San Diego, CA 92116

Started by Gary Beals in 1974, Finderbinder is a group of public relations agencies which are licensed to produce local media directories in their areas. Currently, *over 15 directories* are being published, at about $70 each. Each loose-leaf book includes an annual subscription to a newsletter with updates.

The data for each publication and station include editorial personnel and advertising rates. For example, the Arizona Finderbinder describes about 200 daily and weekly newspapers, wire services, college and military publications and about 100 radio and TV stations. The Denver Metropolitan Media Directory lists, on over 170 pages, about 170 newspapers, 40 magazines, college newspapers, radio and TV stations. The Milwaukee Area Directory (which includes Madison) describes about 95 newspapers, 100 magazines and 50 radio and TV stations.

Other directories are published in Cleveland, Dallas, Houston, Kansas City, Pittsburgh, Portland,

St. Louis, San Diego, Seattle and the states of Indiana, Oklahoma and Louisiana, and new areas are added continually.

Information about the directories can be obtained from Gary Beals Advertising & Public Relations Agency, 4679 Vista St., San Diego, CA 92116, phone (619) 284-1145.

27. Florida Rate Book

Youngblood Publishing
Box 273572, Tampa, FL 33688
$85

Data about 400 Florida publications.

28. Gale Directory of Publications

Gale Research Co.
Book Tower, Detroit, MI 48226
$145

The longest continuously published directory of U.S. magazines, newspapers and other periodicals was acquired in late 1986 by the Gale Research Co., one of the world's leading publishers of reference books.

Now called the Gale Directory of Publications, it was called the IMS Directory, and before that, the IMS/Ayer Directory, and before 1981, the Ayer Directory, which is the name known to thousands of librarians and other users.

The Gale Directory lists more than 24,000 publications, including daily and weekly newspapers, consumer and trade publications. It contains data about address, location (e.g., miles from nearest major city, population, local industry, county) circulation, page size, subject matter, price and other information crammed into its over 1,450 pages. Publications are listed according to the city in which they are published, with an alphabetical index of all publications at the back of the book.

Publicists who try to get by with last year's directory should see the thousands of media additions, deletions and changes that researchers track down each year. Of the 800,000 assorted facts, about 100,000 are new each year, including about 1,200 new publications, which replace about an equal number of periodicals that have expired. Though not thought of as an encyclopedia or gazetteer, the Directory includes over 60 maps and extensive market data.

Returning to the origins of the Directory, the first list of the nation's newspapers was published in 1869 as George P. Rowell's Newspaper Directory, which was continued until 1909. Ayer & Son's Manual for Advertisers, started in 1880, became N. W. Ayer's Directory of Newspapers and Periodicals, and absorbed Rowell's in 1910.

The 1869 edition noted that William Cullen Bryant was one of the New York Evening Post's editors. Harriet Beecher Stowe was listed as editor of a New York weekly called Health and Home. Louisa May Alcott edited a Boston illustrated monthly, Merry's Museum. Godey's Lady's Book had a then huge circulation of 106,000, while Pomeroy's Democrat of New York was the nation's biggest seller.

In 1880, N. W. Ayer started publishing the directory. The purpose was to help advertisers obtain, for the first time, a comprehensive collection of accurate data about media. The publication became so successful that it became a separate operation, called Ayer Press.

In 1979, Ayer Press moved from its long-time office on West Washington Square in Philadelphia to a new suburban building in Bala Cynwyd, and in 1984, it moved again to nearby Fort Washington. In 1981, Ayer Press was sold to IMS Communications, Inc. and it became IMS Press.

In 1987, Gale started a series of enhancements, including a mid-year supplement ($95) with over 2,000 new publications and revisions.

29. Gebbie Press All-In-One Directory

Gebbie Press
Box 1000, New Paltz, NY 12561
Amalia Gebbie, Editor-Publisher
$77

For many years, Con Gebbie published a directory about house magazines and employee publications. Then, he semiretired to his Catskill Mountain home in New Paltz and became a magazine consultant and provider of house magazine mailing lists and related services. In 1972, he introduced the All-In-One Directory. It's a brilliant idea, and the 6 × 9 book has many uses, along with a few shortcomings.

Con Gebbie died in 1974 and the book has been continued by Amalia and Mark Gebbie.

The amazing compact, 507-page, spiral-bound volume literally combines several major directories in its listings of every daily and weekly newspaper, *every* radio and television station, and most consumer, business, trade, farm and black publications. A limited amount of basic data about the 22,000 publications and stations also is included, but the major use of the directory is for its simple, easy-to-use listings of media names and addresses.

The major problem with this directory is that almost all of it has been obtained from other directories. Since every media directory is outdated the day it is published, the Gebbie Directory is additionally outdated. Furthermore, supplements and revisions, such as those provided by Bacon's, are not issued by Gebbie. Users of the Gebbie Directory therefore must not use it as their only source book, tempting though this is for amateurs, librarians and others. However, for what it is, Gebbie is extremely useful and indeed a bargain.

In an attempt to minimize bookkeeping costs, Mrs. Gebbie offers a 10% discount for prepayment.

More good news. The Gebbie Directory now is available on three sets of PC-compatible diskettes, at $105 if billed on $90 prepaid.

Set 1. Daily, weekly papers in fixed or variable lengths, geographic or zip code order.
Set 2. Radio, TV in fixed or variable lengths, geographic or zip code order.
Set 3. Consumer, business, farm publications in variable or fixed lengths.

Con Gebbie's original directory of "house organs" now is called the Internal Publications Directory, and is described later in this chapter.

30. Hispanic Media, USA

The Media Institute
3017 M St., N.W., Wash., DC 20007
$75

250 listings of Spanish-language media (newspapers, magazines, radio, TV) in the U.S., with detailed descriptions of 48 major media, including tips on publicity.

31. Hollis Press & Public Relations Annual

Hollis Directories Ltd.
Contact House, Lower Hampton Rd., Sunbury-on-Thames
Middlesex TW16 5HG, England
Nesta Hollis, Publisher
$70

If you work in the public relations or media fields in the United Kingdom, or if you are an American public relations practitioner or media person with active interests in the U.K., the Hollis book is essential.

Started in 1967, each annual edition has become larger and more comprehensive. The six sections each have a different color.

Grey Pages—Over 1,250 British public relations companies, plus listings of over 2,000 PR counselors in 60 other countries.

White Pages—Several thousand company contacts, many with night telephone numbers.

Pink Pages—Government, association and other information sources.

Green Pages—Media and communications organizations.

Blue Pages—Index.

Gold Pages—Sponsors of events.

Quarterly update supplements are available for an additional $20. The Hollis PR Newsletter no longer is published.

Subscribers can call Mrs. Hollis and her staff for all types of public relations information. The telephone number in Sunbury is 093 27 84781. From London, the number is 76 84781.

In summary, the Hollis Annual is a classified guide to information sources, public relations companies and other data about the United Kingdom. Some information also is included about other parts of the world. Mrs. Hollis is one of the global leaders in the public relations world, and the 600-page book is one of the basic books for anyone involved with international public relations.

32. Hudson's Washington News Media Contacts Directory
Box 311, 44 W. Market St., Rhinebeck, NY 12572
Edited by Howard Penn Hudson and Helene F. Wingard
$99, including revisions

Introduced in 1968 by these experienced public relations practitioners, Hudson's Directory is the most comprehensive compilation of the press corps in our nation's capital. The spiral-bound, annual book includes extensive data about more than 4,000 publications, bureaus, correspondents, editors and freelance writers.

The revisions, in April, July and October, are one of the most up-to-date compilations of any directory and reflect the zeal of the editors.

Howard Hudson also is the publisher of PRQ, a quarterly journal; The Newsletter on Newsletters, a semi-monthly publication; and the Hudson's Newsletter Directory, described later in this chapter.

In 1985, Hudson launched a new book, Hudson's State Capital News Media Contacts Directory ($70), a spiral-bound collection of data about headquarters and bureaus of print and broadcast media. The book combines data also found in News Bureaus in the U.S., Editor & Publisher and Broadcasting, plus considerable new material, including radio and TV talk shows.

Hudson's Yearbook Directory
See listing under Newsletter Yearbook Directory.

33. Illinois Media
Midwest Newsclip, Inc.
425 N. Michigan Ave., Chicago 60611
$95

Newsclip, a regional clipping bureau, has published (since 1958) an annual directory of the radio and TV stations and daily and weekly newspapers in Illinois. In addition to the names of editors, department heads and other personnel at print and broadcast media, there is a unique feature (which other directory publishers should emulate): a separate street index, compiled block-by-block, which enables readers to locate the specific area covered by neighborhood and suburban weekly newspapers.

34. Internal Publications Directory

National Research Bureau
310 S. Michigan Ave., Chicago 60604
$120

The Internal Publications Directory is the one and only source of detailed information about internal and external "house organs" of more than 3,800 U.S. companies, Government agencies, clubs and other groups. The bible of the house magazine industry was founded by Con Gebbie, who defined a house magazine as "a publication issued on a regular basis by a company, firm, association or even an individual. It does not carry advertising, is sent free to readers, and, in one way or another, frankly promotes the interests of its sponsor. A few house magazines accept advertising, a few actually charge subscription prices, and some are issued on a completely irregular basis. But the general rule holds good."

There is no one correct designation. Other terms include house organ, industrial publication, sponsored publication, company publication and industrial magazine. "House organ" is the most widely understood but it also is controversial. Many editors and sponsors feel that "house" is vague and "organ" undignified, but editors do not agree on a substitute. Some state that "industrial publication" is misleading in that it excludes nonindustrial fields, that "company publication" does not take into consideration associations and that "sponsored publication" sounds too commercial. Some favor a definitive term such as "house publication" because it covers the entire field without exception, but others believe that any all-inclusive definition is necessarily vague and not at all necessary.

Regardless of the nomenclature, the directory provides a tremendous amount of information. These publications have a total circulation of more than 180 million (more than twice that of all daily newspapers) and have a remarkably high readership.

In addition to the publication descriptions, which are arranged alphabetically by sponsor name, there also are lists arranged by title, industry and editorial interest.

The Internal Publications Directory is a beautiful, useful book involving an enormous media field which is ignored by many publicists. The book no longer is produced by Con Gebbie (it previously was called The Gebbie House Magazine Directory and was sold for $34.95 in 1975). The publisher, National Research Bureau, sells the book separately, but the unit cost is quite high, $120, and most purchasers buy it as part of the Working Press of the Nation five-volume set for $260. The Internal Publications Directory is the fifth volume of the set.

Names of about 12,500 business and organizational editors and communicators can be obtained from the International Association of Business Communicators, 870 Market St., San Francisco 94102.

The list is $125 a thousand for advertisers (minimum of one page) in the IABC magazine, Communication World, or $150 a thousand for non-advertisers. There is a $25 set-up charge, no discounts or commissions are allowed, the Association must see and "accept" the mailing piece, and the minimum is 5,000 names.

35. International Television and Video Almanac

Quigley Publishing Company, Inc.
159 W. 53 St., N.Y. 10019
Richard Gertner, Editor
$55

Published annually since 1955, the 800-page Almanac includes biographies (more than 6,000 celebrities, with their credits in small type), motion pictures (more than 7,000 titles), TV stations (personnel and other data of all U.S. stations), and other information about television, home video and motion pictures.

The Quigley Publishing Company also issues International Motion Picture Almanac, which also is $55 a copy. Published annually since 1929, this book includes biographies, lists of feature pictures, and many thousands of listings which make it the standard encyclopedia of the motion picture industry. The two almanacs can be purchased for $88.

36. Investment Newsletters

Larimi Communications Associates, Ltd.
5 W. 37 St., N.Y. 10018
$150

Introduced in 1982 by Richard Weiner, Investment Newsletters was completely revised in 1987 by Larimi.

The looseleaf directory contains descriptions and data about 800 investment newsletters—the most comprehensive collection of data ever compiled, including names of influential editors who want to receive news releases and financial reports. Jim Dines, Joe Granville, Harry Browne, T. J. Holt, Howard Ruff, Julian Snyder, Harry Schultz, Martin Zweig and other editors of sizable circulation, influential publications, such as Ruff Times, Value Line and others in the U.S., Europe and Asia. An extraordinary book for investment guidance and publicity opportunities.

The $150 subscription includes monthly updating reports. Subscribers can obtain daily updating by calling (800) 634-4020.

37. Jewish Press in America

Joseph Jacobs Organization, Inc.
60 E. 42 St., N.Y. 10165
Richard A. Jacobs, Editor
$10

The nation's leading Jewish advertising and marketing specialist is an organization founded in 1919 by the late Joseph Jacobs, and is now operated by his son, Richard.

Food, automotive, travel and other major advertisers regularly work with the Joseph Jacobs Organization, headed by Richard Jacobs and David Koch, vice president.

In 1970, Jacobs published the first comprehensive Directory of the Jewish Press in America, containing detailed advertising and publicity information about all Jewish newspapers and magazines in the United States and Canada. The unique book lists the names of editors, editorial requirements, and provides information on publicity and photo needs and special feature issues published by about 160 publications in 65 cities—*almost all of which are in English.*

Among the well-known English language publications in the directory are the Jewish Press (Brooklyn, N.Y., circulation 173,000), B'nai B'rith Jewish Monthly (circulation 169,000) and Hadassah Magazine (circulation 385,000).

Special features in the directory include, "A History of the Jewish Press in America," a short humorous "Yiddish-English Dictionary," containing Yiddish words and phrases that are commonly used in American humor and literature, and an article on ethnic marketing during the past 50 years.

An annual Jewish Media List is free to clients of the Jacobs Organization.

Larimi Communications Associates, Ltd.

5 W. 37 St., N.Y. 10018
Michael M. Smith, Publisher

Formed in 1972, Larimi has become a major company in the field of media publicity directories.

The company moved in 1986 to larger facilities, as it now publishes a greater number and variety of media directories and newsletters than any other company, including Contacts, Investment Newsletters, News Bureaus, Syndicated Columnists, Trade Media News and others, which are described elsewhere in this chapter.

Larriston Communications

Box 20229, N.Y. 10025

Craig Norback, Research Director

Formed in 1979 by Robin A. Elliott, Larriston publishes three directories, which are described individually in this chapter:

Business and Finance News Media
Medical and Science News Media
Travel, Leisure and Entertainment News Media

The company provides 10 percent discounts to nonprofit organizations.

38. Literary Market Place

R. R. Bowker Company

245 W. 17 St., N.Y. 10011

$85

This 900-page directory, revised each November, includes more than 73 sections listing over 25,000 names, addresses and telephone numbers, indicating who's where among publishers, reviewers, agents or book clubs; as well as who will edit a job, translate it, type it, design it, illustrate it, print it, bind or prebind it, promote it, ship it, distribute it and export it.

Published annually since 1940, Literary Market Place is an indispensable aid for anyone in publishing. Among the lists of particular public relations value are literary agents, book columnists and commentators, book review services, literary awards, and writers' associations and conferences.

A unique time-saving section called "Names and Numbers" provides an alphabetical index to the 25,000 entries in the main section, with full name, address and phone number.

For those needing information on publishing and bookselling abroad, Bowker publishes International Literary Market Place, covering 71 countries outside the U.S. and Canada. Published annually each spring, it's $110.

Magazine Information Market Place ($59.95) lists about 18,000 companies and individuals active in the magazine industry. Of special interest to publicists are the listings of small-circulation consumer magazines not included in most other media directories.

Bowker publishes numerous market place directories for specialized industries. These include Audio Video Market Place ($65), The North American Online Directory (previously called Information Industry Market Place, $45) and Microcomputer Market Place ($95).

39. Madison Avenue Handbook

Peter Glenn Publications

17 E. 48 St., N.Y. 10017

$40

This annual volume (started in 1958) is probably the most colorful directory published anywhere. Art, type, paper and other consultants have joined with the publisher to produce a lavish collection of ads and listings of advertising agencies, video and film producers, art and photography studios and other companies in New York, California and elsewhere. The book is used by many producers, art directors, models, artists and photographers and also includes sections of value to publicists.

Peter Glenn Publications also operates Model's Mart, which publishes a Directory of Model-Talent Agencies and Schools ($25) and a variety of books for and about models.

A similar annual directory, called simply The Book, lists suppliers of art, photos, printing and other creative and production services in the Northeast. Published by Heloisa Centner, The Book covers Connecticut primarily, but also includes New England and New York. About 6,000 copies are distributed free to advertising and public relations executives, and other copies are sold at $14 each. The publisher is The Book, Ltd., Box 749, Westport, CT 06880.

NYPG is an annual film and video production guide ($45), published by Richard Babchak at Suite 219, 150 Fifth Ave., N.Y. 10011. Sections of interest to public relations clients include production companies, location finders, sources of props, equipment, costumes and editorial services.

The Creative Directory, Inc., 333 N. Michigan Ave., Chicago 60601, publishes the Chicago Creative Directory, both distributed annually to a total of about 10,000 advertising agencies, production houses and others. The book is sustained by advertisers, though the comprehensive lists of several thousand illustrators, designers, film and videotape producers and other sources also includes non-advisers.

It seems that there is no end to the number of directories in this category. Perhaps a reason for this is that many of these directories sell advertisements, which is a major source of their revenue. The books thus are similar to yellow page telephone directories, though a lot more attractive. For example, Adweek, which has become an extremely important weekly publication in the advertising field, publishes the Adweek/Art Directors' Index, an annual book of over 450 pages of advertisements for photographers, illustrators, video companies and others, as well as about 200 pages of listings of over 22,000 sources, including design, sales representatives, audio-visual producers, printers, sources of talent, props, locations and other creative services. It's $35 from Adweek, 49 E. 21 St., N.Y. 10010.

40. Matthews List and Matthews CATV

Matthews & Partners, Ltd.
Box 1029, Pointe Claire, Quebec H9S 4H9, Canada
Mrs. Robbie Oakley, Pres.
Neil M. Oakley, V.P.

Matthews List and Matthews CATV are indispensible to anyone who is active in Canadian public relations. The directories are completely revised three times a year, which is one of the several extraordinary features of this extremely efficient operation. The basic List is a 360-page collection of data (somewhat like Editor & Publisher and Broadcasting Yearbooks) about 3,600 Canadian daily and weekly newspapers, radio and TV stations, business and consumer publications, news services and other media. Cable and pay TV are included in the 190-page second volume. The two volumes are $190 (including postage). The List is $140. The "Cable list" is $75. Prices are U.S. dollars.

Matthews, which is operated by Neil Oakley and his wife, Robbie, is a subsidiary of Publicorp Communications, Inc., a public relations agency at the same location. Neil Oakley also is the public relations program coordinator at McGill University.

Syd Matthews, a former newspaper editor, and his wife, Ev, started Matthews List in Toronto in 1954. Publicorp purchased the company in 1977. Matthews died in 1984.

MediaMap

A computer media directory, described in the research chapter under Cambridge Communications.

41. Media News Keys

40–29 27 St., Long Island City, NY 11101
Jerry Leichter, Editor

Media News Keys is a weekly four-page newsletter of media personnel changes. An annual subscription is $100. For more information, see the listing under Television Index.

42. Mediamatic Calendar of Special Editorial Issues

Media Distribution Services
307 W. 36 St., N.Y. 10018
$90 (annual subscription)

Introduced in 1972, the Mediamatic Calendar is a unique three-times-a-year compilation of the editorial subjects which major publications are planning to feature in forthcoming issues. If used carefully, this service can be an important placement aid. The name refers to the computerized media system of the publisher (the largest media and mailing services in the publicity field). The president is Hymen V. Wagner.

43. Medical and Science News Media

Larriston Communications
Box 20229, N.Y. 10025
$80

First published in 1982, this annual looseleaf directory provides data about health and science reporters at more than 300 daily newspapers, plus syndicates and other media. The price includes a midyear update.

Metro California Media

See listing under California Media.

Military Publications

See listing under College Alumni & Military Publications.

44. Minnesota Media Directory

Publicity Central
2100 Pillsbury Ave. S., Minneapolis, MN 55404
Twin Cities volume: $65
Minnesota volume: $90

Launched in 1984 by the Brum & Anderson public relations firm, the Minnesota Media Directory was acquired in 1986 by Publicity Central, which is owned by Padilla, Speer, Burdick & Beardsley. The books include media and just about everything you may want to know about the Twin Cities and elsewhere in Minnesota.

45. The National Directory of Magazines

Oxbridge Communications, Inc.
150 Fifth Ave., N.Y. 10011
Matthew Manning, Editor
$125

Launched in late 1987, The National Directory of Magazines is the most comprehensive collection of data about U.S. magazines. The 12,000 magazines are divided into 250 subject areas, with information about editorial, circulation, advertising, personnel, printing and other details. The 500-page 8½″ x 11″ softcover book also is available in computer printouts and tapes, index cards and mailing labels.

46. National Directory of Weekly Newspapers

National Newspaper Association
1627 K St., N.W., Wash., DC 20006
$35

Started in 1920, the National Directory of Weekly Newspapers is the ''advertising bible'' of weekly newspapers with rates and other data about 8,000 weekly, semiweekly and triweekly newspapers. Published by the National Newspaper Association in behalf of American Newspaper Representatives, Inc., the directory is uniquely useful for publicists because of the state maps which enable users to pinpoint the location of the newspapers.

Purchasers of the book may subscribe to Publishers' Auxiliary, the biweekly newspaper about weekly newspapers, for $32.

47. National Radio Publicity Outlets

Public Relations Plus, Inc.
Drawer 1197, New Milford, CT 06776
Harold Hansen, Editor
$159.50, including semi-annual revision

Started in 1971, National Radio Publicity Directory was the first directory exclusively devoted to radio talk-shows. The current edition has 6,800 network, syndicated and local interview programs. U.S. educational and non-commercial listings also are included. That's a lot of talk, and a big opportunity for publicists.

A six-month supplement is provided—actually a completely new edition—which comes as a completely new set of pages that can be inserted in the loose-leaf binder.

Originally published by Peter Glenn, this radio directory was acquired in 1985 by Public Relations Plus, which revised and expanded it.

48. National Survey of Newspapers Op. Ed. Pages

Communication Creativity
Box 213, Saguache, CO 81149
Marilyn Ross, Editor
$15 (plus $2 shipping)

Published in 1986, this unique 32-page guidebook describes the op-ed page policies (pay scale, word length, if writer must live in the area, subjects) of 170 newspapers, including the name of the editor of the editorial page or other appropriate editor.

49. New York Publicity Outlets

Public Relations Plus, Inc.
Drawer 1197, New Milford, CT 06776
Harold Hansen, Editor
$89.50

This spiral-bound 350-page book (first published in 1950) probably is found on the desks of more New York publicists than any other directory. Its success is deserved.

The names of department editors and others on the staffs of the major newspapers and magazines published in New York make this annual book a basic editorial guide. Included also are the names of key broadcasters and contacts at the syndicates and other media in the New York metropolitan area. A semi-annual revision edition keeps the book up-to-date, though most users pencil in their own additions and corrections throughout the year.

The enterprising Mr. Hansen also offers several inducements to subscribers, including a 20 percent reduction for orders of five or more copies (many agencies provide each account executive with a copy). The company, which also publishes other media directories, accepts telephone orders—(203) 354-9361.

50. News Bureaus
Larimi Communications Associates, Ltd.
5 W. 37 St., N.Y. 10018
$98

Published for the first time in 1970, this directory seems to fill a void among the many media aids. It is difficult to be completely objective about this book since the author is Richard Weiner. However, here are the pertinent facts. The unique book lists the names, addresses and phone numbers of the local, state capital, regional and national bureaus of major newspapers, magazines, business publications, wire services and syndicates, including all bureaus, in every state, of The Associated Press, United Press, Reuters, Dow Jones, Fairchild, McGraw-Hill, Copley, Newhouse and other news services. Broadcast media are not included.

The number of newspaper, wire service and magazine news bureaus is increasing and the bureau concept is more important than ever before.

The book includes a listing of bureaus in all major cities. Thus, all of the bureaus of The New York Times, for example, are described in the New York City section, and, in addition, each bureau is listed in the following city sections: Albany, Atlanta, Boston, Chicago, Dallas, Denver, Detroit, Houston, Los Angeles, Miami, Philadelphia, San Francisco, Seattle, Trenton and Washington, D.C.

In 1987, Larimi took over the publication from Public Relations Publishing Company. The new version is vastly expanded—over 500 pages in a three-ring looseleaf binder. New features include descriptions of the editorial needs of each bureau, names of specialized reporters at the bureau, and cross-indexing by city and name of publication.

Most important, the $98 price is for an annual subscription, which includes monthly updates plus a daily updating telephone service.

51. Newsletter Yearbook Directory
Box 311, 44 W. Market St., Rhinebeck, NY 12572
Howard Penn Hudson, Publisher
$90

Howard Hudson has operated for many years The Newsletter Clearinghouse, which provides consulting services to newsletter publishers, and, since 1969, has published the Newsletter on Newsletters. It thus was logical that, in 1977, Hudson launched The Newsletter Yearbook Directory. The sixth edition, published in 1986, lists about 3,400 newsletters in about 165 categories, with addresses, phone number, name of editor and publisher, frequency, subscription price, year founded, circulation and other data (where available—some newsletter publishers are extremely secretive). Text sections include material from the Newsletter on Newsletters.

The actual name of the book is Hudson's Yearbook Directory, but it's generally called by its original name.

The Newsletter on Newsletters, edited by Howard Penn Hudson, is available for $96 a year.

A Newsletter for Newsletters is published ten times a year ($49) by Poll & Erikson, Inc., 1200 S. Aldrich Ave., Minneapolis, MN 55405. Started in 1986. Nancy Erickson is publisher and Donn Poll is editor.

Another publication for editors of newsletters and other publications is Editors' Forum, published 11 times a year ($75) by William R. Brinton and Jay H. Lawrence, at Box 411806, Kansas City, MO 64141. The publication, which started in 1980 as Newsletter Forum, changed ownership and name in 1983.

52. Newsletters Directory

Gale Research Co.
Book Tower, Detroit 48226
Brigitte T. Darnay and John Nimchuk, Editors
$140

Previously called the National Directory of Newsletters and Reporting Services, the third edition of the Newsletters Directory, published in 1987, is vastly improved, with more entries (over 8,000), and in one 1,162-page volume.

Entries are arranged in seven broad categories comprising 31 subjects, with considerable information about each newsletter. Three indexes are arranged by title, publisher and subject. An appendix lists newsletters available online through such services as NewsNet.

The Gale directory is a magnificent reference source and is used by many librarians. It is a very difficult category to compile and none of the newsletter directories are as comprehensive or as up-to-date as other media directories. One of the reasons for this is that many newsletter publishers operate from their homes and other low overhead locations which change sporadically.

53. Oxbridge Directory of Newsletters

Oxbridge Communications, Inc.
150 Fifth Avenue, N.Y. 10011
$125

First published in 1972, this vastly expanded 400-page book lists over 13,000 newsletters in 200 categories. Most are not covered in any of the bibliographic tools concerned with the more conventional types of periodicals. This directory is concerned with the type of publication that is called by a variety of names: newsletter, bulletin, report, fact sheet, information service.

It's hard to keep up-to-date in the newsletter field. Very few accept advertising and therefore are not listed in advertising directories. Many have very small circulations and are not well known. Therefore, none of the newsletter directories are as accurate or comprehensive as other media directories. The other major directories in this field are Howard Hudson's Newsletter Yearbook Directory (described earlier in this chapter) and the Gale Newsletter Directory ($140), published by Gale Research Co. (described in the research chapter).

54. Party Line

PRA Information & Communications Group
330 W. 34 St., N.Y. 10001
Mrs. Betty Yarmon, Mgr. Ed.
$130 for an annual subscription

Party Line is not a directory, but is included in this section because it is devoted exclusively to "placement information and contact leads." This one-sheet weekly newsletter provides inside, advance information about what editors, broadcasters and freelance writers are looking for. Data about new publications, media changes and forthcoming special issues also are included, but the principal content is the terse, informative "contact" items.

Published by PRA, one of the world's largest publicity mailing services, Party Line is printed on white paper. The color probably should be gold because its content can be a goldmine for publicists.

55. Philadelphia Publicity Guide

Fund-Raising Institute
Box 365, Ambler, PA 19002
Cindy Joyce Speaker, Editor
$35.75

The full name of this annual directory is Greater Philadelphia Publicity Guide. With a population of two million, Philadelphia is the fourth largest city in the country. Though not known as a media center, the eight-county greater Philadelphia area has over 500 local publications and stations.

Started in 1967, and published in January, the Greater Philadelphia Publicity Guide has improved with each new edition, and it now is one of the most comprehensive local directories. Dozens of facts, more than in other directories, are provided about each publication, including an impressive section which lists the form in which publishers want advertising and news material submitted. Communities are indexed by name and ZIP code, showing the print media covering each area.

Several of the regional media directories, such as the Greater Philadelphia Publicity Guide, are labors of love. The Fund-Raising Institute proves its belief in its product with a money-back guarantee of satisfaction and an offer of a cash prize to the first person to alert them to a new medium.

The primary business of the publisher, the Fund-Raising Institute, is the publishing of a variety of materials for fund-raisers. Its first (started in 1962) was the FRI Monthly Portfolio, which now includes three sections: a newsletter, Letter Clinic and how-to-do-it bulletin. It's a bargain ($55 a year) and has subscribers all over the country.

The Fund-Faising Institute includes postage in its prices and provides Monthly Portfolio subscribers with a 10 percent discount for orders of three or more publications. In summary—a very well-run operation, and it has a 24-hour phone line, (215) 646-7019.

56. Radio Contacts

Larimi Communications Associates, Ltd.
5 W. 37 St., N.Y. 10018
Michael Smith, Publisher
$222

Annual, 1,300-page directory on local, network and syndicated radio programming. Over 4,000 station listings include network affiliation, news services, personnel, address and telephone numbers, program formats, locally produced programs, guest and information requirements, booking times and contact persons. Network and syndicate listings include personnel, addresses, detailed information on programs and information and guest usage, contact persons for guest placements and affiliate numbers. Four page "Monthly Change Bulletin" updates information on stations, networks and programs. Daily updating service available.

57. R&R Ratings Report and Directory

1930 Century Park West, L.A. 90067
$25

Audience ratings for every commercial radio station (over 1,500) in the 100 largest markets, with easy to understand charts of Arbitron ratings is the major feature of this semi-annual directory. Two issues per year, one published in April and the other in September, so that the most recent fall ratings are available in the April edition and the spring figures are available in the September edition. Other information useful to public relations practitioners and advertisers includes station formats and rankings within age and demographic groups.

The material is provided by Radio & Records, a trade publication.

58. Radio Programming Profile

BF/Communication Services, Inc.
300 S. Oyster Bay Rd., Syosset, NY 11791
Bill Fromm, Editor-in-Chief
$250 (each of two volumes)

This is the most comprehensive radio program directory. Volume One lists the complete program schedules of all (about 1,600) AM and FM radio stations in the top 70 markets, and Volume Two provides the logs of all (almost 1,500) stations in the second tier (markets 71 to 220). Each book is updated, with three editions annually, and costs $250 for an annual subscription. Thus, both services cost $500 with no discount. The service is dispensable for radio advertisers and extremely useful for publicists.

59. Rothman's Guide to Freelance Writers

WRTR Publishing Company
2115 4 St., Berkeley, CA 94710
$75

WRTR Publishing Company (founded in 1982 by freelance journalist Rita Rothman) publishes a unique directory with comprehensive information on 370 California-based freelance journalists and writers. Its 430 pages detail their subject specialties and publication credits, plus addresses and telephone numbers.

The market index cross-references their names into more than 900 local, regional, national and international publications. The subject index pinpoints over 350 topics.

60. The Serials Directory: An International Reference Book

EBSCO Publishing
Box 1943, Birmingham, AL 35201-1943
Emmy Carmichael, Gen. Mgr.
$289

Over 113,000 periodicals are described in this annual directory, which was launched in 1986. A subscription includes quarterly updates.

61. Southern California Media Directory

500 Van Nuys Blvd., #400, Sherman Oaks, CA 91403
$100

Started in 1965 by the Publicity Club of Los Angeles, as a combination membership and media directory, the book was expanded in 1987 and its name changed. The book includes print and broadcast media in Los Angeles and the surrounding counties. PCLA members pay only $50.

62. Standard Periodical Directory

Oxbridge Communications
150 Fifth Ave., N.Y. 10011
Patricia Hagood, Publisher
$295

Listings and descriptions of about 60,000 U.S. and Canadian publications (including 3,300 newspapers) make this 1,500-page annual directory more comprehensive than any other periodical source book.

The Standard Periodical Directory includes newsletters, house magazines and other special-interest publications which are not included in the Gale Directory, though Gale has more newspapers.

The 250 categories range from advertising to zoology and the cross-index—one of the most comprehensive of any directory—includes over 1,000 subjects.

In addition to the name and address of the publication, the Standard Periodical Directory includes a brief description of editorial content, name of editor, frequency, subscription rate, circulation and basic rate for a one-page, one-time, black-and-white advertisement.

Contact Oxbridge for a list of their other reference books, including the Directory of the College Student Press in America, or call Patricia Hagood, publisher, at (212) 741-0231, for costs of mailing lists of libraries and media.

63. Standard Rate & Data Service

Standard Rate & Data Service, Inc.
3004 Glenview Rd., Wilmette, IL 60091
Andrew Snider, Publisher

It is practically impossible for a national advertiser to function without one or more SRDS publications. Since more media data are included in the SRDS "catalogs" than any other directories, many publicists also find these magazines extremely useful.

SRDS publications are sold on an annual subscription basis:

Spot Radio Rates and Data (monthly)	$285
Spot Television Rates and Data (monthly	$260
Newspaper Rates and Data (monthly)	$338
Consumer Magazine & Agri Media Publication Rates and Data (monthly)	$336
Business Publication Rates and Data (monthly)	$374
Print Media Editorial Calendars (monthly)	$195
Canadian Advertising Rates and Data (monthly)	$199
Community Publication Rates and Data (semiannually)	$ 48
Print Media Production Data (quarterly)	$185
Direct Mail List Rates and Data (bimonthly)	$209
Newspaper Circulation Analysis (annually)	$ 93
Co-op Source Directory (semiannually)	$198
Radio Small Markets (semiannually)	$ 94

In 1987, SRDS introduced a directory of special use to public relations people. Called the SRDS Print Media Editorial Calendars, the monthly catalogs provide information about theme issues and special sections of newspapers, 4,200 business publications, 1,500 consumer magazines and 400 farm publications. Since the listings include names of editorial personnel, the catalogs can be used as basic media directories.

The publications are not listed all in one book, however. The newspapers directory is updated and published in March, June, September and December. The business publications directory is updated and published in February, May, August and September. The consumer magazines and farm publications directory is updated and published in January, April, July and October.

Thus, subscribers receive a different directory each month. An annual subscription is $195. Monthly update bulletins for the quarterly directories are available for an additional $50 a year.

International editions are published for the media in various countries. SRDS is a Macmillan company and has offices in London and elsewhere throughout the world.

Obviously, it is not necessary to subscribe to every SRDS publication, but every publicist should be familiar with the subjects covered in the different editions and have access to them via a public library, an advertising agency or another source.

In addition to every detail about advertising, circulation and production, the information also includes key personnel, closing dates, readership analyses and other editorial data.

SRDS subscribers receive a free monthly four-page newsletter, the SRDS Report, with helpful information and comments about media. Started in 1987, the newsletter is extremely useful to market researchers, media planners and buyers.

SRDS operates a mailing list service, called Target Media Group, which sells media lists for $48 per thousand names with a minimum order of $125. Nancy J. Olson is list sales manager.

Among the other advertising basic reference books published by the National Register Publishing Company, Inc., a subsidiary of Standard Rate & Data Service, is the Standard Directory of Advertisers, which is best known as ''The Advertiser Red Book.'' An annual subscription ($352) includes five supplements. The companion book, the Standard Directory of Advertising Agencies is called the Agency Red Book. It's $327 and also includes nine supplements.

In 1985, National Register introduced the Standard Directory of International Advertisers and Advertising Agencies ($177), with data about 1,000 advertisers and 1,000 agencies all in one book, indexed by country (over 60 countries).

64. Syndicated Columnists

Larimi Communications Associates, Ltd.
5 W. 37 St., N.Y. 10018
$120

Former newspaper columnists include Walter Winchell, Dorothy Kilgallen, Red Smith, Walter Lippmann, Ed Sullivan, Amy Vanderbilt, Leonard Lyons and Joseph Alsop—BUT syndicated columnists are far from a dying breed. Hundreds of syndicated columnists still appear in major newspapers, and Jack Anderson, Art Buchwald, Sylvia Porter, ''Abby,'' Marilyn Beck—to mention five completely different types of columnists—are among America's most widely read and influential writers.

Most publicists know this but generally do not work with syndicated columnists. One of the reasons for this is the difficulty in locating the columnist. Editor & Publisher issues an annual directory which is extremely useful but lists the addresses of the syndicates and not the individual columnists. Anderson, Buchwald, Porter, Abby and Beck, for example, do not work at the headquarters office of their syndicates and are not even in the same cities.

The editor of Syndicated Columnists is Richard Weiner, a media buff who also edits News Bureaus in the U.S. and other reference books, including this one.

In 1987, Larimi took over the publication of Syndicated Columnists and vastly expanded and updated it with data about 800 columnists, including types of subjects covered by the columnists.

The annual subscription includes monthly updates. Subscribers can call (800) 634-4020 for daily updates.

The frequency of a column, its size, format and other data are included in the Syndicate Directory which is part of the last weekly issue in July of Editor & Publisher. It is indispensable to publishers, publicists and anyone interested in newspaper syndicates. However, the only addresses in the pull-out section are those of the syndicates. The addresses of columnists are not listed, and this is the principal feature of the Syndicated Columnists Directory.

Publishers' Auxiliary, the biweekly newspaper of the weekly newspaper industry, also publishes a directory of syndicates, which appears in its first issue in August. This directory includes fewer syndicates and less data than in Editor & Publisher.

65. TV News

Larimi Communications Associates, Ltd.
5 W. 37 St., N.Y. 10018
Michael M. Smith, Publisher
$160

A unique annual directory with descriptions of the news departments of all commercial and public TV stations, including names of specialists to whom material should be sent, types of guests for interviews. Useful, hard-to-find information includes night/weekend news directors, bureau chiefs and specialist reporters.

TV Publicity Outlets-Nationwide

In 1986, this directory was expanded and its name changed to All-TV Publicity Outlets-Nationwide. It is described earlier in this chapter.

66. Television Contacts

Larimi Communications Associates, Ltd.
5 W. 37 St., N.Y. 10018
Michael M. Smith, Publisher
$217

Annual directory on national, syndicated and local television programs in the U.S. and Canada, including personnel, program description, booking times, contact person and other data. Four page "Monthly Change Bulletin" updates programs, personnel, editorial requirements and new shows. Daily updating service available.

67. Television & Cable Factbook

Television Digest, Inc.
1836 Jefferson Pl., N.W., Wash., DC 20036
Albert Warren, Editor and Publisher
$265 plus $10 shipping (soft cover, 2 vols.)

This huge (more than 3,200 pages) book (started in 1945) is the most comprehensive authoritative reference for the television industry in the United States. The publisher also issues the weekly Television Digest ($617 a year), and other publications which are used in the advertising, television, and electronics industries, and much of this data is compressed into the Television Factbook.

The principal item of public relations interest probably is the U.S. Television Station Directory, which lists rate digests, personnel, facilities, market maps, network affiliations and other data about every station in the country.

Other sections include information about color and black-and-white sets, national and regional networks, foreign TV stations and sets, independent program producers, research services and hundreds of companies and associations related to television. The Cable & Services volume lists cable systems, alphabetically by state and city.

68. Television Index, Inc.

40–29 27 St., Long Island City, NY 11101
Jerry Leichter, Editor

Every week since 1949, Jerry Leichter has published Media News Keys, a terse collection of extremely useful items about media. Formerly called Publicity Record, this "public relations service paper" crams a tremendous amount of information into its four pages. An annual subscription to Media News Keys is $100.

Network and local radio and television programs are included in the newsletter. This information, which includes a description of the program, name and phone number of the producer or other contact, also is available, as a separate service, on 3×5 index cards. The annual charge for the basic packet and monthly new listings and revisions is $35.

For anyone who works regularly in the broadcast publicity field, Media News Keys and the Radio-TV index cards are basic, indispensable tools.

The energetic Mr. Leichter also publishes Ross Reports ($31.50, a monthly guide for TV actors and writers), which lists program contacts on variety, dramatic and other programs not included in any other directory, and other television services, including:

Television Index: Weekly reports cover network television programming, major independent television production, sponsors, production news and performance records. Has been published weekly since 1949, $230.

Components of the Television Index Information Service can be purchased separately, including the TV Pro-Log ($40), a weekly newsletter on current and future TV production.

In summary, this small operation publishes excellent materials for advertisers, actors, models, publicists and others connected with media (primarily broadcast). Subscribers to Television Index are entitled to call (718) 937-3990 for special information, at no charge.

69. TIA International Travel News Directory

Travel Industry Association of America
1133 21 St. N.W., Wash., DC 20036
$35

This volume lists over 1,000 travel editors, media and sources in the US and 40 other countries and is vital for anyone who regularly works in this field. Association members pay only $20. The book previously was called the Travel News and Publicity Directory, and was published by Discover America Travel Organizations, Inc., which changed its name in 1980 to TIA. Mailing labels are $50.

70. Trade Media News

Larimi Communications Associates, Ltd.
5 W. 37 St., N.Y. 10018
Michael M. Smith, Publisher
$131/year

Launched in 1978, Trade Media News is a semimonthly four-page newsletter with data about new publications, personnel changes, editorial requirements, upcoming special issues and other data about trade, business and professional publications.

Some of the data are included in other publications, including Larimi's Contacts, Bacon's Directory and Media Distribution Services' Calendar of Special Editorial Issues.

71. Travel, Leisure and Entertainment News Media

Larriston Communications
Box 20229, N.Y. 10025
$80

First published in 1986, this annual looseleaf directory provides data about travel, entertainment and related editors and writers at more than 300 daily newspapers, plus syndicates and other media. The price includes a midyear update.

72. Ulrich's International Periodicals Directory

R. R. Bowker Company
245 W. 17 St. N.Y. 10011
$159.95

As a major publisher of books and periodicals (Library Journal and Publishers Weekly, among others) for the professional book world, R. R. Bowker is in a good position to issue a directory in what probably is the most complicated media field—foreign periodicals. Ulrich's International Periodicals Directory lists all types of publications which are issued anywhere from twice a year to five days a week.

Additional information about Bowker is included in the company's listings in the research chapter.

The format and scope of Ulrich's has changed considerably since its first appearance in 1932. Though U.S. publications are now included, the unique value of Ulrich's is its listings and descriptions of foreign periodicals. Each directory entry provides the same complete details that distinguished the original Ulrich's: price (in currency of country of origin, if foreign, with U.S. rate); frequency of issue; whether it is abstracted or indexed in one of the cumulative services; date of origin; circulation figures; whether advertisements are accepted; name of editor, publisher and address; whether the text is in more than one language, and if so, which.

In 1967, Bowker introduced a media reference book which extends the information provided by Ulrich's and records, for the first time, hard-to-locate information about more than 34,500 publications which are issued irregularly or less frequently than twice a year, such as yearbooks, annual and biennial reviews. Titled Irregular Serials and Annuals: An International Directory, the book includes bibliographic and buying information about periodical supplements, reports and other business and professional publications which often are elusive. The directory can be obtained for $159.95 from Bowker Company.

The Bowker International Serials Database Update, formerly Ulrich's Quarterly, is an updating service ($75) to Ulrich's International Periodicals and Irregular Serials and Annuals.

If you're a librarian or in the publishing industry, you may want the entire Ulrich family. If you're a publicist with international business, the key book is Ulrich's International Periodicals Directory.

Among the foreign press directories, the publications of most likely interest to U.S. publicists are International Publicity Checker (described in the section on Bacon's Publicity Checker) and PR Planner, a comprehensive guide to British consumer and trade publications, which lists the business, women's and other editors of every daily newspaper in the United Kingdom. The 400-page loose-leaf book can be obtained ($140) from Media Information Ltd., 290 Green Lanes, London N13 5TP, and from Bacon's, 332 S. Michigan Ave., Chicago 60604.

The World Media To-Day was published in 1985 by Les Temps Medias, 55 rue d'Amsterdam, 75008 Paris, France. The 250-page book ($69) has advertising and editorial data about 1,300 publications, including data not found in Bacon's or Ulrich's. However, the number of publications is relatively small—200 in the U.S. and Canada, 655 in Europe and similarly elsewhere.

73. Vermont Media Directory
Kelliher/Samets Marketing Communications
138 S. Willard St., Burlington, VT 05401
$89

Though Vermont is one of America's smallest states, there may come a time when you have a special campaign in this state. If so, you'll want to know about a 129-page annual directory of *all* media in Vermont.

74. Washington
Columbia Books, Inc.
1350 New York Ave., Wash., DC 20005
Craig Colgate Jr., Publisher
$50

Started in 1966, this annual book has become a useful companion to the Congressional Directory and other reference guides to U.S. Government agencies and is unique in its listings of 16,000 key individuals in governmental and community organizations within the Metropolitan Washington area, including 3,400 businesses, unions, associations, national public interest groups and representatives of international, national and local press, radio and television.

Prior to 1984, it was published by Potomac Books. Other publications of Columbia Books are described in the company's listing in the research chapter.

75. Westchester Media Directory
Rodwick Communications Service
33 S. Broadway, Yonkers, NY 10701
Alan W. Kravath
$4.95

This booklet provides information about all daily and weekly newspapers, radio stations and cable TV systems in Westchester county, which is adjacent to New York City. The most important medium is the Gannett-Westchester Group, headquartered at the White Plains Reporter-Dispatch.

Formed in 1979, Rodwick Communications Service produces newsletters, exhibits, advertising and public relations materials.

76. Willings Press Guide
British Media Publications
Windsor Court, East Grinstead House, East Grinstead
West Sussex, England RH19 1XE
$115, plus $5 postage

First published in 1874, this grandfather of media directories gets bigger and better every year. Primarily for the United Kingdom, the current edition has information about over 11,000 British publications, plus about 10,000 publications elsewhere (about 5,000 in Europe). A key feature in this annual 1,400-page book is a listing of about 2,700 companies that promote services to media and public relations people.

Willings is available in the U.S. from Business Press International (formerly IPC Business Press), 205 E. 42 St., N.Y. 10017.

British Media Publications also publishes several advertising reference books.

Other lists can be obtained from the Foreign Press Association, 18 E. 50 St., N.Y. 10017; United Nations Correspondents Association, United Nations, N.Y. 10017, and Office of Press Relations, Department of State, Wash., DC 20520.

Women's Page Directory
Now called Family Page Directory, see listing earlier in this chapter.

77. Working Press of the Nation
The National Research Bureau, Inc.
310 S. Michigan Ave., Chicago 60604
Sally A. Folkes, Marketing Mgr.
$260 for 5 volumes

Starting in 1946 with one volume of newspaper personnel, Working Press now has grown to five volumes covering print and broadcast media. The company offers a unique bonus, which is a free mailing list (for one-time use) of up to 2,000 names provided to purchasers of at least three of the five volumes. It's possible to buy individual volumes of Working Press for $115 each, or volumes 1, 2 & 3 only for $215. It's also offered on a 30-day free trial basis.

Volume I. Newspaper Directory

The directory includes the names of over 61,000 editors at all daily newspapers, arranged by state and by subjects or departments.

Also included are data about over 5,000 weekly newspapers (more than 3,000 circulation), college, special-interest and foreign-language newspapers, and national and local newspaper supplements and television sections and their personnel.

Syndicates and news services, formerly included in Volume IV, are now listed in this volume.

Volume II. Magazine Directory

Data about 5,400 U.S. trade, consumer, farm, religious and other magazines, including use of by-lined articles, photos, letters to the editor, payment policies for purchased material, charge policies for handling of publicity, readership and editorial analysis, as well as personnel, address, phone number and other details.

Volume III. TV and Radio Directory

Key executives and personnel of over 25,000 programs on over 10,400 TV and radio stations.

Volume IV. Feature Writer and Photographer Directory

This volume lists over 1,900 feature writers and photographers, indexed by subject specialties, including name, address, subject areas of interest and publications that have accepted their work.

Volume V. Internal Publications

Internal Publications Directory was added to the Working Press of the Nation Directories in 1977. This 300-page volume, formerly called the Gebbie House Magazine Directory, lists over 2,800 internal communications publications, with a total circulation estimated at 180,000,000. Included are the companies, clubs, Government agencies and other U.S. and Canadian groups which sponsor them, along with publication titles, addresses, editors, circulation, mechanical information and types of editorial material requested.

78. Writer's Digest

1507 Dana Ave., Cincinnati, OH 45207
Robert Gervasi, Publisher

The largest circulation (220,000) magazine for aspiring and current writers, Writer's Digest is a relatively untapped source of media news for publicists. Included each month are descriptions of many new and offbeat magazines and detailed descriptions of the editorial needs of magazine and book editors. An annual subscription to the monthly magazine is only $21. A special newsstand annual, called Writer's Yearbook, is $2.95, and the annual directory, Writer's Market, is $21.95.

Started in 1930, Writer's Market has become one of the basic books in the publishing field.

Other annual directories patterned after Writer's Market are Photographer's Market, $18.95; Poet's Market, $17.95; Artist's Market, $18.95; Songwriter's Market, $16.95; Summer Employment Directory of the U.S., $9.95; and Internships, $18.95.

The Writer's Directory, a Who's Who-type book with about 16,000 authors from the U.S., Canada, United Kingdom and British Commonwealth, is available for $85 from St. James Press, 425 N. Michigan Ave., Chicago 60611.

79. The Writer's Handbook

The Writer, Inc.
120 Boylston St., Boston, MA 02116
Sylvia K. Burack, Editor
$25.95

More than 100 chapters of advice to beginning and established freelance writers is included in this 800-page annual volume. The chief value to publicists is the listing of more than 2,200 markets for manuscript sales. This section is helpful to anyone interested in learning what publishers are buying, whether you desire to sell or give away a manuscript. Sometimes a publicist can do better by offering an idea, article or book for sale, directly or via a literary agent, rather than trying to give it away free.

The list of markets is based on material from the monthly magazine, The Writer ($20 a year, from the same publisher), the oldest magazine in this field. Founded in 1887, The Writer, Inc. publishes about 20 books for writers.

Though not media directories, three very useful public relations reference books are published by the J. R. O'Dwyer Company, 271 Madison Ave., N.Y. 10016. Under the astute direction of Jack O'Dwyer, the company publishes O'Dwyer's Directory of Corporate Communications (PR departments profiled at 3,000 large companies and 500 trade associations), $90; O'Dwyer's Directory of Public Relations Firms (annual publication started in 1969), data on 1,700 PR firms, $90, and O'Dwyer's Directory of Public Relations Executives, biographies of 4,800 public relations executives, $70, published every third year.

A bibliography of public relations reference books can be obtained from the Public Relations Society of America, 33 Irving Pl., N.Y. 10003.

Following is a list of names, addresses and annual subscription costs of newsletters and magazines in the public relations and communications field. In addition to news about media, these publications include a variety of case histories and other useful information. Descriptions of many of these publications are included in the book, Professional's Guide to Publicity (Public Relations Publishing Co.).

PUBLIC RELATIONS AND COMMUNICATIONS PERIODICALS

AD/PR Agency Report, Box 715, Kentfield, CA 94914, $54
Adweek, 49 E. 21 St., N.Y. 10010, $60
Advertising Age, 740 Rush St., Chicago 60611, $59
The Bottom Line Communicator, 407 S. Dearborn St., Chicago 60605, $49
Broadcasting, 1705 De Sales St., N.W., Wash., DC 20036, $105
Bulldog, The InterCom Group, 2115 4 St., Berkeley, CA 94710, $177
Channels, PR Publishing Co., Box 600, Exeter, NH 03833, $40
Columbia Journalism Review, 700 Journalism Bldg., Columbia Univ., N.Y. 10027, $18
Communications Briefings, 140 S. Broadway, Pitman, NJ 08071, $59
Communications Concepts, 2100 Ntl. Press Bldg., Wash., DC 20045, $97
Communications Week, 600 Community Dr., Manhasset, NY 11030, $65
Community Relations Report, Box 924, Bartlesville, OK 74005, $127
Contacts, Larimi Communications., 5 W. 37 St., N.Y. 10018, $237
Corporate Annual Report Newsletter, 407 S. Dearborn St., Chicago 60605, $197
Corporate Communications Report, 112 E. 31 St., N.Y. 10016, $75
Corporate Public Issues, 219 South St., S.E., Leesburg, VA 22075, $175
The Corporate Shareholder, 230 W. 41 St., N.Y. 10036, $195
Editor & Publisher, 11 W. 19 St., N.Y. 10011, $60
The Editorial Eye, 85 S. Bragg St., Alexandria, VA 22312, $49
Editors' Forum, Box 411806, Kansas City, MO 64141, $75
Editor's Workshop Newsletter, 407 S. Dearborn St., Chicago 60605, $69
The Gallagher Report, 230 Park Ave., N.Y. 10017, $150
High Technology PR News, InterCom Group, 2115 4th St., Berkeley, CA 94710, $245

Hope Reports Briefing, 1600 Lyell Ave., Rochester, NY 14606, $105

Hospital Public Relations Advisor, 1600 Research Blvd., Rockville, MD 20850, $80

IABC Communication World, 870 Market St., San Francisco, CA 94102 (for IABC members), $48

Impact, Box 1896, Evanston, IL 60204, $27

Jack O'Dwyer's Newsletter, 271 Madison Ave., N.Y. 10016, $150

Journal of Communication, Box 13358, Philadelphia 19101, $22

Journalism Quarterly, Association for Education in Journalism and Mass Communication, 1621 College St., Columbia, SC 29208, $35

The Maranto Memo, Box 429, Wilton, CT 06897, $84

MediaFile, Media Alliance, Fort Mason Center Bldg. D, San Francisco 94123, $40

Media Industry Newsletter, 145 E. 49 St., N.Y. 10017, $195

Media News Keys, 40-29 27 St., Long Island City, NY 11101, $100

Media Watch, Gregory Communications, 117 E. Colorado Blvd., Ste. 400, Pasadena, CA 91105, $95

Medical Advertising News, 820 Bear Tavern Rd., W. Trenton, NJ 08628, $50

A Newsletter for Newsletters, Poll Communications Group, 2000 S. Aldrich Ave., Minneapolis, MN 55405, $49

Newsletter on Newsletters, Box 311, Rhinebeck, NY 12572, $96

O'Dwyer's PRServices, 271 Madison Ave., NY 10016, $30

Party Line, 330 W. 34 St., N.Y. 10001, $130

Presstime, American Newspaper Publishers Association, Box 17407, Wash., D.C. 20041, $100

pr reporter, Box 600, Exeter, NH 03833, $145

PR Strategies, 1851A Lawrence Ave. E., Scarborough, Ont. M1R 2Y3, $75

Public Relations Journal, 33 Irving Pl, N.Y. 10003, $32

Public Relations News, 127 E. 80 St., N.Y. 10021, $237

Public Relations Quarterly, 44 W. Market St., Rhinebeck, NY 12572, $20

Public Relations Review, 10606 Mantz Rd., Silver Springs, MD 20903, $33

Publisher's Auxiliary, 1627 K St., N.W., Wash., DC 20006, $25

Publisher's Weekly, 249 W. 17 St., N.Y. 10011, $78

The Quill, 53 W. Jackson Blvd., Suite 731, Chicago IL 60604-3610, $18

The Ragan Report, Lawrence Ragan Communications, Inc., 407 S. Dearborn St., Chicago 60605, $139

Radio Contacts, Larimi Communications, 5 W. 37 St., N.Y. 10018, $229

Social Science Monitor, Communication Research Associates, 10606 Mantz Rd., Silver Springs, MD 20903, $95

The Speechwriter's Newsletter, 407 S. Dearborn St., Chicago 60605, $158

Television Contacts, Larimi Communications., 5 W. 37 St., NY 10018, $233

TJFR, The Journalist & Financial Reporting, 605 W. 112 St., Apt. 4E, N.Y. 10025, $520

TV News, Larimi Communications, 5 W. 37 St., NY 10018, $172

Video Monitor, 10606 Mantz Rd., Silver Springs, MD 20903, $98

WJR Washington Journalism Review, 2233 Wisconsin Ave., N.W., Wash., DC 20007, $22

Writer's Digest, 1507 Dana Ave., Cincinnati 45207, $21

The Writer, 120 Boylston St., Boston 02116, $17

Outside of the U.S., the largest-circulation public relations publication is PR Week, which is published by Rangenine Limited, 100 Fleet St., London EC4Y 1DE.

Chapter 14

Messengers and Air Couriers

There are some things in the public relations field that can be done leisurely, but very few. Whether or not it is justified, there often is a sense of crisis which requires, among other things, rapid delivery of a variety of items. As a result, public relations people and those in related fields, particularly advertising, journalism and entertainment, probably are the largest users of messenger services.

Every client has a favorite messenger story. For example, a group of executives in a New York hotel room probably will never forget that priceless moment at a meeting when they were awaiting an envelope sent by messenger from an accounting office located ten blocks away. After several frantic telephone calls, it was ascertained that the messenger had picked up the envelope at 5 P.M. About 6:30 P.M., a disheveled, feeble-looking old man wandered into the anxiety-ridden room with the greeting, "I'm Speedy."

Whether the messenger service is called Speedy, Mercury, Rapid, Rush, or has some other efficient-sounding adjective in its name, the fact of life with regard to messenger services is that their employees are not Olympic runners. Messenger services do provide an extremely efficient and economical means of picking up and delivering material, however, and the occasional mishap becomes anecdotal, particularly with the passage of time.

One of the delightful names is Heaven Sent Couriers, 53 N. Second St., Philadelphia 19106, phone (215) 923-0929, a specialist in servicing Philadelphia, Baltimore, New York and Washington, DC.

Another offbeat name is Cohen is Goin, a low-cost service in Manhattan, headquartered out of the midtown area at 350 W. 71 St., N.Y. 10023, phone (212) 496-2512.

Every large city has a number of messenger services, and the rate schedule and manner of operation is quite similar, in spite of the claims of those companies which suggest unique facilities and personnel.

Incidentally, there are a few conglomerates in the messenger field. You may fire one service and hire another and not be aware that both are owned by the same company—and use the same personnel. The same situation applies to telephone-answering services.

In cities such as New York, Chicago and Los Angeles, there are messenger services which specialize in communications accounts and offer immediate (relatively immediate, that is) service between publicist and the media, as well as other pickup and delivery points serviced through the day and night.

Messenger delivery generally is better if you are located in mid-Manhattan, Chicago's Loop or other central downtown area. Each messenger service has its own zone schedule. In Manhattan, the central base zone for most messenger services is 34th to 59th Streets, river to river. You generally can expect regular delivery on a non-rain day in the base zone within an hour, and sometimes can obtain "rush" delivery within one-half hour.

Most messenger services generally allow for 15 minutes of waiting time, and then charge for each additional 15 minutes. Extra charges generally relate to weight, pickups before 8 A.M., or after 5:30 P.M. and type of vehicle. Service on foot or bicycle generally is handled within the basic rate, whereas motorcycles (for faster service) and trucks (for heavier packages) are at higher rates. In many cities, a few messenger services maintain motorcycles for airport pickups and deliveries. For example, the charge for pickup or delivery from Manhattan to LaGuardia Airport is about $25 and the charge to Kennedy or Newark airports is about $30.

In large cities, there is rarely a flat fee, but rather the rates depend on distance and time. "Rush service" sometimes is available at premium rates. What this premium service means depends on the company. For example, it can mean the use of a taxicab or the messenger service's own vehicle instead of public transportation. It can also mean the routing of a messenger from the pickup point directly to the delivery point, instead of dropping off the shipment at an intermediate depot. One of the largest messenger services in New York, for example, operates 15 branch offices in the city, which can serve to expedite or delay shipments, depending on the distance and type of service.

A few messenger companies microfilm their records and often can provide fast confirmation of the delivery of your material.

One of the largest on-ground courier messenger services is Choice Courier, 2 Park Ave., N.Y. 10016, phone (212) 683-6411. Formed in 1952, Choice has 14 offices in Boston, Philadelphia, Washington, DC and other cities. In 1986, Choice acquired Copy Clearing House, a messenger service that specializes in media.

A messenger service which specializes in airport pickups and deliveries is Airline Delivery Services, 60 E. 42 St., N.Y. 10017, phone (212) 687-5145, telex 17745. Frank Chivsano is V.P. The company has a branch office at 175 Main Street, White Plains, NY 10609, phone (914) 428-7909. Same day service from Manhattan to White Plains is $24, and overnight service is $14.

Another airport specialist is Martti's Air Cargo, 67-49A 192 St., Fresh Meadows, NY 11365, phone (212) 454-2524. The proprietor is Marty Rye.

No matter how well-organized an executive is, it seems that there is a continuing need for messenger service. This need usually is greatest toward the end of the day, with the greatest rush often on Fridays after 4 P.M. Because of the irregularity in messenger workload, large users of messengers usually have found that it is more efficient and economical to use an outside service instead of maintaining their own staffs.

Many large users of messengers have telephone tie lines to one or more messenger services, and have worked out systems for bunching up pickups and deliveries and effecting other economies and efficiencies.

Rate schedules vary considerably according to the distance, time of day, use of premium, or other special services. A good rule of thumb is to figure that a pickup and delivery will cost about $7 plus carfare or other out-of-pocket transportation costs. Waiting time, out-of-town trips, bulk and truck delivery, and other special situations entail extra charges.

Extra charges for *any* service can be an irritating problem, if they are unexpected and not provided for in the budget. For example, Mobile Messenger Service, 443 W. 54 St., N.Y. 10019, phone (212) 247-7400, provides low-cost speedy service via bicycles, motorcycles and trucks. Its rate schedule is by zone, with the base zone (34th to 59th Streets) $6 for a pickup and delivery. Other zones cost more, ranging from $7 to $10 in lower Manhattan and $7 to $11 in upper Manhattan. More important, here is Mobile's schedule of extra charges:

Rush service . . . . $3.
Oversize or over 15 lbs. $3.
Wrong address . . . . $3.

Waiting (over 15 minutes) $1.50/5 minutes
Night rates .... $3./hr after 5:30 P.M.

In Washington, DC, the Chittenden Press Service in the National Press Building specializes in the pickup and delivery of news releases and other materials to several hundred Government agencies and news bureaus. Telephone David Chittenden at (202) 737-4434 for details of various unique services, including distribution of 450 copies of a news release to the media.

Daily delivery of news releases from the House and Senate press galleries and delivery of releases to members of Congress and the Senate are among the special services of Chittenden and a few other messenger services in the Capital. Chittenden also delivers and mails the Congressional Record and the Federal Register.

For out-of-town shipments of envelopes, publications, cans of film and other small parcels, you can save a lot of time and money by using the terminal-to-terminal package express services of Greyhound and other bus companies. Greyhound, for example, operates around-the-clock, every day including weekends and holidays, to about 25,000 towns and cities. Hourly departures on such routes as New York to Philadelphia, Los Angeles to San Diego, and Chicago to Milwaukee, enable parcels to be shipped in just a few hours at rates of less than $10.

There's also railroad delivery. Amtrak offers special parcel services on some routes.

A few messenger services provide same-day delivery of packages between major cities at extremely low rates. For example, downtown New York to downtown Philadelphia costs $12 from Egbert Messenger Service, 500 8th Ave., N.Y. 10018, phone (212) 947-1750.

Archer Services, Inc., 855 Avenue of the Americas, N.Y. 10001, phone (212) 563-8800, has offices in New York, Connecticut, Virginia, Illinois, California and Washington, DC, and averages over 10,000 deliveries a day.

Other messenger services also have hooked into national truck-air carrier systems which guarantee same-day or overnight delivery, or you can deal directly with the carriers.

In the '70's, Federal Express shook up the industry with its own fleet of trucks and planes and a system of centralizing shipments in the middle of the night at its headquarters airport in Memphis, Tennessee. Federal's toll free number is (800) 238-5355.

Today, the hub system is utilized by many of the air freight carriers and also by the passenger airlines. For example, Airborne has its hub in Wilmington, Ohio.

Since 1980, competition has increased dramatically among the carriers and though off-the-shelf rates of air express have gone up since the initial bargain rates, discounts have deepened, particularly among volume shippers. Furthermore, each of the major companies provide an array of services, so that in some cases bargains can be obtained for light-weight envelopes with one carrier and heavier parcels with another carrier. Each of the major carriers has tremendously expanded its operations. For example, Airborne owns over 26 aircrafts and leases many others, and also has about 1,400 delivery vehicles. The company was formed in 1968 via a merger of Airborne Freight Corporation of California and Pacific Air Freight of Seattle. Both of these companies had routes in the late forties when the post-war boom created a demand for perishable, time-sensitive goods.

Most major airlines provide priority package delivery service (TWA calls it "Next Flight Out"), but you, or a messenger service, must bring the parcel to the passenger check-in counter at the airport, and the recipient or representative must pick it up at the baggage claim area.

United Parcel Service provides Blue Label Air service, which costs less than the post office, Greynound, Federal Express or other carriers. However, Saturday delivery is not available and service generally takes two days, rather than overnight. Emery, Airborne, Federal, Purolator and others delivery on Saturday, but generally charge extra.

Most public relations customers rely heavily on messenger and priority air express services, but are unfamiliar with the details. For example, so-called bonded local messengers generally are insured only up to $100 per parcel. The maximum declared value varies considerably among the major air services. It's $25,000 at Federal Express, from $500 to $300,000 at Emery Air Freight and $25,000 at Airborne for its Express Pack.

Locally, publicists rely on messenger services for the rapid delivery of news releases and other communications to the media, clients and others. However, many large messenger services also offer the use of their personnel for sampling and participation in promotions. An imaginative public relations client can work with a messenger service on an hourly, daily or weekly basis involving the use of messengers who are costumed in accordance with the requirements of the specific promotion.

Several national organizations specialize in the use of temporary personnel who can deliver samples or other items as part of special promotions, and even deliver a "sales pitch." The largest of these companies are Manpower and its subsidiary company, Salespower, and also Kelly Girl, all of which have offices in many cities throughout the country.

One of the most efficient is TempsAmerica, which is headquartered at 41 E. 42 Street, N.Y. 10017, phone (212) 286-0180. The company was purchased by its president, Richard Ross, from the Colonial Penn Group in 1984, which had operated it since 1969 as Mature Temps.

The fastest delivery of printed material (less than three minutes a page) can be obtained via a local or long distance telephone call, using facsimile equipment. The major suppliers of two-way (transmission via a scanner and receiving via a recorder) facsimile equipment are Xerox Corp. (the Telecopier), 3M, and Fujitsu. These companies have sales and service offices in major cities. You can buy or lease the equipment and then pay the regular telephone charges for the time the equipment is in use. It's a fabulous innovation in communications, and the only limitation is that the sender and receiver must have this special equipment.

Telephone facsimile equipment now is almost as common in public relations offices as photocopying machines. However, if you or the intended recipient do not have this equipment, you can use (for a small fee) the Xerox central office in many cities. Several messenger services (including Copy Clearing House, 274 Madison Ave., N.Y. 10016) also provide facsimile transmission.

Incidentally, Fax, Magnafax, Telecopier and other brands are compatible with each other. Information about these companies is included in the chapter on telephone communications.

Messenger services are particularly useful in picking up current and back issues of publications. In New York, Dependable Delivery, Inc., 360 W. 52 St., phone (212) 586-5552, specializes in tracking down hard-to-find back issues.

In summary, messenger service is a vital part of the communications business. There are many alternatives, such as mail, telephone facsimile transmission, Teletype, Western Union Telegrams and Mailgrams, but there's hardly a day which goes by without the need for a messenger to deliver a news release or other public relations material.

Among the frustrating problems of the messenger business, there's not too much you can do about rush-hour traffic jams, but there are at least eleven ways to obtain more efficient and economical use of messenger services.

1. Try to plan pickups early in the day for faster service and to avoid time-and-a half and double rates which generally are charged after 6 P.M. and on weekends.
2. Ask about reduced rates for nonrush calls before 2 P.M. Several messenger services offer lower rates and other incentives to obtain morning business.
3. Call for a messenger while the news release (or whatever the item) is being typed to minimize any delay in pickup.
4. Write the envelope or delivery instructions completely and legibly. Include floor, delivery entrance, or other information which can save precious minutes.

5. Alert the recipient about the anticipated delivery. Items sometimes are delivered within minutes but then are "lost" in the mailroom or receiving point while the addressee fumes about the lack of delivery.
6. Request direct delivery or other individual special delivery, including use of a taxicab or other special routing, but don't use extra-charge services if they really are not needed.
7. In a true emergency, consider other means of delivery such as the use of your secretary. Occasionally, you might try delivering an envelope yourself, in order to see how long it really takes to go from East 59th Street to West 43rd Street in Manhattan at 5:30 P.M.
8. Find out if your messenger service operates at night and on weekends. Some companies do not charge extra for service on Saturdays.
9. Find out about messenger services in New York, Chicago, Los Angeles and elsewhere which make scheduled trips to airports and do not charge extra for these and other long-distance trips.
10. Maintain a list of messenger service phone numbers, particularly those which are in the two preceding categories, in your wallet and at home. Be prepared!
11. And, finally, consider the use of courier firms for rush shipments of important items.

The overnight courier services are so efficient and economical that many clients use them routinely—*even for local delivery*. The term Fed-ex is almost generic, which may or may not please Federal Express.

Public relations practitioners generally are not familiar with the complicated procedures involved in picking up shipments from foreign countries and sending items of commercial value outside the United States. Several of the overnight courier companies handle all documentation, for an additional charge. For example, shipments to Canada which have a commercial value require a commercial invoice attached to the airbill together with a Canada Custom invoice and also a shipper's export declaration (U.S. customs form 7525) if the item is in excess of $640, in the case of Federal Express. The amount varies. With DHL and Purolator, the form is required if the value is in excess of $1,000. "No commercial value" packages simply require an ordinary airbill.

The overnight courier companies now are one of the most frequently used services in the public relations field. They are extraordinarily efficient (though not 100 percent infallible) and their fees are amazingly low.

Companies located in major office buildings enjoy such conveniences as evening pickups (as late as 8 P.M. for delivery the next morning). Federal Express and other companies now have storefront depots throughout Manhattan, Chicago's Loop and elsewhere, and even have easy-to-operate bins in many lobbies of office buildings.

Just about everyone now is familiar with the routing service companies which have proliferated in the long distance telephone business since the breakup and deregulation of AT&T. The same thing has happened on a smaller level in the courier business.

A few companies now provide this special type of routing service. Here is the way they generally operate.

The company, which has its own trucks, picks up all types of parcels from the customer, and brings them to its offices (generally near an airport). Then, depending on the size, and type of shipment destination and other factors, the item is delivered to one of several carriers, such as United Parcel Service, Federal Express or Purolator. In most cases, the "broker" does a large volume of business and gets volume discounts from the carriers. Thus, the customer generally pays the same as the regular price of the carrier. In some cases, some of the volume savings may be passed on to the customer.

A major use of the broker, however, is the selection of the best possible carrier, and also the convenience of a single pickup and a single invoice. Another advantage is the expertise of the broker with international pickups and deliveries, which often requires customs clearances, special forms and has other complications.

In New York, a highly regarded company which operates in this way is Bradish, 10-47 48 Ave., Long Island City 11101, phone (718) 706-0206 and (212) 936-7070.

Formed in the 1940's by John Bradish, the company is now run by the family's third generation. Michel Bayan is executive vice president.

Following is information about the major air courier companies. Each has its bargains and special features. All of them are superb examples of American business at its best. Prices are included as a basis of comparison, though, as with all prices, they are subject to change.

Note: The air courier services generally will not deliver to a post office box, so be sure to include the street address. In most cases, their personnel also will not deliver if the office (or other addressee) is closed and no one is available to accept the item and sign for it. So make arrangements with the recipient (such as alerting a neighbor or doorman, particularly for Saturday deliveries).

1. Airborne Freight Corporation
3101 Western Ave., Seattle, WA 98121
(206) 285-4600, (800) 426-2323
Telex: 32-9543
Kent Freudenberger, Exec. V.P., Marketing Div.

Formed in 1956, Airborne now has over 4,000 employees and is one of the world's largest air express companies. In 1981, the company opened a centralized sorting center at its own airport in Wilmington, Ohio.

Next day service is available to several thousand cities, with morning delivery in major markets and afternoon delivery in smaller cities. Regular customers are provided with a variety of specially designed corrugated boxes and tear-proof water-resistant envelopes, including Express Pack boxes, envelopes and tubes, Letter Express Envelopes (holds up to 15 sheets of unfolded 8½ × 11 sheets), Magnetic Tape Pack Box and padded Ad Pack Envelope (cushioned foam lining, 10½ × 16 inch size accommodates unfolded large sheets).

2. CitiPostal Inc.
421 Seventh Ave., N.Y. 10001
(212) 279-4300
Donald G. Smith, Sr. V.P. Sales

Formerly called Sky Courier Network, Inc. (headquartered in Reston, VA), CitiPostal provides same day and overnight courier services in many major cities.

3. DHL Worldwide Express
333 Twin Dolphin Dr., Redwood City, CA 94065
(415) 593-7474
Charles Lynch, Pres.

DHL Worldwide Express which operates within the United States and its territories, and DHL International, Ltd., which services locations elsewhere, comprise the DHL Corporation, one of the world's largest companies in the air express field. DHL probably has the largest international network, and it is renowned for its service, provided by a staff of about 3,000 individuals, and its fleet of planes, helicopters and trucks. The DHL catalogue provides details of its services to 25,000 communities in the United States and over 20,000 international communities, from Angola to Zimbabwe. The colorful catalogue is a delight, as it includes the flags of such countries as Botswana, Guinea Bissau, Lesotho, Maldives and Tonga. If you are familiar with these countries, then you can get a job with DHL or the United Nations. Of course, DHL also services Canada, England, Japan and other well-known countries, as well as all 50 states.

4. Emery Worldwide

Old Danbury Rd., Wilton, CT 06897
(800) 443-6379
Barbara C. Graves, Mgr. Communications

Emery is one of the largest and oldest companies in the overnight delivery field, particularly in packages in excess of 70 pounds. The company's hub-and-spoke air cargo system at Dayton (Ohio) International Airport handles all types of shipments, ranging from letters and envelopes to small packages to heavyweight cargo. The company also operates hubs in Manchester, England and Maastricht, Holland.

At Emery, the familiar red and white envelopes (the five-ounce Emery Urgent Letter, and two-pound Urgent envelope) are available for same day or next morning delivery and delivery on the second morning (at substantial savings).

5. Federal Express Corporation

Box 727, Memphis, TN 38194
(800) 238-5355
James E. Coleman, Mng. Dir. Public Relations

To many, Federal Express is synonomous with overnight delivery. Like a Xerox copying machine, it's hard to visualize how a public relations department or agency is able to function without it. By now, the story of Frederick Smith's dream of overnight delivery service operating out of a hub airport has become legend.

In case you're not familiar with the legend, here's a brief summary. In the mid-1960s, Fred Smith wrote an economics class paper as an undergraduate at Yale University. The subject was the air shipment of high-priority packages. His grade was a C.

The Federal Express facility at the Memphis airport has been heralded by the media and scrutinized by business visitors from all over the world. The key to the Federal Express success is not its planes, thousands of trucks and other physical facilities; the heart of the company is the extraordinary enthusiasm of its people.

The services provided are various and suited to the numerous needs of communications professionals. They include:

Regular overnight package pick-up and delivery (by 10:30 A.M.) including Saturday deliveries.
Overnight Letters—up to 30 pages in length.
Standard Air—delivery no later than two business days after pickup.
Restricted articles and hazardous materials—Services are within the limits of the code of federal regulations. FE even provides seminars on the restrictions and limits of transporting such materials. To find out if a seminar is in your area, call (800) 238-5355.
Air Cargo Charter—Federal has the largest fleet of air-cargo jet aircraft in the world. They are available to customers for one time or contractual use 24 hours a day, 7 days a week.
Partsbank—combined warehouse and overnight airline. It stores any product for which delivery is time-sensitive. The toll free number for this service is (800) 238-5345.
Canada Service—delivery by 5:00 P.M. the day after pickup, providing there is no delay in customs.

You can count on Federal Express to pick up and deliver to almost any location in the U.S. Its international services extend to Canada, Europe and the Far East.

Federal Express continues to be the leader in overnight deliveries despite abundant competition over the past few years. One reason is the continuing improvement of services.

6. Graf Air Freight, Inc.

10-46 47 Avenue, Queens, NY 11101
(718) 392-6686
Andrew J. Crowley, Mgr.

A specialist in overnight delivery of TV commercials and other advertising and public relations materials, Graf has branch offices in Chicago, Los Angeles, San Francisco and Dallas-Fort Worth, which are the markets it services.

7. Purolator Courier Corp.

131 Morristown Rd., Basking Ridge, NJ 07920-1652
(800) 645-3333
Phyllis H. Gibson, Dir. of Corp. Communications

Purolator started as an air filter company. The courier service originally was simply a way to use its trucks for extra revenue. Today, it's one of the world's largest companies in this business. In fact, its planes and trucks service thousands of small towns (as well as major markets) and Purolator is one of the largest in the overnight delivery of packages.

There's no weight limit for documents sent in the PuroLetter ($9'' \times 12''$) envelopes, and the charge is $13.75 each to more than 23,000 locations from Maine to Alaska and Hawaii.

PuroPak has no weight limit for its $18.50 PuroPak envelopes. Larger packages, up to 125 lbs. and six feet in length, also may be shipped. U.S. shipments are automatically covered for values up to $250. Increased coverage is available to $25,000.

PuroLetter envelopes go to Canada, Mexico, Puerto Rico and London for $24.75 and have no weight limit. Purolator Courier now offers service to 75,000 destinations in more than 165 countries. The automatic liability for international shipments is $100.

Purolator Overnight Package Delivery Centers are centrally located in major metropolitan areas. There are also more than 2,000 Purolator Quickdrop boxes in major office buildings and industrial parks, and packages may be left at the 150 Purolator offices across the country. To arrange shipment, call Purolator Courier to pick up a package at your office, or take the package to one of their drop-off locations. Purolator will not ship to a post office box number.

8. TNT Skypak, Inc.

400 Post Ave., Westbury, NY 11590
(800) 558-5555
Marie Vigliarolo, V.P. Marketing

Whether you're sending a package to Australia or Zimbabwe, TNT Skypak can deliver it. With over 500 offices or representatives in 100 countries, this courier covers the globe. Pickups can be scheduled on a regular or per call basis. The services vary and TNT has an easy-to-read booklet of shipping rates.

9. Sureway Air Traffic Corp.

36-14 32 St., Queens, NY 11106
(718) 937-7600
Tom LoPresti, Pres.

Started in 1975. Sureway provides specialized services, generally at a premium price. For example, Sureway can pickup in New York City as late as 2 A.M. and guarantee delivery to major cities the same morning. Services are available 24 hours a day, seven days a week. In 1986, Sureway acquired the Archer Air Division of the Archer messenger service, a specialist in the New York, Philadelphia and Washington, DC areas.

10. United Parcel Service

51 Weaver St., Greenwich, CT 06830
(203) 622-6000
Joseph C. Tranfo, Ntl. Public Relations Mgr.

Formed in 1907 by two teenagers as a local messenger service, United Parcel Service was a pioneer in the pickup and delivery of small packages. For many years, thousands of department stores and other retailers, and all types of businesses used UPS as their shipping departments. In recent years, UPS added air service to its truck fleet, and today, UPS competes with Federal Express and other companies with UPS ground, next day air and 2nd day air.

UPS employs about 170,000 people in 1,200 locations with 50,000 vans and about 95 airplanes (Louisville, KY is the UPS air hub). About 9 million parcels are delivered daily via its ground fleet!

Note: Don't forget about Expressmail, the guaranteed overnight service of the U.S. Postal Service, with its thousands of Expressmail boxes. In comparison with the private couriers, the Expressmail rates often are lower.

Information about electronic mail is included at the end of the chapter on mailing services.

Chapter 15

Motion Pictures and Video

The videotape has replaced the 16mm film as the most commonly used audiovisual medium in the public relations field. Just about every public relations office has a videotape player (generally ¾-inch, which is the professional width) and millions of schools, offices and homes now have videotape recorders and players. The ½-inch videocassette recorder (VCR) is the hot item in the electronics business and predictions are that it soon will be in most TV homes.

The following chapter deals primarily with 16mm motion pictures. Much of the text also is applicable to videotapes and most of the companies also work with videotape as well as film.

Considerably more time and money often is devoted to the production of a motion picture than to its distribution. While some thought is given to the potential audiences of a public relations film, particularly with regard to the length and other requirements of TV films, it is a sad fact that the details of film distribution usually are not planned until after the film is completed. Film distribution should be planned and budgeted prior to production, so that it does not become a loosely organized afterthought.

Though sponsored films are produced because of the almost limitless audience opportunities available, many films are developed before that is a clear understanding of where they are to be seen and how much will be spent on distribution. The irony is that PR films are produced because of an audience expectation and yet realization of that expectation sometimes becomes an afterthought. Film distribution should be budgeted and planned *prior* to production.

Among the key questions to which thought should be given are:

1. What are the primary audiences?
2. How does this affect the length, subject matter and type of film?
3. Should there be different versions of the same film?
4. How will the film be distributed, how many prints will be required, and how much will it cost?

While television offers the largest audience potential, it should be kept in mind that there is comparatively little time available for public relations films in today's TV marketplace.

Sponsored films sometimes are shown at senior citizen centers and other institutions, resort hotels and other special outlets. Airport showings were tried out in the early 70's but were dropped because they are too expensive and the attention level is low. In the 80's, several companies started systems for showings on airplanes—a modern counterpart of the newsreels and short subjects, which were popular a few decades ago in motion picture theaters. These inflight services are akin to advertising.

An indication of the blurred distinction between advertising and publicity is the variety of films and videotapes which are shown on airplanes, in movie theaters and elsewhere as editorial features, though they obviously are sponsored, and in some cases literally include commercials. In 1984, for example, Music Theater Network launched a project of providing 5-minute rock music video clips which have 15-second commercials (at the end) and are distributed to about 700 movie theaters.

Theatrical film shorts must have strong entertainment appeal, minimum commercial message, high production quality and short running time. Ten minutes and under is best; the shorter the film, the more daily showings it is likely to get. Films for showings in motion picture theaters generally require 35mm prints. Due to improved laboratory techniques, 16mm films often can be blown up to 35mm with satisfactory results.

The opportunity of sponsored films in hardtop theatres and drive-ins is limited. However, the major studios produce very few short subjects and newsreels are no longer being produced. Thus, there is an opportunity to obtain showings in a few hundred (or more) movie theaters.

Another benefit of films produced for theatres is that they also can be shown on television. In fact, theatrical shorts generally are of a higher quality, particularly those with sports, travel and entertainment themes. As a result, they have a better chance of TV station showings.

Traditionally, distributors generate demand for their sponsors' films by sending out catalogs, flyers and other specialized mailing pieces. One distributor, Modern Talking Picture Services, goes a step further. It puts the show on the road and sets up shop in resorts and on college campuses. The services, Resort/Campground Cinema, College, High School and Jr. High School Cinema, supply films (on a continuing weekly basis) and 16mm sound projectors, screens and promotional materials.

As noted in an article on sponsored films in Public Relations Journal (October, 1974), "The sponsorship in *any* film, regardless of the distribution, should be a natural, graceful part of the whole. The commercialism should not intrude or insinuate itself on the audience. Perhaps the question should be: Would you want to see your film in a theater if you were a patron and not a sponsor?"

The size of these audiences is overwhelming, and sometimes confusing because no single film or videotape taps the full potential. Millions of videotape players and film projectors at clubs, churches, schools and other groups use up a lot of audiovisual materials.

The following data about audience size, provided by Modern Talking Picture Service, can be helpful in answering the key question, What can you expect for your AV?

1. Community audiences. Average audience size varies, depending on the type of film and audience specifications. The overall average for community group bookings is about 75. Bookings per print also depend on the film and the audience specifications. As a rule, however, figure on 20 bookings a year for each print. Thus, with 100 prints you could anticipate reaching 2,000 groups annually with a total viewership of 150,000. The actual number of prints recommended would, of course, depend on your budget and distribution objectives.

2. Resorts and campgrounds. Average attendance at resort showings is 40. Prints move at a rate of about 2½ bookings a week. So, with 50 prints in circulation for a 10-week summer season, you can expect about 1,250 showings and some 50,000 viewers.

3. Television. "Free" films are also used to fill out regular programs that run short of normal time breaks, such as movies and sports events, to incorporate into locally produced programs, and to keep on a standby basis for use in case of transmission difficulties or unexpected schedule changes. Performance depends on the individual film. A film that is right for thousands of community groups may have limited success with TV programmers, who think in terms of broad entertainment appeal.

The preferred format for TV is ¾-inch videotape. Many schools, hotels and other places which show public relations materials also have videotape players, though it may be necessary to produce 16mm prints.

Video news releases (about 90 seconds) are shown on many TV stations, often with sizable audiences.

4. Theatres. The average good short can play 1,000 to 1,500 theatres in a year with sufficient prints and will have a total theatre life of about 5,000 bookings over a three to four year period.

A single print can accommodate about 12 theatre bookings per year. The average attendance per booking is 1,200 to 1,500 for all theatres throughout the country and more in major cities with their dense populations. This means 50 prints can reach as many as one million viewers annually.

Because theatrical distribution is so highly organized, both national and regional distribution are easily administered. This enables the sponsor with a limited budget to utilize this channel of distribution. As few as 20 prints will permit strong coverage on a market by market basis, though 50 to 100 prints are recommended for a national program.

Film/video distribution is a complex and important business. To paraphrase the old bromide "Nothing happens until the sale is made," nothing happens to a sponsored film until it is seen. Unlike mailing services that distribute news releases, film distribution has a quantifiable, projectable audience. While distributors don't guarantee showings, they can give sponsors a sound, historically accurate prediction of results. Distributors know, for example, that a given number of prints will result in a specific number of bookings. The number of prints placed in distribution determines the dollars spent because distributors base their charges on monthly bookings. Prints govern budgets.

Despite the fact that videotape has taken over in many situations, film still has many attributes and capabilities that videotape may never attain. Videotape is limited in its tonal range and there are many producers who prefer to work with film because it has a completely different look. There are times when film is easier to use because the location is such that sensitive, bulky and more expensive video equipment would be a hindrance.

Following is a discussion of two other forms of film which are less commonly used by public relations practitioners. The information is based on an interview with Don Phelan, a long-time photographer whose company is described in the chapters on photography and television.

Super 8mm. Many firms and organizations still use Super 8mm film cartridges in Fairchild or La-Belle type projectors. These projectors are simple to use and lightweight to carry. They also are easy to maintain and suffer very few breakdowns. In most cases, the original shooting is done on 16mm film and then edited to master. It's then reduced to Super 8mm format and inserted in the special cartridge which can be set up for repetitive play. Typical uses would be in a booth at a trade show, banks, doctor's offices and for sales calls. No rewinding or threading is required. Costs for Super 8mm production depend on length of the show and many other factors. Average cost per screen minute is $1,850.

35mm Film Production is designed primarily for use in theater, TV commercials or those situations where large audiences will be viewing the film. Production costs throughout are considerably higher than 16mm and release prints are also expensive. A great deal more planning, logistics, talent and equipment usually are required for 35mm production. Usually, costs per screen minute run over twice that of 16mm.

Videotape and film distribution is a complex and important business. Unlike mailing services which distribute news releases, the audiovisual distribution business often is set up on a "nongamble basis," that is, most of the distributors will guarantee showings of your film and you pay only in accordance with the number of bookings. Of course, you can limit the distribution or set up maximum budgets.

Though it is possible to distribute films and videotapes yourself, and some companies and associations do a very successful job of this, it usually is considerably more efficient and economical to utilize the services of a distribution organization. The services include inspection and maintenance of the prints, promotion, certified distribution and the supplying of detailed reports on the showings.

A successful public relations film and/or videotape can entail thousands of school showings and hundreds of television showings, and thus can result in a cost per viewer that is just a few cents. Since the average circulation life of a sponsor's picture is about five years, the distribution can assume greater importance than the production. (Naturally, the better the production, the longer and greater its circulation potential.)

Several companies specialize in the national distribution of sponsored videotapes and films. The next time you contemplate making a film or videotape, talk to two or three distributors before you start the film. Their ideas about content, approach and technique can be helpful to you and the producer, and also will clarify your budgetary requirements with regard to its use after it's produced. A distributor often can predict, with considerable accuracy, the performance and audience potential.

Don't be dazzled by projections of audiences in the tens of millions. It's possible, of course, but potential audiences or other estimates, even when provided with computer readouts, maps and other impressive presentations, can be exaggerated and misleading. Take a look at the inattention of travelers at airplane cinemas or TV viewers at 7 A.M., and think about qualitative analysis linked with accurate audience estimates. Offer a booklet and you'll soon find out which showings pull. However, booklet offers are not the only measurement, since theatrical showings do not generate this type of direct response, but are extremely influential. Booklets are ideal for schools, clubs and television.

Before producing the film or videotape, think about different lengths for different audiences. A half-hour film for clubs and schools can be edited to 10 minutes for theatres, two to 10 minutes for women's TV programs, and a minute or two for TV news programs.

Production costs can range from a few thousand to several million dollars, and depend on length, script, talent, location and dozens of other variables. A rule of thumb which often is cited is $3,500 per minute for a complete color, sound public relations film.

A complete video news release of about two minutes generally can be produced for about $12,000. As for film, a four-person documentary crew going out for one eight-hour portal-to-portal day may cost about $6,250, including 16mm camera, lighting and sound equipment. This budget provides for 800 feet (22 minutes) of color negative film, including processing, rental of a car, crew lunch, crew pension and welfare payments and some petty cash—in other words the multitude of extras which are part of almost every film/video production.

The budget does not include any location fees, since these can vary greatly, though public relations projects are generally less than advertising and may be $250 to $1,000.

Additional rolls of film (they come in 400 ft. rolls of about 11 minutes each) are about $240, including processing and printing. There generally is no reduced rate such as half-day or hourly rates for film crews and equipment, though this is not always the case with video equipment. However, there's no harm in asking! Perhaps the producer can schedule two assignments on the same day.

Studio rentals can be $1,000 a day, plus props or sets. Little or nothing is included when you rent space.

Post-production finishing costs vary widely, depending on the complexity of the optical effects, titles and sound track, and amount of time needed to complete the work. Original music is expensive, so try to stick with "library music".

Does all of the above mean that a 30-minute film, at about $3,500 per minute, will cost over $100,000? Yes and no! These guidelines apply more often to shorter length films. The most important thing to remember is that each film is unique, with its own specifications, amount of labor, creative effort, travel and other factors. To assure that you are getting accurate prices, give your bidding producers as much information as possible about the proposed film. The less they have to guess, the more accurate and fair will be the bid.

Remember that you will be quoted a price through the completion of only ONE color-corrected answer print. Make sure that your budget allows for your print or cassette order and for distribution costs. Too often a beautiful film is made, only to have it sit on the shelf for a year because no budget was established to make and distribute prints.

Here is an extraordinarily detailed price list. Though all prices are subject to change, the charges can be very useful to public relations clients, who generally are less familiar than advertisers and often tend to under-estimate costs.

Studio Daily Rates

Studio
    Studio rental with lights $500

Equipment
    ¾″ control room with Sony master monitor, multi/effects switcher, time code generator,
    sync generator, audio, 3 Sony ¾″ VTR's, time base correction $600
    Sony DXC-M3 cameras .... $300 each
    Digital effects.. $ 50 /hr.
    Chyron .... $ 50 /hr.
    Microphones... $ 65 each
    Computer graphics .... $250 /hr.

Personnel
    Director $500
    Video/audio operator $400
    Cameraman/lighting director $300
    2nd camera operator $200
    Gaffer/electrician $200

Day Rate—One Camera Shoot
    1-camera (broadcast quality)
    1-recorder (broadcast quality)
    1-tripod
    2-light kits
    2-microphones
    crew $1,800

Day Rate—Two Camera Shoot
    2-cameras (broadcast quality)
    2-recorders (broadcast quality)
    2-tripods
    2-light kits
    2-microphones
    crew $2,500

Additional Charges
    Director (per day) $750
    Location (per day/per person) .... $ 50
    Director on location (per day).. $100
    Mileage.. $1.50/mile

Technical ¼″ prints are $23.50 each in small quantities and short duration (10 minutes). A 30-minute print costs $32.30 for less than seven prints and $21.40 for over 100 prints.
Computer graphics services are about $250 an hour. Computer generated slides are about $25 each.

On-line editing ranges from $100/hour for ¾″ Sony to $420/hour for a three-machine system with special effects.

Off-line editing costs less as follows.

A & B roll editorial service	$125/hr.
Digital CEL video effects	$100/hr.
Chyron—record to ¾″	$ 50/hr.
Time coding	$ 35/hr.
Voice-overs	$ 50/hr.
Straight-cut editing without operator with Sony RM 440 Controller	$ 30/hr.
With operator	$ 60/hr.
Screening room	$ 30/hr.

These figures are for production. Now, on to distribution.

A "typical" first year's budget for a 13-minute program could look like this:

Television
  Broadcast,
    50–75 plays
  Cable TV—direct to systems,
    200–300 plays
  Cable TV—via satellite distribution,
    3,000–4,000 plays $15,000–$20,000
Schools, Community Groups, Resorts
    4,000 showings $32,000
Misc. Bookings from Sponsor
    200 $ 2,000
Motion Picture Theaters
    1,000 play dates $25,000–$30,000

With the majority of productions being edited on videotape, the selection of film or video is actually more related to distribution than production. The program above calls for a 50/50 split between filmprints and ½″ (VHS) videocassette dubs. 75–100 16mm prints for the program would run about $5,000–$6,000. The cost of video dubs is the cost of one video master as Modern supplies all necessary tape dubs for TV and manages the program according to demand and budget.

The appropriate audiences reached with this distribution would be:

Television	2 million people
Cable & Satellite TV	4–6 million people
Schools, Community Groups, Resorts	¼ million people
Motion Picture Theaters	1 million

Those elements of a core communications program include TV and community groups, schools and resorts. A budget of approximately $50,000 to reach 6 to 8 million viewers can be worthwhile. Theatrical distribution (if program qualifies) and special audience bookings should be used as distribution extensions.

A preferable approach is to plan the distribution budget *before* producing the film in order to include sufficient funds within the total budget.

Additional information about films can be obtained from the Educational Film Library Association, 43 W. 61 St., N.Y. 10023.

The Official Video Directory & Buyer's Guide ($60 plus $4 shipping) is published annually by Palm Springs Media, Inc., 555 Commercial Rd., Palm Springs, CA 92262. Categories include video equipment, distributors and services.

If you're looking for ways to reduce film costs, talk to one or more producers about using still photos. You can take a collection of good-quality color transparencies and turn them into a 16mm sound, color film by using zooms, pans, dissolves and special effects. You've seen this done creatively with art films and documentaries, and it can be used quite well with sales training and other films. Ask about Film-O-Graph, one of the new equipment systems for producing this type of film. Cost may be about half of conventional film production.

The annual AV Buying Guide, published in October by Audio-Visual Communications, is free to subscribers or can be purchased for $5.75 from United Business Publications, 475 Park Ave. So., N.Y. 10016. The controlled-circulation magazine is free to audiovisual users and producers ($13.50 a year to others), so you may be eligible to receive the directory issue at no cost. Included are descriptions of products and companies, ranging from audio playback systems to video monitors.

If you do maintain a film or videotape library, you'll want to know about Rapid Film Technique, Inc., an unusual laboratory which reconditions old films, including the unscratching of 8mm, 16mm, and 35mm prints. Rapid handles storage, shipping and distribution at 34-54 35 St., Queens, NY 11106, phone (718) 786-4600. Jerome Gober is president.

Projectors and other audiovisual equipment can be bought or rented in every major city. A specialist in New York is Audio-Visual Promotion Aids, Inc., 611 Broadway-Room 841, N.Y. 10021, phone (212) 477-5540. This is *not* a photography store, but rather a source for audiovisual equipment for use at meetings, exhibits, shows and other events.

Publicists often need enlarged still prints made from one or more frames of a 16mm or 35mm TV film or motion picture. Here are hints:

Any good photo lab can print from negative or positive motion picture frames. Enlargements made from motion picture negatives are printed directly from the original, at regular print prices. With motion picture positives, a reverse negative first must be made. To designate the frame in a strip of reel which you want printed, simply tie a thread through the nearest sprocket hole.

The major service with which publicists generally are most concerned in the area of films is the distribution. The following section therefore deals mostly with film distributors, though it includes information about a few producers and other film companies which are oriented to the needs of public relations customers, particularly full-service audiovisual production facilities located *outside* of New York and Los Angeles.

Modern Talking Picture Service is the largest company in this publicity video/film field. Its services and rates are in this chapter and also in the chapter on television.

A few producers maintain libraries and booking facilities. Though these are not as extensive as the companies which specialize in free film distribution, clients occasionally prefer the personalized service which a producer may be able to offer.

Cable TV has become important in recent years, though it still must be considered by public relations and advertising sponsors within the total television spectrum. As such, it must be viewed with some skepticism. Consider this: A cable system subscriber pays a monthly fee to receive improved reception and/or to have access to special programs. The cable subscriber thus can view many TV channels. It is not likely that the viewer will watch a sponsored film, when the choice includes network shows, first-run theatrical motion pictures, sports and special events.

A few cable systems (and also regular TV stations) show sponsored films at the end of sports events and theatrical films in order to round out "the hour." In such cases, the audience may be larger than usual.

Occasionally, a sponsored film is sufficiently institutional or "soft sell" or is so overwhelmingly entertaining, that it can be sold or loaned for a fee rather than lending it free, as a sponsor usually does.

Public relations practitioners can consider a type of distribution arrangement in which the fees can enable the sponsor to get back part or all of the production cost.

Associations and other sponsors with films that seem to offer this type of potential should consult with commercial film distributors, particularly those which specialize in 16mm films.

Paramount, Columbia and other theatrical motion picture studios formerly produced sponsored films, generally related to their production of "short subjects." Some of this work still is done by the Disney Organization, but most of it is produced by independents or companies which specialize in commercials.

Services for the duplication of videotapes now operate in every major city. Most public relations clients generally require only a small number of duplicates, often only one or two. If you are making a large quantity, such as for sales training, a school program or a video news release, shop around, as the prices can vary considerably. You may want to use a laboratory not in your immediate area, such as Video Plus Inc., 201 Arnold Ave., Point Pleasant Beach, NJ 08742, phone (201) 892-7400.

Here then is information about several major film distributors and other video services which are oriented to public relations clients.

1. AVR Enterprises, Inc.
500 Broadway, N.Y. 10012
(212) 226-6358
William R. Jorden, Chm.
Behnam Nateghi, Pres.

A former vice president of Corporate Annual Reports, Bill Jorden heads a video production company, which specializes in video reports to shareholders and employees, videos for training and other business purposes. AVR also produces video news releases.

2. Bergen Expo Systems, Inc.
Box 2109, Main Ave., Clifton, NJ 07015
(201) 472-1154, (212) 564-1195
Carmella Connolly, Mgr.

Formed in 1946, Bergen (the name refers to its location in Bergen County) distributes films, and also has developed considerable experience in front and rear projection systems for conference rooms and exhibitions, including the development of continuous operation 16mm and video cartridges, automatic show programmers and other equipment.

The company now is a major resource in the audiovisual exhibit field and can help in the design, fabrication, installation, operation and maintenance of audiovisual facilities for exhibits, projection rooms and boardrooms.

Bergen has been responsible for over 30 exhibits at all of the recent World Fairs. Its products include the Bergen Eterna (a continuous 16mm cartridge which can be mounted on any 16mm projector), Bergen's quadrapoint (a xenon powered slide projector with a powerful light output), Bergen's mini-X (a 16mm xenon projector) and Bergen's laser pointer (used on front or rear projection). The company was founded by Eugene Demick, a renowned leader in the audiovisual hardware field.

3. Bonded Services
2050 Center Ave., Fort Lee, NJ 07024
(201) 592-7868
Harold J. Eady, Pres.

Bonded, which is a division of Novo Communications, Inc., handles a variety of storage, booking, procurement and shipping services for advertisers and TV program distributors in the United States,

Canada and worldwide. The company has branch offices in Los Angeles, Toronto, London, Amsterdam and Hong Kong.

4. Business Education Films
Box 449, Clarksburg, NJ 08510
(201) 462-3522
Paul Weinberg, Pres.

Films and filmstrips on business subjects, mostly for use in high school and adult commercial courses and vocational education, are rented by the day or week. Also distributes Dartnell Training Films for business and industry.

5. CBS News Archives
524 W. 57 St., N.Y. 10019
(212) 975-2875
Neil Waldman, Director

World renowned 16mm and videotape material produced by CBS News since 1954 is available to "outsiders." Prices depend primarily on the length and use to be made of the material.

6. Centron Productions, Inc.
1621 W. 9 St., Lawrence, KS 66044
(913) 843-0400
Robert Kohl, Pres.

Lawrence, Kansas, is the home of a major producer of sponsored motion pictures, video productions and other business audiovisuals.

Founded in 1947, Centron has its own building, with facilities which are among the most modern and extensive in the country. The sound stage includes a 90-foot cyclorama background and all types of animation, art, camera and sound equipment are used in various studios and editing rooms.

7. Cinemakers Inc.
1974 Broadway, NY 10023
(212) 595-3727
Ed Schultz, Pres.
Carol Hale, V.P.

A specialist in public relations audiovisual communications, Cinemakers produces videotapes, films, filmstrips, slide shows, multimedia kits and other materials.

8. Communications Services Group, Inc.
47 Green St., N.Y. 10013
(212) 226-7837
Jude Quintiere, Pres.

Formed in 1980, CSG is a film and videotape producer specializing in TV commercials and corporate films.

9. Concept/NY, Inc.
156 Fifth Ave., N.Y. 10010
(212) 741-1122
Frank Vince

Video, film and slide presentations.

10. Continental Film Productions Corp.

Box 5126, Chattanooga, TN 37406
(615) 622-1193

Founded in 1951, Continental has offices, studios and production facilities in its own 17,000-square-foot building at 4220 Amnicola Highway, where it produces video programs, multi-image presentations, motion pictures and filmstrips for clients throughout the country.

Besides producing AV presentations for public relations, sales and training, Continental distributes all major brands of AV equipment. Staging and rentals are available.

11. Coronet Film and Video

108 Wilmot Rd., Deerfield, IL 60015
(312) 940-1260, (800) 621-2131

Coronet is a major producer and supplier of 16mm films and video cassettes to schools, hospitals and other groups, specializing in the sale or rental of prints, rather than free distribution.

12. DDC Productions, Inc.

301 E. 22 St., N.Y. 10010
(212) 473-5472
Daniel Dorian, Pres.

Formed in 1980, DDC produces corporate films and videos, news clips and public service announcements.

13. Exar Communications, Inc.

267 "B" McClean Ave., Staten Island, NY 10305
(718) 720-4488
Claire Walsh, Pres.

Real estate is a lot cheaper in Staten Island, as compared to Manhattan, and several motion picture producers and others in the communications business now have their facilities in this borough. In 1982, Claire Walsh and Katherine Finelli, who had been at West Glen Communications, and Frank Cianchetta, who had been at Cine-Mix, formed Exar Communications, which provides a variety of video and film services, including warehousing and distribution to schools and other outlets. The company also markets educational software, does fulfillment for mail order firms and video duplication.

14. Film Counselors Associates, Inc.

630 Ninth Ave., N.Y. 10036
(212) 315-3950
Frank Powers, Pres.

The Film Counselors theater and screening room is well known to PRSA members who use their facilities. The company has over 40 years of experience in the production and distribution of all types of films and videotapes.

15. Films Incorporated

35 S. West St., Mt. Vernon, NY 10550
(914) 667-0800
Phil Goldberg

The company has undergone several changes and now operates as Films Incorporated, a division of Public Media Incorporated. Allen J. Green is president of the entertainment operation, which distributes over 10,000 feature films, many under corporate sponsorship, in the nontheatrical market and is expanding in the repertory theatrical market. Mike Stickney is president of the education operations, which distributes over 2,000 educational films (including sponsored films) in the nontheatrical market (schools, colleges, libraries, companies, associations, government, hospitals, groups and TV stations)!

Charles Benton is chairman of Public Media Incorporated and Wendell Shackelford is president. This is a big company, though generally not as well known to public relations clients as Modern and other competitors.

16. Films of the Nation Distributors
Box 449, Clarksburg, NJ 08510
(201) 462-3522
Paul Weinberg, Mgr.

Also operates Business Education Films (listed earlier in this chapter) and Alden Films, which distributes films of Israel and Judiasm.

17. Alan Gordon Enterprises Inc.
1430 N. Cahuenga Blvd., Hollywood, CA 90078
(213) 446-3561
TWX: (910) 321-4526
Peter Barton

Among the many sources of professional motion picture equipment in the Los Angeles area, one of the largest renters and sellers (in the world) is Alan Gordon. Founded in 1946, the company's six-plant complex stocks just about every type of photo, microfilm and motion picture component and issues a comprehensive catalog, with daily rental rates for every item. The motion picture division is in Hollywood and the aerial and microfilm divisions are in North Hollywood.

18. Sherman Grinberg Film Libraries, Inc.
630 Ninth Ave., N.Y. 10036
(212) 765-5170
Telex: 265823

Branch Office:
1040 N. McCadden Pl., Hollywood, CA 90038
(213) 464-7491
Telex: 269950

Grinberg has an extraordinary collection of film and video material, including Pathe and Paramount Newsreels from 1914 (some even earlier) to 1957, ABC Network News, 20th Century Fox and MGM films, BBC tapes and other programs.

Fees depend on the source, length, format and use. For example, a 16mm newsreel used for a sales meeting costs a minimum of $540 licensing fee plus $45 per foot.

19. Karol Media
22 Riverview Dr., Wayne, NJ 07470
(201) 628-9111
Fontaine (Mick) Kincheloe, Pres.

Karol Media distributes 16mm films, videocassettes, and other audiovisual materials to TV stations, schools and other groups in the U.S. Rates are based on actual usage, as follows:

Television. $60 to $75 for each telecast. Previews that do not result in telecasts are $10 each. Cable systems are $25 to $35 for placement and no charge for previews.

TV news and public service spots, up to 90 seconds, are distributed for $2.50 to $7.50 a station, depending on the number of stations (50 station minimum), plus first class postage. This is a low price, but does not include production of the original film and the prints.

Schools and groups. $6.50 to $7.50 per booking, depending on number of prints and/or videocassettes, plus outbound shipping charges and handling charges for materials (e.g., 50 cents to $1 for teacher's guides and packets).

20. Walter J. Klein Company, Ltd.
6311 Carmel Rd., Charlotte, NC 28211
(704) 542-1403
Walter J. Klein, Pres.

Walter J. Klein and his son Richard and a staff of over 20 photographers and technicians operate one of the country's largest public relations film production and distribution companies from a four-acre site in Charlotte, North Carolina. Very few film producers have their own studios or other facilities as extensive as Klein. The Charlotte building includes a sound stage and two mobile units.

Formed in 1948, the Kleins have produced over 1,000 films in their studio and all over the country. Walter Klein is founder and past president of IQ (International Quorum of Motion Picture Producers), a group of sponsored film producers.

Klein maintains an active TV distribution service. In some cases, prints are supplied to clients at net laboratory cost and *no charge* is made for the distribution service, as it is part of the production package price.

Walter Klein is the author of an excellent book, The Sponsored Film.

21. MG Productions, Inc.
26 E. 64 St., N.Y. 10021
(212) 688-1455
Margie Goldsmith, Pres.

Formed in 1983 and located in an historic landmark townhouse near Madison Avenue, MG Productions specializes in PSAs, VNRs and other film and video production. Facilities include a client screening/living room, a large conference room (for 22 people) and a production area.

22. Modern Talking Picture Service, Inc.
5000 Park St. N., St. Petersburg, FL 33709
(813) 541-7571
Dan Kater, Pres.

Branch Offices:
One Prudential Plaza, Chicago 60601
(312) 337-3252, Ed Swanson, V.P.

45 Rockefeller Plaza, N.Y. 10111
(212) 765-3100, Dan Kater, Pres., Bob Finehout, V.P.

149 New Montgomery St., San Francisco 94105
(415) 777-3995, Steve Mahan, V.P.

1901 L St., N.W., Wash., DC 20036
(202) 293-1222, Robert Kelley, V.P.

Formed in 1937, the only thing old-fashioned about Modern Talking Picture Service is its name, which indicates that the company originated at a time when sound movies were called talking pictures. In fact, the company was started two years earlier, in 1935, as a department of Western Electric when 16mm film was developed. Today, Modern is the largest company in the field of free videocassette and film distribution. Its computers are constantly clicking out information about television and special audience bookings for its hundreds of clients.

In 1979, Modern moved its general offices from New Hyde Park on Long Island to a 105,000 sq. ft. building in St. Petersburg. The operation, with over 100 employees, resembles a TV network.

In 1987, Dan Kater, who has been with Modern since 1954, replaced Bill Oard as President.

The company maintains many film and videocassette service centers, and its people are responsible for several million film and cassette showings in schools, community organizations, resorts, theaters, and TV and distribution of thousands of booklets and other items accompanying the showings.

A full description of the Modern operation appears in the chapter on television.

23. Modern Telecommunications, Inc. (MTI)
1 Dag Hammarskjold Pl., N.Y. 10017
(212) 355-0510
Telex: 422434
Robert C. Weisberger, Pres.
Joe Cohen, Marketing Dir.

One of the largest companies in the film and video production field, MTI facilities include studios at its headquarters in mid-Manhattan (855 Second Ave., which is 1 Dag Hammarskjold Plaza) and also in a large building in upper Manhattan, at 1443 Park Avenue. The uptown building, called MTI Television City, includes two dish antennas for satellite transmission. The building, acquired by MTI in 1980, formerly was the RKO Pathe studios, where many early movies and TV shows were produced. Facilities include computerized graphics and all types of production for advertising and public relations clients.

24. Productions-in-Progress
Box 23562, Wash., DC 20026
(202) 488-0717
Richard M. Huber

Formed in 1987, Productions-in-Progress is a unique databank of TV shows and theatrical motion pictures that currently are in various stages of planning and production. Subscribers, who receive a bi-monthly index, can write or call for detailed reports.

An annual subscription is $250 for corporations (less for nonprofits and independent producers), plus $10 per report. Subscribers include advertising and public relations agencies, as well as media investors, educators, producers and others.

When Richard Huber (B.A., Princeton, Ph.D., Yale) was dean of continuing education at Hunter College in New York, he was producer-host of many public affairs radio and TV programs. He conceived the idea for P-I-P and developed it with funding from several foundations and the partnership of DOCUnet Corporation, an office automation services company headed by Stanley Ross (Ph.D., Harvard).

25. Rafik Film & Video Tape Co.
814 Broadway, N.Y. 10003
(213) 475-8411
Mr. Rafic Azzouny

An increasingly important service in the public relations field is the duplication of videotapes. Costs have come down tremendously in recent years, particularly at those laboratories with two-channel recorders and other special equipment.

In New York, an experienced specialist is Rafik, formed in 1976. The company name is from the proprietor's first name, although the last letter is different. It's pronounced Ruh-feek, and the location is Broadway near 12th Street.

Here's their price list for ¾" videotapes made from one master. The price of ½-inch VHS or Beta is less.

No. of copies	20 Min.	30 Min.	60 Min.
1	$4	$6	$9
2–4	3.50	5.50	8
5–9	3	4.50	7
10–24	2.50	4	6

Plus cost of the tape and assembly charges.

26. Scene East Productions Ltd.
153 Mercer St., N.Y. 10012
(212) 226-6525
Bob Demchuk, Producer
Still and motion picture photography and in-studio and on-site production, ranging from 30-second commercials to full-length feature motion pictures.

27. Science Screen Report, Inc.
2875 S. Congress Ave., Delray Beach, FL 33445
(305) 265-1700
Jerome G. Forman, Exec. Dir.
One of America's most experienced and respected film producers, Jerry Forman previously worked at Telenews (a pioneering TV newsreel company) and operated Allegro Film Productions. Launched in 1970, Science Screen Report is a unique project produced in cooperation with the National Science Teachers Association and the Engineers Council for Professional Development. Each month, SSR produces and distributes a 15-minute motion picture and teacher's guide to science departments in junior and senior high schools. The films are noncommercial and educational and are distributed free. Companies can sponsor the films sent to schools in their area, or any area not already covered by SSR. The sponsor receives an institutional commercial at the beginning and end of each film, at a cost of $1,600 per academic year (eight monthly films) per school.

28. Streamline Film Archives
109 E. 29 St., N.Y. 10016
(212) 696-2616
Mark Trost
Formed in 1983, Streamline Film Archives has collected films and tapes of newsreels, theatrical features, commercials, government and industrial films and a variety of other items, including rare and offbeat footage.

Research fees are $50 an hour, with a four-hour minimum. License fees depend on the use, with an average of $1,400 per minute.

29. Targetron, Inc.
156 Fifth Ave., N.Y. 10010
(212) 463-7668
Steve Gold, Linda Rosenbaum
Targetron distributes materials for schools, colleges and TV stations. For clients who produce their own films and provide prints, Target handles distribution as follows:

Newsclips and public service announcements: $2,800 for the first 100 prints and $1,800 for each additional hundred.
Programs and featurettes: $45 for each confirmed station booking, $30 each cable station booking.
Radio distribution (PSAs): $1,000 first 100 tapes, $750 for each additional 100.
Schools, libraries, colleges: $15 each confirmed booking.

30. Video Cassette Transfers, Inc.
1501 Broadway, N.Y. 10036
(212) 575-8433
Chris Avildsen, V.P.
A specialist in video conversions and duplication, VCT also has facilities for editing and production, as well as slide to tape transfer and film to tape transfer.

31. Video Dub Inc.
423 W. 55 St., N.Y. 10019
(212) 757-3300
Don Buck, Pres.
Video Dub is a sizable laboratory devoted exclusively to video duplication and transfer. The lab also converts from film to tape and duplicates VHS and all types of tapes.

32. W & W Films
1650 Broadway, N.Y. 10019
(212) 541-9441
Richard Winik, Barry Winik
Producer of films and tapes, specializing in sports documentaries and informercials.

33. Worldwide Television News Corporation (WTN)
1995 Broadway, N.Y. 10023
(212) 362-4440
Telex: 285547
Vincent O'Reilly, Library Mgr.
United Press International was a major producer of TV news in the 60's and 70's. WTN owns the UPI film and videotape library, and also sells material from other sources, including England's Independent Television News from 1956 and British Pathe News from 1896.
Prices range from $300 to several thousand dollars.
WTN also covers the world daily and is a prime source of TV news for U.S. and foreign networks and other clients. Bureaus are in many cities including 1705 De Sales St., N.W., Washington, D.C., phone (202) 835-0750.

Other material on this subject is in the chapter on television.

Chapter 16

News Wire Services

Along with the traditional wire services such as Associated Press, United Press International, Dow Jones and Reuters, there is another "wire" that serves almost every major newspaper, wire service and broadcast news room, and is of special importance to the publicists—the "pr wire."

The pr wire actually is a service now provided by several companies around the country, all modelled on the original pr wire—PR Newswire. Still headquartered in New York City and now a national service, PR Newswire was launched in 1954 by Herb Muschel, who pioneered the simultaneous electronic distribution to news media of the full text of press releases and other information from public relations sources. The combined daily output of these wires—about 400 releases a day—is speedily and efficiently disseminated via land lines or satellites to high-speed teleprinters at the media or directly into their editorial computers and is sufficient to fill several large-sized newspapers.

Regardless of the means employed to communicate memos, tips, news and features to the media, the content of the message remains the decisive element in winning space or time. And there still are instances in which the use of messenger, telegram, telephone and mail is preferable to the pr wire services. Exclusive placements, or mailings containing photos, booklets or other material, for example, clearly are not suitable for delivery via teleprinters or into a computer.

But, for distribution of sensitive, time-critical information, especially financial news with its attendant "disclosure" obligations, the pr wire has become an indispensable tool for thousands of publicists.

In the financial field, there is intense pressure from Dow Jones and Reuters to receive information at exactly the same time. In addition, the Securities and Exchange Commission, the stock exchanges and the National Association of Securities Dealers impose their own requirements for media that must be covered to achieve "prompt disclosure to the press." The pr wires provide that simultaneity and serve the media required for prompt disclosure.

The pr wires are not strictly financial. They can be used with equal effectiveness for press conference invitations, photo tips, or general news. Indeed, they all are used frequently by such diverse news sources as colleges, labor unions, philanthropic groups, government agencies, sports organizations and political action groups.

Beyond the expected daily newspapers, wire services and radio-TV outlets, the pr wires also serve a large number of trade, technical and specialized publications, some of which are not served by the regular wire services but which can be very important to specific companies. Each pr wire offers literature listing precisely the media it covers and providing complete information about its services, which it will send you on request.

Publicists should realize, however, that while the names are similar, there are considerable differences in the coverage and services offered by each pr wire. There have been occasions on which clients thought they were dealing with one service and were actually dealing with another. Fortunately, the wires do cooperate with each other.

All the wires operate the same way, following the standards established by Herb Muschel the first day—"Read the copy carefully, catch any error, and get the release out quickly and accurately." All copy is read for typos, grammar, libel, inconsistencies and factual errors. Minor typos are corrected automatically; any factual question is checked with the source. "Speed and accuracy are what we sell," says Dave Steinberg, President of PR Newswire, "but it is accuracy that keeps us in business. There is tremendous pressure on all of our staffs to weed out errors. We're the last pair of eyes that can help keep an embarrassing error from reaching the editors."

In order to maintain good relations with the media, the quality and integrity of their services and also because of certain government regulations, the pr wires reserve the privilege of rejecting copy and occasionally exercise editorial judgment in determining what copy they will transmit on their circuits.

These wires are, of course, commercial and charge for their services. See the individual listings for services and rates.

Most of the private wire services are staffed by former journalists and publicists. Dave Steinberg was a business writer for the New York Herald Tribune and Lorry Lokey, who heads Business Wire, also was a journalist. Both still maintain close friendships with media colleagues.

Shortly after the first few pr wires opened in the United States (New York 1954, Chicago 1956, Detroit 1958) the first such service was launched overseas—in England in 1959 by Alfred Geiringer of Universal News Service.

Subsequently, PR Newswire and Universal News along with Canada News-Wire (in which PRN and UNS are shareholders) introduced international pr wire services, initially featuring their own domestic services plus telex distribution from the UNS desk in London to many other countries, including translation when necessary. Today, through a variety of professional transmission arrangements, high-speed wire coverage is offered to virtually any country in the world, including Eastern Europe, Asia, Africa and Latin America. Immediate international distribution is available to you in the U.S. from most of the pr wires.

In recent years other overseas pr wire operations, sales offices or distribution services have been established in countries such as France, Germany, Spain, Israel, Japan, Hong Kong, Australia and New Zealand. Rates for international services vary widely, depending upon the country, the number of media served and whether or not translation is required.

In the years since the earliest pr wire began, newspapers have moved from teleprinters and linotype machines to the quiet, high-speed efficiency of editorial and typesetting computer systems, and the pr wires have moved with them. The new editorial computer systems require that copy be input electronically, with special formats and protocols and at designated compatible speeds. Today's computerized pr wires enable the public relations professional to deliver the "computer-ready" copy now required by many of the media. The two largest pr wires in the U.S. are PR Newswire and Business Wire. A visit to the PR Newswire headquarters in New York or Business Wire headquarters in San Francisco demonstrates advanced press communications in action. Their editors process press release copy on Video Display Terminals (VDTs) and, with the stroke of a key, dispatch that information via any of their circuits to teleprinters or directly into the media's own editorial computers.

At PR Newswire, for example, its PRONTO computer (actually there are two—one for complete on-line "back up") can simultaneously send and receive different releases at different speeds, ranging from 60 words per minute through 100, 150, 300, 1,200 or 9,600 wpm, each formatted specifically for each speed and line. PRONTO can store millions of words a day, and from that storage automatically transmit a release at a predetermined time to predetermined circuits or other points, even dialing individual telex numbers. The storage capability also means releases can instantly be retrieved for changes or retransmissions if requested by media or required by sources. Indexes of all copy transmitted can be generated automatically for editors on the circuits. The computer also accepts direct transmissions of news releases to be issued from the word processors and computer systems of the public relations agency, corporate and other members.

As a result, you can count in minutes—not hours or days—the time it takes between the end of dictation of a news release to receipt of that copy in newsrooms around the country.

PRN and BW also transmit into a number of on-line data bases where they become accessible for instant retrieval in full anywhere in the world by telephone. (For more on databases, see the chapters on computerized news and research.)

In working with public relations wire services, as with all services, the final responsibility is with you, the client, not the vendor. These services are so speedy and efficient that there's a tendency not to ask questions about details. But ask questions. That way, you won't have any unpleasant surprises about distribution or costs, and you'll probably find new ways to ease your press release distribution problems.

Our annual survey of types of input to the public relations news wires indicates increasing use of word processing computer equipment and decreasing use of telephone and telex. Typed copy, no matter how it's transmitted, is likely to be more accurate than anything read over the telephone. However, few things are perfect in the public relations field, and typed copy can have errors.

Many of the public relations news wire personnel are experienced journalists, and they often detect errors or question items, even when they are transmitted computer-to-computer.

Here's the current estimated breakdown of types of input.

Telephone facsimile	27%
Computer (word processing)	24
Telex (including links with word processing)	23
Messenger (incl. air courier)	15
Telephone	10
Mail	1

About 75 percent of the business is financial news. About half of the input comes from public relations agencies and about half comes from direct sources.

About 2,500 news releases are produced every week on all of the public relations news wires combined. Here's an estimated ranking of the busiest days, starting with the busiest.

Thursday
Tuesday and Wednesday
Monday
Friday
Saturday
Sunday

Very little is transmitted on weekends and off-hours. The busiest times of the day are 11 A.M. to 1 P.M. and 4 to 5 P.M.

Here are some tips on how to use these wires most effectively.

1. Until you are thoroughly familiar with the operations of your specific public relations news wire, always discuss your distribution requirements. All the wires offer a kind of "basic distribution" which may be sufficient for you, but they also offer additional, extended services which you might find useful

routinely or only on certain occasions. If you are especially interested in a specific city or publication, ask if it is covered automatically. If not, how can it be reached? The professional staff of the wires may suggest additional coverage based on the nature of your release—coverage you might not have known was available. Extra distribution, of course, adds to the cost, but it may be worthwhile, and the wires can give you an accurate estimate of your bill.

Some of the services, such as Business Wire, occasionally edit copy and select outlets. This can be very helpful, but you should know in advance what changes are being made and exactly where the news release is to be sent.

In summary, specify the distribution you want. If you do not want distribution to stock brokers, state this. If you do not want national distribution, state this. Otherwise, you may be surprised when you get the bill. The news wire services operate so quickly and efficiently that there sometimes is a tendency for clients to be lulled into ''passive acceptance.''

2. Ask the news wire service for its *current* list of media outlets. The lineup changes frequently, and there may be omissions which you want to cover via messenger, Telex, telegram, telephone or telephone facsimile. Furthermore, don't assume that the receiving or transmitting machines are in constant operation. As super-efficient as they and their operators are, they are fallible.

3. At several media outlets the publicity news wire machine is not in the central wire room, but in the financial news department. That's O.K. for the financial news on the publicity news wire, which is the majority of the news. News for the City Desk or other departments is torn off the news wire machine and routed. It may be delivered to the City Desk a few hours after its arrival in the financial news department. For nonfinancial news, you therefore may want to supplement the news wire with telephone or messenger. It's particularly important to get the time of transmission or transmission number of your release on the news wire, so that you can refer to it when you telephone, as this can help a news reporter to find it. At The New York Times, public relations news wire machines are in the wire room and also in the financial news department.

4. Some of the wires will help you set up ''standing orders'' for distribution of releases. The ''order'' will include the regular wire circuits or other wires you need, other media or individuals such as plant managers or investment bankers. Once the list is made up, distribution to the list is automatic, unless you specify otherwise. This is another good time-saver, though it should be in your budget plan, so there are no irritating surprises when you receive your bills.

5. The public relations news wires provide a way for you to control timing of your release. You may ask them to transmit it immediately (which they will do within minutes), or you may ask them to transmit it at a time you specify, or simply hold it until you phone to release it. Giving them the release in advance can be especially helpful if you're going to be tied up in a news conference, annual meeting or event.

6. If you use Telex, dial the news wire directly. Although they might be cheaper, use of the new ''store and forward'' electronic communications services could delay delivery of your release. Better yet, if you use communicating word processing equipment, check with the public relations wire to see if you can dial from your equipment directly into the wire's computer. That's the most efficient delivery method. Incidentally, if your equipment does not have communicating capability, you should look into adding this feature. It could save you both time and money in the long run. You may, of course, send your release by any of the other ''traditional'' methods—telephone facsimile, messenger or phone dictation.

7. If you dictate a release on the phone, listen carefully when it is read back. Many words sound alike on the phone. And only you know if your client's name is spelled Steven or Stephen.

Do not count on editing as part of the transmission service. In spite of the amazingly high level of competence of these operators, insist that copy be read back to you on the phone and also request a ''hard copy'' (actual copy of the transmission to the media), with the time of distribution.

8. Since wire copy cannot be addressed to individuals—it is slugged ''To Business News,'' ''Sports,''

"City Desk," etc.—occasionally you may wish to phone a personal contact or special editor, such as the science editor, to alert the person that the release is moving on the public relations wire. That way, the editor can either rip it off the printer or call it up on the video display screen if the copy goes directly into the computer.

9. Make sure the person listed as the contact is available and on standby for calls at least an hour after the release has been transmitted, and provide "night numbers" for late-breaking stories.

10. All the services charge an annual membership fee supplemented by charges based on the distribution ordered and the number of words in each release. A visit to the office of one or more news wire services provides an exciting picture of their operations and insights into methods of improving techniques for dealing with them. Most operate Monday through Friday, although some are available 24 hours a day, every day. You usually can make special arrangements for "after hours" services. Peak transmission is in the late afternoon, and while any delay is measured in a matter of a few minutes, arranging for transmission in the morning might give you even faster service—and will be appreciated by the media.

11. Standardize—in advance—the method of transmission to the newswire. Make sure that the secretaries and others are familiar with the complete procedure, which is especially important for use when you are ill, on vacation or otherwise occupied. The ways to reach the newswire are:

Telephone dictation
Messenger
Telex (also called Telex I)
TWX (also called Telex II)
Telephone facsimile
Mail (U.S. or courier service)
Telegram
Direct distance dialing (DDD), which is directly from your processor or computer terminal

So, now are you convinced that the PR wires are not simply sophisticated messenger services!

There are now about a dozen public relations pr wires around the country, listed alphabetically as follows. All but two of them—Business Wire and PR Newswire—are local wires, with some offering varying degrees of regional coverage. All have reciprocal copy exchange agreements with each other. If there is a wire in your city, you should use it for local saturation distribution, and, if required, they can be asked to pass the copy along to other wires for additional coverage. Business Wire and PR Newswire are national lines, with bureaus in a number of cities. Although they appear similar, there are significant differences in the services offered and they should be compared carefully.

Some of the material in the Business Wire and PR Newswire sections applies to the other major news wires. In fact, major clients sometimes are members of more than one news wire, just as they may subscribe to more than one clipping bureau.

1. Business Wire

44 Montgomery St., San Francisco 94104
(415) 986-4422, (800) 227-0845
Telex: 34-828
TWX: 910-372-6135
Lorry I. Lokey, Pres. and Genl. Mgr.

Branch Offices:
1 CNN Center, Atlanta 30303
(404) 688-4422
Mona McGowan, Mgr.

2 Center Plaza, Boston 02108
(617) 720-0012, (800) 225-2030
TWX: 710-321-6317
Barry M. Brooks, V.P.

212 S. Tryon St., Charlotte, NC 28281
(714) 377-0151
Marion Ellis, Mgr.

629 Euclid Ave., Cleveland 44114
(216) 781-0220
Patrick Carpenter, Mgr.

1660 Lincoln St., Denver 80264
(303) 861-8833
Cheryl Malvestuto, Mgr.

672 S. Lafayette Park Place, L.A. 90057
(213) 380-8383, (800) 257-8212
Telex 67-4727
TWX: 910-321-2912
Patricia Canary, Western Div.

555 N.E. 15 St., Miami 33132
(305) 374-3212
Paul Lyle, Mgr.

172 Second Ave., Nashville 37201
(615) 255-3445
Tom Mulgrew, Mgr.

133 Ave. of the Americas, N.Y. 10036
(212) 575-8822, (800) 221-2462
Telex: 14-7158
TWX: 710-581-2432
William D. Dobbins, V.P.-Eastern Div.
Cathy Baron Tamraz, Bureau Mgr.
Anthony P. Galli, V.P. Marketing Director
Deborah E. Pickering, Fin'l. Info. Serv. Mgr.-East

3003 N. Central Ave., Phoenix 85012
(602) 230-0433
Grant Armendariz, Mgr.

1703 Tower Bldg., Seattle, WA 98101
(206) 622-1632
Jodi Beck, Mgr.

The second largest company in the field, Business Wire has expanded considerably in recent years. More important than its growth is its leadership in innovative services and its close rapport with its two publics—working publicists and the working press.

Started in San Francisco in 1961, BW is still actively run by its founder, Lorry Lokey.

In 1969, Lokey set up facilities in his home for off-hours emergency use. The company's expansion has relied on extensive computerized facilities in its offices, and yet Lokey has maintained his personal touch. BW services over 1,200 media outlets in about 300 cities in 48 states and the District of Columbia, plus arrangements with other media throughout the world.

In 1984, BW inaugurated a special package for the Far East (Japan, Korea, China, Taiwan, Hong Kong, Singapore and Australia) via Kyodo News International, a subsidiary of Kyodo News Service. This service is $100 to $350 for up to 300 words.

Innovations include high speed transmission (1,200 baud), computer-to-computer and input to many data bases, including CompuServe, Nexis, X*Press Information Systems, Dialog Information Services, Vu/Text, Dialcom, Infomaster Electronic Library and Desk Top Broker.

The Financial Information Services division recently was set up to reach the investment community with greater speed and accuracy.

Through Analyst Wire, BW transmits financial releases full text to more than 400 brokerage and institutional firms, accessing them electronically via hard copy printer or the Bridge Information System. The Analyst Wire is $60 for up to 400 words.

Another innovation in 1987, was the BW SportsWire to sports editors, both print and broadcast, for $50 to $75 for a region or $150 for all 500 media points across the country.

The newest, and most ambitious, service is BW WirePhotos for electronic transmission of color and black-and-white photos. This supplements BW FeaturePhotos, a bimonthly *mailing* of photos to about 1,500 editors.

Business Wire charges for news distribution begin at $35 and vary with the length of release and geographical coverage. A typical 400-word release sent on the National Circuit costs $225.

Business Wire's coast-to-coast business day extends from 8 A.M. (EST) to 6:30 P.M. (PST). Emergency service can be obtained at other hours for a $100 additional charge by telephoning (415) 343-6212, (213) 541-2428, or (617) 963-3564.

The annual $60 membership includes several unique services at no extra charge. A monthly newsletter is crammed with media and public relations news. BW provides Dow Jones and Reuters financial wire clippings, job placement assistance for employers and toll-free WATS lines both to Eastern and Western offices.

In addition to its own lines, BW transmits copy to other press relations wires and sends releases to individual news media via telex, TWX, Mailgram and telephone facsimile.

In summary, Business Wire has an efficient range of services for a loyal group of clients, and Lorry Lokey is well known in the public relations and journalism fields. Lorry (note the spelling!) was feature editor of the Pacific Stars and Stripes in Tokyo after the Second World War, worked at UPI in Portland, Oregon, and as a newspaper reporter in Longview, Washington, and was in corporate public relations in San Francisco before starting Business Wire in 1961.

2. Canada News-Wire Ltd.
211 Yonge St., Toronto, Ontario M5B 1M4
(416) 863-9350
Telex: 06-22336
Gordon S. Eastwood, Pres.

Branch Offices:
1350 Sherbrooke St., West, Montreal, Quebec H3G 1J1
(514) 842-2520, Telex: 055-60936

165 Sparks St., Ottawa, Ontario K1P 5B9
(613) 563-4465, Telex: 053-3292

Suite 635, 401-9th Ave., S.W., Calgary, Alberta T2P 3C7
(403) 269-7605, Telex: 03-824872

750 W. Pender St., Vancouver, B.C. V6C 2T8
(604) 669-7764, Telex: 04-508529

Just about every professional publicist in Canada uses Canada News-Wire, a comprehensive, efficient operation which provides news wire and other services. Annual access fee of $50 entitles subscribers to use all CNW services.

Formed in 1960, Canada News-Wire operates a private, computerized communications network with printers installed in newsrooms across Canada. Contact with CNW can be by Telex, computer-to-computer, facsimile or courier.

The basic distribution, called the Canadian Basic Network, costs $110 per 100 words and goes to major newspapers, radio and television stations, news agencies and broadcast networks. Transmission to French-language media should be in French, and CNW charges only $19 per 100 words for translation.

All news releases transmitted on CNW networks are automatically and permanently filed in the CNW Database for future reference by reporters, researchers and financial analysts.

CNW rates are based on per 100 word volumes, ranging from $135/100 words for the Canadian Disclosure Network to $35/100 words for Metropolitan Toronto dissemination. CNW also provides translation services at $19/100 words for distribution on the Canadian French Network, which is transmitted at $30/100 words.

The company also has an extensive broadcast division for audio and video news releases.

3. InterMedia Group, Inc.
24500 Southfield Rd., Southfield, MI 48075

Formed as Press Relations Newswire in suburban Detroit, the company expanded by opening newswires in Washington, DC (Press Relations Newswire), Atlanta (Southeastern Newswire) and Cleveland (Ohio Newswire).

In 1986, InterMedia Group, which had been the country's third largest newswire, was acquired by PR Newswire. Its operations are described under Ohio Newswire, Press Relations Newswire and Southeastern Newswire.

4. Mediawire
17 S. 17th St., Philadelphia, PA 19103
(215) 586-6300, (800) 523-4424
Telex I: 83-1853
Telex II: (710) 670-1396
Computer: (215) 864-0999 (300 wpm and 1,200 wpm)
Telecopier: (215) 568-0898
Jane Doner Booth, Mgr.

Branch Office:
300 Sixth Ave., Pittsburgh, PA 15222
(412) 232-3050
Telex: 90-2837
TWX: (710) 664-3707
Computer: (412) 232-3057 (300 wpm and 1,200 wpm)
Telecopier: (412) 232-3053
Pamela Thompson, Mgr.

Mediawire, a regional press release wire service serving five Mid-Atlantic states, was founded in 1976, and in 1983 was acquired by PR Newswire. It continues to operate as a regional service under its own name.

Mediawire transmits more government and political news releases than most other press release wires. Its clients include municipal and state governments, universities, politicians and special interest groups, as well as most of the larger corporations in its region.

Mediawire serves about 70 newsrooms in Pennsylvania for $95; Philadelphia can be ordered separately for $50, Pittsburgh for $50 and the Harrisburg-Lancaster-York area for $35.

Twenty Maryland newsrooms are served for $40; nine in Delaware for $25, and 21 in West Virginia for $40.

Rates are based on releases of 400 words or less, with each additional 100 words costing roughly 20 percent of the posted fee.

The annual membership fee is $60.

The Philadelphia and Pittsburgh bureaus serve as local bureaus of PR Newswire for national and financial public relations accounts.

Mediawire bureaus are open weekdays from 8:30 A.M. to 6 P.M.

5. Newswire
2100 Pillsbury Ave. S., Minneapolis, MN 55404
(612) 871-7201
Telex: 29-0306
TWX: 910-576-2770
Telecopier: (612) 871-1220, (612) 871-0917
Kit Hagen, Genl. Mgr.

In 1973, the Padilla and Speer public relations agency started a private line wire service, called Sports Score Central, to transmit scores from more than 500 area schools to the local media in the Twin Cities area. In 1974, this service was enlarged to Newswire Central, and it now operates as part of Publicity Central (described in the chapter on packaged publicity services).

Newswire transmits news releases to the major news media in the Twin Cities.

The charge is $45 for each use up to 400 words. News conference and other memos up to 150 words are only $25, so if you keep it brief and only want to reach the Minneapolis and St. Paul media, this is a bargain. An Investors Wire to brokerage firms is $10 extra for news releases.

6. Ohio Newswire
815 Superior Ave., N.E., Cleveland 44114
(216) 566-7581
Telex I: 98-0189
*   II: 810-421-8410, 8245*

Computer: (216) 575-0088 (300 wpm)
(216) 575-0366 (1,200 wpm)
Telecopier: (216) 566-1234
John Spetz, Mgr.

Ohio Newswire, which is a bureau of PR Newswire, has a sizable operation in the state. Its basic service is the transmission to 30 newsrooms in the Greater Cleveland area, for $40 for the first 400 words. Additional 100 words are $5.

Additional coverage in Ohio includes:

Ohio State Pack: all major daily papers in the state and wire bureaus in Columbus and Cincinnati.
Northeast Ohio Pack: dailies in Lake, Geauga, Ashtabula counties.
Northwest Ohio Pack: dailies in Lorain, Elyria, Toledo, Sandusky and Medina.
Ohio TV Packs: All major TV stations in the state, available together or by coverage area.
Special City Packs: all major metro areas.

Annual Membership is $60; hours are 9 A.M. to 5 P.M. Monday through Friday; overtime, weekend and holiday service is available by advance arrangement.

7. PR News Service

35 E. Wacker Dr., Chicago 60601
(312) 782-8100
Joseph Reilly, Genl. Mgr.
John Geldmacher, Marketing Dir.

A department of the City News Bureau of Chicago (a cooperative news agency owned by The Chicago Tribune and Chicago Sun-Times), this service charges public relations subscribers an annual fee of $60 plus fees for each transmission. Local rate is $55 for messages up to 400 words; Illinois service is $80. Service to other cities, via affiliated wires, can be obtained.

8. PR Newswire

150 E. 58 St., N.Y. 10155
(212) 832-9400, (800) 832-5522
Telex: 1-2284, 12-6217
TWX: (710) 581-5360
Computer: (212) 832-0347 (300 wpm)
(212) 308-2617 (300 wpm)
(212) 308-2618 (1,200 wpm)
(212) 308-2619 (2,400 wpm)
Telecopier: (212) 832-9406, (212) 832-9408
David Steinberg, Pres.
Roland Eckman, Exec. Editor

Branch Offices:
161 Spring St., Atlanta 30303
(See listing under Southeastern Newswire)

10 Liberty Sq., Boston 02109
(617) 482-5355
Telex I: 94-0906

Telex II: (710) 321-0467
Computer: (617) 542-8717 (300 wpm)
(617) 542-8718 (1,200 wpm)
Telecopier: (617) 423-4157
Robert Davidson, Mgr.

212 South Tryon St., Charlotte, NC 28281
(704) 338-9366
Telex I: 57-5064
Telex II (TWX): (810) 621-0114
Computer: (704) 338-9767 (300 wpm)
(704) 338-9920 (1,200 wpm)
Telecopier: (704) 338-9566
Jerry Mitchell, Mgr.

815 Superior Ave., N.E., Cleveland 44114
(See listing under Ohio Newswire)

370 17th St., Denver, 80202
(303) 592-5077, (800) 843-2495
Telex I: 45-2102
Telex II (TWX): (910) 931-0073
Computer: (303) 893-5426 (300 wpm)
(303) 893-5630 (1,200 wpm)
Telecopier: (303) 592-5078
Sandra Doubleday, Mgr.

24500 Southfield Rd., Southfield, MI 48075
(See listing under Press Relations Newswire)

900 Wilshire Blvd., Los Angeles 90017
(213) 626-5501, (800) 321-8169
Telex I: 67-7512
Telex II (TWX): (910) 321-4420
Computer: (213) 687-4971 (300 wpm)
(213) 687-4580 (1,200 wpm)
Telecopier: (213) 626-5501
Bonnie Nijst, Mgr.

2100 Coral Way, Miami 33145
(305) 856-8885
Telex I: 51-8900
Telex II (TWX): (810) 848-6564
Computer: (305) 858-0259 (300 wpm)
(305) 858-7252 (1,200 wpm)
Telecopier: (305) 856-7118
Wally Machos, Mgr.

117 S. 17 St., Philadelphia 19103
(See listing under Mediawire)

300 Sixth Ave., Pittsburgh 15222
(See listing under Mediawire)

801 Oberlin Rd., Raleigh, NC 27605
(919) 821-4048
Telecopier: (919) 821-4395
Leila Tvedt, Mgr.

50 Francisco St., San Francisco 94133
(415) 986-3400, (800) 334-6692
Computer: (415) 986-6252, (415) 986-6253
Telecopier: (415) 986-6255
David Einstein, Mgr.

1001 Fourth Ave., Seattle 98154
(206) 624-2414
Telex I: 32-6059
Telex II (TWX): (910) 444-0104
Computer: (206) 624-5841 (300 wpm)
*   (206) 624-6118 (1,200 wpm)*
Telecopier: (206) 624-2343
Bonnie Brooks, Mgr.

1301 Pennsylvania Ave. N.W., Wash., D.C. 20004
(See listing under Press Relations Wire)

In 1954, PR Newswire pioneered an ingenious concept—the simultaneous electronic transmission of news releases in full to major media via private teleprinter circuits. On opening day, the "pr wire" reached 12 points in New York City at a then respectable 60 words per minute. Today, PR Newswire is a computerized national and international press communications system with a staff—mostly trained journalists—serving a thousand daily newspapers, wire services, radio-TV outlets, trade and specialized publications in the U.S. by satellite and additional hundreds overseas, at speeds of up to 230,000 words per minute.

Over the years, PR Newswire has been the model for more than a dozen other local "pr wire" with similar names around the United States and overseas—thus creating an "industry" that has become one of the most efficient and effective tools of the pr professional. On an "average" business day, PR Newswire processes over 300 time-critical news releases—each dispatched within minutes!

For four decades, PRN has led the industry it created. It was the first to extend its teleprinter circuits beyond its own city and the first to offer users a choice of "News-Lines" for regional news release distribution. With the encouragement of the New York and American Stock Exchanges, PRN initiated a special line (the Investors Research Wire) to transmit the full text of news releases to banks, brokers and other members of the financial community. And it was the first to transmit news releases directly into newspaper computers and, more recently into the vast electronic retrieval libraries known as databases.

In the technological area, PRN was one of the first wire services anywhere in the world to use electronic editing terminals. PRN observed its 25th anniversary in 1979 by completely computerizing all of its communications operations. In 1984, the service marked its 30th anniversary by introducing satellite transmission from an uplink near its New York headquarters to a satellite and then to rooftop dishes and earth stations around the country—with news releases beamed up and down between them at that incredible 230,000 wpm.

From its headquarters in New York City and bureaus in 14 cities around the country, PRN reaches 1,000 news media in 325 cities across the nation, transmitting to 1,200-wpm teleprinters in newsrooms or directly into the editorial computers of the media. At a number of the most important points—Dow Jones, Reuters, and The New York Times, for example—PRN has installed a second, separate circuit and teleprinter to provide a complete backup facility, and some of the media have as many as six PRN printers in various locations in their offices.

Domestically, PRN offers 50 "NewsLines" tailored to the specific needs of the public relations professional. PRN's premier line—the US1 NewsLine—covers those 1,000 media. Its US2 NewsLine offers, at a lower rate, a more restricted national distribution. Various segments of these national lines can be ordered separately to provide regional coverage; the Northeast NewsLine, for example, covers all media from Washington, D.C., to Portland, Maine; Western covers 240 major news media in eight states from Phoenix to Fairbanks; a number of state NewsLines reach media in individual states and various Metro lines serve media in cities such as New York, Philadelphia, Detroit, Los Angeles and San Francisco.

Several of these NewsLines are the result of major acquisitions made by PRN over the past several years. In 1984, PRN acquired Mediawire, with bureaus in Philadelphia and Pittsburgh, with lines covering Pennsylvania, Maryland, West Virginia and Delaware. A year later, it acquired the InterMedia Group, which operated wires in Detroit, Atlanta, Cleveland and Washington. In 1987, PR NewsWire acquired NewsWire/Denver.

To assure publicly-held companies that they can tell their stories in their own words directly to the financial community, PR Newswire created the Investors Research Wire (originally known as the "Prompt Disclosure Broker Line"). This circuit carries the full text of "immediate release" financial news to leading brokerage firms, banks, insurance companies, mutual and pension funds and others, as well as to the New York, American and Pacific Stock Exchanges and the National Association of Securities Dealers. The PRN-IRW reaches major financial institutions in such important money centers as New York, Boston, Chicago, San Francisco and Los Angeles.

Although PRN is often looked upon as a "financial wire" (the public relations newswires are the recognized and recommended way to meet "prompt disclosure" requirements), it also handles a great many general news stories every day on its regular News-Lines and its special feature wire, which many publicists have used with great success.

PRN also relays copy on request to media not on its circuits or to other local pr wires. International distribution, including translation, and a mailing service to international trade and technical journals are handled through affiliates in Canada, England, Germany, Japan and several other countries. News may be sent to virtually any country in the world, including communist countries and the developing nations of Africa and the Far East.

Anticipating the impact of the "computer revolution" in the nation's newsrooms on press relations, PRN embarked on its own computerization to make publicists' copy compatible with the new electronic requirements of newspapers. Today, PRN's state-of-the-art computer system—with "on line" backup—provides simultaneous transmission of news releases at different speeds, in different formats and various protocols as required by teleprinters or newspaper computers on PRN lines, or via "direct computer dial-up" or the AP DataFeature Service to media not on PRN circuits. PRN employs a full-time staff engineer to maintain its equipment and help clients communicate with PRN.

Also anticipated was another "revolution"—the use of word processors by public relations practitioners. From the beginning, PRN's computers were engineered to receive copy from a wide range of word processors and computers equipped with communications capability. Now, more and more PRN clients use their word processors or computers to transmit directly into PRN's PRONTO computer system. This is by far the fastest way to deliver a release to PRN and on to the media. Transmission can be at 300, 1200 or 2400 wpm. Computer-to-computer transmission also vastly reduces the "turnaround time" at PRN since no rekeyboarding is necessary. PRN suggests you check compatibility of your equipment with a test message first.

You may, of course, deliver your release to PRN by any method—telephone facsimile (from the old-six-minute-per-page to the newest super speeds), TWX, Telex, messenger or telephone dictation.

Another development in the "computer/word processing revolution" has been the growth of databases, those vast electronic libraries that store incredible amounts of information and make it instantly accessible and easily searchable. In 1981, PRN began transmitting every news release to NEXIS, the most comprehensive, on-line, full-text news search and retrieval service in the world. Subsequently, PRN added other databases to its lines and now serves nearly a dozen, including NEXIS, Dialog Dow Jones, News/Ratrieval and NewsNet, a library of industry newsletters.

PRN points out that these databases represent a new form of news release "publication" since the full text remains available to editors and other researchers even if only a small part of the release originally appeared in the papers. And, again, as communicating word processors, computers or table-top data terminals become more commonplace in public relations, more and more publicists are using their equipment to access these databases for their own research or to help prepare sales presentations.

From 1971 to 1982, PR Newswire was owned by Western Union Corporation. In 1982, PR Newswire was acquired by United Newspapers of London, one of England's largest newspaper publishers, whose publications include the Express Newspapers, the Yorkshire Post and Punch magazine. PRN's midtown Manhattan office is well worth a visit to learn more about the latest technology in press communications, to see how databases operate and to meet the staff, most of whom are former financial editors and writers.

Annual membership-retainer fee in PR Newswire is $60 (this also covers the Mediawire and InterMedia Group offices). Rates for the US1 Newsline are $325; US2 NewsLine is $200; the Investor Research Wire is $45; Metro New York, $55, and other regional lines range from rates as low as $45 for local wires to $100 for the Western Newswire. Rates are based on 400 words; there are extra charges for each additional 100 words. Unless otherwise specified, all financial news is automatically transmitted on the IRW.

When PR Newswire was started, it was immediately recognized as a significant technical advance over mailed or messengered press release distribution. Today, with a high-speed technology that makes public relations operations compatible with computerized newsrooms, and with service to databases that make the full text of the news release available to an ever-widening audience, the use of a public relations newswire is literally indispensable to financial and other publicists.

9. Press Relations Newswire

24500 Southfield Rd., Southfield, MI 48075
(313) 557-7474
Telex: 23-5320
TWX: 810-224-4660
Computer 300 baud: (313) 557-9070
David H. Durbin, Mgr.

Press Relations Newswire is the flagship of InterMedia Group, a subsidiary of PR Newswire, which also operates newswires in Atlanta, Cleveland and Washington, DC. Southeastern Newswire and Ohio Newswire are listed elsewhere in this chapter. These are all major media centers, and the company is a thoroughly professional operation.

PRN transmits news releases to 51 points in the metropolitan Detroit area, for $50 up to 400 words. Extra length is $10 per 100 words. The wire includes 8 newspapers, 15 radio stations, 6 TV stations, and 22 other bureaus and points in Detroit, including both the Detroit and Chicago Reuters bureaus. The Detroit News and the Detroit Free Press are served by two teleprinters each—the city desks and financial desks.

A statewide Michigan wire includes the Detroit points, plus nine additional newspapers, two electronic media, the Capital Press Room, Grand Rapids Business Journal and Grand Rapids Magazine. It costs $25 additional for 400 words; and $10 per 100 words for extra length.

Also, the main brokerage houses in Detroit may be served for $5 additional, on the Detroit Investors Research Wire.

Annual membership is $60; hours are 8:30 A.M. to 5 P.M. Monday through Friday. Overtime service for any other time is available by advance arrangement.

10. Press Relations Wire

1301 Pennsylvania Ave., N.W., Washington, DC 20004
(202) 347-5155
Telex: 90-4354
TWX: 710-822-9632
Computer 300 baud: (202) 393-8217
1,200 baud: (202) 393-8243
Dan Selnick, Mgr.

PRW transmits news releases to 65 points in the Capital area, for $60 up to 400 words. Extra length is $15 per 100 words. The wire includes 12 city and suburban newspapers, 9 radio outlets, 9 TV stations, and 35 other media.

A very useful service is the DC Package. News releases are duplicated and delivered by a staff messenger to 185 additional news outlets in the National Press Building, including the Press Club rack, for $45 additional to the wire price. Hand delivery to the House and Senate press galleries (25 copies each) is available for $25.

Annual membership is $60; hours are 8:30 A.M. to 6 P.M. Monday through Friday. The wire is closed on government holidays, but overtime service is available by advance arrangement.

Press Relations Wire is a bureau of PR Newswire.

11. Southeastern Newswire

161 Spring St., Atlanta, GA 30303
(404) 523-2323
Telex: 70-0533
TWX: 810-751-8146
Computer 300 baud: (404) 523-6635
Tom Madden, Mgr.

Southeastern Newswire transmits news releases to 33 points in the metropolitan Atlanta area, for $45 up to 400 words. Extra length is $10 per 100 words. The wire includes 8 newspapers, 9 radio stations, 4 TV stations, and 12 other bureaus and points in Atlanta.

Also available is a Georgia wire, which adds 13 additional newspapers to the Atlanta wire; it costs $15 additional to the Atlanta wire.

Annual membership is $60; hours are 8:30 A.M. to 6 P.M. Monday through Friday; overtime service for any other time is available by advance arrangement.

Southeastern is a bureau of PR Newswire.

12. Southwest Press Relations Newswire, Inc.

2301 N. Akard, Dallas, TX 75201
(214) 871-2940
Telex: 73-0154
TWX: 910-861-4161
James H. Baird

Branch Offices:
2329 W. Holcombe, Houston 77030
(713) 661-4464

621 N. Robinson, Oklahoma City, OK 73102
(405) 236-8615

314 East Commerce, San Antonio 78205
(512) 222-8331

The $75 annual membership fee includes a subscription to Southwest Media/PR Newsletter, a monthly bulletin about editorial personnel changes. Usage per release (up to 400 words) is $50 for the Dallas-Ft. Worth circuit and $50 for the Houston-Austin-San Antonio circuit, or $75 for both circuits. Additional coverage in Oklahoma, Louisiana and elsewhere is available.

13. TRIM International

94 rue Saint-Lazare, 75009 Paris
(33/1) 48.78.38.32
Telex: (842) 290268
Lambert Mayer, Pres.

Launched in Paris in 1981, TRIM International was the first press relations newswire in continental Europe, serving as model for the franchised TRIM operations in several European countries. Communications A.P.U. Inc., CP 628 Mont-Royal, Montreal, QC H3P-3G4, Canada, is the corporate headquarters. A Japan sales office operates in cooperation with Adex Limited Japan, ABS Building 2F, 2-4-16 Kudanminami, Chiyoda-Ku, Tokyo, Japan 102, tel. (81/03) 263-4522.

In the U.S., Business Wire is TRIM's main affiliate, relaying releases to the TRIM Paris office for transmission in Europe. Canada News Wire, Telbec and various regional news wires in North America also accept copy for transmission in Europe via TRIM.

The basic English language service, which goes to computers or printers at Associated Press, AP-Dow Jones, Reuters, UPI and other media in Paris, is $150 for releases up to 300 words. If you provide a French translation, TRIM will transmit it, at no extra charge, to its basic French language network. They can translate releases for $50 up to 300 words.

For business and financial news, TRIM offers an English language Business Capitals of Europe package, covering over 60 key media in 25 major cities in 12 countries, for $600.

In-depth coverage of individual European countries is $325 per country, including translation in the appropriate language.

TRIM's European High Tech pack includes 44 key computer and electronics publications in Europe for $300.

TRIM International's annual membership fee ($100) is waived for clients using Business Wire, Canada Newswire, Telbec or any other TRIM affiliate.

14. Universal News Services

Communications House, Gough Square, Fleet St., London EC4P 4DP, England
01-353-5200
Telex: 266363
Robert Simpson, Mgr. Dir.

Universal News Services is a wire service in the United Kingdom patterned after PR Newswire in the U.S. The company is different from its U.S. counterparts in that it includes editorial and technical services that enable it to function very similarly to nonsponsored news services, and British media have accorded it appropriately high status and acceptance.

UNS is affiliated with PR Newswire, and U.S. clients can use its services via PR Newswire.

Formed in 1958 by Alfred Geiringer, a former Reuters journalist, Universal was acquired in 1986 by the Press Association, Britain's national news agency.

In addition to its private computerized high-speed networks to the national, regional, local and specialized newspapers and radio and television, UNS also provides several other services, including:

Unitel, a nationwide viewdata news service for local media via the British Telecom Prestel system, with copy printout;
Radio Services, the production and distribution of taped interviews and the monitoring of their usage;
All types of mailing, messenger and convention services.

15. U.S. Newswire

1272 Ntl. Pres. Bldg., Wash., DC 20045
(202) 347-2770
Telex: 98-8232
William C. McCarren, Pres.

Formed in 1986, U.S. Newswire transmits to about 40 major print and broadcast media in Washington, D.C., plus the Senate and House press galleries. Cost is $55 up to 400 words and $15 for each additional 100 words.

The U.S. Newswire National Circuit provides service to the same Washington list plus about 70 bureaus of print media in Washington, D.C. The cost is $150 for up to 400 words, plus $40 for each additional 100 words.

Through arrangement with other newswires, service is available elsewhere in the U.S., and other countries. Computer service is available on 300 and 1,200 baud.

Special services include a Daybook of the next day's events and a Recap of headlines of releases transmitted that day. Annual membership is $60.

Chapter 17

Newspaper Services

About 1,650 daily newspapers in the U.S. have a total circulation of about 63 million. Sunday circulation of about 800 newspapers is about 59 million.

About 8,000 weekly newspapers have a free and paid circulation of about 50 million.

In Canada, about 110 daily newspapers have a total circulation of about 5.6 million.

For most public relations practitioners, the greatest amount of activity is geared to daily newspapers though, of course, all media are important and interrelated. The same news release, for example, generally is sent to all print media.

Daily newspapers are read by more than 100 million American adults every day, an average of 2.2 readers per daily newspaper. The typical daily newspaper reader spends an average of 44 minutes a day reading one or more newspapers.

More money is spent by advertisers in newspapers than any other medium, including television, which ranks second.

All of this then is simply a reminder about the medium that is one of the major bulwarks of our free society.

Much of the material in the chapters on clipping bureaus, mailing services, newswires and research relates to daily newspapers. This chapter is primarily about methods of obtaining newspaper publicity via "mat services."

The greatest amount of publicity activity is with newspapers. Every day, thousands of news releases are printed and delivered to various departmental editors at daily newspapers, wire services, syndicates and supplements. Hundreds of news releases are transmitted daily via PR Newswire, Business Wire and other newswires, as well as via messenger and courier services.

Preprinted camera-ready releases are distributed to many thousands of daily and weekly newspapers by specialized companies that many publicists still call mat services, though the word "mat" is an anachronism.

One of the definitions of the word "mat" is "anything densely interwoven or felted or growing in a thick tangle."

To a publicist, the thick tangle of companies which specialize in the distribution of free mats to newspapers often appears to be like a mat of hair or some other thick, imponderable mass. The mat business is ponderable, as it renders a unique, valuable service to both publicist and media. The largest company in this field is North American Precis Syndicate.

As used in the publishing field, a mat is short for matrix, that is, the metal plate, usually of brass, used to mold type. Typesetting and engraving costs are a major factor in the low-budget operations of most small circulation daily and weekly newspapers. As a result, many companies were organized to provide these newspaper publishers with free cardboard mats of cartoons, photos and articles. In addition to the savings in production costs, the publisher also has a handy free source of a variety of features in different sizes and with different illustrations, so that he or she can quickly and conveniently fill in space on the pages.

NOTE: The trend in printing is from letterpress (which uses engravings and mats) to photo offset (which uses photographic negatives). Thus, reproduction proof sheets are provided to offset publishers, and mats are provided only to the few remaining letterpress publishers. However, the term "newspaper mat services" has become generic and is used in this chapter to include all types of color and black-and-white publicity materials provided in *ready-to-print* form.

The *quid pro quo* for accepting camera-ready releases without paying for them, to be blunt about it, is simply that the publisher knows that there is some type of sponsored message involved in the editorial material. However, as with any publicity material, the editor is the final arbiter of what is used and what is not. No editor will accept an advertisement in the disguised form of an editorial mat. The mature public relations practitioner is aware, and appreciative, of the differences between advertising material and editorial matter.

There are more than ten companies throughout the country which specialize in the distribution of ready-to-print publicity mats to newspapers. As with other types of publicity, the client cannot be guaranteed placement. The variables include the content and layout of the mat, total number of mats distributed and the efficiency of the distributor.

The various distributors offer innovations, specialities and other attempts to make their services unique, but their methods of operation and charges often are quite similar. Almost all of them include the provision of clippings as part of the service. The quantity and quality of these clippings vary considerably, but a client can usually expect anywhere from 40 to 400 clippings for a mat mailing which costs about two thousand dollars.

Of these clippings, many are from weekly newspapers whose circulation is less than 10,000. Some of these newspapers have inferior printing facilities so that the clipping often is faded or badly reproduced. However, some of the newspapers have larger circulations and better reproduction facilities, and the total circulation often can be fairly sizable. There are many suburban and other newspapers with circulations in excess of 10,000 which have offset facilities and reproduce from the proof sheets which all of the mat services also provide. A recent development is the use of color by large circulation newspapers in major cities. Two companies now specialize in this type of publicity service.

Many weekly newspaper publishers also do "job printing," and astute publicists, particularly in suburban or rural areas, often turn over booklets or other materials to these printers as a way to obtain low-cost results plus good will. A recent development has been the use by publicists of major newspaper plants, or production companies owned by daily newspaper and magazine publishers. For example, sophisticated phototypesetting from magnetic tape input is offered by Media General Financial Services, 301 E. Grace St., Richmond, VA 23219, phone (804) 649-6736. The company is an affiliate of Media General, publisher of the Richmond Times-Dispatch.

Public relations people involved in the preparation of publications and advertising generally turn over the details of production to printers and designers, and rarely deal directly with typesetters, engravers, binderies and other specialists. (Some printers include these facilities on their premises, others subcontract—you should be aware of what you're paying for and to whom.)

Publicists who prepare their own newspaper mats, or who have other jobs involving newspaper reproduction, must work with printers who are knowledgeable about the variety of newspaper sizes and other requirements.

Ron Levy, founder and president of North American Precis Syndicate, regularly analyzes the different types of mats which are published. There are four principal formats, according to Mr. Levy, who describes them as follows:

> The cartoon generally pulls much more than other formats, and enables you to deliver your sales message with an "imagine that!" impact. If you use a historical approach, your product will look extra modern against the background of its historical antecedents. But don't cheer yet. For all its merit, the cartoon has a big drawback: little space for your message, since the bulk of the release is taken up by artwork. Another drawback is cost, for you will have an art bill to pay.
>
> The photo and caption is the classic approach to camera-ready releases, for good reason. They appeal to an editor mainly because they brighten up the paper with pictures—without having to bear the costs of photography. The drawback to photo-caption mats is that competition is severe; most PR issuers of camera-ready releases use this technique. Also, you run the risk of poor reproduction in some newspapers.
>
> The signed column is growing in popularity because people are eager to get expert advice for nothing. That's why doctors always hear about symptoms at social gatherings. And that's why, if you have a bona fide expert in lawn care, insurance, cooking, or some other widely interesting subject, a signed column can serve the interests of thousands of readers (including you). Curiously, a good series of signed columns tends to increase in circulation like compound interest. You get an average of 2 to 4 percent more clippings with each release. At the end of the year, the increase reaches an impressive figure. But you lose the "compound interest" effect if you don't release at least once a month.
>
> The short feature, illustrated by a photo or a spot of art, gets a circulation proportional to the respect shown by the writer toward smaller papers. If you take the time to research your subject, then present fact-fact-fact as you would in a release to major dailies, you will serve the interests of the small newspaper editor whose time for research is limited. The main advantage of this format is that it permits you a detailed story. The drawback is that it takes more time than cartoons or photo-caption releases.

Whether you are sending conventionally printed news releases or preprints, here are a few comments based on many years of evaluating actual clipping results.

Product Publicity. Among the best-pulling releases are those that offer tips: how to get better results, lower-cost results, or both. The "then and now" approach also pulls well. So do features such as fashion forecasts that help readers choose wisely.

Often, top quality releases can be abstracted from consumer booklets. Or, if you already have completed photography for metro dailies and magazines, the extra photos may create added coverage for you if released to suburban dailies and weeklies.

For releases tied to a holiday such as Father's Day, get them into the mail six weeks before the day. Make it eight weeks before Christmas. And don't get jittery if the Day comes and goes with very few clips left in your hands. It generally takes five or six weeks between the date of publication and the date on which you get your clips.

Corporate Identification. Many companies will turn a security analyst presentation into a major release for suburban newspapers. The idea is to strengthen the investor relations program by supplying the corporate material not only to analysts, but also to investors who get ideas from reading their newspapers.

Sometimes a series of six or eight photo-caption releases can be taken from the annual report to show how the company is serving the public interest. If the illustration on each major division is a picture of the division chief at work, that's not for suburban papers. But if your photos show on-site equipment, a lab scene, or end-products-in-use, and if the words show positive service to the public interest, suburban releases can bring the material to the attention of millions who won't see the annual report. Since camera-ready releases invariably are printed intact, you can use a logo or other corporate identification in the headline and/or photo and obtain added impact. In fact, some editors prefer a logo for easy identification of a regular series of columns.

Public Policy Information. (See the chapter on editorials.) Again, the function of camera-ready releases is not necessarily to go off in a new direction, but to increase the coverage of information you already are disseminating in other ways.

When you are in a situation where the public doesn't understand the situation and doesn't much care about it, you may find that suburban newspapers can be a powerful aid to you in creating awareness of how an issue affects the public interest, and in generating letters to legislators.

A typical camera-ready release, corporate or product, gets 40 to 400 clippings and costs about $2,250. This includes typography, materials, mailing and clippings, all of which are provided by the "mat service."

As in all areas of publicity services, one vendor is not the same as another. Yet many companies and associations that use camera-ready releases as a permanent part of their public relations and marketing programs often continue to use the same format and make little attempt to analyze the results.

Another variable that should be explored is the specific service. Regardless of whether you see few or scores of preprint releases a year, you should be familiar with the different prices and variations in techniques among the major companies.

Most of the distributors are small operations that provide this service exclusively, though a few of them are larger operations offering a variety of related publicity services. Most prices include the writing of the caption or feature article, subject to the approval of the client, and usually include everything from production and distribution of proofs through to the providing of clippings. The sponsor generally provides the photo or artwork or pays an additional small fee for this. *Be sure to ask if the price includes postage.*

Perhaps the greatest advantage of a camera-ready publicity distribution program is that the material is published intact and all of the clippings therefore appear with the client's verbatim message. Preprint publicity thus can play a part in a comprehensive public relations program, particularly if the sponsor is interested in reaching small-town and suburban families.

A few companies have experimented with punched tapes and other electronic materials for the use of major newspapers which have automated printing. Aside from the difficulty in keeping pace with the changing technologies, there is the problem of no single system in use at all newspapers. Though a few food editors and other editors who use a great deal of publicity material might prefer the convenience of electronic news releases, it does not appear to be a necessary service. The subject is discussed in the chapter on computerized news.

The separation between urban, suburban and rural newspapers has become increasingly blurred. There still are newspapers that service mostly farm areas, but there are less of these than a few decades ago. The biggest growth has been in the suburban area, and this includes dailies, weeklies and large-circulation shoppers, many of which use a great deal of preprinted material.

There are over 11,000 newspapers in the U.S., about 1,700 dailies, 8,000 "weeklies" (including those which publish two or three times a week) and over 1,000 free-circulation newspapers called shoppers, generally weeklies. Of course, not all use mats, offset proofs or any type of canned publicity material. But many do. However, be wary of any publicity service which claims mailings to over 10,000 newspapers.

In summary, in exploring ways to produce extra exposure for their top-priority messages, many practitioners have found that more than half the dailies in America, and thousands of weeklies, welcome publicity that arrives in preprinted form.

Again, a reminder! The term "mat service" is becoming anachronistic, for the newspapers that are still printed by letterpress, and require mats, are greatly outnumbered today by offset newspapers that require only camera-ready proofs on coated stock. But the name "mat release" has stuck, though some of the editors who receive it get just a proof and no mat.

A free brochure, Facts About Newspapers, can be obtained from the American Newspaper Publishers Association, the Newspaper Center, Box 17407, Dulles Airport, Wash., DC 20041. It includes data about daily and weekly newspaper circulation, advertising volume, single copy price, newspapers' share of advertising revenue, the 20 largest newspaper companies in the U.S. and the circulation of the nation's 20 largest newspapers.

Several trade associations produce their own newspaper supplements, consisting of an entire section of ready-to-print features. One of the most successful is H.I.T., a semiannual supplement (generally 32 pages) about home improvement, published since 1967 by Home Improvement Time, Inc., Old Steubenville Pike, Oakdale, PA 15071, (412) 787-3220. James A. Stewart heads this private company, which sells space for $2,000 a page in two successive semiannual issues. A ¼-page (16 column inches) is $500.

1. Associated Release Service, Inc.

2 N. Riverside Plaza, Chicago 60606
(312) 726-8693
Ted M. Hathorn, Pres.

It is common practice for a mat release service to insert its own symbol in the illustrations or headlines of the mats it distributes to make it easier for newspaper clipping service 'readers' to spot its releases when they appear on newspaper pages. The Associated symbol, which is ASR, has been appearing on thousands of mats since 1950.

Actually, the company's initials are ARS, but be that as it may, Associated is a sizeable operation in newspaper and broadcast services.

In 1984, Associated changed the column widths of its mat releases to conform to the standard column width adopted that year by the nation's newspaper publishers (following the joint recommendation of the American Newspaper Publishers Association and the Newspaper Advertising Bureau).

To order a mat and offset release, a client indicates the newspaper market coverage desired and sends copy and illustration (photo or line art) to Associated. There is no charge for minor retouching of photos, but where special artwork, combination plates, or other special graphic artwork is required, this is billed at cost. Upon client approval the release is printed on enamel proofing paper in the quantity required for distribution to the newspapers selected. These may include *all* the papers in one or more specific markets, or only the "most frequent user" (MFU) newspapers in these markets. (Currently Associated has identified slightly more than half of the 8,100 small U.S. dailies and weeklies as MFUs.)

Associated recommends 7½ inches as the most editorially accepted length for mat releases and bases its prices on this length, by the number of columns in width, and by the number of newspapers to be serviced. Releases that exceed the 7½-inch standard length incur an oversize charge for each excess inch.

The majority of mat releases are mailed via bulk third class mail (exceptions: releases about a particular event or time period). Approximately five weeks after the mailing, clippings start to arrive and are accumulated monthly for delivery to the client. The fourth and final delivery includes an analysis report that lists the total clips generated by that particular release, the total (combined) newspaper circulation represented by the clippings, and the cost per household reached.

Associated clients have several options in how their releases can be distributed:

1. Individual releases. These are sent to 8,100 small-circulation newspapers in the U.S.; to the 4,000 most frequent users; or to any market or combination of markets. A one-column individual release to 8,100 newspapers is $2,885. A two-column release to 4,000 newspapers is $1,965. A three-column release to 1,000 newspapers is $760. *Postage on individual releases is paid by the client.*

2. Theme pages. These consist of two or more releases and can be distributed together. If the releases have a common theme, they can feature a common headline (running head). Theme page prices are based on size and number of individual features on the page, and the numbers of newspapers to be serviced. For example, for two-column features to 2,000 newspapers is $3,555, and bulk third class postage adds $350 to the cost.

3. Press-ready feature packets. In the fifties, Associated sent mat releases to newspapers in a feature page format, assembling a group of noncompeting articles on a large newsprint page, accompanied by individual copies of the articles on enamel slicks. Eventually, four such feature pages were developed: Successful Lifestyles, which accepted only 'non-brand mentioned' articles; Today's Lifestyles, same distribution as the lifestyles page, but permitting brand mention; Editor's Choice, a variety feature page for small town and rural newspaper distribution, and permitting brand mention; and Monthly Column Syndicate, exclusively devoted to articles in *series*.

In 1981 Associated discontinued the four feature pages and replaced them with a single Press-Ready Feature Packet, which is distributed monthly to the 4,000 editors on the Associated most frequent user list. Non-brand mention features, and articles running in series, continue to be identified as such. The packet is mailed in the form of a booklet containing proof pages, each of which carries up to two mat releases. The features on each page are paired to be noncompetitive with each other—two food releases never appear on the same page; product and service releases are similarly segregated by subject to avoid conflict. A one-column feature 7½ inches deep costs $1,655; a two-column is $1,790, and a three-column release is $1,985. Postage is included in Press-Ready Packet prices.

4. "Hitch-hikers." For clients whose distribution requirements are limited to specific markets, Associated produces hitch-hiker releases separately and mails them *with*—but not *in*—those packets targeted to the desired markets. Such partial mailings are available at reduced cost, depending on the size of the release and the distribution required. For example, a one-column release to only 1,000 editors on the Press-Ready list costs $780; a two-column release to 2,000 editors is $1,405, and a three-column release to 3,000 papers is $2,100. Postage is included.

5. Black press. mailings to 220 U.S. newspapers serving Black communities. When distributed to Black press alone, the cost of a one, two, or three-column release is $395. When sent as an extension of a regular mailing, or as an addition to a Press-Ready Feature Packet distribution, a two-column release is $125, and a three-column release is $145. Postage is additional.

Central Feature News, Inc.

This company is no longer in business and is mentioned here since Bob Altshuler was one of the pioneers in the newspaper mat field.

Alumni include Ron Levy (North American Precis Syndicate), Jerry Multer (Planned Communication Services) and Jim Nesi (National Newspaper Syndicate).

2. Century Features Inc.

Box 597, Pittsburgh, PA 15230

(412) 471-6533

Charles Reichblum

Several companies produce editorial or cartoon columns which are sold to companies for placement as ads (together with the name of the sponsor).

Century provides several features in the sports, home furnishings and other fields, which generally are "leased" exclusively in a market for $11.50 a week.

3. Complementary Color Company, Inc.

Box 2810, Newport Beach, CA 92660
(714) 261-6394, (800) 654-5463
Joseph F. Gotsill, Pres.
Ray Kessell, Mgr.

Complementary is the oldest company in the color newspaper publicity field. Its origins go back to the 50's when it was called Sta Hi. In the 70's, it was sold and became Sun Color Service. In 1986, its ownership and name changed again and the company now is operated by J.F. Gotsill and his wife, Trisha, who is Exec. V.P. Almost all U.S. and Canadian daily newspapers now are equipped to run full color. Though this colorful group does not yet include all of the New York City dailies, the roster features the Chicago Tribune, Los Angeles Times and the newspapers in virtually all other major cities where ROP (run-of-paper) color is used extensively.

Use of a color service, though considerably more expensive than black-and-white services and other conventional newspaper publicity services, can result in exciting large-space clippings, including half- and full-page layouts in the country's top circulation and most influential papers. As with any publicity service, the results may vary, but a good food, fashion, travel or home furnishings color photo feature usually produces 100 to 250 tear sheets.

The procedure is a bit complicated, particularly in requiring more lead time than a conventional black-and-white release. Clients also must be prepared for a budget that will be several thousand dollars, rather than several hundred dollars.

The first step in setting up a color program is to arrange for color transparencies and/or art. Once you have these, Complementary will handle the entire job, starting with preparation of a half- or full-page layout of photos, art, captions and article. After production and approval of color and typography, full-color proof sheets, or preprints, are sent to the chosen department editors of the full ROP list or any portions of it you may select, about two months prior to the most timely period for editorial use. The editors then order reproduction materials on an exclusive in-each-city basis. About 70 percent of the editors who order the preprints use them.

The total budget required for a color release varies with the number of color photos used and the number of screened separations ordered by the newspapers; but when all expenses are in, the overall cost per newspaper is about $100.

4. Derus Media Service, Inc.

500 N. Dearborn St., Chicago 60610
(312) 644-4360
Pat Derus, Pres., Matt McGann, V.P.

Wilbur (Bill) Derus, who died in 1979, was one of the pioneers and long-time leaders in the newspaper mat business. Pat Derus is his daughter.

For more than 40 years, Derus Media Service has provided a variety of illustrated features to newspapers, magazines, radio and TV stations and others in the U.S. and Canada. DMS features are distributed to more than 7,000 newspapers and the DMS keystone symbol appears in hundreds of clippings each week.

Derus Media Service handles all types of offset mailings to newspapers, including customizing on the basis of geographical or other special requirements. DMS' rate structure offers flexibility to clients with limited budgets, with a 1,000 minimum distribution.

The major DMS bonus is via its EDITORIAL PACE magazine, a catalogue which reproduces a variety of DMS features for editors to order. Each client's news feature is included in the catalog and the client is committed to pay only for an initial minimum distribution of 2,500. Art is extra, clipping service is included.

244

The all-inclusive charge for use of the DMS publicity service is $1,875 for a two-column release (up to 7-inch depth) supplied to 2,500 newspapers. The charge for a one-column release is $1,625 for 2,500 newspapers.

Derus Media Service also regularly provides script service to radio program directors for $1,300 to 2,600 stations; slide and script service to 975 TV stations for $1,200; and cable TV service utilizing ¾" cassettes.

Other special techniques include clipsheets, crossword puzzles ($300 for development), distribution to Canadian newspapers and Congressional service. Canadian service to about 1,100 English-language newspapers is $845 for one column, $955 for two columns and $1,190 for three columns. No clipping service is provided, however.

5. Family Features Editorial Services, Inc.
8309 Melrose Dr., Shawnee Mission, KS 66214
(913) 888-3800, (800) 255-6382
David V. Selders, Chm. of Bd.
George E. Selders, Pres.
Dianne Selders Hogerty, Exec. V.P.

Of America's 1,700 daily newspapers, about 90 percent publish color everyday (and not just in Sunday magazine sections). Family Features, which was formed in 1974, is a leader in the ROP (run-of-paper) color publicity field. Family Features differs from the black-and-white mat operations in several distinct ways:

1. Reproducible materials are mailed only to the first editor in a circulation area who requests a specific feature.
2. Payment is based on scheduled circulation of ordering newspapers.
3. The clippings are truly big in size (¼, ½ or full-page) and circulation (major daily newspapers, not small-town weeklies).

David V. Selders, founder of the company, has had extensive experience in advertising, public relations and home economics. Two of his children now carry on the business and are the principals of this sizable operation, which is in mid-America near Kansas City, MO. The portfolio package supplied to editors is beautifully prepared. However, the unique features of the service pertain to the uses of data processing techniques to provide impressive circulation.

With the Family Features pricing formula, the client can control the cost of producing a feature. Based on the total scheduled circulation represented by newspapers ordering reproduction material on a particular release, the total costs to clients consistently range from only $1.75 to $2.73 per thousand circulation. As the budget increases, the final cost-per-thousand is based on scheduled circulation. Thus, on a cost-per-thousand basis, the Family Features price indeed is a bargain.

The client chooses the cost-per-thousand rate based on three factors: the release format most suitable to the subject matter; the newspaper or geographic markets the client wants to reach; and the cumulative circulation goal of ordering newspapers the client wants to achieve with the release. Taking these points into consideration, Family Features can control the cost by imposing a limit on the total circulation to be attained, limiting the release to selected circulation size newspapers. A "typical" feature can be offered to 750 newspapers, representing a potential reach of 30,000,000 in circulation.

Family Features also can supply the ROP color release in black-and-white to meet editors' needs. In addition, the company produces camera-ready features working from the client's black-and-white glossies. The feature is then distributed to newspapers designated by the client's choice of markets.

With each ROP color release, the client receives performance reports, provided weekly during the months following the initial mailing. The computer-generated report indicates the newspapers that ordered and scheduled the feature, including the editor's intended usage date. Statistics on usage can be sorted by Areas of Dominant Influence (ADI), Designated Market Areas (DMA), Metropolitan Statistical Areas (MSA) and by states.

For the ROP color release, the publicist supplies an acceptable full-color transparency with feature story, including, for example, recipes. Family Features can write the feature story and handle photography and recipe development.

In addition, the ROP service supplies the art, matchprint, preprinted feature samples, distribution to client's preselected list of U.S. dailies, merchandising follow-up with editors and computerized performance reporting back to the publicist. Family Features can produce regional releases sent to editors in specific states or regions of the country, if the client prefers. With their ordered materials, editors receive a tearsheet envelope with return postage paid. Tearsheet reminder cards are sent to editors on a regular basis.

Special consideration must be given to color photography for newspaper reproduction so it's recommended to consult with Family Features before the photo session. The staff works with the client to offer advice for quality results in reproduction at no additional charge.

A lead time of twelve weeks before the feature's desired appearance dates in the newspapers is standard. Still, features have been produced and have generated outstanding circulation results in as little as six weeks lead time from beginning date of production to release date. Since editors schedule color subjects weeks in advance, publicists are encouraged to work well in advance to accommodate editor's needs. Articles related to special holidays, themes, seasons and events are especially well received among editors.

Family Features can tailor features to meet the publicist's budgetary limitations. A continuous cooperative search service is available at no charge. This service brings together two or more sponsors and agents on a tie-in basis. A tie-in feature is truly a cooperative effort with both copy and artwork designed to satisfy each of the sponsors involved. In most cases, one of the cooperating agents takes the lead in producing the text and photography.

6. Feature Photo Service, Inc.

216 E. 45 St., N.Y. 10017
(212) 661-6120

In late 1984, American Audio Visual, Inc. a publicity photography company, started a new type of service in which a picture page is distributed monthly to 1,500 daily and weekly college and specialty newspapers in the U.S. and Canada. Editors can order free captioned glossy prints.

The service is produced by Meyer Goldberg, who formerly was at Associated Press and Wide World Photos.

7. (gabriel) graphic NEWS bureau

Box 38, Madison Sq. Stn., N.Y. 10010
(212) 254-8863
Cable: NOLNOEL, N.Y.
Jay Gabriel Bumberg, Dir.

Mr. Bumberg, a veteran printer and graphics expert, operates the (gabriel) graphic NEWS bureau and gabriel graphics, which provide repros, newspaper mats and other publicity, syndication and promotional services. The company, which was founded in 1965, is a very personal operation.

There's no L in his name, and those who misspell it receive various NOEL mailing pieces from Mr. Bumberg, including membership in TCTCTSOCATTY, The Committee To Continue The Spirit Of Christmas All Through The Year.

8. Master Newspaper Syndicate

42 W. 39 St., N.Y. 10018
(212) 719-5888
Morton Lehrer, Pres.

Master has been producing mats for publicists for more than 30 years and offers comprehensive services from writing to clippings. Master mails each client's mat individually and prices therefore vary considerably.

9. Metro Creative Graphics, Inc.

33 W. 34 St., N.Y. 10001
(212) 947-5100
Telecopier: (212) 714-9139
Patricia T. Anwyl, V.P., Sales

Formed in 1909, Metro is well known among several generations of newspaper publishers and editors.

Metro's Publicity Services reaches over 7,000 daily and weekly newspapers with camera-ready editorial publicity through themed sections (Home Improvement, Fashion, Car Care and others) and a monthly editorial service: Prime Cuts (culinary arts). Cost is $96 per column inch. Custom pages and sections also are available.

Metro also has graphics and printing divisions, Mask-O-Neg and Major Press, which provide a variety of artistic and technical production services, including conversions, veloxes, studio photography and one and two color printing.

10. National News Bureau

2019 Chancellor Street, Philadelphia 19103
(215) 569-0700
Harry Jay Katz, Pres.

Formed in 1979, National News Bureau distributes feature articles of 500 to 800 words each to over 1,300 publications, including college newspapers.

11. National Press Service

19 W. 44 St., N.Y. 10036
(212) 391-2076
James Nesi, Pres.
Nancy Glover, V.P.

One of the pioneers in the newspaper mat business, Jim Nesi is renowned for his efficiency, integrity and pleasant personal approach. Mats—or, more accurately, preprinted features—are his only business and he's quite good at it.

The basic service, which includes preparation and distribution of mats and offset proofs and provides all clippings, goes to a select list of about 2,000 weekly and daily newspapers. The cost is $975 for a two-column format and $725 for one column.

The price, which is considerably less than at most other companies, includes production, postage and clippings.

Mr. Nesi also has several specialized services, notably two-column features to a special list of 310 black newspapers. The total cost is $475. All of these newspapers are members of black press associations and are not general newspapers with a concentration of black readers.

National Press also can compose a crossword puzzle to your specifications, which incorporates the name of the client's company or service. The puzzles have unusually high pickup and readership. They are supplied regularly to 2,000 weeklies and small daily newspapers, and invariably result in several hundred clippings. The cost is the regular two-column price, plus $250 for the creation of the puzzle.

One of the many scrupulous aspects of the National Press operation is to eliminate duplicates of clippings. Some of the companies in this field subscribe to two or more clipping bureaus and are intentionally or unintentionally sloppy about sending the same clipping more than once.

12. News Canada Inc.

121 Bloore St. Toronto, Ontario M4W 3M5, Canada
(416) 923-4000
Telex 062-18353
FAX (416) 973-4200
Paul Aunger, Publisher
Hany Kirolos, V.P. Marketing
Lorie Mitchener, Editor

If you are interested in distribution of mats in Canada, the company is News Canada, which produces a monthly tabloid magazine of camera-ready features. Mailings are to about 1,000 newspapers, and the average number of clippings is about 94 per page. Mailings also are made of features in French to about 200 French newspapers (in Eastern Canada), with about 12 clippings.

News Canada can write and illustrate the article or use your prose. Formerly called Power Newspaper Syndicate, News Canada is an extremely efficient operation with dozens of major Canadian and U.S. clients. Rates for 250 words: $413; for 500 words: $660 (English); with quantity and frequency discounts.

Among the frequent users of News Canada features are small circulation weekly newspapers in remote locations and also large-circulation weekly and daily newspapers in Toronto and other major markets. Some of the newspapers have colorful names. (Yellow Knifer, 100 Mile House Free Press, Elk Valley Miner, Grande Cache Mountaineer, Medicine Hat Shopper and Red River Valley Echo.) Large-circulation newspapers (generally with more prosaic names) include the Cross County Shopper (Saskatoon), Winnipeg Free Press, Toronto Jewish Press, Hamilton Spectator, Niagra Falls Shopping News and Catholic Register (Toronto).

13. North American Precis Syndicate, Inc.

201 E. 42 St., N.Y. 10017
(212) 867-9000
Ronald N. Levy, Pres.
John Engel, Candy Lieberman, Francine Lucidon, Exec. V.P.s
Diane Mason, Marilyn Rosenfeld, Claudia Schiff, Jim Wicht, Sr. V.P.s
Kelly Lawrence, Dorothy Levy, Camilla Mendoza, V.P.s

Branch Offices:
333 N. Michigan Ave., Chicago 60601
(312) 558-1200
Jim Brosseau, Nora Lukas, Sr. V.P.s, Bonnie Cassidy Heller, V.P.

1025 Vermont Ave., N.W., Wash., DC 20005
(202) 347-7300
Jake Arnette, Sr. V.P.
Ann Barre, Monty Bodington, Wendy Sollod, V.P.s

248

4209 Vantage Ave., Studio City, CA 91604
(818) 761-8400
Carol Balkin, V.P.

The largest of the newspaper publicity services, North American Precis Syndicate (NAPS) has a staff of over 75 people, which includes several topnotch writers.

There's a tendency for a "mat service" to be a mechanical operation, with emphasis on production and distribution. These aspects are not ignored at NAPS, but the vital ingredient, which may be surprising to some, is creative writing: turning client material into releases that pull well in suburbia.

Some accounts give NAPS releases with instructions to set and distribute "as is" but most accounts either send in material with a "How would this pull?" kind of note, or send background information plus a note requesting a proposal.

Proposals are made without cost or obligation. If only one or two releases are called for, NAPS will write them and submit them for approval. Where a larger number of releases is needed, North American first sends a letter and some rough layouts indicating (1) what kinds of stories are proposed; (2) what results the customer can expect, and (3) what the cost will be.

All releases distributed through NAPS go to 3,800 newspapers, a list which is revised regularly. "Going to more papers doesn't produce enough results to justify the extra cost, and if you go to fewer, results fall off faster than costs," states the articulate proprietor, Ron Levy, who has six staffers and nine computers to keep track of which are the best publications and specific editors to cover.

Including postage, NAPS charges $2,100 for a one-column release, $2,700 if it is two columns wide, or $3,300 if it runs three columns. If releases are more than 7 inches deep, there's an extra charge of $50 for each column inch in excess of the 7-inch depth.

The prices charged by North American Precis Syndicate are somewhat more, per release, than smaller firms charge for covering smaller numbers of newspapers. However, for the additional cost, the practitioner gets to cover not only the 1,000 or 2,000 "biggest users," but also additional newspapers—many with higher circulations and better quality reproduction, including many daily newspapers.

You can give North American information and get back—often in 72 hours—a proposed release or set of releases of the type currently getting the best results in suburbia.

Retouching, if your photo can use it, is free. A line illustration ($65) often brings in considerably more placements than a photo.

At no extra cost, North American will "heavy up" distribution in areas that mean the most to you such as plant towns or key congressional districts.

North American relies on national clipping bureaus for some areas, regional bureaus for others and its own clipping operation.

From North American's computer bank, each customer receives, in addition to the clippings, a printout showing: (a) circulation of each clipping, (b) name and rank of the major market in which each clipping appeared, (c) a map that shows where population is heaviest and placements have been most numerous.

North American has an unusual guarantee: complete satisfaction with the quality, quantity and speed of results—or another release free. Results range from 100 to 400 or more clippings per release.

Additional details about the NAPS operation are described in the chapters on editorials, packaged publicity services, radio and television.

14. Reilly ROP Color Service
812 W. Van Buren St., Chicago 60607
(312) 829-9700
Lynette A. Wood, V.P.

The Milwaukee Journal was a pioneer in run-of-paper (ROP) color in advertising and editorial and operated a color production service for other newspapers. This service was separated from the Journal and later became a part of Reilly Graphics Chicago, a major company which had been producing the reproduction materials for the color features.

Reilly produces full-color features, in full, half and quarter-page format, mails preprints (proofs) to about 1,500 newspapers, with a request form offering a choice of free reproduction material, such as three- and four-color 65 or 85-line separations in film, velos or transparency form, oriented for letterpress, offset or flexography.

The service is a total in-house operation offering top quality craftsmanship from layout and typesetting through color separations and the printed release. Production time for a color release is six weeks. The customers (mostly food, furnishings and fashions) receive a computerized weekly printout of responding newspapers, by state.

A choice of three cost plans is available: Specific, Package Plan and Pay-Only-On-Placement. Specific pricing is based on a basic all-inclusive production charge, then a materials charge for each newspaper order. Postage is customarily the only extra cost. Circulations of up to eight million are possible.

Special Correspondents, Inc.

Special Correspondents was the first major "packaged publicity service." Formed by Bob Maxon in 1941, the company distributed many thousands of news releases.

In 1977, SC was acquired by AD Systems Inc., a newspaper advertising specialist. The publicity mailing service was terminated in 1979. SC is listed here because of its historical importance (the company was headed for many years by Emil F. Stuermer) and also to provide a note about Chicago.

One of the reasons that Chicago has several major mat services is that many public relations agencies and departments are headquartered in the area, but the fact also is that, in the late 19th century and early 20th century, Chicago was the headquarters of Western Newspaper Union and the other newspaper syndicate pioneers.

Stamps-Conheim-Whitehead (SCW)

In 1987, Metro Associated Services purchased SCW, Inc., from the Scripps-Howard Co., and changed its name to Metro Creative Graphics, Inc. The SCW operation was moved from Chatsworth, CA, to New York, and is described under the Metro listing.

Sun Color Service

See listing under Complementary Color Company, Inc.

Newspaper mats are also distributed by many of the companies described under Mailing Services and Packaged Publicity Services.

Chapter 18

Packaged Publicity Services

Several companies provide such a dazzling variety of feature mats, radio scripts, videotapes and other publicity services that it almost seems that these firms have become public relations agencies. Indeed, the comprehensiveness of these companies is indicated by the designation *"packaged* publicity services.''

One major change in the late 70's was the specialization, rather than diversification, of the large ''packagers.'' For example, Planned Communication Services no longer is in the newspaper mat business and works only in the broadcast field, primarily television.

Clients can rely heavily on one or more of the packaged publicity services, some of which are capable of creating and executing comprehensive publicity programs, particularly if they involve the mass media. Though some practitioners make extensive use of the publicity packagers and integrate their services whenever possible into their operations, others shy away from packagers because they believe that they are not creative and can be mechanical, cumbersome and expensive.

Regardless of which of these extreme views you share, you should be familiar with the services offered by the major packagers, so that you can use them whenever it is proper. Obviously, the proper balance, not using any outside services exclusively and yet not ignoring their value and unique facilities, can be achieved only by getting to know these companies.

And, regardless of how frequently you utilize outside services of any kind, the primary responsibility as to content, audience, timing and other major decisions remains yours, and this constitutes the most important part of publicity.

A major difference between a packaged publicity service and a public relations agency or department is that the former is basically a distributor.

A packager generally does not counsel on what to say, how to say it, when to say it—or whether to say anything at all. Instead, once you have made those decisions on your own or with your counsel, using a distributor saves time and money in covering important blocks of media. The distributor also helps to get maximum results by advising on the formats and release sizes that are currently getting the best pickup.

A few companies offer to write news releases and mail them to custom-prepared media lists, together with letters and reply cards—all for a package price of about $200 or less. There's nothing wrong with this, and it can be a wonderful bargain. Indeed, the low price is the problem. The release often is hastily written and the mailing list generally is not totally custom-prepared. This kind of ''package publicity'' can work, but you should be wary of solicitation letters from these companies, several of which thrive on mass mailings to small and new businesses.

The packaged publicity services with their own writers, artists and other specialists rarely create from scratch. Instead, they take information the client has created or assembled, and then put this into the formats that will pull well.

Many successful, competent public relations practitioners can go through their professional lives without knowing anything about animal or prop rentals or other esoteric specialized services. But any publicist involved in a national public relations program which deals with the general public and the mass media cannot claim complete competency without at least being familiar with the packaged publicity services.

The large publicity packagers issue rate cards which are extremely helpful during the planning and budgeting stages of a campaign. Several publicity packagers have operations which are set up like advertising media. In the same way that an advertiser knows that the cost of the time or space is only part of an advertising budget, and must estimate art, talent and a variety of other production charges in contemplating the total budgets, so, too, must the publicist learn what the rate cards of the publicity packagers include and what must be added to them.

For example, some of the packagers publish magazines or offer other techniques which enable them to provide you with requests from editors or broadcasters for your feature articles, scripts or other materials. The price of your listing in the magazine thus is only the first charge. To this must be added the printing, mailing and other production charges necessary to fulfill the requests. Sometimes a publicity packager can produce many hundreds of requests from editors and broadcasters and the client is not prepared to pay the price of this success.

Many of the proprietors of the packaged publicity services started out in the newspaper mat business, and they therefore are still thought of by some publicists as being involved in a prosaic, mechanical aspect of the publicity distribution business. The large publicity packagers today include on their staffs writers, artists, photographers, movie technicians and other people who are capable of rendering creative, exciting projects. Terms such as "boiler plate" and "canned services" no longer are applicable to the professional publicity distribution services whose operations now are a major factor in the publicity service field.

Most of the packagers described in this section also are listed in other chapters, particularly those dealing with literary services, mailing services, newspaper mat services, radio and television.

Public relations agencies are not listed in this directory, though obviously many companies provide "on their own" the services described in this and other chapters. For example, several public relations companies specialize in "media tours," that is, touring an author, performer, hairdresser, physician or company spokesperson to various cities solely or primarily for interviews by broadcasters and other media people. The emphasis generally is on TV talk shows, and the mechanics of scheduling a tour (often only one or two days in each of a dozen cities) require considerable expertise.

1. Associated Release Service, Inc.

2 N. Riverside Plaza, Chicago 60606
(312) 726-8693
Ted M. Hathorn, Pres.

Formed in 1950, Associated Release Service was operated for many years by one of the pioneers in the newspaper mat business, Roger Hathorn, who died in 1983. The company now is operated by Roger's son, Ted. However, it is much more than a family operation and its clients include major companies and associations throughout the country. A description of the basic ASR services appears in the chapter on newspapers. Following are the highlights of the print and broadcast services.

One of the first Associated packages was a feature page called "Successful Lifestyles," on which were "ganged" as many as eight noncompeting articles distributed monthly to Associated's list of frequent mat-using newspapers. The package included all typesetting, production, mailing, postage, clippings and an analysis of use report accompanying the fourth and final monthly delivery of clippings to the client. Subsequent feature pages included Today's Lifestyles, Editor's Choice, and Monthly Column Syndicate.

In 1987, the four feature page packets were combined into one all-inclusive "Press-Ready Feature Packet," distributed monthly to the Associated list of about 4,000 newspapers. As before, non-brand mention and feature articles that run in series are identified as such. A one-column article up to 7½ inches deep costs $1,655; a two-column article is $1,790. A description of the basic Associated newspaper services appears in the chapter on newspapers.

Radio & Television. Associated expanded its publicity package services into radio and television in the 60's. As with newspapers, Associated tracks radio and television stations to identify frequent users of publicity releases. Associated maintains a list of approximately 3,000 radio station that use scripted or recorded releases carrying sponsor mention and a list of over 200 television stations that use sponsor-identified slide/script or videotaped releases.

Scripted Releases. Associated regularly sends one or multipage radio scripts with reply cards to all or part of its list of 3,000 user stations. These packages include retyping and printing client scripts on Associated radio release letterheads, printing station response postcards, distribution and usage reports based on returned cards that identify using stations by call letters and station power, number of times the announcement was aired, and the equivalent cost of such time if purchased at the station's lowest spot rate. The cost of a one-page script, mailed to 1,000 radio stations, is $570; a two-page script to 1,000 stations is $680. *Postage is additional,* but Associated pays the postage on returned response cards.

With slide/script releases for television, the same procedure is followed, with the addition of reproducing duplicate 35 mm slides (one to four different) from original master slides furnished by the client. A slide/script release consisting of a one- to two-page script and up to four slides, to 225 lifestyle programs on U.S. television stations costs $1,475, including first class postage.

Recorded Releases. From master tapes supplied by clients, Associated duplicates recordings in appropriate format for the media to be serviced. For radio, the formats are records, audio cassettes or open reel tapes. One or several announcements totaling up to four minutes on an open reel tape—boxed, labeled and accompanied by a printed script and station response care—to 1,000 radio stations costs $3,800, plus postage. Associated pays postage on returned cards, from which usage reports are drawn and sent to clients, along with the cards containing station comments.

For television, recorded releases are distributed in open reel format or in ¾ inch U-Matic videocassettes, accompanied by scripts and postpaid station response cards. Announcements of up to one minute in length on open real videotape to 300 television stations cost $20 each, plus postage. Up to three minutes of announcements on ¾ inch U-Matic videocassettes to 300 stations cost $26 each, plus postage.

Distribution can be national, to specific markets, or exclusive to one station per market. Costs of any package depend on size of distribution, length of recorded announcement(s), and whether release includes additional material, such as cover letter and literature.

A service unique to Associated is the mailing of association or company literature, product samples, articles, program guides and other materials to 3,200 U.S. Government Extension Home Economists. All of these people constitute a valuable information conduit to consumers in communities throughout the United States; many appear on radio and television and write columns for local newspapers. Associated lists 1,100 that request radio releases, 180 who regularly appear on television. 'Add-on' distribution to these lists in conjunction with regular mailings to radio or television is offered at special rates.

Associated, which formerly was affiliated with PR Aids, now is affiliated with Media Distribution Services, 307 W. 36 St., N.Y. 10018, phone (212) 279-4800.

2. North American Precis Syndicate, Inc.

201 E. 42 St., N.Y. 10017
(212) 867-9000
Ronald N. Levy, Pres.
John Engel, Candy Lieberman, Francine Lucidon, Exec. V.P.s
Diane Mason, Marilyn Rosenfeld, Claudia Schiff, Jim Wicht, Sr. V.P.s
Kelly Lawrence, Dorothy Levy, Camilla Mendoza, V.P.s

Branch Offices:
333 N. Michigan Ave., Chicago 60601
(312) 558-1200
Jim Brosseau, Nora Lukas, Sr. V.P.s, Bonnie Cassidy Heller, V.P.

4209 Vantage Ave., Studio City, CA 91604
(818) 761-8400
Carol Balkin, V.P.

1025 Vermont Ave., N.W., Wash., DC 20005
(202) 347-7300
Jake Arnette, Sr. V.P.
Ann Barre, Monty Bodington, Wendy Sollod, V.P.s

The only anachronistic part of the North American Precis Syndicate operation is its name. Founded in 1958, the company published Precis, a magazine sent to editors with summaries of articles from which they could order the complete articles, with mats, photos, or other materials.

Precis no longer is published, mats generally have been replaced by camera-ready sheets, and many other changes have taken place since 1958; notably, North American Precis Syndicate has become the largest company in the preprinted newspaper publicity field and one of the largest of all public relations suppliers. The staff of over 75 people includes specialists with impressive journalism and public relations backgrounds. NAPS offers three services—newspapers, TV and radio.

Through the newspaper service, clients can send a release to 3,800 papers at a cost (for a two-column release) of $2,700, including postage. You can expect to receive 100 to 400 or more clippings, and NAPS guarantees complete satisfaction with the results of each release or another one free. It's $2,100 for a one-column release and $3,300 for a three-column release.

Through the TV service, clients can send a script and four color slides to 325 TV newscasters and women's talk shows at a total cost of $2,650. Clients can expect usage on upwards of 40 stations, and here again the distributor guarantees satisfaction with results or replacement free. Broadcasters indicate usage of a release on reply cards and these are included in an elaborate report that also contains audience data and a map.

The radio service, which consists of a script sent to 5,000 stations, costs $2,150. The newspaper service is the largest part of the NAPS operation and is the largest in the newspaper mat field.

NAPS offers a multimedia package to newspapers, TV and radio in which the same basic story is adapted to each medium and the total cost is $1,500 less than the combined price of the individual components.

NAPS has analyzed the types of articles which editors actually use. As a result, it not only can estimate which articles will "pull the best," but it also will guarantee satisfaction or provide another insertion free.

This unusual guarantee is typical of the self-confidence displayed by Ron Levy, the energetic, creative proprietor. To clients who scoff at the use of a computer, guarantee, and other techniques involving predictions about the number of clippings, Mr. Levy states that "It's not as hard as it sounds."

"For example," says Mr. Levy, "We have run 34 stories on Avoid These Common . . . . (first-aid, car care, etc.) Errors. Every one of these stories has pulled a massive return. Our 114 Through the Ages stories have also been highly successful. So have 27 stories on Around the World. But all three stories on how a product is made were flops.

"If we run another Errors or History story, is it a certainty that it will be a great success? No. But the probability is superb.

"Might another story on how a product is made hit the top? Perhaps, but we wouldn't recommend this approach.

"In a similar way, we found answers to questions like these:

"What are the best ways of working in a commercial name so that the editor won't delete it?

"Which story elements—leads, structures, endings—get the best pickup?

"Which stories generate the most mail to legislators?

"When is the best time to release various holiday stories?"

Potential clients can obtain reprints of various articles by and about Mr. Levy and NAPS, and a variety of free, useful booklets on Corporate Identification, Public Policy Publicity, Suburban Publicity, Association Publicity, as well as booklets on food, travel, home, industrial and other subjects.

North American Precis Syndicate is operated by Ronald N. Levy, one of the most successful executives in the publicity services field. A graduate of the Wharton School at the University of Pennsylvania, Ron Levy started at Central Feature News, the pioneer company in the publicity mat business.

3. Package Publicity Service, Inc.
27 W. 24 St. N.Y. 10010
(212) 255-2872
Avivah Simon, Pres.

In 1948, theatrical press agent Bernard Simon set up Package Publicity Service to provide professional publicity and advertising materials to amateur and professional theatre people throughout the country. Customers can order a "press-book" for any one of about 725 plays, each containing publicity and advertising material, for $15. Other items, including posters, postcards and lapel pins, also can be purchased for most of the plays, from Absence of a Cello to Zorba.

The company now is operated by his widow, Avivah Simon. A primary service is its booklets, including one on publicity news releases for $1.

4. Planned Communication Services, Inc.
12 E. 46 St., N.Y. 10017
(212) 697-2765
Gerald Jay Multer, Chm.

Formed in 1962 by Jerry Multer and Al Roselin, Planned Communication Services is one of the country's largest producers of publicity materials for broadcast media.

PCS has produced and distributed over 1,800 television public service announcements, news clips, featurettes, industrial and documentary films for television and public service and feature material for radio.

PCS has been extraordinarily successful in producing public service announcements (PSAs) for companies and associations with messages on health, safety, conservation and other public interest issues. The technique is often associated with nonprofit agencies, but PCS has proved that a company or association can get multiple telecasts on a single station, totaling hundreds of telecasts of the same 30- or 60-second spot.

Production of a PSA, from concept through filming, editing, music, narration and preparation of first prints, is $17,500 for a :30 and $20,500 for a :60. Distribution, including preparation of spots in appropriate format and accompanying printed material, selection of stations, mailing and usage reports is $25.50 for :30. Distribution of spots on 2-inch tape is $36.50 for a :30. A :60 is $42.50. Package prices for production and distribution to 200 stations are $25,500 for a :30 and $28,500 for a :60.

TV stations can be reached through the Public Service Communicator, a magazine containing photoboards of PSAs available at no charge to all stations. Public service directors can use the enclosed postage-paid reply card to order those spots best suited to their needs. The Communicator provides a cost-efficient method for expanding the distribution or redistributing a PSA. Typically, 75 to 150 requests are received for any one spot. Preparation of the storyboard, one-page insertion in the magazine and processing of requests is $1,500. Requests then are filled (at the preceding rate schedule) in the formats requested by stations.

PCS produces and distributes video news releases of varying lengths. With a 100-station distribution, the usage generally is over 35 telecasts on local news shows. A video news release with a voice-over can be produced and then distributed on ¾-inch cassette to 100 stations at $19,000 for a :90.

Featurettes, three to five minutes in length, are used extensively on locally produced shows. PCS sends a written inquiry to TV stations and then provides tapes to those who request them.

PCS also produces corporate, sales, training and educational films.

Cable offers another effective outlet for placement of produced materials, such as public service announcements, featurettes newsclips and other sponsored films. However, distribution can be costly since cable systems prefer the more expensive videocassette format. To make cost-effective distribution possible, PCS offers a service where the cost is shared by a number of sponsors. Their film or video materials are transferred to ¾-inch videocassette and distributed to 100 of the largest cable systems and networks. The result is that pickup for any one spot is over 50 percent. Costs including transfer to ¾-inch videocassette, distribution to 100 cable outlets and usage reports is $1,750 for a :30 or :60 spot, $2,500 for both.

Radio PSAs can be distributed on record or tape, sent to selected stations or to those responding to a query. Production of a record with up to 10 minutes of programming per side, query to 2,000 previous users, preparation for distribution on 7-inch disc and fulfillment of first 100 requests is $8,000 for a two-sided record and $4,950 for a one-sided record. Additional records are distributed at $4 per station.

5. Publicity Central
2100 Pillsbury Ave. S., Minneapolis, MN 55404
(612) 871-7201
Telex: 29-0306
TWX: 910-576-2770
Telecopier: (612) 871-1220
Kit Hagen, Genl. Mgr.

Padilla, Speer, Burdick & Beardsley, a Minneapolis public relations agency, has expanded and diversified into several publicity services which are provided independently to many clients. These services are much more than in-house departments which also accept non-agency clients. In recognition of this, in 1984, these companies were grouped together under the name of Publicity Central and moved to a new location.

The companies publish media directories, handle mailings, provide computerized mailing lists, produce and distribute audio news releases, and also operate two divisions, which are described elsewhere in this book:

Broadcast Newsclips: broadcast monitoring
Newswire: newswire service

Publicity Central also represents Media Distribution Services and, in 1986, acquired two directories, the Twin Cities Media Directory and The Minnesota Non-Metro Media Directory.

6. Universal News Services
Communications House, Gough Square, Fleet St., London EC4P 4DP, England
01-353-5200
Telex 266363
Robert Simpson, Mng. Dir.

The comprehensive mailing messenger, radio and other services of UNS in the United Kingdom are described in the chapter on newswires.

Chapter 19

Photo and Fine Art Sources

Many public relations practitioners spend more money on art and photography than any other publicity service. Large corporate public relations departments and a few public relations agencies have graphic arts specialists and photographers on their own staffs. Quite a few commercial art studios, photographers and printers specialize in public relations assignments, with the products varying from a one-page reproduction of a clipping sent to 100 sales representatives to an elaborate annual report sent to 100,000 stockholders.

Just about every experienced public relations practitioner works and is familiar with several artists and photographers and with related services, particularly photo laboratories and printers. For this reason, and also because there are many thousands of companies in these fields, commercial art, photography and printing listings generally have been omitted from this directory.

Publicists often are not too familiar with the various companies which offer an opportunity to buy photos and art already in existence. In addition, the public information departments of many Federal, state and local government agencies, associations, universities and other institutions constitute a major source of *free* photos, as well as posters, booklets and other materials. The U.S. Army and Navy, for example, maintain staffs of experts in many cities who not only are available to provide current and historical photos, but also can serve as technical advisors to check copy and art.

You can sometimes save a lot of money and time by *not* working with an artist or photographer, but instead purchasing a "stock photo."

Various forms of art, particularly old posters, postcards, and other memorabilia, as well as etchings, drawings and photos, can be purchased by publicists, house organ editors and others to illustrate news releases and feature articles. Several private archives have enormous collections of treasures available for sale or loan to the media, advertisers and publicists, as well as private collectors and hobbyists.

Much of this material is historical and thus can add a charming new dimension to publicity material. Stock photos and art also can be purchased for use in booklets, exhibits, displays, direct mail and other public relations and promotion projects.

The staffs of many stock photo and art libraries often are equivalent to museum and gallery curators. They usually are intelligent, sensitive people who are interested in helping you, whether your needs are a single photo or an entire collection.

ASMP—The American Society of Magazine Photographers, 205 Lexington Ave., N.Y. 10016, publishes a free membership directory with several hundred color photos taken by its members. As stated in the directory, "A stock picture is one that is already taken, available on file, and which may be licensed for use or reuse. The photographer may either license its use directly to a client or give permission to a designated representative, such as a stock photo agency, to license the use of the picture to clients in return for a percentage of the license fee. To 'license' means to offer permission for limited use of the photograph which is subsequently returned to the owner or agent after reproduction or projection. While photographers may casually say they 'sell' stock photographs, they mean they are selling the license to use such pictures, ownership of which remains in their possession.''

ASMP also publishes *Professional Business Practices in Photography* ($17.50), which includes stock rates in more than 20 fields. Each market has its own requirements, vocabulary and trade practices, and each applies its own scale of prices to photographs. Reproduction by *any* means is covered by copyright, and stock pictures may not be licensed or used without the permission of the copyright owner.

In the 60's, Dr. Otto Bettmann, the nation's best-known picture retriever, pictured the future of this business as follows:

The picture user in search of 'Melba eating Melba toast' will Teletype his coded request to an electronic picture research pool. After a few minutes' wait, a Western Union messenger will arrive with a fat envelope containing pictures of Melba eating Melba toast, dry, buttered or with marmalade! Only a digit here and there has to be changed should the request happen to be for 'Thomas Jefferson eating spaghetti' or a reproduction of Leonardo da Vinci's 'Mona Lisa.' However, the computer might breathe a little more heavily when fed a request for a profile view of the famous lady with the enigmatic smile.

This Pictorial Futurama is not offered facetiously. We're getting there. Systems have already been developed that have cut picture research time from days to seconds. Even so there will always be room in this field for the personal touch, taste, visual awareness and a Holmesian gift for sleuthing.

Dr. Bettmann's prediction still has not been realized, though we're getting close. (See the listing in this chapter of Photonet Computer Corp.) Indeed, photo and art research offers an exciting potential to public relations clients.

Chase Manhattan, Clairol, IBM, S.C. Johnson, Mead, Phillip Morris and other companies have found a happy marriage of business and fine art. Companies which are aware of the public relations values of fine art projects are sometimes reluctant to enter this field because they think that fine quality paintings and sculptures are too costly.

It is possible to rent or borrow fine art from museums, galleries, artists and private collectors. Another solution is to purchase prints.

A print can be produced in many ways, including woodcut, wood engraving, collotype, etching, engraving, drypoint, aquatint, lithograph and serigraph. One of the excellent American producers of fine art prints is Triton Press, 263 Ninth Ave., N.Y. 10001.

Here then are the details of many photo and fine art sources, for possible use in the publicity business, and also for your personal sleuthing and browsing pleasure. With regard to fine art, almost any gallery will be happy to discuss the rental or sale of art for use by companies in their offices and for public relations purposes.

Many public libraries have excellent photo files. One of the largest is The University of Louisville Photographic Archives, which includes many photo collections. You also might want to consider contributing your own photo collection to one of the public or private archives. Among other benefits, it's a way of getting increased exposure. An illustrated collections guide is $1 from Photo Graphics Archives, Ekstrom Library, University of Louisville, Louisville, KY 40292.

Among the stock art services, one of the largest is the Volk Clip Art, Inc., 1401 N. Main St.,

Pleasantville, NJ 08232, phone (609) 641-8800. A description of Volk and other stock art services is included in this chapter.

Replicas of historical documents can be purchased from Historical Documents Co., 8 N. Preston St., Philadelphia 19104, phone (215) 387-8076. Historic Newspaper Archives, Inc. is described in the back issue section of the chapter on clipping bureaus.

About 100 stock photo agencies are listed in Literary Market Place, published annually by R. R. Bowker Company, 245 W. 17 St., N.Y. 10011.

A directory of libraries, nonprofit organizations, corporations and commercial agencies with stock photo collections is available for $35 from the Special Libraries Association, 1700 18 St., N.W., Wash., D.C. 20009, phone (202) 234-4700. It's called Picture Sources and is edited by Ernest H. Robl.

In 1985, Rohn Engh of PhotoSource International started an unusual service called Photobulletin. Publicists who are seeking a particular photo can call and describe their picture needs. The photo requests are sent out in the form of a three-page newsletter every Thursday evening via MCI MAIL. Photobuyers respond directly to the photobuyer. There is no charge for the initial listing. Publicists also can locate photographers in various cities by making the request on Photobulletin. For a sample issue, write to Rohn Engh at Pine Lake Farm, Osceola, WI 54020.

Many local, state and Federal Government agencies provide free photos, and several of the Federal collections number in the millions of photos, drawings, prints and posters.

As with all Government agencies, the only restrictions are that the photographs not be used in such a way as to imply endorsement by the Government of a commercial product or service.

Many of the Government agencies, libraries and museums can work with you by mail or phone, but each has its own policies. For example, the Museum of the City of New York does not send any material on approval. Black-and-white prints are sold outright for $15 to $45. Color transparencies are rented for $100 for three months.

At the American Museum of Natural History (over 500,000 black-and-white negatives and color transparencies), U.S. and Canadian reproduction fees range from $15 (black-and-white textbook editorial) to $180 (color posters).

Other sources of free photos are chambers of commerce, tourist agencies, trade associations, and, of course, the public relations departments of airlines, automobile manufacturers, food and other large companies.

For example, if you're planning to hold a convention in Chicago, or, for any other reason, you need photos of McCormick Place and other Chicago landmarks, you can get free color and black-and-white photos from the Chicago Convention and Tourism Bureau, McCormick Place on the Lake, Chicago 60616, phone (312) 225-5000.

Several of these sources provide catalogs which are beautiful and informative works of art in themselves. All major public libraries and many museums maintain picture collections, mostly of historical photos.

Be sure to check about reproduction rights and fees as there sometimes are limitations because of copyright and donor restrictions. For example, the Coast Guard generally charges $1.25 for black-and-white prints. The Smithsonian has a permission request form.

Following are a few sources:

Prints and Photography Division, Library of Congress, Wash., DC 20025
Office of Public Information, NASA, Wash., DC 20546
Still Picture Branch, National Gallery of Art, Wash., DC 20025
Office of Printing and Photographic Services, Smithsonian Institution, Wash., DC 20060
Photo Library, U.S. Air Force, 24 & Oklahoma Ave., N.E., Wash., DC 20025

Still Photo Library, Defense Audiovisual Agency, Bldg. 168, Washington Navy Yard, Wash., DC 20374
Picture Librarian, U.S. Coast Guard, Wash., DC 20593
Photography Division, U.S. Dept. of Agriculture, Wash., DC 20250
Photographic Center, U.S. Naval Station, Wash., D.C. 20025
Photographic Collection, American Museum of Natural History, N.Y. 10024
Photo Service, Boston Univ., 270 Bay Side Rd., Boston 02171
Art Div. Picture Collection, Carnegie Library, Pittsburgh, PA 15213
Div. of Photographs, Metropolitan Museum of Art, N.Y. 10028
Dept. of Public Information, Museum of Modern Art, N.Y. 10019
Picture Collection, N.Y. Public Library, N.Y. 10018
Picture Dept., Philadelphia Library, Logan Sq., Philadelphia 19103

Many public libraries now provide computerized literature searches free or at very low cost, often over the phone. For example, The Free Library of Philadelphia, Logan Square, Philadelphia 19103, has access to hundreds of databases through several information vendors. The Information Center phone is (215) 686-2860.

Major libraries maintain separate departments and branches for various specialties, and you should get to know your local library. In addition to libraries, museums and nonprofit agencies, following are descriptions of major photo researchers located throughout the country.

NOTE: Clients are held responsible for any damage or loss of photos. The value of original color transparencies can be $500 each, so handle with care and return promptly, if items are on approval or loan. Valuable items, such as master transparencies and slides, should be returned by bonded messenger or insured mail.

A low-cost, dramatic way to illustrate an annual report, booklet, or exhibit is with an aerial photograph. Information about aerial photographs used by Federal government mapmakers, and views of the earth from satellites, are available from the National Cartographic Information Center, U.S. Geological Survey, 507 National Center, Reston, VA 22092, (703) 860-6045. Simply tell NCIC what type of photograph you have in mind, and the area it should cover. They will select a suitable photograph from their own extensive collection, or from records they maintain about other collections, and tell you how to place your order. An indication of their extraordinary helpfulness is that they also may refer you to any one of several dozen Federal sources or several hundred state agencies or commercial suppliers. NCIC is part of the National Mapping Division of the U.S. Geological Survey, under the Department of the Interior.

Materials are provided on paper, photo negatives or prints and other formats. The unit price is from $5 up. The collection of millions of photographs includes many taken at low altitudes with considerable detail. Some go back to the late 30's, while others are as recent as this year.

Several proprietors of stock photo collections have what could be called "archival personalities." They become extremely knowledgeable in their fields and sometimes are impatient or snobbish to public relations clients and other lay people. They also sometimes have a multitude of restrictions, with regard to the handling, borrowing, lease or purchase of their materials. On the other hand, many proprietors enjoy working with public relations clients because it challenges their creativity and resources.

Many popular magazines include a listing of photo sources. These generally appear in the smallest possible italic type tucked away somewhere in the back of the magazine. This listing usually pertains to outside photographers or photos obtained from agencies, as differentiated from staff photographers whose credits appear adjacent to their photos. The value of these listings to the general reader can be questioned, but there is no doubt that publicists are intrigued by this type of information.

For example, for many years a photo credit seen in almost every top-circulation magazine was that of Underwood & Underwood (established in 1882), which maintained a huge library of black-and-white stock photos for editorial, promotional, publicity and advertising use.

In 1978, Underwood & Underwood was acquired by Hastings Galleries Ltd. The Underwood & Underwood name still appears in thousands of books and periodicals, though today the company is part of the Bettmann Archive. So, for historians, journalists and public relations practitioners, here are descriptions of some of the major sources of photographs and other visuals.

1. American Stock Photography
6640 Sunset Blvd., L.A. 90028
(213) 469-3900
William M. Grabitz, Mgr.

The West's largest and oldest collection of contemporary and historical stock photos. The files consist of about two million black-and-white photos and 300,000 color transparencies, including many old and new movie stills.

2. Peter Arnold, Inc.
1181 Broadway, N.Y. 10001
(212) 481-1190
Telex: 428 281
Ray Pfortner, Connie Chew

Excellent file of color and black-and-white photographs, particularly children, nature, medicine, sports, wildlife and foreign cultures. A specialty is photomicrography and scanning electron micrography.

3. The Bettmann Archive, Inc.
136 E. 57 St., N.Y. 10022
(212) 758-0362
David Greenstein, Dir.

Thousands of art directors and designers, publishers, editors and advertisers use The Bettmann Archive as a vital source.

The Bettmann Archive has assembled and classified, for quick reference, more than 25 million images from the past, all in convenient, glossy form. Here are engravings and woodcuts, cave paintings, tattoo marks and Victorian lantern slides, turn-of-the-century soap wrappers, and 1920 movie stills and photos of memorable events and personalities of the past.

One-time Curator of Rare Books at the Berlin State Art Library, Dr. Otto L. Bettmann started his U.S. business in 1938, with his personal collection of rare prints. In appearance, Dr. Bettmann resembles Sigmund Freud and, as an archivist and graphics expert, he is respected as was the psychotherapist.

Today, a staff of experienced and imaginative librarians is available to help clients and also constantly expand the collection in a discriminating manner. One of the most exciting aspects of the operation is that it is possible to outline the problem by mail or phone and obtain rapid, imaginative service anywhere in the country, sometimes within a few hours.

The Bettmann Archive continues to expand and in 1983 acquired the United Press International Photo Library and Reuters Photo Library, which it operates as a separate division, Bettmann News Photos, at 48 E. 21 St., N.Y. 10010. Mindy Clay is manager of this division, which maintains marvelous hours—8:30 A.M. to 11:00 P.M. on week days and 11:00 A.M. to 7:00 P.M. on Saturday and Sunday. Can you imagine if public libraries operated with the same hours!

The News Photos phone number is (212) 777-6200, and is available to send a selection of photos or photocopies to enable you to make a selection and then order the specific prints.

Bettmann is the North American agent for the entire BBC Hulton Picture Library, for Great Britain's largest picture agency, and for a number of other well-known collections, including the news features and scenic views of Underwood & Underwood (with many photos of the late 19th century) and the color and black-and-white movies stills from the John Springer and Penguin collections.

The Bettmann Archive itself currently has about 3,000 subject categories.

You will be charged a fee only for those you reproduce in printed material or other media. There is a slight charge for use of the prints in presentations and for photostating. Fees are reasonable and are designed to make the use of Bettmann prints feasible within the budgetary limits of your medium. The research fee (minimum of $35 for black-and-white, $50 for color) is deductible from the usage fee in most cases.

The reproduction fees in the public relations field start at $55 per print. A publicist who is interested in adding a "then and now" historical comparison to an otherwise ordinary product news release thus can inexpensively use one or two Bettmann prints.

Whether or not you use, or contemplate using, The Bettmann Archive, you'll want to see the Bettmann Portable Archive, a book which represents a sampling of this company's resources. This $35 volume could be a copious source of ideas for those who create with pictures and love the graphic arts. Published by Picture House Press, Inc., a subsidiary of Bettmann, the 232-page volume was created by Dr. Bettmann and Herbert Migdoll, a talented young photographer and art director. This unique encyclopedia includes 3,669 miniatures of pictures and other items from the Bettmann Archive, 5,000 cross references and an "Idea and Image Index."

Dr. Bettmann now is adjunct professor of history at Florida Atlantic University.

4. Black Star Publishing Co., Inc.
450 Park Ave. South, N.Y. 10016
(212) 679-3288
Benjamin J. Chapnick, Exec. V.P.

The Black Star photographers handle a tremendous number of assignments from Fortune, National Geographic, Newsweek and other magazines in the U.S. and other countries, as well as industrial photography for clients all over the world.

The Black Star stock file includes thousands of contemporary color transparencies and black-and-white prints, available for one-time use.

5. Brown Brothers
Sterling, PA 18463
(717) 689-9688
Meredith Collins, Pres.

It seems inconceivable that so many of the firms described in this section possess photo collections each of which number in the millions, yet it is true. Brown Brothers, for example, owns about five million photos and three million woodcuts and engravings.

One of the nation's oldest photographers and photo illustrators, Brown Brothers has been supplying publications and commercial clients with pictures for many years.

In 1972, a monumental move took place in the photo archive world, when Harry and Meredith Collins supervised the transfer of eight million negatives, photos, woodcuts and engravings from 220 West 42 Street in Manhattan to an all-metal fireproof building on the Collins farm in the Poconos.

Established in 1904 by the brothers Arthur R. and Charles Brown, who were photographers, the company's specialty is its collection of many original glass plates taken by its photographers. Note that some of the photos can *not* be used for publicity.

6. Camera Hawaii, Inc.

875 Waimanu St., Honolulu, HI 96813
(808) 536-2302
Errol De Silva, Pres.

Established in 1950 by photographer Werner Stoy, Camera Hawaii serves Hawaiian and mainland accounts from its studio and elsewhere.

In 1983, Camera Hawaii moved to a new studio. It has a staff of studio and location photographers and maintains a stock library of over 300,000 photos of Hawaii and many other areas.

7. Camerique Stock Photography

Box 175, 1701 Skippack Pike, Blue Bell, PA 19422
(215) 272-4000
Orville Johnson, Mildred Johnson, Chris Johnson

Formed in 1974, Camerique has a large collection of color and black-and-white photographs, particularly contemporary people. The Johnson family also owns American Stock Photography in Los Angeles, which is described earlier in this chapter, and is represented by:

Bert Eccles, 245 Newbury St., Boston 02116, (617) 267-6450
Howard Cox, 233 E. Wacker Dr., Suite 4305, Chicago 60601, (312) 938-4466
Roberta Groves, 1181 Broadway, N.Y. 10001, (212) 685-3870
Judy Boundy, 180 Bloor St., W., Tornoto M5S 2V6, (416) 925-4323

8. Walter Chandoha

287 Springhill Rd., Annandale, NJ 08801
(201) 782-3666

Flora and fauna are Walter Chandoha's specialty. His stock file of over 200,000 color transparencies and black-and-white negatives includes one of the world's largest collections of cat and dog pictures, as well as photos of other animals, fruits, flowers, vegetables, gardening and all types of nature scenes. Service charge of $15 to $50, plus fee according to use.

Mr. Chandoha is a renowned photographer of animals, and his pictures have appeared in many magazines, as well as in his books.

9. Click/Chicago Ltd.

213 W. Institute Pl., Chicago 60610
(312) 787-7880

Click has about 790,000 images—the midwest's largest collection of color transparencies and black-and-white prints.

Price depends on the photo and its use: A research fee is charged (unless you do your own research), but it's refundable if you use any of the pictures. Clients can examine pictures for up to 30 days. Thereafter, a holding fee is charged of $5 per week per photo. All photos must be returned in person, by registered mail or bonded carrier. As will all stock photo services, Click values its collection, and charges $1,500 for a lost or damaged transparency and $100 for a lost or damaged B/W print.

It's worth a visit to Click to see their collection and meet their capable staff. Connie Geocaris works with advertising and public relations clients. Brian Seed handles assignments (Click also represents many photographers) and media clients.

When you visit Click, stop in to meet the staff of Special Events Report, a newsletter that is in the same charming building.

10. Bruce Coleman Inc.

381 Fifth Ave., N.Y. 10016
(212) 683-5227
Telex: 429 093
Norman Owen Tomalin

Branch Office:
17 Windsor St., Uxbridge, Middlesex UB8 1AB, England
(011) 44-895-57094
Telex: 932 439

Founded in 1970 as a specialist in travel and natural history, Bruce Coleman now stocks over 750,000 original color transparencies on a variety of subjects.

11. Compu/Pix/Rental

22231 Mulholland Hwy., Woodland Hills, CA 91364
(818) 888-9270
Bert Eifer, Pres.

A freelance photographer for over 15 years, Bert Eifer launched, in 1972, Associated Photographers International, which now has about 30,000 members throughout the world. He still is president of the association, and thus was able, in 1983, to set up an unusual type of stock photo agency, which enables clients to have access to the over 600,000 photographs in the collections of the members of Associated Photographers International.

Specifically, what Eifer has done is to list the subjects (not each of the photos) of the various members in a computerized databank. Clients are provided free with the names of one or several photographers whose specialties match the needs, or who have the subject categories. Payment then goes direct to the photographer, who remits a commission to C/P/R.

12. Comstock

30 Irving Pl., N.Y. 10003
(212) 889-9700, (800) 225-2727

The Comstock catalog is used by thousands of art directors and others. This free 132-page 9 × 12 magazine has several hundred color photos, from among Comstock's enormous collection of color transparencies.

13. Creative Color, Inc.

4911 W. Grace St., Tampa, FL 33607
(813) 879-5680
Burton McNeely, Pres.

A photographer for over 30 years, Burt McNeely specializes in underwater and outdoor scenes. His company also provides all types of laboratory services, including machine prints, and also stock photos.

14. Culver Pictures, Inc.

150 W. 22 St., N.Y. 10011
(212) 645-1672
Harriet Culver

Since 1926, the Culver family and staff have amassed an antiquarian's dream, with a picture research service based on more than nine million photos and other historical items. Culver's headquarters is stacked

12 feet high, with more than 50 tons of materials. The filing cabinets include some current material, such as movie stills, but the collection consists mostly of photos, engravings, posters and other illustrations of Americana and various subjects.

Companies and communities celebrating their 50th, 100th, or even 350th anniversaries are among Culver's nostalgia-conscious clients. Many book and magazine editors regularly dip into Culver's repository of illustrative material. American Heritage, for example, is liberally sprinkled with Culver credit lines.

Pictures are submitted on approval and rates vary according to the item and its use. The Culver Picture Guide (free to clients; $2.50 to others) is easy-to-use and extremely attractive.

15. Design Photographers International, Inc. (DPI)
19 W. 21 St., N.Y. 10010
(212) 627-4060
Alfred W. Forsyth, Pres.

The DPI Library includes a large variety of color photographs. A network of domestic and foreign photographers also is available for assignments. Fee dependent on use and rights.

16. Leo de Wys Inc.
1170 Broadway, N.Y. 10001
(212) 689-5580
Telex: 238 667
Leo de Wys, Pres.
Deborah Clickenger, Sales Mgr.

A variety of subjects, particularly animals, babies, children, industrial, people, recreation, scenics, sports, transportation and travel.

17. Four By Five Inc.
11 W. 19 St., N.Y. 10011
(212) 633-0300,
Deborah Levinson

Branch Offices:
5215 N. O'Connor Rd., Irving, TX 75039
(214) 556-2444

The Penthouse, 99 Osgood Pl., San Francisco
(415) 781-4433

Full-color stock photography on virtually every subject. Color catalog is available.

18. FPG International
251 Park Ave. South, N.Y. 10010
(212) 777-4210
Jessica Brackman, Pres.

Established in 1938, FPG's network of 500 photographers has produced one of the country's largest libraries of quality transparencies and prints. Clients can choose from among two million color transparencies and about three million black-and-white photos.

19. Ewing Galloway
100 Merrick Rd., Rockville Centre, NY 11570
(516) 764-8620
Tom McGeough

One of the most popular photo source credits in major magazines is Ewing Galloway, whose files of black-and-white photos probably are more extensive than any other commercial source. Included in the Galloway collection are more than 200,000 color transparencies.

Ewing Galloway founded the company in 1920 and after his death in 1956 the company was operated by 3 partners. Two have retired and the third is Thomas McGeough, who has been part of the Galloway company since his discharge from the U.S. Navy in 1946.

Recent catalogs of representative photos can be obtained at no charge. Fees for purchase or one-time reproduction of photos vary, according to the photo and media in which it will appear. Public relations rates are lower than those for advertising and often are considerably less than if one attempted to recreate the same scene.

Galloway is affiliated with three other companies that house large collections of photos:

American Stock Photos, 6842 Sunset Blvd., Hollywood 90028, (213) 469-3908

Campbell Stock Photo Services, 28000 Middlebelt Rd., Farmington Hills, MI 48018, (313) 626-5233

E. P. Jones, 45 Newbury St., Boston 02116, (617) 267-6450

20. Globe Photos, Inc.
275 Seventh Ave., N.Y. 10001
(212) 689-1340
Mary Beth Whelan
Raymond Whelan

Branch Office:
8400 Sunset Blvd., L.A. 90069
(213) 654-3350, Dick De Neut

Founded in 1939, Globe represents many internationally famous photographers. Clients include magazines, advertisers and publicists.

The Globe stock file of over 10 million transparencies and black-and-white historic and contemporary photos includes the collection of Rangefinder Photo, Camera Clix and Alpha.

21. Peter Gowland Productions
609 Hightree Rd., Santa Monica, CA 90402
(213) 454-7867

America's most prolific photographer of young women, Peter Gowland sells photos that he has taken during the last 35 years. Included are many photos of models with the "California look." Gowland also has photographed the models on the famous calenders distributed to plumbers by Ridge Tool Company.

22. The Granger Collection
1841 Broadway, N.Y. 10023
(212) 586-0971
William Glover, Dir.

267

Woodcuts, engravings, lithographs, tintypes and old silent movie stills are among the more than five million black-and-white prints and color transparencies available from The Granger Collection for reproduction, exhibition and reference. Fees are determined by the use made of the illustrations. A free illustrated folder describing the collection is available.

Mr. Glover welcomes visitors who desire to share, in pictures, the people, places, things and events of the past. He possesses an overflowing cornucopia of rare woodcuts and engravings, famous paintings and sculpture, and antique tintypes of times gone by, all of which are available to publicists, at a moment's notice, for reproduction and reference.

23. Historic Newspaper Archives, Inc.
1582 Hart St., Rahway, NJ 07065
(201) 381-2332
Sue MacGregor

Formed in 1963, Historic Newspaper Archives sells actual newspapers (not reproductions and not just front pages) of major cities of the U.S. and other countries.

In addition to The New York Times (1880–1985), Wall Street Journal (1955–1971), Washington Post (1953–1974) and other major newspapers, the archives (over 1.5 million newspapers!) have many hard-to-find defunct newspapers, including the Washington (D.C.) Star (1890–1971), Chicago Daily News (1875–1910), Chicago Herald (1915–1918), Chicago Examiner (1903–1922), Boston Post (1896–1935), Brooklyn Eagle (1880–1934), New York Globe (1904–1923), New York Herald Tribune (1880–1965), New York Sun (1947–1949) and the Cleveland Press (1926–1943).

Newspapers are sold "as is" or in presentation cases, which are delightful gifts for books, anniversaries and other occasions.

In fact, Historical Newspaper Archives is not really a back-issue clipping bureau. The price varies, depending on the newspaper and the presentation case, but it's generally *$34.50 per newspaper*, in a vinyl case.

24. Keystone Press Agency, Inc.
202 E. 42 St., N.Y. 10017
(212) 924-8123
Brian Alpert, Managing Editor

Keystone is a relatively small, but lively, international operation involving the sale of news and stock pictures and features, as well as assignments that are handled by local photographers affiliated with the agency. Keystone maintains its own offices in Paris, Munich, Rome, Tokyo, Montreal, Hamburg, Vienna, Zurich and Rio de Janeiro, and has correspondents in other major cities abroad. It is able to handle photo publicity assignments in these places at standard rates and also is interested in receiving photos from publicists. which it regularly distributes, at no cost, as part of its regular photo service to media.

The agency has an extensive collection of contemporary black-and-white and color photos, which can be purchased for editorial and commercial use.

25. Harold M. Lambert Studios, Inc.
2801 W. Cheltenham Ave., Box 27310, Philadelphia 19150
(215) 885-3355

Over a million color and black-and-white photos are in the Lambert collection. Rates vary with the use to be made of the photo. The minimum charge is $50 for a black-and-white photo and $150 for a color transparency. The company maintains sales offices in several cities to service its many customers.

26. Frederic Lewis, Inc.
134 W. 29 St., N.Y. 10001
(212) 594-8816

The Lewis Library, established in 1938, includes over a million historic and contemporary color and black-and-white photos and engravings, including early scenes of many American and European cities. The four-color catalog features detailed listings, from accidents to zoos.

27. Life Picture Service
2858 Time & Life Bldg., N.Y. 10020
(212) 522-4800
Telex 126767
Marthe M. Smith, Mgr.

Several million color and black-and-white photos, taken on assignment for Life Magazine, are card-catalogued and cross-referenced under 9,000 subject headings. Services charges are $100 an hour and license fees start at $175.

When possible, specify the page number and date of the issue of Life in which the photograph appeared. The collection also includes photographs which have not appeared in Life.

Formed in 1974, this major photographic resource (a lifetime of imagery) has been relatively unused by public relations clients.

28. The Map Store, Inc.
1636 Eye Street, N.W., Wash., DC 20006
(202) 628-2608

The Map Store is an excellent source of maps and related materials in Washington. They stock travel maps from all over the world, physical maps of the world and U.S., black-and-white market maps of all varieties, NOAA and DMA nautical charts and aeronautical charts and U.S. maps, state maps and city maps from around the country. If you want to order by mail, the shipping charge for almost all single packages is $2.50 (no credit cards, please). Sorry, but they do not publish a catalog.

29. Memory Shop
109 E. 12 St., N.Y. 10003
(212) 473-2404
Mark Ricci

Located near Fourth Avenue, this store has over three million photos, mostly related to movies and TV. Prices range from $3 to $15. The movie collection also includes posters, lobby cards, press books and other materials.

30. Movie Star News
134 W. 18 St., N.Y. 10011
(212) 620-8160
Paula Klaw Kramer

If you need a photo of Marie Dressler in Mack Sennett's ''Tillie's Punctured Romance,'' or just about any other old or contemporary movie still, chances are you can find it here.

Founded in 1940 by the late Irving Klaw, Movie Star News, now operated by his sister, Paula Klaw Kramer and her son, Ira Kramer, still is an essential resource for film buffs and researchers. Stills from films produced before 1950 often are better photographs than those from recent films. The explanation is that the earlier pictures were taken by specially hired still photographers, rather than excerpted from the actual movie frames.

A few blocks away is Cinemabilia (611 Broadway, NY 10012, phone 533-6683), which has U.S. and foreign still photos, back issues, posters, autographs and lots of other material for the collector and researcher.

Also nearby is the aforementioned Memory Shop (109 E. 12 St., phone 473-2404), a basement treasure trove run by Mark Ricci, who has organized his collection of photos, posters, press books and other items in file cabinets.

As mentioned in the preface to the chapter, researchers must be familiar with the picture collections of public libraries. In the film and show business fields, major collections are at the New York Public Library and the libraries of New York University, University of Southern California and the University of California at Los Angeles.

31. NYT Pictures
229 W. 43 St., N.Y. 10036
(212) 556-1243
Jack Topchik, Mgr.
Barbara Mancuso

Several publications sell pictures from their morgues. One of the largest and finest collections is the 500,000 black-and-white photographs taken since 1920 by photographers of The New York Times. You can dip into this archive by mail or phone. Note that only pictures published in The Times are available.

32. National Oceanic and Atmospheric Administration
National Ocean Service
Rockville, MD 20852
(301) 436-6990

If you need environmental data, aerial photographs, nautical maps and charts, or the names, dates and locations of the most famous shipwrecks, the National Oceanic and Atmospheric Administration, part of the U.S. Department of Commerce, is the best source. For a free catalog, write to Distribution Branch, N/CG33, Office of Charting and Geodetic Services, National Ocean Service (NOAA), Riverdale, MD 20737. You also can get a free catalog of Aeronautical Charts and Related Publications.

33. John Neubauer Photography
1525 S. Arlington Ridge Rd., Arlington, VA 22202
(703) 920-5994

This full-service studio also maintains an extensive color and black-and-white collection. Formerly located in Washington, D.C.

34. The Old Print Shop, Inc.
150 Lexington Ave., N.Y. 10016
(212) 683-3950
Kenneth M. Newman

Established in 1898, this store (at 30th Street) specializes in old original American prints, maps and paintings, including, of course, Currier & Ives.

35. Photography for Industry
1697 Broadway, N.Y. 10019
(212) 757-9255
Charles E. Rotkin

Formed in 1950, Photography for Industry provides stock photos and also publishes The Rotkin Review, a direct marketing book review journal.

36. Photonet

1001 S. Bayshore Dr., Miami, FL 33131
(305) 374-0074, (800) 368-6638

Photonet is a computer network for picture researchers, publishers, advertising agencies, stock photo agencies and photographers in the U.S. and overseas. The subscriber may send and receive a variety of information quickly, with almost any kind of terminal or computer.

For those who need photos quickly but don't have a computer, Photonet can be accessed via a national toll free number, 800-FOTONET.

Photonet's specialty is picture research. The user logs onto Photonet and selects the Photo Research Directory from the main menu. The user's photo requests can be transmitted simultaneously to numerous stock picture agencies in the U.S. and Europe. For picture researchers, Photonet can be the answer to tight deadlines and long-distance phone bills. It has dozens of online services, including the photo sources directory, electronic mail and bulletin boards.

Corporate subscriptions cost $300 (one-time fee) and include monthly billing, discounts on additional ID numbers and an unlisted ID option. Individual subscriptions, especially for photographers and freelance picture researchers, are billed monthly to a credit card account and have a one-time subscription fee of $125. Photonet's network access charge is $24 per hour, with a monthly corporate minimum of two hours and a monthly individual minimum of one hour.

37. Pictorial Parade, Inc.

130 W. 42 St., N.Y. 10036
(212) 840-2026
Baer M. Frimer, Pres.

A leading seller of photos to Life, Newsweek, The New York Times Magazine and other media, including book publishers and TV networks.

The usual arrangement for companies such as Pictorial Parade is to split the sales price with the photographer on a 50/50 basis.

38. Photo Researchers, Inc.

60 E. 56 St., N.Y. 10022
(212) 758-3420, Telex 428532
Bob Zentmaier, Pres.

Though its initials are PR, Photo Researchers does relatively little work for public relations clients, which is surprising. It currently maintains the collections of more than 3,000 photographers and sells their color and black-and-white photos to a large number of major book and magazine publishers, as well as advertisers and advertising agencies. However, the company is happy to deal with publicists, and it often is possible to obtain, for a relatively modest fee, the one-time reproduction rights to photos taken by some of the world's outstanding journalistic and scenic photographers.

Close to two million original transparencies and black-and-white prints are available for immediate viewing, including famous people and places of a more contemporary and artistic nature than is found in many stock photo collections.

In 1975, Photo Researchers acquired Rapho Guillumette Pictures, a famous name in the photography field, and also the renowned collection of the National Audubon Society.

In 1983, Photo Researchers became the U.S. representative for the Vandystadt Photo Agency of Paris, which specializes in sports coverage, and also launched a new division, called Science Source, which maintains a collection of photos in the medical, high technology and science fields. The company also is the U.S representative for the Science Photo Library of London and the Explorer and Jacana agencies in Paris.

39. Photo Source, International
10 W. 20 St., N.Y. 10011
(212) 633-0200
Daryl Murray, Gen. Mgr.
 A comprehensive stock photography agency, Photo Sources includes the color and black-and-white photos of the venerable Three Lions Photo Service.

40. PHOTRI (Photo Research International)
505 W. Windsor Ave., Alexandria, VA 22303
(703) 836-4439
Telex: 899 167
Telecopier: (703) 836-6572
Jack Novak
 Extensive library, specializing in military and aerospace, with over 500,000 images.
 PHOTRI has representatives in major cities including:

Atlanta (404) 588-9609
Chicago (312) 726-0433
Dallas (214) 641-6049
Los Angeles (213) 622-4220
New York (212) 926-0682

 The mailing address of PHOTRI is Box 26428, Alexandria, VA 22313-6428. Mr. Novak is also a photographer.

41. Reference Pictures
119 Fifth Ave., N.Y. 10003
(212) 254-0008
Doris Denhil
 A collection of over seven million clippings and photos. Rental fee is $23 per category for one to ten pictures or other items.

42. H. Armstrong Roberts
4203 Locust St., Philadelphia, PA 19104
(215) 386-6300

Branch Offices:
233 E. Wacker Dr., Ste. 4305, Chicago 60601
(312) 938-4466

1181 Broadway, NY 10001
(212) 685-3870

272

Nearly a million *contemporary* and historical color and black-and-white photos can be purchased, with the price related to the intended use. The company was founded in 1920.

Selections are sent on 10-day approval. Catalog available.

43. Anna Sosenko, Inc.
76 W. 82 St., N.Y. 10024
(212) 799-1357
Anna Sosenko

Memorabilia of the performing arts, mostly autographs, but also photos, programs, letters, posters and manuscripts, are the specialty of this little museum/shop.

Other caches of theatrical graphics can be uncovered in dozens of delightful shops in New York, Boston, Chicago and Los Angeles.

44. Stock Boston, Inc.
36 Gloucester St., Boston 02115
(617) 266-2300
Martha Bates, Mgr.

Extensive files of over 500,000 tightly edited contemporary color and B/W images, representing hundreds of photographers and subjects, both domestic and foreign.

45. The Stock Market
1181 Broadway, N.Y. 10001
(212) 684-7878, (800) 999-0800
Telex: 4973082
Telecopier: (212) 532-6750
Richard Steedman, Pres.

Formed in 1981 and operated by Richard Steedman and Sally Lloyd, The Stock Market has about 900,000 color transparencies from photographers in all fields.

The company is affiliated with major photo agencies throughout the world, including Granata Press, Milan, Italy; Masterfile, Toronto, Ontario, Canada; The Stock House, Hong Kong; Stock Photos, Victoria, Australia; Zefa, London, England; Imperial Press, Tokyo; and Zefa, Dusseldorf.

46. Studio Archives
Box 1041, Studio City, CA 91604
(213) 464-3244
Len Miller, Marilyn Blair

Old comedy movie stills, with full reproduction rights, can be obtained from these experienced archivists, who have been in business since 1969.

Three Lions, Inc.
See Photo Source, International

47. Uniphoto Picture Agency
Box 3678, 1071 Wisconsin Ave., N.W., Wash., D.C. 20007
(202) 333-0500, (800) 345-0546
William L. Tucker, Director

Extensive stock photo collection (over 500,000 images) plus network of over 200 photographers in major cities for all types of assignments. In 1984, Uniphoto and Meta Media Systems, Inc., combined to form the Photo Store, in which the original color transparencies in the Uniphoto Archives have been converted to video disks for use in video productions. In addition, the library can be accessed via the Image Search software, which is compatible with IBM-PC and interactive with most video disk players.

48. Volk Clip Art, Inc.
Box 347, Washington, IL 61571-0347
(609) 641-8800

Monthly camera-ready art service in easy-to-use 5″ x 8″ booklet size. Each monthly shipment consists of two 8-page and two 12-page clip books dealing with a single theme, such as family, winter sports, plus a 6-page supplement on current issues. $17.50 monthly cost includes postage and handling.

49. Wide World Photos
50 Rockefeller Plaza, N.Y. 10020
(212) 621-1930

The commercial division of The Associated Press—a huge and fascinating operation—is described in the following section. The stock photo library is the largest contemporary collection in the world.

Chapter 20

Photography

A single fashion photo for a magazine advertisement can cost over a thousand dollars. Photography for an annual report can entail several weeks, with extensive travel, and can cost several thousand dollars. Most public relations assignments to photographers, however, are not in this league. For example, Martha Holmes, a former Life photographer, charges $500 a ½-day for a collection of candid photos to illustrate a magazine article or other publication. She is at 161 W. 75 St., N.Y. 10023, phone (212) 874-3242.

Since several volumes would be required to describe the operations of photographers with such specialties as architecture, beauty, fashion, food, new products and other subjects, and several more volumes would be required to describe photographers categorized by such specialties as mail order catalogs, industrial, editorial, commercial, advertising and publicity, this directory must omit a comprehensive chapter on photography. (The Manhattan classified telephone book lists more than 1,000 commercial and portrait photographers and more than 500 photo labs!)

It is assumed that every publicist regularly uses one or more photographers, and you are capable of finding specific specialists whenever your needs cannot be handled by your regular roster. The Professional Photographers of America issues an annual directory which indicates the specialties of its members. For a free copy of the directory, write to Professional Photographers of America, 1090 Executive Way, Oak Leaf Commons, Des Plaines, IL 60018. In addition to the 550 commercial photo studios and other members of the Association, arranged geographically, alphabetically and by specialty, the book includes sources of quantity prints, photomurals and other photography services.

Another directory lists, alphabetically and geographically, about 3,000 top freelance photographers who are members of the ASMP—The American Society of Magazine Photographers. The ASMP Membership Directory is available free from the Society at 205 Lexington Ave., N.Y. 10016, phone (212) 889-9144.

Another professional association is APA—Advertising Photographers of America, 45 E. 20 St., N.Y. 10003.

Publishers Network, Inc., 828 Charcot Ave., San Jose, CA 95131, publishes The Editor's Guide to Freelance Photographers and Photojournalists, a 516-page book ($95) with descriptions and photographs by top photographers. The format is one page per photographer, arranged by state.

Several major hotels have resident photographers who cover conventions and other events at the hotel and elsewhere. For example, Christina Krupka is the person to contact at Darlene Studios, the Plaza Hotel, NY 10022, (212) 755-4320.

Many photographers who work from their homes are thoroughly professional and experienced in coverage of public relations events. Two in Westchester county are Bill Donovan, 165 Grand Blvd., Scarsdale, NY, (914) 472-0938, and Harold Hechler, 67 Gladstone Rd., New Rochelle, NY, (212) 654-8199.

The relatively few photographers and photography service organizations which are described in this chapter are included because they are unique or so large or unusual that they could be of value to many publicists. Attention also is given to aerial photography and other specialties which are rarely used by public relations clients in spite of their seemingly high publicity potential. Finally, the prices of a few photography organizations are included, in order to provide a guide to the use of commercial photographers.

Many newspapers sell photos as a service to readers and advertisers, but few are in the photography business in as big a way as the Copley News Service in San Diego, California. Copley Photos, operated by Al Sund in the Union-Tribune Bldg., 350 Camino de la Reina, San Diego 92108, phone (619) 293-1838, sells quantity photo prints and provides other commercial photography services.

The New York Times operated a portrait studio for many years, but closed it in 1974.

United Press International no longer has a publicity photography operation, but the Wide World commercial photography division of The Associated Press still is one of the largest and most efficient networks in the world.

PhotoDataBank is a database of over 35,000 entries, submitted by several hundred photographers, with their specialties, special-interest photos, plus states and countries where they have a good supply of photos. To tap this information and locate either a photographer or a particular photo need, call (715) 248-3800. The service is free.

Photographers who are listed in the PhotoDataBank are subscribers to Rohn Engh's PhotoSource International (established in 1976) service which includes a semi-monthly Photomarket ($20 per month) and a weekly Photobulletin ($35 per month) which he transmits to his subscribers electronically from his 120-acre farm near Osceola, Wisconsin 54020.

Engh's services are on NewsNet (PB12), MCI Mail (189-2053) and General Electric GEnie network (PSI).

Publicists often can use this system to glean photo opportunities for acquiring photos and placing them. Publicists also can search the NewsNet database (on the NEWSFLASH services) for key words, such as products or trade names, for photo buyers who are searching for these photos.

Potentials In Marketing, a monthly magazine totally devoted to publicity about new products and services, publishes a booklet, How to Get Your Publicity Into Print. You can get the free booklet and a sample copy of the magazine from them at 731 Hennepin Ave., Minneapolis, MN 55403. Most of the items in this excellent magazine include photos, and the booklet requests good-quality, glossy photographs . . . "not a printed halftone clipping or mass-produced print. Send color (4 × 5 color transparencies are preferred) only when requested."

Seems like a reasonable request! However, many professional publicists still have vast areas of ignorance or inexperience with regard to photography and photoprints. If you are in this category, here are a few things you can do.

1. Spend a few hours with a professional photographer and learn, from the beginning if necessary, about cropping, retouching, mass vs. original prints, types of color (negatives, slides, prints) and lots of other details related to public relations.
2. Read books and magazines available on photography at bookstores and libraries. If you're active in photography, you may want to take a course.
3. Subscribe to photography periodicals specifically oriented to public relations and media people. For example, Hope Reports is crammed with audiovisual data and commentary by Tom Hope,

who since 1970 has operated a market research and publishing company which specializes in the audiovisual industry. Hope is at 1600 Lyell Ave., Rochester, NY 14606.

The use of freelancers or semiprofessional photographers often is a false economy. Illness, lateness, difficulty in getting prints and other problems are more likely to make a one-person photography operation a potential disaster for the client. Whether you use an independent photographer or photo service, here are several tips for better-quality photography.

When a publicist refers to an inferior photograph for publication, it does not necessarily mean that the picture is photographically bad. Errors in lighting or focus should not be a factor.

An inferior photo can have many things wrong with it and still be a pretty picture to hang on the wall. The editor, whose job it is to come up with a graphically perfect page, as well as one that makes good news sense, does not judge a photo on quality alone. It simply must make sense and justify its publication.

To illustrate, let's start with an executive appointment or promotion.

Most portraits are deadly. They are low-key lighted and soft-focus. A formal portrait for publication should be dead-sharp focus all the way through and strongly lighted. Your best bet is a candid close-up, if possible shot under available light in the subject's office. But even this must be sharp, have good clear detail and be well exposed. It should be printed on single-weight glossy paper only. Matte or textured paper is magnificent for display, but not for reproduction. Above all, do not use a Polaroid photo or a copy of one (because of printing problems).

The next type of photograph most frequently published in the award or presentation shot, and it too is abused by many publicists.

This photograph should be kept as newsy as possible. This means tightness; that is, limit the picture only to the people actually involved in the award or event. In many of those photographs, a simple presentation ceremony has evolved into a graduation group. Never pose more than three persons in the shot, always keep the grouping tight with shoulders touching if possible ("Think Two Columns"), and always keep the grouping away from walls, as far as possible, to eliminate black blob shadows forming behind the subjects.

The committee photo or society grouping also can be deadly, if not handled properly. Avoid photos of large groups or even small groups staring at the camera. The decision must be made to cut the group down to three or four people in a working group.

Be aware of the techniques in shooting speakers. This is best accomplished by using a 35mm camera and a long lens which reduces the angle between the camera and the speaker, eliminating the flash which either distracts the speaker and causes her to lose her lines or leaves moons and stars dancing in front of her eyes. This technique also affords the opportunity to get background identification behind the speaker.

What happens when the photographer plants himself in front of the dais and pops flashes? He annoys the speaker and winds up with the hackneyed up-the-nostril shot of a hard-to-recognize subject behind a podium.

If you're planning to photograph a meeting, exhibit, party or other event, go over your goals with the photographer. Instead of asking the photographer to roam around and shoot a lot of pictures, explain what you hope to achieve, in terms of mood and impact and not just content.

One aspect of photography which often is overlooked by clients is model releases. Model agencies and professional photographers usually handle details, such as clearances from the people who are photographed. The question of whether clearances are required of participants at news events and other "amateurs" who are photographed should be considered by public relations practitioners, in consultation with their attorneys. A public relations department should have an established policy with regard to clearance forms, compensation and related matters, and not abdicate this responsibility to the photogra-

277

pher. Following is a suggested model release form, which can be used even when the compensation is a token $1.

> For good and valuable consideration, I hereby consent to the reproduction and/or use of my photograph in all manners and for all purposes including advertising, trade, display, exhibition and art, and also to the use of my name in connection herewith. I also consent to my photograph and name appearing in any and all legitimate periodicals, pamphlets, booklets, etc. in connection with the aforementioned uses.
>
> I am over 21 years of age and have read the above authorization and release prior to its execution.
>
> Signature . . . .
> Address . . . .
> City and State . . . .
> Witness . . . .

In working with nonprofessional "models," the publicist must balance the fact that the longer the release form the more apprehensive the person may become, against the need to protect the client. For example, the following phrases may result in the refusal of the subject to be photographed, and yet the clauses have merit.

> I hereby waive any right to inspect or approve the finished photograph or advertising copy or printed matter that may be used in conjunction therewith or to the eventual use that it might be applied.
>
> I hereby release, discharge and agree to save harmless the photographer, his representatives, assigns, employees or any person or persons, corporation or corporations, acting under his permission or authority, or any person, persons, corporation or corporations, for whom he might be acting, including any firm publishing and/or distributing the finished product, in whole or in part, from and against any liability as a result of any distortion, blurring, or alteration, optical illusion, or use in composite form, either intentionally or otherwise, that may occur or be produced in the taking, processing or reproduction of the finished product, its publication or distribution of the same, even should the same subject me to ridicule, scandal, reproach, scorn or indignity.

Food, beauty, fashion, home furnishings, industrial and other photography often require an expert in the specific field to assist the photographer. A food stylist, for example, can "create" food with a variety of skills and artifices, which is beautifully photogenic.

Food photographers generally work with home economists or others who are experienced in cooking and baking foods which are gorgeous, though sometimes inedible. In the Chicago area, food stylists include Monica Baxendale Cooper, 1017 Vine St., Winnetka 60093, phone (312) 446-6882; Caroline Kriz, 100 E. Walton, Chicago 60611, phone (312) 751-2655; Jane Kuoni, 111 E. Chestnut St., Chicago 60611, phone (312) 787-9669; Carol Smoler, 1825 N. Sedgwick, Chicago 60614, phone (312) 266-1133; and Judy Vance, 720 S. Stone, La Grange 60525, phone (312) 354-6196.

Many food, fashion and photo stylists are available as media spokespeople, helpers in finding props and other public relations assignments.

Some of the fashion and home furnishings consultants are experienced shoppers of props and literally are set designers. A few are in such demand that they have unlisted telephone numbers!

A wedding specialist is Dennis Reggie, 1512 Monarch Office Plaza, 3414 Peachtree Road, N.E.,

Atlanta, GA 30326. He has produced wedding photo albums for many prominent people all over the country, and also covers other special events.

A guide to color print, slide, and movie processing, Kodak Processing Lab Services, A3-21, is available free from Eastman Kodak Company, Photo Information Department, 343 State St., Rochester, NY 14650. Included are descriptions of processing services, such as announcements, copyrights and other special color and black-and-white processing services.

You can also send for a catalog of Kodak books and pamphlets, the Index to Kodak Photographic Information, L-1, which lists more than 400 publications on the use of Kodak photographic products. Send $1 to Eastman Kodak Company, Dept. 412-L, Rochester, NY 14650. Residents of Canada may order from Kodak Canada Inc., 3500 Eglinton Ave. West, Toronto, Ontario M6M 1V3, Canada.

Most professional photographers use 35mm cameras and Tri-X black-and-white film exposed at its recommended rating of 400 ASA and developed with D76 developer. United Press often prefers color transparencies and Associated Press prefers color negatives.

The following guide to color photography is adapted from the catalog of K + L.

There are three basic color print mediums available for the reproduction of color photography.

1. Maximum Quality

Reproduction dye transfer, can be made from—any positive color transparency (Kodachrome, Ektachrome, Ansochrome), any color negative material (Ektacolor, Kodacolor), any type of original color art.

A dye transfer is an opaque color print made from any type and size of color film or art. This medium is the finest and most versatile method of color reproduction. One that permits a wide range of color correction during the laboratory process or a match to the color of the original. Color corrected separation negatives enlarged to the size of the desired image on matrix film to form a gelatin relief image (positive). Each matrix then is dyed with its respective dye (cyan, yellow, magenta). The dye image is transferred in register to a single sheet of mordanted white photographic paper to form the final image. The ultimate in the preparation of the multiple element illustration brought into a common focus for mechanical reproduction; eliminates cost of separate sets of separation negatives at the printing stage.

2. Maximum & Medium Quality

(Type "C") Ektacolor prints, can be made from the same type of original materials listed above although this process yields maximum quality when made from original negative color film exposed in the camera. Quality of "C" from original negatives in some cases is comparable to Dye Transfer.

Ektacolor print paper essentially consists of three emulsions—sensitive to blue, green and red light, respectively. Coated on a medium weight paper, this material is exposed from a color negative film image via "white light" exposure or by three separate exposures through red, green and blue filters. Ektacolor prints, commonly referred to as type "C" prints, will yield maximum reproduction quality when made from original color negative film exposed in the camera, although color internegatives are readily made from positive transparencies or flat art which can be used for prints of any size and in any quantity. Color stats are made via this internegative means. This negative—positive system of color print making is essentially a one-step process offering limited color correction and retouching possibilities.

3. Fair Quality

Colorstats, commonly known as Ektacolor or Ektachrome stats, can be made from positive color transparencies for full color art, for use as stats or layout prints, etc.

Color stats have been used most successfully for comprehensive layouts, sales meetings, presentations and other applications requiring color impact. These prints are dry mountable, retouchable and have white whites. Perfect for comps and presentations.

Here is additional information about dye transfers.

The dye transfer process exceeds all other techniques in its ability to control and enhance the image. Only a few custom laboratories in the country can produce the ultimate in color photographic reproduction—the dye transfer print.

In this process, images are enhanced, endowed with red or blue tones, altered shades of light and dark, heightened or reduced in color contrast, mounted and prepared for gallery exhibition or other uses produced to sell the world's goods.

The dye transfer process utilizes three colors. Because the dyes are so concentrated, no black printer or matrix is required. The resulting prints have the longest known permanency.

The dye transfer is essentially a hand-crafted process. Each color is controlled individually. Color shifts and corrections can be made in large areas. It is possible to selectively mask and change the color density of an area, retouch, or alter other areas completely. Such modifications can enhance the detail and tonal qualities of the original. Additional images can be combined together to produce a multiple-image dye transfer print.

Dye transfers are widely acknowledged by most professional photographers, art directors and retouchers as the photographic ultimate reproduction process.

Dye transfer prints yield the best results for printing reproduction, and dye transparencies used as back-lit displays include a "fail-safe" benefit of a quality print even without rear illumination.

A print can be called the sum total of a photographer's reputation. Many magazine photographers and other top-notch professionals turn over all of their darkroom work to custom laboratories. Some publicists, on the other hand, often try to save pennies and mail out prints with varying grades of quality.

It is possible to turn out "usable photos" by low-cost mass production methods, and there are times when such facilities are in order. However, every publicist should know the difference between poor and top-quality photo prints and should be familiar with the best possible photo laboratory services so that they can be used whenever possible. A really good lab, for example, develops by inspection, to give the finest possible grain with maximum shadow detail. More important than routine service is the ability to force development of underexposed negatives and to otherwise correct inferior negatives. The charges for these custom services vary, of course.

If you are interested in placing a photo or set of photos with a magazine or other publication which looks for excellence in photography, it is almost always essential to utilize a custom photo laboratory which offers special printing services. Whenever possible, prints should be semigloss or matte finish.

Many photo laboratories offer only a limited amount of color facilities. Most color processing of Kodachrome film, including professional work, is handled directly by Eastman Kodak and other film manufacturers. In a few cities, motion picture and still film laboratories have been set up to specialize or handle color work exclusively.

Except for those who are experienced amateur photographers, most publicists are relatively unfamiliar with color photography and still work almost entirely with black-and-white prints. Since many major newspapers now use color, publicists should become familiar with the color print media available for the reproduction of color photography.

Many trade and business publications now use color photos on their covers and inside, but often lack the budgets of consumer magazines and thus are extremely receptive to quality color transparencies from publicity sources. The old photo case history has changed, with the emphasis today more on photos, including color, than text. When assigning a photographer for a major project, it generally is preferable to request several formats, including black-and-white, color transparencies and color negatives or prints.

Modernage Photographic Services, an internationally renowned lab (described later in this chapter), provides the following advice in its catalog:

If you shoot 2¼ × 2¼ negatives and want your finished 8 × 10 prints to be a vertical or horizontal format, indicate how to crop, preferably on a contact sheet, so that the technician will not crop important parts of the subject. The same holds true for 35mm negatives which will have to be cropped slightly if you want the full paper size on 8 × 10, 11 × 14 or 16 × 20 filled out. A full negative 35mm will give an image of 6½ × 9½ on 8 × 10 paper when printed with a border. Use the marking instructions to indicate possible lightening or darkening desired. In general, keep the following in mind: For general pictures, let the image fill the frame, without crowding. This means minimum enlargement to reach the desired print size. If your camera format is square, allow room for the part that must be lost in cropping when you want vertical or horizontal prints. Always hold the camera level so that the horizontal lines will be straight. Straightening lines in a picture uses up corner space in the negative. Give consistent correct exposure, preferably through the use of an exposure meter. When you are not sure, expose so that any errors will be slightly on the overexposure side. Negative films should have more latitude in that direction. When shooting color negative films, use the film balanced for the color temperature of your illumination and if you have to mix, use the correct light balancing or color temperature correction filters. Also, use the correct film for the length of exposure. (For example, EKTACOLOR and VERICOLOR L films are to be used for long exposure time, 1/10 to 60 seconds only.) Exposure times shorter or longer than a film is made for can result in "crossed curves," color errors that cannot be corrected in printing.

For best results in custom color printing, try to include a KODAK NEUTRAL DENSITY CARD in at least one exposure, if the light remains the same for the rest of the roll. This helps our technicians arrive at the correct color balance faster and with precision.

Most publicity pictures still are produced in black-and-white. However, here's an indication of the importance of color: In late 1987, all Associated Press bureaus in the U.S. were set up to use color photos.

Several photographers, printers and photo laboratories in the midtown Broadway area of Manhattan and Sunset Blvd. areas of Hollywood specialize in extremely low-cost photography, photo postcards and machine print glossy photos. Much of this work is for models, actors and actresses, but others can take advantage of these bargain sources.

Here are several in the Times Square area:

Cogliano Benedict Photographics, Inc., 1472 Broadway, N.Y. 10036, (212) 391-0141
Eljay Photo Service Co., 42 W. 48 St., N.Y. 10036, (212) 869-5149
Franklin Photos, Inc., 370 W. 35 St., N.Y. 10001, (212) 279-1950
Ideal Photo Service, 145 W. 45 St., N.Y. 10036, (212) 575-0303

Ideal was formed in 1948 and currently is operated by Carl Canizares.

These suppliers include such large well-established photo labs as JJK, which is a division of James J. Kriegsmann, a company founded in 1934 and located at 165 W. 46 St., N.Y. 10036, phone (212) 382-0190. Other specialists in machine print photos are described later in this chapter.

Ted Kraskow operates Color Slides, Inc., 383 Fifth Avenue, N.Y. 10016, phone (212) 679-2344. 35mm slides are $4 for the first copy, 90¢ for 2–10 prints, 85¢ each for the next 11–25. You might want to look into 45mm super-slides, which are $6 for the first copy and $2.50 each for two to ten copies.

Chicago area photographers who specialize in photojournalism and public relations assignments include (all are area code 312):

Nick Ambrosia, 1100 W. Washington St., Chic. 60607, 666-9200
Lee Balgemann, 725 Monroe Ave., River Forest 60305, 771-9427
Baver Studio, 2923 W. Touhy, Chic. 60645, 338-4595
Les Boschke, 806 N. Peoria, Chic. 60622, 666-8819
Donald Bromley, 4455 N. Ashland, Chic. 60622, 334-3340
Cable Studios, 2212 N. Racine, Chic. 60614, 525-2240
Mike Camacho, 124 W. Maine, W. Dundee 60118, 428-3135
Rees and Michael Candee, 1212 W. Jackson, Chic. 60607, 829-3188
Dave Chare, 1045 Northwest Hwy., Park Ridge 60068, 696-3188
Thomas Cindman, 2141 N. Hoyne, Chic. 60647, 276-4188
Bill Crofton, 326R Linden Ave., Wilmette 60091, 256-7862
Janet Davis, 1 S. 035 Euclid Ave., Oak Brook Terrace 60181, 495-3345
Charles Hodes, 233 E. Erie St., Chic. 60611, 951-1186
Debbie Leavitt, 2756 N. Pine Grove Ave., Chic. 60614, 348-5862
Stef Leinwohl, 439 W. Oakdale Ave., Chic. 60657, 327-3669
Don Mally, 20 W. Hubbard St., Chic. 60610, 644-4367
Milton & Joan Mann, Box 413, Evanston 60204, 777-5656
Photo-One, 7000 W. Carol Ave., Niles 60648, 965-5289
Victor Powell, 59 W. Hubbard St., Chic. 60610, 836-0261
Jim Vaughan, 321 S. Jefferson St., Chic. 60606, 663-0369

Several of the large-sized mailing companies, notably PR Aids, produce their own prints.

The mass photo print business has become so important to advertising and public relations clients that several large laboratories operate in various parts of the country.

The usual procedure is to make an 8×10 "copy negative" from one print, and then mass produce prints from the copy negative. Since there is an intermediate photography step, the quality of the print not only depends on the quality of the original print but also on the fidelity of the copy negative.

Check the price lists carefully. In some cases, there is little or no saving by ordering less than 100 prints.

There is a trend toward the use of 5×7 prints, which are particularly useful for portrait photos. Some editors still prefer the 8×10 size, probably because it may be easier to file. A few publicists are using the 4×5 size, which can be mailed in regular business envelopes.

A few comments about slides.

35mm slides proportion out approximately 2 to 3. Keep your artwork and your cropping of transparencies and slides in this proportion to avoid taping or black areas. Keep under $20'' \times 30''$ in size to avoid additional costs.

Super-slides proportion out 1 to 1. Keep material under $20'' \times 20''$ to avoid additional costs.

TV slides are approximately ⅛" less on the longer dimension than the standard 35mm slide . . . Format must be *horizontal* . . . TV title area must be ⅛" from the top and bottom of slide and approximately ¼" from the sides.

Leave extra background area on all slide art . . . keep lettering as large as possible for legibility . . . keep subjects simple to avoid confusion.

Photostats (or, as they generally are called, stats) still are a basic product in the advertising, printing and graphics fields. Public relations people often need the sharpness of a stat for reproduction purposes. Furthermore, a stat machine can be used to enlarge or reduce to exact dimensions. Stats are made by specialists, though photography labs, design studios and other companies often have stat machines. In New York, Adams Photoprint Co. is one of the largest stat companies. The main office is at 250 W. 57 St., N.Y. 10107, phone (212) 247-4637, and branches are located throughout Manhattan.

And finally, here's a cost-savings tip. Print two, three or four different 4×5 photos on one 8×10 sheet. You save on prints, captions and mailing costs. In fact, you can gang up four 4×5 prints of the same photo on one 8×10 sheet and then cut them yourself. Get yourself a paper cutter, which has many other uses, and you'll be doing what the lab charges you for.

So much for miscellaneous photo tips. Following are descriptions of several of the largest publicity photography operations throughout the country.

1. Adams Studio Inc.
1523 22 St., N.W., Wash., D.C. 20037
(202) 785-2188
Jon Francis, Pres.
Jerry Mesmer, V.P.

Colorful location with a courtyard, studio and darkrooms, and, more important, experienced photographers.

2. American Audio Visual, Inc.
216 E. 45 St., N.Y. 10017
(212) 661-6100
Bob Goldberg, Pres.

Founded in 1966 as B & G International Photos by former AP and UPI wirephoto photographers, American Audio Visual is a major company in publicity photography. The company was at one time known as Compix of New York, when it was affiliated with UPI's commercial photography division. The name change occurred in 1978.

In 1980, American AV bought Gary Wagner's well-known Wagner International Photos, and now handles all photography and related services through Wagner International Photo Service. The New York office has a staff of five publicity photographers and support personnel. A network of photographers around the U.S. and countries around the world provide photo coverage out of New York. Gary Wagner serves as a consultant and Bob Goldberg, one of the company's original founders, is President. Sid Birns (the B of B & G) is no longer with the company.

American AV also provides slide shows and multi-media presentations, and has extensive in-house facilities.

3. Apco Apeda/Rik Shaw
525 W. 52 St., N.Y. 10019
(212) 586-5755
Paul Stein, Pres.
David Stein, Sales Mgr.

A merger of three well-known photographic services, Apco Apeda/Rik Shaw produces prints and countless other standard services, plus its own light boxes and other special items.

The company publishes one of the most comprehensive rate schedules in the photography business, with dozens of pages that describe close to 200 photographic services (all produced by Shaw). The catalog is helpful to anyone needing a primer in this field.

In addition to the services, Mr. Shaw and his associates are available to give publicists the benefit of their many years of photographic know-how with regard to any type of project involving art and photography. If you supply the script, Shaw will produce artwork and photography for films and film-strips.

4. Atlas Photo, Inc.

45 W. 27 St., N.Y. 10001
(212) 683-6590
Don Bell, Ray DeLessio

Studio photography and very low prices on quality/quantity prints, black-and-white and color, has developed a sizable business for Atlas since the company was started in 1947.

5. Audio Visual Promotion Aids Inc.

611 Broadway, N.Y. 10012
(212) 477-5540
Rosemary Heath

All types of audiovisual equipment, including slide and film projectors, recorders, lecterns, special effects lighting.

6. Bachrach, Inc.

48 E. 50 St., N.Y. 10022
(212) 755-6233
Kenneth R. Carpenter, V.P.

Branch Offices:
647 Boylston St., Boston, MA 02116
(617) 536-4730
Audry Weber, Mgr.

12 South St., Morristown, NJ 07960
(609) 267-2006
Janice Bordeaux, Mgr.

1611 Walnut St., Philadelphia, PA 19103
(215) 563-0551
Marie Baldino, Mgr.

104 S. Michigan Ave., Chicago 60603
(312) 236-1991
Victor de la Puenta, Mgr.

Bachrach probably is the world's most famous portrait photographer. There certainly are other well-known studios, such as Karsh of Ottawa and Pach Brothers in New York, but Bachrach is the oldest and largest operation of its kind. Yousuf Karsh, who resides in Ottawa, Canada, travels to clients all over the world and maintains a studio at 18 E. 62 St., N.Y. 10022, phone (212) 838-4565. Pach Brothers is at 16 E. 53 St., N.Y. 10022, phone (212) 758-3366.

Founded in 1868 by David Bachrach, and continued by Louis Fabian Bachrach, and then Bradford Bachrach, the company now is headed by Louis Fabian Bachrach III and his brother, Robert.

In much the same way that some people will look for the Tiffany emblem on personal letterheads and envelopes (though there certainly are other purveyors of fine quality stationery), so too, do clients and editors respect the Bachrach name on portrait photographs. It's possible to take top-quality photo portraits in an executive's office, on location, or in the studios of dozens of other experienced photographers, but there is something about the Bachrach name which gives its pictures a special appeal.

Special attention is given to the print reproduction qualities of the photos, and top-quality paper and other products are used. More than 150 employees operate the New York studios and laboratories. Bachrach no longer maintains studios in Hartford; Baltimore; Washington, D.C.; Atlanta, and Providence, and now sends photographers to company offices throughout the country.

Bachrach portraits are not as expensive as one might think A studio sitting and six black-and-white glossy prints costs $137.50. From the moment of arrival in the crystal-chandeliered New York reception room, a Bachrach appointment is a pleasant, personalized experience. Allow about an hour for a sitting.

If you're interested in portrait painting, the man to see at Bachrach is artist Arthur Pyykko, who uses photos as guides; prices are $6,000 and up.

With regard to portraiture, which has aesthetic vanity, and public relations values, you should visit several art galleries and arrange to meet with artists whose work appeals to you in terms of style and fee.

One of the best known specialists in the field is Portraits, Inc., 985 Park Ave., N.Y. 10028, phone (212) 879-5560. Founded in 1942, the company works with many painters and sculptors and maintains an exhibition gallery exclusively devoted to portraits. Rutgers Barclay is President.

7. Bel-Air Co. Photographers
2511 W. Holcombe, Houston, TX 77030
(713) 666-1511
Ben Smusz

A commercial photographer for over 20 years, Ben Smusz handles studio work and assignments throughout the world.

The company was acquired in 1986 from veteran photographer Stan Began.

8. Alan Berliner Studios
Box 480066, L.A. 90048
(213) 857-1282
Alan J. Berliner, Pres.

Since 1969, Alan Berliner has operated a full-service studio and lab, specializing in public relations clients. Rates are $75 to $125 per hour, plus film and mileage.

9. Brilliant Image
141 W. 28 St., N.Y. 10001
(212) 736-9661
Jerry Cahn

State-of-the-art business slides is the specialty of this full-service computer graphics firm, which produces slides, overhead transparencies and photo prints.

10. Burton Photo Industries, Inc.
3332–44 Rorer St., Philadelphia 19134
(215) 425-8940, (800) 523-3225
Scott Segen

Founded in 1945, Burton Photo Industries, Inc., is a full service commercial photographic lab source. Services include quantity photos (including display size) in color and black-and-white, duplicate slides and transparencies, display prints, transparencies and duratrans up to 6' × 15' in one piece.

11. Chase Studios, Inc.

1220 19 St., N.W., Wash., DC 20036
(202) 338-2400
Brooks Blunck

Branch Office:
5019 Wilson Lane, Bethesda, MD 20014
(301) 986-1050

Chase primarily is a photography studio specializing in portraits, ranging from passport photos to elegant color renditions of executives and Government officials.

12. Citiphoto Ltd.

320 E. 42 St., N.Y. 10017
(212) 692-9427
Ed Peters, Dick Lewis

Formed in 1983 by Ed Peters (former Director of Photography of the NY Daily News) and Dick Lewis (also a News veteran), Citiphoto provides studio and location photography to advertising and public relations clients. Basic ½-day rates are $300 (black-and-white) and $400 color.

13. Color Film Corporation

777 Washington Blvd., Stamford, CT 06901
(203) 327-7050, (800) 243-9022
C. Nelson Winget, Pres.

An indication of the national clientele of Color Film Corporation is its toll-free 800 number. The company specializes in video cassettes, filmstrips and slides. The filmstrip process starts with photography of a master negative from camera-ready original material. Thereafter, a detailed price list includes the cost of double exposures, frame numbers, split frames and other services.

Other services include film and slide to tape transfer and all types of video duplication.

14. COMPOA (Commercial Photographers of America)

339 Blvd. of Allies, Pittsburgh, PA 15222
(412) 281-2774
Jack Lever, Director

This network of commercial photographers serves over 1,000 cities in the U.S. and Canada.

15. Creative Technologies, Inc.

7630 Little River Turnpike, Annandale, VA 22003
(703) 256-7444
Roy T. Fell, Jr.

Branch Offices:
801 Stephenson Hwy., Troy, MI 48083
(313) 589-3100
Jo Ann Fell

1010 Vermont Ave., N.W., Wash., DC 20005
(202) 783-5477
Janet Quinn

Established in 1973, Creative Technologies is a full service audiovisual firm headquartered in the Washington, DC metropolitan area. Areas of specialization include computer-generated 35mm slides, graphic arts and photo special effects.

16. Crown Photo Service
370 W. 35 St., N.Y. 10001
(212) 279-1950
John V. Taranto, Sales Mgr.
Martin Richman, V.P.

An experienced maker of black-and-white prints and postcards, Crown also operates Colorama Labs, a specialist in quantity and custom color prints, murals and display transparencies.

The single-weight glossy or matte print price schedule is:

Size	25	50	100	250	500	1000
4x5	$12.50	$18.50	$30.00	$ 65.00	$115.00	$190.00
5x7	$13.75	$20.50	$32.00	$ 70.00	$125.00	$200.00
8x10	$15.75	$24.50	$37.00	$ 85.00	$150.00	$280.00
8½x11	$31.25	$24.50	$37.00	$137.50	$250.00	$450.00

Note, as with all machine prints, a copy negative first must be made from an original print. The copy negative cost is $6.50 for all sizes, except 11×14, which is $8.25. Overnight rush service is also available for color and black-and-white prints.

17. Du Art Film Laboratories, Inc.
245 W. 55 St., N.Y. 10019
(212) 757-4580, (800) 223-9730
Telex: 640253
Robert M. Smith, Exec. V. P.

Branch Office:
39 Chapel St., Newton, MA 02158
(617) 969-0666

A major laboratory in the motion picture and TV industries, Du Art processes "dailies" during shootings and provides other production and post-production services to customers throughout the world.

Services relevant to public relations clients include film-to-tape and tape-to-film transfers, videotape editing ($220 an hour, with two VTRs) and videocassette duplication ($13 to $25 for five minutes tapes; $36 to $75 for 60-minute tapes, depending on quantity).

18. Flying Camera, Inc.
114 Fulton St., N.Y. 10038
(212) 619-0808
Allan J. Litty, Pres.

Mr. Litty is an aerial photography specialist with considerable publicity experience and is capable of taking photos of a news event, printing and captioning them, and delivering them to media within a few hours.

In the Chicago area, aerial photography specialists include Bill Arsenault, 1244 W. Chicago Ave., Chicago 60622, phone (312) 421-2525, and Steve Brown, 107 W. Hubbard St., Chicago 60610, phone (312) 467-4666.

19. Fotos International

4230 Ben Ave., Studio City, CA 91604
(818) 762-2181
Telex: 65-1489
Max B. Miller

A specialist in the entertainment industry, Fotos International is a photo news agency which covers "Hollywood" for many publications and other clients. The company has a sizable business throughout the world and has affiliates in 46 countries. Its New York representative is Pictorial Parade, Inc., 130 W. 42 St., N.Y. 10036, phone (212) 840-2026; Baer Frimer, president.

20. Gamma Photo Labs

314 W. Superior St., Chicago 60610
(312) 337-0022
Benjamin Lavitt, Pres.
Shirley Wright, Sales Mgr.

Founded in 1959, Gamma is a full service custom photographic lab with basic film processing and printing, computerized slide graphics, overhead transparencies, and giant display murals in black & white and color. Housed in its own six-story building, Gamma operates one of the country's largest professional photo labs with such distinct features as its own radio-dispatched vehicles, an after-hours dropbox, night and Saturday services, preprinted order forms, free film mailing bags, and free parking in a lot on Superior Street just west of Orleans. Special services include photo restoration, Ektachrome processing on Saturday, a creative laminating and mounting department and a Cibachrome Copy Center.

A suburban facility is at 500 N. Mannheim Rd., Hillside, Il 60162, phone (312) 544-1331.

21. Alan Gordon Enterprises Inc.

1430 N. Cahuenga Blvd., Hollywood, CA 90078
(213) 466-3561
TWX: (910) 321-4526
Peter Barton

Among the many sources of professional motion picture equipment in the Los Angeles area, one of the largest renters and sellers (in the world) is Alan Gordon. Founded in 1946, the company's six-plant complex stocks just about every type of photo, microfilm and motion picture component and issues a comprehensive catalog, with daily rental rates for every item. The motion picture division is in Hollywood and the aerial and microfilm divisions are in North Hollywood.

22. Bob Graves Photo Printers, Inc.

40 Hathaway Dr., Stratford, CT 06497
(203) 375-7034

Complete photographic service includes an extensive mail business in machine prints. 100 8 × 10 glossy prints are $34.50 plus $6.50 for the copy negative, plus postage.

23. K & L Custom PhotoGraphics

222 E 44 St., N.Y. 10017
(212) 661-5600
Peter Lichtiger, VP Sales

K & L, one of New York's largest custom laboratory for professional photographic services, provides a complete range of products around-the-clock in one midtown New York facility.

Established in 1948 the company was acquired in 1966 by Berkey Photo, Inc. K & L is a leader in product and technical innovations. Acquisitions have included Manhattan Color Laboratories, 1966 (filmstrip and quality slides); Bernard Hoffman Laboratories, 1967 (custom black & white processing and printing); and Peterson Color Laboratory, 1974 (expanded dye transfer prints).

K & L products include black-and-white and dye transfer prints, slides, color and display prints (as big as 6× 22 feet in one piece) and custom mounting and installation.

24. Ken Lieberman Laboratories, Inc.
118 W. 22 St., N.Y. 10011
(212) 633-0500
Ken Lieberman, Pres.

Formed in 1984 by Ken Lieberman (who has had over 30 years of experience), this custom lab provides services to photographers and designers throughout the world. The staff of over 40 people produces color prints, transparencies and slides, ranging from one item to an entire exhibit.

25. Mass Photo Company
1315 Waugh Dr., Houston, TX 77019
(713) 523-4503
Tom Darling, Pres.

In business since 1952, Mass is one of the nation's largest producers of quantity contact prints. Black-and-white orders require two days, plus mailing time; color requires an extra day. 8×10 black-and-white prints are about 34 cents each.

26. Media Photo Group Inc. (MPG)
311 W. 43 St., N.Y. 10036
(212) 582-6880

In 1978, Mel Nudelman and Michel Legrou opened a fully equipped studio and lab geared to public relations clients. Today, the company maintains a studio in mid-Manhattan, and also in lower Manhattan, at 105 E. 16 St., enabling it to provide studio and on-site assignments for many public relations clients. In addition to its still photographers, Media Photo Group also handles videotaping, quantity prints and other laboratory services, and works with a network of photographers around the world.

27. Merrill Photos Corp.
1501 Broadway, N.Y. 10036
(212) 221-8211
Mel Golomb

A complete photographic reproduction organization, Merrill produces a variety of still photo items including glossy prints, color prints, transparencies, slides and filmstrips.

28. Modernage Custom Darkroom, Inc.
1150 Ave. of the Americas, N.Y. 10036
(212) 997-1800
Harry Amdur

Founded in 1944, this is one of the city's superior darkrooms, specializing in custom film processing. In fact, Modernage has advertising, media, and public relations clients all over the world. A lower Manhattan branch in located at 150 Fulton St., N.Y. 10038, phone (212) 227-4767, and an East side branch is at 239 E. 53 St., N.Y. 10022, phone (212) 752-3993.

The Modernage price list includes a section with extremely useful tips on the handling of contact proof sheets, as follows.

Mark your contact proofs with red crayon right on the print. (It can be taken off again.) Never mark or tape negatives. Use the following code marks to order prints and indicate cropping:

For burning in:	Cross-hatch or slanting lines indicate "make darker."
For dodging:	Small circles indicate "make lighter."
For routine cropping:	Wiggly lines where they can vary to suit paper size, or mark: "crop for subject matter," "use your judgment" "full negative" "full paper size" or similar.
For specific cropping:	Straight lines where outer limit is desired.

Modernage also provides guidelines on preparing negatives, slides, and the like. Here's an excerpt from one of their brochures:

A 35mm negative or slide is longer in proportion to its width than 8×10, and when 8×10 or larger print sizes are ordered cropping cannot be avoided. The full 35mm negative cannot be enlarged to a full size 8×10, 11×14, 16×20, or 20×24 without cropping.

If you order *full negative*, here are the image sizes:

8×10 will have an image	$6\frac{3}{4}'' \times 10$
11×14	$9\frac{1}{4}'' \times 14$
16×20	$13\frac{1}{4}'' \times 20$

Mail negatives in flat lengths—120 in strips of 3 or 4; 35mm in strips of 5 or 6 exposures. Where possible, include uncut contact proof of sheets with all enlarging orders. These will be returned with your order.

Be sure that the photo used for quantity reproduction is slightly on the soft side in appearance. The making of a copy negative increases the contrast. Therefore, a snappy (contrasty) looking original photo will produce a final print that may be too contrasty and harsh in appearance.

Modernage offers its exclusive "dry mat" finish. It means the prints have a smooth, lustre finish rather than the slick glossy. Here's the cost:

Print for copy	$ 7.50
Copy Negs $8 \times 10/5 \times 7$/Postcard	9.00
10×12	12.00
Litho Negative 8×10	10.00
Color Neg from slide	9.00
Stripping per element	5.00
Hot Press Lettering (name)	8.00
Retouching (minimum)	25.00

29. National Color Laboratories, Inc.

306 W. First Ave., Roselle, NJ 07203

(201) 241-1010

Vince Gallo, Tech. Sales/ Marketing Dir.

One of the country's largest color laboratories, National conducts an extensive business by mail. Customers receive mailing envelopes and other items to facilitate the ordering of proofs, prints and transparencies. Many professional photographers use this service, as prices are competitive and quality is excellent.

30. National Photo Service, Inc.

114 W. Illinois St., Chicago 60610

(312) 644-5211

Milton Rubin, Steve Rubin, Berry Rubin

National Photo Service mass produces thousands of color and black-and-white 8×10 glossy photos for clients throughout the country. The charges, which are similar to those of other operations of this kind, are $7.50 for the copy negative and 38 cents for each photograph in quantities of 100. The price is a bit higher in smaller quantities, but still lower than many other machine print labs.

Color is available with a minimum order of $15, and the cost of an 8×10 copy negative is $15. 100 8×10 color prints are available for 88 cents each, with a choice of matte or glossy.

Special services include captions or titles on the photos for $6, and production of composite negatives (an economical means of combining two or more photos on one print). National also does studio and location photography.

31. Ornaal Color Photos Corp.

24 W. 25 St., N.Y. 10010

(212) 675-3850

Neil M. Locker

$10. is the cost of a color negative from your photo, art or transparency. The cost for "C" prints is $1. for 8×10s. 70¢ for 5×7s, and 55¢ for 4×5s (in quantities of 100). Ornaal also operates a machine print company, called Ornaal Glossies, Inc., which does quantity black & white work in both contact and enlargement prints. Negatives cost $8. for 8×10's and $7.25 for 5×7 and smaller. 100 8×10 contact prints are only $30., all on RC paper.

32. Pach Brothers

16 E. 53 St., N.Y. 10022

(212) 758-3366

Oscar White, Pres.

Established in 1867, Pach Brothers is one of the oldest and best-known photographic studios in the country. Pach Brothers has photographed every U.S. President since Ulysses Grant, and its slogan is "Photographers To Those Who Make History."

Whether or not your client is of historical importance, you'll be pleased at the relatively low price schedule for a studio portrait.

Photography, including one 8×10 glossy print, about $80, depending on number of poses and proofs, plus $39.75 for six additional prints.

33. Don Phelan Inc.

311 W. 43 St., N.Y. 10036

(212) 586-2541

Branch Office:
114 Abbott St., N. Massapequa, NY 11758
(516) 249-3615

A long-time photographer for UPI and other companies, Don Phelan started his own company in 1980. Services include still film and video photography and distribution. The TV services are described in the TV chapter.

Services in New York are $85 an hour, $600 a day. Outside of New York, arrangements are made with photographers with whom Phelan has worked for many years.

In 1984, Don Phelan provided a summary of his career which is fascinating in its indications of the changing picture of the photography field.

> My background covers 43 years beginning with the Daily Reporter in White Plains, New York, in 1938, which was then taken over by the former Westchester Macy Chain of 16 papers. It was nothing in those days to cover 8 to 10 assignments a day at $18 per week with 3½¢ per mile for car use. I went into the US Navy in 1942–46 as a petty officer assigned to cover FDR in the White House and on his various trips . . . then out to the Pacific as a combat photographer. In 1946 after the war, I went to work as a photographer for the old Acme Newspictures division of NEA. We were taken over in 1952 by United Press and we in turn took over International News Pictures in 1956, when I went on the desk as an editor. In 1958, I gave up the desk for a sales post, eventually becoming New York Regional Manager. I left UPI in 1972 to take a VP job at American A/V and formed my own company in 1980.

34. Photo Replicas Corp.
239 W. 39 St., N.Y. 10018
(212) 354-5280
Donald Scal

Photo Replicas, as indicated by its initials, specializes in PR services, including photography and photo reproduction and other conventional services, plus a complete publicity mailing department, which is unusual. The company's Photorama divisions are at 239 W. 39 St., N.Y. 10018.

Photo Replicas acquired two other companies, which operate independently elsewhere in Manhattan:

Alfred Miller, 47 Ann St., N.Y. 10038, phone (212) 349-4443, Abby Marquez
Photorama, 108 W. 40 St., N.Y. 10018, phone (212) 382-1993, Bill Boyd

35. QPI
7050 Village Dr., Buena Park, CA 90620
(213) 655-4322, (714) 522-8255
Michael O'Neal, V.P.

A specialist in custom color laboratory work, QPI (Quarterly Professionalism Innovation) has facilities for rapid production of slides, C prints, photocomposites and other photography products.

36. Jean Raeburn Studio
205 E. 42 St., N.Y. 10017
(212) 697-8696
Lester Cole, Pres.

Since 1948, the Jean Raeburn Studio has specialized in executive photos for publicity uses. A sitting, including three glossy prints is only $140.

37. Reiter-Dulberg Laboratories Inc.
250 W. 54 St., N.Y. 10019
(212) 582-6871
Abe Dulberg

Custom photographic services, from a location on the West Side of Manhattan, has made this a mecca for many of the city's top photographers for over 30 years.

38. Kay Reese & Associates, Inc.
175 Fifth Ave., N.Y. 10010
(212) 598-4848
Telex: 238 790
Kay Reese, Pres.

Formed in 1971 by a group of Life magazine photographers, Kay Reese & Associates now represents about 20 prominent photographers for corporate photojournalism assignments all over the world.

39. Sickles Photo-Reporting Service
Box 98, 410 Ridgewood Rd., Maplewood, NJ 07040
(201) 763-6355
Gus Sickles

Since 1938, Sickles has operated a network of about 500 photographer-reporters who can obtain anything from a single on-location photo to a complete article, interview or case history. Prices range from $200 to $1,500.

40. Skyviews Survey, Inc.
1 E. Main St., Ramsey, NJ 07446
(800) 247-5949
William J. Fried, Pres.

Skyviews specializes in illustrated aerial photography in black-and-white and color and also maintains a computer-accessed stock file of aerial photographs which can be loaned or purchased, with or without reproduction rights. The 180,000 stock photos are coded by subject matter and location.

41. Speed Graphics Inc.
342 Madison Ave., N.Y. 10173
(212) 682-5861

Rush services include same-day C prints, stats and other photographic items. The company also has a lab at 150 E. 58 St., N.Y. 10155.

42. Stewart Color Laboratories Inc.
563 Eleventh Ave., N.Y. 10036
(212) 868-1440
Jerry Schochet, Pres.

Formed in 1964, Stewart is a major company in the field of custom photographic laboratory services.

43. Taylor-Merchant Corporation
212 W. 35 St., N.Y. 10001
(212) 757-7700
Harvey B. Schneider, Pres.

A few of the items produced by Taylor-Merchant (formed in 1952) are exclusive with the company, while others can be obtained from many motion picture and slide film producers and photographic laboratories throughout the country.

The most popular T-M package is its "Sell-o-Vue," a cardboard viewer which can be folded, with a strip of 35mm transparencies. If the client provides the original art or photos, Taylor-Merchant then charges $145 to produce a master photographic negative. The cost of 300 Sell-o-Vues, which is the minimum quantity, would be $675.

There are many extras available, such as special envelopes and vinyl imprinted wallets (at various prices, depending on quantity) to hold the viewers and slides. Stereo presentations are more expensive, with individual units varying from $1.95 to more than $2.95, depending on type and quantity.

T-M sales representatives are eager to develop new customers and new uses for their services and often will work with publicists to adapt their visual techniques to public relations needs. Taylor-Merchant provides a free kit which bulges with samples of its 35mm and stereo slide viewers and other fascinating visual aids. But the kit is really bursting with ideas, rather than materials, pertaining to the adaptation of visual aids as selling tools. For example, one client recently distributed an eight-frame color film clip, together with a portable cardboard viewer, to editors, in order to supplement its news release with a unique, dramatic visual presentation. The same kit was provided to the company's sales force, as part of its "news release of the future" campaign.

Whether you use this firm for conventional film and slide duplication services or for a publicizable adaptation of its pocket projectors and other visual tools, you are likely to be interested in the Taylor-Merchant Idea Kit.

44. Vanguard Photography
3371 Cahuenga Blvd. West, Hollywood, CA 99068
(213) 874-3980
Wayne Seidel. Pres.

A publicity specialist since 1954, Vanguard has a simple schedule for location still photography—$75 an hour, minimum of one hour, additional time in ¼-hour increments, plus film, travel time and mileage.

45. Wagner International Photos, Inc.
216 E. 45 St., N.Y. 10017
(212) 661-6100

For several decades, Gary Wagner operated one of the country's best-known publicity photography companies, renowned for its long-time, extensive, capable services and also for its free seminars on publicity. The company was acquired in 1980 by American Audio Visual, Inc., and is described earlier in this chapter.

A unique service is called Feature Photo Service, which distributes a sheet of about 20 photos to 1,500 newspaper editors who can order free captioned prints. Cost is $3 per photo insertion. Another service, started in 1986, is called Business News Pictures, which is geared for use by the wire services.

46. Wide World Photos, Inc. (Subsidiary of The Associated Press)
50 Rockefeller Plaza, N.Y. 10020
(212) 621-1930
James M. Donna, Dir.

Branch Office:
Box 5309, Hacienda Heights, CA 91745
(818) 968-4118

Wide World handles hundreds of commercial photography assignments a week, through its own and affiliated photographers in every major city in the U.S. In addition, its world headquarters in New York

City coordinates assignments in more than 100 countries. The parent company, The Associated Press, services about 8,500 newspapers, radio and TV stations throughout the world and 700 wirephoto subscribers.

It seems inconceivable, but Wide World's black-and-white and color transparency picture files contain more than 50 million photos taken during the last 50 years, and this is only one part of the Wide World operation.

The commercial operation is completely separate from the editorial side. The Associated Press photo editors are interested only in news value and not whether the picture was processed by a "sister company."

One of the many benefits of working with Wide World is the 24-hour, 7-day-a-week service. It sometimes costs a bit more than the minimum rate, of course, but there is no other photography operation which can match Wide World in the extensiveness of its facilities, including wire, radio and satellite transmissions.

Chapter 21

Press Associations

Many of the associations of newspaper publishers issue directories (often free), operate mailing services (generally at very low rates), place advertising, maintain clipping bureaus, and, in general, provide so many services that the following list could be repeated in almost every chapter of this book.

Several associations, such as the Inland Daily Press Association in Chicago, offer associate memberships, which includes access to advertising comparison reports, bulletins and workshops.

Two lists of press associations follow; the first is by state, and the second is by region.

STATE NEWSPAPER ASSOCIATIONS

	MANAGER	TELEPHONE
Alabama Press Association, Box 1800, Tuscaloosa, AL 35403	William B. Keller	(205) 345-5611
Alaska Newspaper Association, 2425 W. 67 Ave., Anchorage, AK 99502	Lew Williams	(907) 248-4808
Arizona Newspaper Association, 2303 N. Central Ave., Suite 102, Phoenix, AZ 85004	Ted L. Hecht	(602) 277-3600
Arkansas Press Association, 1701 Broadway, Little Rock, AR 72206	Dennis Schick	(501) 374-1500
California Newspaper Publishers Association, Inc., 1127 11 St., Sacramento, CA 95814	Everett Bey	(916) 443-5991
Colorado Press Association, The Press Bldg., 1336 Glenarm Pl., Denver, CO 80204	William F. Lindsey	(303) 571-5117
Connecticut Daily Newspapers Association, c/o Record Journal, Meridan, CT 06450	Forrest C. Palmer	(203) 235-1661
Florida Press Association, 306 S. Duval, Tallahassee, FL 32301	Dick Shelton	(904) 222-5790
Georgia Press Association, 1075 Spring St., N.W., Atlanta, GA 30309	Kathy Chaffin	(404) 872-2467
Hoosier State Press Association, 115 N. Pennsylvania St., Indianapolis, IN 46204	William Connelly	(317) 637-3966
Idaho Newspaper Association, Inc., Box 1067, Boise, ID 83701	Bob C. Hall	(208) 343-1671
Illinois Press Association, 929 S. Second, Springfield, IL 62704	David R. West	(217) 523-5092
Inland Daily Press Association, 777 Busse Highway, Park Ridge, IL 60068	R. E. Ivory	(312) 696-1140
Iowa Newspaper Assn., 319 East Fifth St., Des Moines, IA 50309	Bill Monroe	(515) 244-2145
Kansas Press Association, Box 1773, Topeka, KS 66601	Mike Harris	(913) 233-7421
Kentucky Press Association, Inc., 322 Capitol Ave., Frankfort, KY 40601	Lewis Owen	(502) 223-8821
Louisiana Press Association, 680 No. 5th St., Baton Rouge, LA 70802	Jill Wilson, Mgr.	(504) 344-9309
Maine Press Association, University of Maine at Orono, 107 Lord Hall, Orono, ME 04469	Robert G. Drake	(207) 581-1283
Maryland-Delaware-D.C. Press Association, University of Maryland, College Park, MD 20742	Winston Taylor	(301) 454-0245
Massachusetts Press Association, Journalism Dept., Suffolk University, Boston, MA 02108	Robert Finneran	(617) 723-4700
Michigan Press Association, 827 N. Washington Ave., Lansing, MI 48906	Warren M. Hoyt	(517) 372-2424
Minnesota Newspaper Association, 84 S. Sixth St., Minneapolis, MN 55402	Linda Falkman	(612) 332-8844
Mississippi Press Association, 2720 N. State St., Jackson, MS 39216	Rebecca Simmons	(601) 981-3060
Missouri Press Association, 802 Locust, Columbia, MO 65201	William A. Bray	(314) 449-4167
Montana Press Association, 1900 No. Main, Ste. C, Helena, MI 59601	Mrs. Joan G. Jenewein	(406) 443-2850
Nebraska Press Association, 1120 K St., Lincoln, NE 68508	Ken Kauffold	(402) 476-2851
Nevada State Press Association, Box 137, Carson City, NV 89702	Andrea (Ande) Engleman	(702) 882-8772
New England Press Association, Northeastern University, 360 Hunting Ave., Boston, MA 02115	Loren G. Ghiglione	(617) 437-2896
New Jersey Press Association, 206 West State St., Trenton, NJ 08608	Walter Worrall	(609) 695-3366
New Mexico Press Association, 117 Richmond NE, P.O. Box NNN, Albuquerque, NM 87196	Mary Lee Quinalty	(505) 265-7859
New York Press Association, 10 Thurlow Terrace, Albany, NY 12203	Donald J. Carroll	(518) 465-2285
North Carolina Press Association, Box 2598, Raleigh, NC 27602	Joe Doster	(919) 821-1435
North Dakota Newspaper Association, Box 8137, Grand Forks, ND 58202	Eugene G. Carr	(701) 777-2574
Northwest Daily Press Association, 84 S. 6 St., Minneapolis, MN 55402	Bruce Peck	(612) 338-7128

STATE NEWSPAPER ASSOCIATIONS (con't.)

	MANAGER	TELEPHONE
Ohio Newspaper Association, 145 E. Rich St., Columbus, OH 43215	R. Victor Dix	(614) 224-1648
Oklahoma Press Association, 3601 N. Lincoln, Oklahoma City, OK 73105-5499	Larry Wade	(405) 524-4421
Oregon Newspaper Publishers Association, Inc., 7150 S. W. Hampton St., Ste. 232, Portland, OR 97223	Pat Patterson	(503) 684-1942
Pennsylvania Newspaper Publishers Association, 2717 No. Front St., Harrisburg, PA 17110	Milton D. McLean	(717) 234-4067
Publisher's Bureau of New Jersey, Inc., 1979 Springfield Ave., Maplewood, NJ 07040	David J. Winkworth	(201) 762-8080
South Carolina Press Association, Box 11429, Columbia, SC 29211	Reid H. Montgomery	(803) 254-1607
South Dakota Press Assoc., Box 2230, Brookings, SD 57007	Keith M. Jensen	(605) 692-4300
Southern Newspaper Publishers Association, Box 28875, Atlanta, GA 30328	Reed Sarratt	(404) 256-0444
Tennessee Press Association, Inc., Box 8123, Knoxville, TN 37996	Don R. McNeil	(615) 974-5481
Texas Press Association, 718 W. 5 St., Austin, TX 78701	Norris Monroe	(512) 477-6755
Utah Press Association, Inc., 467 E. Third St., Salt Lake City, UT 84111	Glen Curtis	(801) 328-8678
Vermont Press Association, Journalism Dept., St. Michael's College, Winooski, VT 05404	Alex Nagy	(802) 655-2000
Virginia Press Association, Inc., 300 W. Franklin St., Ste. 101E, Richmond, VA 23220	Ray Carlsen	(804) 648-8948
Washington Newspaper Publishers Association, Inc., 3838 Stone Way N., Seattle, WA 98103	Jerry Zubord	(206) 634-3838
West Texas Press Association, 2502 Ivanhoe, Abilene, TX 79605	Joyce Lowe	(915) 692-1087
West Virginia Press Association, Inc., Level B, Hoyer Bldg., Charleston, WV 25301	Delbert Benson	(304) 342-1011
Wisconsin Newspaper Association, Box 5580, Madison, WI 53705	Jane Slaats	(608) 238-7171
Wyoming Press Association, 710 Garfield, Ste. 248, Laramie, WY 82070	Mike Sellet	(302) 745-8144

REGIONAL AND NATIONAL NEWSPAPER ASSOCIATIONS

	MANAGER	TELEPHONE
American Newspaper Publishers Association, 11660 Sunrise Valley Drive, Reston, VA 22091	Jerry W. Friedheim	(703) 620-9500
Canadian Community Newspaper Association, 88 University Ave., Ste. 705, Toronto, ON M5J IT6, Canada	Kevin Hamm	(416) 598-4277
Canadian Daily Newspaper Publishers, 321 Bloor St. East, Ste. 214, Toronto, ON M4W IE7	John E. Fay	(416) 923-3567
Inland Daily Press Association, 777 Busse Highway, Park Ridge, IL 60068	R. E. Ivory	(312) 696-1140
National Newspaper Association, 1627 K Street, N.W., Ste. 400, Washington, DC 20006	James H. Roberts	(202) 466-7200
New England Press Association, Northeastern University, 360 Hunting Ave., Boston, MA 02115	Loren F. Ghiglione	(617) 437-2896
New Mexico Press Association, Box 11278, Albuquerque, NM 87192	Mary Lee Qunialty	(505) 299-7542
New York Press Association, The Carriage House, 10 Thurlow Terrace, Albany, NY 12203	Donald J. Carroll	(518) 465-2285
Northwest Daily Press Association, 84 S. 6 St., Minneapolis, MN 55402	Bruce Peck	(612) 339-7128
Publisher's Bureau of New Jersey, Inc., 1979 Springfield Ave., Maplewood, NJ 07040	David J. Winkworth	(201) 762-8080
Southern Newspaper Publishers Association, Box 28875, Atlanta, Ga 30328	Reed Sarratt	(404) 256-0444

Chapter 22

Press Weeks

A nightmare which haunts many publicists revolves around calling a news conference and then waiting, with the client, for the distinguished members of the news media to arrive—and no one turns up. At one time, a group of publicists considered forming a service called "Bodies Incorporated" which would provide people who look like reporters (yes, there is a certain look about reporters) to turn up at news conferences. However, this deception might serve to fill the conference room but would not result in any publicity.

There are several organizations which can *guarantee* to deliver bona fide members of the press to a news event. These services do not think of themselves in this manner, but that is exactly what they do—and it's legitimate.

Most publicists, particularly those who deal with business news, know that companies can be invited to make presentations to groups of financial analysts, such as the New York Security Analysts Society, and that these events "automatically" will be covered by the press. However, it is perhaps surprising to note that all financial publicists are not aware that the business editors have their own association (founded in 1963) and that it is possible to arrange for a company president or other executive to speak to these business news writers. Called The Society of American Business Writers, the group meets annually in a different city each spring.

The Society does not have an office and, to track down information, you'll have to contact one of its 100 members, who are the business editors of most of the big city newspapers.

In the women's interest field, there are several associations with annual meetings that are regularly attended by large numbers of editors. The largest of these press functions are in the food and fashion fields, including men's fashions.

Publicists often strain to find an offbeat site for a press party or other event. If you're thinking of holding a wedding in a vineyard, a corporate dinner in a planetarium or a party in a greenhouse, in New York and elsewhere, your job will be made easier by Tenth House Enterprises, Inc., Box 810, N.Y. 10028, which publishes Places, a biannual directory of public places for private events and private places for public functions. The book is $18.95. Call (212) 737-7536 if you're in a hurry to find out the details about renting an armory, pier, school or simply a hotel or conference center.

In New York, a unique private facility for presentations, press conferences and events, particularly those related to food, was opened in 1984 at 47 E. 34 Street. Called Yellowdot Meetings, it consists of a floor in a small building and a rooftop area. Facilities include an audiovisual installation and a kitchen. It is necessary to bring in your own caterer, so Yellowdot is useful for food demonstrations. The New

York Party Directory, with information about caterers, facilities, party planners and other sources, is $9.95 from 12 E. 54 St., N.Y. 10022, (212) 486-0410.

The Hotel and Motel Red Book (published annually since 1886) includes U.S. and foreign listings plus a Meeting Planners Guide and travel services sections. Published annually in June, the Red Book is available for $45 from Pactel Publishing Co., 1600 S. Main St., Walnut Creek, CA 94596.

The Directory of Hotel & Motel Systems (published annually since 1931) includes companies that own, operate or manage three or more lodging accommodations. Published annually in May, the Systems Directory is available for $31.50 from the American Hotel Association Directory Corp., 888 Seventh Ave., N.Y. 10106.

For many years, the name Eleanor Lambert was synonymous with Press Week, a project she originated for the New York Dress Institute in 1942. After Ms. Lambert withdrew from the Dress Institute in 1960, it merged with the Couture Business Council which continued to hold press weeks. Ms. Lambert then organized American Designer Showings, in which a group of about 50 influential American designers and fashion manufacturers held semi-annual showings for the press.

The event was discontinued in 1982. Ms. Lambert continues to guide many important fashion events, including the International Best Dressed Women polls.

1. American Home Economics Association

2010 Massachusetts Ave., N.W., Wash., DC 20036
(202) 862-8300

One of the 20 largest professional organizations in the U.S., the American Home Economics Association has a membership of more than 27,000 men and women.

The AHEA annual convention is held late in June in a different major city each year. Many home furnishings, food and other companies rent exhibit space and participate in press events at the convention. Attendance is more than 5,000 home economists and others with related interests.

Membership lists can be purchased, and other products and services are available from the Association.

The National Association of Extension Home Economists, 300 Lincoln Street Center, Lawrenceburg, KY 40342, also conducts an annual convention with exhibits and other opportunities.

2. American Women in Radio and Television, Inc.

1101 Connecticut Ave., NW, Ste. 70, Wash., DC 20036
(202) 429-5102
Susan Kudla, Exec. Dir.

AWRT has about 3,000 members in 60 chapters across the country. Public relations professionals can join AWRT and participate in regional and national conventions.

3. International Food Media Conference

Primavera PR
Yorktown Heights, NY 10598
(914) 245-5390
William Primavera, Pres.
MIchael Pierce, VP

For over 40 years, the Newspapers Advertising Sales Association conducted an annual Newspaper Food Editors Conference. The project evolved into the International Food Media Conference conducted by William J. Primavera, President of the Culinarians and head of a public relations firm.

The four-day conference attracts food editors and broadcasters from a variety of media throughout the country. Events and other participations are available for sponsorship.

299

4. Men's Fashion Association of America

240 Madison Ave., N.Y. 10016
(212) 683-5665
Norman Karr, Exec. Dir.

Formerly The American Institute of Men's and Boy's Wear, the MFA is the consumer promotion arm of the men's apparel and textile industry. Members may sponsor fashion shows and participate in the semiannual press weeks, attended by about 200 men and women, mostly from newspapers, who cover men's fashions.

Chapter 23

Printing

Almost all public relations practitioners work with printers. However, it is a regrettable fact that most public relations practitioners are ignorant about many aspects of printing. Some of us are only vaguely aware of the different types of printing (e.g., letterpress, offset) and the steps in the printing process. Each step (e.g., galley proofs, page proofs, blueprint) involves time and money, and the more you know about the technical details, the more you are likely to work with a printer speedily, economically and with less aggravation.

There are thousands of printers in the U.S., and this chapter is not a listing of specific companies. Typesetting, design and binding are specialized aspects of the graphic arts, and these services are handled by specialists, sometimes separately, sometimes subcontracted by the printer and sometimes all within the premises of the printer.

A recent development is the printing cottage industry—the setting up of electronic typesetting and design studios in homes and apartments. Some of these operations provide professional service at low prices and others are erratic and unpredictable, as sometimes is the case with one-person home businesses.

The following comments are not a printing primer, but they may be useful to public relations people. The material was prepared with the assistance of George Weiner, who for 40 years operated Weiner Press, a letterpress printing company in lower Manhattan. Yes, he is related to the author of this book, who here thanks his father.

In the mid-15th century, it took Johann Gutenberg five years of sacrifice to typeset, print and bind 200 copies of his majestic Bible.

As astonishing as his achievement appears to our current computer-age reader, in its day the feat was incredible. An army of monks could scarcely have duplicated similar production in their collective lifetimes. The rush to discard tradition and copy the new method quickly spread throughout Europe.

Late in the 19th century, after 400 years of what then was described as conventional printing, mechanical devices brought about through the industrial revolution could cast type at the rate of five characters per second. Thus, the second major innovation in printing occurred with comparable astonishing significance.

Phototypesetters brought the state of the art to 30 type characters of output per second by the mid-20th century. Today, printing has been revolutionized by computer.

The primary function of the computer is the processing of information and that of the printing industry is the duplication of information. A marriage was inevitable, and typesetting now can take place at the rate of up to 1,000 characters per second.

In the seventies, the high technology revolution took place in the printing industry. Many public relations agencies and departments installed a variety of copiers and printing equipment and made more extensive use of outside printing services. For example, over 15,000 ''quick printers'' now exist throughout the country, so that it is possible to get low-cost same-day service of printed news releases and other items.

The major new developments relate to photocomposition and other automated typesetting equipment, mailing/word processing services, microprocessor software and hardware, high speed copy duplicating services and laser color separation.

Large public relations operations, particularly those which are involved with newsletters, employee magazines and other periodicals, now have a variety of typesetting systems, either on their premises or by service agreement. One of the largest suppliers is the Compugraphic Corporation, which has a variety of systems, ranging from a basic one terminal configuration to a multiterminal system.

R. R. Donnelley & Sons, Chicago, the nation's largest printer, developed typesetting systems which are linked with other printers. Several networks have been set up which include printers and typographers, in which the linkage is by telecopy machines.

Several large companies also are in the typesetting business. InfoConversion is a division of CallData Systems, Inc., which in turn is a division of Grumman Data Information Services, Inc., a Grumman Company. The company developed a remote automated text editing systems, called Remotext, which uses video display terminals or word processing equipment and a telephone link to directly link its computer and photo composition equipment with clients, particularly those which produce directories and reference publications. InfoConversion is located at 280 Crossways Park Drive, Woodbury, NY 11797, phone (516) 682-5200.

''The Use of Typography in Office Communication'' is one of the free booklets available from Compugraphics Corp., 200 Ballardvale St., Wilmington, MA 01887.

The increased application of science to all stages of printing has resulted in increased specialization and a higher level of graphic arts techniques.

In particular, the specialty of financial relations involves the typesetting, printing and distribution of Securities and Exchange Commission (SEC) documents under extremely tight production schedules. Customer requirements involve the preparation of prospectuses, indentures, proxy and registration statements, listing applications, annual reports and other related printed materials produced under deadline pressure. An up-to-date, top printer can save time and countless dollars by utilizing technology that was not available a few years ago.

Financial printing is a specialized industry serving publicly-held corporations and others such as municipalities and public agencies raising money through the sale of stocks, bonds or other offerings. These printers, knowledgeable in SEC regulations and procedures, as well as those of other regulatory bodies in banking, insurance and municipal bonds, should be familiar to the financial and investor relations practitioner.

Their sales and customer service staffs can be a tremendous resource in a crisis, as these specialists are accustomed to overnight deadlines and must meet strict criteria for error-free production, often in conditions of top secrecy, utilizing advanced printing technology.

Let's examine this operation: A secretary starts the process by typing, either on a typewriter, or more typically today, into a word processor. If these keystrokes (the input) are captured by a word processor, the printer does not have to duplicate the input, at considerable cost savings to the client. These keystrokes, retained on a diskette or tape, are sent to the printer in one of two ways. The disk or tape may be sent directly by courier or express mail and converted at the plant via media reading. Only the top printers have the software to do a wide variety of media reading. Alternatively, the in-house word processor can be connected to a modem, a black box interface with a telephone, and the data sent over phone lines (telecommunication) to the printer's own modem and computer.

A modern financial printer employs electronic photocomposition and can set type directly from this input, whether received through media reading or telecommunications, at speeds of up to 1,000 characters per second. This "type" is stored in a computer and output onto photo-sensitive paper, ready for proofs of platemaking for printing.

Within the next few years, typecasting will be laser-burned right onto a printing plate, eliminating the "film to plate" process.

Direct savings now are achieved with computer-based photocomposition because the original words do not have to be keyed again, authors' alterations are dramatically reduced and so are proof cycles.

Commercial printers which specialize in annual reports generally have high-speed web presses and other equipment for producing press runs in the hundreds of thousands. Laser scanners for color separation, computerized page makeup equipment and other modern technology require sizeable investments. Printers throughout the country, and not just in New York, have these capabilities. One of the largest is Case-Hoyt of Rochester, NY. In the Boston area, three major printers are Acme Printing Co. of Medford, W. E. Andrews Co. (owned by Graphic Industries of Atlanta) of Bedford, and Daniels Printing Co. of Everett.

The type commonly used in books (including this one) and all classes of ordinary reading matter is known as roman. Although all roman types are essentially the same in form, there are two fairly well-defined divisions or styles.

The older form is called "old style" and is characterized by strength and boldness of feature, with strokes of comparatively uniform thickness and with an absence of weak hairlines. The serifs (the short cross-lines at the ends of the main strokes) are rounded, and the contour is clear and legible. Caslon is an example of an old-style face. The other style is called "modern" and is characterized by heavier shadings, thinner hairlines and thin, straight serifs. Bodoni is an example. The typeface in this book is Times Roman.

For a comprehensive and compact discussion of type, typesetting and the graphic arts, the publicist is referred to International Paper Company's outstanding Pocket Pal, A Graphic Arts Production Handbook. Now in its 13th edition, the bestseller is available by sending $4.25 to Pocket Pal, Box 100, N.Y. 10008-0100.

The following advice was prepared by Sorg Printing Company, one of the nation's leading financial printers. Sorg has its headquarters at 111 Eighth Avenue, N.Y. 10011, phone (212) 741-6600. The advice, from David L. Rosenstein, vice president, corporate communications, of Sorg, is oriented to the financial relations and investor relations practitioners but also is of value to any printing client.

1. Make sure that you select a printer who has the "know-how," mechanical capacity and skilled personnel to do the job for which you have selected him. Everyone who claims to be a financial printer is not necessarily one. Make sure your printer does all his work "in house" and does not have to rely on outside suppliers, who may not be available when you need them! It's a problem when you need something at 3 A.M., and it isn't there. Make sure that the printer you have selected is familiar with S.E.C. requirements, practices and procedures. Discuss your time schedules, and any expected problems, with the printer. This prior planning may afford savings in labor and paper costs.

   Be sure to ask for references. A good financial printer has a roster of Fortune 500 clients. Many claim the title "financial printer" who are not true specialists. Mistakes can be costly in the extreme.

2. If you supply the printer with hard (typed) copy, prepare it in as neat and final form as possible. Always double-space pages and type only on one side of the sheet of paper. This facilitates typesetting and makeup, no matter what the composition system.

3. If you have a word processing system, by all means, use it. But, be sure your printer can

directly translate its "floppy disc" output electronically into printed pages, in order to save you much on original composition costs. Sorg, for example, converts any word processor's output sent over phone lines and has written systems to convert several dozen types of diskettes on-site at its plants.

4. It is best to have one control person in charge of communication with the printer. This helps to avoid confusion, duplication of instructions and concerned people working from differently dated proofs.

5. Make sure that a sufficient number of proofs have been ordered. Reordering is more expensive than requesting a few extra copies at the start.

6. When substantial changes are to be made, try to avoid marginal notations. Neatly typed and numbered riders, attached to the changed pages, are the best way to make large changes, saving both time and money in composition and makeup.

7. Never make editing marks within the body of the copy unless you clearly indicate in the margin that there is a change in that line. Your clear red-inked comma will not stand out on a Xerox copy when it turns black.

8. Do you know how to read a blue line (or, blue print)? Ask your printer to show you how to find the color "breaks," the subtle differences in shading that indicate where a second color is intended to appear. Be sure to check those color breaks; it's a lot less costly than discovering a wrong color on an actual press sheet.

9. Keep one master copy, the "bible," and only retain the latest proof in that master. Retain a Xerox of marked up pages that are in for AA's (author's alterations) in your master copy. Check new proofs against that marked copy and then replace them with the new proofs.

10. Allow extra time for the printer to set tabular material. Tabular material takes more time to put into type than narrative material.

11. If possible, inform the printer as to quantities of documents and delivery instructions prior to final "okays." For a lengthy document, consider lighter paper stock to save on mailing costs.

12. If you plan additional financial printing in the near future, and may be able to use the type from the current job, request the printer to hold the magnetic tapes. This will enable you to save on composition costs in the new job, as well as reducing your proofreading time.

13. Caution typists to use the numeral key for number one, not the lower case "L" as each has a different code.

14. Avoid hyphenation. When possible, keep copy ragged right.

15. Footnotes should be sequential from beginning to end of each division or section and should be gathered together at the end of the section. The printer will distribute them properly at the bottom of each page if that is required.

16. Finally, don't be fooled by a "low-balling printer" who quotes an unusually low price in the knowledge that you or your attorneys will double or triple the final bill with AA's. Ask to be given cost-to-date information as the job progresses.

Those seeking the names of reliable printers, typographers, binders and suppliers of other graphic arts services may contact the Association of the Graphic Arts at 5 Penn Plaza, N.Y. 10001, William Dirzulaitis, president, (212) 279-2100 or, in other areas of the country: The Printing Industries of America, (703) 841-8100.

Several large printers, particularly the specialists in periodical publishing and financial materials, have regional plants and offices. For example, Packard Press, which was founded in 1876, is headquartered at 10th & Spring Garden Sts., Philadelphia 19123, and has facilities in Boston, Los Angeles, Miami, New York, Pittsburgh, San Francisco, Washington, DC, and Wilmington, Delaware.

In New York, Chicago, Los Angeles, San Francisco and a few other cities, typographers and printers operate 16 hours a day, in order to provide speedy service to advertising and other customers. In New York, for example, I, CLAUDIA Inc., a design and typography firm is open throughout the day and much of the night at 15 W. 26 St., N.Y. 10010, for typesetting via Compugraphic Quadex system, disk conversion and telecommunications. A clear, professional operation, and a pleasure to see in action anytime. Phone (212) 889-9460 and talk to the proprietor, Claudia Moran.

Prices for a one-column (2½ inches wide) galley of 17 inches is about $75. Thus, the cost to set type for a two-page (one sheet) 8¼ × 11 newsletter with a two-column format would be about $90, plus about $95 for makeup for camera-ready mechanicals. Plus, author's alterations!

Somehow, it always seems to cost more, but it can be done!

Many low-cost, creative typesetting design, production and printing operations are located in semi-residential neighborhoods, often near campuses. These cottage industries often can produce anything from Xerox copies to newsletters and entire publications. For example, Quad Right, 711 Amsterdam Ave., N.Y. 10025, phone (212) 222-1220, is able to read computer disks from over 200 different computers and output high-resolution copy in a selection of 800 typefaces.

The partnership of the graphic designer and printer is essential. Some printers have in-house design departments or can arrange for freelance designers or design studios.

Mike Spett of Spett Printing Company, 155 E. 38 St., N.Y. 10016, notes that the earlier the designer and printer are involved in a project, the less likelihood of "technical" production problems later on. Experienced graphic artists often can determine the success of the campaign. Good design will create and convey the image, message and intent desired, whether by printing, in all its various forms and aspects, or by video and other media, or in combination.

The means by which a designer can convey an idea through visual and tactile means in printing are myriad. Techniques include Duotone and process color reproduction, silhouetting, mezzotints and screens; proper selection of paper and colors; finishing effects, such as lamination, varnishing, embossing, metallic foil staining, raised printing, die cutting, gluing, special folds and other variations.

Many word processing programs can be coded and adapted for transmission to typesetters, either directly from the user's disc or over the telephone, with a modem.

One of the oldest companies in automated publishing is Inforonics, Inc., 550 Newtown Rd., Littleton, MA 01460, phone (617) 486-8976. It provides a complete range of text processing services to publishers all over the country. Services include information gathering, such as working with publishers of directories and reference books to arrange, index and typeset entries and updates. Write to Robin Humes for various free booklets about directories, journals, and abstracts, indexes, typesetting by authors and editors and on-line access to text.

A variety of low-cost, handy, easy-to-use time-savers for anyone involved in producing newsletters, sales bulletins or any aspect of graphics can be obtained from The Type Aids Company, 238 Merrydale Rd., San Rafael, CA 94903. Most of the items were developed by James Mennick in the 50's, cost only a few dollars each, and once you see them, you'll wonder how you ever got along without them. Among the miracle aids are:

Character Counters (for both elite and pica typewritten copy), which easily and quickly determine the number of typewritten characters and word space on a page for copy-fitting purposes with no, or little, figuring to do, $5.50 each.

Inch-Pica Conversion Rulers (12" or 18"), which accurately combine both inch and pica scales for instant conversion from one to another; the reverse side provides type measurement gauges of agate, 7, 8, 9, 10, 11, 13 and 15 points, 12" size $4.50, 18" size $6.35.

Photoguides (either inch or pica calibration), which provide fast four-sided cropping of photographs, squares copy at a glance, checks engraver's proof for size and square, measures any two dimensions of a proof at the same time, 8½ × 11" size $3.95, 15 × 19⅜" size $7.75.

Photoscalers, which quickly enlarge or reduce any number of different size photographs or artwork to a standard proportion for reproduction, in either 5 × 7″ or 8 × 10″ proportions $3.95.

Type-Line Gauges, which are used for copy fitting in determining the exact line spacing required to fill a given depth, for determining the line spacing of printed type when the type size is known, for making layouts and quickly ruling off any number of type lines in any point size you will need from agate through 16 point, set of 5 cards $5.95.

A significant development for editors of newsletters, employee magazines and other publications is the use of personal computers for typesetting, graphics and layout. Called desktop publishing, it indeed is becoming popular with associations and nonprofit organizations.

A list of financial printers appears in the financial chapter.

Chapter 24

Prizes, Promotions and Potpourri

Art exhibitions, concerts, professional and amateur sports competitions, festivals, fairs, shows and tours of all kinds often are created, conducted and promoted by public relations people. Sometimes the event, promotion or project is set up solely or primarily for publicity and other public relations values, with the audience at the site of minimal importance. Often the event, such as the Olympics, involves many millions of dollars spent by many co-sponsors for advertising and other promotion.

In 1982, a newsletter was started solely devoted to special events. Called Special Events Report, the newsletter (described in this chapter) describes the costs and other details of sponsorship by companies, cities, chambers of commerce and other organizations, including behind-the scenes information not reported elsewhere.

Arts Management (edited by Alvin Reiss at 408 W. 57 St., N.Y. 10019), Public Relations News (particularly its two-page case studies, which are in every issue of this venerable weekly) and other publications also provide how-to-do-it information about events and promotions. The bigger the project, the more likely it is to require a variety of specialists.

A few public relations practitioners, particularly those involved with consumer products, occasionally set up contests and are involved with premiums and other aspects of marketing and merchandising. Others occasionally work with organizations which create contests from the viewpoint of providing them with prizes.

Nationally advertised contests often are created and administered by companies which specialize in this type of activity. The advertising agency or contest sponsor usually pays a fee to the contest organization, which includes a budget for the purchase of prizes. The exact price paid for such expensive prizes as automobiles and vacation trips is a closely guarded secret, as it involves "delicate negotiations" in which the contest organization offers product identification in the magazine advertisements, display materials and other contest promotion materials.

Publicists who are interested in this exposure for their clients' products often will offer the products free to the contest organization or at prices considerably less than wholesale cost.

This chapter includes data about a few of the companies which set up contests involving many millions of dollars worth of advertising each year. Several of these companies also purchase items for use as premiums, create contests and promotions, and conduct surveys, sampling and other marketing activities. Most of the clients are major advertisers and advertising agencies, though a few specialize in radio and TV giveaway programs and broadcast promotions and thus deal with publicists.

More detailed information can be obtained from the annual directory issues of Premium Incentive Business, Advertising Age, Adweek and other trade publications.

Advertising Age, Sales & Marketing Management and other publications list forthcoming conventions, special weeks and other information which can be helpful with regard to news "pegs," tie-ins and other publicity and promotion.

Successful Meetings publishes an annual guide for meeting planners, with advice about site selection, hotels, hospitality suites and speakers. The monthly magazine, including supplements, is free to meeting and convention planners, from Bill Communications, 633 Third Ave., N.Y. 10017. Others may obtain a single copy for $5 and an annual subscription for $41. The International Facilities Directory is published in March. Other relevant Bill publications are Directory of Conventions ($90) and Exhibits Schedule ($95). Additional information is included in the chapter on clubs.

The alert, imaginative public relations practitioner should get to know some of the prize, promotion, premium and related companies because they often can be helpful in the development of major projects. Of course, your most important resource for promotions and other ideas must be yourself. Since few ideas are completely original, the alert practitioner should be familiar with what others are doing, in order to adapt their products, services and ideas to your specific needs.

One technique is "barter time," which is an arrangement whereby a company can purchase commercial time on radio and television stations by providing its products instead of, or partly in lieu of, cash. The commercials are broadcast in the same way as other advertisements and the rates are less than the published schedules.

Though not all stations accept barter arrangements, the practice has become an accepted part of the broadcast business. The stations use the products on their own give-away programs and other local promotions, resulting in added publicity exposure for the barter advertiser.

Somewhat related to "barter time" is an offbeat technique of purchasing broadcast time on a payment-for-results basis. Called Per Inquiry, the P.I. system is used by various companies, particularly those in the book, record and mail order fields, to advertise and pay the stations a fee for each inquiry or sale resulting from the spot announcements.

If you're looking for T-shirts, banners, trophies and other items used by public relations and promotion people, the single best reference book is the classified telephone book. Reminder: Ask if the company is a manufacturer or a broker. There's nothing wrong with a broker or other intermediary, but you're entitled to know the facts.

Awards, scrolls, plaques can be produced in many cities. You'll generally save time and money by dealing with the actual supplier and not a broker. If in doubt, ask to see the facility. In New York, an excellent calligrapher is the Gilbert Weiss Studio, 370 Lexington Ave., N.Y. 10017, phone (212) 532-7269.

A major part of this chapter is devoted to television programs that use products as prizes, as this is an area of great interest to many publicists.

Airlines, hotels, manufacturers of appliances, wristwatches, apparel and automobiles and other companies are major clients of "prize brokers." These companies generally deal directly with the networks and major syndicators, and TV viewers are accustomed to seeing audio and video credits on all of the game shows. Indeed, there are so many plugs on some of the game shows that the impact and value of this exposure can be questioned.

There's often a set fee schedule for the plugs, though it's negotiable, particularly on a long-term contract basis. A daytime plug might be listed for $600 and a nighttime plug might call for $3,000. Part of this can be paid for in merchandise (at wholesale cost) and the rest is in cash, so the lower the cost of the item, the more the cash payment.

One thousand dollars might be considered a bargain by advertising rate standards, but multiply this by one or more times a week and the total is prohibitive for most publicists. Which is just as well because these plugs are often annoying. There's nothing illegal or improper about any of this—the producer must acknowledge the "promotional consideration" on the program and disclose the source in statements provided to the Federal Communications Commission.

The names of the programs change a bit from season to season, but it doesn't make too much difference because most of them look alike, and the prize concept remains the same. Also, several variety programs use prizes, and these often can have more impact for the prize donors, particularly with celebrity hosts.

All this considered, participation in prize programs can be useful but, as with all areas of merchandising, it's not as simple as the promoters claim.

Game show spots generally consist of seven to 10 seconds of visual and 20 to 25 words of announcer-read copy. The sponsor supplies the visual, typically a 11 × 14-inch color print or art in a horizontal format with the company name or other copy overprinted, using press-down letters or color cells. Reminder: Keep letters at least 1½ inches from the borders because of cropping effect on many TV sets.

Advertisers who regularly use game shows obviously find them cost-efficient. A study by Dupont revealed that a surprisingly high percentage of viewers are able to recall the prizes 24 hours after the telecast.

And don't forget radio, particularly stations which run disc jockey promotions, often involving pickups of buttons, entries or other items at retail stores.

Prize specialists add on a service fee, generally $50 for a daytime and $100 for nighttime programs.

Note that these costs are *per program*. Contracts generally are required, with a minimum of one participation per week for 13 weeks.

Many clients prefer to use the services of a prize specialist, either on the basis of a service fee per show or a retainer fee. One advantage is that the promotion agency helps to select the specific programs.

The services provided by a specialist include:

Negotiating with producers to gain the best possible presentations; arranging for the visual display (either live or flip-card); writing of copy if required; supervising program tapings; providing off-the-air monitor reports as proof of performance; notifying you of advance air dates; sending shipping notices for awards to contestants; assisting in tie-ins with other promotional material; maintaining prop control, and coordinating new product changes.

Following are a few companies which can be helpful in the development of new ideas, as well as in special events and promotions, particularly those involving prize contests.

1. American Slide Chart Corporation
Box 111, 445 Gundersen Dr., Wheaton, IL 60187
(312) 665-3333, (800) 323-4433
David Johnson, Sales Mgr.

The largest designer and manufacturer of slide-charts, this company can convert formulas, graphs and other data into a slide chart (circular or other shapes) for use by salespeople, dealers, customers and others. Though essentially this is a sales promotion or advertisement specialty item, it is possible to use this type of mailing piece to obtain publicity and other public relations goals.

2. Associated Film Promotions, Inc. (AFP)
11331 Ventura Blvd., Studio City, CA 91604
(818) 762-2141
Robert H. Kovoloff, Pres.

Formed in 1977, AFP is the world's largest company in the field of product placement in theatrical motion pictures and TV shows. Most clients are on an annual retainer fee ($25,000 and up), which provides for a guaranteed number of placements in movies and television.

3. Bigger Than Life Inc.
Box 191189, 1327 Fayette St., El Cajon, CA 92020
(619) 449-9988, (800) 221-3304
Telex: 188912
R. T. Dickson, Pres.

Inflatables—the really big ones for parades, trade shows and special events—are produced for sale or rental by this big company, which was formed in 1985.

4. D. L. Blair Corp.
1051 Franklin Ave., Garden City, NY 11530
(516) 487-9200
Tom Conlon, Pres.

Professional contest entrants study the fine print of major contests and often claim that they can predict the winning jingles or other information about the winners, based on which professional contest organization is retained to handle the judging.

Whether it's a jingle or some other contest requiring "skill," or a nationally advertised sweepstakes or other lucky drawing, one of the names you'll see most frequently is that of D. L. Blair. The company constantly is on the lookout for offbeat products suitable as contest prizes or premiums.

5. Capital Sports, Inc.
805 Third Ave., N.Y. 10022
(212) 319-7770
Robert J. Arrix, Pres.
Mark Brickley, Dir., Public Relations

Founded in 1973, Capital Sports is a sizable producer of sports events, promotions, TV programs and other sports marketing.

6. Carlson Marketing Group, E. F. MacDonald Motivation
12755 Highway 55, Minneapolis, MN 55441
(612) 540-5208
James K. Pfleider

MacDonald has offices throughout the U.S. and in many other countries. Chances are, therefore, you'll find a MacDonald representative in or near your city. MacDonald is recognized by thousands of advertising and sales managers for its motivation programs which use merchandise and travel.

7. Delta Consultants, Inc.
333 W. 52 St., N.Y. 10019
(212) 245-2570
Don Marks, Pres.
Paul Stewart, Exec. V.P.

Don Marks spends most of his time arranging for products to be used in motion picture, theatrical and television productions, in which he is paid a fee either by the producer or the publicist who provides the products. He has been doing this since 1957 and is generally acknowledged to be the leader on the East coast, where his greatest activity is with stage productions. In fact, he operates a subsidiary specializing in this area, called Omicron Production Services Corp. Most of the clients are on an annual retainer fee basis, though per project representation also is available, generally with a minimum fee of $1,250.

8. Exposure Unlimited
15840 Ventura Blvd., Encino, CA 91436
(818) 995-0983
Started in 1977, Exposure Unlimited is operated by two women with broadcasting backgrounds—Sheila Ray and Neila Sisskind.

9. Edward E. Finch & Co., Inc.
220 Fifth Ave., N.Y. 10001
(212) 532-5030
Edward Finch, Pres.
Daniel Finch, V.P.

Branch Office:
6464 Sunset Blvd., Hollywood 90028
(213) 462-7426
Jack Finch, V.P.

Finch has been merchandise consultant to dozens of TV programs for more than 35 years. The Finch company has contracts with network, syndicated and local TV shows to provide prizes for on-the-air use. In addition to providing merchandise, clients also must pay a fee, which varies from $500 to $2,500 or more per telecast, depending on the program and the prize value. Contracts are flexible, usually for 13-week periods.

10. Daniel Fox & Associates, Inc.
4421 Riverside Dr., Burbank, CA 91505
(818) 841-3221
Dan Fox, who was director of program merchandise at NBC-TV for 15 years, started his company in 1977.

11. Game-Show Placements, Ltd.
7011 Willoughby Ave., Hollywood, CA 90038
(213) 874-7818
Robert A. Robertson, Pres.
Game-Show Placements is one of the largest companies in the TV prize field, and Bob Robertson is a leading proponent of this type of promotion. He describes the awesome sales power of prizes on network and syndicated television game shows as follows.

You will reach a mass audience of approximately seven million viewers per daytime program. If such 10-second spots were available on a commercial basis, the cost would be many thousands of dollars.
Through Game-Show Placements, you can reach these millions of viewers at a fraction of this amount. And remember, these 10-second presentations are well integrated into the program format and studies have shown viewer awareness to be extremely high.

Clients receive Arbitron ratings and other data, and a newsletter, Spot-Watch.

12. Martin Greenfield Associates, Inc.
MGA Plaza at Urban Ave., Westbury, NY 11590
(516) 334-7100
Burt Fischler, Pres.

As part of Martin Greenfield's successful sales training, promotional and marketing program, the company has developed a unique project called the Expectant Mother Giveaway Contest. The contest is of a six-month duration. The contest begins on September 1, culminating on February 28, and then a new contest starts March 1 and culminates on August 31—thus the program is one of continuity.

Banks, insurance companies and manufacturers of products for the baby and infant market, who are interested in obtaining the rights to mailing lists of the names of expectant mothers, help underwrite the cost of the promotion in each marketing area where the contest is conducted. The materials consist of placards and ballot boxes, display units, brochures and entry blanks. The procedure entails the registration of expectant mothers who are eligible for monthly drawings of free prizes that are shipped directly from the manufacturers to each expectant mother.

The cosponsoring manufacturers, those that offer their products as prizes, receive space on the displays in thousands of drug, food, department and other retail outlets.

No competitive products are involved in any contest. Sponsors must be prepared to supply sizable quantities of prizes and take care of the shipping costs. A company with a product that retails at a low price such as $1 could possibly become part of the package program by agreeing to furnish 1,000 prizes that would be shipped directly to the winners.

13. International Management Group
22 E. 71 St., N.Y. 10021
(212) 772-8900
H. Kent Stanner, Sr. V.P.

A division of Mark McCormack's extensive International Management Group (offices in Cleveland, New York, Los Angeles, Toronto and throughout the world), IMG specializes in sports and leisure-time promotions.

14. International Sport Summit
372 Fifth Ave., N.Y. 10018
(212) 500-5308
Monica de Hellerman, Pres.

Formed in 1973, International Sport Summit conducts an annual conference on sports events and facilities and also provides a variety of sports marketing services.

In 1987, its Sports Summit Publications published three directories, Sports Media Buyer's Guide, Sport Construction Buyer's Guide and Sportbil, which includes biographies of sports industry executives. All of the publications accept advertising and are distributed free to advertisers, advertising agencies and others.

International Sport Summit is a division of de Hellerman & Co., which produces conferences in finance and other fields.

15. Don Jagoda Associates, Inc.
One Underhill Blvd., Syosset, NY 11791
(516) 496-7300
Don Jagoda, Pres.

Don Jagoda Associates started in 1960 as a specialist in sweepstakes promotions and has evolved into a full-fledged marketing services company, with offices in a 50,000 square-foot facility on Long

Island and a staff of over 200 people. Services include the development and execution of consumer promotions, sweepstakes, instant winner games, contests, sales and dealer incentive programs, rebate and premium offers, and fulfillment programs.

16. Licensing Company of America
75 Rockefeller Plaza, N.Y. 10019
(212) 484-8807
Joseph P. Grant, Chm.

Branch Office:
3903 W. Olive, Burbank, CA 91522
(818) 954-6640

A Warner Communications Company, LCA is the largest company in the licensing field, with a multiplicity of products and fictional characters, plus sports representation which includes endorsements by Major League Baseball, National Football League Players Association, National Hockey League Players Association, National Hockey League and other associations and individuals.

If you are a licensee or a licensor, or simply interested in local or national merchandising, LCA may have a tie-in, or premium.

17. Marden-Kane, Inc.
410 Lakeville Rd., Lake Success, NY 11402
(516) 326-3666
Robert Bell, Pres.

Branch Offices:
20 Park Plaza, Boston 02116
(617) 542-8942, Hillary Etkin

505 N. Lake Shore Dr., Chicago 60611
(312) 644-5433, Walt Kaiser

3435 Branar, Houston, TX 77027
(713) 850-8663, Foster Wick

4800 Lincoln Blvd., Marina del Rey, CA 90292
(213) 578-5802, Robert Buenzli

666 Fifth Ave., N.Y. 10103
(212) 765-5390, Inez Apley

1255 Post St., S.F. 94109
(415) 771-2489, Myron Wacholder

Marden-Kane is one of the country's leading consultants in consumer contests and sweepstakes, games and incentive programs. Established in 1958, it is one of the oldest companies in these various promotional fields.

18. Merchandising Enterprises, Inc.

9250 Wilshire Blvd., Beverly Hills, CA 90212
(213) 858-1115
Charles M. Forman, Pres.

Branch Offices:
35 E. Wacker Dr., Chicago 60601
(312) 444-9777

400 Madison Ave., N.Y. 10017
(212) 223-1322

ME represents many major companies in the field of prizes on TV programs and in contests and promotions, particularly with TV and motion pictures.

Charles Forman, who started in 1949 as merchandising director of Queen For A Day, states that game show audiences tend to be more attentive, interested and emotionally involved than other TV viewers, and repeated exposure of a prize message is translated sooner or later into sales.

19. David Mirisch Enterprises

280 S. Beverly Dr., Beverly Hills, CA 90212
(213) 275-9485
David Mirisch, Pres.

A sports promotion agency, this company specializes in producing sponsored sports events for charities involving theatrical and sports celebrities.

20. Jack Morton Productions, Inc.

830 Third Ave., N.Y. 10022
(212) 758-8400
Bill Morton, Pres.
Jaye Hewitt, V.P. & Gen. Mgr.

Branch Offices:
233 Peachtree St., N.E., Atlanta, 30303
(404) 659-2262

666 North Lake Shore Dr., Chicago 60611
(312) 440-9700

31500 Northwestern Hwy., Framington Hills, MI 48018
(313) 851-5600

The Warwick, Houston 77001
(713) 526-3475

110 Pine Ave., Long Beach, CA 90802
(213) 436-6363

350 Townsend St., San Francisco 94107
(415) 546-0800

314

1825 Eye St., N.W., Wash., DC 20006
(202) 296-9300

Founded in 1960, Jack Morton Publishing (JMP) provides full service capabilities in meeting communications (notably audiovisuals, multi-media, videoconferencing and entertainment).

21. Motion Picture Placement (MPP)

Suite 404, 9250 Wilshire Blvd., Beverly Hills, CA 90212
(213) 858-3083
Joel S. Henrie, V.P.

Formed in 1982, MPP places products in theatrical feature films, TV shows and music videos.

22. The National Football League Alumni

2866 E. Oakland Park Blvd., Fort Lauderdale, FL 33306
(305) 564-6118
Vic Maitland, CEO

Formed in 1967, the NFL Alumni is a national service fraternity of several thousand former professional football players.

The nonprofit educational association owns Pro Legends, Incorporated, a sports marketing firm operated by Bill Palmer and Gene Felker.

23. Orbito Associates

4446 Carver St., Lake Worth, FL 33461
(305) 967-7597
Herman Secolsky

Orbito has a continuing need for products to be used as props in motion pictures and as prizes on game shows and other TV programs, and also people for placement on television interview programs. Fees vary according to type and length of exposure.

24. PIC-TV Incorporated

10933 Camarillo St., N. Hollywood, CA 91602
(818) 985-1100
Robert J. Murphy, Pres.

Branch Office:
11 E. 47 St., N.Y. 10017
(212) 308-6464
James Perkins, V.P.

One of the largest companies in "TV promotional advertising" (i.e., prizes on TV game shows), PIC-TV handles all of the production, fulfillment and other details. Fees depend on the program, value of prize and length of schedule.

Prizes range from the major prize (actually shown in the program) to low-priced "consolation prizes" (flipcards or tape with about 20 words of audio copy).

25. Product Exposure Co., Inc.

7855 Grosspoint Rd., Skokie, Il 60077
(312) 675-2330
Grace J. Nathan, Pres.

In addition to its handling of consumer sweepstakes and contests, sales incentive and other trade programs and specialized premium promotions, Product Exposure arranges for products to be used as prizes on TV programs.

26. Promotional Advertising Services

342 Madison Ave., N.Y. 10017
(212) 986-5950
Robert I. Feinberg, Pres.
Scott H. Kramer, V.P.

Founded in 1958, PAS does product promotion via TV game shows, talk shows and other programs, as well as sporting events and other projects. The company also provides arrangement and fulfillment of premium and sales incentive programs. Its principals are among the most experienced and knowledgeable in this business.

27. Promotion Finders

230 Pan Am Bldg., 200 Park Ave., N.Y. 10166
(212) 972-1212
Ron Rosenberg, Pres.

Formed in 1975, this unusual company provides a free, source-finding service, a "living Yellow Pages." Marketers can get to the right source for premiums, incentive programs, business gifts, a-v consultants, agencies, meeting needs and direct response suppliers.

28. ProServ

888 17th St., N.W., Wash., DC 20006
(202) 457-8800
Donald L. Dell, Chm.
Jerry Solomon, Exec. V.P.
Stephen Disson, Sr., V.P.

One of the largest companies in sports marketing, ProServ creates and manages events, exhibitions, clinics, TV shows and other productions, and is heavily involved in product merchandising, sales promotion, celebrity appearances and corporate sponsorships.

ProServ also represents clients in various sports, including tennis, basketball, football, cycling, baseball, golf and volleyball.

Among its TV programs is Tennis Magazine Reports, shown on the ESPN Cable network, and syndicated documentaries.

A free newsletter, ProServ News, is published twice a year and is available to clients.

29. Bob Rose & Associates

9300 Wilshire Blvd., Beverly Hills, CA 90212
(213) 274-7117

Bob Rose has had over 35 years of working with TV shows, including Ralph Edwards' Truth or Consequences and Art Linkletter's Houseparty and People are Funny. The company provides prizes to over 20 TV programs.

30. Science Faction Corporation

333 W. 52 St., N.Y. 10019
(212) 586-1911
Richard C. Sandhaus, Pres.

Founded in 1978, Science Faction Corporation manufactures laser scanning systems for laser graphic displays and produces shows for trade and industrial presentations, sky shows, discos, theaters, TV, film and advertising. Chances are that you've seen some of its large-scale laser shows at state and world's fairs and other major events. The company's free quarterly newsletter is called The Successful Event Report.

31. G. Smith & Company
221 W. Alameda, Burbank, CA 91502
(818) 848-6651
Gary S. Smith, Pres.

Started in 1966 as Bresee, Smith & Associates, the company was one of the pioneers in the merchandising of products on radio and television programs. Gary S. Smith was the director of merchandising at Queen For A Day.

The Smith company excels in creating merchandising projects which make a prize giveaway part of a total promotion. For example, they created play-at-home, board-game versions of The Dating Game, The Newlywed Game and other TV shows for use by companies, with dealers and others to promote their TV exposure.

32. Shopping Center Network, Inc.
11410 N. Kendall Dr., Miami, FL 33176
(305) 595-0201
Joel Benson, Pres.

Branch Offices:
10920 Wilshire Blvd., Suite 1110, L.A. 90024
(213) 824-0595, Lynn Gahagan

50 W. 34 St., N.Y. 10001
(212) 714-2121, Scott Lange

Founded in 1975, Shopping Center Network is a unique company which creates events, exhibits, promotions and attractions and arranges for them to be set up at shopping centers. Fees vary, depending on the cost of producing and transporting the project, and can range from a small display to a mobile unit with permanent personnel.

If you are active in shopping center promotions, you may be interested in the publications of the International Council of Shopping Centers, 665 Fifth Ave., N.Y. 10020, and the National Research Bureau, 310 Michigan Ave., Chicago 60604. NRB publishes the basic encyclopedias of the industry. The Shopping Center Directory, a five-volume set (East, Midwest, South, West and National Summary) with data about over 23,000 centers, maps, glossaries, new centers under construction or planned. The $265 price includes two supplements. Individual regional volumes are $125 each, so there is an incentive to buy the complete set. Actually, you don't buy the books, National Research Bureau leases them to you and they must be returned if the subscription is not renewed. How's that for clever marketing!

Another shopping mall promotion specialist is Axiom Marketing Inc., 666 Old Country Rd., Garden City, NY 11530, (516) 222-8070, headed by Myron Charnless.

33. Special Events Report
213 W. Institute Pl., Chicago 60610
(312) 944-1727
Lesa Ukman

Sports, arts, cause and music marketing is the subject of this biweekly newsletter, which was launched in 1982. It covers who is sponsoring what and why. Founder Lesa Ukman and her staff have made it into an extremely important newsletter for public relations practitioners. An annual subscription ($240, $140/

nonprofits) is essential for anyone involved in sponsoring or producing special events. In addition, the subscription includes the Directory of Sports, Festivals and Special Events, which costs $100 if purchased by itself.

The Directory, which was started in 1984, includes listings of 3,000 events, cross indexed by subject, date, attendance and location. The unique 400-page book also includes a Yellow Pages section with sports marketing, music marketing and special events specialists, as well as suppliers of fireworks, sound, stage, lighting and others involved in the production of special events.

Send for a sample copy so that you can see how beautiful and useful this newsletter is.

34. Television & Radio Features, Inc.

550 Frontage Rd., Northfield, IL 60093
(312) 446-2550
Morton Small, Pres.

Television and Radio Features is retained by radio and television stations to set up contests and program promotions and to provide them with prizes. Stations pay a fee, and it thus is possible to obtain exposure on top-rated programs in major markets, merely by providing products for use as prizes. The exposure usually consists of a 25-word announcement and a photo or other visual credit. Previously located in Chicago's Loop, the company now is in a nearby suburb.

35. Video Enterprises, Inc.

8721 Sunset Blvd., L.A. 90069
(213) 659-4311
Philip J. Lane, Pres.

A well-established (1958) specialist in placing promotional spots in TV giveaway, talk, variety and sports programs, Video Enterprises represents many clients and TV programs on a service-fee basis.

Since this chapter is a potpourri, following are a few tips about new services and miscellaneous information.

Public relations agencies occasionally place advertising. As an advertiser, you not only can obtain commissions, but also a few privileges not available to publicists. For example, most magazines will send you complimentary subscriptions if you are an actual or prospective advertiser. Some publications will send you copies, by mail or messenger, prior to their general distribution. Some publications (for example, The New York Times) provide free messenger pickup of advertising materials. Most newspapers, and a few magazines, set type (often at no charge) so all you have to do is send an insertion order and typed copy. Advertising is much more complex than this, but this saves a lot of time and usually is the preferred procedure for financial, recruiting and other types of advertising which are likely to be handled by a public relations agency.

Information about translators, typists, videotaping and other convention services is included in several other chapters.

Movie premieres, parties and special events which call for red carpets, carbon-arc searchlights and other items are the speciality of Edward LaPidus, of A-1 Premieres, Inc., 141 W. 54 St., N.Y. 10019, phone (212) 247-3829. His slogan is "If a press agent can dream it up, I can make it work."

Whether or not you handle your own travel arrangements, you may find it handy to carry with you a Pocket Flight Guide or other publications from Official Airline Guides, Inc., 2000 Clearwater Drive, Oak Brook, IL 60521. Each of the editions (North American, European and Pacific/Asia) is about $50. The company also publishes the OAG Travel Planner/Hotel/Motel Redbook ($75). Airline and hotel information is available to your personal computer or other computer terminals by subscribing to the OAG Electronic Edition.

The Reuben H. Donnelley Group, comprised of Donnelley Directory, Donnelley Information Publishing, and Donnelley Information Technology, is responsible for the sales, marketing, and publishing of Yellow Pages directory products and other related information products and services.

In 1886, Reuben Donnelley was the first to publish a classified telephone directory to contain advertising. In 1961, the company was acquired by The Dun & Bradstreet Corporation. In addition to its Yellow Pages Services, Donnelley publishes Promotion Power, a newsletter for promotion and graphic arts professionals. For a copy, contact the editor, Tibor Taraba, director of communications, Reuben H. Donnelley, 287 Bowman Ave., Purchase, N.Y. 10577.

Gift-Pax, Inc., 25 Hempstead Gardens Drive, W. Hempstead, N.Y. 11552, is well-known to advertisers for its product sampling to students, newlyweds, expectant mothers, new mothers, senior citizens, homeowners and others. Call Wally Scofield, president, at (516) 485-0660, or one of the company's branch offices (Chicago, Memphis, Los Angeles, Toronto).

The American Society of Association Executives, 1575 Eye St., N.W., Washington, D.C. 20005, provides a great deal of information about meetings and meeting facilities. Nonmembers may subscribe to the monthly Association Magazine for $24. Included are such helpful items as a suggested detailed letter of agreement with a hotel for the use of convention facilities.

One of the many benefits which association executives receive as members of the American Society of Association Executives (ASAE) is *editors' news*, a monthly newsletter filled with useful advice about publicity, printing, mailing, advertising and other communications subjects. Nonmembers can subscribe for the bargain price of $10 a year.

A Tradeshow Calendar is included in every issue of Tradeshow Week, a newsletter ($237 a year) published at 12233 W. Olympic Blvd., Suite 236, L.A. 90064, phone (213) 826-5696.

In regard to fund raising, a variety of fund-raising publications, including extensive data about foundation grants, is published by Taft Corporation, 5130 MacArthur Blvd, N.W., Wash, D.C. 20016.

Prentice-Hall (Englewood Cliffs, NJ 07632) publishes a Nonprofit Organization Handbook, 333 pages in a loose-leaf binder, for $35.

The most extensive library about fund raising and philanthropy is maintained by The Foundation Center at 79 Fifth Ave., NY 10003. The Center also has libraries at 1001 Connecticut Ave., N.W., Wash. DC 20006; 312 Sutter St., San Francisco 94108 and 1442 Hanna Bldg., 1422 Euclid Ave., Cleveland 44215. The headquarters (located for many years at 888 Seventh Avenue, N.Y.) were moved in 1984 to Fifth Avenue and 16 Street.

Regional depositories of foundation information, which are open to the public, are at over 75 major libraries.

The Public Management Institute, 358 Brannan St., San Francisco 94107, publishes the Computer Resource Guide for Nonprofits, a directory ($175) of software designed for nonprofit and granting agencies, and Corporate 500: Directory of Corporate Philanthropy, which describes the top 500 companies in the U.S.

The Society for Nonprofit Organizations, 6314 Odana Rd., Madison, WI 53719, has a variety of services (individual membership is $75 a year) and publishes a bimonthly magazine, Nonprofit World ($39 a year to non-members).

Want to see your name in lights? Nonprofit organizations can obtain public service space on the moving news signs that light up many downtown areas by contacting the outdoor advertising company or owner of the sign.

Spectacolor operates the full-color animated space on the building at 1 Times Square, N.Y. 10036. Publicists can set up public service or other announcements, limited to a few words, for low fees, by contacting George N. Stonbely, President, at (212) 221-6938. Clients are informed of the time when the message will be shown so that arrangements can be made for a photograph, which often can be useful in publicity and promotion.

Here's a guaranteed way to get your client's name in newspaper headlines. Contact Times Square Publishers, 200 W. 48 St., N.Y. 10036, phone (212) 246-5762, and they'll set and print two-line headline (up to 40 letters) on a "dummy" newspaper. The cost is $7 for the first copy, $2 for extras. A nifty idea for sales meetings and presentations, though not too useful for filling a publicity scrapbook.

Special regulations and techniques, as well as specialized media, exist with regard to accounting, architecture, law, medicine and other fields, and professional associations in these fields provide public information materials to members and nonmembers.

In the medical field, current guildelines on press relations and standards of professional responsibility are published in the Current Opinions of the Judicial Council of the American Medical Association. The bulletin (OP-122/6) is $9.50 from the AMA, Box 10946, Chicago 60610.

With regard to associations, here is information about the two largest associations in the public relations field.

International Association of Business Communicators
870 Market St., 940, San Francisco, CA 94102
(415) 433-3400

Over 11,000 editors, public relations directors and other business communicators belong to the International Association of Business Communicators, which during the last decade has grown tremendously in numbers and influence. The $135 annual membership dues includes a subscription to Communication World, a lively monthly magazine which changed its format from a tabloid to a full-color magazine in 1983. Members also received an annual directory.

Formed in 1970, IABC now provides a variety of services, including regional seminars, annual international conference (at which its Gold Quill Awards are presented), Job-line and a Communication Bank which includes videotapes and other audiovisuals, as well as publications.

The accreditation program provides an IABC as a recognition of professional achievement to communicators who have taken written and oral examinations and submitted a portfolio evaluation. IABC has a United Kingdom office, headed by Marian G. Hawkins at 46-48 Osnaburgh St., London NW1 3ND.

Public Relations Society of America
33 Irving Pl., N.Y. 10003
(212) 955-2230

PRSA is the leading (about 14,000 members) public relations association in the world. Services include annual conferences, workshops, Research and Information Center, monthly magazine (Public Relations Journal), membership directory and awards (the Silver Anvils are the "Oscars" of the public relations field). There are also awards for individuals, films/video, educators and public service, and other services relating to all aspects of public relations. For example, a voluntary accreditation program, with a vigorous test procedure (examination fee $125), has enhanced the respect for professionalism in public relations.

In addition to an initiation fee ($50) members pay annual dues ($150) and chapter dues (set by chapters). Professional interest sections, such as the Counselors Academy, charge additional dues.

In 1987, PRSA moved from mid-Manhattan to the Gramercy Park area. 33 Irving Place is between 15 and 16 Streets, east of Park Avenue S.

The New York University/PRSA Program conducts workshops (generally two-days) in New York, Washington, DC, and other cities. The Program is administered by Al Horowitz and Don Bates, at 310 Madison Ave., N.Y. 10017, phone (212) 682-1435.

A smaller operation, not connected with PRSA, is The Professional Development Institute, 2472 Fox Ave., Baldwin, NY 11510, phone (516) 868-5757, which conducts two-day programs in New York. Jerome Prager is managing director.

320

Chapter 25

Props and Animals

Many trade associations and companies provide products to photographers, advertising agencies, television shows and motion picture studios. Companies often are less inclined than associations to distribute their products as free "props," particularly if the item is costly or not easily recognizable, as the company generally wants an audio or video credit. Even without the credit, though, the exposure itself or the exploitation of the tie-in can be valuable.

As any "property man" can tell you, "prop" is theatrical slang for property. In working with property people and others who collect props (scenery designers, wardrobe mistresses, stage managers, photographers), publicists must be prepared to provide a good quantity of merchandise to allow for breakage and pilferage. Of course, prop people rarely can guarantee that the product will be shown. Even when the script calls for a close-up of a specific product, the donor of the product must anticipate that the scene may be cut out or revised so as to exclude the product.

Perhaps this is the reason that many public relations practitioners ignore prop publicity or prefer to deal with an agency.

As might be expected, several companies specialize in the placement of products as props in Broadway plays, television shows and motion pictures. Some of these are discussed in the preceding chapter. This chapter deals with the use of products as props, rather than prizes, and also the rental of items for use as props. Related to this is the rental of animals.

Let's start with the placement of products in plays, movies and TV shows. Be wary of the "entrepreneurs" who often charge extravagant fees and dazzle prospective clients with the glamorous possibility of obtaining a fantastic amount of "free advertising." Often these promoters are unsuccessful, not necessarily due to any dishonesty. For example, a scene showing the use of the product might end up on the cutting room floor of a motion picture studio, thus canceling the otherwise successful efforts of the prop promoter.

For this reason, and also in order to give a certain amount of business stability to this field, several companies often arrange for the placement of products in shows on a contingency or "C.O.D." basis, that is, payment only if successful.

The C.O.D. arrangement protects your cash investment, but you still can waste a lot of time with fly-by-night promoters and others who seem to have theatrical, TV or motion picture connections.

There are only a few companies which have been in the business for many years. Each of these has survived the murky problems of this field by evolving techniques by which trusting suppliers and receivers of props can work with them on a business-like basis.

In 1985, Denise Harbin introduced the TIPPS Directory, an acronym for Talent Information, Props, Places and Services. The 4½ × 7-inch spiral-bound book is $35 from Box 7420, N.Y. 10150. The 1987 edition includes a California section, in addition to NYC.

More than 50,000 musical items, from antique Chinese gongs to tuned water glasses, are available for sale or rental from Carroll Musical Instrument Service, 351 W. 41 St., N.Y. 10036, phone (212) 868-4120. Mr. Carroll Bratman delights in requests for unusual noises, though he'll also rent conventional instruments.

What do you do with an antique curio after you've used it as a prop? The more exotic the item, the more likely it is to end up as an office or home decoration.

Many of the costume companies are family operations. For example, Rubie's Costume Co. was organized by Rubin & Tillie Beige in 1951 and now is operated by their four children. Marc Beige is head of the company, and his brother, Howard, is Vice President in charge of sales. The factory and showroom is located at 1 Rubie Plaza in the Richmond Hill section of the borough of Queens, NY and the warehouse is nearby at 101-10 Van Wyck Expressway, Queens 11419. As with most costume companies, a major business consists of directing theatrical costumes, particularly for high school and college productions. Rubie's also has a variety of costumes related to specific products, such as Fruit of the Loom, Wonder Bread and Kool Aid.

Check the yellow pages of the telephone book under Costumes for sources of props, uniforms, costumes, wigs and other items for sale or rental. In the New York City area, there are several major masqueraders:

Animal Outfits For People Co., 252 W. 46 St., N.Y. 10036, (212) 840-6219

Chenko Studio, 167 W. 46 St., N.Y. 10036, (212) 944-0215

David's Outfitters Inc., 36 W. 20 St., N.Y. 10011, (212) 691-7388

Eaves Costume Co. (established 1870), 21-07 41 Ave., Queens, NY 11103, (718) 729-1010

House of Costumes, Ltd., 166 Jericho Turnpike, Mineola, N.Y. 11501, (516) 294-0170, Ferne Tita

Lane Costume Co. (specializes in Santa Claus suits), 234 5 Ave., N.Y. 10010, (212) 684-4721

Cathy Lazar, 155 E. 23 St., N.Y. 10010, (212) 473-0363. (Cathy and Jeffrey Lazar create special costumes and life-size "soft props" for events, product identification and other uses.)

Lillian Costume Co., 226 Jericho Turnpike, Mineola, N.Y. 11501, (516) 746-6060, Ron Greco

Rubie's Costume Co. (specializes in Revolutionary War period), 120-08 Jamaica Ave., Queens, N.Y. 11418, (718) 846-1008 (Ask Marc Beige for the colorful catalog.)

Universal Costume Co., 535 8 Ave., N.Y. 10018, (212) 239-3222

Among the many sources of props in the Los Angeles area, the following do a sizable business with public relations and advertising clients:

House of Props, 1117 N. Gower, L.A. 90038, (213) 463-3166

Don Post Studios, 8211 Lankershim, N. Hollywood 91605, (818) 768-0811

Hollywood Fancy Feather, 220 W. 5 St., L.A. 90013, (213) 625-8453

If feathers are your fancy, Hollywood is the place to buy all colors of natural and dyed quills and feathers from pheasants, ostriches and other birds.

Further down the California coast is a major resource, San Diego Costume Co., 7899 Clairemont Mesa Blvd., San Diego, CA 92111, phone (619) 560-9161.

Are you more interested in renting a live animal than a stuffed one?

An adage in the publicity business states that "You can't miss with animals, sex or children."

Though most adages, including this one, can be disputed, it is true that many press agents have set up successful situations for newspapers and television which have involved the rental of animals.

Whether or not one desires exotic or ordinary horses, dogs and other animals, it is preferable to secure animals from a professional organization. Zoos, circuses, pet shops and animal trainers sometimes are available as sources of "professional animals," but it definitely is more efficient to work with the organizations which specialize in animals for use in advertising, publicity and promotions.

There is a temptation, perhaps, to save money or, due to lack of experience, to call a zoo, circus, pet shop, farmer, museum, college biology department, or simply a friend who owns animals. Don't!

Patricia Poleskie, who operated Animal Talent Scouts in New York, provided this advice a few years ago. It's still extraordinarily valid.

1. There are no experienced, reliable, professional trained animals or animal trainers in zoos. Zoos are the keepers and the kept. The keeper never handles or trains the animals and the animals are, therefore, wild (uneducated). Zoo directors and other zoo personnel are endlessly annoyed by those people who try to wrangle a "cheap job," (no insurance) and sneak an animal out on the vague promise of possible publicity coverage for the zoo and maybe expenses covered. They want no part of this and, actually, it's against their municipal and society charters and bylaws. The responsible zoo director, when confronted by this type of person, always refers him to the theatrical animal agencies.

2. A circus has animals that are trained to a "routine" and know little else. They work well in the security of repetition. They are not professional theatrical animals and have little to offer a client in the way of spontaneous cueing. No client would look forward to spending time and money trying to chase an "ever mobile" circus, in pursuit of, say, an elephant, when he can call an animal agency and book one that is "in residence and, therefore, always available" within an hour or two from any given job site.

3. Pet shops are in the business of selling animals, not renting them. Profit is their aim, and there are no trained animals in pet shops. No animal should ever go out on a job without its owner, trainer or handler.

4. Animal trainers are not freewheeling entities, floating around with their animals in tow. They are in permanent residence and, because they are professionals, they either work in circuses under contract for a year (or a season) at a time, run their own agencies, or book themselves and their animals through agencies.

5. Professional (experienced) animals are owned and live with professional trainers who work through a professional agency.

6. Beware of "wild" animals. "Wild" is a state of animal psychology and not a description of type. A horse or pig can be "wild" and do a lot of damage, if it's never had human handling. A tiger can have better manners and be more tractable and predictable than the horse or pig, if it's had the handling and training. A truly "wild" animal has no business being in any place other than a zoo or jungle (and certainly not out among the public).

If an animal is truly "rare," there is a 99 percent possibility that it is on the U.S. Government's list of "endangered species" and, therefore, would be illegal to harbor, much less rent out.

Chapter 26

Radio

In this television era, the medium of radio is alive and well. Surprisingly, public relations people frequently ignore the enormous publicity possibilities presented by the more than 10,000 radio stations within the country. There are over 500 million radios in the U.S., and there are many times when more of them are turned on than television sets. There are over five radio sets per home!

During the summer, for example, the millions of transistor radios used at beaches and other public places, plus automobile radios, result in larger audiences for radio programs than for TV. Throughout the year, there are heavy concentrations of radio listeners during the day, particularly the early morning and late-afternoon travel periods.

In 1987, the U.S. had considerably more radio stations than ever before—over 4,800 AM and 5,200 FM stations (about 4,000 commercial and 1,200 noncommercial).

The radio medium is stronger and more vital than ever before in its history, but its programming has changed considerably. The emphasis has switched from network dramatic and comedy programs to music and news programs, mostly local.

Radio has changed considerably during the last 20 years, including the development of all-news stations, telephone call-in programs, late-night talk programs and big-audience FM stations.

FM radio now has about half of the radio audience. However, the publicist should not be fooled by this. One great value of FM is its "clear sound." Thus, FM stations use more music, particularly classical, rock and disco. AM stations reach larger geographical areas and are more likely to have news, interview and talk shows—which generally are of greater interest to most publicists.

Do *not* be fooled by audience figures in publicity directories. Radio audiences of individual programs are smaller than the cumulative figures which often are listed. In fact, the circulation of a major daily newspaper still is larger than any single radio interview program in the same city.

Of course, radio is an important part of a public relations program. However, it may be more cost-efficient to arrange for long-distance phone interviews, or to arrange for radio interviews on a media tour only after booking TV and newspaper interviews, or, most important, to know the medium and to zero in on those radio programs which are relevant to you. For one client, an early morning farm news program may be important; for another, it may be a late-night talk show.

Sophisticated advertisers know that radio station demographics range considerably. In New York, for example, publicists should listen to and appreciate the lineup of interview programs on WMCA or WOR, and also understand the general composition of each interviewer's audience.

Though there are now relatively few network interview programs, there are hundreds of local broadcasters, disc jockeys and announcers who regularly conduct interviews. These local programs have a continuing need for scripts, interview records, promotion ideas and programming suggestions. For placement of guests on the few network programs and the many top-rated local programs in major cities, the best approach is the same as with any other medium—that is, the direct approach, by mail, phone or in person, to the producer or other contact at the program.

In addition to the direct approach, publicists should consider using one or more of the many services which specialize in the distribution of scripts and records to radio stations. Since these services rarely offer their scripts and records on an exclusive basis, most of their users are relatively small stations. However, a modest expenditure with one of these services can result in exposure of several hundred small stations, and occasionally one or more of the very big stations also make use of the material, thus adding an extra frosting to the cake.

Because of the importance of the radio medium, the use of these services is strongly recommended to those clients interested in reaching large audiences, particularly teenagers and housewives.

Several of the services provide usage maps and statistical tabulations based on the postcards returned by the broadcasters. Caution is suggested in the interpretation of these statistics. In many cases, the numbers refer to the total population or total radio listeners in the market area. In other cases, the numbers refer to the peak audiences of the particular radio station. In no cases can these numbers be considered to be the actual audiences of the specific program on which the publicity material was broadcast. Therefore, the time-cost figures supplied by some of the radio publicity services often are exaggerated or not too meaningful.

Occasionally, a radio station (or other service) will provide grossly inaccurate data, such as padded reports. These services *can* be reliable, efficient and useful, but clients sometimes must be skeptical, particularly if the reports include many top-market stations.

Furthermore, while it is true that many broadcasters use publicity scripts complete and verbatim, there is always the possibility that the broadcast omitted the name of the company or product and had other deletions of vital significance to the client.

There are times when publicity exposure is considerably more valuable than the equivalent advertising time or space, but the reverse also may be true, which makes advertising time-cost figures for publicity exposure a dangerous practice. In spite of these reservations, one still can't help but be impressed by the figures relating to the number of radio stations, radio sets and listeners, and a comprehensive consumer public relations program must include consideration of the radio publicity programming and distribution services.

Those publicists who remain unimpressed by exposure on such stations as KSEW, Sitka, Alaska; KTLO, Mountain Home, Arkansas, and WZEP, Defuniak Springs, Florida, still must acknowledge that radio stations do reach a fair number of listeners, when judged collectively, and the list occasionally includes such stellar stations as WSB, Atlanta, Georgia.

Many radio and TV stations offer their personnel and facilities for use by advertising and public relations clients. A few of the large stations operate talent bureaus which enable clients to hire professional announcers for use at news and entertainment events. Though the use of station personnel in no way influences acceptance of this material, it usually does guarantee good quality at reasonable rates and with services which often can be quicker than that provided by a commercial studio.

If you are particularly active in the broadcast field, you may want to join the National Association of Broadcasters, which offers an associate membership. The Association, which is located at 1705 De-Sales Street, N.W., Wash., DC 20036, provides its members with weekly and monthly newsletters and other publications and services. Furthermore, as a member you can attend the association's annual convention.

You can learn a lot more about radio by sending for Radio Facts, a free 48-page booklet published annually by the Radio Advertising Bureau, Inc, 304 Park Ave. S., N.Y. 10010. For example, the booklet includes data about the increased number of radios, where they are (41 percent of all rooms have radios), who listens (slightly more men than women, which is significant to many public relations people), when they listen (the largest number listen in the morning drive time, much more than in the afternoon drive time), when radio listening exceeds TV viewing, types of station formats and much more.

In addition to the following specialists, many creators and distributors of radio publicity materials also are described in the sections on mailing services, packaged publicity services, prizes and television.

1. Ads/BBS Audio Visual Productions, Inc.

100 N. Washington St., Falls Church, VA 22046
(202) 536-9000
Blake B. Stamler, Exec. Producer

Founded in 1962 by Arthur D. Stamler (hence Ads), Audio Visual Productions is a very big operation with a unique specialty—radio and TV spots for nonprofit organizations, associations and Government agencies.

Various distribution plans are available, from individual states, to selected markets, to and including all on-air commercial stations and systems.

2. Accent on Broadcasting, Inc.

165 W. 66 St., N.Y. 10023
(212) 362-3616
Miss Randie Levine, Pres.

Placement of guests on radio and television programs throughout the country, on a per program or project basis, is the specialty of this publicist.

3. Audio/TV Features, Inc.

149 Madison Ave., N.Y. 10016
(212) 889-1327
Alan Steinberg, Chmn.
Robert Kimmel, Pres.

Formed in 1979 by two experienced broadcast newsmen, Audio/TV Features produces brief radio news and feature reports and also radio and TV public service announcements. Distribution is via the satellite broadcast facilities of the AP and UPI Radio networks. Services include scripting, production, recording and distribution.

A PSA or a brief interview to 2,000 radio stations via satellite is $750, including script, production and distribution.

The company's TV services are described in its listing in the television chapter.

4. Broadcast Interview Source

2500 Wisconsin Ave., N.W., Wash., DC 20007
(202) 333-4904
Mitchell P. Davis, Editor

Broadcast Interview Source publishes the annual Talk Show Guest Directory, a unique list of interviewees, that is, individuals who are available as guests on radio and TV talk shows. The directory is sold and also sent free to program directors and brief listings for public relations sources are free. Advertising is available for $95 a quarter page.

The directory is $25. The company also publishes Talk Show Selects, a directory of talk show hosts and producers. Updated quarterly, it's $185 for an annual subscription.

5. News/Radio Network, Inc.
9431 W. Beloit Rd., Milwaukee, WI 53277
(414) 321-6210

Branch Offices:
644 Danbury Rd., Georgetown, CT 06829
(203) 762-8065, Michael Hill, V.P.

800 Ogden Rd., Downers Grove, IL 60515
(312) 963-4455, Robert Hill, V.P.

204 W. 4 St., Claremont St., Claremont, CA 91711
(714) 621-6903, Thomas Hill, V.P.

3136 N. 10 St., Arlington, VA 22201
(703) 243-2929, Burke Walsh, Sales Mgr.

The Hill family, assisted by a large experienced staff of reporters, editors and technicians, covers major sports, farm, business and all types of conventions and events for public relations clients, via their Audioline satellite service or other news feeds, or by tape. Costs range from a few hundred to a few thousand dollars, depending on the place, number of broadcasts and stations.

The recent boom in sponsored special events in the sports and entertainment fields and the use of satellite and high tech methods for distributing sponsored materials are among the reasons for the tremendous expansion of the News/Radio Network. The company now has active offices in suburban Chicago, Los Angeles, New York and Washington, D.C.

6. North American Precis Syndicate, Inc.
201 E. 42 St., N.Y. 10017
(212) 867-9000
Ronald L. Levy, Pres.

Branch Offices:
333 N. Michigan Ave., Chicago 60601
(312) 558-1200
Jim Brosseau, Nora Lukas, Sr. V.P.'s Bonnie Cassidy Heller, V.P.

1025 Vermont Ave., N.W., Wash., DC 20005
(202) 347-7300
Jake Arnette, Sr. V.P.
Monty Bodington, Wendy Sollod, V.P.'s
Anne Barr, Lynne Dean, Washington Representatives

4209 Vantage Avenue, Studio City, CA 91604
(818) 761-8400
Carol Balkin, V.P.

The NAPS radio service consists of a script prepared, printed and mailed to news and talk programs on 3,000 stations, for a total cost of $2,150 for one release or $1,850 each for 12. You can expect usage on more than 200 stations. The results report includes audience data and a map.

Additional information about NAPS is included in the chapters on newspapers and packaged publicity services.

7. Planned Communication Services, Inc.
12 E. 46 St., N.Y. 10017
(212) 697-2765
Gerald Jay Multer, Chm.

Formed in 1962, PCS is one of the country's largest producers and distributors of publicity materials for radio and TV stations. Radio interviews, features or PSAs can be distributed on record or tape, sent to selected stations or to those responding to a query.

News: Radio stories produced with "actualities" are a fast, cost-effective way to get broad exposure for new product, issue-related and other messages. Spokespeople are recorded, stories are written and produced quickly, and fed in one day over the phone to news services, national and regional networks, and local stations. A story can be produced and fed to newsrooms covering 2,000 to 4,000 stations on a budget of $2,500 to $3,000, including comprehensive report of pickup.

Public Service Announcements: Radio public service campaigns, usually consisting of both recorded spots and "live-copy" scripts in multiple lengths, can receive considerable "free airtime" on budgets of $10,000 to $20,000. PCS has one of the most complete and up-to-date radio databases, with capability to target stations based on market rank, station rating or format, and ethnic and demographic factors.

8. Planned Television Arts
25 W. 43 St., N.Y. 10036
(212) 921-5111
Mike Levine, Pres.; Richard Frishman, V.P.

The only confusing aspect of Planned Television Arts is its name. The company is a super-specialist in placement of guests on TV programs, but PTA also places guests on radio programs. Payment is on a per placement basis. Details are in the PTA listing in the chapter on television.

9. Public Affairs Satellite Systems, Inc. (PUBSAT)
1012 14 St., N.W., Wash., DC 20005
(202) 628-3600

See description in TV chapter.

10. Public Interest Affiliates
666 N. Lakeshore Dr., Chicago 60611
(312) 943-8888
Brad Paul, Pres.
Sandra Kramer, V.P.

Branch Office:
12 W. 31 St., N.Y. 10001
(212) 714-9550
Susan Null

Founded in 1980, Public Interest Affiliates has become the largest company in the field of public relations radio. It produces several weekly radio programs and sponsored "specials" with unusually high programming quality, and a variety of radio contests and programs that offer public relations sponsorship opportunities.

The programs are generally provided free to participating radio stations (including many major stations) together with commercial spots (from which PIA derives its income).

Information about PIA video services is included in the TV chapter.

11. Radio & TV Roundup Productions
426 Sunset Blvd., Cape May, NJ 08204
(609) 884-0620, (212) 749-3647
Bill Bertenshaw, Exec. Prod., Bobbie Cherrelle, TV Dir., Fred Long, Radio Dir.

Starting in 1956 with a tape recorder and with himself as announcer, engineer and the entire staff, Bill Bertenshaw has developed a sizable syndicated broadcast operation which today includes a greater variety of regularly scheduled radio programs than almost any other company in the radio publicity business. The Bertenshaw current "roundup" comprises nationally distributed radio and TV programs, ranging from 30 seconds to 60 minutes, on travel, business, religion, gardening, health, agriculture and other special-interest subjects.

The significant aspect of Bertenshaw's prolific operation is that many of the programs are broadcast on major stations on a regularly scheduled basis, including "suggested solutions" and various public service programs. Special programs are produced with Spanish, Yiddish, Italian, black and other commentators for ethnic radio stations.

Bertenshaw hosts some of the programs, including a Sunday morning program which mixes popular music and religious messages, produced in cooperation with the Council of Churches of the City of New York and New Jersey Council of Churches.

12. Sheridan-Elson Communications, Inc.
20 W. 37 St., N.Y. 10018
(212) 239-2000
William Sheridan and Robert Elson

Formed in 1967, Sheridan-Elson Communications offers complete creative and technical services in the broadcast and audiovisual areas. This material includes a regular monthly radio program, Audio Newsfeatures, which is distributed to 400 stations. Each program on the disc has its own theme and format.

13. J & J Ziehl Radio
Box 25, Greens Farm, CT 06436
(203) 259-7697, (800) 451-4453
Joe Ziehl, Joan Ziehl

Mr. & Mrs. Ziehl (she uses the nom de plume of Kate Forbes) produce and distribute several recorded radio series which are broadcast on a regular basis by many stations. Some of the stations list these programs on the schedules which are published in newspapers and, as a result, the zealous Ziehls are able to provide more exact figures than many other broadcast publicity services.

The Ziehls estimate that their oldest program, Around the House (started in 1963), is broadcast by about 300 stations. The current daily lineup includes many major cities, thus enabling many clients and prospective users to actually hear the program, which somehow creates more of an impact than any amount of postcards and tabulations.

A four-minute Around the House show is $1,200 and there are similar rates for other Ziehl programs, including Consumer Hot-Line.

The Ziehls also produce custom radio programs and work exclusively for public relations clients.

Chapter 27

Records and Tapes

Several thousand public relations practitioners spend the major part of their time in the creation and development of newsworthy events and projects and the subsequent publicizing of these activities. Too little time is devoted to the presentation and merchandising of results and the integration of public relations into sales, marketing, stockholder, employee and other functions.

The public relations professional who takes pride in ability to write a good news release, combined with knowledge of the media, also should be familiar with the enormous range of audiovisual techniques which can be used to merchandise publicity.

Many directories can be consulted for the names of companies which specialize in motion pictures, slide films, records and other audiovisual techniques. As usual, the classified telephone directory can be extremely helpful, as well as the many trade publications and reference books.

Recording services, materials and products are available in every major city in the country and occasionally are utilized by publicists, particularly for the production of tapes and records which are distributed to radio stations. A few practitioners also use records to merchandise their publicity results and for other forms of direct communication, particularly in connection with sales promotion.

Almost all radio and television stations offer their facilities to publicists and other commercial users for studio recording, editing, disc cutting, sound tape duplication, and the production of other radio and television materials. Among the commercial studios, several are oriented to the needs of public relations clients. Prices vary considerably.

In sizable quantities, records should be purchased from the custom divisions of RCA, Columbia and other record manufacturers. Most public relations clients usually require relatively small quantities and prefer to deal with local recording studios.

The rate cards of most recording studios frighten many clients who only occasionally use these services. Don't be afraid to ask if sleeves and labels are included (they usually are), and ask about the cost of jackets, mailing envelopes and other extras which you might have to obtain from printers and other suppliers. Sophisticated buyers sometimes goof in their budgets, forgetting mastering, processing, shipping and other costs that take place before and after the pressing of the records or the duplication of tapes.

The leading manufacturer of flexible vinyl records is:

Eva-Tone Inc.
4801 Ulmerton Rd., Clearwater, FL 34622
(813) 577-7000, (800) EVA-TONE
James M. Dunne

Eva-Tone Soundsheets has been producing high quality, low cost flexible vinyl phonograph discs for more than 20 years. These Soundsheets are used in direct mail, magazines (advertising and editorial), employee communications, education, and as premiums. They also are used as audio pages in corporate annual reports. Eva-Tone has recently expanded its capabilities in printing, bindery and lettershop services, and can provide turnkey service from mechanical art to mailing. High speed, quality audio cassette duplicating is now available also, plus the unique capability of machine inserting audio cassettes into 10 envelopes for mass mailing.

Products and services of Eva-Tone include various sizes of Soundsheet, audio cassettes, printing, bindery, lettershop and all associated services. Creative consultation and production is also available.

The music on the Coca-Cola, Pan Am and other successful television commercials has been broadcast by many disc jockeys—at no charge to the sponsor and to their considerable delight. Various sponsors and publicists occasionally endeavor to create a popular record which includes a commercial reference or feature the music from a commercial. Most advertisers and publicists who try the Tin Pan Alley gambit usually fail to create a popular tune, as the mysteries of the popular music field are almost imponderable.

Attempts to create a tuneful ditty which incorporates a commercial plug or is linked to the music of a radio or TV commercial not only are likely to be unsuccessful, but also may occasionally backfire in terms of criticism from stations, particularly those which are not included on the advertiser's schedule. Still, the lure of cracking the "hit charts" is exciting, and publicists occasionally retain songwriters, vocal or instrumental groups and assorted agents and agencies in the entertainment business.

Most of the music campaigns are created for advertisers or advertising agencies. Occasionally, the client is wholly or partly from the public relations area. An excellent company which has the patience and expertise to work with neophytes is Purcell Productions, 484 W. 43 St., N.Y. 10036, phone (212) 279-0795. Don Purcell and his partner, Lou Carter, have created many successful singing commercials and other audio campaigns.

Here is an excerpt from the Purcell booklet, which is helpful to clients with limited advertising experience.

Pricing Policy

There are fixed costs: Studio fees and tape, plus union fees for musicians, singers, actors and announcers. Do not let the "Union" label scare you. Rates for local and regional usage are quite realistic. Using union people you are assured a choice of the best. Other than "name" artists, we can obtain the finest talent at scale rates. This little extra expenditure assures you performance that will make your commercial stand out from the run-of-the-mill.

We try to relate creative and production fees to usage, reach and frequency. We charge the small market client less than a major market client. Our fees are higher for regional and national accounts. We consider our contribution to the sales effectiveness of your broadcast campaign as important as the media on which it will be played and that there should be a relationship between cost and effective use.

Purcell charges a minimum of $1,000 for a development fee. Upon approval of the lyrics and music, the fee for production generally is a few thousand dollars.

The Purcell Client Background Questionnaire and Creative License also are extremely useful to public relations clients with limited experience in advertising. For example, the questionnaire discusses the variety of formats, including contemporary, standard pop, march, a cappella, country, jazz, show-tune, hard rock, soft rock, dixie, nostalgia and others.

Here, in full, is the licensing agreement used by Purcell.

Creative License

TO: AGENCY _____ CLIENT _____

ADDRESS _____ ADDRESS _____

We at Purcell Productions are pleased to prepare Creative Material in Sound for the above-named client/ agency, as follows: Singing Commercial(s)_____Comedy/Production Campaign____Underscoring(s)__ A/V Sound Track(s)____Corporate Song(s)____Other_____

For use in the following medium: Radio (   ) TV (   ) Other (   )

In consideration of the sum of $_____, we license you to exclusive use of the above material for the period of one year from the date of the first air use on the indicated medium in the following trade and marketing territory_____

This license shall be extended to use on an additional medium (radio _____ TV _____) in the same marketing territory for an additional fee of $_____ for the first year.

This license shall be extended beyond the first year for a continuance fee of $_____ for radio, and $_____ for TV for each successive year.

Since the material we develop is created exclusively for you, and is so personalized as to be unusable for resale, we must request an advance payment of $_____ prior to the submission of either demonstration or finished material. Upon your final approval of the material subjected, this advance payment will apply to the full licensing fee specified above. Payment is due within ten business days of the date of approval.

Unless otherwise specified, Purcell Productions owns the copyright or has usage rights to any musical material used in the above described production. We have exclusive authority to grant the above-stated license(s). All copyright (including performance rights) remains the property of Purcell Productions. Any changes in the above are subject to acceptance by an officer of Purcell Productions.

FOR: PURCELL PRODUCTIONS, INC.   FOR: LICENSEE

Representative _____ Date _____   By _____ Title _____

Accepted by _____ Title _____   Date of Agreement ___ Date of Final Approval ___

Chapter 28

Research

The most significant result of the "information explosion" of the 70's was the development of information databanks and other services which are directly oriented to the needs of public relations clients.

In the 80's, the Information Age really arrived. Thousands of public relations practitioners now use a dazzling variety of research services and techniques, ranging from computer scanning of publications to focus groups, opinion surveys and dozens of other forms of quantitative and qualitative research.

The biggest changes relate to computers and database research services. However, not all research requires a computer, nor are large expenditures the sine qua non of research. (Have you noticed that the subject of research inevitably produces esoteric vocabulary?)

The public library, the telephone (particularly free 800 numbers) and hundreds of associations and other resources are easy to use and require a minimum of time and money. All you need is the orientation to appreciate the value of research and an awareness of the ways to get help.

Many Government agencies provide free and low-cost information. For example, the Commerce Department operates the New Product Information Service and the World Trade Data Reporting Service; the Bureau of Economic Analysis publishes Business Conditions Digest and Survey of Current Business, and the Library of Congress issues Science Tracer Bullets.

It sometimes takes many weeks to receive data, however, and public relations clients often prefer to pay a Washington researcher or other intermediary. Now, database services have changed this, and information can be obtained in a few minutes.

In fact, some newcomers to computers go overboard and become overly dependent on their terminals. The result can be too much time seeking out unnecessary or redundant data. You can run up a bill of several hundred dollars for a bibliographic compilation and still not know what to do about the specific public relations assignment.

In the 50's and 60's, several public relations counselors heralded the era of scientific communications and the marriage of public relations and the social sciences. Predictions were made about the harnessing of computer technology and anticipated breakthroughs which would enable the successful engineering of consent.

In the 70's, the use of opinion research, focus groups and many types of surveys progressed in advertising and marketing. They were utilized by a few public relations professionals, notably in politics.

Now, in the 80's, the public relations field is a major user of research techniques. However, many practitioners who acknowledge the need for research still claim that they lack the time and money to research and analyze a problem before recommending a solution.

One of the country's leading public relations researchers is Sharyn Mallamad Sutton, Ph.D., who is senior vice president in charge of the research departments of Doremus Porter Novelli (described later in this chapter). She notes that research can be a significant component of several major areas of a public relations program, including:

Identifying and defining the right audience;
Developing strategies and positioning for issues, products, services and organizations;
Identifying message concepts and refining executions;
Tracking progress and measuring program effectiveness.

Here's her view about tracking publicity within a public relations program:

The ultimate goal is not simply to obtain a large number of clippings and other publicity, but rather to communicate an image or information to a target audience through the media. However, by quantifying and evaluating the publicity process and outcome, we understand the current media environment for planning purposes, track progress and assess what message gets out there. Once we quantify the publicity effort, we can relate it back to our audiences to measure our contribution and impact.

Research services also are useful in identifying and analyzing media outside of the U.S.

International online news products have become increasingly important and accessible. The major American vendors offer overseas newspapers or newswires, in full text or concise abstract. For example, DataTimes provides full-text coverage of some Australian newspapers and the Canadian newspapers carried by Infomart. Several vendors offer the Kyodo News Service from Japan, as does NewsNet, which also carries the Xinhua English Language News Service, China Express, Japan Weekly Monitor and Asian Intelligence. Information Access Co. presents the U.K. Finsbury Data Services databases. Finsbury's Textline is a compendium of 120 newspapers from Europe and other continents.

VU/TEXT makes available Canadian databases and the far-reaching Datasolve World Reporter. Datasolve includes the BBC Summary of World Broadcasts, the World Importer file of overseas periodicals, the World Exporter business file on companies and products, and Magic, the public relations and marketing file.

Other international services worth noting include Data-Star, the Swiss database vendor that, in addition to providing extensive international business and wire service files, carries the full text of some publications that cannot be found elsewhere online, and the Nikkei Telecom Service, a thorough source of English-language Japanese business and financial news.

Many database services offer some of the same materials, such as the major wire services. Usually, there's not much duplication in coverage of major newspapers, since exclusive arrangements are made between the vendors and the newspapers. A notable exception is The Washington Post, part of which is available on several vendors, including The Source. (The databases containing The Post usually carry only material generated by Post writers, not other wire service stories printed in the newspaper.) Information Access, on DIALOG, and BRS provide a time-saving index to several newspapers, including The New York Times, The Wall Street Journal, Los Angeles Times, Christian Science Monitor and Washington Post.

Doris Lindell of Doremus Porter Novelli, New York, is one of the most experienced researchers in the entire public relations field. That's a broad statement. Its validity is confirmed by the following extraordinarily useful advice about saving time and money with database services.

Before you set up your computerized library, try to assess your needs by keeping a record of visits to libraries, telephone inquiries, purchases of back copies and requests made to research companies.

Obtain comprehensive brochures and spec sheets from database services, particularly the ones that are popular with public relations clients, such as VU/TEXT, DataTimes, DIALOG, Dow Jones News/ Retrieval, NewsNet, NEXIS and The Source.

Find out about free trial or short-term service. Some vendors provide option plans depending on your anticipated usage. When signing up for the service, choose the option requiring no minimum usage. When your needs for the material provided have increased, ask the vendor to switch you to the cheaper, pay-as-you-use, option. (In this case, you generally will want to guarantee the provider you will use the service a minimum amount of time each month, usually about one hour.) Occasionally, a vendor, such as NewsNet, will permit you to pay the subscriber fee on a yearly basis, rather than monthly. If you've clearly established your use of this database, a yearly fee can represent a savings. Sometimes the services, such as The Source, offer sign-up specials and discounts on user guides. Some database producers and the major vendors provide classes at selected locations at reasonable fees and, in some instances, for free. Another producer has a self-instruction videotape available.

Make sure you have compatible equipment and the correct software with proper settings. The modem should operate at 1,200 baud if using Dialnet. Use a data grade phone line. There should be no interruption by incoming telephone calls. Your costs for a search could double if you are bumped off the line in the middle of a search. Don't let other people talk to you or distract you while searching. Remember, time spent on line is money: One database costs $300 an hour. If you are having trouble getting online and you've verified all protocol settings, it may simply be a problem with the packet-switching network. Have your database vendor give you the telephone number of another network. Try to use the system at a time of day when everyone in your area is not attempting to log on at once. (Some vendors provide discounts between 6 P.M. and 8 A.M.) Download material, when you can, to save online time.

When you start using the services, monitor the costs carefully. Study the procedures and practice the log-on routines. Memorize the network telephone numbers and your passwords for each system. The numbers and procedures for using the packet-switching networks (e.g., Telenet and Tymnet), as well as the access methods may be changed, supplemented or streamlined every few months so it can be a waste of time and money to use out-of-date instruction sheets. When in doubt, call the toll-free 800 number the vendor maintains for customer service.

DIALOG also provides "Blue Sheets" of database descriptions of the actual database products. These sheets contain considerable information for the searcher, including the address and phone number of the producer, contents, date range available and the correct formats to use, depending on whether you want a citation or full text. (Costs of formats selected can vary tremendously, from no charge to $100 for special items.)

Prepare the assignment before you turn on the meter. Each online minute adds to the cost, so compile a list with all of the key terms, search strategy and proper names with spelling variations before you go online. It would be helpful to jot down how much time you expect the search to take in advance. If the search is taking too long, perhaps the database won't be loaded with the material you want until early the next day, or possibly you've been given the wrong spelling of proper names. The "Expand" feature on DIALOG can help you quickly locate how a company name, for example, is spelled in a particular database.

The more advanced systems (VU/TEXT, for example) let you key in your reference code at the beginning of the search. When your project is completed, it will print out your reference and time and charges online. The next time you do a similar search, you can try to accomplish it in a shorter time.

Remember that most systems are designed and searched differently. The search strategy that works in one may have to be changed for the next database you use. The rules of one vendor differ greatly from another. One provider charges the searcher an additional three dollars every time one letter in a search is modified. Another vendor permits up to two hundred modifications in the search without additional charge. DataTimes charges for time spent on menus; Vu/Text does not.

Information-gathering is now automated, but the most important component is the live person who is the researcher.

Originally the vendors designed databases to accommodate searchers in the social sciences. Now the needs of public relations clients are being met with increasing competitiveness among the vendors. New databases and new services are added each month. Global searching of several newspapers and many magazines at once has become available.

A pleasant, easy-to-read introduction to the various services is provided in Online Access Guide magazine, available on newsstands or by subscription ($24.95 for one year) from Online Access Guide, 5615 W. Cermak Rd., Cicero, IL 60650.

For new subscribers, the first database to try could be The Source and, second, NewsNet. You will receive a few major wire services, The Washington Post, columnists (e.g., Jack Anderson), publications such as The American Banker, and timely newsletters on many industries and topics. Then, consider VU/TEXT and DataTimes, which are two of the most innovative full-text newspaper and wire service vendors in the U.S.

Next on the agenda should be DIALOG, which offers a great variety of all kinds of information, including the index and full text of consumer and trade publications. DIALOG charges $25 yearly and provides its own network for access time at a more nominal cost than either Telenet or Tymnet. If you have built up a sufficient budget for online research, then bring in the broad, retrospective range of coverage that NEXIS provides.

Be careful when signing up for overseas services. Your need for these may be only occasional, especially in the beginning. One or two requests for information on European or Japanese companies does not establish a clear need for the service of foreign vendors. It may not be essential to pay the sign-up fee required by one overseas database service, or the ongoing monthly minimum for yet another, if your usage is only sporadic. (A monthly subscription fee can add up to more in a year's time than the one-time sign-up charge asked by another vendor.)

Password access that you would pay for now may come to you for free if you shop around or wait a few months until additional inducements are offered to new subscribers. An American vendor, VU/TEXT, offers a free password to Datasolve and the QL Canadian databases. DataTimes provides some Canadian newspapers, such as The Vancouver Sun, and three Australian newspapers without charging an additional subscriber fee. If you are convinced you'll need abundant overseas materials, look into Datasolve, Finsbury's Textline and Data-Star.

The wire services are almost immediately accessible on the database services. For example, Reuters financial and around-the-world news is now delivered via satellite to DIALOG (File 611). It is available within two hours of release with "flashes" announcing important news during the day.

If you've scheduled a morning news conference that will be attended by reporters from the wire services, here is a practical procedure to follow to pick up the articles you anticipate. First, the day before the conference, put your search terms in the NewsFlash section of NewsNet. By this method, you can monitor PR Newswire and United Press International. Later in the afternoon of the conference day, search The Associated Press and UPI on The Source. (There used to be a 48-hour embargo on Associated Press stories on the database services. This has gradually given way.) If your article is not sufficiently national in scope to be on The Source, then you may want to wait until early the next morning and search AP on VU/TEXT.

You can easily and inexpensively search national, regional and state UPI wires on The Source. It is often possible to locate an article on a state UPI wire when the search on the national wire hasn't been productive. Select the state that might have contributed the dateline. If your client is headquartered in another state, or if an important part of the client's research was done elsewhere, or if a reporter was in attendance from another state, don't be satisfied with just checking the national wires. The chances are the story may originate at the state level and then possibly be carried nationally later.

With DIALOG's addition of the First Release news service (Files 600, 610, 611 and 613), real time wire service news releases are available for Reuters, Business Wire, PR Newswire, McGraw-Hill and other major newswires. The databases are updated every 15 minutes. To use the latest update of a file, simply key in UD=9999.

Then, within 24 to 48 hours after your news event, look on NEXIS, where you'll find newspapers such as The New York Times and the major wire services. Your Dow Jones News/Retrieval and Wall Street Journal articles can also be found on DataTimes. By monitoring the media in this way, you can find out quickly the initial range of print coverage you've generated.

Thank you, Miss Lindell. Now that you have become a "computerized researcher," let's not forget the noncomputer resources!

Research still can encompass spending a few hours reading back issues of newspapers, magazines and other publications in a nearby public library. A similar type of background research consists of going through corporate files, publicity scrapbooks and correspondence. This type of research may provide helpful information and clues to problem solutions, but it is more in the nature of background briefing rather than exploring new areas.

Too many public relations practitioners rely on their own well-stocked memories and files and lack basic reference books. Almost every office includes an abridged dictionary as its primary reference book, but even a small publicity operation should consider one or more of the following reference books as being equally essential.

(1) Unabridged Dictionary. There's quite a difference between Merriam-Webster and Random House, as well as distinct variations among other well-known unabridged dictionaries, and purchasers should consider convenience, number of words, style and other factors which are considerably more important than price.

The dictionary most commonly used by media people (such as the wire services) is Webster's New Ninth Collegiate Dictionary of the English Language (Merriam-Webster). Another popular, easy-to-read book is the American Heritage Dictionary. Of course, lexicographers prefer the unabridged Webster's Third New International and the Oxford English Dictionary, and major offices should consider this investment. You can join the Book-of-the-Month Club and get the two-volume compact edition of the Oxford at a bargain price.

(2) Encyclopedia. A journalistic axiom is "check your facts." You may not need a complete set of the Encyclopaedia Britannica in your office, but there are several handy, low-cost sources of statistics and other factual data which should be available to you. Take your pick, for example, between the World Almanac and Book of Facts and the Information Please Almanac or, since they are so cheap and handy, buy both. Another bargain is the one-volume Concise Columbia Encyclopedia.

(3) Word Books. For speech writers and all types of authors, Bartlett's Familiar Quotations, Roget's Thesaurus and other classics not only are indispensable reference sources but also provide reading pleasure. As with all reference books, each edition includes a considerable amount of revision and new material and usually is preferable to outdated editions.

Though not as well known as Roget's, a treasure of a thesaurus is The Synonym Finder (Rodale Press), originally edited by J. I. Rodale and revised by Laurence Urdang.

Other books for writers and editors include The Oxford Dictionary of Quotations, Oxford Reference Dictionary, The St. Martin's Press Dictionary of Biography, The Penguin Dictionary of Quotations, The Penguin Dictionary of Proverbs and Harper & Row's International Thesaurus of Quotations. The Oxford University Dictionary of Information Technology ($29.95) provides comprehensive coverage of technical jargon and computerese.

Major public libraries have most of these books. Take a look at them to help you decide which books to purchase.

(4) Stylebooks. These are discussed in the chapter on literary services. If you want to research the subject, consult American Usage and Style: The Consensus ($12.95, Van Nostrand Reinhold) by Roy Copperud, the journalism professor at the University of Southern California who wrote many hundreds of columns on usage for Editor & Publisher.

In summary, the increasing use of database research services by public relations people is commendable and necessary. But print reference publications still are vital. Besides it's a lot easier, cheaper and more fun to browse through an encyclopedia or other reference book and use it as an idea stimulator and not just for fact-checking.

During the last few years, several major publishers have issued readable, attractive, useful reference books of the Whole Earth Catalog type. Some of these are more entertaining and less comprehensive than "standard" reference books, while others are original and fill a need.

The National Directory of addresses and Telephone Numbers ($34.95), edited by Geri Hardy, pulls together more than 150,000 numbers of Government offices, media, hotels, hospitals, carriers and other agencies and companies. (See alphabetical listing.)

Names and Numbers, compiled by Ron Nordland, lists over 20,000 names with direct lines and home phones ($59.95, John Wiley & Sons, N.Y., 1986). Bantam and other paperback publishers have lower-priced directories of this type, and one simple, pleasant way to select the book or books which meet your needs and budget is to visit a bookstore. If you are searching for out-of print books, try Book Look, 51 Maple Ave., Warwick, NY 10990, phone (914) 986-1981.

The well-stocked public relations library can include dozens of other atlases, lists and reference books. However, the resources of the largest corporate research department do not equal the facilities of major public libraries. Some practitioners also have access to private, business and other specialized libraries, such as the Morgan Library, 29 E. 36 St., N.Y. 10016, and the Engineering Societies Library, 345 E. 47 St., N.Y. 10017.

The Public Relations Society of America maintains an Information Center for its members at PRSA headquarters, 33 Irving Place, N.Y. 10003. Contact the Center for professional help. PRSA members, and others, also are urged to supply the Information Center with copies of books, annual reports and other materials.

Many public libraries now provide computerized literature searches free or at very low cost, often over the phone.

Major libraries maintain separate departments and branches for various specialties, and you should get to know your local library.

Many private libraries are open to the public, for example, the library of the Chemists' Club, 52 E. 41 St., N.Y. 10017, is available for use by the business researcher Monday through Friday, 9 A.M. to 5 P.M., at no charge.

Who's Who in Special Libraries is a useful and inexpensive resource at $25, available from the Special Libraries Association, 1700 Eighteenth St., N.W., Washington, DC 20009.

Associations offer a variety of free publications and reference aids. The standard directory of associations is the Gale Research Co. Encyclopedia of Associations, which is described in this chapter.

Columbia Books, 1350 New York Ave., N.W., Washington, DC 20005, publishes National Trade and Professional Associations, an annual collection (about 400 pages, $50) of data about 6,200 U.S. associations. (See separate listing.)

The U.S. Chamber of Commerce conducts studies and sells reports to nonmembers. The Chamber's Survey Research Center is at 1615 H St., N.W., Washington, DC 20062.

The catalog of the American Bankers Association, 1120 Connecticut Ave., N.W., Wash., D.C. 20036, phone (202) 663-5221, includes the following publications (the price is for nonmembers; ABA members pay less):

Effective Public Relations and Communications ($49.90)
How to Determine Your Image and Your Competitor's ($25)
Sales Promotion for Banks ($35)
Selling Bank Services (seminar, $18)
Thesaurus of Financial Services Marketing Terms ($30)

A Directory of Public Information Contacts in Washington, DC, is published annually by Martin Marietta Corporation, 6801 Rockledge Dr., Bethesda, MD 20817. The 80-page booklet is free!

Several services and directories about the Federal Government are listed in this chapter. The Capital Source, a directory of 7,000 individuals in Government, media, associations and other groups, is published ($20) by the National Journal, 1730 M St., N.W., Washington, DC 20036.

The Federal Database Finder, a directory of 4,200 databases or files available from the Federal Government, is published ($125) by Information USA, 4701 Willard Ave., Chevy Chase, MD 20805.

Research is vital to fund raisers.

The standard reference book for fund raisers is The Foundation Directory, which lists more than 5,500 foundations, including name, address, officers and directors, aims, activities and financial information, arranged by state. The eleventh edition was published in the fall of 1987 by The Foundation Center, 79 Fifth Ave., N.Y. 10003. The $85 price is a bargain.

Other publications of The Foundation Center include Foundation Grants to Individuals (fifth edition, 1986, $18) and computerized listing of foundation grants by subject ($18 per category). The computerized files of the Center are available through DIALOG Information Services. Associate membership in the Center ($325 a year) provides telephone reference and computerized search services.

The Council on Foundations publishes Foundation News ($29.50 a year), which includes in each bimonthly issue grant-making plans and developments in the nonprofit sector.

Note that the Council on Foundations is a separate organization and is located at 1828 L St., N.W., Washington, DC 20036, phone (202) 466-6512. (The Council and Center previously were in the same building in New York.) Additional information about The Foundation Center is included in a separate listing in this chapter.

Information and ratings of nonprofit organizations can be obtained from the National Charities Information Bureau (formerly National Information Bureau), an independent agency formed in 1918 and now located at 19 Union Square West, N.Y. 10003, phone (212) 929-6300. This extraordinary organization provides, on written request, a current copy of its Wise Giving Guide and up to three of its reports on individual nonprofit organizations. The material is provided without charge. Contributors to NCIB may request unlimited reports on the phone or by mail. The NCIB Standards of Philanthropy are described in a 40-page booklet which is available for $4. Other useful publications include A Grantmaker's Guide ($7.50) and the Volunteer Board Member in Philanthropy ($4).

Following is a summary of the NCIB Basic Standards in Philanthropy:

1. **Board**—An active and responsible governing body, holding regular meetings, whose members have no material conflict of interest and serve without compensation.
2. **Purpose**—A clear statement of purpose in the public interest.
3. **Program**—A program consistent with the organization's stated purpose and its personnel and financial resources, and involving interagency cooperation to avoid duplication of work.
4. **Expenses**—Reasonable program, management and fund-raising expenses.
5. **Promotion**—Ethical publicity and promotion excluding exaggerated or misleading claims.
6. **Fund Raising**—Solicitation of contributions without payment of commissions or undue pressure, such as mailing unordered tickets or merchandise, general telephone solicitation and use of identified government employees as solicitors.

7. **Accountability**—An annual report available on request that describes program activities and supporting services in relation to expenses and that contains financial statements comprising a balance sheet, a statement of support/revenue and expenses and changes in fund balances, a statement of functional expenses and notes to financial statements, that are accompanied by the report of an independent public accountant. National organizations operating with affiliates should provide combined or acceptably compiled financial statements prepared in the foregoing manner. For its analysis NCIB may request disclosure of accounting treatment of various items included in the financial statements.

8. **Budget**—Detailed annual budget approved by the governing body in a form consistent with annual financial statements.

Douglas M. Lawson Associates, Inc., is a fund-raising organization at 39 E. 51 St., N.Y. 10022, phone (212) 759-5660, which publishes The Foundation 500 ($32.50), a triennial directory that analyzes grants given by the top 500 foundations, and The Philanthropic Trends Digest, a bimonthly newsletter ($48 a year). Dr. Lawson conducts workshops and provides fund-raising counsel. Craig A. Harris is director of client services.

A variety of extremely useful fund-raising publications is published by the Taft Corporation, 5130 MacArthur Blvd., N.W., Washington, DC 20016, (202) 966-7086. Ask for a catalog.

The Taft organization is one of the most creative and successful fund-raising counselors, and its orientation often is to set up newsworthy events in behalf of universities and other large clients.

Another type of company, The Fund-Raising Institute, publishes several publications that are relatively low-priced and particularly helpful to small, nonprofit organizations and neophyte fund raisers. FRI, which is at Box 365, Ambler, PA 19002, phone (215) 628-8729, also publishes the Greater Philadelphia Publicity Guide ($35.75) and its publications are described in the chapter on media directories.

The membership lists of associations often can be obtained free, and these can be useful items for your reference files. Many publishers, outdoor and transit advertising companies, and radio and television stations, publish promotional brochures that often include market data and other valuable reference material.

McGraw-Hill will contract to do research studies for a fee. Contact the director of research, at 1221 Ave. of the Americas, N.Y. 10020, phone (212) 512-3517.

Several publishers of trade publications also issue directories and other reference books. For example, Crain Communications, 740 N. Rush St., Chicago 60611, publisher of Advertising Age, operated Crain Books, which publishes books on advertising, marketing and communications. In 1985, Crain Books became an imprint of NTC Business Books, published by National Textbook Co., 4255 W. Touhy Ave., Lincolnwood, IL 60646, phone (800) 323-4900.

Leo Shull Publications, 1501 Broadway, N.Y. 10036, publisher of Show Business ($35 a year; $55 for two years) since 1941, publishes:

Film Angels. Annual list of names and addresses of investors in films and shows, including amounts. Useful in fund raising. $75.
Theatre Angels. $75.
Models Guide. Agencies, photographers and producers who use models. $5.
Summer Theatre Directory. Published annually in March. $12.
How to Break into Show Business. $5.
Show Kids. $5.

A few major newspapers also maintain libraries and reference departments which are open to the public. In the 70's, the New York Daily News and The New York Times closed their free information services.

The Wall Street Journal Index is available monthly and in annual volumes from Dow Jones Indexes, Box 455, Chicopee, MA 01021, phone (413) 592-7761. The Monthly WSJ Index is $410, the WSJ/ Barron's Annual Index, $375, or $685 for both.

Books which are "directories to directories" are:

Guide to American Directories, a 600-page description of 8,000 directories of Government agencies, business reference books and other information sources, published by B. Klein Publications, Box 8503, Coral Springs, FL 33065, phone (305) 752-1708, for $75. Bernard Klein also publishes Guide to American Educational Directories and Guide to American Scientifica and Technical Directories.

American Reference Books Annual, edited by Bohdan S. Wynar and published every spring since 1970 by Libraries Unlimited, Inc., Box 3988, Englewood, CO 80155, phone (303) 770-1220. For $70, you can obtain critical reviews and appraisals by 325 specialists of over 1,700 reference books, arranged by categories, including advertising and public relations. Libraries Unlimited also publishes Fund-raising, Grants and Foundations: A Comprehensive Bibliography ($27.50) and Educational Media Yearbook ($50).

Business Information Sources ($40, University of California Press) is an annotated guide to books and reference sources; phone (800) 822-6657.

An offbeat directory, unknown to most city slickers, is the County Agents Directory, published annually since 1915. The book lists Extension personnel including county agricultural agents, home economists, 4-H agents and university specialists who act as consultants to farmers. Many of these people conduct radio programs and use booklets and publicity materials. The book is $19.95 from Century Communications, Inc., 6201 W. Howard St., Niles, IL 60648, phone (312) 647-1200.

Another bargain is Statistical Abstract of the U.S., prepared by the Bureau of the Census of the U.S. Department of Commerce and available for $22 from the Superintendent of Documents, Government Printing Office, Washington, DC 20402, (202) 275-2051.

For general information about Government agencies and sources of help, telephone (202) 245-6000, and also see the listing, later in this chapter, for the U.S. Government Printing Office. Books and pamphlets may also be ordered from the Superintendent of Documents through an office of the U.S. Government Printing Office in New York, Room 110, 26 Federal Plaza, N.Y. 10278-0081, phone (212) 264-3825. For example, the Standard Industrial Classification Code directory is $24. A Consumer's Resource Handbook, giving addresses of numerous agencies, is free from the Consumer Information Center, Pueblo, CO 81009.

In addition to thousands of U.S. Government publications, countless directories and other publications are produced by state and local governments. For example, the City of New York publishes an annual Green Book, a pocket-size directory with more than 6,000 names, numbers and addresses of officials at 900 units of city, state and Federal government offices. It's $8.50 from Citybooks, 2223 Municipal Building, N.Y. 10007.

The same office also publishes The City Record, a five-times-a-week newspaper with announcements of legislation, proposals and other notices. An annual subscription is $250.

A similar type of publication also is published by the Federal Government, as well as many cities and states. New York City also issues a Directory of Women's Organizations ($7.50). Again, this type of book is available from other cities throughout the country. While you are buying your collection of New York City publications, please consider a Big Apple pin ($4) and an I Love New York T-shirt ($4).

Here's a list of Washington, DC, phone numbers (all are area code 202), which are particularly useful to public relations people.

White House	456–1414
President's Schedule (recording)	456–2343
First Lady's Schedule (recording)	456–6269
Capitol Hill	224–3121

Democrat Congressional News (recording)	225–1600
Republican Congressional News (recording)	225–2020
Foreign Press Center (recording of events)	724–1635

Many colleges conduct market research and other services for outside clients. For example, the Center for Business Research of Long Island University, Brookville, NY 11548, phone (516) 299-2833, sells copies of its studies, as described in its free monthly newsletter, Business Alert.

Reference books which provide detailed information about publications, radio and TV stations are described in the section on media directories. The Public Relations Society of America and the Publicity Clubs in Boston, Chicago and Los Angeles conduct many courses and workshops on an immense variety of subjects and also include reference data in their newsletters.

The aforementioned books and services are found in very few corporate or agency libraries, but they are commonplace in public libraries. A writer should be familiar with the resources of the public library, because they are almost limitless with regard to public relations usefulness.

In addition to The New York Times Index and Wall Street Journal Index, the most common ''jumping-off point'' generally is the Reader's Guide to Periodical Literature. Two other valuable indexes which are not as commonly known are the Business Periodicals Index and the Funk & Scott Index (business articles, including newsletters and other special sources).

To take advantage of the axiom that ''man bites dog'' is news, publicists often look for offbeat facts, anecdotes and colorful material. To this end, useful reference books are Kane's Famous First Facts; The Guinness Book of Records; old editions of encyclopedias, such as the famous eleventh edition of the Britannica; Facts on File (available in almost every public library), and The People's Almanac (plus its various extensions, such as The Book of Lists).

One of the largest publishers of reference books is Gale Research Co., Book Tower, Detroit, MI 48226, phone (800) 223-GALE. Gale publishes many books which are useful to public relations people. One of them, the Encyclopedia of Associations, is absolutely indispensable. That's a bold statement, so here's a description of it. (A description of other Gale books appears in its alphabetical listing later in this chapter.)

The Encyclopedia of Associations is published in four volumes:

1. National Organizations of the United States. Detailed descriptions of national trade, professional and other organizations. This volume now is about 2,000 pages and actually appears as three books, Volume 1, part 1, part 2, and part 3, the index for Volume 1.
2. Geographic and Executives Indexes. Refers to material in Volume 1 and is arranged by states and also by names of executive directors and other individuals.
3. New Associations and Projects. Periodic reports listing additional associations.
4. International Organizations. Detailed descriptions of international trade, professional and other organizations.

In summary, Gale's Encyclopedia of Associations is one of the finest reference books of any type. Congratulations to Karin E. Koek and Susan Martin, editors, and the others at Gale Research Company.

Gale also publishes the Subject Directory of Special Libraries and Information Centers, which describes 18,000 facilities in five volumes ($160 each, $685 for the set). The five volumes are:

Business and Law Libraries, Education and Information Science Libraries, Health Sciences Libraries, Social Sciences and Humanities Libraries, and Science and Technology Libraries.

One of the reference books that is absolutely delightful to read is Celebrity Register. Published in 1985 by Doubleday, the 550-page book is more than worth its price. This is the fourth edition and, since about 10 years have elapsed between editions, do not wait for the next volume, and make the investment in this extremely useful book. The concept was originated by Cleveland Amory and Earl Blackwell, and the editor is Earl ("Mr. Celebrity") Blackwell. It's $75 from Celebrity Register, 1780 Broadway, N.Y. 10019.

Newspaper obituary writers, journalists, publicists and just plain hero-worshippers use Celebrity Register as an adjunct to Who's Who in America. Only about 1,800 people are listed in Celebrity Register, but each is shown with a photo and a biography which is an extremely well-written short essay, often with quotations, anecdotes and items which reflect the individual's distinctive personality.

Of course, the most famous reference books of contemporary biography are those published by Marquis Who's Who (founded 1899), 3002 Glenview Rd., Wilmette, IL 60091. The 1986–87 edition of Who's Who in America describes over 75,000 prominent men and women in two volumes, for $250.

Several of the Marquis Who's Who directories, including Who's Who in America, and Who's Who in Frontier Science and Technology, are available as outline databases through the DIALOG Information Services of Lockheed Corp.

Other Marquis biographical guides are published for regions of the U.S., lawyers, doctors, online and computer graphics professionals, women and other categories. There's also a Who Was Who in America and Who's Who in the World. The 1987–88 edition of Who's Who in Finance and Industry has over 21,000 biographies and is $165.

The name of the R. R. Bowker Co. is inseparable from the book trade in the United States. Its publications include Books in Print, Literary Market Place and Publishers Weekly—all essential tools of the industry.

In 1967, Bowker became a unit of the Xerox Corp. and increased and diversified its publications. Bowker was purchased, in 1985, by Reed Publishing U.S.A. Following are several Bowker reference books of value to public relations people. Standing order prices generally are 5% less.

American Book Trade Directory, annual, $149.95
American Library Directory, $149.95
Audio Video Market Place, annual, $65
The Bookman's Glossary, 6th edition, $29.95
Books in Print, annual, 7-volume set, $237.45
International Literary Market Place, annual, $110
Irregular Serials and Annuals, biennial, $159.50
Literary Market Place, annual, $75
Magazine Industry Market Place, $59.95
Publishers, Distributors & Wholesalers of the U.S., Annual, $85
Subject Guide to Books in Print, biennial, 3 volumes, $179.95
Ulrich's International Periodicals Directory, annual, $159.95
Who's Who in American Politics, 11th edition, $149.95
Who's Who in American Art, biennial, $94.50

The R. R. Bowker Company was founded in 1872 by Frederick Leypoldt, named after Richard Rogers Bowker who headed it until 1933, and currently Ira Siegel is president. Many of the Bowker publications are available online, in microfiche or CD-ROM, including Books in Print, which is updated throughout the year.

The checking of facts and other information searches constitute the day-to-day reference part of the research function of most public relations practitioners. Social scientists and other academicians are more inclined to stress a broader kind of research, and many who are concerned with advertising, marketing and sales consider the lack of adequate evaluation methods to be one of the major shortcomings in public relations.

Advertising professionals are more conditioned toward objective research, testing and evaluation than are public relations people. Several thousand psychologists, sociologists, statisticians, librarians and other professionals are engaged in staff or freelance work involving market research, consumer interviews, motivation analysis, testing and other research projects which are commonplace in the advertising field.

These same techniques can be extremely helpful in the public relations field, and practitioners should work with specialists in these research areas whenever possible. In addition to research companies, many business and social science professors and academicians are available for freelance assignments. For names of professional research organizations, consult with their various professional associations or check the classified telephone directory.

The Council on Economic Priorities, 30 Irving Place, N.Y. 10003, conducts research projects and publishes reports on corporate philanthropy, national security, environment and other significant issues. Individual donors ($25 to $100 a year) receive CEP studies, reports and newsletters. Alice Tepper Marlin is the founder and editor-in-chief of the CEP Newsletter.

Periodicals of Public Interest Organizations, a 58-page booklet that describes over 100 publications, was published ($6) in 1982 by the Commission for the Advancement of Public Interest Organizations, 1875 Connecticut Ave., N.W., Washington, DC 20009.

The Philip Lesly Company, 303 E. Wacker Dr., Chicago 60601, publishes Managing the Human Climate, a bimonthly newsletter which deals with sophisticated aspects of communication and public attitudes. Started in 1970 by one of the world's renowned public relations counselors, the newsletter is $22.50 a year. It's now a bargain as it's included as a supplement to pr reporter (Box 600, Exeter, NH 03833).

Ray E. Hiebert, a prominent public relations educator, is president of Communication Research Associates, Inc., which publishes Social Science Monitor ($85) and Public Relations Review ($29). The company is at 10606 Mantz Rd., Silver Spring, MD 20903. (See separate listing.)

The "Green Book," an international directory of marketing research companies, is published by the New York chapter of the American Marketing Association. The 500-page book is free to members and $50 to others, from the AMA at 310 Madison Ave., N.Y. 10017.

MacFarlane & Co., 1 Park Pl., Atlanta, GA 30318, publishes the International Directory of Market Research Organizations ($90), which lists 1,300 firms in 64 countries, and the International Directory of Published Market Research ($148), which lists 11,500 case studies.

A biweekly newsletter, started in 1984, on consumer marketing studies is "research alert" ($170 per year), at 30–87 37 St., Queens, NY 11103.

Several market and opinion research companies are described in this chapter. Following are summaries of 10 major companies in this field.

A. C. Nielsen Co., Northbrook, IL. Founded 1923. Since 1984, a subsidiary of Dun & Bradstreet. Renowned for supermarket audits and TV audience measurements.

IMS, N.Y. Founded in 1954. Specialists in drugs and health care throughout the world. IMS America is headquartered in Ambler, PA.

SAMI/Burke, Cincinnati. Founded in 1966. Subsidiary of Time Inc. Selling Areas-Marketing Inc. (SAMI) acquired Burke Marketing Services in 1986. The company provides data on the movement of food and drug products in 54 market areas, called SAMI markets.

Arbitron Ratings Co., N.Y. Founded in 1949. Since 1967, a subsidiary of Control Data Corp. Radio and TV audience data. In 1986, acquired Broadcast Advertiser Reports (BAR) and Radio-TV Reports.

Information Resources Inc., Chicago. BehaviorScan test market system and other services related to consumer products.

MRB Group, N.Y. Subsidiary of JWT Group (J. Walter Thompson advertising). Includes Simmons Market Research Bureau, founded in 1978, which is renowned for media studies.

M/A/R/C, Irving, TX. Founded in 1965. Survey research. Renowned for its panel of about 300,000 households.

NFO Research, Toledo, OH. Founded in 1946. Since 1982, a subsidiary of AGB Research. Renowned for its mail panel of about 900,000 individuals in 350,000 households. Specializes in apparel, beverages, carpeting, mail order and toys.

Market Facts, Chicago. Founded in 1946. Shopping mall interviews, mail interviews of a panel of 235,000 households, telephone and other market research.

NPD Group, Port Washington, NY. Founded in 1953. Diary panel of 14,500 households, including meal usage information.

Following are summaries of other market and opinion research companies of particular interest to public relations clients.

Maritz Marketing Research, Inc., St. Louis. Founded in 1973. Renowned for automotive and agriculture studies.

Yankelovich, Skelly & White/Clancy, Shulman, Westport, CT. Subsidiary of Saatchi & Saatchi. Shared-cost consumer surveys include Youth Monitor and Pacific Basin Monitor.

Chilton Research Services, Radnor, PA. Founded in 1957. Since 1979, subsidiary of Capitol Cities/ ABC. Conducts ABC election polls and a variety of custom research projects.

ASI Market Research, N.Y. Founded in 1962. Since 1983, a subsidiary of IDC Services. Specializes in testing of advertising and pilots of TV shows and movies.

Louis Harris and Associates, N.Y. Founded in 1956. Since 1975, a subsidiary of Gannett Co. Mr. Harris is a renowned pollster and syndicated columnist.

Opinion Research Corp., Princeton, NJ. Founded in 1930. Since 1975, a subsidiary of Arthur D. Little Inc. Surveys in which costs are shared and conducted biweekly and quarterly.

Gallup Organization, Princeton, NJ. Founded in 1935, headed by George Gallup Jr., son of the founder. Renowned for its Gallup Poll, which appears as a column in many newspapers.

Starch INRA Hooper, Mamaroneck, NY. Founded in 1923. Renowned for its audience studies of print advertising and media. Includes the Roper Organization.

J. D. Powers & Associates, Westlake Village, CA. Founded in 1968. Specializes in automotive studies.

A free copy of Agencies and Organizations Represented in AAPOR Membership can be obtained from the American Association for Public Opinion Research, Box 17, Princeton, NJ 08542, (609) 924-8670.

Dun & Bradstreet Corp., N.Y., which is best known for its credit reports, has acquired several companies of interest to public relations practitioners, including Moody's Information Services (described in the financial chapter). In England, D&B acquired (in 1984) Datastream, a major supplier of financial futures data and other financial information. In 1984, D&B also acquired the A. C. Nielsen Co.

Many shopping malls have meeting rooms, test kitchens, focus group rooms and other facilities. A chain of such facilities is operated by Quick Test Opinion Center, 400 Ernest Barrett Pky., Kennesaw, GA 30144, (404) 423-0884.

Many associations, universities and nonprofit organizations provide opinion research consultation and several actually conduct surveys for outside clients, including:

American Medical Association, 535 N. Dearborn St., Chicago 60610, (312) 645-5160, Mary Lou White, director of dept. of Survey Design and Analysis.

Behavior Science Laboratory, Institute for Policy Research, Univ. of Cincinnati, Cincinnati 45221, (513) 475-5028, Alfred J. Tuchfarber, dir.

Center for Public and Urban Research, Georgia State Univ., Atlanta, GA 30303, (404) 658-3523, John D. Hutcheson Jr., dir.

Center for Survey Research, Univ. of Nevada, Las Vegas 89154, (702) 739-3322, Donald E. Carns, co-dir.

The Eagleton Poll, Eagleton Institute of Politics, Rutgers Univ., New Brunswick, NJ 08901, (201) 828-2210, Cliff Zukin, dir.

Institute for Social Science Research, Univ. of California-Los Angeles, 405 Hilgard Ave., L.A. 90024, (213) 825-0712, Marilynn Brewer, dir.

National Network of State Polls, Univ. of Alabama, Box 587, Tuscaloosa, AL 35487, (205) 348-3824, Dana Stone.

Northwestern University Survey Lab, 625 Haven St., Evanston, IL 60201, (312) 491-5625, Paul Lavrakas, dir.

SRI International, 333 Ravenswood Ave., Menlo Park, CA 94025, (415) 4164, Susan Russell, dir. Formerly Stanford Research Institute.

Survey Research Center, Univ. of California-Berkeley, 2538 Channing Way, Berkeley, CA 94720, (415) 642-6594, Percy Tannenbaum, dir.

Survey Research Center, Institute for Social Research, Box 1248, Ann Arbor, MI 48106, (313) 764-8365, Howard Schuman, dir.

Survey Research Center, Univ. of Maryland, 1103 Art/Sociology Bldg., College Park, MD 20742, (301) 454-6800, John Robinson, dir.

Survey Research Laboratory, Univ. of Illinois, 910 W. Van Buren St., Chicago 60607, (312) 996-6130, Richard Warnecke, dir.

Wisconsin Survey Research Laboratory, Univ. of Wisconsin-Extension, 610 Langdon St., Madison, WI 53703, (608) 262-3122, Harvey Sharp, dir.

Outside of the U.S., many research organizations are familiar with U.S. techniques and conduct projects for U.S. clients. Here are two:

Datos, C.A., Apartado 5957, Zona 1010A (Carmelitas), Caracas, Venezuela, phone 979-5611, Andrew Templeton and Edmund Saade, managing directors. The largest market research company in South America.

Decision Marketing Research Limited, 661 Queen St., E, Toronto, Ontario M4M 1G4, Canada, (416) 469-5282, John Gonder, pres.

After many years of tests, videotext appears to be a useful communications and marketing medium. Among the commercial services are:

Agridata Network, a news service for farmers, produced since 1982 by Agridata Resources, Milwaukee, WI, and

Videolog, a service for the electronics industry, produced since 1984 by Videolog Communications, Norwalk, CT.

The most frequently used computerized database vendors include Lockheed's DIALOG, the National Library of Medicine (MEDLARS), Mead's INFOBANK (including the former New York Times Information Bank) and NEXIS, The Source, DataTimes, Dow Jones News/Retrieval, VU/TEXT, CompuServe, BRS and NewsNet. The following descriptions of these and other companies is the most comprehensive ever published in the public relations field. Other research services are listed in the financial chapter, and, of course, reference books are listed in the media directories chapter and throughout this book.

For example, Advertising & Marketing Intelligence (AMI) is an online database containing abstracts of articles from over 60 advertising, marketing and public relations publications. Subjects include new products, sales promotions and consumer trends. The database is available through Mead Data Central, which is described in this chapter. As with all listings, prices and other details change frequently.

The MARS (Marketing and Advertising Reference Service) database online with Predicasts is an excellent source for marketing information on many companies and products, including existing and planned campaigns.

For neophytes and others, some of these descriptions may be too technical. For example, many of the database services are available in different speeds, such as 300, 1200 or 2400 baud. And baud is simply a unit of speed in data transmission, as one bit per second for binary signals. If you still are confused about bits and bytes, don't be afraid. Computers do not bite, and most researchers (including salespeople for research services) will be happy to explain.

Also included in this chapter is information about management consultants who specialize in public relations. The largest company is this field is CommuniCorp.

So, here is the largest chapter in this book. You do not have to memorize it; you will not be quizzed; you do not have to read it in its entirety. Scan it with an eye to discovering nuggets of special relevance to your needs. Welcome to the public relations research era!

1. Katherine Ackerman and Associates
Box 1707, 403 Oxford, E. Lansing, MI 48823
(517) 332-6818
Katherine Ackerman

Katherine Ackerman is a former reference librarian for The Chicago Tribune. She now conducts computer-based research on a per-project basis for clients. Projects include document retrieval and online searches of over 300 databases, current awareness services for particular fields of interest, library research and the creation of targeted mailing lists.

Online database searches are $60 per hour plus computer costs and information consulting is $60 per hour, with a one-hour minimum. Ms. Ackerman offers seminars, from San Francisco and New York to London, on information brokering and databases for personal computer users. She previously published the newsletter, Modem Notes, which has been incorporated by Link-Up, published by Learned Information. (See separate listing.)

2. Advertising Age Research Service
Crain Communications Inc.
740 Rush St., Chicago 60611
(312) 649-5476, (800) 621-6877
Betty Betz

This service offers the most detailed index of Advertising Age available—the entire library of back issues. Each issue has been cross-indexed by category, product and subject. The service advises you on which date and page number you'll find the article needed and, if you don't have the back issue, an article copy is provided for 50 cents a page.

If you plan to use the service frequently and want to prepay, the $250 Search Package entitles users to $300 worth of searches and 25 pages of articles. The $500 Search Package provides $600 in searches and 25 copies of articles. For occasional users, the fee structure depends on how many years back your search goes; one year is $35 and two years, $40.

3. American Society for Information Science (ASIS)

1424 Sixteenth St., N.W., Wash., DC 20036
(202) 462-1000
Linda Resnik, Exec. Dir.

ASIS is a membership organization dedicated to the advancement of information science and technology.

Many of its members manage information programs, services and databases, or are in consulting and programming.

Members may join any of more than 20 special-interest groups to exchange ideas and information about developments in their subject areas. These groups range from office automation to international information issues, management, technology and society.

Membership dues are $75 per year, which includes the ASIS Bulletin, a bimonthly magazine, and the ASIS Journal, a bimonthly journal in information science and related fields. ASIS currently has more than 25 chapters in the U.S., Canada, Europe and Taiwan.

4. American Society of Association Executives (ASAE)

1575 Eye St., N.W., Wash., DC 20005
(202) 626-2723
Elissa M. Myers, Dir. of Member Services
Chris Condeelis, Mgr., Research and Information

If you are on the staff of an association, or work closely with trade, professional and other types of associations, you are familiar with ASAE and its catalog, Membership Services. Members pay considerably less (generally half) for dozens of publications, mailing lists and others services.

Who's Who in Association Management, a directory of 15,000 members of ASAE, $75
Editing Your Newsletter: A Guide to Writing, Design and Production, $20
How to Conduct Association Surveys, $30
How to Speak TV: A Self-Defense Manual When You're in the News, $15
Teleconferencing, $35
Association Communications in the 1990's, $30
Association Public Relations, $40
Readership Surveys, $40

5. Arbitron Ratings Company

142 W. 57 St., N.Y. 10019
(212) 887-1300
Anthony J. Aurichio, Pres.

For over 35 years, Arbitron, a division of Control Data Corp., has provided radio and television audience research to broadcasters, advertisers and agencies. In 1949, as the American Research Bureau, Arbitron was the first to use the written diary as a way to collect information on television viewing. By the late 1950s, the company had changed over from hand tabulation to computer data processing.

Arbitron measures audiences in 213 television markets and 259 radio markets. Arbitron first began to measure television audiences by an electronic meter system in 1958. Arbitron uses household meters to track television viewing on a continuous basis in 14 major markets.

In 1984, Arbitron developed the ScanAmerica Network, a syndicated research service that uses a people meter to electronically track television viewing of each individual and a portable UPC scanner to record product purchases by the household.

In 1986, Control Data acquired Broadcast Advertiser Reports, Inc. (BAR), a television commercial monitoring service. BAR provides competitive expenditure information and monitoring of network and spot broadcast advertising.

6. Ayer Information Center
1345 Ave. of Americas, N.Y. 10105
(212) 708-5181
Holly Bussey, Mgr.

Several public relations and advertising agencies provide research services to "outsiders" on special request. One of the best-organized operations is the Ayer Information Center, which started in 1965 as a department of the N W Ayer advertising agency. The Ayer Information Center has handled many assignments involving public relations, and coordinating and disseminating secondary sources and surveys. The basic fee structure is $80 per hour plus out-of-pocket expenses.

Founded over a century ago in Philadelphia as N W Ayer & Sons, the company is one of the oldest advertising agencies in the country. The Ayer public relations operation is a separate entity, located primarily in New York. The corporate name is now N W Ayer, Inc. (the only period is at the end).

7. BRS Information Technologies
1200 Route 7, Latham, NY 12110
(518) 783-1161, (800) 468-0908, (800) 553-5566, (800) 345-4BRS
Debbie Hull, V.P., Marketing

BRS, formed in 1976, is a subsidiary of Thyssen/Bornemisza, Monaco. This large online information utility has more than 140 databases, including business, education, science and medicine. The BRS Search System is a retrieval program that offers users an advanced way of acquiring information. It provides numerous business databases such as ABI/INFORM, Management Contents, Predicasts Annual Reports Abstracts and PTS PROMT and Industry Data Sources. BRS has the Harvard Business Review/ Online as well as other business publications.

The BRS Open Access plan costs $25 per hour connect time and a database royalty fee (varies with the database) plus telecommunications charges. The annual fee is $75. There are also various advance payment options reducing time charges to $12 per connect hour. Database royalties, network charges and offline printing are extra with these pricing plans.

BRS/After Dark is an evening hours, lower-cost service giving a condensed version of BRS databases in the social sciences, business and finance, and science and technology. It includes the Academic American Encyclopedia. After Dark is available through Tymnet and Telenet Networks. A $75 sign-up fee applies and there are $6 to $35 per hour connect-time charges, plus a monthly minimum for two hours' usage.

BRS/Colleague provides the full text of medical journals, Medline and other hard-to-find medical and pharmaceutical sources. For information call (800) 468-0908.

8. Daniel H. Baer, Inc.
3738 Glenridge Dr., Sherman Oaks, CA 91423
(818) 981-9030
Daniel H. Baer, Pres.

A long-time executive with the public relations firm of Harshe-Rotman-Druck, Dan Baer has been a management consultant to public relations agencies and companies since 1971. Most of his projects have centered around conducting attitude and communications audits in industry, government and the health-care field.

Mr. Baer is also involved in the development of first-time public relations programs; evaluations of existing programs and projects; locating, screening and hiring firms and personnel; structuring research and providing other services, including feasibility studies, acquisition and merger assistance, and helping to establish affiliate relationships, and time and cost controls.

9. Boeing Computer Services Company (BCS)

2800 160 Ave., S.E.., Bellevue, WA 98008
(206) 865-5166
Joseph L. Holmes, Dir. of Communications

Branch Office:
7980 Boeing Ct., Vienna, VA 22180
(703) 821-6505
John Alter, Communications Mgr.

Boeing Computer Services (BCS), a division of The Boeing Company, was created in 1970, consolidating 13 separate computing organizations. Six data centers are spread around the country. With 11,000 employees and more than $800 million worth of computing equipment, Boeing products and services cover the entire field of information.

Evans Economics Service provides over one million forecast and historical timeseries which cover the economy as a whole and specific sectors, and supplies the data needed to track the performance of the U.S. economy.

EIS includes data such as the Department of Commerce National Income and Product Accounts and Business Conditions Digest.

10. R. R. Bowker Company

245 W. 17 St., N.Y. 10011
(212) 337-6989
Ira Siegel, Pres.
Anthony Ferraro, V. P. Electronic Publishing

R. R. Bowker Company opened in 1872 in the offices of Publishers Weekly, the trade journal of the publishing industry. In 1968, Bowker became part of the Xerox Publishing Organization and was acquired in 1985 by Reed Publishing USA.

The company maintains the largest databank of U.S. bibliographic information on books, periodicals and microcomputer software. It is the U.S. headquarters for the International Standard Book Numbering Agency and the Standard Address Numbering System. The International Standard Book Number (ISBN) is printed on the copyright page of most books (including this one) as a convenience to librarians and book-buyers.

In 1982, Bowker expanded its database information system and, in 1984, established an electronic publishing division to facilitate the storage and retrieval of information in formats other than print and to provide related services. Most recently, Bowker began offering its products on CD-ROM (compact discs with read-only memory).

R. R. Bowker products include data on books, periodicals and microcomputer software; institutional, biographical and marketplace directories; handbooks and guides for the publishing, library and information fields; professional magazines and newsletters, and mailing list services.

Robert Allen is director of sales for Bowker Electronic Publishing. The Bowker directories now available electronically are:

Books in Print. A major source of trade information on books currently published and in print (as well as books going out of print) in the U.S. The file includes scholarly, popular and children's books, and scientific, technical and medical books. It contains records from 1900 to the present and lists books produced by 12,000 publishers. The database is available on DIALOG at $65 per online connect hour and at approximately the same cost on BRS. BOOKS IN PRINT is also available in CD-ROM.

American Men and Women of Science. A biographical registry of prominent, active American and Canadian scientists, this file includes about 130,000 scientists in over 65 broad scientific disciplines and 1,100 specialties. It is available on DIALOG at $95 per hour and BRS at $70 per hour.

Ulrich's International Periodicals Directory. The database version contains over 135,000 records and offers the R. R. Bowker Ulrich's print publication plus the contents of Irregular Serials and Annuals, Sources of Serials and Ulrich's Quarterly, with references to the publications of 65,000 publishers in 181 countries. Ulrich's can be used to verify titles and addresses, to build a publicity campaign or to give current awareness in broad subject areas. It is $65 per connect hour on DIALOG and about the same for an average user of BRS. Ulrich's is also available on CD-ROM.

The Microcomputer Software and Hardware Guide. This is a constantly updated record of virtually every microcomputer software program and hardware system available in the U.S. More than 30,000 entries from some 3,500 software publishers—with 4,000 new entries each year—cover all areas, including business and professional, educational, consumer, and utility programs. Microcomputer hardware and peripherals are also included in this database, which is available on DIALOG at $60 per connect hour.

Directory of American Research and Technology. This online database provides complete detailed listings of more than 11,000 R&D organizations in the U.S. One can locate laboratories, colleagues, clients and other data concerning them. The online charge is $95 per connect hour on Pergamon's InfoLine.

American Library Directory. This online service provides various information on American and Canadian libraries. Personnel, addresses, special collections, budget and other parameters are listed for over 34,000 libraries. The database is on DIALOG.

Publishers, Distributors, & Wholesalers of the U.S. This directory had the complete addresses and numbers for more than 44,000 U.S. publishers, 1,500 distributors, 1,500 wholesalers, 1,800 associations, 3,000 software publishers and more. It is updated monthly and is available through DIALOG Information Services at $66 per connect hour.

11. The Bureau of National Affairs, Inc. (BNA)

1231 25 St., N.W., Wash., DC 20037
(202) 452-4200, (800) 372-1033, (800) 862-4636
Telex: 89-2692
George Knight, V.P., Sales and Marketing

The Bureau of National Affairs, Inc. (BNA) is one of the nation's largest private publishers. For more than 50 years, BNA has provided information services in the fields of law, labor relations, tax, business and economics, environmental protection and other public policy issues.

BNA also provides business professionals with customized research; issue monitoring, and document delivery services, plus access to their collection of published and unpublished documents and electronic information services.

12. Cambridge Communications

7 Central St., Arlington, MA 02174
(617) 643-5700, (617) 646-4800
Steven Factor

In 1986, Cambridge Communications launched Media Map, a unique quarterly directory for public relations people in the computer field.

Each issue (a 700-page report in a three-ring binder) describes *in depth* computer publications and organizations, as well as other media.

Service for one year is $1,200.

13. Cambridge Reports, Inc.

657 Massachusetts Ave., Cambridge, MA 02139
(617) 661-0110
Gene Pokorny, Pres.

Several research firms provide opportunities for multi-client participation in their surveys. This often is particularly appealing to public relations clients because of the savings in time and money. One of the most successful companies in this arena is Cambridge Reports, which, of course, is in Cambridge, MA, a citadel of all types of research.

Formed in 1973, Cambridge Reports, Inc., conducts in-depth national consumer and public opinion surveys based on 1,500 interviews with scientifically selected samples of Americans. Each survey includes about 200 questions that measure public perceptions and attitudes about a spectrum of economic, public affairs, business and consumer issues. Each quarter, Cambridge Reports uses the collected data to produce three syndicated research programs (Cambridge Report, Quarterly Opinion Review and Quarterly Opinion Briefing) that are available on a modular subscription basis, allowing selective access.

The Omnibus and Consumer Public Opinion Surveys are conducted eight times a year, four are in person and four are by telephone. They measure public reactions to events, monitor trends and test reactions to alternate advertising themes, among other things. Each questionnaire contains questions purchased by individual clients for their proprietary use. Clients' results are analyzed by demographics, including household income, age, sex, marital status, education, locality (urban, suburban, rural) and geographic region. Printouts of a client's data are available about three weeks after completion of interviewing. The basic fee schedule for participating in an Omnibus survey is: one to 10 questions, $1,000 each; 11 to 20 questions, $950 each, and, 21 or more, $900 each. Discounts are given to clients who subscribe to the Cambridge Report, Quarterly Opinion Review or Quarterly Opinion Briefing.

14. Columbia Books, Inc.

1350 New York Ave., N.W., Wash., DC 20005
(202) 737-3777
Craig Colgate Jr., Chm.
Arthur C. Close, Pres.
John J. Russell, V.P.

A highly respected publisher for over 20 years of directories mostly related to our nation's capital, Columbia Books publishes an annual book titled Washington (followed by the year), which is described in the chapter on media directories. Other Columbia annual directories are:

National Avocational Organizations of the U.S. Information about 2,500 avocational, cultural, civic and recreational organizations. Published since 1981. $30.

National Directory of Corporate Public Affairs. Information about 11,000 public affairs people at 1,500 companies—lobbying, political actions, contributions. Published since 1982. $65.

National Trade and Professional Associations of the U.S. Information about 6,300 associations, societies and unions, plus 200 management firms. Published since 1946. $50.

Washington Representatives. Information about 11,000 lobbyists and other agents and advocates. Published since 1977. $50.

Compared with other reference books of this type, the prices of Columbia books are very low. Discounts are provided for prepaid orders and purchases of two or more books.

In 1987, Columbia Books launched Baltimore/Annapolis, a unique directory about 1,600 companies, associations and organizations in Maryland. It's $40. The data in this book, and other Columbia books, is available in mailing list form.

352

15. Communication Research Associates, Inc.

10606 Mantz Rd., Silver Spring, MD 20903
(301) 445-3230
Ray E. Hiebert, Pres.

Communication Research Associates is headed by Ray Hiebert, a professor of journalism and public relations at the University of Maryland. The company publishes Public Relations Review (a quarterly journal sponsored by the Foundation for Public Relations Research and Education, $29), Social Science Monitor (a monthly newsletter), Video Monitor (a monthly newsletter) and Hi-Tech Alert for the Professional Communicator.

Hi-tech Alert is a report on new technologies for public relations and advertising and is available in both print and electronic database form. It provides ''how to'' information for corporate communications executives and public relations agencies, as well as forecasting of long-term trends in such new technologies as cable TV, satellite, videotext and teletext, videoconferencing, computer applications and low-power TV.

The electronic version is available on NewsNet at $36 per connect hour for nonsubscribers to the publication and $24 for subscribers. CompuServe offers it online for the Public Relations Special Interest Group (PRSIG). (See separate listing.)

The print edition of the monthly Hi-Tech Alert costs $98 for an annual subscription.

16. CommuniCorp, Inc.

171 Madison Ave., N.Y. 10016
(212) 725-0000
Bill Cantor, Chmn.
Alfred Geduldig, Pres.

In 1982, Chester Burger & Co. merged with The Cantor Concern, an executive recruiter specializing in public relations. The combined company now is called CommuniCorp.

The Chester Burger division is the largest management consultant firm specializing in public relations. Its partners, particularly founder Chet Burger, are among the most prominent individuals in the communications field.

For corporate public relations, the firm assists in strategic communications planning (themes, issues), measuring performance, organization, budgeting and agency selection. For public relations agencies, it counsels on a variety of management problems. Its innovations include the development of media interview training in 1967 and video annual reports for employees.

Prior to starting the company in 1964, Chet Burger was national manager of CBS Television News and an executive at two public relations agencies.

17. CompuServe Information Service (CIS)

Box 20212, 5000 Arlington Centre Blvd., Columbus, OH 43220
(800) 848-8199
Charles W. McCall, Pres. and CEO
David J. Kishler, Supvsr., Corporate Communications

CompuServe, an H&R Block company, has a vast array of online services, including computerized clubs catering to people in a particular industry or affinity group, electronic conferencing, electronic mail, Standard & Poor's, Value Line, The Associated Press, The Washington Post and other resources.

It also offers company-sponsored electronic bulletin boards for Lotus, Microsoft, Borland and other computer products, as well as the Official Airline Guides Electronic Edition.

The CompuServe Information Service Subscription Kit retails at $39.95 and includes a $25 connect time credit, which may be necessary to wade through what is online with CompuServe.

The CompuServe Information Service has no monthly fees or dues. The Executive Service Option has a $10 per month minimum. Payment is for time used, with 300 baud prime daytime usage costing $6 an hour.

18. The Conference Board

845 Third Ave., N.Y. 10022
(212) 759-0900
Linette Waters, Supervisor, Fee-paid Information Services

The Conference Board, a research organization founded in 1916 and long known for its excellent membership library used by many corporations, also offers the Conference Board Data Base, which is available through the following vendors:

Data Resources Inc., (617) 863-5100
Interactive Data Corp., (800) 621-5103
Cornell University, (607) 255-5513

The database includes The Conference Board economic projections and forecasts, consumer attitudes and buying plans, business executives' expectations, capital expenditures and appropriations of the 1,000 largest manufacturers and investor-owned utility companies, as well as financial and labor market indicators. It also is available on diskettes for use with a PC.

The annual fee for online usage is $500 for Associates of The Conference Board and $650 for Non-Associates, plus computer usage fees paid to the timesharing vendor.

19. Consumer Pulse, Inc.

725 S. Adams Rd., Birmingham, MI 48011
(800) 336-0159
Ron Korno Kovich

Consumer Pulse is a Network of focus group rooms, telephone interviewing rooms, test kitchens and other research facilities in shopping malls and other sites.

20. Control Data/Business Information Services (BIS)

Box 7100, Greenwich, CT 06836
(203) 622-2070
Judith Rothrock, Public Relations, Mgr.

Control Data Corporation's Business Information Services (BIS) group provides software and computer services to major companies.

BIS develops and offers large application systems called Management Application Systems (MAS), which integrate and share specific data with multiple users at various locations to support management decision-making. In 1982, BIS introduced its MARKSMAN, designed for use by marketing professionals. BIS products can be delivered remotely or through a customer's in-house IBM mainframe or minicomputer.

21. Corporate Technology Information Services, Inc. (CorpTech)

Box 281, Wellesley Hills, MA 02181
(617) 237-2001
Telex: 497 2961
Andrew Campbell, Pres.
Charles T. Peers, Jr., Mng. Ed.

Formed in 1984, CorpTech publishes the Corporate Technology Directory and Corporate Technology Database, which lists over 17,000 U.S. manufacturers and researchers of high technology products. Companies can be referenced via company name, location, parent/subsidiary and product manufactured. CorpTech has developed the CorpTech Codes to classify high tech into over 4,000 product areas. The four-volume directory is available for $795, and the database, which is available on hard card or magnetic tape, retails for $7,500. The company is located in the Babson Building on Market Street.

22. Corsearch
19 W. 21 St., N.Y. 10010
(212) 627-0330

The Library of Congress in Washington, DC, does copyright searches for a small fee. Among the firms that do trademark searches is Corsearch. They offer Federal, state, common law, corporate name and drug name searches. Fees depend on which files are searched.

23. Cuadra/Elsevier
52 Vanderbilt Ave., N.Y. 10017
(212) 916-1180, (212) 916-1010
David Dionne, Marketing

The Cuadra/Elsevier Directory of Online Databases lists more than 3,400 online databases offered through over 500 services. Two main issues are provided each year, plus two updates. A one-year subscription is $130. It's also available online through WESTLAW and ORBIT.

The Directory is a joint venture of Cuadra Associates, Inc., and Elsevier Science Publishing Co., Inc. The editorial office is located at 11835 W. Olympic Blvd., Los Angeles 90064, (213) 478-0066, where Carlos A. Cuadra is president of Cuadra Associates.

24. DATANETWORK, Inc.
400 Embassy Sq., Louisville, KY 40299
(502) 491-1050
Don Brady, Pres.

For companies with test kitchens, DATANETWORK offers an online Nutrition Analysis System which gives a quick and reliable means of calculating the amounts of each nutrient in a given recipe or meal without the expense of laboratory processing. Within seconds, the analysis, including caloric content, is received directly on your terminal listing nutritional information per serving and per 100 grams. The price on the system is $3 per completed recipe with a $100 minimum per month.

DATANETWORK purchased the Pillsbury system from the Honeywell DATANETWORK time-sharing service in 1983.

25. DataTimes
14000 Quail Spring Pky., Oklahoma City, OK 73134
(405) 751-6400, (800) 642-2525
Brad Watson, Natl. Sales Mgr.

Formed in 1981 as a timesharing company, and acquired in 1983 by Oklahoma Publishing Co., DataTimes has become one of the nation's leading online information providers. They combine local, national and international newspaper databases with financial and economic sources.

Subscribers can access the databases of major metropolitan and national newspapers, including The Washington Post, USA Today, Chicago Sun-Times, The Daily Oklahoman, The Dallas Morning News, The Record, Houston Chronicle, The Minneapolis Star & Tribune, The Orange County Register, San Francisco Chronicle, The Seattle Times, St. Petersburg Times, plus Dow Jones News/Retrieval (which includes The Wall Street Journal), Barron's, Forbes, Financial World, Dow Jones News, Kyodo Newswire (Japan Economic Daily), Gannett News Service, PR Newswire, seven Canadian newspaper and financial databases, and three Australian newspapers.

There are two payment options. The first is $75 per hour of online time with minimum monthly usage of one hour. The second option is $105 per hour online time with no monthly minimum and a $12 per month service fee. A one-time sign-up fee of $75 applies to both options. International databases and Dow Jones News/Retrieval services cost about $160 per hour. DataTimes is available 24 hours a day, seven days a week.

26. Delphi

3 Blackstone St., Cambridge, MA 02139
(617) 491-3393, (800) 544-4005
Rusty Williams, Marketing Mgr.

Delphi was an ancient city in Greece. Its wise women (oracles) had the reputation of being obscure or ambiguous. Be that as it may (or may have been), Delphi today is a company that offers online access to databases of finances, stock quotes, investments, commodities, securities and travel. It is the information utility of General Videotex Corp.

It offers Naico-net, of the North American Investment Corp., an online brokerage permitting users to buy and sell securities. Delphi also provides current financial news and a gateway to DIALOG's research library. Electronic mail services are available to subscribers.

Connect time rates are $17.40 per hour from 7 A.M. to 6 P.M. and $7.20 per hour on evenings and weekends. There are no charges for telecommunications via Tymnet and Telenet and no monthly minimum. A price package is available for $49.95 providing two free hours, a command card and handbook. The $29.95 package offers one free hour and a command card.

27. Dialcom, Inc.

6120 Executive Blvd., Rockville, MD 20852
(301) 881-9020
John Morris, Pres.
Marilyn Bardsley, V.P., Marketing & Sales
Karen Chun, Dir., Marketing Services
Mandy Pritchett, Dir., Intl. & Industry Marketing

Branch Offices:
124 Mt. Auburn St., Cambridge, MA 12138
(617) 576-5752

1001 E. Touhy Ave., Des Plaines, IL 60018
(312) 694-2536

5300 Hollister, Houston, TX 70040
(713) 690-6311

1 Penn Plaza, N.Y. 10019
(212) 947-7995

555 Montgomery St., San Francisco 94111
(415) 445-1335

600 Maryland Ave., S.W., Wash., DC 20023
(202) 488-0550

Founded in 1970 and acquired by British Telecom in 1986 from ITT Corp., Dialcom was a pioneer in electronic mail services. It is a leading provider of worldwide electronic messaging between dissimilar systems and with all electronic messaging and information services for government, associations and companies.

In 1987, Dialcom announced the commercial availability of its X.400 Message Handling System, Dialcom400 (sm). This product is based on the international standard designed to permit worldwide exchange of electronic messaging between dissimilar systems and with all electronic mail systems throughout the world.

Dialcom Services are accessible through U.S. and international public data networks from personal computers, word processors and other computer terminals.

In addition to electronic messaging, several other value-added products are available, including electronic publishing for news releases, newsletters and other publications; public and private bulletin boards; electronic forms processing and forms for library management; text and spelling editors; word processor and personal computer interfaces; file transfer (ASCII and binary, with error checking), and a variety of news and information services.

An electronic clipping service, NEWS-TAB, allows the user to create a personal index of key words and phrases. The program then continuously searches news wires (UPI, AP and others) and automatically deposits all stories containing those key words into the user's electronic mailbox.

Dialcom also offers Dow Jones News/Retrieval; ABI/INFORM, the leading abstract business database; ABA/net, the Lawyer's Network, stock reports from UPI and Bunker Ramo, and BNA, the Bureau of National Affairs news database. Dialcom news services combine the speed of computer-based news services with electronic mail package. Through its menus and keyword searching, users select the information needed, whenever it is needed.

Dialcom also offers access to the electronic edition of the Official Airline Guides (OAG) and Eaasy Sabre (American Airlines' travel information and reservation system). Dialcom is capable of gatewaying to all commercial and public databases available via the public data networks.

Dialcom's pricing is comprised of base usage plus telecommunications charges (which range from $9.55 to $21 per hour, depending on volume and peak/non-peak hours), and a kilocharacter transmission rate of five cents per 1,000 characters. The value-added products have an additional premium charge that depends on the service used. There is no start-up fee, but there are minimum usage charges that vary according to the price plan selected.

The company is a wholly owned subsidiary of British Telecom, the U.K.'s main supplier of telephone services, and domestic/international telex and data communications services.

28. DIALOG Information Services, Inc.
3460 Hillview Ave., Palo Alto, CA 94304
(415) 858-3785, (800) 3-DIALOG
Telex: 334499, TWX: 910-339-9221
Dr. Roger K. Summit, Pres.

Branch Offices:
3 Cambridge Center, Cambridge, MA 02142
(617) 494-1114

75 E. Wacker Dr., Chicago 60601
(312) 726-9206

5858 Westheimer Rd., Houston 77057
(713) 789-9810

4640 Admiralty Way, Marina del Rey, CA 90291
(213) 827-0055

200 Park Ave., N.Y. 10166
(212) 682-4630

2100 Arch St., Philadelphia 19103
(215) 977-8161

1901 N. Moore St., Arlington, VA 22209
(703) 553-8455

DIALOG Information Services, Inc., a subsidiary of Lockheed Corporation, has been in commercial operation online since 1972, when it offered access to two databases covering education and technology. Since that time, the service has grown to become one of the world's largest databanks, providing over 280 databases containing more than 120 million items of information. Subjects covered include business, economics, marketing, current affairs, law, medicine, science, technology, social sciences, patents and trademarks. In late 1984, DIALOG II, with enhanced search features and Dialmail, providing electronic communication services, were introduced.

DIALOG is currently used by more than 80,000 customers in 80 countries. International representatives are located in Canada, Japan, Korea, Australia, Mexico, and Europe. Typical applications include competitive intelligence, tracking company and product mentions in publications, secondary market research, product development and obtaining comprehensive financial data on companies. Many of the databases are bibliographic, providing citations or abstracts rather than full-text. Full-text databases include Magazine ASAP, Trade & Industry ASAP, McGraw-Hill Business Backgrounder and several news services.

Databases of particular interest to public relations professionals include The Associated Press, UPI News, Reuters, First Release, PR Newswire on NEWSEARCH, Businesswire, Encyclopedia of Associations, National Newspaper Index, Magazine Index and Facts on File. One special group of databases is called Medical Connection. It provides databases ranging from Medline and Drug Information FullText to Magazine Index and Books in Print.

The Reuters library wire, receiving about 225 selected articles a day from about 100 bureaus, as well as late-breaking financial news, is online with DIALOG (File 611) at $120 per connect hour.

Some of DIALOG'S databases and approximate prices per online connect hour are as follows:

ABI/INFORM . . . . $96 (File 15)
Academic American Encyclopedia . . . . $45 (File 180)
Associated Press News . . . . $84 (Files 258, 259)
Biography Master Index . . . . $63 (File 287)
Books in Print . . . . $65 (File 470)
D&B Million Dollar Directory . . . .$100 (File 517)
DISCLOSURE II . . . . $45 (File 100)
D&B Dun's Electronic Yellow Pages Index . . . . $35 (File 500)
Encyclopedia of Associations . . . . $54 (File 114)
Facts on File. . . . . $60 (File 264)

Harvard Business Review .... $96 (File 122)
Magazine Index .... $84 (File 47)
Management Contents .... $90 (File 75)
Marquis Who's Who .... $95 (File 234)
National Foundations .... $60 (File 78)
National Newspaper Index....................... $84 (File 111)
NEWSEARCH ....$120 (File 211)
NTIS (National Technical Information Service)........ $69 (File 6)
PTS PROMPT ....$126 (File 16)
Standard & Poor's News .... $96 (File 132)
Trade & Industry Index .... $84 (File 148)
Ulrich's International Periodicals Directory .... $65 (File 480)
UPI News .... $85 (Files 260, 261)
Washington Post Electronic Edition .... $87 (Files 146, 147)

"Files" refers to the contents of a database. For example, UPI File 261 is the current file with daily updates offering the most recent three months (up to 48 hours before the present date). UPI File 260 is the back file going back to April 1983.

There is no initiation fee for beginning service and no monthly minimum charge; customers pay only for actual use of the system. However, potential users are advised to purchase DIALOG's basic documentation package at $50 and attend at least the initial training seminar ($125). Additional seminars are also offered in some special-interest areas. The databases are all priced individually with an average hourly cost of about $75. Usage charges are prorated to the fraction of a minute, with a typical inquiry taking 10 to 15 minutes.

With the OneSearch service, users may search up to 20 different files with a single command.

DIALOG may be accessed using virtually any personal computer, terminal or communicating work processor, plus a modem and standard telephone line. DIALOG is available at 300, 1200, or 2400 baud. (Baud is the unit measuring speed of transmission of data and refers to the number of times the communications line changes states each second and, although not technically identical, is sometimes referred to as bits per second.)

In most databases, small additional charges apply for online typed displays and printing or for offline prints sent by mail. Telecommunications network charges are approximately $11 an hour for Tymnet and Telenet, and $8 per hour for DIALOG's Dialnet. These charges are included in the monthly bill.

29. Disclosure
5161 River Rd., Bethesda, MD 20816
(301) 951-1300, (800) 638-8241, (800) 843-7747
Telex: 89-8452
Steven I. Goldspiel, Pres.

Branch Offices:
161 William St., N.Y. 10038
(212) 732-5955

10 So. Riverside Plaza, Chicago 60606
(312) 902-1550

5757 Wilshire Blvd., Los Angeles 90036
(213) 934-8313

37–39 Oxford St., London, W1, England
01-434-1788

Since 1968, Disclosure has been providing a variety of services involving the dissemination of information filed at the S.E.C. by corporations and other organizations. It is the number-one source worldwide for S.E.C. data on public companies.

The services include the Disclosure online computer database of information extracted from original reports including 10K, 20F, 10Q, 8K, Proxy and Registration Statements and tender offer and acquisition reports. The database is available on the following retrieval systems: ADP Network & Financial Services, BRS Information Technologies, CompuServe Executive and Business Information Systems, Datext, DIALOG Information System, Dow Jones News/Retrieval, Lotus Development Corp. One Source, Quotron Systems, I.P. Sharp and Warner Computer System. Information from the database is also available on COMPACT DISCLOSURE, a CD-ROM product.

Disclosure Information Centers deliver paper or microfiche copies of documents to clients who need data on public companies, and orders can be placed by a toll-free phone call to (800) 638-8241.

Disclosure also offers, on Dow Jones, DIALOG, BRS and CompuServe, the Disclosure/Spectrum Ownership database of detailed corporate ownership information for over 5,500 companies. Detailed stock information, such as latest shares traded, total shares held and latest trade data are included for three categories of owners: Institutional Holders, Five-Percent Holders and Inside Owners. This information is also available on CD-ROM.

Other databases include Disclosure/Europe (profiles and financial statements for over 2,000 European companies), Disclosure/Canada and Disclosure/Mutual Funds.

Disclosure has offices in Washington, DC; Chicago; Los Angeles; New York, and London, England.

30. Dixon & Turner Research Associates
4801 Broad Brook Ct., Bethesda, MD 20814
(301) 530-4178
Edward Dixon, Ellis Turner, Sr. Associates

Library and archival research, annotated bibliographies, document and data retrieval, literature searches, indexing of manuscripts and other bibliographic and research services, at inexpensive hourly rates.

31. Doremus Porter Novelli
1001 30 St., N.W., Wash., D.C. 20007
(202) 342-7000
Sharyn M. Sutton, Ph.D., Sr. V.P.

One of the country's largest public relations agencies, Doremus Porter Novelli is a leader and innovator in public relations research. DPN has one of the largest research staffs of any public relations agency, with departments in Washington, DC, New York, Chicago and Los Angeles.

One of the firm's research systems, PRESS (Public Relations Evaluation Support Services) measures the performance and results at each stage of the strategic public relations process, beginning with planning, through program development and implementation and, finally, with program assessment and evaluation.

DPN's PRESS includes unique methods to address the special needs of public relations programs resulting from limited budgets, unusual audiences (CEOs, legislators, media) and the vast array of communication tactics and channels.

PRESS services make use of online computer databases, as well as proprietary data from an annual lifestyle survey among 6,000 consumers. This national survey has trendline data on consumer attitudes, interests, opinions, purchase habits and media use.

Another major service is Publicity Evaluation and Tracking (PET), a computerized clipping analysis. While most clipping analyses are restricted to measures of circulation, PET assesses reach against the client's target audience and generates a "quality" index that measures the effectiveness of the placement on five different dimensions (e.g., Was the article on strategy? Was it attention-getting? Were key visuals/captions used?)

This sophisticated DPN system for tracking publicity and studying its impact has four major functions:

1. Summary statistics—measures of volume (e.g., clips, inches, circulation).
2. Target audience impressions—an assessment of publicity placements against a specified target audience.
3. Strategic contact analysis—a comparison of communicated messages against campaign strategy.
4. Quality placement points—quality evaluation of a placement effort along five dimensions.

The PET service allows establishment of a publicity baseline in terms of volume and measures current messages and images communicated through the media.

32. Dow Jones & Company, Inc.

Box 300, Princeton, NJ 08543-0300
(609) 452-1511, (800) 257-5114
William L. Dunn, Publisher
Carla L. Gaffney, Sr. Marketing Coordinator

Dow Jones News/Retrieval provides more than 40 databases with a variety of business, financial and general information that includes Dow Jones News, DISCLOSURE Online (10K extracts), Media General Financial Service (financial information on about 4,300 companies), as well as the Academic American Encyclopedia. The databases include current and historical stock quotes, investment forecasts and company earnings. Items from Barron's, the Dow Jones News Service and The Wall Street Journal are abstracted online for 90 days and can be found using stock symbol and industry access codes.

In 1984, the full text of The Wall Street Journal became available to subscribers of Dow Jones News/Retrieval. An electronic archive of news, The Wall Street Journal Full-Text database provides the contents of The Journal at 6 A.M. on the day of publication.

The database has news articles, editorials and other features that have been published in the newspaper starting with January 3, 1984. It is updated every business day and provides reference sources of interest to public relations departments, librarians, and legal and financial departments, as well as private investors.

The full-text Journal is part of News/Retrieval's Text-Search Services, which also provide parts of Dow Jones News Service, Barron's and The Wall Street Journal dating back to June 1979. The Services also include the full text of selected articles from the Washington Post since January 1984 and over 140 business publications and PR Newswire since January 1985.

Dow Jones News/Retrieval offers three membership rates, Standard, Blue Chip and Executive, one of which can be selected depending on amount of usage. The Standard Corporate Offer has a start-up fee of $49.95 per location. Eight free hours must be used within 30 days of receipt of password. The $12 service fee is waived the first year. The Blue Chip membership has a $95 annual subscription fee, in addition to the start-up fee of $49.95. There's a 33-⅓ percent discount on non-prime usage. The Executive membership carries a $50 monthly subscription fee with a 33-⅓ percent discount on prime and non-prime usage. Per-minute usage charges range from $0.10 to $1.20, depending on the database. Fees and usage costs may be tax-deductible in some instances.

33. The Dun & Bradstreet Corp.

299 Park Ave., N.Y. 10171
(212) 593-6800
Robert S. Diamond, Sr. VP, Corporate Communications
Walter F. Giersbach, Mgr., Internal Communications

Dun & Bradstreet is well-known as a provider of information to the business community. Now D&B also supplies information through its online utilities.

The Dun & Bradstreet Corporation's 25 operating units are grouped into three business segments: Business Information Services, Publishing and Marketing Services. Many of the units are well-known business names, such as Donnelley Directory, Dun & Bradstreet Credit Services, McCormack & Dodge, Moody's Investors Service, Nielsen Marketing Research, Nielsen Media Research and Official Airline Guides. The company's customers find D&B's resources essential in making credit, marketing investment, data processing, insurance and general management decisions.

A D&B company of interest to public relations clients is Market Data Retrieval, 16 Progress Dr., Shelton, CT 06484, phone (203) 926-4800, (800) 243-5538. This company, which acquired Educational Directory, has over 600,000 names of college faculty and administrators in the U.S. and Canada.

Following is information about a major D&B operation of particular interest to public relations clients. For additional information, see also the separate listing in the financial chapter.

34. Dun's Marketing Services

49 Old Bloomfield Ave., Mountain Lakes, NJ 07046
(201) 299-0181, (800) 526-9018, (800) 223-1026, (800) 526-0651
Patricia Mallon, V.P., Business Reference
Rick Clark, Dir., Online Services

Dun's Marketing Services (part of Dun & Bradstreet) provides both electronic and hard-copy business directories from their well-maintained, huge database of eight million companies.

Dun's Market Identifiers, online, gives detailed information on more than two million public and private U.S. business establishments having 10 or more employees and at least $1 million in sales. The current address, product, financial and marketing information for each public and private company, as well as all types of commercial and industrial establishments are included.

DMI records have more than 30 searchable and sortable fields, making questions like who are the key companies in certain industries, and within certain states, counties or cities, and who are those key company's other corporate family members easy to answer. The cost is $100 per online connect hour on DIALOG plus record charges. The database is updated quarterly.

The Canadian Dun's Market Identifiers (CDMI) contains corporate profiles on 350,000 Canadian establishments. Records are searchable and sortable by name, address, size, line of business, executive name, parent company, sales or employee growth or decline trend. It is updated quarterly and costs $100 per connect hour on DIALOG plus record charges.

D & B-Million Dollar Directory, online, carries comprehensive business information on 160,000 U.S. companies from the four-volume Million Dollar Directory Series. Companies with a net worth of $500,000 or more are listed with hard-to-find information on businesses privately held, as well as publicly owned companies. MDD records contain full addresses and county, SIC codes, sales and number of employees, as well as executives, stock exchanges and ticker symbols for the public companies. On DIALOG, the database is $100 per connect hour plus record charges.

In hard-copy form, Dun's Million Dollar Directory Series is the authoritative source of marketing data on the most prosperous U.S. companies—ones with a net worth over $500,000. Manufacturers, wholesalers, retailers and industrial concerns, and transportation, financial and service companies are included. The Directory provides data on 160,000 firms and contains addresses, telephone numbers, names of principal officers, division names, lines of business, stock ticker symbols, and names of principal banks, accounting firms and legal counsel. Cross-referencing is alphabetic, by SIC code and by geographical location in the four-volume set.

Details on more than eight million U.S. establishments, regardless of size, are available through DIALOG and CompuServe via EasyNet in Dun's Electronic Yellow Pages (DEYP). Public and private companies are searchable by SIC code, name, size of business, geography and telephone number. The cost is $60 per hour plus record charges.

Who Owns Whom (WOW) is a database providing corporate relationships down to 10 percent ownership. It covers approximately 25,000 parent companies with their 275,000 subsidiaries and associates. Records are searchable by company name, county of incorporation, company relationship, address, SIC codes, history and parent country of incorporation. This database is updated monthly and is available through Pergamon InfoLine. WOW costs $198 per connect hour.

Key British Enterprises (KBE) gives information on the United Kingdom's top 20,000 companies. It is searchable by company name, address, telephone number, trade type, sales, export sales, markets, directors, employee size, parent company and trade awards. Available through Pergamon InfoLine, it is $105 per hour plus record charges.

Two directories, America's Corporate Families and America's Corporate Families and International Affiliates, provide cross-linkage information, a "who owns who" of relationship marketing. These directories explain which companies are related to each other, where their subsidiaries are located, what their divisions are, their lines of business, who owns and runs them, and what their products and services are.

America's Corporate Families includes detailed information on more than 8,000 U.S. parent companies and on 45,000 U.S. subsidiaries and divisions they own. These companies report annual sales of $50 million or more and maintain a controlling interest in one or more subsidiary companies.

International Affiliates includes detailed information on U.S. ultimate parent companies and their Canadian and foreign subsidiaries, and U.S. subsidiaries and their ultimate parent companies outside the U.S. To be included, they must have a U.S. family member and one or more family members elsewhere. This volume covers 22,000 companies, including more than 1,800 U.S. parent companies.

The America's Corporate Families two-volume set is $725. The domestic version alone is $425 and the International affiliates version is $375.

Other publications available from Dun's Marketing Services include:

Reference Book of Corporate Managements/America's Corporate Leaders—$695 per four-volume set. Three volumes contain the A-Z listings and the fourth volume, cross-referencing.

Principal International Businesses—$550

Dun's Business Rankings—$395

Europe's Largest Companies—$425

Dun's Industrial Guide (manufacturers)—$695

Who Owns Whom

Individual volumes: North America, $375; United Kingdom and Republic of Ireland, $325; Continental Europe, $355, and Australasia and Far East, $325.

35. Facts On File

460 Park Ave. S., N.Y. 10016
(212) 683-2244
Telecopier: (212) 213-4578
Howard Epstein, Pres.

Started in 1940, Facts On File publishes a weekly digest and index of national and international news, which is provided to thousands of librarians, editors, researchers and others. An annual subscription ($465) includes a semimonthly cumulative index, desktop binder and 32-page world atlas. Facts on File is online with NEXIS, DIALOG and VU/TEXT.

The company also publishes Editorials On File, a semimonthly compilation of editorials and editorial cartoons from about 150 U.S. and Canadian newspapers available for an annual subscription of $275.

One of its reference books is the Facts On File Yearbook, $95. In addition, the company publishes a variety of nonfiction and reference books. It has a major subsidiary in the United Kingdom, located on Collins St., Oxford, England OX4 1XJ.

36. Federal Document Retrieval
514 C St., N.E., Wash., DC 20002
(202) 628-2229
Linda Futato, Marketing

Federal Document Retrieval is one of the best-known of the document-locating firms in Washington. It provides research and documents on legal, securities, banking, legislative, corporate and governmental matters.

37. FIND/SVP
625 Ave. of the Americas, N.Y. 10011
(212) 645-4500
Telex: 148358
Andrew P. Garvin, Pres.
Kathleen S. Bingham, Exec. V.P.
Anthony Zeidler, Dir., Business Development Group

FIND/SVP offers a total information resource that now is one of the largest in the business field. Its Quick Information Service provides direct phone access to a comprehensive information center for quick answers to business and general questions, as well as computer database searches. More extensive research assignments are performed by FIND'S Strategic Research Division. Project fees are estimated in advance.

The company also produces a variety of publications, including market studies and contents publications. FIND/SVP is a member of the international network of SVP information services. (SVP was founded in Paris in 1935.)

Born in 1945, Andy Garvin graduated from Columbia University Graduate School of Journalism and started FIND in 1969 as "The Information Clearing House." The company now has over 90 employees.

Following is a summary of FIND/SVP.

1. The Find/SVP Quick Information Service. Provides direct telephone access to a comprehensive information center. Available on a monthly retainer basis (plus out-of-pocket charges). Clients have a full range of FIND resources at their disposal including telephone discussion, articles, reference works, files, computer databases, information specialists and the network of SVP information centers. The service handles questions requiring under two hours of research time. Turn-around time varies depending on the request. Inquiries requiring more in-depth research are referred to the Strategic Research Division.

    Information Cards, entitling a client (and designated colleagues) to use the Quick Information Service are automatically issued.

    The Quick Information Service is offered on a flexible retainer basis and the fee is adjusted up or down based on average usage of the service. FIND/SVP's retainer agreement and fact sheet contain an outline of policies on out-of-pocket expenses, rate revisions and cancellations.

2. Strategic Research Division. Handles more extensive research and information gathering needs,

including custom market and industry studies, surveys and large information-gathering tasks beyond the scope of the retainer. Cost estimates are provided for approval before these assignments are undertaken and this service is available on an individual project basis.

3. Computer Database Search Service. Searches of more than 300 computer databases are part of the Quick Information Service but also are available to non-retainer clients on a per search basis.
4. Information Tracking Service, Retrieval and Consulting Services
5. Publications.

The Information Catalog: A free catalog of studies, reports and information products. Includes available company and industry reports prepared by Wall Street investment firms and marketed by FIND/SVP by special arrangement.

Management Contents, Computer Contents: Legal Contents. Each Contents publication offers a wide selection of tables of contents from hundreds of trade, scholarly and government periodicals. Published bimonthly, the three publications are available as yearly subscriptions. Subscribers can source articles represented through their own libraries or through FIND/SVP's document retrieval service. FIND/SVP also publishes special market studies and reports.

6. Online Search Service. FIND/SVP provides access to over 1,000 different databases on a variety of systems, including:

BRS
CompuServe
Control Data/Business Information Services
Derwent Inc.
DIALOG Information Services
Dow Jones & Company
Finsbury Data Services Ltd.
Mead Data Central
National Library of Medicine
NewsNet
Pergamon-InfoLine-ORBIT
Source Telecomputing
Textline

7. FIND's Document Retrieval Service. Documents may be ordered by mail, phone, telex or via terminal through Lockheed's DialOrder. Regular service $10 per article plus 30 cents per page and rush service is $16 per article plus 30 cents per page. Deposit accounts (at least $250) are required. Orders are accepted from customers without a deposit account but the regular service price is higher per article. Other materials are available.

Special research/verification is billed at $40 an hour with a two-hour minimum. Other miscellaneous expenses may include postage charges, toll calls, computer charges, couriers, facsimile and royalty payments. Royalty payments are made to Copyright Clearance Center, Inc., where appropriate.

38. The Foundation Center
79 Fifth Ave., N.Y. 10003
(212) 620-4230, (800) 424-9836
Thomas R. Buckman, Pres.

Branch Offices:
1442 Hanna Bldg., 1422 Euclid Ave., Cleveland 44115
(216) 861-1933
Patrica Pasquale, Dir.

312 Sutter St., San Francisco 94108
(415) 397-0902
Roberta Steiner, Dir.

1001 Connecticut Ave., N.W., Wash., DC 20036
(202) 331-1400
Margot Brinkley, Dir.

The Foundation Center, established by several major foundations in 1956, is the national nonprofit clearinghouse for information on foundations and their grant-making activities. The Center offers a variety of services and publishes a wide range of reference books to help grantseekers and others.

All community and private foundations actively engaged in grantmaking, regardless of size or geographic location, are included in one or more of the Center's publications. There are basically three kinds: *directories* that describe specific grantmakers, characterizing their program interests and providing fiscal and personnel data; *grants indexes* that list and subject classify recent foundation awards; *guides* and related materials about funding research, elements of proposal writing and other topics of interest to nonprofit organizations.

The Center also operates an extensive public service and education program through its four libraries and its national network of over 170 cooperating library collections. The libraries provide free public access to all of the Center's publications, plus a wide range of other books, services, periodicals and research documents relating to foundations and philanthropy.

Foundation Center Publications:

The Foundation Directory, Biennial. Comprehensive profiles of over 5,100 of the largest U.S. foundations (those that have over $1 million in assets or make annual grants of $100,000 or more). Includes foundation address and telephone number; application guidelines—including contact person and giving limitations; complete financial data; donors, and officers, directors, and trustees. $85.

The Foundation Directory Supplement. Updates Directory entries for about 2,000 of the foundations. Published in non-Directory years. $35.

National Data Book, Annual. Brief listings for all of the 25,000 active U.S. foundations that give more than $1 per year. Includes address, principal officer, asset and annual grant amounts. $60.

Source Book Profiles. Comprehensive profiles of the 1,000 largest U.S. foundations, published on a two-year cycle. 500 foundations profiled each year in quarterly, cumulative volumes. Entries for all 1,000 foundations are continuously updated. Includes analyses of actual foundation grants with breakdowns by subject area of giving, type of grant support awarded and type of recipient organizations. Annual subscription, $285.

Corporate Foundation Profiles. Detailed information on 230 of the largest company-sponsored foundations, plus brief descriptions of an additional 490 corporate foundations. Includes extensive information on company locations, board affiliations, and limitations on giving, as well as address, telephone, contact person and application guidelines. $55.

Foundation Grants Index, Annual. Indexes over 40,000 actual grants of $5,000 or more awarded by 460 major foundations. Fully indexed by subject areas, recipients, key words and geographical focus. $46.

Foundation Grants Index, Bimonthly. Subscription service lists over 2,000 recent foundation grants in each issue. Also includes details on foundation and corporation publications; updates on new foundations and reports on foundation changes. Annual subscription: $28 for 6 issues.

COMSEARCH: Printouts. Computer printouts of recent foundation grants in 92 subject areas; 26 broad topics, 20 geographic areas, 66 specific subject categories, and three special, often-requested topics. Indexed by foundation, recipients and subject. Subject COMSEARCH available on microfiche. Broad Topics, $38; Geographic, $30, and Subjects, $18.

Foundation Grants to Individuals, Biennial. Details of foundation grant programs for individual applicants. Over 1,041 foundations awarding grants to individuals are described. Includes address and telephone, contact person, application procedures, limitations on giving. $18.

Foundation Fundamentals. This guide for grantseekers discusses the foundation funding process step-by-step. It has illustrations, worksheets and checklists provided to help the grantseeker. Comprehensive bibliographies and detailed research examples. $9.95.

39. GPO Monthly Catalog
Library Division
Superintendent of Documents
U.S. Government Printing Office, Wash., DC 20401
(202) 275-1121

The U.S. Government Printing Office now is electronic. Its file, online with DIALOG, indexes public documents which are produced by the legislative and executive branches of the Federal Government. It corresponds to the hard-copy Monthly Catalog of U.S. Government Publications. The database is $35 per connect hour. It is also available through BRS.

Additional information about free and low-cost publications appears in the listing of the U.S. Government Printing Office.

40. Gale Research Company
Book Tower, Detroit 48226
(313) 961-2242, (800) 521-0707 (editorial), (800) 223-GALE (customer services)
David Bianco, Publicity Mgr.

Stepping off the elevator into the offices of Gale Research Company is like stepping into a museum of library objects and lore. Gale is one of the nation's major publishers of library reference books, and the halls and offices of its headquarters are lined with prints, paintings, signs and other objects from libraries and bookstores.

Started in 1955 by Frederick G. Ruffner, Gale was acquired in 1985 by the International Thomson Organisation Ltd. This enormous operation, now a Thomson subsidiary, has over 500 employees and annual sales of about $45 million.

Gale publishes encyclopedias, bibliographies, indexes, concordances, directories, almanacs and who's whos that cost from $50 to over $400 each. Among the most widely used titles are the Encyclopedia of Associations; the Acronymns, Initialisms and Abbreviations Dictionary, and Contemporary Authors.

The company was started when Mr. Ruffner found that there was no single source of information about the trade associations and professional societies. He rented desk space and began to compile what was to become the Encyclopedia of Associations (EA). The first edition of EA, published in 1956, contained 6,000 entries. The current edition contains detailed descriptions of more than 20,000 associations.

Book Tower is named after a prominent Detroiter and does not refer to Gale or its books. In fact, the company's principal offices are no longer in the Book Tower building, though it still uses it as its mailing address. The company also has offices in New York, Fort Lauderdale and Minneapolis.

The Encyclopedia of Associations is typical of many Gale books. Like others, such as the National

Directory of Newsletters and Reporting Services, Medical and Health Information Directory, Statistics Sources and the Encyclopedia of Business Information Sources, EA provides the private and public sectors with valuable information about where to look for more comprehensive information. EA is the most widely distributed of Gale's reference books. The 21st edition is $220.

The Acronymns, Initialisms and Abbreviations Dictionary (AIAD), which also receives widespread distribution, contains more than 375,000 terms that reflect our society's penchant for verbal and written shorthand. This is a significant jump over the 12,000 entries that appeared in the first edition 24 years ago. "The growth in acronymic forms has been necessitated by breakneck progress in electronics, space exploration and data processing," explains Ellen T. Crowley, editor of AIAD. "The acronym and abbreviation saves precious inches of newsprint and precious seconds of broadcast time. They are so prevalent that they have formed their own new language."

Gale also publishes many titles that serve academe. Contemporary Authors (CA), for example, which is second in company sales to EA, is a bio-bibliographical guide to current writers in fiction, general nonfiction, poetry, journalism, drama, motion pictures, television and other fields. CA's 120 volumes (45 books), which contain information about more than 90,000 writers, can be found in most libraries. Also serving the academic community are other publications such as Contemporary Literary Criticism, Twentieth-Century Literary Criticism, Dictionary of Literary Biography, and Something About the Author, a series of volumes presenting facts and pictures about contemporary authors and illustrators of books for young people.

Among Gale's other publishing projects are a series of books on weather and meteorology; numerous books on publishing, and the sales of rare books, such as Bookman's Price Index, and many, many, more, including, of relevance to this chapter, an annual Research Centers Directory ($355) with a supplement.

A true bibliophile, Mr. Ruffner has collected tens of thousands of books in pursuit of his combined vocation and avocation. These interests are reflected in a travelling collection of art on libraries and books that is displayed in libraries around the nation.

Also on display in many libraries are sculptures of literary figures and other outstanding men and women that are part of The Gale Gallery—a collection of sculpture reproductions that Gale provides to libraries.

"The key to progress is information," says Fred Ruffner. "It is our business to help people know where to find that information and to help them move forward."

Other Gale books which are relevant to public relations include Publishers Directory (two volumes, $275), Book Review Index ($170), Consultants and Consulting Organizations Directory (over 12,000 entries, $380), and The Directory of Directories ($195). A cumulation and revision of the Directory Information Service, the Directory of Directories (launched in 1980) provides updated information on more than 10,000 directories! The Directory Information Service, which appears between biennial editions of DOD, is $135.

Encyclopedia of Information Systems and Services ($400) describes over 30,000 information systems, products, services and programs in the U.S. and other countries, including more than 1,000 computerized searching services and over 1,000 publications. Revisions are listed in New Information Systems and Services ($260).

As stated in the introduction to this chapter, *the* Gale book is the Encyclopedia of Associations, which now is published in four volumes. Volume 1 provides extensive information about *national* organizations and is very easy to use because of a keyword alphabetical index. Many users purchase only Volume 1, which is the basic book and is one of the most important reference aids in terms of relating to publics. A seven-volume Regional, State and Local Organizations was launched in 1987.

National Faculty Directory. An alphabetical list with addresses, of about 650,000 faculty members at United States and selected Canadian junior colleges, colleges and universities. Four volumes, over 4,000 pages, $500.

Statistics Sources. A Subject Guide to Data on Industrial, Business, Social, Educational, Financial and Other Topics for the United States and Selected Foreign Countries. Thousands of sources of statistics on about 20,000 subjects. $280.

Gale Research Co. has put three of its most popular books online with DIALOG.

Book Review Index (File 137) offers a reference guide to locating the sources of published reviews of books and periodicals titles. It indexes reviews published in 460 periodicals from 1969 to the present, including the New York Review of Books, Publishers Weekly, Business Week and the London Times Book Review. The database is $48 per connect hour on DIALOG.

Biography Master Index (File 287) provides biographical information from over 600 source publications on over six million prominent persons. This database corresponds to Gale Research Co.'s eight-volume Biography and Genealogy Master Index. It is available online at $63 per connect hour on DIALOG.

The Encyclopedia of Associations (File 114) is a comprehensive source of information about 20,000 associations, societies, unions and other organizations. Foreign and international associations of interest to Americans are listed, as well as citizen action groups. The database costs $54 per connect hour on DIALOG and 75 cents per record displayed, typed or printed offline. John Schmittroth is online coordinator.

41. The Gallup Organization, Inc.
53 Bank St., Princeton, NJ 08540
(609) 924-9600
George Gallup, Jr., Chm.

This world-famous marketing and attitude research firm was founded in 1935 by George Gallup, who died in 1984. In addition to its Gallup Poll and other ongoing projects, the company handles assignments for public relations clients.

42. Gannett New Media
Box 450, Wash., DC 20044
(703) 276-5945
Phil Fuhrer, V.P.

Gannett New Media can deliver a variety of news summaries to your computer terminal daily at 8 A.M. These are Gannett wire service briefings on topics of the day, ranging from business and marketing to health. For a charge of $250 minimum per month, subscribers receive five hours of online material. It can then be downloaded and distributed to as many as 50 persons.

43. GE Information Services
401 N. Washington St., Rockville, MD 20850
(301) 340-4000, (800) 638-9636

GEnie, begun in 1985 by General's Electric's Information Services, is a service for online communicators. Appealing to special-interest groups and E-mail users, the expenses are reduced by making use of GE's large teleprocessing network in non-prime time hours. The rate is about $5 per hour for access at 300 or 1200 baud. More than five dozen cities also have the service at 2400 baud. It has 550 telephone nodes so the network portion of the cost is not more than the price of a local call. GEnie (GE network for information exchange) offers GE Mail (a simplified consumer version of GE's business-oriented QUIK-COMM System), a stock market analysis database called VESTOR, Dow Jones News/Retrieval, USA Today Update Decisionlines, a real-time news service called NewsGrid and other services.

44. Edward Gottlieb, Inc.

169 E. 69 St., N.Y. 10021
(212) 772-7226
Edward Gottlieb, Chm.
Janet Laib Gottlieb, Pres.

One of the country's renowned public relations counselors, Ed Gottlieb has been in the public relations field for over 35 years. During much of this time he operated his own international public relations agency, which he sold to Hill & Knowlton. After a few years at Hill & Knowlton, he became a partner of Chester Burger. In 1983, Janet Laib, who headed her own PR firm for many years, joined him as president and partner. Clients include companies, public relations and advertising agencies, and related communications firms. The Gottliebs counsel on internal and external communications, mergers and acquisitions, search for advertising and public relations agencies, and also conduct opinion and marketing research.

45. Grolier Electronic Publishing, Inc.

95 Madison Ave., N.Y. 10016
(212) 696-9750

Grolier's Academic American Encyclopedia is now on CD-ROM (compact disc, read-only memory). The 21-volume set takes up less than one-third of a CD-ROM, yet there are some 32,000 articles on many topics. In case you don't have CD-ROM equipment, the encyclopedia is also available through several database vendors.

46. Harkavy Information Service

33 W. 17 St., N.Y. 10011
(212) 206-7746
Michael Harkavy, Pres.
Ruth Tenenbaum, Dir.

Harkavy Information Service provides a variety of services of special interest to public relations clients. Services, which have a basic fee of $45 an hour, include all types of library and online research, industry and market reports.

The scope of a search determines cost and turnaround time. Questions are handled within 48 hours and sometimes in less than an hour.

In 1984, Harkavy started a new service, SKIM, which:

Surveys current news in your field of special interest.
Keeps tabs on late-breaking developments.
Informs you of the latest Federal Government publications.
Mails you photocopies of this information every week.

The electronic clipping service monitors over 500 publications, including Advertising Age, Barron's, Forbes, Fortune, Harvard Business Review, Inc., Newsweek, New York, The New York Times, Publishers Weekly, Time and The Wall Street Journal.

47. Harvard Business Review Database

John Wiley & Sons, Inc.
605 Third Ave., N.Y. 10158
(212) 850-6331
Patricia Howe, Assoc. Product Mgr.

Produced by Wiley Electronic Publishing, the Harvard Business Review Database consists of citations and abstracts to HBR articles from 1971 to the present, plus 800 classic earlier articles. Records from 1976 forward include the full text of the article. In addition, 8,000 cited references from HBR articles are included in the file. It covers a wide range of management subjects, from industry analysis, time management and economic outlook, to marketing and advertising.

HBR Database is available online through BRS, DIALOG, Data-Star, NEXIS, Human Resource Information Network and EasyNet. On DIALOG, it is $96 per connect hour.

48. The Human Resource Information Network

Executive Telecom System, Inc.
9585 Valparaiso Ct., Indianapolis, IN 46268
(800) 421-8884
Patricia Peets, Marketing Dept.

A subsidiary of the Bureau of National Affairs, Inc., HRIN provides online databases for human resources professionals in the areas of public information, census data, studies and surveys, occupations, administration and tax, benefit compensation, employment and labor relations. An annual subscription ranges from $2,720. Average online charges are $66 per hour.

49. Idea Generation, Inc.

220 E. 73 St., N.Y. 10021
(212) 472-1015
Alexa Smith, Pres.

The major technique used in qualitative research is the focus group. Public relations people often find that this type of market research is an extremely efficient and economical way to determine the strategy, theme and other components of a public relations plan. A focus group simply is a group of individuals, perhaps about 10, gathered together in a room for a discussion, lasting about an hour or two, focused on a specific topic. The moderator is extremely important in helping bring out the opinions of the participants, without influencing them. The participants have similar characteristics, such as the same age group, occupation or other demographics.

The people who conduct groups generally are part of large market research firms or, in a few cases, are simply small firms or individuals who specialize in this activity.

The way that a focus group often works is for the client and agency to observe the discussion through a one-way window. The discussion generally is audio- or videotaped. Costs vary in accordance with the location and the participants. The participants are paid a fee, which may be relatively small with general consumers and may be larger with physicians or management executives. The total cost of a focus group may be about $3,000, and possibly four groups may be required in order to provide a geographical or other mix.

One of the country's renowned focus group specialists is Alexa Smith. Though she operates a relatively small company, she has major clients throughout the country.

50. Industry Data Sources

Information Access Co.
11 Davis Dr., Belmont, CA 94002
(415) 591-2333, (800) 227-8431
Susan Higgins, Marketing Mgr.

Formerly Harfax Industry Data Sources (owned by Harper & Row), this database was acquired in 1984 by Information Access Co. (owned by Ziff-Davis).

Industry Data Sources provides access to industry-intensive data on 65 major industries, including banking, communications equipment, computers, foods and beverages, insurance, printing and publishing, retail and wholesale trade and transportation. It is designed for those who need financial and marketing information on an industry or a specific product. On DIALOG, it is $75 per connect hour.

51. INFO/DOC

INFORMATION/DOCUMENTATION, Inc.
Box 17109, Dulles Intl. Airport, Wash., DC 20041
(703) 979-5363, (800) 336-0800
Telex: 90-3042
Albert A. Paschall, Research Group

INFO/DOC, a Wash., D.C.-based information broker, is an authorized distributor for National Technical Information Service (NTIS) products, Government Printing Office (GPO) publications and other organizations. They retrieve documents and reports from Government departments, agencies, businesses, trade associations and professional societies. Current awareness profile searches with regularly scheduled updating, as well as retrospective searches on all the literature indexed on a topic, are available. Users may request custom computer searches that are used to identify news stories, corporate filings, market analysis, patents and advertising on a particular product.

Orders can be placed by electronic mail, telecopier, telex or toll-free call.

52. Info Globe

444 Front St. West, Toronto, Ont. M5V 2S9, Canada
(416) 585-5250
Telex: 06-219629
Rick Noble, Sales Mgr.

One of North America's major daily newspapers is The Globe and Mail. Published in Toronto, it is renowned for its financial news section called Report on Business.

Info Globe is the electronic publishing division of The Globe and Mail and, since 1977, has been one of the pioneers in developing information and services. By 6 A.M., Eastern time, each day's edition of The Globe and Mail has been incorporated into online files containing all the articles published in The Globe since November 1977. The database includes Report on Business since January 1, 1976. All are fully indexed.

Among the databases that can be accessed by using Info Globe are The Canadian Financial Database, which has information on 500 Canadian corporations; Report on Business Corporate Database, which contains financial information on more than 1,800 Canadian companies; Canadian Periodicals Index; Who's Who Online; Key Government documents and Marketscan, an online stock service with quotations from six North American stock exchanges. Info Globe also represents Textline—world business news from 100 respected sources including newspapers and business journals such as The Economist, the Financial Times and Japan Economic Journal—and Datasolve World Reporter, significant overseas news sources and publications.

The Info Globe databases are online through Datapac (in Canada), and Telenet or Tymnet, from 6 A.M. to 3 A.M., weekdays, and, on Saturdays, from 6 A.M. to midnight and, on Sundays, from 8 A.M. to 3 A.M., Monday. The rates vary from about $0.50 to $3.20 per minute, depending on what is accessed. The Globe and Mail full-text file has a connect fee of $2.82 per minute. Sign-up fees also apply to some of the databases. High-speed offline printing costs $10 per thousand lines. Custom searches are $90 per hour. Most telephone-compatible computer terminals or word processors can be used with Info Globe.

53. Information Access Co. (IAC)

11 Davis Dr., Belmont, CA 94002
(415) 591-2333, (800) 227-8431
Susan Higgins, Marketing Mgr., Online Services

Information Access Co, a division of Ziff-Davis Publishing Co., supplies databases especially relevant to public relations. For example, PR NEWSWIRE releases are now included in four IAC databases on DIALOG:

1. NEWSEARCH (File 211) can be used for searching the full text of the most current news releases (the last two to six weeks) and is updated each day. (However, there can be a 24- to 48-hour delay in putting a release on the system so don't expect to find a release sent out by PR NEWS-WIRE today.) The hourly connect rate is $120.
2. Trade & Industry Index (File 148) can be searched for the bibliographic records corresponding to PR NEWSWIRE releases going back to January 1983. The text may be typed, displayed or printed provided that a banner appears on the screen next to the accession number indicating: For full text, type Format 9. The hourly connect rate is $84.
3. Trade & Industry ASAP II (File 648) can be used for full-text (and bibliographic) searching of PR NEWSWIRE releases back to January 1983. The hourly connect rate is $96.
4. Newswire ASAP (File 649) contains texts of releases from PR NEWSWIRE, Reuters and Kyodo.

IAC's NEWSEARCH is a daily index of more than 2,000 news stories, articles and reviews from over 1,900 significant newspapers, magazines and periodicals. There is thorough cross-indexing by industry, geography, SIC code and individual name. At the end of each month, NEWSEARCH's PR NEWSWIRE releases are moved to IAC's Trade & Industry Index file.

The magazine article data in NEWSEARCH is moved, also monthly, to the Magazine Index (File 47) database, and the newspaper coverage is transferred to IAC's National Newspaper Index (File 111) database which provides front-page to back-page indexing and abstracting of The Christian Science Monitor, The New York Times, The Wall Street Journal, Washington Post and Los Angeles Times.

Magazine Index provides a comprehensive index to more than 435 well-known magazines published in the U.S. and Canada. Magazine ASAP II (File 647) offers the complete text and indexing of over 60 publications selected from Magazine Index such as Dun's Business Month, Forbes, Science and Smithsonian.

Trade & Industry Index carries the PR NEWSWIRE releases more than one month old, plus indexing and abstracting of over 330 trade, business and industry journals, as well as selective coverage of over 1,200 newspapers, magazines and journals.

The Trade & Industry ASAP II database offers the full text and indexing of over 100 publications from the American Banker to Women's Wear Daily.

IAC also has The Computer Database, which is $96 per connect hour on DIALOG.

The Legal Resource Index (File 150) indexes the key law-related literature including the Harvard Law Review. On DIALOG, it is $90 per connect hour.

DIALOG's automatic selective dissemination of information (SDI) service is available for Magazine Index, National Newspaper Index, Trade & Industry Index and Legal Resource Index. Simply save your search using the END/SAVE command and DIALOG will run the strategy once a month and mail the results. If you don't want to wait a month for results but need daily or weekly updating, the NEW-SEARCH file is the place to look as it updates these four databases plus Management Contents (see separate listing) and the Computer Database every day.

DIALOG prices are also available online using ?RATESn, where *n* represents the file number (e.g.,

?RATES648). The charges for a record displayed or typed online or printed offline range from $0.10 to $2 depending on the database and format needed. Several of the files are now available through Mead Data Central. (See separate listing.)

54. Information for Public Affairs, Inc. (IPA)
1900 14th St., Sacramento, CA 95814
(916) 444-0840
William Hauck, V.P., Marketing

The Information for Public Affairs (IPA) databases, called State Net, give the current status of all bills and proposed regulations in every state and in Congress. They are indexed, cross-referenced and searchable by one of 1,200 key words or topics. Costs of annual subscriptions vary but range from $3,000. The databases are available to clients over Telenet at 300 or 1,200 baud. IPA can track bills and generate reports for clients, customized to meet clients' needs.

55. Information on Demand, Inc.
Box 1370, Berkeley, CA 94701
(415) 644-4500, (800) 227-0750
Christine Maxwell, Pres.

Formed in 1971, Information on Demand (IOD) provides research services and document delivery to clients all over the world. Resources include access to over 400 computer databases and a network of information centers.

Documents are delivered for a base fee of $15 per item (includes first class delivery and up to 20 pages/document; 25 cents per page therafter). Clients may utilize this service by supplying IOD with as complete a bibliographic citation as possible. IOD retrieves the requested documents from its field network of 17 "runners" who access major library centers within the U.S. and outside information centers worldwide. Orders may be placed by phone, mail, facsimile or electronically over a number of online services, including IOD's own electronic ordering service, IOD DIRECT.

Research services are $75 per hour, plus costs, with a two-hour minimum. Translation services are also available. IOD is associated with the Pergamon Group of Companies.

56. InfoServe
360 W. 21 St., N.Y. 10011
(212) 807-0529
Elaine Snow

Elaine Snow combines a library science and public relations background in a consulting business, which ranges from setting up routine information management systems to handling individual research assignments. Her specialty is identifying spokespeople and other experts, compiling bibliographies and preparing abstracts and indexes.

57. Institute for Scientific Information/ISI
3501 Market St., Philadelphia 19104
(215) 386-0100, (800) 523-1850
Dr. Eugene Garfield, Pres.

ISI is well known for providing products, services and research in the arts and humanities and in the scientific disciplines. They include the publication, Current Contents ($298); citation indexes, such as the Arts and Humanities Citation Index ($3,200 per year); Social Sciences Citation Index ($3,350 per year), and online citation indexes which include SciSearch and Social SciSearch. ISI also offers document delivery services: The Genuine Article costs $8 per article up to 10 pages.

58. Interactive Market Systems (IMS)

55 Fifth Ave., N.Y. 10003
(212) 924-0200, (800) 223-7942
Richard Makely, Pres.

IMS stores over 300 databases, including multimedia marketing studies, such as Simmons; broadcast studies, such as Nielsen; marketing, such as PRIZM, and opinion surveys, such as Roper, as well as related international databases, used primarily by broadcasters, publishers and advertisers. Rates decrease for clients with annual minimum usage commitments. There may be extra subscription fees, depending on the database required. A number of IMS programs for analyzing these databases also are available on diskette for use with data downloaded to a personal computer.

59. Knowledge Index

DIALOG Information Services, Inc.
3460 Hillview Ave., Palo Alto, CA 94304
(415) 858-3785, (800) 334-2564, (800) 3-DIALOG
Libby Trudell, Mgr., Mktg.

You can use your home computer *after working hours* to bring in portions of DIALOG's smorgasbord of databases.

Knowledge Index carries such online business information as ABI/INFORM, Trade & Industry Index, and Standard & Poor's News (giving extensive coverage of the corporate world with financial reports). In fact, information is divided into several subject sections: Magazines, News and Books; Business News and Information; Medicine and Psychology; Legal; Agriculture; Computers, Electronics and Engineering, and Education and Government. Information Access Co.'s databases contain PR NEWSWIRE releases and cover-to-cover indexing The New York Times, The Wall Street Journal, The Washington Post, Christian Science Monitor and Los Angeles Times, as well as over 400 magazines and journals.

Available after regular business hours and on weekends, Knowledge Index has a start-up fee of $35 which provides a User's Workbook and two free hours of connect time. Access costs are $24 per hour, including network charges and billing is to your credit card.

60. Knowledge Industry Publications, Inc.

701 Westchester Ave., White Plains, NY 10604
(914) 328-9157
Marc Weinstein, Pres.

A respected publisher of newsletters in the educational and publishing fields, Knowledge Industry Publications was one of the first to predict the database research explosion. The company has taken its own advice with its DataBase Service, directory of computer databases which may be cost-effective because it helps the online searcher get to the right information source quickly. The annual fee is $222.

The company also publishes DataBase Alert, a monthly newsletter. The DataBase Directory Service is available online from BRS.

The Knowledge Industry Publications Database Directory ($195) lists over 3,000 databases.

61. Learned Information

143 Old Marlton Pike, Medford, NJ 08055
(609) 654-6266
Jacqueline Trolley, Marketing Mgr.

Since we live in a modern world, someone in your organization may want to be familiar with Link-Up, the bimonthly newspaper of online communications, published by Learned Information. Eleven issues cost $24.

Learned Information also publishes the monthly Information Today ($27.50 for 11 issues) and sponsors the National Online Meetings, gatherings of companies and people involved in online databases and communications services. They also sponsor an annual Optical Publishing seminar and an International National Online Meeting in London.

62. Arthur D. Little/OnLine

Arthur D. Little Decision Resources
Acorn Park, Cambridge, MA 02140
(617) 864-5770
Anne V. Quinn

Arthur D. Little/OnLine provides coverage of industries, management topics and technologies. The database includes economic forecasts, market overviews and company assessments. Industries covered include health care, telecommunications, information processing, office automation, chemicals, energy and biotechnology. On DIALOG, it is $114 per connect hour. Selected records have a $100 surcharge.

63. McBer and Company

137 Newbury St., Boston, MA 02116
(617) 437-7080
Robert F. Ryan, Pres.

This Boston-based behavioral science research firm was founded by David McClelland of Harvard University. It was sold to Saatchi & Saatchi in 1984.

McBer offers a full array of human resource research and consulting services to industry and government clients.

64. McGraw-Hill Publications Online

1221 Ave. of the Americas, N.Y. 10020
(212) 512-2911
Telex: 127960, 232365 (International)
TWX: 7105814849
Patricia Markert, Mgr., Editorial Licensing
Andrea Broadbent, Mgr., Marketing Services

McGraw-Hill distributes the full text of 30 of its leading publications through two online information retrieval services: DIALOG Information Services and Mead Data Central's NEXIS.

On DIALOG, 17 publications are available as McGraw-Hill Business Backgrounder—File 624. Searchable fields include byline, dateline, section heading, title, journal name, journal code, publication date and ISBN.

Access to the DIALOG database requires a password issued to the user by DIALOG Information Services. The price is $96 per online connect hour. There is no extra charge for online printing of the complete text of the article.

On NEXIS, 30 McGraw-Hill magazines and newsletters are available. They can be accessed through the Business, Finance, Magazine, Newsletter, and Trade/Technology group files or individually by specifying the publication name.

McGraw-Hill publications available on DIALOG and NEXIS include Aviation Week, Business Week, Chemical Week, Electronics, Engineering News Record, Securities Week and others.

65. Management Contents/Information Access Co.

11 Davis Dr., Belmont, CA 94002
(800) 227-8431
Susan Higgins, Mgr., Marketing

The Ziff-Davis Publishing Co. database, Management Contents, is an excellent place to search for all kinds of business-related topics. It is a bibliographic database providing citations and abstracts from 700 current and historical publications, starting in 1974. It includes journals, books, conference proceedings and course material. Among the publications are Across the Board, Business Month and Wharton Magazine. Aid in searching is available in Access to Access: An Online User's Guide to IAC Databases, priced at $125.

The database is up on DIALOG at $90 an hour, on BRS at about $75 an hour and on Data-Star at $84 an hour.

The current month's Management Contents information is available on NEWSEARCH, another Information Access database.

66. Mead Data Central
Box 933, Dayton, OH 45401
(513) 865-6800, (800) 227-9597, (800) 227-8379
Jack W. Simpson, Pres.

Branch Offices:
Harris Tower, 233 Peachtree St., N.E., Atlanta 30303
(404) 577-1779

Old City Hall, 45 School St., Boston 02108
(617) 367-8427

135 So. LaSalle St., Chicago 60603
(312) 236-7903

Cincinnati Commerce Center, 600 Vine St., Cincinnati 45202
(513) 721-8565

Eaton Center, 1111 Superior Ave., Cleveland 44114
(216) 566-7819

One Main Place, Dallas 75250
(214) 742-4394

Petro-Lewis Tower, 717 17 St., Denver 80202
(303) 298-8693

100 Renaissance Center, Detroit 48243
(313) 259-1156

1200 Milam St., Houston 77002
(713) 655-3400

611 W. Sixth St., Los Angeles 90017
(213) 627-1130

710 Miami Center, 100 Chopin Plaza, Miami 33131
(305) 358-1388

727 First Bank Place W., Minneapolis 55402
(612) 333-4886

1971 Pan Am Life Center, 601 Poydras St., New Orleans 70130
(504) 525-2958

200 Park Ave., 43rd fl., N.Y. 10166
(212) 309-8100

Two Mellon Bank Center, Philadelphia 19102
(215) 564-1788

One Oxford Center, 301 Grant St., Pittsburgh, PA 15219
(412) 261-5595

101 California St., San Francisco 94111
(415) 781-1707

1050 Connecticut Ave., N.W., Wash., DC 20036
(202) 785-3350

Mead Data Central Intl.:
Sun Life Centre, 200 King St. W., Toronto, Ont. M5H 3T4
(416) 591-8740

Intl. House, One St. Katherine's Way, London, England E19UN
(001) 441-488-9187

Mead Data Central, Inc. (MDC), a leader in instant information and a wholly owned subsidiary of The Mead Corporation, has developed the world's largest online, full-text database of business, legal, medical, general news and information. Mead has been a pioneer in electronic publishing, the rapidly growing information-based technology.

Formed in 1970, MDC provides nine major information services to subscribers in the U.S. and overseas. Two well-known services are LEXIS and NEXIS. The services are licensed overseas through Butterworth (Telepublishing) Ltd., in the United Kingdom, Tele-Consulte in France and Nihon Keizai Shimbun, Inc., in Japan. In addition, Mead Data Central International handles subscriptions worldwide with offices in London and Toronto.

LEXIS, a full-text, computer-assisted legal research service, was introduced in 1973. It includes the laws of all 50 states, Federal and state statutes and court cases, codes and regulations, as well as libraries of English and French law. It also contains law libraries concerned with securities, tax, labor, energy, bankruptcy, trade regulations, banking, international trade, admiralty, blue sky law, environmental law, transportation, military justice, law reviews, communications, public contract, insurance and patents, trademarks and copyrights. LEXIS has about 53 billion characters of information, equivalent to over 11 million documents. Supreme Court cases are usually added within 24 to 48 hours of decision.

NEXIS, a general and business news and information service, was introduced in 1980. It contains the full text of about 160 publications, including leading newspapers, magazines, newsletters, wire services and reference materials. It ranges widely from The Almanac of American Politics to the Xinhua (New China) News Agency and includes The New York Times, Fortune, The Associated Press, United

Press International, Reuters, Newsweek, Time, Sports Illustrated and the complete Encyclopaedia Britannica, as well as PR NEWSWIRE, among other resources.

About 14 million articles, or approximately 31 billion characters of information, are on NEXIS. Each week, about 17,000 articles are added.

Public relations and advertising agencies and departments, broadcast and print news media, publishers, government agencies, corporate planners and executives, investment bankers, and law and accounting firms are among the major users of NEXIS.

According to the results of a survey on newspapers' use of commercial databases taken by the Automation/Technology Committee of the Special Libraries Association Newspaper Division, NEXIS is used more frequently than any other database service.

In 1983, Mead Data Central added The Information Bank, a library of news summaries and abstracts originally created by The New York Times Information Service.

MDC also offers The New York Times in full text from June 1, 1980, to the present; the Advertising and Marketing Intelligence database (AMI); Kaleidoscope (data on economy, government, geography, population, culture, political party systems, for states, countries and world organizations), and other databases.

INFOBANK and NEXIS are excellent sources of biographical material and business news. Material from magazines and newspapers in addition to The New York Times is available, such as from The Wall Street Journal, The Washington Post, Business Week and the Financial Times (London), as well as Facts on File.

Following are some of the current publications abstracted in INFOBANK. This list also contains publications which may be researched in full text in NEXIS (marked with an asterisk). It is reprinted here as an aid to occasional users of INFOBANK and NEXIS. Perhaps no public relations professional reads all or most of these publications, but every professional should have a degree of familiarity with many of these newspapers and magazines.

General Circulation Newspapers

    Atlanta Constitution
    Chicago Tribune
   *Christian Science Monitor
    Houston Chronicle
    Los Angeles Times
    Miami Herald
  *The New York Times
    San Francisco Chronicle
    The Seattle Times
 *Washington Post

Business Publications

    Advertising Age
  *American Banker
    Automotive News
    Barron's
    Business Month
  *Business Week
 *Daily Report for Executives
    Editor & Publisher

Financial Times (Canada)
*Financial Times (London)
*Forbes
*Fortune
*Harvard Business Reviews
*Japan Economic Journal
Journal of Commerce
*Oil and Gas Journal
Oil Daily
Platt's Oilgram
The Wall Street Journal
Women's Wear Daily

International Affairs

Far Eastern Economic Review
Foreign Affairs
Foreign Policy
*Latin America Weekly
*Middle East Executive Reports
*The Economist
World Press Review

Science Publications

Astronautics
*Aviation Week & Space Technology
Industrial Research
Science
Scientific American

Other Periodicals

Atlantic
California Journal
Consumer Reports
Current Biography
Current News
*National Journal
National Review
*Newsweek
*Sports Illustrated
The New Yorker
*Time
*U.S. News & World Report
Variety
Washington Monthly

In addition, NEXIS has, in full text, many other publications such as Public Relations Journal, Harvard Business Review, Inc., InfoWorld, FEDWATCH and seven Time Inc. publications, including

People, Money, Discover and Life. The Executive Speaker newsletter offers tips for corporate spokespersons.

Another element of NEXIS is the EXCHANGE service, containing financial and trend analysis of thousands of companies and industries written by leading researchers and analysts at top brokerage and investment banking firms. The full text of 10K and 10Q filings with the Securities & Exchange Commission are also available.

INFOBANK Abstracts is a computerized information store of about 2.5 million abstracts on business, social and political topics prepared from over 60 publications. It provides detailed, informative abstracts of newspaper and magazine articles. An inquirer can specify the topics to be covered: broad or narrow, a single name or a combination of subjects. Each one retrieved is displayed on the computer terminal, along with a complete bibliographic citation from the original articles. Subscribers may use their own personal computers or terminals and high-speed printers or ones leased from Mead Data Central. On large reports, the basic bibliographic information is printed below the abstract.

The largest single source is the final Late City Edition of The New York Times. The Times files (abstracts, not full text) go back to January 1, 1969, and include Sunday and regional sections. Complete editions in full text are added 24–48 hours after publication.

NEXIS has also added selected full-text articles from hundreds of magazines and trade and industry journals in Magazine ASAP II and Trade & Industry ASAP II, provided by Information Access Co. These range from Chain Store Age to Modern Office Technology.

AMI contains a great number of advertising and marketing journals and magazines that are not abstracted in the regular ''Information Bank'' database. AMI and Deadline Data are especially helpful to professionals in public relations and advertising.

Another service of interest to communicators in health care institutions or businesses is MEDIS, medical information service. MEDIS contains the full text of dozens of leading clinical journals, including the publications of the American Medical Association (AMA). MEDIS also provides access to leading abstract databases of medical information.

The AP Political Service, also available in NEXIS, contains information on election campaigns, political issues, national polls, Congressional ratings, as well as events relating to past, present and future elections.

There is no one-time sign-up charge for subscribing to NEXIS. There are, however, installation and leasing charges if you obtain your terminal and printer from Mead. You may prefer to use your own equipment. NEXIS is available on most PCs, including IBM, Apple, Wang and DEC. MDC also supports Maryland Computer Service's terminal for the visually impaired.

There is a $50 monthly subscription charge and connect time charge of $20 per hour plus $15 per hour for the telecommunications network. The per search charges vary from $7 to $30, depending on the file being used. For example, the price for searching the full text of The New York Times is $7 per search. The file charge for searching the AMI database or the INFOBANK Abstracts database is $9 per search, while you may search both simultaneously for $15. It costs $9 to search Deadline Data on World Affairs. The Associated Press Political Service file (used extensively by newspapers) costs $12 to search. These search charges are 30 percent off between 7:30 P.M. and 7:30 A.M., local time.

67. Mediamark Research, Inc.
341 Madison Ave., N.Y. 10017
(212) 599-0444
Jack Nephew, V.P., Marketing

Mediamark is a superb resource for people in marketing. Among its tools are the MRI 10 Mediamarkets. This is a database of media and marketing information on 10 of the major markets in the country, New York, Los Angeles, Chicago, Philadelphia, San Francisco, Boston, Detroit, Washington, Cleveland and St. Louis.

Audience estimates for television news programs, newspapers, radio stations and radio station formats (e.g., top Country Western), are included, as well as user patterns for many products and brand names, and valuable demographics on survey respondents in these markets.

In MRI's Business-to-Business database, demographic information is available on 4,000 business professionals and managers MRI interviews. Included in survey results are their product purchases, such as advertising and equipment, and 200 magazines. Resulting demographics are provided on the professionals and their companies.

68. Monitor Publishing Co.
1301 Pennsylvania Ave., N.W., Wash., DC 20004
(202) 347-7757
Louis Isidora, Pres.

If you're involved with governmental relations and public issues, you'll want to know about these publications: The Federal Yellow Book is an organizational directory of the top-level decision-makers in the Federal departments and agencies. Each of the 29,000 listings includes titles, direct addresses, room and telephone numbers. The Federal Yellow Book is updated four times a year and costs $130 plus $10 postage and handling. The Congressional Yellow Book is a directory of members of Congress, their key staff aides and their committees and subcommittees. The Congressional Yellow Book is updated in its entirety four times a year and costs $107 plus $10 postage and handling.

Monitor also publishes Access Reports/Freedom of Information Newsletter and Reference File. The biweekly Newsletter is $250 a year; the Reference File is $375 for one year, or $475 for one year for the combined services. Other publications include quarterly directories of major companies.

69. The Naisbitt Group
1101 30 St., N.W., Wash., DC 20007
(202) 333-3228
John Naisbitt, Chm.
John Elkins, Pres.

John Naisbitt, author of several popular books about trends, publishes a newsletter ($98 a year) and operates a research firm that identifies and analyzes the effect of social, political, economic and technological trends in order to help clients respond to change. Services include:

Business Intelligence—environmental analysis tailored to client-identified issues. Findings published quarterly, $25,000 per year; $15,000 for six months.

Future Focus—a program integrating The Naisbitt Group trend analysis, industry-specific data, and personal interviews with company decision-makers, enabling executives to develop plans that account for the threats and opportunities affecting their company over the coming decade. Tailored to company needs and agendas, they are $30,000 and up.

Custom research, executive briefings, seminars and speakers also are available.

70. National Directory of Addresses and Telephone Numbers
General Information
401 Park Place, Kirkland, WA 98033
(206) 828-4777
Geri Hardy, Editor

Of special interest to public relations practitioners planning media tours, this directory includes guides to the top 50 cities, listing airports, car rentals, hotels and restaurants, and has sections on media and information sources. There are ZIP and area code guides, as well as hard-to-locate phone numbers.

The directory lists over 80,000 corporations in 300 categories, both alphabetically and by industry.

Included are all S.E.C. registered companies, banks and financial institutions, and major law and accounting firms. More than 6,200 government offices, Federal agencies and information centers, and 9,000 toll-free phone numbers are listed.

Copies are $39.95 each plus $4 for postage and handling. Discounts apply when ordering two or more copies.

71. National Library of Medicine

8600 Rockville Pike, Bethesda, MD 20894
(301) 496-6308, (301) 496-6095 (reference)
Dr. Donald A. B. Lindberg, Dir.

The National Library of Medicine (NLM), established in 1836, is the largest research library in a single scientific field. It collects materials in all major areas of the health sciences as well as in botany, chemistry, physics and zoology. There are over four million items housed in the library including rare medical manuscripts. It is open to researchers Monday through Saturday.

The library's computer-based Medical Literature Analysis and Retrieval System (MEDLARS) was a pioneer in the early 1960's for rapid retrieval and bibilographic access to NLM's storehouse of biomedical information. MEDLARS has evolved into a group of over 20 online databases of which the MEDLINE database is the most well-known. MEDLINE uses NLM's controlled vocabulary, MeSH (Medical Subject Headings), and searcher training is advisable.

72. National Technical Information Service (NTIS)

U.S. Department of Commerce
5285 Port Royal Rd., Springfield, VA 22161
(703) 487-4600, (800) 336-4700 (rush orders)
Joseph F. Caponio, Dir.

The National Technical Information Service, an agency of the U.S. Department of Commerce, is the central source for the public sale of information on U.S. Government-sponsored research and development and engineering reports. It serves as a clearinghouse for scientific data that are made available on paper, in film and machine-readable formats, as well as in online databases.

NTIS publications include the Government Reports Announcements & Index ($379), 26 Abstract Newsletters, six-volume GRA&I Annual Index ($479) and the Corporate Author Authority List ($175). Free catalogs are available on request.

The NTIS Bibliographic Database has been in existence since 1964 and is searchable through several commercial computer services, including BRS Information Technologies, Inc. (BRS); DIALOG Information Services, Inc., and ORBIT Search Service. It contains material on business procedures, urban and regional planning, regulatory matters, energy and the environment, behavior and society, and technological research. The database is comprised of summaries of more than one million technical reports prepared by Federal agencies and, annually, about 70,000 new citations are added.

73. NewsNet, Inc.

945 Haverford Rd., Bryn Mawr, PA 19010
(215) 527-8030, (800) 345-1301
John H. Buhsmer, Pres.
Andrew S. Elston, Exec. V.P.
Robert M. Hunsicker, Marketing Dir.

One of the most popular information retrieval services among public relations practitioners, NewsNet is owned by Independent Publications, a company with diversified interests in the information field and publisher of the Philadelphia Bulletin until 1980.

Specializing in newsletters, NewsNet focuses on 35 specific industry fields, including:

Telecommunications
Electronic/Computers
Investment
Finance & Accounting
Taxation
Energy
Publishing/Broadcasting
Government
Aerospace
Defense
Advertising
International Business
Law
Social Sciences

TRW Business Profiles is also available. This service monitors over 10 million business locations nationwide to give instant business credit information.

NewsNet indexes meaningful words for keyword scanning; it keeps back issues of publications on-line for reference and search. NewsNet's SEARCH commands include flexible date-range searching, proximity searching, string searching, wildcarding, and the Boolean operators AND, OR and BUT NOT.

NewsNet subscribers also have access to NewsFlash, its electronic clipping service, to allow continuous monitoring of all new material added to NewsNet for information of interest to the subscriber.

The database is a valuable resource for public relations clients because its specialized newsletters provide information from more than 320 services that contain in-depth, industry-specific news that is unavailable in newspapers or trade journals.

Ten news wire services, delivered on a 24-hour basis, are available on NewsNet. They include Associated Press (USA), UPI (USA), Reuters (Europe), Jiji (Japan), Xinhua (China) and PR Newswire (USA).

PR Newswire has news releases from over 8,500 sources, and it is more economically retrieved on NewsNet than through most electronic databases.

NewsNet's basic connect charges are : 300 and 1,200 baud, $60 per hour and, at 2,400 baud, $90.

A subscription fee, payable annually ($120), semiannually ($75), or monthly ($15) is applicable at time of sign-up.

NewsFlash has a delivery charge of 50 cents per captured news article.

NEXIS
One of the most widely used database services, NEXIS is described in the listing on Mead Data Central, the division of The Mead Corporation. It's indeed a reflection of the computer age that this venerable paper company now provides general major electronic "paperless" services.

74. Nielsen Marketing Research
Nielsen Plaza, Northbrook, IL 60062
(312) 498-6300
Steven J. Weinberg, V.P.

Is there a TV viewer who has not heard of Nielsen ratings? The A.C. Nielsen Co. (which merged in 1984 with Dun & Bradstreet) is one of the world's largest research companies.

Following are some of the Nielsen Marketing Research services. SCANTRACK Service is a weekly database of consumer sales through scanner-equipped supermarkets, measuring 38 major metropolitan areas and the total U.S.

The Retail Index is a record compiled for the drug/health and beauty aids, and food and alcoholic beverage industries on point-of-sale purchases and consumer response. The information is based on reports by Nielsen auditors who visit selected stores in each category.

A subscriber to Nielsen can see information on brand distribution, prices and trade support, consumer sales, inventories, competitive sales performance and market share. This is available in printed reports, charts and online via Nielsen's INF*ACT.

This retail index database can be accessed on an office or home computer. Costs vary depending on specific client requirements. Nielsen also offers other services, including test marketing.

75. Online

Online, Inc.
11 Tannery Lane, Weston, CT 06883
(203) 227-8466
Helen Gordon, Editor

Online, Inc., publishes professional journals and books and holds well-attended conferences in the online database industry. Its best-known publication is Online, which appears six times a year ($42.50). Database, a quarterly, is $42.50 a year, and there are Database Search Aids available.

76. Opinion Research Corporation

Box 183, N. Harrison St., Princeton, NJ 08540
(609) 924-5900
Andrew J. Brown, Pres.
Harry W. O'Neill, Vice Chm.
Henry L. Dursin, Sr. V.P.

Founded in 1938, Opinion Research Corporation conducts research for corporate, government, association and agency clients in a wide variety of areas. The Corporate Research Group, one of a number of operating groups within the company (others include Organizational Research, Marketing Research, Public Policy Research), conducts both customized and multi-client research projects in such fields as corporate reputations research, advertising and media research, financial and investor relations, community relations, media relations and public relations, and provides expert testimony in litigation.

ORC conducts two Omnibus surveys:

(1) Executive Caravan Surveys, quarterly telephone omnibus interviews with 500 top and middle management executives of the largest U.S. corporations, and (2) the bimonthly telephone Caravan survey among the general public.

ORC also has offices in New York, (212) 557-6616; Washington DC, (202) 484-5992; Chicago, (312) 828-9780, and San Francisco, (415) 421-1198.

77. ORBIT Search Service

Pergamon ORBIT InfoLine, Inc
8000 Westpark Dr., McLean, VA 22102
(703) 442-0900, (800) 421-7229
Michael Jones, Marketing

ORBIT offers access to over 70 databases in specialized technical fields. Pergamon InfoLine provides access to several million abstracts and references to journal articles, conference papers and technical reports. The databases also cover the biosciences and occupational safety and health. Prices per online connect hour range from $30 to $168.

78. Oxbridge Communications, Inc.
150 Fifth Ave., N.Y. 10011
(212) 741-0231
Patricia Hagood, Pres.

Oxbridge has the largest list database of U.S. and Canadian periodicals. Called Select Periodical Data, it covers 65,000 consumer and business magazines, trade and professional journals, as well as newsletters, newspapers and directories, and is available on labels, index cards, tape or printout. The periodicals lists have 245 subject classifications and can be requested by category and ZIP code selection, or by circulation, frequency, type of periodical, print method and other selections.

The lists can be addressed, for example, to the editor, publisher, advertising director, circulation director or art director. Lists of phone numbers also are available.

Labels, by category and ZIP selection, are $60 to $100 per thousand for Cheshire and $10 extra per thousand for pressure-sensitive labels. Select Periodical Data can be tapped with custom searches. These lists may be especially productive for news releases and estimates are available on request. Oxbridge guarantees its service by refunding 25 cents for each piece of undeliverable mail.

Oxbridge's eleventh edition of the Standard Periodicals Directory costs $325.

79. Packaged Facts Information Services
274 Madison Ave., N.Y. 10016
(212) 532-5533
David Ansel Weiss, Pres.

In 1958, Mr. Weiss took a look at the several hundred files, envelopes, shoe boxes and miscellaneous containers which were filled with books, clippings and other fact files which he had collected as a publicist for Universal Pictures and decided that he could go into business supplying facts to other publicists. Starting on a part-time basis, he quickly developed procedures which enabled him to delve into his own files and also tap the multitude of research sources in New York City. It's no coincidence that the company's offices are located near the New York Public Library.

In 1962, Mr. Weiss became a full-time researcher and Packaged Facts thus may be the oldest "information service" in the public relations field. Originally established to research colorful trivia and "believe it or not" historical facts for use in advertising promotion and publicity, Packaged Facts now offers a dozen different other research services, ranging from "information packages" on specific subjects to anniversary facts geared to companies and organizations celebrating anniversaries.

Packaged Facts is totally oriented to public relations needs, and you should talk with David Weiss about any problems which could be solved via research.

Packaged Facts operates a unique "back-dated" clipping service, and it also checks advertisements and editorial coverage as far back as the 1880's for trademark and other legal purposes. It operates on an assignment basis and is not confined to its own library resources (which are extensive), but utilizes the services of a large network of private and public information sources it has built up through the years. Another difference between Packaged Facts and other information sources is that it is staffed by professional writers who, because of their writing ability, can evaluate the research in terms of the use to which it will be put—and also, if desired, write whatever is required from a fact news-letter or magazine article to a full-length book.

80. PaperChase
Beth-Israel Hospital
330 Brookline Ave., Boston, MA 02215
Patricia Ryan, Marketing Mgr.
(800) 722-2075

With the help of a grant from the National Library of Medicine, the PaperChase service first became available to the public in 1984. It provides online searchers with menu-driven access to citations and abstracts in the 4,000 biomedical journals of NLM's Medline. The connect fee is $23 per hour plus 10 cents per reference printed. There's no subscription charge or monthly minimum.

Any reference can be flagged for the complete article which can be copied and mailed. The cost is $6 per article.

81. Pharmaceutical News Index (PNI)

UMI/Data Courier
620 S. Fifth St., Louisville, KY 40202
(800) 626-2823
Susan Baker, Editor

Pharmaceutical News Index (PNI) is an online citation source of current news about pharmaceuticals, cosmetics, medical devices and related health fields. Its records are drawn from such sources as Biomedical Business International, SCRIP World Pharmaceutical News, "Clinica," Pharma Japan and the seven FDC Reports. On DIALOG, PNI is $129 per connect hour.

82. Predicasts, Inc. (PTS)

11001 Cedar Ave., Cleveland, OH 44106
(216) 795-3000, (800) 321-6388
Telex: 985 604
Paul Owen, V.P., Online Services
Don Lensner, Dir. of Marketing

Predicasts was founded in 1960 as a research company and went online in 1974. The firm is a subsidiary of Thyssen/Bornemisza, Monaco.

The Predicasts Terminal System (PTS) is one of the largest online sources available for business information. Consisting of 10 databases, it can be used to obtain information about mergers and acquisitions, market data, management trends, economic environment, growth markets, international activities, new products and technologies, government regulations, and social and political climates. Many documents cited in the databases are available through Predicasts' Articles Delivery Service (PADS). Predicasts also produces much of this same information in hard-copy publications.

Marketing and Advertising Reference Service (MARS) is a Predicasts database that focuses on the advertising, promotion and marketing of consumer products and services. It contains abstracts of articles from over 120 key publications, including Adweek, Chicago Tribune, Jack O'Dwyer's Newsletter, The New York Times, Public Relations Journal, Marketing, Campaign and Advertising Age. Predicasts uses nine specific search codes for public relations topics and over 40 advertising and marketing concept codes for searching related topics.

Predicasts databases also include PROMT, an excellent resource for information on companies—their products, technologies and industries—abstracting articles from worldwide trade and business journals, business newspapers, research studies, brokerage reports and many local U.S. and Canadian publications.

PROMT Daily is a business news database that is updated every business day with the same broad source and subject coverage as PROMT, including abstracts from The New York Times online within 24 hours and other key publications within 48 hours of receipt.

Aerospace/Defense Markets & Technology (A/DM&T) provides abstracts from the world's leading aerospace, defense and commercial aviation publications containing information on company and market activity.

New Product Announcements (NPA) contains the full-text of news releases detailing the introduction of all types of new products and services as submitted by the issuing company or organization.

Annual Reports Abstracts (ARA) contains key information from the annual reports of more than 4,000 leading U.S. and selected foreign companies.

F&S Index offers concise (one- or two-line) summaries of articles covering companies, business and financial activities, demographics, government regulations, economic and other issues affecting business. F&S Index covers hundreds of other sources not covered in PROMT.

Forecasts and Time Series are invaluable for providing projection and historical statistics—with emphasis on product data—especially helpful when evaluating size and trends of an industry, product or market.

All Predicasts files are available through DIALOG; selected files are available on BRS, Data-Star and VU/TEXT. A user can establish an account with the vendor directly or contact Predicasts Customer Service Dept. for information. The price structure varies according to the Predicasts database and vendor. For example, on DIALOG, PROMT is $126 per online connect hour plus 73 cents per full record printed offline, or 63 cents per full record typed or displayed online.

PTS Online News, a Predicasts newsletter, is available at no charge.

83. QL Systems Ltd.
1 Gore St., Kingston, Ont. K7L 2L1, Canada
(613) 549-4611, (800) 267-9470
Adrienne Herron, V.P., Marketing

Branch Offices:
250 Sixth Ave., S.W., Calgary, Alberta T2P 3H7
(403) 262-6505

1819 Granville St., Halifax, Nova Scotia, B3J 1X8
(902) 429-3725

275 Sparks St., Ottawa, Ont. K1R 7X9, Canada
(613) 238-3499

355 Burrard St., Vancouver, British Columbia V6C 2G8
(604) 684-1462

QL Systems Ltd., which developed out of a project begun in 1968 by law students at Queens University, Kingston, was incorporated in 1973, offering the first Canadian commercial information retrieval system, QL/Search.

QL/Search provides online retrieval of over 100 databases concerning news, business, environment, energy, government and Parliament, law, mining and related subjects. In 1984, Canada News-Wire Database became available on QL Systems with full-text, next-day access to all news releases transmitted by the wire service.

Users are required to have an ASCII terminal that will communicate at 300, 1,200 or 2,400 baud through Telenet or Tymnet (in the U.S.). Access charges are $75 per hour (QL/Search subscribers in Canada pay $150 per hour on VU/TEXT). Addition royalty or copyright charges may apply to some databases.

84. Research & Forecasts, Inc.
301 E. 57 St., N.Y. 10022
(212) 593-6400, (212) 593-6424
Steve Barnett, Chm.
Frank Walton, Pres.

Formed in 1968, Research & Forecasts is owned by Ruder Finn & Rotman, one of the world's largest public relations agencies, so that the initials R & F were perfectly chosen. With offices in New York and Chicago and a staff of over 14 professionals who handle assignments for many ''outside clients,'' including other agencies, R & F has become one of the largest public relations research organizations in the country. Facilities include an in-house WATS line center with over 30 stations, an array of computers and other equipment. Omnibus services include:

Physicians Omnibus—a quarterly multi-client survey involving a national sample of about 300 physicians.
Communications Omnibus—a monthly multi-client, shared-cost survey.
Business Leaders Omnibus—a quarterly multi-client survey.

R & F conducts routine searches, as well as a variety of other studies and surveys, the most famous of which are its corporate-sponsored, public issue research projects.

85. The Reuter NewsFile
Reuters Information Services
1700 Broadway, N.Y. 10019
(212) 603-3575
Jim Outman

Reuters, one of the world's leading suppliers of business and financial news to investment professionals and the news media, has been transmitting the news since its founding in 1851.

In 1986, Reuters introduced Reuter NewsFile, a key-word monitoring program that runs on personal computers (IBM compatible). The program allows the end user to choose a list of up to 315 key words or phrases. The computer then monitors incoming Reuters and other news wires. When it finds one of the designated key words or phrases, the entire story containing the item is saved on the PC's disk for instant access.

NewsFile is designed for information professionals who wish to track specific issues, companies or persons in the news, without wading through the many thousands of words a day issued by Reuters. The program operates ''in background,'' allowing the PC to be used simultaneously as a word processor.

Developed by News Technology Corp., of Mountainview, CA, NewsFile runs with a variety of Reuter news services: The Reuter News Report (general world and national news); the Reuter Financial Report (a broadtape of U.S. corporate news), and The Reuter Business Report (U.S. and international business news edited for the news media).

The software retails for $1,250. Additional charges include a monthly subscription fee of about $550.

See the financial chapter for information on The Reuter Monitor, the interactive system used by the financial and business community.

86. The Roper Center for Public Opinion Research
Box 440, Storrs, Ct 06268
(203) 486-4440
John M. Barry, Mgr., User Services Development

The Roper Center is the world's largest library of public opinion data. A nonprofit library with offices on the campus of the University of Connecticut, the Roper Center is affiliated with Williams College and the University of Connecticut. It was founded in 1946 by George Gallup and Elmo Roper.

The Roper Center has over 11,000 surveys conducted during the last 50 years, including over 1,400 Gallup polls, plus material from the Roper Organization; Yankelovich, Skelly and White; the National Opinion Research Center (NORC); CBS News and The New York Times; ABC News and The Washington Post; NBC News; Market Opinion Research International (MORI), in Great Britain; Canadian Gallup; Brule Ville Associes in France; Social Surveys (Gallup Poll) Ltd., in Great Britain, and many others.

Members can charge services against their annual membership fee ($2,000). Services generally are $27 an hour for members and $36 an hour for nonmembers. Other fee schedules, including access charges, also vary for members and nonmembers.

87. Search/INFORM

UMI/Data Courier
620 Fifth St., Louisville, KY 40202
(800) 626-2823, (800) 626-0307 (Canada)

Search/INFORM, by the producers of ABI/INFORM, is a two-volume loose-leaf user aid for searchers. It contains a thesaurus of more than 6,000 controlled vocabulary terms for the searcher. Search tips for the electronic systems that offer ABI/INFORM are included with a chart of each system's protocols and "how-tos" on ordering documents. Search/INFORM is $65.

88. I.P. Sharp Associates Ltd.

Exchange Tower, 2 First Canadian Place, Toronto, Ont. M5X 1E3, Canada
(416) 364-5361, (800) 387-1588
Telex: 06-22259
I.P. Sharp, Chmn.
Irene Shimoda, Marketing Services

U.S. Headquarters:
1200 First Federal Plaza, Rochester, NY 14614
(716) 546-7270

Many newspapers, such as Newsday, print graphs and charts, with the source of the data attributed to I.P. Sharp. The company is not as well known to consumers as Nielsen, Gallup, Harris, NEXIS and DIALOG, though it is used by many researchers.

I.P. Sharp Associates is an international communications and software company which provides a variety of software products for both mainframe and personal computers, a private international packet-switched telecommunications network (IPSANET), one of the world's largest collections of online numeric business data (InfoService), and SHARP APL (a powerful, concise, highly productive programming language). With corporate headquarters in Toronto, the company has over 40 offices in 25 countries, and provides local dial-up access to IPSANET from more than 600 cities worldwide, either directly or through interfaces to most public networks.

Comprehensive data, provided through I.P. Sharp's InfoService, includes over 60 million time series of public data in more than 120 databases. Information covers the areas of aviation, economics, energy and finance. Complete flexibility in time series analysis and report generating is available, along with portfolio analysis and plotting capabilities. Users can combine InfoService data with their own private data using the I.P. Sharp Online service, or data can be retrieved from InfoService using a personal computer and downloaded for local analysis by user programs or software systems such as LOTUS 1-2-3, VisiCalc or Compu Trac.

89. Softwhere?

Box 3336, Yuba City, CA 95992
(916) 674-3688
David Peterson, Marketing Mgr.

This company helps to locate software and also offers over 6,000 inexpensive public domain software programs for many applications.

90. The Source

Source Telecomputing Corporation (STC)
1616 Anderson Rd., McLean, VA 22102
(703)734-7500, (800) 336-3366, (800) 336-3330
Nancy Beckman, Mgr., Corporate Communications

The Source information network was founded in 1979. Previously a subsidiary of The Reader's Digest Association, it was purchased in 1987 by Welsh, Carson, Anderson & Stowe.

The first online information service designed for the individual, The Source offers an array of hundreds of features, such as information retrieval, electronic messaging and computing. Like CompuServe and Dow Jones, it is a menu-driven system that asks the user questions on screen and has a command-driven system for expert users.

The Source is one of the most economical of the database research services and is particularly useful to public relations practitioners who are just getting started with computerized research. It provides reference and news databases, such as the United Press International wire service, Associated Press, The Washington Post, Scripps-Howard News Service, United Media Features (75 columns and features including Jack Anderson's "Washington Merry-Go-Round") and Academic American Encyclopedia online.

The Source carries financial information, including real time stock market quotes; consumer information services, including movie reviews, restaurant and hotel guides; communications services, such as electronic mail and bulletin boards, and general entertainment, including games.

The UPI Newswire has online the latest news, business features, sports, regional and state news. Features and syndicated columns can be searched by author or keyword. UPI material is retained online for seven days after being filed. Current stores can be obtained more economically on The Source than on some other electronic services, and there are about 2,500 UPI stories each week.

Commodity World News (CWN) watches news and price activity on all major commodity exchanges. Market quotes are available from the UPI Unistox service and include stocks, bonds, commodities, money markets, Government paper and metal. Stockvue, provided by Media General Financial Services, retrieves current and historical information on 4,000 stocks.

The Official Airline Guides Electronic Edition lists fares and schedules from 750 airlines and information is updated continually.

The Mobil Restaurant Guide includes over 6,000 listings in U.S. and Canadian cities. The printout includes a restaurant review, driving directions, phone number and credit card information. Reservations for hotels, airlines, car rental and tours can be made online.

Source subscriptions and manuals are available through The Source or at computer stores. The Source charges a one-time sign-up fee of $49.95. The fee includes ID and password, user's manual and subscription to the monthly Sourceworld newsletter. There's a $10 per month minimum usage fee.

The Source is online 24 hours a day. At 300 baud, it is $0.36 per minute and, at 1,200 baud, $0.43, from 8 A.M. to 6 P.M. Weekends, evenings and holidays cost $0.14 per minute at 300 baud and $0.18 at 1,200 baud.

Value-added services, including Media General (with the Stockvue Service) are $39.75 per hour on 300 baud, Monday through Friday, 7 A.M. to 6 P.M., and $34.75 from 6 P.M. to 7 A.M., and on weekends and holidays.

91. Standard & Poor's COMPUSTAT Services, Inc.
7400 S. Alton Ct., Englewood, CO 80112
(800) 525-8640
Frank Hermes, V.P., Marketing

Branch Office:
121 Ave. of Americas, N.Y. 10020
(212) 512-4900

COMPUSTAT, a subsidiary of Standard & Poor's, is a database of standardized financial statistics on more than 7,000 companies. It is gathered from public source documents and updated daily, and is one of the most widely used financial databanks.

The data generally cover two decades of annual and one decade of quarterly income statements and balance sheets and market statistics. The database has two major classifications, Industrial and Nonindustrial, with the Industrial containing information on U.S. and Canadian companies, and the Nonindustrial encompassing U.S. bank holding companies, utility and telephone companies. A "Comparative Analysis" service provides client-selected criteria reports.

The database includes specialty files such as Prices-Dividends-Earnings (PDE), a Business Information file with geographic and industry data, a Research file covering companies no longer actively filing reports with the S.E.C., and the Aggregate file, with data on industries.

COMPUSTAT is furnished on magnetic tapes, hard disk cartridges, floppy diskettes for microcomputer usage and through timesharing access over several commercial systems, such as CompuServ, Interactive Data, Data Resources (owned by McGraw-Hill) and ADP Network Services. A new product, PC Plus, presents the COMPUSTAT database on a CD-ROM (Compact Disc-Read Only Memory).

92. Survey Research Corporation
1331 Pennsylvania Ave., N.W., Wash., DC 20004
(202) 662-7358
Philip W. Steitz, Pres.

Founded in 1974 to conduct studies of public opinion, Survey Research Corp. is operated by people with considerable public relations experience. One of the founders, Paul M. Lewis, now retired, was cofounder of Press Intelligence, a clipping bureau. Phil Steitz was managing editor of Publishers Newspaper Syndicate and directed communications for VISTA and recruitment for the Peace Corps.

The company conducts national polls, national image surveys, focus groups and creates studies.

93. Technical Library Service, Inc.
213 W. 35 St., N.Y. 10001-1996
(212) 736-7744
Mrs. Elaine Haas, Pres.

Several very sizable business libraries have been set up in New York, Chicago and a few other cities to supply the needs of private subscribers. In addition, most public libraries maintain reference departments in which the librarians usually welcome intelligent inquires from publicists and other local residents. Several of the public libraries provide encyclopedia information and answers to questions over the telephone.

Technical Library Service is a group of professional librarians who are specialists in many areas of business, science and technical subjects. They are available for all types of literature research and information assignments for fees of about $15 per hour, with special rates for long-term projects.

94. Toll-Free Digest

Toll-Free Digest Co., Inc.
Box 800, Claverack, NY 12513
(518) 828-6400, (800) 447-4700
Paul Montana, Editor

Is there a public relations person who can work without a telephone? Here's a book which definitely will save you a tremendous amount of time and money. The Toll-Free Digest, which is published annually for $17.95, lists over 43,000 toll-free numbers in about 500 pages.

Note that in many areas it may be necessary to dial "1" or "O" before beginning the call and that some companies have an 800 number for a limited time only or for a brief promotion.

Should you have a toll-free number and want it listed in Toll-Free Digest, send the necessary information on your letterhead to Paul Montana. Include your company address, the category, the number and geographic areas from which the number may be dialed. There is no charge for the listing.

95. TRINET

Nine Campus Dr., Parsippany, NJ 07054
(201) 267-3600, (800)-FOR-DATA

Trinet produces the U.S. Business Information databases about companies with over 20 employees. Comprehensive and well-researched, they provide company specifics, including market share, annual sales volume, number of employees, SIC Codes, ticker symbols and geographic codes, among other searchable fields. They are useful for market research and analysis, merger and acquisition analysis and prospect lists. This database is available online through DIALOG, Mead Data Central, Data Resources Inc., M.A.I.D. and Control Data Business Information Services. Offline, the information is available directly through TRINET in various formats such as diskettes, magnetic tape, standard reports, mailing lists, lead cards and custom reports.

96. TRT Telecommunications Corporation

1331 Pennsylvania Ave., N.W., Wash., DC 20004
(202) 879-2200
Telex: 197779

Branch Office:
26 Broadway, N.Y. 10004
(212) 635-2680
Fred Kossar, V.P.-Voice Services

Through an operating agreement with British Telecom International, TRT provides international direct distance dial telephone service, and voice/data service for businesses in New York and London. Called Citydirect, this innovative service adds a new dimension to transatlantic communications by providing an attractive cost-effective alternative to regular telephone service and dedicated private lines for banks, brokerage houses, hotels and multinational companies.

TRT also has partnerships with COMSAT, International Satellite, Inc., Pacific Satellite, Inc. and other companies to provide a variety of telex and telecommunications services.

97. Tyson Capitol Institute

7735 Old Georgetown Rd., Bethesda, MD 20814
(301) 652-4185
Charles M. Tyson, Pres.

A subsidiary of Tyson, Belzer & Associates (formed in 1965), Tyson Capitol Institute conducts research and development of computer systems and databases for use by lobbyists, Government relations and public affairs specialists. Its Congressional District/ZIP Code System permits associations, companies, unions, special-interest groups and others to identify membership, employees, stockholders and manufacturing plants by Congressional district of location by using the ZIP code in the address.

Other database services include:

Congressional District/Newspapers: Computer system and publication which identifies the newspaper coverage within each Congressional district. Particular emphasis on weekly newspapers. State Legislators database: Computerized data file on 7,500 state legislators. Addresses are home or business addresses. Cross-referenced legislative district locator maps identify geographic area represented by legislator.

Available on magnetic computer tape, diskettes and in book form, the systems are provided at discounts to members of the Institute. Membership is $995 per year, plus separate charges for the various systems: $750 for the newspapers and $675 for the state legislators system.

98. U.S. Bureau of The Census

Data Users Services Division
Wash., DC 20233
(301) 763-4100

If you're searching for census data, Cendata offers online demographic information compiled by the U.S. Bureau of the Census. It gives economic data in many areas including manufacturing. Cendata offers domestic demographics, containing excerpts from the Current Population Reports. It also carries press releases issued on housing starts, the balance of trade and other items. Updated daily, Cendata can be found on DIALOG.

99. United States Government Printing Office

Wash., DC 20402
(202) 783-3238

The world's biggest bookstore and publication research source is the U.S. Government. Best sellers (over 10 million copies) include Infant Care (number-one best seller), Prenatal Care and Postage Stamps of the U.S.

Books of special interest to public relations readers include:

Statistical Abstract of the United States
GPO Style Manual
National ZIP Code Directory

The U.S. Government Manual ($20) is a 900-page index to Federal offices throughout the country and is the basic source for many other directories.

The more than 14,000 different Government publications are sold by the Superintendent of Documents—*not* the individual Government agencies. More than 2,000 orders are processed a day, so the more you know about the government's bookstore, the faster the service to you and everyone else.

The most complete list of currently issued Government publications is the "Monthly Catalog of U.S. Government Publications," available on subscription at $141 a year, which lists the publications of all departments issued during the month, whether for sale or otherwise.

There is no free distribution by the Superintendent, nor is there any credit or c.o.d., though a prepaid deposit account may be established for a minimum of $50. Quantity discounts are available. Publications may be charged to VISA and Mastercard accounts.

The sale of Government publications is largely a mail-order business, but the Superintendent of Documents operates a modern bookstore in the Government Printing Office at North Capitol and G Streets in Washington just a few blocks from the Capitol. It is open from 8 A.M. to 4 P.M., Monday through Friday. On display are over 2,000 of the more popular Government publications. Bookstores are located in two locations in Washington and in Chicago, Kansas City, San Francisco, Boston, Los Angeles, Dallas, Atlanta, New York City, Milwaukee, Seattle, Pueblo, Philadelphia, Birmingham, Detroit, Columbus, Houston, Denver, Cleveland, Jacksonville and Pittsburgh.

If you are a frequent user of Government publications, you may wish to request U.S. Government Books, a quarterly catalog about 1,000 new and popular publications and New Books, a bimonthly listing. Both are available at no charge from the Superintendent of Documents, U.S. Government Printing Office, Washington, DC 20402.

The National Technical Information Service of the U.S. Department of Commerce is the central source for Government and Government-sponsored research reports, available in print, microfiche and via computer. For a catalog and price list, write NTIS at 5285 Port Royal Rd., Springfield, VA 22161. (See separate listing in this chapter.)

The Consumer Information Center in Pueblo, CO 81009, provides free booklets from various Federal agencies.

Government information can be located using indexes published by Congressional Information Service, Inc. (CIS), 4520 East-West Highway, Bethesda, MD 20814. Selected searches also may be conducted online through the computer facilities of CIS and Lockheed's DIALOG, and the documents identified may be obtained in microfiche format from CIS. Call Richard K. Johnson at (301) 654-1550 for more information.

100. United States Institute of Marketing

221 Penn Towers, 1100 Penn Center Blvd., Pittsburgh 15235
(412) 824-2022
Robert C. Steckel, Pres.

This marketing consulting firm publishes 130- to 300-page studies about the current print orchestrating (including samples and evaluation) in various categories, including banking, computer, health, real estate and retirement. Each report is $135.

101. The United States Trademark Association

6 E. 45 St., N.Y. 10017
(212) 986-5880
Douglas Barden, Dir. of Membership Services

An excellent trademark library is maintained by the U.S. Trademark Association, a nonprofit organization with a worldwide membership of more than 1,800 corporations, professional associations and individuals interested in the protection and development of trademarks.

The USTA, through its news bulletins, keep members posted and provides A Guide to the Care of Trademarks, which offers such tips as "since a trademark is not a noun, it should never be used in the plural form," and "trademarks are proper adjectives and should never be used as common descriptive adjectives."

Public relations firms qualify as Associate Members. Dues are $600 a year and include a subscription to the bimonthly The Trademark Reporter, the preeminent publication in the field, and about 50 bulletins a year on developments in U.S. and international trademark law and related articles in the press.

102. VU/TEXT Information Services, Inc. (a Knight-Ridder Company)

325 Chestnut St., Philadelphia, PA 19106
(215) 574-4400, (800) 323-2940
Donna Willmann, Dir. of Marketing

VU/TEXT provides full-text access to such national publications as The Washington Post and The Los Angeles Times; regional newspapers including The Philadelphia Inquirer, The Detroit Free Press, Philadelphia Daily News, The Sacramento Bee, The Anchorage Daily News, Lexington Herald-Leader, Houston Post and The Miami Herald; sources of business and financial information such as The Wall Street Transcript, The Journal of Commerce and VU/QUOTE. The Tribune Company has selected VU/TEXT to provide full-text electronic library retrieval services for its eight newspapers, including The Chicago Tribune and New York Daily News.

In 1984, VU/TEXT added access to article summaries from hundreds of business publications, such as Forbes, Fortune and Advertising Age, through the business-oriented databases of PTS PROMT and ABI/INFORM. VU/TEXT also offers several wire services, The Associated Press wire, Knight-Ridder Financial News, Knight-News-Tribune News Wire, Business Wire and PR Newswire.

In 1986, Business Dateline was added, offering full-text articles from 140 regional publications in the U.S. and Canada.

VU/TEXT is accessible via any PC or communicating terminal with a modem. It is command-driven.

There are two payment options for subscribers to VU/TEXT—the first is a contract rate plan requiring $90 minimum per month in connect time billing. The other is an open rate plan, which costs more per hour but the subscriber is only charged if the service is used. For example, on Option I, The Philadelphia Inquirer is $90 an hour and, on Option II, $105 per hour. Actual charges vary according to the database accessed. There is no additional charge for 1,200 baud access. One definite plus is that VU/TEXT is available 23-½ hours a day, seven days a week.

103. WSY Consulting Group, Inc.

1350 Ave. of the Americas, N.Y. 10019
(212) 247-2690
Daniel Yankelovich, Chm.
Florence Skelly, Vice Chm.
Arthur White, Pres.

Formed in 1987, WSY Consulting Group includes the Van Dyk Associates of Washington, D.C., consultants on public policy and government affairs; the Futures Group of Glastonbury, CT, and Washington, which does marketing studies, and Stockman & Associates of Greenwich, CT, consultants in international marketing, technology transfer, brokerage and distribution. Daniel Yankelovich was founder and chairman of Yankelovich, Skelly & White.

104. Washington Post Index

Research Publications, Inc.
12 Lunar Dr., Woodbridge, CT 06525
(203) 397–2600
Helen Greenway, Marketing V.P.

The Washington Post Index covers all "significant" material appearing in the final edition of each day's Washington Post, as well as the three regional weeklies: Virginia, Maryland and District of Columbia. The index includes business and finance, commentary and opinion, national and international news, sports, entertainment, religion, real estate, Washington area news and travel. Items under two column inches are not included, nor are question-and-answer advice columns and other "routine" items. An annual subscription is $350.

The Washington Post is available online in full text on NEXIS VU/TEXT, The Source and Data Times.

105. Washington Researchers, Ltd.
2612 P St., N.W., Wash., DC 20007
(202) 333–3499
Leila K. Kight, Pres.
Dania Fitzgerald, Office Admin.

Started in 1974 as a customized research service, Washington Researchers has grown into a major publisher and research firm. Some of its publications are:

How to Find Information About Companies: The Corporate Intelligence Source Book, $125.
Who Knows: A Guide to Washington Experts, $125.
Federal Fast Finder (where to locate Federal departments, agencies, commissions, boards), $15.
The Information Report (a monthly newsletter), $120.
Business Researcher's Handbook: The Comprehensive Guide for Business Professionals, $65.
How to Find Business Intelligence in Washington, $95.

The company, which also conducts a variety of seminars, was founded by Leila Kight and Matthew Lesko. Note that her name does not have an N in it.

106. Washington Service Bureau
655 15th St., N.W., Wash., DC 20005
(202) 833–9200, (800) 828–5354
Jeanne M. Carroll, Marketing Mgr.

Washington Service Bureau has a library of government documents, available on a same-day basis, including S.E.C. reports such as: 13Ds—Williams Act filings, 10Ks, 10Qs, proxies, registration statements, Investment Company Act filings, releases and no-action letters.

Documents cost 45 cents per page, $25 minimum. Research is available at any Federal agency for same-day service ($65), 24-hour service ($45), or one-week service ($35), plus photocopying charges of 65 cents per page.

A monitoring service is available to watch for filings at Federal government agencies. Information can be sent by facsimile. A daily watch costs $8.50 per day per company, a weekly watch is $35 and a monthly watch, $70.

Washington Service Bureau also can provide publications that specialize in various areas, including immigration law, ERISA, energy, communications, securities and banking.

107. WESTLAW/West Publishing Co.
Box 64526, 50 W. Kellogg Blvd., St. Paul, MN 55164
(800) 328–0109
D. D. Opperman, Pres.

WESTLAW is renowned as a law-related online service. It carries Federal and state cases, statutes, current awareness services like CCH's Tax Day, and Tax Notes Plus. It also has services such as Insta-Cite (West's Case History and Citation verification service), law reviews, the Forensic Services Directory and Cuadra-Elsevier Directory of Databases, as well as the American Bar Association summaries and related sources. Subscribers can lease or buy equipment to connect, through a telephone data line, to the WESTLAW computer in St. Paul, and charges vary by type of account and amount of usage.

108. The H.W. Wilson Company

950 University Ave., Bronx, NY 10452
(212) 588–8400, (800) 367–6770
John L. Clayborne

Wilson publications and WilsonLine databases are well known to researchers. Online files include Readers' Guide to Periodical Literature, at $45 per connect hour, and Business Periodicals Index, $65 per connect hour. Prices are somewhat lower for subscribers to Wilson publications and those who prepay for searches. Telecommunications through Telenet or Tymnet packet-switching networks are $10 per hour. The user's guide costs $55. The company was started in 1898.

109. World Wide Information Services, Inc.

360 First Ave., N.Y. 10010
(212) 677–7839
Richard W. Hubbell, Pres.

In May 1958, United Press and International News Service merged, and a lot of people, particularly from INS, suddenly found themselves out of work. Within a few days after the merger, World Wide Information Services was formed with a nucleus of former INS staffers. The initial intent was to provide competent reporting and research to commercial clients, making use of the several thousand INS personnel throughout the world.

Today, the World Wide Information Services network includes more than 14,000 reporters, photographers, editors, analyists and other specialists who handle assignments in just about every city in the U.S. and 142 other countries.

In addition to interviews and writing assignments, WWIS has developed an Intelligence Service. Confidential information, feasibility analyses and other research reports are filed by WWIS correspondents for dozens of commercial clients. In many cases, these correspondents are employed by newspapers and other media and thus have ready access to publication morgues, public records and other information sources, in addition to being trained in interview techniques.

Assignments range from print or broadcast monitoring, and other specific, one-time, easy-to-do projects, to confidential, comprehensive investigations, interviews and evaluations. Fees generally start at $1,000 in the U.S. and $2,500 elsewhere.

110. Yankelovich Skelly and White/Clancy/Shulman, Inc.

Eight Wright St., Westport, CT 06880
(212) 752–7500, (203) 227–2700
Kevin Clancy, Chm.
Robert Shulman, Pres.

Branch Offices:
822 Boylston St., Chestnut Hill, MA 02167
(617) 739–1112

567 San Nicolas Dr., Newport Beach, CA 92660
(714) 759–1425

Yankelovich Skelly and White/Clancy/Shulman is a full-service market research and consulting firm using marketing models, sophisticated analysis techniques and proprietary databases to provide "marketing intelligence." The firm is divided into three business units: Consumer Research, Consumer Marketing Consulting and Business to Business Research and Consulting.

Chapter 29

Schools

More than 59 million students and educators spend a good part of their lives in about 110,000 public and private schools in the United States, ranging from nursery schools to universities. Enrollment figures shift each year. An upward trend is the number of adults enrolled in nondegree, continuing education programs. Since one out of four Americans is a student, one way to reach the group is via the general media, as well as the campus media, particularly high school and college newspapers and college radio and TV stations. Services which include these media in their distribution are discussed in the chapters on newspapers, radio and television.

Many public relations clients, particularly associations and companies in the health, cosmetics and youth-oriented fields, operate school programs, which include posters, films, speakers and other techniques to reach students inside their schools.

Videocassette players and recorders are now widely used in schools and industry. Filmstrips and slide film projectors are a vital piece of equipment in almost every primary and secondary school classroom. Many thousands of business, Government, religious and other organizations own or have access to projectors. As a result, videotapes, slides and filmstrips can play an important part in almost any public relations program. Government agencies, associations, companies and others have made a valuable educational contribution by distributing thousands of educational filmstrips to schools.

Most motion picture producers and still photographers produce filmstrips. However, many public relations clients prefer to deal with filmstrip specialists, particularly since there are some companies which have established channels of distribution to schools and other key audiences.

Though filmstrips are cheaper than films, videotapes and motion pictures generally are more effective, and since more schools have videotape players and 16mm sound projectors than ever before, the trend is moving toward these media among public relations sponsors. However, slide programs and filmstrips certainly are not outmoded or unacceptable. An educational consultant generally considers budget and other factors before selecting one or more techniques.

Schools offer sponsors one of the most important channels of communication, because motion pictures have become an integral part of class study. A well-made film can become part of a young person's learning experience, particularly if it is introduced by the teacher and then discussed by the class. Many sponsors send out teachers' guides, booklets, wall charts and other supplementary materials to be used with their films.

Sponsors interested in reaching school audiences should take advantage of the new research material that is available. Recent studies address such questions as: *What sponsored film subjects are of greatest interest? What is the best length (running time)? Which format is preferred (16mm film, videocassette, other)? What kind of collateral materials are needed?*

The size of the market makes it impossible for any one client to cover all schools, and the best technique may be a teacher's guide or teacher's program, with no student materials, or perhaps a live program (one unusual company specializes in live shows in "school assemblies"), or one or more of an array of materials, including comic books, booklets, posters, charts, records, samples, as well as films and filmstrips.

Among the services provided by a film or filmstrip distributor are reports of numbers of showings, numbers of students, their ages, comments of the teachers and other data. One print of a filmstrip often is viewed by more than 500 students per school during the first year of its use and frequently is used for several years, and films reach even larger audiences.

The cost of a filmstrip depends a great deal on the amount and quality of photographs or artwork provided by the client. In most cases, it is necessary for the producer to create all of the photography and artwork and also to write the script. A filmstrip accompanied by a record or audio cassette costs more than one accompanied by a printed script. The nature of the teacher's or speaker's guide and materials distributed to the audience also affect the production cost.

Multimedia kits are common. They generally include a set of slides or filmstrip, audio cassette, transparencies, poster, booklets for the students and teacher's guide. The cost can be quite high, and many sponsors charge $10 to $50 per kit, in order to recover some of the production costs.

A filmstrip generally is 60 to 120 frames, if it is to be useful as an instructional item and not merely decorative or promotional. A shorter filmstrip of 30 to 50 frames can be used for testing or review of material that previously was presented in a filmstrip or other format.

Filmstrips are more effective if used with audio cassettes and supporting printed materials.

It therefore is impossible to estimate the cost of a filmstrip except that it costs considerably less than a motion picture of the same length. Among the variables contributing to the budget is whether the filmstrip is sold, donated on a permanent basis, or loaned but returned to the producer.

In the school field, a good filmstrip program could result in several thousand requests a year from schools throughout the country. Clients who are budget-conscious (who isn't?) can set a ceiling on a number of requests per year.

Several companies in the school audiovisual field are experienced and reliable, and a potential client should meet with more than one producer before making a decision.

In the youth-marketing field, particularly on the college level, the situation is more erratic. Several well-known companies, such as Go Publishing Company and Student Marketing Institute, no longer are in business. In some cases, their problems were not solely a result of the economic recession, but rather were a reflection of shabby management. The financial ups and downs of National Student Marketing Corporation and other "youth conglomerates" were widely publicized in the 70's.

Prospective clients of *any* company in the youth-marketing field are advised to check carefully about the *specific* facilities and services, as distinguished from claims and promises. The field had been particularly chaotic and filled with promoters whose dazzle has been greater than their delivery.

Youth organizations often sell membership mailing lists, convention exhibition space and other services. Several advertising, promotion and marketing agencies feature departments which specialize in student programs. For example, Gift-Pax, Inc., 25 Hempstead Gardens Drive, West Hempstead, NY 11552, distributes millions of cosmetic and other product samples to high school and college students, as well as other groups such as brides, mothers, mothers-to-be and others.

One of the most efficient and economical arrangements is offered by the National 4-H Council. Their magazine is distributed to the professional volunteer 4-H leaders who guide the activities of five million 4-H boys and girls. Advertisers can list booklets, posters, films and other materials, available free or for sale, in the "Leader Aids" section. A full-page ad generally is the minimum for one listing. Details can be obtained from the Advertising Department of 4-H Leader, 7100 Connecticut Ave., Chevy Chase, MD 28015, (301) 961–2892.

Other magazines, particularly special-interest publications, offer similar promotional tie-ins to advertisers.

Following is information about several leading school and youth-marketing specialists. Many other companies, particularly film producers and audiovisual services, advertise in educational journals, and information about these companies often can be obtained from school film reviews, as well as the ads.

National On-Campus Report is an excellent biweekly newsletter ($68) published by Magna Publications, 2718 Dryden Dr., Madison, WI 53704.

The Intercollegiate Broadcasting System, Box 592, Vails Gate, NY 12584, is an association of school and college radio stations. Contact Jeff Tellis, president, for information about mailing services.

1. CASS Communications Inc.
1633 W. Central St., Evanston, IL 60201
(312) 475–8800, (800) 323–4044
Mark Rose, V.P.

Branch Offices:
5455 Wilshire Blvd., L.A. 90036
(213) 937–7070, Craig Krugman

369 Lexington Ave., N.Y. 10017
(212) 986–6441, Mark Businski

Basically a publisher's representative of high school and college newspapers, CASS also distributes news releases to 3,600 high school and 1,200 college newspapers. If the client provides the release and envelopes, the cost is only 50 cents per school plus postage.

The 1987 edition of the National Rate Book and College Newspaper Directory, published by CASS and distributed free to advertisers, provides extensive data about its 1,200 newspapers with a total circulation of over nine million.

2. CMG Information Services (formerly College Marketing Group, Inc.)
50 Cross St., Winchester, MA 01890
(617) 729–7865
David Wetherell, Pres.

Founded in 1968, the principal business is marketing services to publishers, including mailing lists of college faculty, and other mailings lists and computerized marketing services to colleges, libraries and other categories.

Other details are in the chapter on mailing services.

3. College News Bureau
141 E. 33 St., N.Y. 10016
(212) 684–2208
Jean Green, Exec. Dir.
Herbert Green, Mgr. Dir.

A unique service that provides sponsored news releases to college radio stations (*not* newspapers, though). An annual fee of $250 entitles "members" to service releases to 564 radio stations at a cost of

$200 per release. Clients simply provide one copy, and CNB edits (to one or two pages), prints and mails.

CNB also can include tapes at modest extra costs.

4. College Press Service

2505 W. 2 Ave., Denver, CO 80219

(303) 936–9930

Formed in 1962 and originally operated by the now-defunct U.S. Student Press Association in Washington, DC, College Press Service is an independent higher education news agency.

It operates College Press Service, the largest news and graphics syndicate for college and university publications. It publishes twice weekly during the academic year, and five times during the summer. Approximately 600 publications subscribe to the service.

Subscribers pay $225 to $405, depending on publication size.

The company also publishes High School News & Graphics, which services about 200 senior high school publications, which pay $150 a year.

Public relations clients can make mailings to college and high school newspapers at varying rates.

Interrobang, Inc., CPS' parent, also operates an electronic news service aimed at individual students, faculty members and administrators. Readers receive the latest in national college news and trends via their microcomputers when they subscribe to several commercial databases, such as CompuServe and NewsNet or via a password to CPS directly.

The company updates this nationwide electronic newspaper for American colleges weekly and adds National Campus Classifieds, in which advertisers can place messages of events, housing, jobs and services.

Bill Sonn is editor and publisher.

5. Educational Directories, Inc.

Box 199, Mount Prospect, IL 60056

(312) 459-0605

Lloyd Moody, Publisher

Published annually, Patterson's American Education lists names and addresses of school superintendents and principals of high and junior high schools, along with other data about school systems and colleges at a cost of $47.50 a copy, plus $2 postage and handling.

A mailing service provides lists, primarily in the educational, health and religion fields. As with most mailing services, EDI rents the lists on pressure-sensitive or Cheshire labels, for one-time use.

6. GM Associates/Consultants

Box 1441, N.Y. 10150

(212) 595–5459

George Mihaly

George Mihaly was president of Gilbert Youth Research, which was one of the pioneer marketing companies in the high school and college field. Founded in 1944 by the late Gene Gilbert, the company had several changes of ownership until it faded away in the late 70's.

Mr. Mihaly thus has had tremendous experience in surveying and marketing to students.

7. The Glick & Lorwin Group

1633 Broadway, N.Y. 10019

(212) 887–8690

Ira Glick, Group Exec.

Boris Lorwin, Mgr. Dir.

Founded in 1953, Glick & Lorwin are education specialists who have developed, produced and distributed booklets, books, posters, filmstrips, films and other school materials, and also materials for use at clubs and various organizations. Another specialty is the health care field, particularly patient and physician education materials.

The group is part of Creamer Dickson Basford, a major public relations agency.

8. The JN Company
510 Broadhollow Rd., Melville, NY 11747
(516) 752–8800
Jerry Naidus, Pres.

Produces sponsored educational and employee communications materials of a very high quality.

Karol Media
Information about the school services of Karol is included in the company's listing in the chapters on motion pictures and television.

9. Rick Trow Productions
Box 717, 2539 Aquetong Rd., New Hope, PA 18938
(215) 862–0900
Rick Trow, Pres.

Formerly called School Assembly Service (founded in 1927), this dynamic company (in suburban Philadelphia) is a multimedia education specialist, primarily in the school field, and also producing films, filmstrips, posters, booklets and other materials for all types of clients.

The unique business, for which Rick Trow is justifiably famous, is involved in the creation, production, booking and touring of *live*, multimedia assembly programs which are put on by talented young people in elementary, junior high and high school auditoriums. Audiences, which range from several hundred to over two thousand, avidly respond to these entertaining, educational programs. The enthusiastic reaction is unlike anything accorded a film, filmstrip or other conventional class program.

Thousands of these inspiring, high-quality programs are presented in schools. In 1970, SAS initiated a service of free programs to schools. These programs are sponsored by companies and associations. Costs, including personnel, travel and bookings, range considerably, depending on the number of programs, geographical area and other factors. Since this enables a message to be presented live to many thousands of students, the projects offer immense public relations value, and the total cost can be from $1,000 to $1,000,000.

10. The Rand Youth Poll
404 E. 55 St., N.Y. 10022
(212) 752–3489
Lester Rand, Pres., Robert Williams, Exec. Dir.

The Rand Youth Poll, an opinion research operation conducted on a continuing basis, appears as a syndicated column in many newspapers. Mr. Rand's organization (also called Youth Research Institute) specializes in market research surveys conducted among high school students and young marrieds and singles, ranging from 13 to 35 years old.

Prices range from $500 to $1,500. The company was formed in 1953 and was one of the pioneers in this field.

Other school services are included in the chapters on filmstrips and motion pictures.

Chapter 30

Skywriting

The *biggest* communications medium in the world is the sky. Though some advertisers use banners towed by airplanes and skywriting, most communicators completely ignore this medium.

The Goodyear blimp is perhaps the best-known promotional use of the sky. If public relations people were to turn their creative vision toward the sky on occasion, many novel and newsworthy uses of this medium undoubtedly would be developed.

For example, suppose an executive has been promoted to a new position, such as vice president. Can you imagine the executive's surprise if you broke the news by announcing it in the sky?

Maybe it wouldn't work with everyone, but most people would never forget the thrill of looking up and reading on a banner, or by means of skywriting, a message such as, "Congratulations, you're now a vice president."

And wouldn't this also be newsworthy?

For $500, for example, a message of up to 12 letters can be written about three times over a 2,500-square-mile area. With letters twice the size of a city block, the message will be read by quite a few people. However, note that one plane usually is limited to about 112 letters. Longer messages require additional planes.

More common than skywriting planes are planes which tow banners. Most bannertowers include the cost of the banner in their rates. Letters usually are five feet high with a 40-letter maximum. Costs usually start from the time the banner is picked up and end when it is dropped. Three days' notice usually is required. Rates usually are based on a minimum of two hours. Some companies include a photo of the banner being towed as part of the job.

There are only a few full-time skywriters in the country. It's quite a difficult art and requires working quickly from a pattern so that the feathery letters, which are sprayed backwards and upside down, can be read before the wind erases them.

The first commercial smoke sign was seen in England in 1922. Today's skywriters make their marks in the wild blue yonder with Skytyping, which generally involves several planes flying in formation and releasing staccato puffs via computer programmed signals.

While looking to the sky as a promotional medium, think also about the *weather* as a public relations opportunity. One way to capitalize on the universal interest in weather is to retain the services of a private weather forecaster. A few are listed in the classified phone books of major cities under "Weather Forecast Service."

Contact Barry Schilit, Pres., Weather Trends, Inc., 156 Fifth Ave., N.Y. 10010, phone (212) 463–

7594 for samples of monthly forecasts. The four-page monthly weather report is colorful and fascinating, and sponsors, who purchase copies for exclusive mailings in their category, are able to use a portion of pages one and four for selling messages. Basic cost is $310 for the first thousand copies, and $110 for each additional thousand.

Another publicizable use of the sky pertains to the rental of airplanes. Fashion shows and other events have been held aboard chartered aircraft. Press junkets, particularly to factories in small towns or offbeat locations, can be enhanced by the use of private aircraft.

For companies who cannot afford the several million dollars required to own a jet plane, and for public relations clients who cannot afford the several thousand dollars required to charter conventional aircraft, the use of helicopters should be considered. In many cities, Santa Claus arrives at department stores and shopping centers via helicopter. (For details about aerial photographers, see the section on photography, and also check the classified telephone directory under ''Aircraft Charter and Rental Service.'')

Almost every major city has a private airplane operator with equipment available to tow banners. In a few cities, skywriting and other aerial techniques are also available. Following is information about several companies to give an idea of the rates involved for these services.

1. Continental Camera Systems, Inc.
7240 Valjean Ave., Van Nuys, CA 91406
(818) 989–5222
John Carroll

Started in 1972 and located at the Van Nuys airport in suburban Los Angeles, Continental produces and rents camera systems for special purpose photography, particularly aerial and underwater uses, table and miniature photography.

2. Joe C. Hughes Air Shows
Box 1253, Santa Ana, CA 92702
(714) 752–7777
Joe C. Hughes

An aerobatic pilot, Joe C. Hughes pilots all types of aircrafts and performs wingwalking and other spectacular gymnastics which are useful for promotions and publicity. His sponsors include Penzoil, Champion and Goodyear.

3. Paramount Air Service
Box 155, Rio Grande, NJ 08242
(609) 344–3777, (215) 988–0753

Started in 1946, Paramount Air Service is one of America's oldest and largest aerial advertising companies. Its tow banners regularly fly over the beaches in Atlantic City and Cape May and the stadiums in Philadelphia and elsewhere.

4. Skytypers, Inc.
145 S. Gene Autry Trail, Palm Springs, CA 92262
(619) 320-8800
Greg Stinis

Operating out of Long Beach Airport (near Los Angeles), Stinis covers the sky over America, puffing out five-mile long messages for suntan lotions, soft drinks and other advertisers. The company does conventional skywriting but most of its business is Skytyping, with five airplanes flying in formation. In fact, it has the patent for this technique.

The charge is a minimum of $650 per 20-letter message when the planes are flying in the area. Depending on location, Skytypers can reach up to two million people with a single message. Its slogan is "Make the whole sky your billboard."

5. World Balloon Corporation
4800 Eubank N.E., Albuquerque, NM 87111
(505) 293–6800
Sid Cutter, Pres.

There are some who maintain that a hot-air balloon should be the symbol of public relations. Be that as it may, hot-air balloons are useful for promotions and special events and have been used successfully by Budweiser and other companies.

WBC can provide a fully equipped hot-air balloon and crew for a day, at rates which start at $650 on up, for cross-country promotions, races and other spectacular ballooning events. Up, up and away.

Chapter 31

Telecommunications

The telephone is one of the indispensable items in almost all businesses and notably in the public relations field. Telephone service is the single largest monthly bill at many public relations departments and companies.

One of the many significant changes resulting from the 1982 Modified Final Judgment (MFJ) agreement between AT&T and the Department of Justice is the requirement for *all* telephone consumers to choose a primary long distance company from among those serving their area.

The MFJ required that AT&T divest itself of the local Bell Operating companies (BOCs) and also that the BOCs make changes in their switching machines and transmission facilities to allow any long distance carrier to be connected to local lines in the same manner as AT&T.

In 1984 and 1985, a bewildering array of these common carriers purchased access to local phone company central offices to enable them to be reached by any type of telephone by dialing 11 digits on long distance calls (1 + area code + local telephone number).

Blame it all—or thank—Judge Harold Greene. In the 80's, millions of companies and individuals changed their view of telephone equipment and services. Many public relations people now own telephone equipment purchased from NEC, Northern Telecom, Rohm and other companies, ranging from conventional instruments to complex computerized systems with video terminals and other attachments.

Perhaps the greatest change has been with long-distance telephone service. MCI, the David who challenged the Bell giant, now is a giant itself with strong competition from ITT and other giants, plus dozens of mavericks.

Indeed, the decade of the 80's is spawning the long-awaited telecommunications explosion, resulting in the linking of computers, television and telephone for data transmission, video conferences, automatic teleprinters and, in general, the "international electronic office."

One of the buzz words in telecommunications is LANs. A LAN, or Local Area Network, is a system for moving information (data, voice, text, graphics, image or you-name-it) among devices (computers, printers, telephones, scanners, files, sensors, actuators, PBXs) on the same premises. In other words, a LAN is a way of connecting together various communications devices such as interconnecting personal computers or linking personal computers, microcomputers and main frame computers.

In 1988, the computer is being linked with the telephone more than ever before, particularly with regard to Voice Mail. Systems, such as the Wang DVX voice processing system, enable clients to call into the system using a pay telephone in an airport terminal, or any touch-tone telephone. Clients simply enter an identification number and optional password and then are asked to select from among a variety of services.

According to Wang Information Services Corp. (described in this chapter), DVX Voice Mail provides these benefits:

Improve communications regardless of time or location.
Complete your telephone transactions first time, every time.
Reach "hard-to-contact" employees or clients easily.
Conduct business conveniently.
Transmit information with total accuracy.
Be assured of message security and confidentiality.
Eliminate costly "telephone tag" and reduce the writing of memos.
Decrease communications costs.

The International Business Satellite Service (IBS Service) sends computer data and voice messaging overseas and is used for teleconferencing in less busy times of the day. Such leased channels are used to transmit entire newspapers and for videoconferences as well as for data and voice transmission. These digital channel services, leased through carriers such as RCA, have brought international communications costs down to about one-third of what they were.

Fiber optic digital cables now span the Atlantic and Pacific oceans, offering better service and reducing the costs of cable facilities. The costs of this cable-laying are being borne by the major U.S. and overseas communications carriers. With fiber optic cable, many more circuits can be squeezed in. Because it is a digital system, not analog, information is conveyed more accurately.

If you are as bewildered about telecommunications as most consumers and professionals, you should consider retaining a telecommunications consultant. Ideally, such a consultant should be completely objective and not be an employee or agent of a telephone, Teletype, telegraph or other company or type of service.

One of the leading consultants is William I. Schwartz of Computoll Services, 171 Madison Ave., N.Y. 10016, phone (212) 725–2000. The following section is based on material provided by William Schwartz.

The optimal long-distance carrier is a complex issue involving not only analysis of usage and rates, but also the telephone equipment to be utilized at each end of the service, and the quality of derived service depending on the client and customer locations.

It is a sophisticated and fascinating field and it is essential that public relations practitioners, who are major users of the telephone service, understand and gain greater control of communication systems. You, or someone in your organization, must know about the relative cost and effectiveness of numerous telephone companies and other services, including WATS lines, recorded announcement services, 900 services, 800 telemarketing services, as well as a host of written telecommunications forms, such as Electronic Mail, Telex, Packet Communications and Computer-to-Computer Communications.

The introduction of personal computers used as word processors and list management systems adds to the utility of telecommunications systems. There is a significant symbiosis in the combination of these services.

The bill back of telecommunication charges to clients becomes a very tedious expense item in running the modern public relations office. The proper selection of PBX or terminal equipment by a public relations office can aid in the accounting necessary to perform this record keeping efficiently. A consultant can help in the selection of a telecommunications accounting system which might include facilities to pick up time charges for professionals. Law firms pioneered in the development of these integrated professional billing packages and these packages may have much to offer to public relations agency executives and others.

Regarding the long distance area, the Federal Communications Commission in conjunction with the Antitrust Federal Courts mandated an Equal Access Plan guaranteeing it will be as easy to reach non-AT&T common carriers for long distance service as it was to reach AT&T. Under the Equal Access Plan, customers select a primary long distance carrier. This selection is made at the time the local central office is converted to an equal access basis. Once the selection is made, any user dialing "one" for a long distance call is automatically routed to the carrier of choice. This eliminates the need for very long dial stream or a large number of digits to be dialed in order to reach the long distance carrier and specify the number called. Depending upon the location, if no positive action is made by the customer to select a carrier, the default carrier becomes AT&T.

Under the equal access provisions, once a customer has specified the prime long distance company it still is possible to reach other long distance companies by dialing a special three digit code indicating the company selected. Calls are automatically routed to the selected carrier and the calling party's number is identified. At any time, customers can change their selected long distance carriers for a nominal five dollar registration fee. When calls are routed to a carrier, the carrier automatically decides whether or not to handle them, depending on whether or not credit has been arranged between the customer and the carrier.

Finally, some carriers may choose to have the local operating telephone company do their detailed billing for them. This is an arrangement between the telephone company and the long distance carrier. Many carriers own their long distance billing.

There is little effective federal regulation of these carriers. This complicates the decision making but creates a greater opportunity for cost savings or service improvements by selecting a carrier who best fits your business needs.

Some of the factors, in addition to price and quality that affect carrier choice, are time of day discounts, universal service, and whether the carrier provides service to all points in the United States, whether the carrier provides special discounts to certain major cities where call volumes are high, and whether carrier timed calls are based upon actual connected time (some carriers actually charge for busy signals and ring-no-answer calls). Many carriers allow the service to be used not only from a company's offices but also from coin phones and other points using a special identification number. This can be a real benefit to travellers but it also opens up the possibility of abuse if employees learn they can use the special identification numbers for personal calls made from home.

On many of the special services such as credit card calls or calls billed to a third party, the telephone company treats calls as an operator handled call. This can greatly increase the cost of a call, especially calls made by employees at night from home. If these calls are placed on a credit card, or billed to a company's main number, they are treated as operator handled third party calls at a premium cost. On the other hand, if calls are billed directly to the employee's home, they are charged as direct dialed calls and may be subject to a time of day discount, as high as 65 percent depending upon when calls are made. One way to reduce the cost of calls made by employees from their homes is to have employees make calls on their regular long distance bills and simply submit copies of their bills with reimbursable business calls circled. This reduces cost and adds to the control of long distance costs.

In addition to independent telecommunications experts, such as Computoll, most telephone companies also provide systems analysis and consulting, though it is likely to be biased.

The breakup of the Bell Telephone System has enabled AT&T and the seven new regional companies to diversify their telecommunications services, including transmission of data and TV, cellular phones, business and telecomputing equipment.

The seven companies still are working at popularizing their names, which are: NYNEX, Bell Atlantic, Bellsouth, Ameritech, Southwestern Bell Corp., U.S. West and Pacific Telesis. For more information, call your local company.

Another recent change is the assignment of new area codes in New York City and other high-population regions. For example, New York City is 212 for Manhattan and the Bronx and 718 for the other three boroughs, Brooklyn, Queens and Staten Island. The Los Angeles area now is 818 and 213.

Only a very small number of companies are able to "bypass" their local telephone companies, such as by setting up a private microwave network. What is more common are systems of drastically reducing local and long distance phone costs. New technologies include use of cable television, cellular mobile radio, digital termination systems, end-to-end satellite links and teleports. Cable TV may be useful in popularizing the long-discussed photo telephone, as well as in two-way voice and data transmission.

Cellular phones, which now are used by individuals in their automobiles, undoubtedly will decrease in price and become even more popular.

Digital termination systems (DTS) are point-to-multipoint microwave systems, which are used with satellites for long-haul links. Point-to-point satellite communications can be effectively used with the dish antennae which now are seen on the roofs of some office buildings.

A teleport is simply a collection of telecommunications facilities at a site. It's linked, such as via optical fiber, to a nearby concentration of customers. An example is the teleport on Staten Island across the bay from Manhattan.

It's a sophisticated, fascinating field, and it's essential that public relations practitioners—who are major users of telephone services—understand and gain greater control of communications systems, including knowing about the relative costs and efficiencies of tie lines, WATS lines, recording of usage by individual and department, computer-controlled routing of calls and other telecommunications procedures.

In New York and other major cities, entrepreneurs have opened offices which provide desk or other space to executives on an hourly, daily, weekly or monthly basis, and also offer access to messengers, Telex, copying machines, telephone facsimile and other equipment, as well as secretarial and other business services.

Television Digest, Inc., 1836 Jefferson Place, N.W., Wash., DC 20036, publishes Telecom Factbook ($125), an extraordinary encyclopedia about common carriers, independent satellites, data communications, organizations, regulators and others in telecommunications.

Toll-Free Digest, an annual directory of toll-free telephone numbers is $17.95 on newsstands, in bookstores and from the publisher, Paul Montana, Box 800, Claverack, NY 12513. Add $2 for shipping.

Note: It's not generally known, but you can find out if a company has an 800 number by calling the telephone company at (800) 555–1212. In 1987, Gale Research Co. published the National Business Telephone Directory, a 1,900-page directory with addresses (including zip codes) and telephone numbers of 350,000 companies and organizations. The companies are listed alphabetically so that it is easy to obtain information when their headquarters location is not known. Listings also include branches and subsidiary companies. This superb book is $95 from Gale Research Co., Book Tower, Detroit, MI 48226.

Some telephone companies sell "reverse phone directories," which list by address instead of the conventional alphabetical list of names. Cole Directories, which are published for about 2,100 cities, are indexed by address and also by telephone numbers. These directories, used by detectives and other sleuths, are compiled from telephone books and other sources. Many market research, direct marketing, banking and credit people also use the Cole Directories because they include zip codes, the year a telephone was installed and whether a phone number is a new listing. They also include numbers which are unlisted in the phone company directories.

Cole Directories are in a few major public libraries. They can be leased for an annual fee, ranging from about $100 for a small city to $380 for Manhattan. Cole Publications is at 529 Fifth Ave., N.Y. 10017, phone (212) 599–2616.

Telephone answering services and equipment (live and recorded) are more popular than ever before, particularly at small-size offices.

Compare several companies with regard to rates, hours and other details and make a few trial calls to check on the operators. They should be intelligent, courteous, relaxed, accurate and cheerful—and some of them are, sometimes! Rates vary considerably and depend on your proximity to the answering service. For example, Executive Telephone Answering Service at 314 West 53 St., N.Y. 10019, phone (212) 246–7676, provides a discount to clients who mention The Professional's Guide to Public Relations Services. The company, in business since 1939 and operated by Allan Lynn and his son Rocky, charges $59.50 a month for 9 A.M. to 5 P.M., Monday to Friday service, and $79.50 for 24-hour, seven-day service. Other services provide Tele-copier (FAX) service, secretarial, dictation, toll-free 800 numbers, order taking, telephone sales solicitations and more.

Independent consultants are available to compare your telephone bills with your telephone equipment. If you are paying for signal lights, phone extensions and other items which you do not have (perhaps you once did), the consultant will get a refund for you. The fee generally is simply half of any savings obtained by the consultant. In New York, contact Ronald Chernow, phone (212) 662–0200.

Have you ever read your phone book?

The Manhattan directory, published for New York Telephone by NYNEX Information Resources Company, has over 55 pages preceding the listings with a tremendous amount of useful information, including:

Emergency Care Guide (first-aid tips).
Manhattan postal ZIP code map.

And following the directory listings is a blue page section of frequently called local, state and federal offices. Other cities also have telephone directories with maps and useful information.

Calls to telephone information are not free, so get extra copies of the directory for use throughout your office. Out-of-town directories (which are not free) also may be useful, particularly for addresses.

Free booklets about telephone companies and other services can be obtained from many Better Business Bureaus.

An excellent guide for consumers, "How to Buy a Telephone" is available free (stamped self-addressed envelope) from the Consumer Electronics Group of Electronic Industries Association, Box 19100, Wash., DC 20036. The booklet answers these questions:

How much money can I save by buying my own phone?
Is it legal to own my own phone?
What should I do if my phone doesn't have a registration number?
What do I do with my rented phone when I buy a new one?
What kinds of phones are available?
What should I consider when I buy a phone?
Should I buy a "tone" or "pulse" phone?
What are all those extra buttons on the new telephones?
What phone accessories are available?
How do I select a cordless phone?

AT&T publishes a Business Directory of 800 Phone Numbers (listing manufacturers and wholesalers) and a Consumer Directory of 800 Phone Numbers (listing services aimed toward the public). The Business Directory is $9.25 and the Consumer Directory, $6.75, including postage. The annual directories include advertisements. You can order them by writing to the 800 Directory Service, AT&T Customer Information Center, Box 19901, Indianapolis, IN 46219. But why write! Call (800) 242–4634.

The New York City Department of Consumer Affairs has a free booklet with a list of questions to be asked when choosing a long-distance telephone carrier. The Department is located at 80 Lafayette St., N.Y. 10013, phone (212) 566–0414. The Better Business Bureau of Metropolitan New York, 257 Park

Ave. So., N.Y. 10010, phone (212) 533–6200, offers a free checklist for selecting a service. Simply send a stamped (40¢) self-addressed envelope. Consumer Checkbook, 806 15th St., N.W., Wash., DC 20005, (202) 347–7283, offers a consumer guide on telephones for $6.95 and can analyze which carrier is best for your needs—for a fee.

A major development of the 70's was facsimile equipment, which transmits printed material via telephone lines. There now are more than 500,000 facsimile machines in the U.S. The cost is that of a local or long-distance call, plus the rental or purchase of the equipment. The tabletop machine, which transmits via a scanner and receives via a recorder, is easy to use and can be set up anywhere.

Telephone facsimile transmission equipment now includes portable machines (ideal for news conferences, conventions and special events, particularly in remote locations) and machines which can receive unattended at night or other times.

In 1987, RCA Global Communications introduced RCA Thrufax, a service that delivers telex messages to facsimile terminals.

In the 80's, U.S. and foreign companies introduced high-speed equipment that takes a few seconds per page! Here are some of the major companies in the field and their product names.

Fujitsu Imaging Systems of America, Danbury, CT 06810, (203) 796–5581, (800) 243–7046 (dex).
Panafax Corp., (Division of Matsushita Graphic Communications Systems, Inc.), 10 Melville Park Road, Melville, NY 11747, (516) 420–0055 (PX-200, MV-3000, PX-100, UF-400, MV-1200).
Rapicom, Inc., 7 Kingsbridge Rd., Fairfield, NJ 07006, (800) 631–1155 (Rapifax).
Ricoh Corporation, 5 Dedrick Pl., W. Caldwell, NJ 07006, (201) 882–2000.
3M Co., 3M Center, St. Paul, MN 55101, (612) 733–1110 (3M 9600).
Xerox Corp. Direct Marketing, 1350 Jefferson Rd., Rochester, NY 14623, (800) 828–6014 (Telecopier).

Check with the local sales offices of these companies and ask about:

1. Is machine compatible with other companies? If not, how much is adaptor?
2. Rent or purchase?
3. Speed of transmission (new models transmit at two minutes a page, or less)?
4. Service costs?

Many communications companies now offer facsimile services—transmission of photocopies of printed materials from one location to another within one to two hours. Several courier services also provide these services. They are described in the chapter on messenger services.

The telephone has not replaced the telex machine. In fact, more public relations people are involved in activities in foreign countries than ever before and many are using telex machines for the first time. Telex can be economical, convenient for time zone differences and efficient, particularly for transmission of news releases and other hard copy.

Note: Many public relations people (and others) receive throughout the year invoices for listings in telex directories. Though some of these are legitimate, many of these so-called invoices actually are unauthorized, unsolicited attempts to obtain advertising and the publishers are boiler-room-type operations.

The most significant new developments relate to computerized telephone systems and the long-distance telephone companies. The installation of sophisticated telephone equipment enables users to rent or purchase phone systems from independent interconnect companies instead of AT&T or other telephone companies.

Perhaps of greatest interest to public relations practitioners, and other big users of long-distance phone service, has been the phenomenal development of companies which provide long-distance service at less than regular rates.

In 1969, the Federal Communications Commission (FCC) authorized a small company, Microwave Communications of America, Inc. (MCI), to set up a communications service between Chicago and St. Louis. In 1975, MCI (the company now is called MCI Communications Corporation) introduced Execunet, a service which links cities via MCI's microwave lines and uses regular local telephone lines for access.

The Southern Pacific Communications Company followed with a similar service called SPRINT and, in 1979, the International Telephone and Telegraph Corporation introduced its City-Call.

In the 80's, over a dozen other companies entered this field—and the consumer benefited as the companies improved their transmission quality and territories *and* actually lowered their prices.

Note: These systems thus are useful only for station-to-station or other calls which do not require operator assistance. They cannot be used for collect calls, for example.

However, the calls are charged in units of considerably less than three minutes, and most subscribers find that it's worth taking a chance with station-to-station calls instead of person-to-person calls.

Most of the long-distance communications networks offer the following features (some at extra, optional cost):

800 Service. An alternative to collect calls, inward WATS and remote call forwarding. It works simply by calling the local access number and then dialing a special code which completes the call automatically to the headquarters or other "base" telephone.

Abbreviated Dialing. Reduces the number of digits necessary to complete frequently called numbers.

Accounting Codes. Helps to keep track of users by assigning codes.

Reminder: You must have a touch-tone phone!

There are problems, such as an occasional hollow sound or busy signal from the system. And you do have to punch out carefully and accurately—you generally can't complain to the phone company about wrong numbers.

In the domestic and international public switched telephone network (PSTN) voice world, the main companies are AT&T, GTE, the Baby Bells, MCI, Sprint, ITT's USTS and Contel.

Telegraph and telex are the oldest forms of electronic mail. Both still are alive and well and have not been replaced. There are about 1.5 million telex subscribers in the world, and about 180,000 are in the U.S.

The leading companies are RCA, ITT, Western Union International (now part of MCI), Western Union Domestic, TRT and FTC (McDonell-Douglas). International telex, which includes telex and cablegram via satellite or undersea cable, has become less popular because international phone calls have become easier to make (direct dial) and less expensive.

If you do not have your own telex machine, you can use one of the many telex services in most major cities. You can put their telex number on your stationery and use them like a telephone answering service. In New York, major companies are:

Executive Telex, (212) 732–2252, started in 1939

National Teletype Corp., 207 Newtown Rd., Plainview, NY 11803, (516) 293–0444, (212) 239–8750

Rapid Relay Telex, (718) 380–4500

Swift Telex, (212) 432–2680, (800) 645–3348

One of the most exciting developments in the communications field is the transition from wires to satellites. The telegraph—the first device to use electricity for communications—was invented by Samuel

F. B. Morse in 1835. The famous first message, ''What Hath God Wrought!'' was tapped out in 1844. The Western Union Telegraph Company was formed in 1856 as a union of several companies. Early in the 20th century, the teletypewriter replaced the Morse key and sounder. In recent years, many public relations people drifted away from use of Western Union Telegrams and the company was dubbed by some as old-fashioned. Actually, Western Union was the first company to adopt multiplex telegraphy, microwave transmission and message-switching computers. Recently, with the advent of the computer and the communications satellite, and the growth of data communications, a new era began. Telegraphy has become telecommunications.

Following is a list of long-distance carriers, selected from the hundreds who operate around the country. Most of these carriers provide universal service to all points within the United States. In some cases, regional companies operating in only one small market may offer more attractive rates. There also are suppliers for direct line services, if there is great volume between an agency and its client, for instance. Direct line services, if warranted on the basis of volume, can often cost far less than per call or time services. Several large companies use them to link branch offices. Most of the companies on this list are described in greater detail later in this chapter.

Allnet Communication	(800) 982–8888
AT&T Long Distance Service	(800) 222–0300
Garden State Long Distance (Reseller)	(201) 539–6900
U.S. Sprint Long Distance Service	(800) 521–4949
ITT U.S. Transmission Systems	(800) 526–3000
MCI Telecommunications Corporation	(800) 624–2222
R.C.I. Corporation	(800) 458–7000
Starnet Division, American Network	(619) 569–4022
TDX Systems, Cable and Wireless Communications	(800) 368–4729
Western Union Long Distance Service	(800) 527–5184

AT&T and ITT provide service to the largest number of countries.

A resale carrier (reseller) leases or rents from AT&T, MCI or other long distance carriers. Customers receive least-cost routing in which calls are routed over the cheapest available system. In some cases, computerized choices include land lines or satellites via the company's own equipment or others.

Several cable TV system operators have developed telecommunications services. For example, digital electronic message service (DEMS) is available from American Cable-systems Corp., 55 Tozer Rd., Beverly, MA 01915, phone (617) 921–0080.

Outside the United States, telecommunications generally is handled by a governmental agency. Here are a few of the major operators in Canada and the United Kingdom.

Canadian Satellite Communications Inc. (Cancom), 50 Burnhamthorpe Road West, Mississauga, Ontario L5B 3C2, phone (416) 272–4960
British Telecom, 81 Newgate St., London, EC1A 7AJ, (01) 356–5000. (U.S. office is at 150 E. 52 St., N.Y. 10022.)
Cable & Wireless Public Ltd. Co., Mercury House, London WCIX 8XR, (01) 242–4433
ITT Commercial Cable Co., Melbray House, London EC1V 3PH, (01) 251–1577
Eastern Telegraph Company Ltd., Mercury House, London WC1X 8RX, (01) 242–4433
Mercury Communications Ltd., 90 Long Acre, London WC2E 9NP, (01) 836–2449

Here then are descriptions of a variety of telecommunications companies, starting with AT&T.

1. AT&T

550 Madison Ave., N.Y. 10022
(212) 605-5500

The long distance phone company that's been in service for a century reaches out and touches someone through the millions of calls it handles each day. It's had some stiff competition in the past few years, but the company has expanded its services to keep up with the competition for long distance customers. Among the numerous services AT&T provides are voice, data, and image telecommunications and many products and services.

2. Allnet Communication Services, Inc.

30300 Telegraph Rd., Birmingham, MI 48010
(313) 647–6920, (800) 982–8888
Lou Tazioli, District Mgr.

Allnet is a wholly owned subsidiary of ALC Communications Corp. It is the nation's fourth largest long-distance telephone company.

It offers a spectrum of telephone services and a graduated schedule of volume discounts that may appeal to business customers. WATS and WATS-like services are available for high volume users ($500 and up per month) at money-saving rates. For example, a discount of 11 percent may be applied to bills over $2,000.

Allnet's dial-up long-distance services are billed in one-minute increments. There's no monthly or minimum charge, or start-up fees. Volume discounts can apply for the individual user after meeting a minimum usage level of $20. Calls from states ranging from Illinois to Texas earn a two percent bonus on all interstate long-distance calls.

3. The Computoll Group. Ltd.

171 Madison Ave., N.Y. 10016
(212) 725–2000
William I. Schwartz, Pres.

One of the leaders in integrated telecommunications services, Computoll Group provides a variety of services, including cost reduction and consulting about telemarketing, telephone equipment, integrated data and voice communications, as well as telecommunications systems design. Computoll utilizes computer models for analysis of long distance services and other problems.

4. Graphnet, Inc.

8230 Boone Blvd., Vienna, VA 22180
(703) 556–9397, (800) 336–3729

Branch Office:
329 Alfred Ave., Teaneck, NJ 07666
(201) 837–5100
John Reese, Gen. Mgr.
Mary Beth Lane, Marketing Services

Graphnet, a subsidiary of Graphic Scanning Corp., of Teaneck, NJ, offers a variety of communications services through its Freedom Network. Interactive and instant communications are available on the Network through a terminal, computer or dataphone to any other asynchronous device operating between 50 and 1,200 baud. The Network has both domestic and international service, via telex and TWX, plus direct communications to any international public network terminal. Messages are transmitted in real time using English-language codes and message delivery is immediately confirmed.

Graphnet's 108 service is for international Telex calls and FAXGRAM is the electronic mail service. The store-and-forward system permits messages to be delivered by hand, phone, through the U.S. Postal Service or to a terminal, with verification of receipt.

The Freedom Network has advanced message-handling services, including the ability to send a single communication to hundreds of addresses, and the system can insert names into the message. The edit function can add or subtract words, sentences or paragraphs. Subscription can be via direct line of DDD/WATS. A typical domestic message costs 30 cents per 100 words. Service charges, above actual transmission time, are about $5 per month. A 10-page business document can be sent at about the same cost as Express Mail with delivery in seconds rather than the next day.

Graphnet provides a 24-hour toll-free service hot line for questions. Access to the Freedom Network via the customer's regular DDD phone line is on a subscription basis. There are no other start-up fees and no deposit is required. Graphnet supplies itemized and department billing on request.

International rates to the United Kingdom, for example, are $1.86 per minute; to Europe, $1.74 per minute, and to the Far East, $2.15 per minute. The rates compare favorably with ITT, RCA and MCI, as well as with Western Union's Easylink, Telex and TWX.

5. ITT U.S. Transmission Systems Inc.

100 Plaza Dr., Secaucus, NJ 07096
(201) 330–5000, (800) 526–3000
Christopher Hoppin, Dir. of Corp. Relations

ITT offers a spectrum of communications services primarily for business.

1. ITT SMART WATS service can be integrated into any telephone (even rotary) and provides direct lines from your office to ITT for fast, direct connections. ITT will design a system to meet the needs of your business and incorporate the services of speed dialing (4 digits), conference calls (up to 5 parties) and more. ITT also will program three digit codes to indicate on your bill the client, department, employee or whatever you choose, for an additional fee. And, ITT has a 24-hour maintenance service.

2. ITT Longer Distance designed specifically for reducing business costs.

6. MCI Communications Corporation

1133 19th St., N.W., Wash. DC 20036
(202) 872–1600, (800) 624–2222
Roy Gamse, V.P., Marketing

The pioneer in discount long distance phone service, MCI is the largest alternative long distance carrier.

MCI offers discount service that reduces long distance phone costs from 5–24 percent. The *lowest* rates are on calls made anytime Saturday and Sunday until 5 P.M.; rates are considerably decreased weekdays, particularly after 5 P.M.

Along with regular discounts there is a bonus plan for calls in excess of $50 a month. All calls can be charged to major credit cards or you can receive a bill directly from MCI.

MCI even has its own directory assistance—at a discount, of course!

The free MCI calling card allows for discount service on calls made away from your home. Monthly bills include a free MCI newsletter with information on the latest developments in telecommunications and the newest MCI services.

MCI International is headquartered at Two International Dr., Rye Brook, NY 10573, phone (914) 937–6000, (800) 826–6300.

7. RCA Global Communications, Inc.

201 Centennial Ave., Piscataway, NJ 08854
(800) 526–3969
Alan Garratt, Mgr., Public Affairs

RCA Globcom has been a pioneer in communications, including the use of satellites for improved international telex and telegram service, radio communications between the U.S. and London, international leased channels, international telex and data transmission services, and high-speed, high-quality international digital facsimile service from the U.S. to points overseas.

Among RCA's services are:

International and Domestic Telex—available via three access methods: *personal computers with modems,* DDD 50 Telex (which can connect your owned telex machine to a phone, eliminating the ever-increasing costs of a private leased line from the telephone company), and RCA PTL (private leased tie-line telex which attaches your terminal to the RCA telex exchange).

AIRCON—provides larger firms the benefits of a store and forward message-switching system, centralizing communications without capital investment.

ExpressNet—provides domestic leased channel service at costs 30 to 40 percent less than comparable services.

RCA Mail—offers interoffice electronic mail service and the ability to access the RCA Telex Network and all of its services.

Telex delivers a typewritten message across the nation or across the world in only a few minutes but, unlike a telephone, no one has to be present to answer a telex terminal. In the last decade, using computers, many new store and forward features have been added to telex service, and these features are available to any telex terminal because they reside in the system, not the terminal.

There are over 1.5 million telex terminals around the globe, some 200,000 of them in the U.S. Major businesses and government agencies have at least one telex or telex-compatible terminal. Each of these can send or receive a telex with any other terminal, regardless of what carrier supplies service or the type of telex terminal used.

Two types of telex service are available: real time, online service providing direct connection to another telex terminal for live, typewritten conversation, and store and forward telex offering the ability to send a telex message, have the telex exchange hold it until the specified terminal is free (or some other user-specified condition is met) and then deliver the message. Telex is a 50-baud service.

The cost of telex is competitive with other forms of communication. Real time domestically is 46 cents a minute. Store and forward is 61 cents a minute. (These costs assume the message is going to an RCA terminal.) Typical store and forward overseas rates, per minute, are: London, $1.30; Paris, $1.81; Tokyo, $2.19 and Rio, $2.70. (Real time rates are about 20 cents a minute higher.)

A news release can be sent out to those on your release media list simultaneously by using their telex numbers, to the attention of the editors you specify, all for the regular cost of a store and forward telex. Time of delivery can be stated, and if one of the releases is not delivered for any reason by that time, you will get notification back on your terminal and delivery can be made in another way. There is no regular subscription charge for using the telex—only the actual cost of the telex. There is a $25 a month minimum billing.

An optional Databank Mailbox allows you to call up at your convenience on your terminal incoming "mail" held for you.

There are three warnings in telex use from a computer through DDD: Do not exceed a format of 69 characters per line; do not use underscoring as it does not translate well into telex, and do not use five consecutive periods in the middle of a message since this will terminate the message.

From outside the U.S., you can use your telex keyboard to access many online database services. The access is via Tymnet, Telenet and other networks. RCA packages this operation as Datalink. Here are some of the details.

Most databases in the U.S. and their host computers are connected to either the Tymnet or Telenet packet switching network. These networks provide access to a variety of databases, and RCA Globcom's Datalink gives overseas telex subscribers this same access, as easily as sending an ordinary telex.

All that is necessary is to have a telex machine and make a prior agreement with a data host on the Telenet or Tymnet network or one directly connected to RCA's Datalink node. Charges for access to the database and the packet switching network will be billed by the database company. Charges for the telex call to Datalink will be billed at the regular telex message rate.

If using Telenet, you acquire a user name and password from the host database to be accessed. The host will invoice for both its computer service and Telenet. When using Tymnet, both a Tymnet user name and password and a database (host) user name and password are required. These are supplied by the database selected.

Advertising, bibliographic information on many subjects, business information, economics, finance, flight planning, magazine and newspaper articles, marketing, medical pharmaceutical, research and forecasting are among the U.S. data resources available via Datalink. Once you locate the data needed, if time is not a problem, you can usually request to have a printout of the material airmailed to you and save online time charges.

RCA Globcom has a Hotline Telex News Service which offers the closing prices on leading stocks in 13 world markets, commodities reports, the latest world news bulletins and the news from Washington, international financial news bulletins, international sports reports, general-interest information and worldwide weather reports. To access the Hotline, type 12 + on your RCA telex terminal. For more information, call RCA's Customer Care Center at (800) 526–3969.

If you are planning to send and receive telex messages from a computer, RCA's booklet, "Introducing Telex Communications from Your Personal Computer, Word Processor or Terminal via RCA Computer-Originated Telex Service" will provide information concerning requirements and all the options currently available.

8. RCI Corporation
333 Metro Park, Rochester, NY 14623
(716) 475–8000, (800) 458–7000
James Geiger, Dir. of Marketing

RCI, a subsidiary of Rochester Telephone Corp. (one of America's oldest independent telephone companies), offers an integrated digital network telephone system. This system provides crystal-clear transmission, free from static and echoes.

Unlike analog transmission, signals on a digital network are transmitted long distances without error-causing line noise so data correctly reach their destination as intended.

9. U.S. Sprint
700 Airport Blvd., Burlingame, CA 94010
(415) 692–5600
Jacques Hoppus, V.P. Sales

Branch Office:
211 E. 43 St., N.Y. 10017
(212) 557–0700

Sprint offers 24-hour long distance savings for calls made anywhere in the U.S. Volume discounts are applied in excess of $25 and there is no installation fee. For travellers, Sprint has Telecode, a 2-digit access number that allows calls to be made from any push-button phone in the country and charged to your personal or business phone. In-Sprint serves as a toll-free number for businesses or customers who phone-in from out of state. The charge is $5 for installation and a $15 monthly service charge. Phone calls for this service must total $500 monthly.

10. Swift Global Communications, Inc.

997 Glen Cove Ave., Glen Head, NY 11545
(516) 676–8000, (800) 645–3348
Telex: 645924
TWX: (510) 222–9435
George Abi Zeid, Pres.

Branch Offices:
17 Battery Pl., N.Y. 10004
(212) 514–6006
Richard Costa, Dir. of Marketing

949 S. Detroit St., L.A. 90036
(213) 934–4435
Michael Pairn, District Sales Mgr., V.P., Western Region

2441 Springs Rd., Vallejo, CA 94591
(707) 643–7087
Joanne Robinson, District Sales Mgr.

If you are a major user of domestic or international telex, you can save money by using a computerized routing company, which works akin to the telephone routers. Access is via any telex, TWX, DDD, microcomputer, word processor or just about any "intelligent terminal or keyboard." One of the dynamic companies in this field is Swift Global.

11. Wang Information Services Corp.

One Industrial Ave., Lowell, MA 01851
(617) 967–7500, (800) 835–5389
Frank A. Calabrese, Marketing Mgr.
Jan Bergeron, Marketing Communications

The Wang DVX Voice Communications System, which is available on a time-shared basis, enables clients who call in, via any touch-tone telephone, to use a variety of services, including:

Mailbox access allows you to listen to any messages that have been deposited for you. After listening to your voice message, you can send a reply to the message originator without entering any telephone address; you can also forward messages and add introductory comments or store messages for future reference.

Message creation allows you to create, review and, if necessary, rerecord messages prior to sending. You can also specify time and date of message delivery. Additionally, individual voice messages can be specified for delivery to a single party, to multiple parties, or to two distribution lists.

Message confirmation allows you to determine if your intended message recipients have accessed and listened to their messages. If a voice message has not been accessed, you can review its contents and refresh your memory. As a system user, you can activate this function anytime following the creation and distribution of a message.

12. Western Union Corporation
1 Lake St., Upper Saddle River, NJ 07495
(201) 825–5000
Warren Bechtel, Asst. V.P.-Corporate Communications

One of the world's best known corporate names, Western Union used to be synonymous with telegrams. The company has changed tremendously in recent years (does anyone remember Western Union "messenger boys?") and now is a major factor in telecommunications, notably its Westar satellites, transcontinental microwave system and other facilities.

Most of the company's services are provided through its principal subsidiary, The Western Union Telegraph Company, a leading carrier of record message and data traffic. These services include:

Network services, principally Telex I and Telex II, which constitute a core network for rapid written communications among business firms in the United States. Previously restricted to domestic operations, Western Union inaugurated its WorldWide Telex service in 1982. A new network service, EasyLink, enables communications terminals (including telex), personal computers and word processors worldwide to communicate with each other through regular telephone connections.

Communications systems and services tailored to the special needs of business and government users, including systems that carry both data and voice traffic. Some of these services, such as transmission of television and radio broadcasts, are made possible by Western Union's Westar satellite system.

Public message services such as Money Transfer service and individual Mailgram, Telegram and cablegram messages.

Priority mail services, including volume handling of computer-originated Mailgram messages and Western Union Priority Letter and Computer Letter service.

Western Union long distance telephone services.

Following are the details about some of these services. Others, such as telegrams, are described in the chapter on mailing services. Satellite services are detailed in the chapter on teleconferencing.

Telex is an automatic teletypewriter network that operates either at 66 words per minute (Telex I) or at 100 words per minute (Telex II, formerly TWX). It allows subscribers to communicate in writing and with other subscribers on a direct dial (conversational) or store-and-forward basis. Telex services include:

> *WorldWide Telex*. Enables Telex I and II customers to Dial 100 and access telex terminals anywhere in the world.
> *Telephone Acceptance of Telex Traffic*. Available to telex subscribers who need to send a Telex message when their terminal is not available.
> *Public Telex*. Public use of telex equipment at selected Western Union offices to reach another domestic or overseas telex.
> *Tel(t)ex*. Telephone or messenger delivery of a telex message.
> *Telex Editor*. On-line editing capability with quieter, remote-controlled operation.

Ancillary Telex services include:

> *RediList*. Transmission of messages to up to 250 computer-stored addresses.
> *NiteCast*. Low-cost transmission of multiple address messages to other telex subscribers between 8 P.M. and 8 A.M.

Datagram. Messages telephoned toll-free by field personnel are sent directly for printout at the subscribers' terminals; often used for order entry.

FYI News. Informative reports in a wide range of categories, including news, weather and stock market; available on a dial-in or subscription basis.

News Alert. Printout of United Press International bulletins as events occur.

Teletex service is a document transfer service about 45 times the speed of telex. It offers letter format printout, automatic memory and text-editing capabilities. Western Union provides Teletex service between the U.S. and Germany, Canada and other countries, and among major U.S. cities.

EasyLink Instant Mail enables communications terminals (including telex), personal computers and word processors worldwide to communicate with each other through regular telephone connections. EasyLink subscribers can reach EasyLink subscribers in the United Kingdom and France, access all domestic and overseas telex stations and tap Western Union's wide array of message services. The EasyLink computer-based electronic message service enables subscribers to send and receive messages from their personal computer or word processor, originate Mailgram, telegram, Computer Letter and cablegram messages for transmission to those without communications terminals and access the Western Union FYI News for stock quotations, currency reports and other news.

InfoMaster Database Service provides instant access to one of the largest, most comprehensive electronic libraries in the world. Subscribers can use their communicating terminals to access business periodicals, financial information, engineering reports, legal abstracts and more than 800 other databases without having to maintain separate subscriptions or use separate log-on procedures and multiple command languages.

Data Services (private data transmission networks):

Low-Speed Leased Transmission service, offered for series 1000 teleprinters, transmits at 300 bps and is available in two-point or multipoint configurations.

DataCom, a multiplexed data transmission service, is available in two- and three-point arrangements and allows for mixing codes and speeds from 75 to 1,200 bps. DataCom equipment is housed and maintained on Western Union's premises.

Medium Speed Leased Transmission service operates from 2,400 to 4,800 bps and meets the majority of today's communications needs.

High-Speed Leased Transmission service, capable of transmitting from 9.6 Kbps to 56 Kbps, is tailored to user requirements. InfoCom private wire customers share circuits and switching facilities to send a variety of internal messages and data without incurring the expense of operating a private message-switching system of their own.

Hot/Line point-to-point voice service is designed for low-volume users who need to call a pre-designated number frequently. It can connect individual phones, PBS/PABX equipment and data terminals.

Westar high-volume point-to-point voice service, transmitted via Westar satellite, offers voice, data and video transmission. It can connect individual phones, PBXs or facsimile terminals and can also be used for off-premises extension and foreign exchange service.

Western Union Long Distance Services is an economical long-distance telephone service for business and residential subscribers. Businesses may select Dial Access or Dedicated Access service.

Here is a list of some of the subsidiary companies.

The Western Union Telegraph Company
One Lake St., Upper Saddle River, NJ 07458
(201) 825–5000

Western Union Electronic Mail, Inc.
1651 Old Meadow Rd., McLean, VA 22102
(703) 821–5800

Western Union Equipment Services, Inc.
One Lake St., Upper Saddle River, NJ 07458
(201) 825–5000

Western Union Teleprocessing, Inc.
82 McKee Dr., Mahwah, NJ 07430
(201) 529–6000

If you're still uncertain about which phone service you should use, you may want to consult Telecom Library, Inc. 12 W. 21 St., N.Y. 10010, phone (212) 691–8215. The library publishes Teleconnect Magazine and a book which may provide savings on telephone systems for public relations offices: Which Phone System Should I Buy? ($39.95)

Telemarketing—the use of the telephone as a direct marketing medium—is not included in this book. However, many of the major companies in this field are available for fundraising, opinion and market research and other subjects of interest to public relations people.

For example, CCI Telemarketing Corporation, 555 W. 57 St., N.Y. 10019, phone (212) 957–8520, has a tremendous amount of varied experience relevant to public relations. The company was founded in 1967 by Murray Roman, one of the pioneers in telemarketing, who died in 1984. CCI now is headed by Fred B. Tregaskis, president.

Chapter 32

Teleconferencing

Videoconferencing, also known as closed-circuit television or teleconferencing, was originally developed by NASA for visually tracking spacecraft. The introduction of the simple concept of television delivered by satellite revolutionized communication. The commercial use of videoconferencing was perfected by heavyweight boxing promoters to create box office events. Prior to the introduction of satellites into the communications arena, all television, radio and data transmissions utilized telephone long lines. Satellites allowed a very cost-effective technology, as well as increasing the clarity and quality of the transmission. In fact, it's difficult to imagine American business today operating without satellite communications.

In an article published in 1945 in a British publication, Wireless World, Arthur C. Clarke put forth the idea that it was possible to completely cover the earth with telecommunications service by placing three space stations in geosynchronous orbit. They had to be positioned equidistant from each other and each 22,300 miles above the equator (one-tenth of the way to the moon). This was based on laws of orbital mechanics and captured the attention of scientists. The first geosynchronous satellite, Syncom II, was launched by Hughes in 1963.

From those early experiences, satellite communications literally has taken off. The application would have developed long ago if the industry had the capability; the technology has existed for a long time. But it had not been intergrated into a complete usage package. Now, major corporations are using some form of satellite communications, whether videoconferencing or related applications of data and high speed facsimile, as well as "private" telephone systems. As the distribution services and equipment packages become more reduced in cost, the satellite industry will continue to grow. Costs must come down still further in the future in order for videoconferencing to become truly popular. Most experts agree that closed circuit television will become as common as our use of long distance telephone lines. The industry will truly explode when equipment is reduced to simple installation, usage and maintenance.

Some public relations practitioners still are ignorant about videoconferencing or think it's only in the realm of show-biz. As long as that casual attitude exists, videoconferencing will be limited to that kind of usage. But improving the package and costs will gain the recognition that videoconferencing is used not only in an entertainment environment, but is an important day-to-day tool married to other office procedures.

Many corporations have moved ahead with building their own videoconferencing inhouse facilities. Most experts agree that usage isn't as high as it should be from these facilities. Most public relations

423

clients use ad-hoc transportable networks, rent a transportable earth station or TVRO (television receive only).

Transportable uplinks are also available to make transmitting available from anywhere in the United States and Canada. The international system, of course, is not as flexible due to government technicalities. Based on each country's regulations, private vendors can access the Intelsat system with transportable or fixed (in one place) facilities.

Until 1984, even satellite videoconferencing (two-way, full motion audio and video) was rather expensive. One hour between New York and London cost around $10,000. Today that same videoconference costs $1,600 and less, depending on the service selected.

Bruce Pennington (described later in this chapter) credits principally two organizations for the technological initiatives that generated this dramatic cost reduction. One is SBS (Satellite Business Systems), which introduced and advocated Ku-band transmission—using smaller less-expensive uplink and downlink dishes made possible by more powerful transponsers on the satellites. Television broadcasters and ad hoc videoconference networkers were using C-band transmission—larger, more expensive dishes, supported by less-powerful transponders.

The other technological advance is the video codec, pioneered by Compression Labs in California. The device "compresses" the band-width required by the video signal for transmission, then expands it when it reaches the receiving site. The one drawback is a slight delay in video signal, distracting only in the case of quite rapid movements or gestures. It's a small price to pay for the significant reduction in transmission cost—and one of which the user becomes unaware after the first few minutes of conferencing.

For public relations purposes, the era of pure ad hoc videoconference networks is virtually at an end. The cost of rolling in uplink and downlink dishes can, in most cases, be avoided. A few companies now have permanent Ku-band uplinks and downlinks. With the basic systems in place, it is possible to access any number of "public rooms" for those locations where it is not practical to install permanent up-and-down links.

International videoconferencing, the area in which the economies of the electronic travel alternative are most apparent, is growing significantly. Intelsat's multinational satellite exclusivity may give way to the efficiencies and securities of the fiber optic cablescrawling across the Atlantic Oceanbed. And the U.K.'s Docklands project, promising to become the "electronic gateway between the U.S. and Europe," may increase competition and help to reduce further the transatlantic interconnection costs.

The two ends of the networking spectrum are (1) a dedicated, private videoconference network, and (2) use of public videoconference rooms. For most public relations purposes, for the next few years, it is a combination of elements from the two that will deliver the most effective conferences.

The two ends of the content spectrum are (1) an event, with most of the information going one way, to a large, geographically dispersed group, and (2) a meeting, with continual back-and-forth information exchange.

In many cases, the interrelationships among these four facets have not been clear, because the public relations person has been dealing with a single supplier who specializes in perhaps only one of the four. A news conference, for example, contains elements of an "event"—in presenting the information—and elements of a "meeting"—in answering questions by media people.

The following section was provided by Michael Clifford, president of Victory Communications of Scottsdale, Arizona. This company has created, planned and executed videoconferences for fund raising, public relations, sales training and other clients throughout the world.

Here's how videoconferencing works.

There is a need to communicate a message not necessarily intended for public distribution.

Closed circuit satellite broadcasts can be transmitted to meeting facilities across the county or around the world.

It is done with transportable receive-only earth stations, wide-screen color television projectors and a local representative at each site.

A local representative opens the meeting, coordinates any materials distributed or collected, closes the meeting and transports any materials to the central hub.

Every meeting is treated as if each individual were in a personal meeting with the organization's personalities.

Two-way audio interaction via telephone for questions/answer segment add a unique production dimension as well as selected inserts from personalities as video telegram endorsements, either live from around the world or on tape endorsing a specific program.

A concentrated follow-up program to the videoconference is launched immediately after the broadcast.

How much does all this cost? The range is tremendous, but a rough estimate is $5,000 per site, which includes:

Transportable satellite receive-only earth stations with site clearances (fixed down links where possible)
Terrestrial facilities where needed
Wide screen color television projection systems
Uplinks
Space segments
Production
Travel arrangements
Materials transportation
Training material
Site facility rentals averaging 750-1,000 seats per site
Producer's fees and coordination expenses
Public affairs, promotion and advertising

Teleconference projects range considerably in cost, depending on the number of locations and a multitude of other factors which relate to transmission, reception, meeting facilities and the production costs, including producing pre-taped portions of the event, as well as coverage of the event itself. Production costs can be as little as $3,000 or well over $100,000, so that it is impossible to provide even a ball park estimate for a typical videoconference. It is possible for a one-hour conference involving 50 locations to cost only a few thousand dollars for the transmission and about $60,000 for the reception. However, these costs are only part of the total budget.

Videoconferencing can be a powerful medium, particularly for organizations to communicate one-on-one with their constituencies. Organizations are using videoconferencing for membership recruitment, new product introduction, public relations, fund raising and other major purposes. Videoconferencing can allow an organization the opportunity to speak privately (scrambling the signals for security purposes are available) and directly to an entire constituency live via satellite to share a common cause or need. Whether for strictly entertainment purposes (such as the Rolling Stones closed circuit world-wide rock box office event) or for fund raising (such as Christian Broadcasting Network's successful fund raising videoconferences), this now is a valid medium. Videoconferencing can be used for small groups, even on a point-to-point basis. For example, President Reagan used this technology to speak from the White House to a single location in the West to address his supporters. This technology also can be used to produce what is referred to as mega-events. For example, an event produced in 1984 by Victory Communications entailed over 200 international receive sites, including Radio City Music Hall in New York.

This special tool allows an organization to move from a passive relationship to an active relationship.

By utilizing the state of the art technology, a message can be communicated to a qualified (by RSVP invitation only) participant. This makes the individual feel special, creates the right for two-way interaction and is cost-effective. Leaders in this industry agree that conferencing the satellite way will eventually greatly reduce travel among business executives. Conferences, seminars, conventions, and symposia involving city-to-city participants are easier and more economical with videoconferencing services.

This particular use of technology allows an organization's host or personality to be simultaneously multiplied live in numerous locations. Meeting facilities are selected in close proximity to the constituency. Sometimes in the corporate structure (as with Hewlett-Packard), transportable down links are put in place at factories once a month with large 15×20 color television projection screens utilized for the chairman of the board and other key executives to help motivate employees. This message obviously is broadcast privately and is not intended for public distribution.

Participants for an event or conference may be selected from a specialized profile. Meeting facilities can be enlarged, added, deleted, or cancelled, based on RSVP participation until the night or day of the event. As the lights are dimmed, the live satellite signal is transmitted from the origination point or points to the satellite 22,700 miles above the earth to the down links, whether transportable or fixed, on the medium facility. The signal transmission happens within seconds and the clarity of transmission can be superior to broadcast television because of no tape generation losses.

Outlined below are some of the most used terms in videoconferencing.

Antenna (dish)—primary earth station component. Used for receiving or down linking the satellite transmission.

Down link—reception of signal from the satellite. (Also the equipment used to receive the signal.)

Earth Station—the antenna or dish used to send or receive satellite signals in the associated electronics.

Encryption/Decryption—technical term for scrambling or unscrambling a satellite signal to ensure security.

Full motion video—image presents live, complete video action rather than a "snapshot-like" picture.

Slow scan transmission—"snapshot" transmission. Slow scan usually does not utilize satellite transmission but digitizes existing telephone lines. Full color image or black and white appears approximately every 30 seconds on screen with live audio.

Fully interactive audio—all sites of the videoconference have voice interaction with each other via speaker phones hooked up to long distance telephone lines and/or a bridge network.

Bridge network—a sophisticated conferencing unit for teleconferencing (teleconferencing literally means use of telephones, not video).

Satellite technician—skilled operator of earth station equipment. Should be on site for duration of videoconference.

Space segment (satellite time)—channel time booked on a communications satellite.

Site clearance check—inspection of meeting locations to be sure clear reception of the satellite signal will be possible.

Terrestrial facilities—land lines, long lines. Where microwave interference makes it impossible to receive a satellite signal, long distance telephone lines must be ordered to deliver signal. This is extremely expensive and unadvisable.

TVRO—Television Receive Only earth station.

Transponder—a channel on a satellite.

Transportable TVRO—earth stations that are mounted on a trailer and can be moved from site to site.

Uplink—transmission of earth station signal to the satellite. Can be a transportable moved from site to site.

Video display (projection equipment)—equipment utilized for viewing the video conference. Sizes range from 19" TV monitor to large-screen television projection systems up to 34' wide.

Following is a description of a few companies involved in varied aspects of teleconferencing. Several hotels are in this business, notably Hilton and Holiday Inn.

The Video Register and Teleconferencing Resources Directory, a 450-page directory of studios and other facilities and services, is published ($74.50) by Knowledge Industry Publications, 701 Westchester Ave., White Plains, NY 10604.

1. American Video Teleconferencing Corp. (AVTC)
110 Bi-County Blvd., Farmingdale, NY 11735
(516) 420-8080
Gary Lewis, V.P. Marketing

This teleconferencing company has combined a personal computer with a videoconferencing system to create Inforum.

Computer images and video pictures are distributed on the same communications line to an unlimited number of videoconference facilities.

The two technologies, information processing and videoconferencing, thus are merged for information exchange. A unique software package, designed for this particular source, and used with an IBM personal computer allows for any combination of text, graphs, spreadsheets and user-created drawings within a single visual frame.

2. Connex International, Inc.
12 West St., Danbury, CT 06810
(203) 797-9060, (800) 243-9430
Susan Pereyra, Pres.
Bobbi Heyel, V.P.
Patti Bisbano, V.P.

Founded in 1981, Connex International is an independent telephone conferencing service that provides bridging capabilities to link multiple locations for audio teleconferences domestically and internationally. It also offers audio-graphic conferencing, audio connections for video conferences, user training and other conferencing services.

Charges are $10 per half-hour for each calling location. Participants dial in individually to be connected to the teleconference; therefore each incurs telephone long-distance charges. Tape recordings of conferences available for $15 per 60-minute cassette. Discount rates are offered to volume users of the services.

3. The Meeting Channel
1815 Century Blvd., Atlanta, GA 30345
(404) 982-1555, (800) 241-8470
Telex: 543024
Ken Van Meter, Dir. Teleconferencing

Conceived in 1982 by Isacomm Inc., The Meeting Channel now is owned by US Sprint Communications Company and has become one of the world's largest videoconferencing networks.

The Meeting Channel provides two-way audio and video links to over 250 sites in the U.S. and elsewhere, plus about 5000 analog sites in the U.S.

Hourly usage for U.S. conferences are only about $400.

Modern Telecommunications, Inc. (MTI)
See listing in chapter on motion pictures and video.

4. Bruce Pennington Associates, Inc.
1180 Avenue of the Americas, N.Y. 10016
(212) 391-1234
Bruce Pennington, Pres.

Since producing the first nationwide videoconferences in 1971, Bruce Pennington has continued to pioneer in the field with the first corporate video annual report, distributed via cable-TV; the first international video security analysts presentation via satellite, among the first video news releases; the first video of an annual meeting expressly for shareholders who were unable to attend; the first videotaped executive roundtable to clarify corporate policies, positions and operations for both internal and external audiences.

Formed in 1985 (at that time, in partnership with Huber Wilke, a pioneer in the design of electronic communications systems), Pennington specializes in integrating video applications into comprehensive corporate communications programs.

5. Private Satellite Network (PSN)
215 Lexington Ave., N.Y. 10016
(212) 696-9476
Marc Porat, Chm.
Richard Verne, Pres.
Richard Neustadt, Sr. V.P.

Branch Offices:
2232 N. Seminary St., Chicago 60614
(312) 248-3799
Jonathan Sendor

3403 Gallows Rd., Falls Church, VA 22042
(703) 560-0821
Jim Knickle

Formed in 1983, PSN is a large company in the field of business television and satellite communications.

Using Ku band satellite technology, PSN installs and operates business television networks domestically and internationally and provides creative, production and networking services for events.

PSN also owns and operates professional programming networks specifically targeted to the investment, legal and MIS communities.

6. Public Affairs Satellite System, Inc. (PUBSAT)
1012 14 St., N.W., Wash., DC 20005
(202) 628-2600
See description in TV chapter.

7. Satellite Conference Network, Inc.
200 Park Ave., N.Y. 10166
(212) 351-2700
A. Reza Jafari, Pres.
Jennifer A. Joffrey, Exec. V.P.

SCN was founded in 1983 and is an affilitate of Primerica (formerly American Can).

The company offers comprehensive custom-designed video-teleconferencing, including program development and meeting planning.

SCN also designs, installs, and operates private, dedicated satellite TV networks.

8. Satellite Theater Network
6069 Arlington Blvd., Falls Church, VA 22044
(703) 241-2363, (800) 423-8907

Formed in 1986, Satellite Theater Network is a network of movie theaters in major cities equipped as downlinks for Ku-band satellite transmissions. Each theater has a large-screen video projection system that provides a picture on the theater screen of up to 250 inches measured diagonally. The network is used primarily for video conferences of all types, such as news conferences, product introductions, stockholder meetings, seminars, training programs, political membership meetings. Each theater rents for $1,900 per day (New York City $2375), which covers everything except catering and the cost of the telephone line to the originating site.

9. Victory Communications International
6617 N. Scottsdale Rd., Scottsdale, AZ 85253
(602) 951-8444
Michael K. Clifford, Pres.

Formed in 1983, Victory Communications International combines the full services of a teleconferencing company with promotional and marketing activities. Victory specializes in developing and producing major media and fund-raising events for nonprofit, religious and political organizations. Since the company's formation, Michael Clifford has developed and produced major media events for many world-renowned individuals and organizations.

Victory broadcasts teleconferences to national and international locations and handles all details, from technical aspects to scouting sites for each broadcast. Victory can develop a complete marketing and promotion package for each client, including creative idea development through broadcast and follow-up.

Victory also has a radio division that syndicates live radio programs via satellite.

10. Video Star Connections, Inc.
3490 Piedmont Rd., Atlanta, GA 30305
(404) 262-1555, (800) 241-8850
Ken Leddick, Pres.

Branch Office:
475 Fifth Ave., N.Y. 10019
(212) 684-2121

Formed in 1980 by engineers Ken Leddick (Georgia Tech) and Jim Black (M.I.T.), who had worked together at Scientific Atlanta (a pioneer in the manufacture of earth stations), Video Star Connections has become a major company in satellite transmissions. The company operates earth stations at many hotels, including Marriott, Sheraton and Westin facilities, and also has its own fleet of transportable earth stations.

VideoStar Connections is a satellite communications company which provides complete communications services for satellite videoconferencing to first-class hotel meeting rooms throughout the U.S., and also to college and university sites through an agreement with the National University Teleconference

429

Network (NUTN). The company takes total responsibility for transmission of domestic or international events, including all the necessary satellite communications facilities and the voice return circuits for two-way audio if desired. VideoStar's services include booking satellite time, arranging satellite facilities from the conference origination point, providing satellite receiving stations at the various meeting locations and large screen video displays in the meeting rooms.

Using a combination of fixed and transportable satellite earth stations, VideoStar's Tele-Meeting Network now serves all major cities. In addition to hotels, videoconferences can be delivered to some convention centers, civic auditoriums, and even directly to the client's offices.

11. Western Union Corporation
1 Lake St., Upper Saddle River, NJ 07458
(201) 825-5000
Warren Bechtel, Asst. V.P.

Western Union's Westar satellites and earth stations are integrated with the company's transmission system to deliver a wide range of satellite-based communications services.

Broadcast services include audio and video transmission for radio and television broadcasters and cable operators. Transatlantic delivery of video programming via Westar satellite is handled by Brightstar Communications Ltd.

Transponder Sales and Leases include sale of full or partial transponders and transponder leases on monthly or two-year terms for audio, video or data transmission. Partial lease services give customers access to shared transponders for audio and data services.

Video Channel service offers a full range of video services to major cities, including uplinking, space segment, downlinking, local channels, remote program pickups and video tape playbacks.

Facsimile transmission of pages via Westar satellite is used by magazine and newspaper publishers.

12. Wetacom, Inc.
428 National Press Building, Wash., D.C. 20045
(202) 737-2500
Ellen Belkin, Nancy Fearhely, Jane Symons

Major producer of video conferences throughout the world, as well as other video projects.

13. Wold Communications, Inc.
10880 Wilshire Blvd., L.A. 90024
(213) 474-3500
TWX: 910-342-6977
Robert N. Wold, Chm.
Bill Hynes, Exec. V.P.

Branch Offices:
875 Third Ave., N.Y. 10022
(212) 832-3666
Keitha Fairhurst, Account Executive

8150 Leesburg Pike #910
Vienna, VA 22180
(703) 442-8550
Diana Calland, Account Executive

Founded in 1971 as a subsidiary of Robert Wold Company, Wold Communications is the world's largest single user of satellite communications facilities for the transmission of radio and television programming. A pioneer in satellite communications, Wold services include:

Point-to-point-multipoint television program distribution and network interconnection via the Wold Satellite TV Network (a live, nation-wide program distribution system providing syndicated television program distribution in monaural or high-fidelity stereo).

Fixed satellite transmission and reception in New York, Los Angeles and Washington, DC.

Mobile uplink and microwave services throughout the United States via seven fulltime satellite transponders, a nationwide network of satellite earth stations owned and operated by Wold Communications, and other facilities for videoconferencing and/or related services. For example, you can distribute a video news release or PSA for only a few hundred dollars.

Chapter 33

Television

In 1986, of America's 1,702 television stations, 548 were commercial VHF, 451 commercial UHF, 109 noncommercial VHF and 187 noncommercial UHF. In addition, over 7,000 cable systems reached about 48 percent of the 87 million TV homes.

Marshall McLuhan called television the medium that controls our environment, simultaneously influencing and typifying the new electronic age.

But Dr. McLuhan stated that the program content of television has little or nothing to do with the real changes television has produced. The basic message of television is television itself, where everything is happening at once, instantaneously. As Professor McLuhan said, "The medium is the message."

Whether television is hot or cold, inept or informing, inferior or superior, *it's big* and *important*.

Among the recent changes in the ways in which public relations practitioners relate to television are:

1. Setting up events at times of the day and in specific places which are most likely to attract TV news coverage. Other media are invited, or course, but the orientation often is to TV.
2. Touring authors, executives, performers and other spokespeople for the sole or primary purpose of interviews on TV programs. They're called "media tours," and generally include radio, newspapers and magazines, but the emphasis frequently is on TV.
3. Increased use of specialists to provide and distribute one-minute news clips and feature films geared specifically to TV.
4. Coaching of spokespeople prior to TV appearances.

Some industrial and other public relations practitioners still devote more attention to the print medium than to television. The reasons for this probably include a combination of "old-fashioned" print orientation combined with a sense of being overwhelmed by television. The reality indeed is that it's generally much harder to obtain significant publicity results on television than with print media which use a much greater amount of publicity material.

Though it is possible to reach Government officials, stockholders, executives and other special audiences which often are the "targets" of public relations campaigns by means of television, many practitioners prefer to pinpoint their efforts by concentrating on speeches, events and news releases which are likely to be of interest to editors of newspapers, trade publications and other print media. It is simpler, more economical, and usually more effective to distribute reprints of print articles as compared to films and other means of merchandising television publicity.

Newspapers and other publications vastly outnumber TV stations and offer a considerably larger number and variety of publicity opportunities. During the evening hours, when more people are seeing television than any other medium, the programs usually consist of situation comedies, theatrical motion pictures and other shows which seem to offer no opportunities to publicists.

However, there are quite a few network programs which offer publicity opportunities, in addition to hundreds of local news, women's and other programs to which public relations clients could have access. America's TV stations beam their programs to almost every man, woman and child in the country, and television is *the* mass medium.

On the network level, NBC's Today show and the other morning programs have a constant need for authors and other news guests. As with any other television program, the best way to identify the program's needs is to look at it yourself. Then contact the producer or other staff member of the program, whose name you can obtain from various media directories or simply by looking at the credits at the end of the program. A new opportunity is the recent proliferation of "Live at 5"-type magazine-style TV programs.

Of course, most public relations clients are not sufficiently renowned to be of interest to network news programs. In addition, nonpolitical, commercial clients often are reluctant to be interviewed on programs which thrive on controversy. An exception is the author of a book or magazine article, and this is a major category of TV publicity.

The creative publicist must adapt "print themes" so that they are logical and appealing to the many daytime game shows, interview programs, documentaries and variety shows which offer network publicity opportunities. It generally is more difficult to work with these programs than with print media, but it is too important to be ignored.

For example, many millions of viewers watch the Tonight Show and other network and syndicated talk shows. Some of these viewers are sleepy-eyed. Others are semihypnotized by the electronic medium, but that still leaves millions of people from all socioeconomic groups receptive to your publicity message.

Public broadcasting stations have become increasingly important, as a result of their sizeable audiences, which generally are upscale and of considerable interest to a variety of companies, and also because of "enhanced underwriting," which permits on-air credits from "sponsors," rather than simply a corporate identification. The name and description of the products, often including a logo, is akin to a brief commercial. However, these projects often are handled by public relations practitioners, rather than advertising agencies, and they are not commissionable.

Communicators no longer can ignore the importance of cable as a medium. Modern and other distributors supply many public relations films to cable stations. However, it is not likely that cable subscribers are paying for the privilege of receiving, or viewing, this type of program.

In summary, cable should be considered as part of the total TV medium. Similarly, many UHF stations and the campus and school district stations are a specialized, relatively minor part of the TV picture, when compared to the VHF stations and public stations in major markets.

Videotex and teletext are remote communications services that combine graphics and text in efficient digital form over a television screen or terminal.

Videotex are telephone-based, two-way interactive services and include transactions (electronic mail, reservations, banking, shipping), and retrieving information (such as news and the weather) and computing (interactive games or financial analysis), and telemonitoring (such as providing security for offices and homes).

Videotex and teletext both originated in the United Kingdom. Teletext is noninteractive. Services are usually page-oriented and repeat after a given cycle. Teletext is commonly found on cable TV systems. Some of these services are described in the chapter on research.

In 1987, the long-predicted videotex boom still had not materialized. Instead, the VCR era has developed. The videotape cassette recorder (VCR) has become, during the last few years, basic equipment in most public relations offices. It is used mostly to record and play back TV programs and thus serves as a record and also a means to study performance. When used with a camera, the system enables speakers to prepare and be coached for interviews and public speeches, and for many other purposes.

Public relations people involved with closed-circuit TV, videotapes for training and other nonbroadcast uses of television should be familiar with *The Video Source Book,* which describes over 50,000 prerecorded (tape and disc) video programs. It's $199 (plus $6 mailing) from National Video Clearinghouse, Inc., 100 Lafayette Dr., Syosset, NY 11791.

Many public relations operations now have on their premises a variety of audiovisual equipment, including videotape and audiotape recorders, slide and film projectors. No matter how much equipment you own, it seems there always are occasions when you don't have the necessary equipment. If you have a ¾-inch videotape player (the professional size used by TV stations), a client will send you a ½-inch videotape (the lower-priced home version). If you have an audio cassette player, a radio station will send you a reel. If you have a 16mm sound film projector, a theatrical producer will provide you with a 35mm print.

Here's one solution. Buy your equipment from a professional audiovisual company, ask them about what to buy and set up an arrangement for rapid, low-cost delivery of rental items.

Los Angeles, Chicago, New York and other cities have several of these companies. In New York, audiovisual specialists include Reliance Audio Visual, 623 W. 51 St., N.Y. 10019, (212) 586-5000, and MPCS, 514 W. 57 Street, N.Y. 10019, (212) 586-3690. MPCS Video Industries, Inc., one of America's largest video sources, also provides production services.

A few individuals and firms specialize in television publicity campaigns. These specialists know the TV programs and their personnel, but they usually cannot be expected to know your public relations needs, objectives, orientation and sensitivities. Therefore, public relations clients are more likely to keep to themselves any work involving broadcast interviews and publicity on major TV programs. The most important form of contact consists of personal communication with the producers and staff personnel of network and local news and interview programs. "Outside" services can be useful in tapping the enormous publicity potential of the many hundreds of local TV programs.

The most common types of "packaged TV services" are:

1. Script accompanied by photos, slides or props. Merely sending a press release or script, unattached to these items, usually is wasted if sent to TV stations, though many publicists persist in this extravagance.
2. News clips (video news releases).
3. Features.

Do not try to save money by sending a news release or script with no visual. Videotape (sound and color, of course) is preferable. And, the professionals use ¾-inch, not ½-inch.

In the past few years, the term "chroma key" slide has been heard with increasing frequency. Completely opaque except for a small "window" in which your picture appears, the chroma key slide makes your picture appear on a screen behind the newscaster or talk show hostess. Therefore, you also can do well with slides.

There are two basic ways to get your story on TV. Each offers an important advantage.

1. *The basic TV news release* (four slides and a script). The advantage of this technique is that your message is delivered not by an actor or an industry spokesman, but by the viewer's own broadcaster. The cost of producing and distributing a basic TV release through a distribution service is relatively low when you consider audience size. For about $2,500 to $3,000, you can typically appear on 40 stations that go into over 10 million TV homes with 29 million viewers. The dollar

434

cost of using a service is usually no more than that of approaching stations directly—and the time cost is substantially less. In addition, the typical distributor has an ongoing research apparatus to keep track of which stations—and which people at those stations—are most receptive to receiving TV slides and scripts.

2. *The interview* between a talk-show personality and a spokesperson. A typical interview lasts five to 15 minutes, yielding the advantage of more in-depth coverage of a subject than is practical with basic TV news releases. However, there are many more potential interviewees than there are talk shows, so competition for air time is keen. But your spokesperson will have a competitive advantage if you offer prospective interviewers not only the guest, but also a set of supportive pictures in color. These can come from the annual report, from consumer booklets or, if you send our slide-and-script releases which use cartoons in color (very much in demand), have extra sets of slides made for use with interviews.

In creating a basic TV news release, slides or tape, here is the benefit of Ron Levy's wisdom and experience in terms of a list of themes which generally produce the best results (Levy's company, North American Precis Syndicate, is described in this and other chapters):

1. *History:* The latest development tends to look extra modern when it is described with copy and slides on its historical antecedents.
2. *Tips:* There is a demand for information on increasing safety, saving money and getting things done more efficiently around the house.
3. *Straight product news:* This is effective if you have a new and noteworthy product. However, if what you have is really a new model rather than a new idea, this is not the technique of choice.
4. *Travel:* Even if you do not represent a destination or a carrier, by fitting your message into a travel format, you can get an abundant volume of usage.
5. *Superlatives:* If your development is "the most" in some respect—the biggest, fastest, lowest-cost, or whatever—letting the script include three unrelated superlatives will mean more exposure for the one you want people to know about.
6. *Public policy questions:* Many PR people assume that because of the "equal time" doctrine, TV cannot be used for publicity on a public policy question. It is true that you *can't* get air time for what amounts to an editorial for or against a course of public action. However, you *can* get air time—and a great deal of it—for a feature on the subject. For example, if resolution of the public policy question will have an effect on the prices consumers pay, you can do a feature on the history of inflation, tips on coping with inflation, inflation around the world or superlatives connected with inflation. In each release you can make known the key reality—that if such-and-such happens, it stands to cost the viewer money.

A word of caution about placements. According to Ron Levy, when a story mentions no commercial names and is the kind of thing that would benefit the public, there is a "temptation to direct it to the public service director of TV stations. *This is wrong.* We have tested the concept repeatedly. Virtually without exception, the material, though public service in nature, attracts a bigger volume of returns when addressed to news directors and news program managers—not public service directors. Also, you get a substantially larger audience on a news show than if the release runs on public service time."

And finally, here is Ron Levy's list of specific suggestions to obtain maximum results with slide scripts. The same concepts apply to TV tapes, except that the cost of inefficiencies is greater.

1. *Use only color visuals.* Most TV stations no longer even consider the use of black-and-white photos or drawings except for old prints, historic photos or other special artwork. Color is essen-

tial. If you do not have color photos or artwork from which to have slides made, you can usually get drawings in color for about $100 each.

2. *Keep your script short.* Ten to 50 words per slide is about right. Anything shorter and your visual will not be on screen long enough to register in the minds of viewers; anything longer and you will have trouble holding the attention of viewers on a single idea.

3. *Keep pictures horizontal and subject matter centered.* Since all TV screens are horizontal, TV pictures should be too. Most TV sets tend to crop the picture sent out by the station—as much as 15 percent on all slides. Therefore, be sure your subject matter is centered. "Live" material should *never* stray into the outer 15 percent of your artwork.

4. *Avoid type in art.* Then, if a slide is inadvertently reversed, a "lost" placement is "saved." If type must be used, be certain that lables on the slide mount clearly orient it.

5. *Never request return of transparencies.* Make 35mm slides—which are relatively inexpensive—and calculate their cost as part of the cost of the release.

6. *Always enclose two copies of the script.* Most stations want one script for the announcer and another for the control room.

7. *Keep track of which news directors use your material.* If a station's news director consistently fails to return your use cards, try addressing your next release to someone else—the program director.

8. *Keep track of results.* You should typically get 5–10 percent return on a release. If you are getting less, take a critical look at story ideas and presentations, and review your mailing list to make sure you are properly directing your efforts.

Another long-time practitioner in TV services is Don Phelan, whose company is listed in this chapter. He also operates Doncorps TV News at the same location (311 W. 43 St., N.Y. 10036) and is an expert on producing and distributing public relations materials to TV stations. Following is an interview with Don Phelan about video news releases.

Q: Is the Video News Release a new technique for gaining time on TV news program?

A: Really no. A VNR (video news release) is simply an extension of the old reliable 16mm film clip service that was first offered to the trade in 1957 by UPI's commercial department. It was a very simple service utilizing silent B&W film, no graphics and no voice over. TV news programming was still in the infancy stage and most stations had little means of producing their own programs. Film clips were usually well received by most TV news departments.

Q: What advantage does videotape have over film?

A: Film is too complex to process and edit and far more time consuming. By 1974 many stations around the country had purchased their own ENG video equipment and had expanded their staffs to include camera operators and video editors. The first commercial video news service was started by Phelan in the same year and by 1978 film became a rarity for distribution to TV. Videotape can also be shot under reduced available light conditions more so than film. It can be edited quickly and distributed the same day.

Q: What does a VNR entail and how complicated is the production?

A: A VNR is ideal when a public relations agency or corporate public relations department has a meaningful story to tell that lends itself to TV news. The original scripting is very important and the actual production should be in the hands of people with previous experience in TV news production and distribution. Copy must be crisp and there should be adequate visuals throughout. Unless the story is of exceptional merit, the release should not exceed 1:30 min. In any event, the product or company name for the client should be in the beginning or middle . . . never near the end. With a good production staff, a story can be shot in the morning, edited in 2–3 hours and distributed by satellite or ¾″ video cassette that afternoon so news directors can use it in their TV news programming that or the following evening.

Q: When are VNR's used most often?

A: It depends on the content and the subject matter and also the volume of news traffic on that particular day. If the release is not topical news—but well done and interesting—it will be held for a filler on weekend news programs. If the release relates to current events, it usually appears on the evening prime time news programs. If a station has a specific business news show and the VNR is business or financially oriented, that's where it will show up.

Q: Does it make any difference whether the VNR is distributed electronically by satellite or by ¾″ cassette using express courier service?

A: From a quality point of view it makes no difference although the satellite signal usually is received on one-inch videotape and the end product is closer to broadcast quality. Also, satellite transmission avoids the tedious production of duplicate tapes, labelling and packaging for express shipment. And some news directors may be more inclined to review a satellite release since it implies important news. On the other hand, it's easier for a news director working under deadlines to get to a ¾″ playback tape deck for viewing the material since all TV news departments have machines nearby. Also, the original script and postage paid return use card can be included with the tape in the same package. The script for the satellite tape must be sent by TWX and may arrive on the news director's desk before or after the one-inch satellite tape. Or it can be scrolled at the end of satellite-transmitted tape so technicians at TV stations can freeze frame it for their use. Rule of thumb is to use satellite if the story is current news and ¾″ cassette tape for "evergreen" material.

Q: What topics are most popular?

A: Generally speaking, anything to do with new business trends are of considerable interest as well as items that relate to science, medicine, health, consumer safety, sports and food.

Q: Which TV stations should be considered when planning a VNR release?

A: Start with the top 100 markets, if your budget permits. Select a network affiliate and independent station in each market. Better still send an *exclusive* VNR to one station in each of 150 markets.

Q: How many plugs for the product, company name or special technique/service can one expect on a single VNR?

A: As a general rule, one is considered safe. However, if the plug is in the audio track, a second visual plug can usually be included if not to long or obvious.

Q: Should stations be advised in advance that a VNR is being sent to their news departments?

A: Absolutely. This is true no matter how the VNR is sent. If time permits, send first class letters of notification to the news directors with all possible details one week in advance. On the day before the actual distribution, it's best to send a TWX message to remind all concerned at each station news department. If the transmission is by satellite, the script must be sent at the same time by computerized TWX. Some people involved in this field go to the long distance phones to alert news directors. This is often expensive and frustrating. Many key news people at TV news stations can't be reached in the morning. In the afternoon, they are busy preparing their evening news shows and unavailable to anyone except close associates.

Q: How will a PR client know the results of a VNR distribution?

A: As with anything in public relations, this can often be a difficult result to fully tabulate. When we use satellite, we sometimes add a short section at the end of the TWX script permitting the news director to fill in a use report and mail back to us for tabulating. Some do and some don't for various reasons. Many simply forget or company policy precludes their affirmative response. As a result, two weeks after the transmission, we send a first class follow-up letter with stamped, addressed reply card requesting their cooperation in compiling our report. If the distribution is by express courier, we include the postage paid reply card with the ¾" tape cassette and then follow the same procedure two weeks later as we do with satellite.

Q: What percentage of stations generally use VNR's and what size audience can one expect?

A: Fifteen years ago, the average known TV station usage of a distributed PR press release either by film or tape was 45 percent. Currently, it averages about 25 percent. This is still a good number though. Assuming that the VNR has been sent to 100 stations, it means that it will be viewed by at least 5,000,000 TV households. It also means that another 10–12 stations have probably used the tape but have not advised us adding about 980,000 TV households to the audience.

Q: When you refer to TV households, what do you mean?

A: A household is a single dwelling unit, which may be a house, apartment or a group of two or more rooms. It can have one or more TV sets and in most cases, probably does. In compiling our final report on usage by TV stations of a particular release, we use the current TV factbook which is considered the most authoritative reference for the advertising, public relations, television and electronics industries. In listing a TV household audience for each reporting station, we use the current Arbitron circulation estimates which are rounded off to the nearest hundred. The ADA (average daily audience) is the estimated average number of television households reached by a particular station on each day of the week, sign-on to sign-off. Usually, in each household, there are more viewers but there is no way of determining this number.

Q: Can you relate the cost for producing and distributing a VNR to media cost per thousand?

A: As a general rule, if you have a well produced VNR with good sharp copy and interesting visuals, the cost per thousand runs about $2.09 which compares very favorably with any other media. It's probably the best value around today.

Q: Will anything else help to get your VNR used on television news?

A: Yes. Keep the content simple and straightforward and be sure to include a "super" list at end of script with all names and titles of persons shown as they appear on tape. Another good idea is to add about two minutes of "B" roll material so the news director can construct his or her own show. This would be extended scenes of footage already included or scenes not used in your original edited version.

Thank you, Don Phelan! His companies, Don Phelan, Inc. and Doncorps, are described under P in this chapter.

Many companies which specialize in other types of television publicity projects, including arranging for products as prizes on programs and distribution of scripts and films to local TV stations, are described in the sections titled Mailing Services, Motion Pictures, Packaged Publicity Services, Prizes and Radio.

If you are particularly active in the broadcast field, you may want to become an associate member of the National Association of Broadcasters, 1771 N Street, N.W., Wash., DC 20036. Dues start at $350 a year, and are in a variety of categories depending on gross broadcast-related income or number of professionals in the firm or department.

Associate members receive a variety of publications, including the weekly Radio/TV Highlights and monthly RadioActive, and also can attend the annual convention and other meetings.

More companies, including several formed in 1986, now produce more video news releases than ever before. Here are descriptions of several of these companies, as well as other companies and organizations involved in the public relations aspects of television.

1. Accent on Broadcasting, Etc., Inc.
165 W. 66 St., N.Y. 10023
(212) 362-3616
Miss Randie Levine, Pres.

438

A specialist in booking guests on TV and radio programs, Randie Levine is sufficiently confident of success that she generally operates with a "package guarantee" of a minimum number of interviews. For example, a tour of five major cities generally is handled with a minimum guarantee of 25 radio and television placements. The minimum often is exceeded, and if it isn't met, there's no payment required! A former talent coordinator at several radio and television programs, Miss Levine is particularly adept at creating interview themes and coaching interviewees. Authors are a specialty, and though she can handle print interviews, her expertise is with the radio and television media, including, of course, corporate spokespeople.

2. Armstrong Information Services, Inc.
141 E. 44 St., N.Y. 10017
(212) 986-0910
Willa L. Z. Armstrong, Pres.
Robin Bossert, V.P.

Founded in 1979, Armstrong produces public service announcements, video news releases, corporate films, training videos, sales promotion tapes, PBS documentaries, theatre shorts, airline shorts and the full range of sponsored film and video.

3. Audio/TV Features, Inc.
149 Madison Ave., N.Y. 10016
(212) 889-1327
Alan Steinberg, Chm.
Robert Kimmel, Pres.

Branch Office:
National Press Club, Wash., DC 20045
(202) 662-7596
Lee Shephard, V.P.

Formed in 1979, Audio/TV Features has considerable experience in all types of radio and TV services, including media training ($850 for one person for ½ day, $450 for a full day) and video news release production.

The company has a VNR package that is extraordinarily low in cost ($1,950), which includes telex notification to 600 TV stations, phone notification to "hot prospects," satellite distribution, follow-up phone calls, monitoring and usage report.

4. Broad Street Productions
50 Broad St., N.Y. 10004
(212) 480-8031
David H. Dreyfuss, Pres.
Jeanette M. Theroux, Dir. of Sales

Video has come to Wall Street.

Formed in 1981 as the in-house video department of Drexel Burnham Lambert (the investment banking and brokerage firm), Broad Street Productions (originally called DBL Video Network) has become one of America's largest and most respected producers of video projects which are primarily for financial and corporate clients.

Among the types of productions (minimum cost generally is $30,000) are shows for annual meetings, corporate and product profiles, documentaries, initial public offering profiles, marketing presentations, real estate, music and entertainment videos, as well as TV programs and commercials.

Production facilities include six editing suites, studios, a large stock footage library, audio and video duplication equipment, as well as film and video cameras and equipment.

Indeed, this division of Drexel is a major independent facility for just about any type of audiovisual project.

5. CWI Productions, Inc.
Box 606, Armonk, NY 10504
(914) 921-0318
Carolyn Worthington

Carolyn Worthington worked for the Burson-Marsteller public relations agency and was public relations director of Foremost-McKesson Wine and Spirits Group. In 1984, she and Elizabeth Hoskinson formed CWI Productions to produce and distribute films, video and audiotapes, primarily for public relations clients.

6. Caplin Communications
120 E. 79 St., N.Y. 10020
(212) 570-1688
Jo Ann Caplin, Pres.

Formed in 1985 by former TV news producer Jo Ann Caplin, this firm specializes in VNRs.

7. DWJ Associates, Inc.
1 Robinson Lane, Ridgewood, N.J. 07450
(201) 445-1711
Daniel Johnson, Pres.
Michael Friedman, V.P.

Branch Offices:
295 Madison Ave., N.Y. 10016
(212) 684-4000

1730 Rhode Island Ave., N.W., Wash., D.C. 20036
(202) 457-0884
Lynn Sullivan

Formed in 1973, DWJ is one of the largest producers of VNRs and other sponsored video projects. Partners Dan Johnson and Mike Friedman have considerable experience in broadcasting and public relations. Production facilities are in northern New Jersey.

8. Dee Gee Productions
295 Lafayette St., NY 10012
(212) 334-8181
Gigi Pritzker, Deborah Delprete

Video news releases (60 to 120 seconds) produced (about $8,500) and distributed ($40/market). The company is located in The Puck Building, a landmark in lower Manhattan that once housed Puck, one of the first newspaper supplements.

9. The Executive Report
Station KWHY-TV
5545 Sunset Blvd., L.A. 90028
(213) 466-5441
John Nelson, Sales Mgr.

KWHY-TV is a UHF (Channel 22) station that specializes in business news. The Executive Report is a daily morning program featuring an interview with an executive. The cost is $400 for a 10-minute segment.

10. The Fourth Network, Inc.
141 E. 33 St., N.Y. 10016
(212) 684-2208
Jean Green

Founded by George Green (a long-time broadcast publicist), the company now is operated by his widow. The specialty is the creation, production and distribution of a variety of radio and TV materials.

11. GHA Film & Tape
1170 Broadway, N.Y. 10001
(212) 683-6304
George Hudak

GHA specializes in public relations services in the video field, including video news releases distributed to TV stations, public service announcements, as well as employee training, documentaries and other productions. The company was formed in 1975 by George Hudak, who studied communications at Fordham University and film and television at New York University, and has had extensive experience as a film maker, producer and director.

Production of a video news release or public service announcement costs about $6,000, including script consultation and production, three person crew, four hours of editing and all talent. Distribution can be handled by the client or arranged through a distributor, and costs about $6,000, depending on the number of stations.

12. Hollywood Newsreel Syndicate, Inc.
1622 N. Gower St., Hollywood, CA 90028
(213) 469-7307
Rick Spalla, Pres.

More television and theatrical films are produced in Los Angeles than any other city. Several of the studios can be utilized for public relations films. A publicity specialist is Hollywood Newsreel Syndicate, a subsidiary of Rick Spalla Video Productions. $1,275 is the charge for a one-minute videotape with script serviced to Los Angeles TV stations, and additional stations are $30 each. A five-minute videotape is about $8,500.

13. KEF Media Associates, Inc.
213 W. Institute Pl., Chicago 60610
(312) 951-5894
Kevin E. Foley, Pres.

Formed in 1986, KEF (Kevin E. Foley) produces VNRs and other video materials at the adjacent studios of Media Process Group.

14. Karol Media, Inc.

22 Riverview Dr., Wayne, NJ 07470
(201) 628-9111
Fontaine (Mick) Kincheloe, Pres.
Carol Kincheloe, Eugene Dodge, Carl Sallach, V.P.s

Karol Media maintains company-owned libraries in Wayne, NJ: Smyrna, GA; Des Plaines, IL: Kansas City, MO and Fullerton, CA. Karol distributes 16mm films, videocassettes, film-strips, slides and printed materials to TV stations, schools and community groups, such as clubs, religious, business, and medical organizations and campgrounds.

Rates are $60 to $75 per broadcast placement (one or more airings by the station) plus a $10 preview charge when no airing results. Cable TV is $25 to $35, with no preview charge.

PSAs and other materials also are distributed to radio and TV stations.

Formed in 1976 by Mick Kincheloe (who had been with Modern Talking Pictures for 19 years), Karol Media has become a major company in the distribution of sponsored film and video materials. Mick's wife, Carol, and their son, Mark, head a large team of library and computer managers and other personnel.

15. Killingsworth/O'Neil Assoc.

356 Sixth St., Atlanta 30308
(404) 876-1744
Ngaio Killingsworth, Cecil O'Neil

Formed in 1980 by two former broadcasters, Killingsworth/O'Neil produces VNRs and other film and video products. Killingsworth is the director and O'Neil is the cameraman and editor.

16. Lee Martin Productions

3 Dallas Communications Complex, Irving, TX 75039
(214) 556-1991
Lee Martin, Pres.

A former TV sports broadcaster and director, Lee Martin formed a TV production and syndication company in 1979. The company now produces and distributes a variety of video news releases and programs. A typical production or live interview, including satellite feed, results in coverage by a minimum of eight TV stations and one cable TV network for about $5,500, plus travel expenses.

17. Martin Video Productions Incorporated

458 W. 144 St., N.Y. 10031
(212) 283-5237
Telex: (910) 997-6661
Sigrid E. Martin, V.P.

Martin produces a variety of news releases and other public relations videotapes and films, and operates the Evergreen Satellite Network for distribution to TV stations. She also has a working kitchen studio.

18. Neal Marshad Productions

76 Laight St., N.Y. 10013
(212) 925-5285
Neal Marshad, Pres.

Formed in 1974, Neal Marshad Productions produces all types of film and video for advertising and public relations clients.

19. Media Enterprises Inc.

175 Fifth Ave., N.Y. 10010
(212) 254-6310
Eugene Marlow, Pres.
Sylvia Hack, V.P.

Formed in 1979, Media Enterprises produces video news releases and a variety of video, film and multi-media presentations.

20. Medialink

Video Broadcasting Corp.
708 Third Ave., N.Y. 10017
(212) 682-8300, (800) 843-0677
Larry Moskowitz, Pres.
Robert R. Frump, Exec. V.P.

Launched in 1987, Medialink is a significant new development in TV news. The Medialink System solves the problem of how to inform TV stations about video news releases and other video materials. The solution was to install teleprinters at TV stations, akin to newswires. In fact, Larry Moskowitz started Mediawire in Philadelphia, which was sold to PR Newswire, and then worked for PR Newswire.

Public relations clients can subscribe for $250 a year. An arrangement with Nielsen tracks the usage of VNRs. Notification services can be as low as $250 per message, and VNR distribution prices range from $2500 to $3750.

The message is sent via satellite to the high-speed teleprinters which Medialink has installed at TV stations. The message alerts the TV stations to news events, and the availability of TV materials, such as the forthcoming transmission of a video news release. Medialink can handle the transmission of the video news release, or you can handle it. If Medialink handles it, their service also includes Nielson research to confirm active broadcast. The telefeed is about $2,500 to over 100 stations. Additional stations can be reached via satellite, air courier or mail.

The Medialink System, which is being expanded to many other TV stations, is installed and serviced by SATNET, a subsidiary of The Associated Press.

21. Mobile Video Service, Ltd.

2139 Wisconsin Ave., N.W., Wash., DC 20007
(202) 944-2800
Steve Meeks

Since 1974, Mobile Video Services has provided a variety of creative, technical and production video services. Its facilities include a studio, post-production editing, as well as mobile equipment. Projects range from relatively simple video coverage of events to the production of television programs. The company also provides multiple-camera video teleconferencing services. Distribution is via messenger, mail and also microwave transmission, including satellite.

22. Modern Talking Picture Service, Inc.

5000 Park St. N., St. Petersburg, FL 33709
(813) 541-7571
William M. Oard, Pres.
Patrick M. Swonger, Div. Mgr.

Branch Offices:
2020 Prudential Plaza, Chicago 60601
(312) 337-3252, Ed Swanson, V.P.

45 Rockefeller Plaza, N.Y. 10111
(212) 765-3100, Dan Kater, Pres., Bob Finehout, V.P.

149 New Montgomery St., San Francisco 94105
(415) 777-3995, Steve Mahan

1901 L. St., N.W., Wash., DC 20036
(202) 293-1222, Robert Kelley, V.P.

Modern is the world's largest distributor of sponsored films and video features and its services are described in the section on motion picture distribution. Following is a description of the services of the Modern Television division.

Features (generally 5 to 28 minutes) provided to Modern are distributed to television stations, and sponsors pay only for results, at the rate of $45 per broadcast ($25 for cable).

Clients also can provide Modern with a public service announcement package (videotape, script, business reply card, letter). Modern duplicates the printed materials (clients must provide nonreturnable videotape) and services to TV stations at a cost of $800 for 100 stations, and $3 per additional station on the same order. Unlike Modern's other services, the charge is for distribution and not total broadcasts.

Modern Satellite Services (MSS) offers sponsors of programs, PSAs, featurettes and other A-V material an opportunity to be included in the daily programming schedule of a basic cable service. Currently MSS is carried by more than 775 cable systems nationwide. A typical broadcast day includes a business news program, sponsored films, made-for-cable specials and other programming of an informational or educational nature. Sponsored programs are packaged in the series, World In Motion. PSAs and commercials are acceptable.

Rates:

Full Year Distribution (4 Network Airings): $2,000 entry fee plus $200 per minute running time, PSAs are $750 for programs supplied on ¾" or 1" tape.

Single Placements: $450 entry fee plus $55 per minute running time.

Note: Deadline for entry of programs is eight weeks prior to telecast date.

Sponsored films and videotapes are distributed to cable systems on an individualized basis.

23. National Television News, Inc.
23480 Park Sorrento, Calabasas Park, CA 91302
(818) 883-6121
Howard Back, Pres.

Branch Office:
13691 W. Eleven Mile Rd., Oak Park, MI 48237
(313) 541-1440
Jim O'Donnell, V.P.

NTN is one of the most experienced public relations oriented video and film groups in the country. Howard Back worked in corporate public relations for Chrysler Corporation, after several years in local and network broadcasting; he is an accredited member of PRSA and of the Counselors section. Jim O'Donnell has had Signal Corps, corporate, and television experience in film and video.

The company produces a wide variety of information video and film materials. The Michigan operation features the professional quality half-inch RECAM system. Company specialties are TV news reports, TV public service spots and video for employee and management communications.

Producing a TV news report generally costs $9,000 to $13,000 plus servicing stations at $40 per outlet.

Public Service spots for television range from $9,000 to $13,000 for production. Distribution is $8,000 for 300 stations, or $12,000 for 500 stations. Included in both news and PSA distribution are the tapes, scripts, follow-up cards and follow-up reports. A new service is the NTN Video Backgrounder, a cassette with about 10 minutes of B-roll footage. Production is about $15,000 and distribution is $45 per cassette.

Founded in 1961, NTN was located for many years in Woodland Hills and moved in 1984 to Calabasas Park. Both are near Los Angeles.

NTN publishes a free newsletter that is crammed with news personnel changes, comments about trends in broadcasting and other helpful material.

24. Newsfilm, USA
2 Beechwood Rd., Hartsdale, NY 10530
(914) 684-0110
Richard S. Milbauer, Exec. Producer

One of the pioneers in the production and distribution of TV news films, Newsfilm, USA, also produces motion pictures and videotapes, for television stations and theaters. The firm has affiliates in Washington, DC, Chicago and has its own and freelance crews throughout the country. Production costs average about $5,000 per minute for sound, color film or tape.

25. Newslink, Inc.
205 Lexington Ave., N.Y. 10016
(212) 725-0783
Bryn Jones, Pres.
Bradley B. Niemcek, Sr. V.P.

Branch Office:
122 C St., N.W., Wash., D.C. 20001
(202) 737-9454
Peter Ettinger, V.P.

Formed in 1982, the company has expanded considerably, and now has over 60 people. Art Browne formerly was national editor of ABC-TV News and others have impressive news and public relations backgrounds. In 1987, Newslink acquired Avatar Satellite Corp., which had been headed by Peter Ettinger. Mr. Ettinger now heads Newslink's Creative Media Division, which produces video press kits, teleconferences, satellite media tours and other TV projects.

Distribution of a five-minute video to about 650 TV stations is $2,500.

26. NewsTeam
53 E. 34 St., N.Y. 10016
(212) 683-5219
Richard Stern, Pres.
Jane A. Zamost, V.P.

Formed in 1984, NewsTeam covers major conventions, particularly medical meetings, with a variety of services, primarily the production of video news releases and other audiovisual materials. The reporters also cover seminars and prepare reports and other editorial services.

27. North American Precis Syndicate, Inc.

201 E. 42 St., N.Y. 10017
(212) 867-9000
Ronald N. Levy, Pres.
John Engel, Candy Lieberman, Francine Lucidon, Exec. V.P.'s
Diane Mason, Marilyn Rosenfeld, Claudia Schiff, Jim Wicht, Sr. V.P.'s
Kelly Lawrence, Dorothy Levy, Camilla Mendoza, V.P.'s

Branch Offices:
333 N. Michigan Ave., Chicago 60601
(312) 558-1200
Jim Brosseau, Nora Lukas, Sr. V.P.'s, Bonnie Cassidy Heller, V.P.

4209 Vantage Ave., Studio City, CA 91604
(818) 761-8400
Carol Balkin, V.P.

1025 Vermont Ave., N.W., Wash., DC 20005
(202) 347-7300
Jake Arnette, Sr. V.P.
Ann Barre, Monty Bodington, Wendy Sollod, V.P.'s

Though best know for its newspaper service, North American Precis Syndicate also has a sizeable broadcast operation, including the largest script-slide TV service.

NAPS writers prepare the script and set of four color slides and distribute them, with a reply card, to 325 TV programs, mostly news.

The total cost is $2,650, including materials, distribution, usage cards and reports.

Clients must provide the original art or photos in color, or you can pay $100 per drawing provided by NAPS.

Although product publicity often requires pictures of the product in use, NAPS reports that artwork in color often is quite well received, and good artwork can often be picked up from booklets or other consumer literature.

An advantage of stills is that your message is given to the viewer not by an actor but by the viewer's own newscaster. Another advantage is that extra sets of slides can be made up for use by company representatives in the field who may give speeches or appear on TV interview shows.

Drawbacks to the use of news slides include inability to show motion or to create moods with talent and music, but relative to film, slides offer the advantage of speed and economy.

NAPS guarantees customer complete satisfaction with the results of each release or another one free.

28. Northeast Video, Inc.

420 Lexington Avenue, N.Y. 10017
(212) 661-8830
Henry Steiner, Pres.

Formed in 1980, Northeast Video provides video production and post-production services, including tape duplication, editing, animation, and conversions.

29. Orbis Productions, Inc.

3322 N. Lakewood Ave., Chicago 60657
(312) 883-9584
Jeff Bohnson, Pres.

Formed in 1983, Orbis produces and distributes a variety of film and video products. The company has considerable experience in the health care field and operates a medical news division.

30. Don Phelan, Inc.
311 W. 43 St., N.Y. 10036
(212) 586-2541
Don Phelan, Pres.

Branch Office:
114 Abbott St., N., Massapequa, NY 11758
(516) 249-3615

During his many years at United Press International, Don Phelan helped to develop the country's first sponsored film clip service and other services to TV stations. He started his company in 1980 and provides an extensive variety of TV production and distribution services: general on-location and studio still photography services; audiovisual services; video production in all formats. Most of his clients are public relations agencies and departments. For example, the Phelan Video News Release consists of a one-minute edited videotape with two minutes of rough edited "B" roll sound bites added on at the end to permit a news director to edit. The complete tape is sent on ¾" cassette by overnight express courier or by same-day satellite feed. This service is produced and distributed by Doncorps TV News, a division of Don Phelan, Inc.

Basic cost of the service, including scripting, production, editing and distribution (100 stations by cassette; 650 stations by satellite) is $9,050. Out-of-pocket expenses for director fee, local travel, materials, voice-over narration, printing, express shipping or satellite time, postage, phone calls is about $2,150 by courier express and $2,900 by satellite.

General photography assignments in most major cities run $450 for a half-day. New York City rates for half-day service are $350. Out-of-pocket expenses for materials, processing and travel are extra.

31. Planned Communication Services, Inc.
12 E. 46 St., N.Y. 10017
(212) 697-2765
Gerald Jay Multer, Chm.

PCS is one of the country's largest producers and distributors of sponsored materials for television, including public service announcements, VNRs, news clips and featurettes.

Production of a PSA, from concept through shooting, editing, music, narration and titles is $18,500 for a 30-second spot and $23,000 for a :60. Distribution, including preparation of spots in appropriate format and accompanying printed material, selection of stations, mailing and usage reports is $40 for one spot and $60 for two spots.

PCS's computerized station profiles allow distribution choices based on previous use of similar spots, market or station rankings, network affiliation, length and format preferences and other factors. The system produces detailed usage reports that include Arbitron audience estimates and other data.

PCS produces and distributes hundreds of video news releases. The usage generally is over 35 telecasts on local news shows. A video news release with a voice-over can be produced and then distributed on ¾-inch cassette to 100 stations at $19,500 for a :90. show. PCS sends a written inquiry to TV stations and then provides tapes to those who request them. Satellite distribution also is available.

Cable is another effective outlet for placement of produced materials such as public service announcements, featurettes, newsclips and other sponsored films. PCS offers a service where the cost of distribution is shared by a number of sponsors. Their film or video materials are transferred to ¾-inch (the preferred cable format) and are distributed to 100 of the largest cable systems and networks. Costs, including transfer to ¾-inch videocassette, distribution to 100 cable outlets and usage reports, is $995 for one spot.

Jerry Multer is one of the best-known people in the public relations service business. In 1987, his long-time partner, Alvin Roselin, retired.

32. Planned Television Arts Ltd.
25 W. 43 St., N.Y. 10036
(212) 921-5111
Mike Levine, Pres.; Richard Frishman, V.P.

PTA is a unique important resource for live and taped radio and television interviews, and Mike Levine and Rick Frishman are two of the country's most experienced and capable broadcast publicists.

The firm's specialty consists of the booking of live appearances of guests on local and network TV programs—on a payment-per-telecast basis. PTA can handle a comprehensive national tour of a client spokesman, involving dozens of live program interviews, within a relatively brief period, or it can make arrangements for salespeople and local representatives to appear on television programs in their own communities.

The virtue of this operation is that it results in exposure on live interview programs, which frequently have much bigger audiences than the programs on which sponsored films frequently are shown. The charge is $300 to $500 per telecast (according to size of market) which includes preparation of scripts or interview ideas, distribution of props to accompany the interviews and all other details. An estimate of the value of local interview programs can be determined from Nielson and Audience Research Bureau figures which indicate that many local interview programs have audiences which are the largest, or close to the largest, of any network or local programs in their markets.

PTA also operates a tour program for authors and other guests with "news pegs," whereby print interviews are included with saturation radio and TV bookings—all on a pay-for-success only basis, but with a lower price per interview.

33. Potomac Communications, Inc.
444 N. Capitol St., N.W., Wash., DC 20001
(202) 783-8886
Karen Weinstein, Steve Hellmuth

Potomac comprises several divisions, including Video Services, Potomac News Service and American News Bureau, which produce and distribute news reports to many TV stations around the country.

Potomac's Daily Business Satellite produces and transmits sponsored news reports (90 to 180 seconds) and other public relations material to TV stations. Transmissions are twice daily—late morning and mid-afternoon. The basic rate (up to two minutes) is $1,900 per feed and $8,900 for a complete package, including 10-minute transmission.

34. P. R. Connection
Box 691, Bala Cynwyd, PA 19004
(215) 664-3198
Hal Platzkere, Pres.

An experienced broadcaster (reporter, producer, writer, cameraman) for networks and local stations, Hal Platzkere formed PR Connection in 1983 to provide a variety of radio and television services, particularly in relation to special events and promotions. The company is located in suburban Philadelphia, and serves clients throughout the country with video news releases, satellite media tours, video conferencing and other TV projects.

35. Professional Communications Services

1776 Broadway, N.Y. 10019
(212) 24/-7965
Joe Feurey

A former newspaper reporter and editor, Joe Feurey is a popular lecturer on video. The company produces and distributes VNRs, PSAs and other broadcast materials. It operates the National Television News Syndication Service.

36. Projection Systems International, Inc.

219 E. 44 St., N.Y. 10017
(212) 682-0995, (800) 223-5753
Allan A. Armour, Pres.
Roland R. Blackway, Production Supervisor

PSI is one of the largest companies in the audio-visual field. Its full range of equipment and services is described in the motion picture chapter.

Following are representative prices of videotape duplication, a service of particular interest to public relations clients.

	10-Minutes		30-Minutes	
	Under 7 copies	Over 100 copies	Under 7 copies	Over 100 copies
1/2″ VHS	$23.50	$16.25	$32.30	$21.40
1/2″ Beta I	$22.55	$15.35	$30.25	$19.65
1/2″ Beta II	$21.90	$14.90	$29.35	$19.10
3/4″ U-Matic	$24.75	$17.75	$38.00	$25.25

37. Pro Video News Service, Inc.

303 S. Crescent Heights Blvd., L.A. 90048
(213) 655-4774
Telex: 188208
Gail Cottman, Pres.
D. Elayne Angel, Exec. V.P.

Formed in 1984, by public relations counselor Gail Cottman, Pro Video has become a sizeable full-service video operation, with production and satellite services in behalf of TV stations, as well as public relations clients. Semiweekly 30-minute news feeds include a variety of sponsored segments, with rates starting at $600 for a 2-minute segment.

Pro Video also conducts live satellite TV tours, with individual interviews broadcast from studios in Los Angeles and New York. The company also covers events and provides other video services.

38. Public Affairs Satellite System, Inc. (PubSat)

1012 14 St., N.W., Wash., DC 20005
(202) 628-2600
Telex: 466160
Caren Kagen, V.P., Client Services
Robert N. Bass, Exec. V.P.

Video news releases generally are transmitted during two half-hour satellite feeds. Placement services generally involve call, to 150 stations, from which PubSat projects usage on the 650 stations. Total cost is about $15,000.

In late 1987, PubSat and PR newswire started PR/TV Newswire, which transmits news releases on United Press International printers to more than 500 TV stations.

39. Public Interest Affiliates, Inc.

666 N. Shore Drive, Chicago 60610
(312) 943-8888
Brad Saul, Pres.
Sandra Kramer, V.P.

Branch Office:
12 W. 31 St., N.Y. 10001
(212) 714-9550
Susan Null

Founded in 1980 as a producer of public affairs radio programs (described in the radio chapter), PIA has expanded into video news releases and other video services, notably inflight video features for American Airlines and inflight audio programs for several airlines. Segments are available to sponsors.

40. Rowland Industries, Inc.

Box 941, Teaneck, NJ 07666
(201) 833-0501
Jack Brooks, Pres.

A long-time producer of syndicated radio and TV shows, Jack Brooks produces the Joan Fontaine show, which is distributed via satellite to cable TV stations throughout the country. For $2,250, clients receive a 10 to 15 minute interview with the renowned actress, color videotape and black-and-white photo.

The same radio format, and the same price structure, is used for the Rita Gam show, which also is distributed as a five-minute radio program to 400 stations, at a fee of $650.

41. Sheridan-Elson Communications

20 W. 37 St., N.Y. 10018
(212) 239-2000
William R. Sheridan, Robert E. Elson and Paul Gourvitz

Formed in 1968, Sheridan-Elson produces and distributes TV news films and featurettes and other materials. The cost for a 90-second video news release, with production and distribution, is about $20,000.

The company is unusual in that it has many production facilities on its premises and is able to design film and video projects to meet the specific needs of clients. In-house video for corporate clients has also become a speciality of the firm.

Sheridan-Elson also produces and implements videotape training programs and audio-cassette libraries in addition to their broadcast projects.

42. DS Simon Productions

159 W. 85 St., N.Y. 10024
(212) 580-3614
Douglas S. Simon, Pres.

Formed in 1986, Simon produces and distributes VNRS (about $14,000 for the basic package) and other video materials.

43. Targetron Inc.

156 Fifth Ave., N.Y. 10010
(212) 463-7668
Steven Gold, Linda Rosenbaum

Targetron produces and distributes film and tape releases to schools, colleges and TV stations.

Public service announcements and VNRs (30, 60 and 90 seconds): $2,800, for the first 100 cassettes and $1,800 for each additional hundred.

Sponsored shorts and features (5 to 60 minutes): $45 per confirmed booking on TV, $30 for cable and $15 for schools and colleges.

44. Teatown Video, Inc.

165 W. 46 St., N.Y. 10036
(212) 302-0722
Marlene Hecht, Pres.

Formed in 1979, Teatown has considerable experience in producing and distributing all types of film and video products. The company name refers to Ms. Hecht's interest in Japanese culture.

45. Television Digest, Inc.

1836 Jefferson Pl., N.W., Wash., DC 20036
(202) 872-9200

If you are active in the television field, you must have one or more of the encyclopedia publications of Television Digest. They range from a daily newsletter to an annual directory. None are cheap; one of the lowest price books is the annual Television & Cable Factbook ($235). The "3,200-page" two-volume set probably is of greatest interest to public relations people, as compared to the more specialized publications, which are:

Common Carrier Weeks $9
Communications Daily $1,595
Early Warning Report $75
Public Broadcasting Report $88
Satellite Week $626
Space Commerce Bulletin $96
Television Digest with Consumer Electronics $617
Television Digest with Consumer Electronics and TV & Cable Action Updates $89
TV & Cable Updates $307
Video Week $623

46. Tower Intermark

1481 Broadway, N.Y. 10036
(212) 764-1602
Thomas Alison, Chm.
Donald Roosa, Pres.

A specialist in public service video, Tower produces and distributes VNRs, PSAs and other broadcast materials. The VNRs for public television often are much longer than commercial VNRs.

47. VICAM

1853 Post Rd., E., Westport, CT 06880
(203) 259-1560
Harry Eggart, Pres.

A former CBS and NBC network producer and director, Harry Eggart operates a full-service film and video production company (formerly called Video Profiles).

48. Video Base International
200 W. 57 St., N.Y. 10019
(212) 541-5611
Sally Hunter, Pres.
Bernard Shusman, Dir.
Alumni of Newsweek Broadcasting Service (Sally Hunter was general manager and Bernard Shusman was V.P. at Newsweek, Inc.), Video Base (formed in 1983) produces video news releases and other film and tape materials.

49. Videocorp Communications Co., Inc.
213 E. 21 St., N.Y. 10010
(212) 254-9306
Douglas L. Evans, Pres.
Formed in 1986, Videocorp produces and distributes video news releases and other TV materials.

50. Video Monitor
Communications Research Associates, Inc.
10606 Mantz Rd., Silver Spring, MD 20903
(301) 445-3230
Ray E. Hiebert, Publisher
Video Monitor is a report on television for public relations and advertising. It provides "how to" information for corporate communications executives and public relations agencies, as well as forecasting of long-term trends in such new technologies as cable TV, satellite, videotext and teletext, videoconferencing and low-power TV.
Video Monitor costs $98 for an annual subscription.

51. Video Planning/Carob Video
250 W. 57 St., N.Y. 10107
(212) 582-5066
Marc Wein, Pres.
A major part of its business is with public relations clients, so that Video Planning is able to provide speedy, economical, efficient and creative services for video news releases, public service announcements, coverage of events and production of all types of video.
Its facilities include a fully equipped studio, broadcast quality cameras, lighting packages, smaller setups for spokesperson training sessions and teleprompters. Editing facilities, which are in midtown and lower Manhattan, include one-inch editing suites, multiformat editing suites, digital effects, offline editing and large and small volume tape duplication and distribution.

52. Visnews International
630 Fifth Ave., N.Y. 10111
(212) 698-4500
Telex: 239875
Gwendolyn Jefferson, Marketing Coordinator
The U.S. subsidiary of Visnews Limited (headquartered in London), Visnews is one of the world's largest producers and distributors of TV news and feature programs. Services include video news releases,

video conferences and other video projects. Visnews also sells stock films and tape from its news library and provides crews for studio and location work.

53. Visual Concepts
85 N. Main St., East Hampton, CT 06424
(203) 267-0262
Steve Shaw, Pres.

Formed in 1986 by Steve Shaw and Ric Serrenho, Visual Concepts produces and distributes video news releases and other video materials. The company is located in Connecticut, not Easthampton, Long Island.

54. West Glen Communications, Inc.
1430 Broadway, N.Y. 10018
(212) 921-2800
Stanley S. Zeitlin, Pres.

Established in 1970, West Glen is a leading producer and distributor of sponsored educational programs, specializing in:

Video News Releases (90-second inserts for use on local live news shows), public service announcements, daytime talk shows (three to five minute how-to featurettes), and library programs (five to 28-minute films/videos to broadcast and cable stations). In addition to its television projects, West Glen produces and distributes free and rental films to schools and other organizations, and distributes sponsored theatrical short subjects to movie theatres.

55. You're On/Access to Television and Radio
19 Madison Ave., Beverly, MA 01915
(617) 927-6768
Richard M. Goldberg, Pres.

Established in 1979, You're On helps public relations people communicate their messages more effectively on television and radio news broadcasts, talk programs, and public service announcements. Goldberg is a former TV news managing editor, producer, and writer who uses an insider's perspective to get you to work more effectively with broadcasters.

In 1983, he produced an audio cassette album of tips and tactics called The Success System For Getting Television Coverage ($49 plus $2 shipping). The album's three tapes cover TV news, talk programs, and cable television. Tip sheets, sample cover letters to assignment editors and talk show producers, and a reference guide are included.

Though Richard Goldberg also does communications coaching, what he specializes in is assisting public relations people in broadcast publicity.

Note that his Madison Avenue address is *not* in New York.

Television services are discussed in several other chapters, notably broadcast monitoring, communications consultants, packaged publicity services, radio, teleconferencing and VIP services.

Chapter 34

Translations

Though many public relations practitioners confine their activities almost exclusively to their local communities, an increasing number work on a global basis. As American companies expand their marketing in foreign countries, a large number of people are involved in sending and receiving correspondence, news releases, publications and other communications in foreign languages.

Many offices include foreigners, linguists, and others who have a familiarity with one or more foreign languages, which is sufficient for most correspondence. However, it often is of tremendous importance to be absolutely precise, particularly with regard to technical language and current idioms. The use of a professional translation service is highly recommended, and often is considerably superior to the translating services provided by students and other *"laissez faire"* freelancers.

Professional translators are slowly developing into a profession, with higher standards as well as fees, though there still is a high degree of looseness in the field. The International Association of Conference Interpreters is helping to set standards for its 1,500 members (of whom about two-thirds work on a freelance basis).

The Association is at 14, rue de l'Ancien Port, 1201, Geneva, Switzerland. Conference interpretation, as defined by the Association, may be performed by either of two techniques.

> *L'interprétation consécutive:* l'interprète, assis à la table de conférence, interprète lorsque l'orateur a terminé son intervention. Il s'aide généralement de notes.
> *L'interprétation simultanée:* l'interprète, assis dans une cabine entend l'intervention au moyen d'un casque d'écoute et en fait au fur et à mesure une interprétation transmise par microphone aux écouteurs des délegués.

In case you don't understand French, here's a translation:

> *Consecutively:* the interpreter is seated at the conference table and reproduces the statement in another language after the speech, usually with the help of notes.
> *Simultaneously:* seated in soundproof booths, the interpreters receive a speaker's statement through the headphones and deliver a running interpretation into another language which is relayed through their microphones to the delegates' headphones.

454

For more information, contact Diane G. H. Cook, exec. director, at the Translation Center, 307A Mathematics Blvd., Columbia University, N.Y. 10027, phone (212) 280-2305. Founded in 1972, the Translation Center promotes excellence in the art of literary translation. Its magazine, Transalation ($16.50), publishes translations of foreign contemporary literature.

About 2,000 translators belong to the American Translators Association, 109 Croton Ave., Ossining, NY 10562, and about 550 translators belong to the American Literary Translators Association, Box 688, Richardson, TX 75080. A listing of close to 200 translators and interpreters is published in Literary Market Place, the encyclopedia-directory published annually by R. R. Bowker Company, 205 E. 42 St., N.Y. 10017.

Several typographers specialize in foreign languages. The king is King Typographic Service, 300 Park Ave. South, NY. 10010 phone (212) 254-7421. The company was acquired by TGC, a 24-hour-a-day typesetting operation which specializes in overnight jobs from advertising and public relations companies. King can handle about a thousand languages and dialects. The cost of a "difficult language," such as Russian or Chinese, may be double the English language cost.

Somehow one might think that the translation business is more cultural and gentle than other public relations services, and it perhaps is a surprise to note the intense competitiveness in this field. One company, All-Language Services, advertised as follows:

> Did you ever visit a translation bureau? You'd be shocked if you did! There are thousands of "translation bureaus" in the United States. If you asked them to show you their German or Japanese department, library and staff, or those in Russian and other major languages, they have almost nothing to show you. Virtually 100 percent of such translation "bureaus" are mere brokers, operating without the essential facilities, qualified staff or reference library which only All-Language Services has. By resorting primarily to freelancers working at home, mostly ill-prepared, without quality control or accountability, they have produced the most substandard translations with resultant havoc, apart form hazardously having unknown persons become privy to privileged corporate information.

Many of the companies in this field are small offices which make use of foreign students and other multilingual freelance personnel. For most purposes, these operations are satisfactory, though service sometimes is unpredictable, unreliable and "emotional." For major assignments, it's a good idea to visit the office and talk with the proprietor.

Following are a few organizations scattered about the country which specialize in commercial translation work. Several universities, including Carnegie-Mellon and the University of Pittsburgh, provide translation services. To find translation services outside of the U.S., ask your bank or other companies with foreign offices. In Singapore, Peace Translation & Clipping Services (listed in the clipping bureau chapter) provides English, Chinese, Malay and other translations and copywriting.

Many other translators and interpreters are listed in Literary Market Place (described in the media chapter).

1. AD-EX Translations International/U.S.A.
525 Middlefield Rd., Ste. 150, Menlo Park, CA 94025
(415) 854-6732, (800) 223-7753
Telefax: (415) 325-8428
Robert L. Addis, CEO
Robert Abilock, Dir. of Operations

Founded by Robert L. Addis in 1957, AD-EX is a major company in the field of translation for industry, government and other clients. Located in the Silicon Valley, the company specializes in translation from and into English of technical, promotional, legal and other specialized literature and documentation. Its facilities include word-processing and phototypesetting equipment.

2. All-Language Services, Inc.

545 Fifth Ave., N.Y. 10017
(212) 986-1688
Telex: 852929
John Tansey

With a staff of over 150, All-Language is one of the largest translation companies in the country. The 24-hour-a-day service relies on bilingual teams of writers, attorneys, accountants, engineers and other experts.

On relatively short notice, this agency can supply interpreters in any one of 59 languages. Fees vary, starting at $85 an hour.

3. The Berlitz Translation Services

866 Third Ave., N.Y. 10022
(212) 486-1212
David Laube

Professional translators handle commercial, promotional, legal, scientific and technical material from and into all major languages. Service is accurate, fast and confidential.

Formed in 1878 in Rhode Island by Maximilian Berlitz, this company name is synonymous with foreign languages. It's part of Macmillan, as are the Berlitz Language Centers. Berlitz translation branches are in major cities including Chicago, Houston, Los Angeles, Philadelphia, San Francisco, Washington, DC and Miami.

4. Bertrand Languages, Inc.

370 Lexington Ave., N.Y. 10017
(212) 685-9772
Rochelle L. Uffner, Mng. Dir.

Formed in 1936 by Lewis Bertrand, the company now is operated by a group of professional translators who provide interpreting and translations from and into dozens of languages. Related services are typing in foreign languages and transcription of foreign-language tapes.

5. Conway Associates International, Inc.

104 E. 40 St., N.Y. 10016
(212) 682-6970
Leonard E. Coplen

Specializes in copywriting into foreign languages. All major languages, including Chinese, Japanese, Korean and Russian.

Also provides simultaneous and consecutive interpreters and equipment for symposiums, trade shows, business tours and conferences.

Divisions are FAM Translations, The George Bellido Company and Translating Associates.

6. GFE Translation Co.

6807 Winter Lane, Annandale, VA 22003
(703) 354-0491
Harry Julich

A staff of six carries out professional and mainly technical translations in all fields and in the languages of the developed countries. The company was started in 1971 by Mr. Julich, who is an engineer.

7. Language Translation Services, Inc.

319 S. Limestone St., Lexington, KY 40508
(606) 233-4154
Terry K. Parks, V.P.

Founded in 1974 by Stanley S. and Terry K. Parks, LTS is a highly professional operation located in a community not noted for its foreign expertise. However, the company has an excellent track record with clients all over the country. Facilities include a reference library for translators and marketing researchers, phototypesetting interfaced to wordprocessing, and a complete graphic arts/photographic department.

Services include foreign language marketing communications for the U.S. Hispanic and most major international markets. LTS produces promotional and technical information in camera-ready form for printing or for audiovisual presentation. Informational services include two studies, The English, Spanish, French, and German-speaking World Markets and The U.S. Hispanic Market ($20 each) and Expansion, a quarterly international marketing publication ($5 a year). Market research and consultation are provided on a fee basis.

The typesetting, graphic arts and photgraphic services operate as a separate company, LTS/C Corp. The audiovisual services, which operate as AV International, include a sound track recording system which records several languages in synchronization.

8. Lindner Translations, Inc.

29 Broadway, N.Y. 10006
(212) 269-4660
Mrs. V. E. Lindner, Pres.

In 1966, after 15 years of professional experience, Mrs. Lindner formed her own translation and interpreting company. Interpreting rates start at $50 an hour and vary according to the language, location and time of day. Translation rates start at $10 per 100 English words.

9. Linguistic Systems, Inc.

116 Bishop Allen Dr., Cambridge, MA 02139
(617) 864-3900
Martin Roberts, Pres.

Formed in 1967, Linguistic Systems is a full-service translation company which provides translating, interpreting, audiovisual, information gathering, typesetting and other services to clients throughout the world. One of the largest companies in the field, LSI has typing (e.g., Chinese and Japanese typewriters) and typesetting equipment for many languages.

10. Nation-Wide Reporting & Convention Coverage, Inc.

350 Broadway, N.Y. 10013
(800) 221-7242
Lori Ungarsonn, Pres.
Harry Ungarsonn, V.P.

Interpreters in New York and elsewhere (through affiliates). Also stenotypists, video- and tape-recording, typed transcripts from recorded media and a variety of secretarial and other services.

11. Rennert Bilingual Translation
2 W. 45 St., N.Y. 10036
(212) 819-1776
Telecopier: (212) 921-7666
Erick Derkatsch, Catherine Godbille

A division of the Bilingual Institute, Ltd., Rennert can handle translations, narrations, typesetting, printing, interpreting, bilingual tour and shopping guides, foreign-language courses and other services.

Chapter 35

VIP Services

Some journalists, clients and others have the idea that public relations practitioners can "fix" parking tickets, arrange for admission to "very important person" events and obtain theater tickets to sellout hit shows. Though there are occasions when a public relations person has the "right contacts," it usually is impossible to fulfill assignments of this type.

Still, clients and friends persist in the notion that a public relations person can get a hotel room or airline reservation when nobody else can—and at a special price!

Perhaps the most common requests involve theater tickets. Undoubtedly, press agents who represent Broadway shows or handle theatrical clients can be helpful in obtaining tickets to hit shows. "House seats," which are reserved for the producers, stars and others connected with the show, sometimes can be purchased. However, theatrical publicists find it almost impossible to obtain front-and-center tickets to Saturday night performances of hit musical comedies.

This directory has no magic solution to this problem. Undoubtedly, there are contacts at ticket agencies who often have supplies of "impossible to get" tickets—for a premium price. Rather than encourage this practice, we offer the following suggestion.

Many churches and temples, women's auxiliaries of hospitals and other charities purchase thousands of tickets to Broadway shows, films, concerts and other events. The more popular the show, the more likely there are to be many theater benefits.

The Sunday Society section of The New York Times provides extensive listings of forthcoming benefit performances, usually including the name, address and telephone number of the ticket source. Many of these organizations are quite willing to sell tickets to nonmembers and, though arrangements usually are made several weeks in advance, it occasionally is possible to pick up a ticket with relatively short notice.

Benefit tickets cost $5 or more than the regular price, but the surcharge goes to a worthy cause. It is a tax-deductible means of solving what otherwise can be an extremely time-consuming and frustrating chore.

So much for the theater ticket problem. We offer no suggestion with regard to parking tickets, except to advise the offender to "pay the $2" (or more).

With regard to tickets to Tonight and other television shows which are popular with out-of-towners, it usually is possible to obtain them by writing to the guest relations department of the network. Advertising agencies and network advertisers often can help with last-minute requests.

The large temporary employment agencies, such as Manpower, can provide party hostesses, tour escorts or other VIP services. The chamber of commerce or convention bureau in the city in which your event is being held can provide information about local sources.

Incidentally, with regard to airlines, you no longer have to be a celebrity to become a member of an airline VIP Club. Annual membership dues in the TWA Ambassadors Club, American Airlines Admirals Club, Northwest Airlines Top Flight Club, Eastern Airlines Ionosphere Club and other airline VIP clubs are about $100 a year.

And, a final shopping note. Most major department stores offer free shopping services, often including multilingual guides. A few stores add a small service charge.

As always, the classified telephone book can help you find chauffered limousines, escorts and other services for VIPs. Charter bus and limousine companies often have vehicles with special facilities for public relations and promotion purposes. For example, Short Line, which operates in the Metropolitan New York area, has a luxurious customized coach called the Flagship. It has plush swivel chairs for 20 people and is equipped with TV and audio-visual facilities, as well as a bar, kitchen, restroom and tables, so that it is superb for press conferences, seminars, meetings and V.I.P travel. Contact Joann Sadowski at Shortline, 17 Franklin Turnpike, Mahwah, NJ 07430, phone (201) 529-3666.

The nation's "media centers" are New York, Los Angeles and Washington, DC. More national media and bureaus are located in these cities than any others. In New York, it literally is possible to *walk* from one interview to another. The New York Times, New York News, United Press, Associated Press, Reuters, NBC network and local stations, WPIX-TV, McGraw-Hill, Time, Newsweek and dozens of other major media are in the midtown area.

In other cities, however, the distances are considerably greater. If you ever have been on one of the Los Angeles freeways at rush hour, you know the problem! So it's a delight to note that several enterprising individuals in major cities have started "media escort services."

Information about where to find VIPs is included in the chapter about celebrities.

The Social Register, a directory of about 33,000 socialites and their clubs, is published by Carrier Pidgeon, 40 Plimpton St., Boston, MA 02118. It's $54.50, including updates.

1. Muriel Brown Services
19500 Turnberry Way, Ste. 2E, N. Miami Beach, FL 33180
(305) 932-7076
Muriel Brown
Since 1983, Muriel Brown has been an escort in the Miami, Ft. Lauderdale and Palm Beach area.

2. Chicago Media Tours
54 W. Park Ave., Cary, IL 60013
(312) 639-2440
Dennis R. Frisch
An experienced broadcaster (including production staff of WMAQ-TV in Chicago), Dennis Frisch started a publicity tour service in 1984 which includes much more than a luxury car and chauffeur. For example, he is familiar with production schedules (some tapings are flexible, changes can be made, even at the last minute; some shows frequently run late) and also can help in contacting producers before the interview and after (for feedback).

3. Creative Food Service
14 Lawton St., New Rochelle, NY 10801
(914) 235-1421, (212) 772-0514
Mrs. Sylvia Schur, Dir.

460

A former editor of Look and other magazines, Sylvia Schur is a consultant to food companies and associations, as well as advertising and public relations agencies. Her versatile staff provides an inventive expansion of the services offered by several food editors, home economists, cooking schools, and other culinary experts. CFS services food photography, works in new product identification and development and develops new recipes which make use of commercial products, writes recipe books and booklets, handles all of the details, except the eating, for press parties and other events which make use of food.

4. Gallery Passport Ltd.
1170 Broadway, N.Y. 10001
(212) 686-2244
Bunny Mautner, Pres.

Since New York is the art capital of the Western world, this company fills a genuine need by conducting gallery and museum tours for clubs, conventions and other groups. Guides also are available for trips to art landmarks in Pennsylvania, Connecticut and the surrounding areas. Fees are quite low and vary according to size of group and type of transportation.

Gallery Passport was founded in 1960 by Caroline Lerner Goldsmith, a well-known fine arts public relations consultant.

5. Sandi Kopler
2512 College Park Rd., Pittsburgh, PA 15101
(412) 486-5804

An experienced publicist and tour escort, Sandi Kopler charges $125 a day (eight hours) for chauffering, and $350 to set up a day of interviews.

6. Locations, Inc.
445 Fifth Ave., N.Y. 10016
(212) 481-9111
Susan Johnson, Pres.

Do you need help in finding a location for photographic or promotional use? Miss Johnson knows about several thousands lofts, mansions, farms and castles, primarily in New Jersey, New York and Connecticut.

7. Media Escort Service of Detroit
27887 Zelton, Madison Heights, MI 48071
(313) 548-2875
Linda Tomcko

Particularly experienced with authors. Rates are $90 a day (eight hours), plus .25 a mile for a chauffeured Cadillac.

8. Places
Box 810, Gracie Station, N.Y. 10028
(212) 737-7536
Hannelore Hahn, Pres.

Places, an unusual directory of about 2,000 public places for private events and private places for public functions in the New York City area and elsewhere, is published ($18.95) biannually by Tenth House Enterprises. The company also consults about special locations throughout the country, including boats, lofts, landmarks, mansions, meeting rooms, party and performance places. In fact, the consultations are free to purchasers of the book.

Index

B

C

H

I

J

K

N

O

P

S

About the Author

Richard Weiner is a public relations consultant in New York. Mr. Weiner began his communications career at a radio station in Madison, Wisconsin, where he produced the nation's first broadcast description of a childbirth.

He was one of the first members of the Public Relations Society of America to be accredited and has been responsible for several programs which received Silver Anvil Awards from the Society. In 1984, he received the John Hill Award. He is a frequent lecturer and has conducted seminars for public relations organizations, companies, associations and government agencies, and courses at several universities.